Blackstone's

Police Investigators' Manual

Blackstone's

Police Investigators' Manual

2009

Paul Connor
Glenn Hutton
David Johnston
Gavin McKinnon

OXFORD
UNIVERSITY PRESS

OXFORD
UNIVERSITY PRESS

Great Clarendon Street, Oxford OX2 6DP

Oxford University Press is a department of the University of Oxford.
It furthers the University's objective of excellence in research, scholarship,
and education by publishing worldwide in

Oxford New York

Auckland Cape Town Dar es Salaam Hong Kong Karachi
Kuala Lumpur Madrid Melbourne Mexico City Nairobi
New Delhi Shanghai Taipei Toronto

With offices in

Argentina Austria Brazil Chile Czech Republic France Greece
Guatemala Hungary Italy Japan Poland Portugal Singapore
South Korea Switzerland Thailand Turkey Ukraine Vietnam

Published in the United States
by Oxford University Press Inc., New York

First edition 1998
Eleventh edition 2008

British Library Cataloguing in Publication Data

Data available

Library of Congress Cataloging in Publication Data

Data available

Typeset by Laserwords Private Limited, Chennai, India
Printed in Italy
on acid-free paper by
Legoprint S.p.A.

ISBN 978–0–19–955294–8

10 9 8 7 6 5 4 3 2 1

Contents

How to use *Blackstone's Police Investigators' Manual 2009*

The National Investigators' Examination (NIE) contains questions based solely on the text within the *Police Investigators' Manual*.

Any feedback regarding content or editorial matters in this Manual can be emailed to police.uk@oup.com.

Table of Cases

Tables of Primary Legislation

EU Legislation

Tables of Secondary Legislation

Codes of Practice

Home Office Circulars

PART ONE

Evidence

1.1 State of Mind

1.1.1 Introduction

It is traditional when studying or explaining criminal law to strip out the main concepts of *mens rea* (state of mind) and *actus reus* (criminal conduct) at the beginning, followed by a few other key areas such as general defences and incomplete offences (attempts, conspiracies, etc.). This is because these concepts apply across the board and, as such, are fundamental to an understanding of all offences and the idea of criminal liability generally.

In this Manual, the 'state of mind' is considered first, followed by the notion of criminal conduct.

There is a cardinal rule in the criminal law of England and Wales that acts alone cannot amount to a crime unless they are accompanied by a 'guilty mind' or '*mens rea*'.

The idea of 'guilty knowledge' suggested by the original Latin terminology is misleading and there are many different mental states which will fulfil the requirements of many different offences which have nothing to do with 'guilty knowledge' or, sometimes, any other kind of 'knowledge'.

The key to proving *mens rea* in any criminal charge is to show that a defendant had *the required state of mind at the required time*. If you are going to do that, you need to know what the relevant state of mind for the offence is. The coincidence of the state of mind with the criminal act (the *actus reus*) is critical and is dealt with in the next chapter.

1.1.2 Strict Liability

Some criminal offences are said to be offences of 'strict liability'. This expression generally means that there is little to prove beyond the act itself and that the state of mind of the defendant is immaterial. However, in most cases it is more accurate to say that there is no need to prove *mens rea* in relation to one particular aspect of the criminal activity or behaviour. There have been isolated instances in which the courts have held that an offence does not require any *mens rea* to be proved. An example relates to the offence of driving with excess alcohol, contrary to the Road Traffic Act 1988, s. 5, which was stated in *DPP* v *H* [1997] 1 WLR 1406 not to require proof of any *mens rea*.

In some other, albeit rare, cases absolute liability is imposed, reducing even further the burden on the prosecution.

Situations where strict or absolute liability is imposed are usually to enforce statutory regulation (e.g. road traffic offences), particularly where there is some social danger or concern presented by the proscribed behaviour. So, where a defendant was charged with possessing a 'prohibited' weapon the court held that it did not matter whether he *knew* he had the weapon—a CS gas canister—in order to prove 'possession' (*R* v *Bradish* [1990] 1 QB 981).

Some other offences such as public nuisance at common law require only strict liability in relation to some elements of the criminal conduct.

As a general rule, however, there is a presumption that *mens rea* is required for a criminal offence unless parliament clearly indicates otherwise (see *B (A Minor)* v *DPP* [2000] 2 WLR 452). This rule should be borne in mind, not only when approaching the rest of the material in this Manual, but also when considering criminal law in general.

1.1.3 States of Mind

Criminal offences generally can be classified in terms of the level of *mens rea* required. In descending order they are:

1.1.3.1 Offences Requiring a Particular *Mens Rea*

These are often referred to in legal textbooks as crimes of *specific* intent or *ulterior* intent, a distinction which is important when considering defences. In policing terms the important thing is to note the specific requirements that must be shown in order to prove that the defendant was guilty of the particular offence, and then to gather any evidence that tends to support or undermine that proposition. In summary, crimes of specific intent are only committed where the defendant is shown to have had a particular intention to bring about a specific consequence at the time of the criminal act. Murder is such a crime, requiring proof of an intention to kill or seriously injure. Other examples would be offences such as:

- wounding or inflicting grievous bodily harm *with intent* (Offences Against the Person Act 1861, s. 18);
- blackmail (Theft Act 1968, s. 21);
- contamination of goods (Public Order Act 1986, s. 38(1)).

Ulterior intent means an intention beyond the basic intent of carrying out the core criminal act. For example, where a defendant is charged with burglary under the Theft Act 1968, s. 9(1)(a), you must show the intention, not just to enter a building as a trespasser, but also to *inflict grievous bodily harm, cause damage, or steal*. The italicised intention makes this a crime of ulterior intent.

1.1.3.2 Offences of Basic Intent

Many criminal offences require no further proof of anything other than a basic intention to bring about the given circumstances.

Whereas an offence of burglary under s. 9(1)(a) of the Theft Act 1968 requires proof of the ulterior intent described above, burglary under s. 9(1)(b) simply requires proof that the person entered the building/part of a building as a trespasser and that he/she went on to commit one of the prohibited acts (theft/attempted theft; inflicting/attempting to inflict grievous bodily harm). As well as easing the burden of proof on the prosecution in cases of basic intent, the distinction can also be significant when dealing with possible defences.

A further important difference in offences of specific or ulterior intent and those requiring only basic intent is that, in the case of the latter type of offence, *recklessness* will often be enough to satisfy the mental element. Recklessness is a particularly important concept in the area of *mens rea* and is dealt with at **para. 1.1.4.2.**

1.1.3.3 Negligence

Although many commentators argue that, by definition, negligence should not appear alongside discussions of *mens rea* as it is not a 'state of mind', it is useful to include it here. Negligence is generally concerned with the defendant's compliance with the standards of reasonableness of ordinary people. Like strict liability, the concept of negligence focuses on the consequences of the defendant's conduct rather than demanding proof of a particular state of mind at the time. Unlike strict liability, negligence still ascribes some notion of 'fault' or 'blame' to the defendant who must be shown to have acted in a way that runs contrary to the expectations of the reasonable person.

The most important criminal offence that can be committed by negligence is manslaughter (manslaughter by gross negligence), which is also one of the only offences to include specific reference—at common law—to the word 'negligence'. The requirement to show that an *individual person* was negligent has been one of the main problems in the development of 'corporate manslaughter'. Other offences that can be committed by negligence do not usually contain the word itself but attract that test in relation to the mental element. Good examples are offences involving the standard of driving.

1.1.4 Statutory Expressions

Statutory offences use a number of different terms to describe the respective states of mind which must be proved. The more common expressions are:

- intent
- recklessness
- wilfully
- dishonestly.

These have been developed through our common law system and now have the following meanings:

1.1.4.1 Intent

Like many other concepts of *mens rea* 'intention' is not defined by any statute. If a defendant intends something to happen, he/she wishes to bring about certain consequences. In some offences, say burglary under s. 9(1)(a) of the Theft Act 1968, the defendant's *intention* may be very clear; he/she may enter a house as a trespasser *intending* to steal property inside. As a crime *of ulterior* intent (**see para. 1.1.3.1**), it would need to be proved that the defendant not only entered the house or part of it in such a way, but that at the time he/she also *intended* to steal. Provided there is enough admissible evidence (e.g. the possession of article for use in the theft, a 'shopping list', an admission by the defendant and an arrangement for the disposal of the property once stolen), this element of the defendant's intention is relatively straightforward.

However, there will often be consequences following from a defendant's actions that he/she did not *intend* to happen. An example might be where, in the above burglary, it was late at night and the householder came across the burglar and suffered a heart attack as a result of the shock. In such an event it would be reasonable to suggest that it was the defendant's behaviour or actions that had brought about the victim's heart attack. The defendant, however, may well argue that, although he/she intended to break in and steal, there had never been any *intention* of harming or frightening the occupant. At this point you might well say that the defendant should have thought about that before breaking into someone else's house in the middle of the night. This then brings in the concept of *foresight*, a concept that has caused the courts considerable difficulty over the years—for a number of reasons.

First, there is the Criminal Justice Act 1967 which says (under s. 8) that a court/jury, in determining whether a person has committed an offence:

(a) shall not be bound in law to infer that he intended or foresaw a result of his actions by reason only of its being a natural and probable consequence of those actions; but
(b) shall decide whether he did intend or foresee that result by reference to all the evidence, drawing such inferences from the evidence as appear proper in the circumstances.

Secondly, there is the body of case law which has developed around the area of 'probability', culminating in two cases in the House of Lords (*R* v *Moloney* [1985] AC 905 and *R* v *Hancock* [1986] AC 455). Following those cases it is now settled that foresight of the probability of a consequence *does not amount to an intention to bring that consequence about, but may be evidence of it*.

In other words, you cannot claim that a defendant *intended* a consequence of his/her behaviour simply because it was virtually certain to occur. What you can do is to put evidence of the defendant's foresight of that probability before a court which may infer an intention from it. In proving such a point the argument would go like this:

- at the time of the criminal act there was a *probability* of a consequence;
- the greater the probability, the more likely it is that the defendant *foresaw* that consequence;
- if the defendant foresaw that consequence, the more likely it is that the defendant *intended* it to happen.

Whether or not a defendant intended a particular consequence will be a question of fact left to the jury (or magistrate(s) where appropriate). Most of the problematic cases in this area have arisen in relation to murder. In such circumstances, where death or serious bodily harm was a *virtual certainty* from the defendant's actions and he/she had appreciated that to be the case, the jury *may* infer that the defendant intended to bring about such consequences (*R* v *Nedrick* [1986] 1 WLR 1025). Therefore, where the defendant threw a three-month-old baby down onto a hard surface in a fit of rage, the jury *might* have inferred both that death/serious bodily harm was a virtual certainty from the defendant's actions and that he must have appreciated that to be the case; they should therefore have been directed by the trial judge accordingly (*R* v *Woollin* [1999] 1 AC 82).

Finally, the relevant intent may have been formed, not of the defendant's own volition, but influenced in some way by other external factors. An example is where the defendant's thinking is affected by duress.

1.1.4.2 Recklessness

The concept itself goes beyond a statutory expression and has probably become more important in proving criminal offences than the concept of 'intent' above as proof of recklessness is often enough to fulfil the requirement of *mens rea* (although not in offences requiring 'dishonesty').

The good news is that, following decades of complex differences between objective and subjective recklessness (the former applying only to a very limited number of offences), the law was eventually clarified.

An advantage of recklessness over intention is that the former is easier to prove by the attendant circumstances; a disadvantage is the different elements attributed to the word 'reckless' by different courts considering different offences—there are different sorts of recklessness.

EXAMPLE

Consider a schoolgirl who throws a stone into a neighbour's garden, breaking the glass of a greenhouse window. She tells you that she was only 'having a laugh' and did not stop to think of what damage might be caused by the stone. Does the fact that she gave no thought to the consequences of her actions make her 'reckless' or blameless? Had she stopped to think about the possible consequences, would she have seen the risk? Does that matter?

If some reasonable person walking past at the time had seen her about to throw the stone, would that person have realised the possible risk? What if the person walking past had been another schoolgirl of the same age and understanding as the one who threw the stone? Are these questions relevant in determining recklessness?

Taking the last question first, yes—all of the above deliberations can be relevant, both to the type of recklessness involved and the liability of the defendant.

In addition, there are not only different types of recklessness, but they are *applied* in different ways to different offences.

Take the example of assault occasioning actual bodily harm. In such an offence recklessness can suffice in proving the mental element (*R* v *Venna* [1976] QB 421). But recklessness as to what? The defendant may have been reckless as to the assault itself and/or to the *harm* that was actually caused *by* the assault. The courts have held that assault occasioning actual bodily harm only requires proof of recklessness *as to the assault* and there is no need to show that the defendant was reckless as to the extent of the harm caused by his/her assault (see *R* v *Savage* [1992] 1 AC 699).

In offences of criminal damage, the situation is slightly different. It is in this context that the concept of 'objective' recklessness caused the most problems for the courts. In such cases, so-called Caldwell recklessness (from the House of Lords decision in *Metropolitan Police Commissioner* v *Caldwell* [1982] AC 341) applied. This gave rise to difficulties of proof where the defendant failed to consider an *obvious* risk and then went on to damage property. In those cases a defendant was not allowed to claim to have had no *mens rea* simply because he/she had not thought the matter through and if the prosecution showed that the relevant risk (in our schoolgirl example above, the risk to property) would have been apparent to a reasonable person, it was not necessary to show that the defendant realised that risk. Of course if a defendant *did* in fact see the risk then clearly this strengthens the prosecution's case in any event. But this notion of obvious risk presented some real problems in practice, for instance, where the defendant, because of his/her mental condition or personal attributes, would not have been able to appreciate the risk *even if he/she had stopped to consider the consequences*. This meant that a defendant could be held criminally liable for the consequences of his/her actions even where he/she could not have foreseen those consequences and the strict application of the rule resulted in some 'harsh' decisions (*Elliot* v *C* [1983] 1 WLR 939; *R* v *R* (*Stephen Malcolm*) (1984) 79 Cr App R 334). The abolition of the old *doli incapax* rule meant that, where objective recklessness was the appropriate test—e.g. manslaughter and criminal damage—children who were incapable of appreciating the risks arising from their actions could still be found guilty. Similarly, adults whose mental characteristics prevent them from appreciating the risks created by their behaviour were not able to raise those characteristics as a defence to charges requiring objective recklessness.

Although this type of recklessness was generally confined to offences under the Criminal Damage Act 1971, it still caused concern among practitioners and academics alike. It is not surprising perhaps that it was a criminal damage case involving children, who did not think that their actions would lead to the ultimately disastrous consequences, that changed the law. In *R* v *G & R* [2003] 3 WLR 1060—the House of Lords decided that the former *Caldwell* decision should be departed from. Their Lordships held that a person acts recklessly for the purposes of criminal damage on the following basis: a person will be 'reckless' as to circumstances when he/she is aware of a risk that existed or would exist. A person will be 'reckless' as to a result or consequence when he/she is aware of a risk that it would occur and it is, in the circumstances known to him/her, unreasonable to take the risk.

Whilst the House of Lords has concluded (*R* v *Reid* [1992] 1 WLR 793) that the word reckless may not have exactly the same meaning in all statutory provisions (a viewpoint that has caused problems to practitioners and students alike), in offences that can be committed 'recklessly' the test will generally be *subjective*.

The requirements of subjective recklessness can be found in the case of *R* v *Cunningham* [1957] 2 QB 396 and are satisfied in situations where the defendant foresees the consequences of his/her actions as being probable or even possible. In cases requiring subjective recklessness, the fact that the consequences *ought to have been foreseen* by the defendant will not be enough. The most important group of offences where this will be the case is those requiring 'malice' under the Offences Against the Person Act 1861. In such cases the term 'malice' is misleading. What the prosecution will need to show is that the defendant either intended to do harm to the victim or that he/she *foresaw that harm* (though not the extent of that harm) *may be caused but nevertheless went on to take that risk* (*R* v *Savage* [1992] 1 AC 699).

A good operational example of these issues in action can be seen in *D* v *DPP* [2005] Crim LR 962. In that case a police officer attending a domestic incident arrested a man in order to prevent a breach of the peace. During a subsequent struggle the defendant bit the officer on the hand. The magistrates' court convicted the defendant of assaulting the officer in the execution of his duty (**see para. 3.2.13**) on the basis that the biting of the officer had been 'reckless'. The defendant appealed, arguing that a bite could not be reckless; either it was deliberate or it was accidental. The Divisional Court dismissed the appeal and held that the test of recklessness in this case involved the defendant having foreseen the risk that the victim would be subjected to unlawful force and having gone on to take the risk. While the case endorses the view that there can be a reckless 'battery' (**see para. 3.2.4**) the facts of it are not so convincing as, say, an occasion where the defendant causes injury by thrashing his arms around to avoid being handcuffed or by attempting to throw away some property during an arrest.

1.1.4.3 Wilfully

This term implies that a defendant must be shown to have desired the consequences of his/her actions or at least to have foreseen them (subjective recklessness). The term 'wilfully' however is *not* restricted to such occasions and has been taken to include *objective* (*Caldwell*) recklessness (*R* v *Sheppard* [1981] AC 394; *R* v *Newington* (1990) 91 Cr App R 247).

'Wilful' can also mean simply that an action was voluntary, that is, it describes the criminal conduct (*actus reus*) rather than the state of mind (*mens rea*).

1.1.4.4 Dishonestly

The concept of 'dishonesty' is of great importance to a number of mainstream offences, including theft and deception. In proving many of the offences under the Theft Acts 1968 and 1978 you will need to show that the defendant acted dishonestly. This expression is defined for certain purposes within the 1968 Act itself. However, it has also been extended by common law decisions of the courts and it is critical, in dealing with offences requiring proof of dishonesty, that you identify the nature of the state of mind required and the ways in which it can be proved/disproved.

1.1.5 Transferred Malice

The state of mind required for one offence can, on occasions, be 'transferred' from the original target or victim to another. Known generally as the doctrine of 'transferred malice' because it originates from a case involving malicious wounding, the doctrine only operates if the crime remains the same. In other words, a defendant cannot be convicted if he acted with the *mens rea* for one offence but commits the *actus reus* of another offence. For example, in the original case (*R* v *Latimer* (1886) 17 QBD 359) the defendant lashed out with his belt at one person but missed, striking a third party instead. As it was proved that the defendant had the required *mens rea* when he swung the belt, the court held that the same *mens rea* could support a charge of wounding against any other victim injured by the same act. If the *nature of the offence* changes, then the doctrine will not operate. Therefore if a defendant is shown to have thrown a rock at a crowd of people intending to injure one of them, the *mens rea* required for that offence cannot be 'transferred' to an offence of criminal damage if the rock misses them and breaks a window instead. The House of Lords has acknowledged that this doctrine is somewhat arbitrary and is an exception to the general principles of law (*Attorney-General's Reference (No. 3 of 1994)* [1998] AC 245).

The issue of transferred *mens rea* (which is really what this doctrine amounts to) can be important in relation to the liability of accessories. If the principal's intentions are to be extended to an accessory, it must be shown that those intentions were either contemplated and accepted by that person at the time of the offence, or that they were 'transferred' by this doctrine.

EXAMPLE

A person (X) incites another (Y) to assault Z. Y decides to attack a different person instead. X will not be liable for that assault because it was not contemplated or agreed by X. If, however, in trying to assault Z, Y happens to injure a third person inadvertently, the doctrine of 'transferred malice' may result in X being liable for those injuries even though X had no wish for that person to be so injured.

1.2 Criminal Conduct

1.2.1 Introduction

Having considered the concepts that arise out of the relevant state of mind that must exist before a defendant can be found guilty of a criminal offence, the next key element is that of the criminal conduct. Although this may sound an easy concept at first, and many statutory offences spell out exactly the sort of behaviour that will attract liability, there are some important general rules that need to be considered.

For a person to be found guilty of a criminal offence you must show that they:

- acted in a particular way
- failed to act in a particular way (omissions) or
- brought about a state of affairs.

Known as the *actus reus*, this essential characteristic of any offence is the behavioural element.

1.2.2 *Actus Reus*

Mens rea is what a defendant must have had; *actus reus* is what a defendant must have done—or failed to do.

When proving the required *actus reus* you must show:

- that the defendant's conduct was voluntary and
- that it occurred while the defendant still had the requisite *mens rea*.

1.2.2.1 Voluntary Act

Other than in the few specific instances where an 'omission' will suffice (**see para. 1.2.3**), you must generally show that a defendant acted 'voluntarily', that is, by the operation of his/her own free will.

If a person is shoved into a shop window, he/she cannot be said to have damaged it for the purposes of criminal liability, even though he/she was the immediate physical cause of the damage. Similarly, if a person was standing in front of a window waiting to break it and someone came up and pushed that person into the window, the presence of the requisite *mens rea* would still not be enough to attract criminal liability for the resultant damage. In each case, the person being pushed could not be said to be acting of his/her own volition in breaking the window and therefore could not perform the required *actus reus*.

This aspect of voluntariness becomes important, not just when considering offences committed under physical compulsion, but also where the defendant has lost control of his/her own physical actions. Reflexive actions are generally not classed as being willed or voluntary, hence the (limited) availability of the 'defence' of automatism.

Likewise, the *unexpected* onset of a sudden physical impairment (such as severe cramp when driving; actions when sleepwalking) can also render any linked actions 'involuntary'. If the onset of the impairment could reasonably have been foreseen or anticipated (e.g. where someone is prone to blackouts) the defendant's actions may be said to have been willed in the respect that he/she could have prevented the loss of control or at least avoided the situation (e.g. driving) which allowed the consequences to come about.

1.2.2.2 Coincidence with *Mens Rea*

Generally it must be shown that the defendant had the requisite *mens rea* at the time of carrying out the *actus reus*. However, there is no need for that 'state of mind' to remain unchanged throughout the entire commission of the offence. If a person (X) poisons another (Y) intending to kill Y at the time, it will not alter X's criminal liability if X changes his mind immediately after giving the poison or even if X does everything he can to halt its effects (see *R* v *Jakeman* (1983) 76 Cr App R 223). Similarly, if a person 'appropriates' another's property while having the required *mens rea*, giving it back later will not prevent them from committing theft (*R* v *McHugh* (1993) 97 Cr App R 335).

Conversely, if the *actus reus* is a continuing act, as 'appropriation' is, it may begin without any particular *mens rea* at the start but the required 'state of mind' may come later while the *actus reus* is still continuing. If this happens, whereby the *mens rea* 'catches up' with the *actus reus*, the offence is complete.

This principle can be seen in the offence of rape. The sexual intercourse may be consensual at the time it starts but, if that consent is later withdrawn, any continued intercourse will amount to an offence (*Kaitamaki* v *The Queen* [1985] AC 147).

A further illustration can be found in a case where a motorist was being directed to pull his car over to the kerb by a police officer. In doing so, the motorist inadvertently drove onto the officer's foot. Having no *mens rea* at the time of driving onto the officer's foot, the defendant was not at that point guilty of battery. However, once the situation was pointed out to him, the fact that he left the car where it was (the *actus reus*) was then joined by the appropriate *mens rea* and he was convicted of assault (*Fagan* v *Metropolitan Police Commissioner* [1969] 1 QB 439).

1.2.3 Omissions

Criminal conduct is most often associated with *actions*: damaging or stealing property, injuring or deceiving others. In some cases more than one action is required to give rise to criminal liability (e.g. harassment). But occasionally liability is brought about by a failure to act.

Most of the occasions where failure or omission will attract liability are where a *duty to act* has been created. Such a duty can arise from a number of circumstances, the main ones being:

D The creation of a Dangerous situation by the defendant. See, for example, *R* v *Miller* [1983] 2 AC 161 where the defendant, having accidentally started a fire in a house, moved to another room taking no action to counteract the danger he had created.

U Under statute, contract or a person's public 'office'. Examples would be where a police officer failed to intervene to prevent an assault (*R* v *Dytham* [1979] QB 722) or where a crossing keeper omitted to close the gates at a level crossing and a person was subsequently killed by a train (*R* v *Pittwood* (1902) 19 TLR 37).

T Where the defendant has Taken it upon himself/herself to carry out a duty and then fails to do so. Such a duty was taken up by the defendant in *R* v *Stone* [1977] QB 354 when she accepted a duty to care for her partner's mentally-ill sister who subsequently died.

Y In circumstances where the defendant is in a parental relationship with a child or a Young person.

Whether or not there is a sufficient proximity between the defendant and the victim brought about by a duty to act will be a question of law (see generally *R* v *Singh* [1999] Crim LR 582 and *R* v *Khan* [1998] Crim LR 830). A graphic and topical example of where such a duty can be created by the defendant is in the case of a lorry driver smuggling illegal immigrants in the back of his vehicle (*R* v *Wacker* (2003) 2 WLR 374).

In such situations there may be a *duty* to act. Having established such a duty, you must also show that the defendant has *voluntarily* omitted to act as required or that he/she has not done enough to discharge that duty. If a defendant is unable to act (e.g. because someone else has stopped them) or is incapable of doing more because of their own personal limitations, the *actus reus* will *not* have been made out (see *R* v *Reid* [1992] 1 WLR 793).

Some statutory offences are specifically worded to remove any doubt as to whether they can be committed by omission as well as by a positive act (e.g. torture under the Criminal Justice Act 1988, s. 134). Other offences have been held by the courts to be capable of commission by both positive acts and by omission (e.g. false accounting under the Theft Act 1968, s. 17).

The distinction between acts and omissions was considered by the High Court in a case concerning withholding medical treatment from chronically ill patients (*NHS Trust A* v *M* [2001] 2 WLR 942).

An interesting and highly practical issue arose in this area in a case where the defendants' dogs barking in the night were claimed to have caused a neighbour harassment under the Protection from Harassment Act 1997. The defendants argued that their failure to stop the dogs barking could not amount to a 'course of conduct' for the purposes of that Act. The prosecution argued that the defendants incited the dogs to bark and this was more than a mere failure to act. Although the Divisional Court was not prepared to state that inciting dogs in this way could never amount to a course of conduct, the issue of whether failing to stop the dogs' behaviour could support a charge of harassment was not resolved—*R* v *Tafurelli* (2004) unreported.

1.2.4 Causal Link or Chain of Causation

Once the *actus reus* has been proved, you must then show a *causal link* between it and the relevant consequences. That is, you must prove that the consequences would not have happened 'but for' the defendant's act or omission.

In a case of simple criminal damage it may be relatively straightforward to prove this causal link: a defendant throws a brick at a window; the window would not have broken 'but for' the defendant's conduct. Where the link becomes more difficult to prove is when the defendant's behaviour triggers other events or aggravates existing circumstances. For example, in *R* v *McKechnie* [1992] Crim LR 194 the defendant attacked the victim, who was already suffering from a serious ulcer, causing him brain damage. The brain damage prevented doctors from operating on the ulcer which eventually ruptured, killing the victim. The Court of Appeal, upholding the conviction for manslaughter, held that the defendant's criminal conduct had made a significant contribution to the victim's death even though the untreated ulcer was the actual cause of death. In some cases a significant delay can occur between the acts which put in train the criminal consequences. An example is where a defendant transported an accomplice to a place near to the victim's house some 13 hours before the accomplice shot and killed the victim. Despite the delay and despite the fact the accomplice had not fully made up his mind about the proposed shooting at the time he was dropped off by the defendant, there was no intervening event (**see para. 1.2.5**) that diverted or hindered the planned murder—*R* v *Bryce* [2004] 2 Cr App R 35.

In a case which had similar facts to our 'simple damage' example above, the defendant entered the house after throwing the brick through the window. Although the defendant did not attack the occupant, an 87-year-old who died of a heart attack some hours later, the Court of Appeal accepted that there could have been a causal link between the defendant's behaviour and the death of the victim. If so, a charge of manslaughter would be appropriate (*R* v *Watson* [1989] 1 WLR 684).

1.2.5 Intervening Act

The causal link can be broken by a new intervening act provided that the 'new' act is 'free, deliberate and informed' (*R* v *Latif* [1996] 1 WLR 104).

If a drug dealer supplies drugs to another person who then kills himself/herself by overdose, the dealer cannot, without more, be said to have *caused* the death. Death would have been brought about by the deliberate exercise of free will by the user (see *R* v *Armstrong* [1989] Crim LR 149). Although the Court of Appeal has accepted that, under certain circumstances, where a person buys a controlled drug from another and immediately injects it, resulting in his/her death, the supplier *can* attract liability for bringing about the person's death (*R* v *Kennedy* [2005] EWCA Crim 685), this was an odd and much criticised decision. The general view is that the supplier is unlikely to be held liable for *causing* death in such a case unless he/she actually takes a more active part in the administering of the drug (see *R* v *Dias* [2002] Cr App R 5).

If the medical treatment which a victim is given results in their ultimate death, the treatment itself will not normally be regarded as a 'new' intervening act (*R* v *Smith* [1959] 2 QB 35). However, in *R* v *Jordan* (1956) 40 Cr App R 152, where the defendant had stabbed the deceased, it was held that death could not be attributed to the defendant. In this case the actual cause of death had been the administration of a drug (terramycin) after the deceased had shown he was intolerant to it (treatment described as 'palpably wrong' by the court) and when his original wound had nearly healed. *R* v *Jordan* has been described as a very particular case, depending on its exact facts. The basic rule is that an intervening act will not generally break the causal link/chain of causation.

There is also a rule which says defendants must 'take their victims as they find them'. This means that if the victim has a particular characteristic—such as a very thin skull or a very nervous disposition—which makes the consequences of an act against them much more acute, that is the defendant's bad luck. Such characteristics (e.g., where an assault victim died after refusing a blood transfusion on religious grounds (*R* v *Blaue* [1975] 1 WLR 1411)) will not break the causal link.

Actions by the victim will sometimes be significant in the chain of causation such as where a victim of a sexual assault was injured when jumping from her assailant's car (*R* v *Roberts* (1972) 56 Cr App R 95). Where such actions take place, the victim's behaviour will not necessarily be regarded as introducing a new intervening act. If the victim's actions are those which might reasonably be anticipated from any victim in such a situation, there will be no new and intervening act and the defendant will be responsible for the consequences flowing from them. If, however, the victim's actions are done entirely of his/her own volition (as in *Armstrong* above) or where those actions are, in the words of Stuart-Smith LJ 'daft' (see *R* v *Williams* [1992] 1 WLR 380), they *will* amount to a new intervening act and the defendant cannot be held responsible for them.

1.2.6 Principals and Accessories

Once you have established the criminal conduct and the required state of mind, you must identify what degree of involvement the defendant had.

There are two ways of attracting criminal liability for an offence: either as a *principal* or an *accessory*.

A principal offender is one whose conduct has met all the requirements of the particular offence. An accessory is someone who helped in or brought about the commission of the offence. If an accessory 'aids, abets, counsels or procures' the commission of an offence, he/she will be treated by a court in the same way as a principal offender for an indictable offence (Accessories and Abettors Act 1861, s. 8) or for a summary offence (Magistrates' Courts Act 1980, s. 44). The expression 'aid, abet, counsel and procure' is generally used in its entirety when charging a defendant, without separating out the particular element that applies. Generally speaking, the expressions mean as follows:

- aiding = giving help, support or assistance
- abetting = inciting, instigating or encouraging.

Each of these would usually involve the presence of the secondary party at the scene (unless, for example, part of some pre-arranged plan):

- counselling = advising or instructing
- procuring = bringing about.

These activities would generally be expected to take place before the commission of the offence. These are purely guides by which to separate the elements of this concept and will not necessarily apply in all cases. However, if you are trying to show that a defendant *procured* an offence you must show a causal link between his/her conduct and the offence (*Attorney-General's Reference (No. 1 of 1975)* [1975] QB 773). 'Counselling' an offence requires no causal link (*R* v *Calhaem* [1985] QB 808). As long as the principal offender is aware of the 'counsellor's' advice or encouragement, the latter will be guilty as an accessory, even if the principal would have committed the offence anyway (*Attorney-General* v *Able* [1984] QB 795).

1.2.6.1 State of Mind for Accessories

Although the concept of 'state of mind' was addressed in the previous chapter, it is necessary to consider the particular requirements in relation to accessories here.

Generally, the state of mind (*mens rea*) which is needed to convict an accessory is: 'proof of intention to aid as well as of knowledge of the circumstances' (*National Coal Board* v *Gamble* [1959] 1 QB 11 at p. 20). The *minimum* state of mind required of an accessory to an offence is set out in *Johnson* v *Youden* [1950] 1 KB 544. In that case the court held that, before anyone can be convicted of aiding and abetting an offence, he/she must at least know the essential matters that constitute that offence. Therefore the accessory to an offence of drink/driving must at least have been aware that the 'principal' (the driver) had been drinking (see *Smith* v *Mellors and Soar* (1987) 84 Cr App R 279).

There must also be a further mental element, namely an intention to aid the principal. Whether there was such an intention to aid the principal is a question of fact to be decided in the particular circumstances of each case. An example of such a case can be seen in *Gillick* v *West Norfolk & Wisbech Area Health Authority* [1986] AC 112. The case concerned the question as to whether a doctor who prescribed a contraceptive pill for a girl under the age of 16 could be charged with being an accessory to an offence by the girl's partner of having unlawful sexual intercourse.

You can see from this requirement that the wider notions of recklessness and negligence are not enough to convict an accessory.

Occasionally statutes will make specific provision for the state of mind and/or the conduct of accessories and principals. An example can be found in s. 7 of the Protection from Harassment Act 1997.

1.2.6.2 Joint Enterprise

If an accessory is present at the scene of a crime when it is committed, his/her presence may amount to *encouragement* which would support a charge of aiding or abetting. However, mere presence at the scene of a crime will not usually be enough evidence of guilt (see *R* v *Coney* (1882) 8 QBD 534).

Enormous problems have been encountered where one person involved in a joint venture goes beyond that which was agreed or contemplated by the other(s).

EXAMPLE

A person (the 'accessory'), accompanies a friend (the 'principal'), to a public house where the principal intends to attack a third party. When the two arrive at the public house, the principal produces a knife and stabs the third person. Is the accessory liable for the wounding of the victim? The answer will depend on a number of things. The main features that will determine the accessory's liability will be:

- the nature and extent of the offence that was agreed upon and contemplated by the two of them when they set out on their joint enterprise;
- whether the accessory *knew* that the principal had a knife;
- whether the principal used *a different weapon* than the one that the accessory knew about;
- whether the principal *used the knife in a different way* from that agreed upon.

If the accessory knew that the principal intended to attack the victim, but knew nothing about a knife or any intention to stab the victim, the accessory may be liable for the resultant injuries caused by the principal if the joint venture envisaged a physical attack on the third person and the stabbing was simply an 'unusual consequence' arising from the execution of that enterprise (see *R* v *Anderson* [1966] 2 QB 110). If, however, the principal used a different weapon from the one that the accessory knew about or he used it in a wholly different way (e.g. using rope to strangle a victim when the agreed plan was to tie the person up with it), the accessory would not generally be liable for the consequences of the principal's actions (see *R* v *English* [1999] 1 AC 1).

What would be the liability of the accessory if, in the above example, the victim had subsequently died from his injuries? This situation has caused further problems for the courts and there are many authorities setting out the liability of accessories in such cases. The overall conclusion appears to be that, if at the time they set out on their joint enterprise, the accessory realised:

- that the principal *might* kill someone and
- that, when killing, the principal might have the *intention* to kill or
- an intention to cause *grievous bodily harm*

then the accessory *may* be liable for murder (*R* v *Powell* [1999] 1 AC 1), subject to the other considerations in *English*. These evidential issues are fairly complex and will usually be a matter for the Crown Prosecution Service. The Court of Appeal confirmed the law in relation to joint enterprise in *Attorney-General's Reference (No. 3 of 2004)* [2005] EWCA Crim 1882. It was alleged that the defendant had recruited two co-defendants to scare someone with a loaded firearm, but one of the co-defendants subsequently went on to shoot the victim dead. The issue turned on whether the first defendant could be convicted of manslaughter on the facts. The primary question raised by the Attorney-General was whether a secondary party to a joint enterprise was guilty of manslaughter if he had contemplated an unlawful act to frighten the victim and the principal carried out that act with the necessary intention for murder.

The court held that the test was whether the secondary party had foreseen the possibility that the primary party would do what he had done. In this case the act done by the primary party (shooting the victim) was of a fundamentally different character from any act contemplated by the person who had recruited him—he had not foreseen the possibility of *any* harm to the victim, let alone any intentional harm. These principles were in accordance with *Powell* which was to be regarded as representing the law.

In proving joint enterprise in assaults, the intentions of the defendants will be highly relevant, but so too will any foresight of probable or likely consequences. It will not only be necessary to gather any evidence of what harm a defendant or his/her colleagues *intended* to do; it will also be critical to obtain any evidence showing that a defendant envisaged a degree of harm being caused by the others, even though he/she did not wish to bring harm about themselves. The Court of Appeal has held that the issue in joint enterprise generally is not a 'state of mind' or intention, but an objective act which it was contemplated by a defendant would or might be done (*R* v *Day* [2001] Crim LR 984). There are areas of concern in this approach (see the comments in the *Criminal Law Review* accompanying the case report) but, so far as investigations are concerned, the need to establish any available evidence of foresight or contemplation of the consequences is probably the most important point.

The evidential and practical issues become further complicated where the accessory or secondary party is not present during the substantive offence. In such circumstances involved in the example above, the position can be summarised as follows:

> Where the principal (P) relies on acts of the accessory (D) which assist him/her in the preliminary stages of a crime later committed in D's absence, it is necessary to prove

intentional assistance by D in acts which D knew were steps taken by P towards the commission of the crime. Therefore the prosecution must prove:

- an act done by D;
- which *in fact* assisted the later commission of the offence;
- that D did the act deliberately realising that it was capable of assisting the offence;
- that D, at the time of doing the act, contemplated the commission of the offence by P, (e.g. he/she foresaw it as a real or substantial risk or real possibility); and
- that when doing the act D intended to assist P.

(see *R* v *Bryce* [2004] 2 Cr App R 35).

Another practical consideration arises, not from the absence of the accessory, but the failure to trace the *principal.*

If the principal cannot be traced or identified, the accessory may still be liable (see *Hui Chi-ming* v *The Queen* [1992] 1 AC 34). Similarly, an accessory may be convicted of procuring an offence even though the principal is acquitted or has a valid defence for his/her actions. The reasoning for this would seem to be that the principal often supplies the *actus reus* for the accessory's offence. If the accessory also has the required *mens rea*, the offence will be complete and should not be affected by the fact that there is some circumstance or characteristic preventing the principal from being prosecuted.

Additionally, if the accessory had some responsibility and the actual ability to control the actions of the principal, his/her failure to do so may attract liability (e.g. a driving instructor who fails to prevent a learner driver from driving without due care and attention (*Rubie* v *Faulkner* [1940] 1KB 571)).

It is possible for an accomplice to change his/her mind before the criminal act is carried out. However, the exact requirements of making an effective 'withdrawal' before any liability is incurred is unclear. Evidence such as how far the proposed plan had already proceeded before the withdrawal and the amount and nature of any help or encouragement already given by the accessory will be very relevant. Simply fleeing at the last moment because someone was approaching would generally not be enough. In the absence of some overwhelming supervening event, an accessory can only avoid liability for assistance rendered to the principal offender towards the commission of the crime by acting in a way that amounts to the *countermanding* of any earlier assistance such as a withdrawal from the common purpose. Repentance alone, unsupported by any action taken to demonstrate withdrawal, will not be enough (see e.g. *R* v *Becerra* (1975) 62 Cr App R 212 and *R* v *Mitchell* (1999) 163 JP 75).

Particular care needs to be taken when charging defendants with joint enterprise in outbreaks of public disorder (see *R* v *Flounders and Alton* [2002] EWCA Crim 1325).

A person whom the law is intended to protect from certain types of offence cannot be an accessory to such offences committed against them. For example, a girl under 16 years of age is protected (by the Sexual Offences Act 2003) from people having sexual intercourse with her. If a 15-year-old girl allows someone to have sexual intercourse with her she cannot be charged as an accessory to the offence (*R* v *Tyrrell* [1894] 1 QB 710).

1.2.7 Corporate Liability

Companies which are 'legally incorporated' have a legal personality of their own, that is they can own property, employ people and bring law suits: they can therefore commit offences. There are many difficulties associated with proving and punishing criminal conduct by companies. However, companies have been prosecuted for offences of strict liability (**see para. 1.1.2** and *Alphacell Ltd* v *Woodward* [1972] AC 824); offences requiring *mens rea* (*Tesco*

Supermarkets Ltd v *Nattrass* [1972] AC 153); and offences of being an 'accessory' (*R* v *Robert Millar (Contractors) Ltd* [1970] 2 QB 54—aiding and abetting the causing of death by reckless (now dangerous) driving). There are occasions where the courts will accept that the knowledge of certain employees will be extended to the company (see e.g. *Tesco Stores Ltd* v *Brent London Borough Council* [1993] 1 WLR 1037).

Clearly there are some offences that would be conceptually impossible for a legal corporation to commit (e.g. some sexual offences) but, given that companies can be guilty as accessories (see *Robert Millar* above), they may well be capable of aiding and abetting such offences even though they could not commit the offence as a principal.

A company (OLL Ltd) has also been convicted, along with its Managing Director, of manslaughter (following the school canoeing tragedy at Lyme Bay in 1994) (*R* v *Kite* [1996] 2 Cr App R (S) 295). From 6 April 2008, companies can be prosecuted for such offences under the terms of the Corporate Manslaughter and Corporate Homicide Act 2007.

1.3 Incomplete Offences

1.3.1 Introduction

There are circumstances where defendants are interrupted or frustrated in their efforts to commit an offence. Such circumstances might come about as a result of police intervention (e.g. where intelligence suggests that a serious offence is to take place on a given date) or as a result of things not going as the defendants had hoped (e.g. the property which they intended to steal not being where they thought it was). In these and other cases several general offences, often called inchoate or incomplete offences, may be used to ensure that the defendant's conduct does not go unpunished.

1.3.2 Encouraging or Assisting Crime

The common law offence of inciting an offence has been abolished by the Serious Crime Act 2007. Incitement has been replaced by the offences under ss. 44, 45 and 46 of the Act.

OFFENCE: **Intentionally Encouraging or Assisting an Offence—*Serious Crime Act 2007, s. 44***

• Triable in the same way as the anticipated offence • Where the anticipated offence is murder the offence is punishable by life imprisonment • In any other case a person is liable to any penalty for which he would be liable on conviction of the anticipated offence

The Serious Crime Act 2007, s. 44 states:

(1) A person commits an offence if—
  (a) he does an act capable of encouraging or assisting in the commission of an offence; and
  (b) he intends to encourage or assist its commission
(2) But he is not to be taken to have intended to encourage or assist the commission of an offence merely because such encouragement or assistance was a foreseeable consequence of his act.

KEYNOTE

This offence requires the defendant to *intentionally* encourage or assist an offence. As such, s. 44(2) makes it clear that foresight of a consequence is not sufficient to establish intention.

OFFENCE: **Encouraging or Assisting an Offence believing it will be committed—*Serious Crime Act 2007, s. 45***

• Triable in the same way as the anticipated offence • Where the anticipated offence is murder the offence is punishable by life imprisonment • In any other case a person is liable to any penalty for which he would be liable on conviction of the anticipated offence

The Serious Crime Act 2007, s. 45 states:

(1) A person commits an offence if—
  (a) he does an act capable of encouraging or assisting in the commission of an offence; and
  (b) he believes—
    (i) that the offence will be committed; and
    (ii) that his act will encourage or assist its commission.

KEYNOTE

This section creates an offence of encouraging or assisting an offence *believing* it will be committed. The person commits the offence if he does an act capable of encouraging or assisting an offence and believes *both* that the offence will be committed and that his act will encourage or assist its commission.

OFFENCE: **Encouraging or Assisting Offences believing one or more will be committed—*Serious Crime Act 2007, s. 46***

• Triable on Indictment • Where the reference offence is murder the offence is punishable with life imprisonment • In any other case a person is liable to any penalty for which he would be liable on conviction of the reference offence

The Serious Crime Act 2007, s. 46 states:

(1) A person commits an offence if—
  (a) he does an act capable of encouraging or assisting the commission of one or more of a number of offences: and
  (b) he believes—
    (i) that one or more of those offences will be committed (but has no belief as to which); and
    (ii) that his act will encourage or assist the commission of one or more of them.
(2) It is immaterial for the purposes of subsection (1)(b)(ii) whether a person has any belief as to which offence will be encouraged or assisted.

KEYNOTE

Under s. 46, the defendant must do an act capable of encouraging or assisting *one or more offences* believing that one or more offences will be committed and that his act will encourage or assist one or more of them.

General Points

Section 47 of the Act sets out what needs to be proved in order to establish guilt for each of the above offences.

There are some similarities between ss. 44, 45 and 46 and their predecessor, the offence of incitement. For instance, s. 49(1) of the Act states that offences can be committed regardless of whether or not the encouragement or assistance has the effect which the defendant intended or believed it would have.

EXAMPLE

D, a dentist, wishes to sexually assault his patients whilst they are unconscious under anaesthetic. To do so D will need the co-operation of his assistant, V. D puts his idea to V while they are having a drink in a pub, intending to encourage V to take part in the offences. V is outraged and wants nothing to do with D's plan. In this situation, the fact that V is not remotely interested in D's plan and is not encouraged to take part in it will not alter the fact that D has committed an offence under s. 44 of the Act.

A person can be convicted of more than one of these offences (ss. 44, 45 or 46) in relation to the same act (s. 49(3)).

Section 50 of the Act sets out that it will be a defence to the offences under sections 44, 45 and 46 if the person charged with those offences acted reasonably, that is in the circumstances he was aware of, or in the circumstances he reasonably believed existed, it was reasonable for him to act as he did.

Section 51 limits the liability of the offence by setting out in statute the common law exception established in the case of *R v Tyrrell* [1894] 1 QB 710. A person cannot be guilty of the offences in sections 44, 45 and 46 if, in relation to an offence that is a 'protective' offence, the person who does the act capable of encouraging or assisting that offence falls within the category of persons that offence was designed to protect and would be considered as the victim.

EXAMPLE

D is a 12 year old girl and encourages P, a 40 year old man to have sex with her. P does not attempt to have sex with D. D cannot be liable of encouraging or assisting child rape despite the fact that it is her intent that P has sexual intercourse with a child under 13 (child rape) because she would be considered the 'victim' of that offence had it taken place, and the offence of child rape was enacted to protect children under the age of 13.

The offences under sections 44, 45 and 46 do not apply to the offence of corporate manslaughter. This means an individual cannot be guilty of an offence of encouraging or assisting the offence of corporate manslaughter (s. 62 of the Act).

1.3.3 Conspiracy

Conspiracies can be divided into statutory and common law conspiracies.

1.3.3.1 Statutory Conspiracy

OFFENCE: **Statutory Conspiracy—*Criminal Law Act 1977, s. 1***

• Triable on indictment • Where conspiracy is to commit murder, an offence punishable by life imprisonment or any indictable offence punishable with imprisonment where no maximum term is specified—life imprisonment • In other cases, sentence is the same as for completed offence

The Criminal Law Act 1977, s. 1 states:

(1) Subject to the following provisions of this Part of this Act, if a person agrees with any other person or persons that a course of conduct will be pursued which, if the agreement is carried out in accordance with their intentions, either—

(a) will necessarily amount to or involve the commission of any offence or offences by one or more of the parties to the agreement; or
(b) would do so but for the existence of facts which render the commission of the offence or any of the offences impossible,

he is guilty of conspiracy to commit the offence or offences in question.

KEYNOTE

A charge of conspiracy can be brought in respect of an agreement to commit indictable or summary offences. Conspiracy is triable only on indictment even if it relates to a summary offence (in which case the consent of the Director of Public Prosecutions will be required). Offences of conspiracy are committed at the time of the agreement, therefore it is immaterial whether or not the substantive offence is ever carried out.

Agreeing with Another

For there to be a conspiracy there must be an agreement. Therefore there must be at least two people involved. Each conspirator must be aware of the overall common purpose to which they all attach themselves. If one conspirator enters into *separate* agreements with different people, each agreement is a separate conspiracy (*R* v *Griffiths* [1966] 1 QB 589).

A person can be convicted of conspiracy even if the other conspirators are unknown (as to the affect of the acquittal of one party to a conspiracy on the other parties, see the Criminal Law Act 1977, s. 5(8)).

A defendant cannot be convicted of a statutory conspiracy if the only other party to the agreement is:

- his/her spouse (or civil partner)
- a person under 10 years of age
- the intended victim (Criminal Law Act 1977, s. 2(2))

A husband and wife can both be convicted of a statutory conspiracy if they conspire with a third party (not falling into the above categories) (*R* v *Chrastny* [1991] 1 WLR 1381). A person is not guilty of statutory conspiracy if the only other person with whom he agrees is his civil partner. A civil partnership is a same-sex partnership registered under the Civil Partnership Act 2004. The 'end product' of the agreement must be the commission of an offence by *one or more of the parties to the agreement*. Once agreed upon, any failure to bring about the end result or an abandoning of the agreement altogether will not prevent the statutory conspiracy being committed.

Note that if an agreement to commit a *summary offence which is not punishable by imprisonment* is made in contemplation or furtherance of a trade dispute, it must be disregarded (Trade Union and Labour Relations (Consolidation) Act 1992, s. 242).

1.3.3.2 Common Law Conspiracies

OFFENCE: **Conspiracy to Defraud—*Common Law***

- Triable on indictment • Ten years' imprisonment and/or a fine

Conspiracy to defraud involves:

> ... an agreement by two or more [persons] by dishonesty to deprive a person of something which is his or to which he is or would or might be entitled [or] an agreement by two or more by dishonesty to injure some proprietary right [of the victim] ...

(*Scott* v *Metropolitan Police Commissioner* [1975] AC 819).

(See also Blackstone's Criminal Practice 2008, section A6.25.)

KEYNOTE

This offence has been endorsed by senior judges as representing an effective—if not *the* most effective—means of dealing with multiple defendants engaged in a fraudulent course of conduct.

The common law offence of conspiracy to defraud can be divided into two main types. The first is contained in the *dictum* of Viscount Dilhorne in *Scott* above, the second involves a dishonest agreement to *deceive* another into acting in a way that is contrary to his/her duty (see *Wai Yu-Tsang* v *The Queen* [1992] 1 AC 269).

Although the requirement for an agreement between at least two people is the same, this offence is broader than statutory conspiracy. There is no requirement to prove that the end result would amount to the commission of *an offence*, simply that it would result in depriving a person of something under the specified conditions or in injuring his/her proprietary right.

You must show *intent* to defraud a victim (*R* v *Hollinshead* [1985] AC 975).

You must also show that a defendant was dishonest as set out in *R* v *Ghosh* [1982] QB 1053 **(see para. 2.1.3.)**.

Clearly there will be circumstances where the defendant's behaviour will amount to both a statutory conspiracy and a conspiracy to defraud. The Criminal Justice Act 1987, s. 12 makes provision for such circumstances and allows the prosecution to choose which charge to prefer.

Examples of common law conspiracies to defraud include:

- Buffet car staff selling their own home-made sandwiches on British Rail trains thereby depriving the company of the opportunity to sell their own products (*R* v *Cooke* [1986] AC 909).
- Directors agreeing to conceal details of a bank's trading losses from its shareholders (*Wai Yu-tsang* above).
- Making unauthorised copies of commercial films for sale (*Scott* above).

A further example can be found in *R* v *Hussain* [2005] EWCA Crim 1866 where the defendant pleaded guilty to conspiracy to defraud after a widespread abuse of the postal voting system. In that case the defendant, an official Labour party candidate, collected uncompleted postal votes from households and completed them in his own favour.

1.3.4 Attempts

The Criminal Attempts Act 1981, s. 1 states:

(1) If, with intent to commit an offence to which this section applies, a person does an act which is more that merely preparatory to the commission of the offence, he is guilty of attempting to commit the offence.

...

(2) A person may be guilty of attempting to commit an offence to which this section applies even though the facts are such that the commission of the offence is impossible.

(3) In any case where—
  (a) apart from this subsection a person's intention would not be regarded as having amounted to an intent to commit an offence; but
  (b) if the facts of the case had been as he believed them to be, his intention would be so regarded, then, for the purposes of subsection (1) above, he shall be regarded as having had an intent to commit that offence.

(4) This section applies to any offence which, if it were completed, would be triable in England and Wales as an indictable offence, other than—
  (a) conspiracy (at common law or under section 1 of the Criminal Law Act 1977 or any other enactment);
  (b) aiding, abetting, counselling, procuring or suborning the commission of an offence;

(c) offences under section 4(1) (assisting offenders) or 5(1) (accepting or agreeing to accept consideration for not disclosing information about a relevant offence) of the Criminal Law Act 1967.

KEYNOTE

Most attempts at committing criminal offences will be governed by s. 1. Although some statutory exceptions apply, the sentence generally for such attempts will be:

- for murder—life imprisonment
- for indictable offences—the same maximum penalty as the substantive offence
- for either way offences—the same maximum penalty as the substantive offence *when tried summarily.*

If the attempted offence is triable summarily only, it cannot be an offence under s. 1. However, if the only reason the substantive offence is triable summarily is because of a statutory limit imposed in some cases (e.g. criminal damage to property of a low value) the offence can be attempted. Some summary offences include an element of attempt (e.g. drink drive offences).

If the offence attempted is triable only on indictment, the attempt will be triable only on indictment. Similarly, if the offence attempted is an 'either way' offence, so too will the attempt be triable either way (s. 4(1)).

Many other statutory offences contain references to 'attempts', including:

- Theft Act 1968, s. 9 (burglary)
- Firearms Act 1968, s. 17 (using firearm to resist arrest)
- Official Secrets Act 1920, s. 7 (encouraging others to commit offences).

Section 3 of the Criminal Attempts Act 1981 deals with such statutory provisions and they will generally be governed by the same principles as those set out here.

More than Merely Preparatory

A defendant's actions must be shown to have gone beyond mere preparation towards the commission of the substantive offence. Whether the defendant did or not go beyond that point will be a question of fact for the jury/magistrate(s). There is no specific formula used by the courts in interpreting this requirement. An example of where the defendant was held to have done no more than merely preparatory acts was *R* v *Bowles* [2004] EWCA Crim 1608. In that case the defendant had been convicted of several offences involving dishonesty against an elderly neighbour. The neighbour's long-standing will left her estate to charity but, following his arrest, police officers searched the defendant's premises and found a new will, fully complete except for the signature. The defendant and his wife were named as the main beneficiaries and were to inherit the neighbour's house. Although the defendant's son was said to have been heard making reference to the fact that he was going to inherit the house, the 'new' will had been drafted over six months earlier and there was no evidence of any steps to have it executed, nor was there any evidence of it being used. On this basis the Court of Appeal held that the making of the will was no more than merely preparatory and the defendant's conviction for attempting to make a false instrument was quashed. Courts have accepted an approach of questioning whether the defendant had 'embarked on the crime proper' (*R* v *Gullefer* [1990] 1 WLR 1063) but there is no requirement for him/her to have passed a point of no return leading to the commission of the substantive offence. However, to prove an 'attempt' you must show an *intention* on the part of the defendant to commit the substantive offence.

This requirement means that a higher level or degree of *mens rea* may be required to prove an attempt than for the substantive offence. For instance, nothing less than an *intent* to kill can support a charge of attempted murder (*R* v *Whybrow* (1951) 35 Cr App R 141), while in proving the substantive offence, an intention to cause grievous bodily harm will suffice. A defendant's intention may be *conditional*, that is, he/she may only intend to steal from a house if something worth stealing is later found inside. The conditional nature of this intention will not generally prevent the charge of attempt being brought and the defendant's intentions will, in accordance with s. 1(3) above, be judged *on the facts as he/she believed them to be*. However, careful drafting of the charge may be required in cases where there is doubt as to the precise extent of the defendant's knowledge at the time he/she was caught (see *R* v *Husseyn* (1977) 67 Cr App R 131n).

Although 'intent to commit' the offence is required under s. 1(1), there are occasions where a state of mind that falls short of such a precise intention may suffice. For instance, in cases of attempted rape the courts have accepted that recklessness as to whether the victim is consenting was (under the earlier sexual offences legislation) sufficient *mens rea* for attempted rape because it is sufficient for the substantive offence (*R* v *Khan* [1990] 1 WLR 813).

In proving an 'attempt' it is enough to show that a defendant was in one of the states of mind required for the substantive offence and that he/she did his/her best, so far as he/she was able, to do what was necessary for the commission of the full offence (*Attorney-General's Reference (No. 3 of 1992)* [1994] 1 WLR 409).

1.3.4.1 Interfering with Vehicles

OFFENCE: **Interfering with Vehicles—*Criminal Attempts Act 1981, s. 9***

- Triable summarily • Three months' imprisonment and/or a fine

The Criminal Attempts Act 1981, s. 9 states:

(1) A person is guilty of the offence of vehicle interference if he interferes with a motor vehicle or trailer or with anything carried in or on a motor vehicle or trailer with the intention that an offence specified in subsection (2) below shall be committed by himself or some other person.

(2) The offences mentioned in subsection (1) above are—

(a) theft of the motor vehicle or trailer or part of it;

(b) theft of anything carried in or on the motor vehicle or trailer; and

(c) an offence under section 12(1) of the Theft Act 1968 (taking and driving away without consent);

and, if it is shown that a person accused of an offence under this section intended that one of those offences should be committed, it is immaterial that it cannot be shown which it was.

(3)–(4) ...

(5) In this section 'motor vehicle' and 'trailer' have the meanings assigned to them by section 185(1) of the Road Traffic Act 1988.

KEYNOTE

'Interference' is not defined and there are no conclusive cases on the subject at the time of writing. This offence is one of specific intent and you must prove that the defendant interfered with the vehicle, etc. with one of the intentions listed—(note, however, that it is not necessary to show which *particular* intention).

Where a person suspected of committing this offence has any articles with them, the further offence of going equipped (s. 25 of the Theft Act 1968) should be considered. The above offence is a specified offence for the purposes of the Vehicles (Crime) Act 2001, s. 3(4)(b).

1.3.5 Impossibility

Practical difficulties have arisen where, despite the best (or worst) efforts of the defendant, his/her ultimate intention has been impossible (such as trying to extract cocaine from a powder which is, unknown to the defendant, only talc). Impossibility is now far clearer following the Criminal Attempts Act 1981 and its interpretation through the courts. It differs however in some incomplete offences.

EXAMPLE

Taking an example of someone who tries to handle goods which are not in fact stolen, the following rules would apply:

- A defendant could *not* be guilty of inciting another, nor of common law conspiracy to defraud in these circumstances. The *physical* impossibility of what they sought to do would preclude such a charge.
- A defendant *could* be guilty of a statutory conspiracy with another to handle 'stolen' goods and also of attempting to handle 'stolen' goods under these circumstances. The physical impossibility would not preclude such charges as a result of the Criminal Attempts Act 1981 and the House of Lords' decision in *R* v *Shivpuri* [1987] AC 1. The only form of impossibility which would preclude liability under the Criminal Attempts Act 1981 or for a statutory conspiracy would be the *legal* impossibility.

1.4 The Regulation of Investigatory Powers Act 2000

1.4.1 Introduction

The 2000 Act addresses the interception of communications and the covert acquisition of information about people. The Act is intended to make sure that these activities, when carried out by public authorities, are subjected to a robust statutory framework which allows for proper independent control and monitoring. A further reason for the legislation is the need for such practices to conform to the European Convention on Human Rights, particularly since the former regulatory provisions were held to be inadequate in this regard (see *Khan* v *United Kingdom* [2000] Crim LR 684).

The 2000 Act appears in five parts:

- part I—the interception of communications and the acquisition/disclosure of data;
- part II—surveillance and use of covert human intelligence sources (informers, agents and undercover officers);
- part III—the investigation of electronic data (e.g. encrypted files);
- part IV—the supervision of investigatory powers and Codes of Practice;
- part V—miscellaneous provisions.

1.4.2 Purpose of the Act

The main purpose of the 2000 Act is to control the use of surveillance and Covert Human Intelligence Sources operations by public authorities. Breach of the Act's provisions in a policing context will have three main consequences. The first consequence is that any evidence obtained may be excluded by any court or tribunal as being unfair. The second consequence is that the breach may give rise to proceedings under the relevant police conduct regulations. A third consequence is that a person may make a claim before the Investigatory Powers Tribunal in London. Such a claim can generally be made where the conduct complained of occurred within one year of the complaint, though the Tribunal may consider claims outside this time limit. Claims made to the Tribunal will be separated into those relating to an alleged infringement of a person's human rights by the intelligence services, the police and HM Revenue and Customs and those falling into broader, non-human-rights cases against other public agencies. The Tribunal will investigate whether the relevant authority has carried out any activities in relation to the complainant, their communications or property and, if so, whether the proper authorities were obtained. The Tribunal will then consider whether the complaint or claim is justified and will advise the person whether or not it has found in their favour as soon as possible. If it finds in the person's favour, the Tribunal *may* provide a summary of its findings and, after hearing representations from the person, order such remedial action as it considers appropriate (see generally the Investigatory Powers Tribunal Rules 2000 (SI 2000/2665)). Leaflets advising people how to bring a claim before a Tribunal are available from HMSO.

On a further practical note, most, if not all, police services have an identified bureau or department that deals centrally with the procedures under the 2000 Act and any queries as to the practical implementation of what follows in this section should be directed to them. Under s. 71 of the Act, the Secretary of State must draw up Codes of Practice and these must be taken into account by anyone exercising powers or authority given by the Act (s. 72). Breach of the Codes of Practice is not of itself an offence but the Codes will be admissible in evidence. Although the rest of this chapter sets out some of the key *legal* features, the Codes of Practice make significant additions (particularly in the requirements for authorisation levels) to the practical implementation of the Act and should be referred to in any practical context.

1.4.3 Independence and Safeguards

Taking the regulatory framework first, part IV of the 2000 Act provides for a number of independent public appointments, giving the relevant postholders clear duties and powers. The Chief Surveillance Commissioner and the Interception Commissioner are among the key postholders tasked with ensuring the proper supervision of the Act and currently these posts are held by very senior judges. Other appointments include ordinary and assistant Surveillance Commissioners and these posts will generally be held by circuit judges or their equivalent. Part IV also sets up a tribunal with a very wide remit to consider, among other things, complaints arising from the application of the Act.

1.4.4 Surveillance and Human Intelligence Sources

Part II of the 2000 Act sets up a system for the authorisation and monitoring of various methods of surveillance and the use of 'covert human intelligence sources'. These activities, which are a significant feature of modern crime management, were formerly governed by agreed codes of conduct and guidelines. Now, in the wake of the Human Rights Act 1998, they have been placed on a firm statutory footing. Failure to follow the statutory requirements will render the relevant public authority liable to an action for breaching the 1998 Act and will also risk any evidence that has been obtained as a result being excluded by the courts.

Part II deals with three main types of activity by the police (and other investigators), namely:

- covert human intelligence sources
- directed surveillance and
- intrusive surveillance (s. 26(1)).

Although only the first of these expressly uses the word 'covert' for the nature of the activity, it is relevant to *all three* of these areas. Part II is concerned with *covert* activity and so, as a general rule, if it is not covert, it is not covered.

Some law enforcement activities fall outside the scope of the Act—an example is 'property interference' which is a very intrusive form of intelligence gathering such as attaching listening devices within people's homes. This type of activity is covered by part III of the Police Act 1997 and is beyond the scope of this Manual.

1.4.5 Covert Human Intelligence Sources

The 2000 Act introduces the concept of a 'covert human intelligence source' (CHIS). As with the legislation regulating surveillance (see below), it is the *covert* nature of this type of activity that the Act is concerned with. This is because of the effect of such activity on an individual's rights under the European Convention *when carried out by public authorities* (e.g. the police). As the decided cases show, the use of human intelligence sources has been a significant feature of crime detection and management for many years. However, the various types of activity involving informers, test purchasers and undercover operatives have not been subjected to open statutory regulation. The lack of clear legal regulation of such activity raises the risk of incompatibility with the European Convention and, with the arrival of the Human Rights Act 1998, a robust statutory framework was needed if the activities of the police and other agencies in this area were to avoid fundamental challenge. It is worth noting that, apart from the many other considerations of using CHIS, the police owe a duty to take reasonable care to avoid unnecessary disclosure to the general public of information which an informant has given to them—*Swinney* v *Chief Constable of Northumbria Police (No. 2)* (1999) *The Times*, 25 May.

1.4.5.1 What is a CHIS?

Broadly, a covert human intelligence source is someone who establishes or maintains a relationship with another person for the *covert* purpose of:

- obtaining information
- providing access to information

or who *covertly* discloses information obtained by the use of such a relationship.

The full definition is set out in s. 26(8) of the 2000 Act. Clearly this definition would cover the types of police operation involved in the decided cases. A purpose is 'covert' here only if the relationship (and the subsequent disclosure of information) is conducted in a manner that is calculated to ensure that one of the parties is unaware of that purpose (see s. 26(9)). Therefore the definition would not usually apply to members of the public generally supplying information to the police. Similarly, people who have come across information in the ordinary course of their jobs who suspect criminal activity (such as bank staff, local authority employees, etc.) do not have a covert relationship with the police simply by passing on information. Great care will be needed, however, if the person supplying the information is asked by the police to do something further in order to develop or enhance it. Any form of direction or tasking by the police in this way could make the person a CHIS and thereby attract all the statutory provisions and safeguards.

Practically there are two broad areas to be considered when considering covert human intelligence sources: 'use' of a CHIS and acting as a CHIS. Both areas are strictly controlled by the legislation and require the relevant authorisation if they are to be lawful. 'Using' a CHIS includes inducing, asking or assisting someone to act as such and obtaining information by means of such a source (s. 26(7)(b)).

Generally, covertly recording conversations and other personal information about a particular person will amount to some form of 'surveillance' (and therefore will be governed by the strict rules regulating such operations: see below). However, such use of a CHIS will not amount to 'surveillance' (s. 48(3)).

1.4.5.2 Who can authorise a CHIS?

Section 27 of the 2000 Act provides that activity involving a CHIS will be lawful for all purposes if it is carried out in accordance with a properly granted authorisation. Such authorisation can cover activity in the United Kingdom or elsewhere.

The people who can grant authorisations for a CHIS are prescribed by s. 30 and the relevant order(s) made by the Secretary of State. The power to authorise the use of a CHIS extends to public authorities far beyond the police (see sch. 1 to the Act). The Regulation of Investigatory Powers (Directed Surveillance and Covert Human Intelligence Sources) Order 2003 (SI 2003/3171), as amended, sets out the relevant people who can authorise the activities of a CHIS. The schedule to the Order identifies the relevant roles and ranks of people in a whole series of public authorities, from the Serious Organised Crime Agency to the Egg Marketing Inspectorate! In the case of police services in England and Wales, the relevant rank is superintendent and above. However, where

- it is not reasonably practicable
- to have the application considered
- by someone of that rank in the same organisation
- having regard to the urgency of the case

then an inspector may generally give the relevant authorisation (see r. 6 of the Order). As with other parts of the Act, however, the Codes of Practice place further restrictions on this area and must be consulted. For example, in the case of a juvenile CHIS or a situation where the CHIS may obtain confidential material, the Code does not allow an inspector to give the relevant authority. Given that this issue will most commonly arise where the police are trying to adduce evidence obtained by a CHIS, it will normally fall to the officer seeking the authorisation to prove that all the above ingredients were in fact present.

1.4.5.3 How long will an authorisation last?

Unless it is renewed, the authorisation given by a superintendent will ordinarily cease to have effect after 12 months beginning on the day that it was granted (s. 43(3)(b)). If that authorisation was given orally by the superintendent in an urgent case, it will only last for 72 hours unless renewed (s. 43(3)(a)(i)).

Where the case was urgent and the authority was given by an inspector, it will cease to have effect 72 hours later unless renewed (s. 43(3)(a)).

Special provisions exist where the CHIS is under 18 (see below).

A single authorisation can cover more than one regulated activity (e.g. the use of surveillance—see below—and the use of a CHIS) but they operate independently of each other. This means that when one authorisation lapses, any other authorisation made at the same time does not necessarily end as well.

1.4.5.4 When and how can a CHIS be used?

A designated person must not authorise any activity by a CHIS unless he/she believes it is necessary:

- for the purpose of preventing or detecting crime or of preventing disorder
- in the interests of national security, public safety or the economic well-being of the United Kingdom

- for the purposes of protecting health or collecting or assessing any tax, duty, etc.
- for any other purpose specified by an order made by the Secretary of State

and that to do so is proportionate to what is sought to be achieved (s. 29).

It will not be enough for a designated person to show that he or she thought the use of a CHIS would be very useful or productive in achieving one of the above purposes; he/she must *believe* that is both *necessary* and *proportionate* to the legitimate objective of the operation. Both the requirements for necessity and proportionality are key features of the European Convention. In *R* v *Winter* [2007] WLR (D) 314 it was held the police must act within the statutory provisions and not go beyond what was acceptable. Police conduct that brought about state-created crime was not acceptable except where the accused took the opportunity to break the law of his/her own free will, unless that conduct brought the administration of justice into disrepute.

Generally, the authorisation must be given in writing but, in urgent cases involving superintendents' authority, it may be given orally (s. 43(1)).

In addition to the requirements surrounding authorisation, the 2000 Act makes provisions for the independent management and supervision of a CHIS. A Code of Practice, together with a number of statutory instruments set out clear guidelines for the control and monitoring of CHIS activities and the keeping of records (see, for example, the Regulation of Investigatory Powers (Source Records) Regulations 2000 (SI 2000/2725)). These provisions set out detailed requirements which replace any former rules governing the recruitment and handling of informants. This regulatory framework sets out specific conditions in relation to the deployment of different types of CHIS, from undercover operatives who change their entire identity in order to infiltrate criminal organisations, to 'decoys' who have no direct communication with suspects.

The Code of Practice sets out the requirements of key personnel in the recruitment and management of CHIS such as *handlers* (broadly the person dealing with, directing, monitoring and recording the activities of the CHIS) and *controllers* (the person with the relevant experience who oversees the use of the CHIS); it also defines some core activity that will be caught by the legislation such as the 'tasking' and 'cultivation' of a CHIS.

In addition, the Code sets out the form and content of the records that must be kept when applying for, authorising, using and maintaining a relationship with a CHIS. Among other things, these records will contain the confidential details of the CHIS's true identity, their given name or reference and a risk assessment of their deployment. Details of payments or rewards made along with all information provided by the CHIS must also be recorded.

Very strict controls have been put in place where the CHIS is under 18 years of age (see the Regulation of Investigatory Powers Act (Juveniles) Order 2000 (SI 2000/2793)). One such control is the time for which a written authorisation will last; in the case of a juvenile it is reduced from 12 months to one month. Further restrictions are imposed by the Code of Practice.

This discussion is merely a summary of the key aspects of this legislation. To find the full extent of the powers and duties under part II, the statutory text should be used, along with the relevant Code of Practice in force at the time.

1.4.6 Covert Surveillance

Along with the deployment of CHIS, covert surveillance has become a vital method of obtaining evidence and intelligence in the reduction of crime and the investigation of offences. Surveillance will only be covert for the purposes of part II of the 2000 Act if it is carried out in a manner that is calculated to ensure that people subject to it are unaware that it is (or might be) taking place (see s. 26(9)). Surveillance includes monitoring, observing, listening to and recording people and their conversations, activities and communications (see s. 48(2)). So, if the police are monitoring a person's movements and are trying to do it without that person knowing, the activities will usually amount to 'covert' surveillance. General monitoring of a particular area such as a shopping precinct by CCTV will not usually be covert and therefore will not be caught by the provisions of part II. There are, however, exceptions (see below). The proper use of covert TV detector equipment is neither directed nor intrusive surveillance (s. 26(6)).

1.4.6.1 Directed surveillance

It can be seen from s. 26(1) that there are two particular types of surveillance for the purposes of part II—'directed' and 'intrusive'. It is clear from the wording of s. 26 that surveillance must be one or the other; it cannot be both. Why does it matter? Because the controls surrounding *intrusive* surveillance are far tighter than those imposed on *directed* surveillance. If surveillance is:

- covert (but not 'intrusive'—see below)
- for the purposes of a specific investigation or specific operation
- likely to result in the obtaining of private information about a person (including information about their family life)
- whether or not that person has been specifically identified for the purposes of the investigation/operation, and
- not carried out in immediate response to events/circumstances where it would not be reasonably practicable to seek prior authorisation

it will generally be 'directed' surveillance (s. 26(2)).

Therefore, if in the example cited above, the police *specifically* use the CCTV camera in connection with a planned operation or they are covertly filming an area in a way that is likely to result in the obtaining of private information about someone, these may amount to directed surveillance. On the other hand, if a police officer in immediate pursuit of a suspect conceals himself/herself behind an obstacle in order to watch that person briefly, this would not amount to directed surveillance—because the activity was carried out in immediate response to events/circumstances where it would not have been reasonably practicable to seek prior authorisation.

Note that the *use* of CCTV footage, even if lawfully obtained in the first instance, can potentially give rise to a serious infringement of a person's right to private and family life (under article 8 of the European Convention) and its disclosure should be carefully considered in every case (see *Peck* v *United Kingdom* (Application No. 44647/98) ECHR [2003] EMLR 15).

The interception of a communication in the course of its transmission by a postal or telecommunication system will be 'directed' surveillance if the communication is sent or intended to be received by someone who has consented to its interception and there is no interception warrant (as to which, see below) (s. 48(4)). However, the use of a CHIS (see above) to record or obtain information will not usually amount to 'surveillance' (s. 48(3)).

1.4.6.2 Authorising directed surveillance

Directed surveillance must be authorised by a designated person (see below) and the authorisation can cover activity in the United Kingdom or elsewhere. The person must not grant the authorisation unless he/she believes that it is *proportionate* to what is sought to be achieved and *necessary* on the specified grounds (s. 28). These specified grounds are the same as those for 'communications data' (see s. 22) with the exception that there is no provision for emergency actions.

The people who can grant authorisations for directed surveillance are prescribed by s. 30 and the relevant order(s) made by the Secretary of State. The power to authorise directed surveillance extends to other public authorities (see sch. 1 to the 2000 Act). The Regulation of Investigatory Powers (Directed Surveillance and Covert Human Intelligence Sources) Order 2003 (SI 2003/3171) as amended, sets out the relevant roles and ranks of the people in those public authorities who can authorise directed surveillance. In the case of police services, the relevant rank will generally be superintendent and above. However, where it is not reasonably practicable:

- to have the application considered
- by someone of that rank in the same organisation
- having regard to the urgency of the case

then an inspector may give the relevant authorisation (see r. 6 of the Order).

Authorisations must generally be made in writing but, in urgent cases, a superintendent may give an oral authorisation (s. 43(1)(a)).

Additional procedural safeguards are made by the Codes of Practice. For instance, if the material sought by the surveillance is subject to legal privilege, is confidential personal information or some journalistic material, the authority of the relevant chief officer will be needed.

1.4.6.3 How long will an authorisation last?

Unless it is renewed, the authorisation given by a superintendent will ordinarily cease to have effect after three months beginning on the day that it was granted (s. 43(3)(c)). If that authorisation was given orally by the superintendent in an urgent case, it will only last for 72 hours unless renewed (s. 43(3)(a)(i)).

Where the case was urgent and the authority was given by an inspector, it will cease to have effect 72 hours later unless renewed (s. 43(3)(a)).

1.4.6.4 Intrusive surveillance

Intrusive surveillance is broadly what it says—surveillance activity that immediately intrudes on someone's private life (as protected by article 8 of the European Convention). The statutory regulation of this activity is concerned as much with the intrusive *effects* of such surveillance as the means by which they are carried out and is designed to keep such intrusions by public authorities to an absolute minimum. If surveillance is:

- covert,
- carried out in relation to anything taking place on any *residential premises* or in any *private vehicle*, and
- involves the presence of an individual on the premises or in the vehicle, or is carried out by means of a surveillance device

it will generally be 'intrusive' surveillance (s. 26(3)).

The definition of residential premises extends much wider than a conventional home. Covert rural surveillance operations and the use of specialist devices in houses or hotel rooms will generally fall into the category of intrusive surveillance. In addition to the activities authorised under part II of the 2000 Act, the Police Act 1997 makes further provision governing the interference with property for the purposes of evidence/intelligence.

These highly specialised areas of property interference are beyond the scope of this Manual.

The elements of intrusive surveillance listed above require the presence of people or devices on the relevant premises/vehicle. However, if the surveillance:

- involves a surveillance device and
- relates to activities taking place on residential premises or in private vehicles
- but without the device being present on the premises or in, on or under the vehicle

it will still be 'intrusive' if that device *consistently* provides information of the same quality and detail as might be expected from a device that was actually present on the premises or in the vehicle (s. 26(5)). An example would be long-range audio equipment monitoring conversations or powerful lenses used to watch people inside a house and giving the same quality and detail of image as if a camera had been placed in the premises. This is in keeping with the aims of part II of the Act in this area, namely to minimise the intrusive effects of such surveillance on people's legitimate right to conduct their private and family life without interference from the State.

Surveillance carried out by means of a device for the purpose of providing information about the location of a vehicle (e.g. a tracking device) is not 'intrusive' (s. 26(4)(a)).

1.4.6.5 Authorising intrusive surveillance

Given the type of activity that is covered by this category, the restrictions on its authorisation are very tight. In addition, many types of activity under this heading will involve applications for 'multiple' authorisations and specialist advice must be sought.

Generally, the person who will authorise intrusive surveillance by the intelligence services, the armed forces and other specified bodies is the Secretary of State. In relation to the police (including the armed services police) the authority will be sought from senior authorising officers. Broadly these will be chief officers, the Commissioners/Assistant Commissioners of the Metropolitan and City of London Police and the Director-General of the Serious Organised Crime Agency (SOCA) (s. 32). Provision is also made for authorisations by designated deputies in some cases. In keeping with the tenor of the Act, these officers must not grant the relevant authorisation unless they believe that it is necessary and proportionate to do so:

- in the interests of national security;
- for the purpose of preventing or detecting 'serious crime', for example, offences for which a person aged 21 or over could reasonably expect to be sentenced to at least three years' imprisonment on his/her first offence, or offences resulting in substantial financial gain, involving the use of violence or a large number of people pursuing a common purpose (s. 81(3));
- for the purpose of safeguarding the economic well-being of the United Kingdom.

These are very similar to the grounds on which an interception warrant may be authorised (see below). The 2000 Act makes detailed provision for the recording and notification of authorisations. Anyone granting a police, SOCA or Revenue and Customs authorisation for intrusive surveillance must notify a Surveillance Commissioner (as to which, see above) in writing as soon as reasonably practicable (s. 35). This is because, except in urgent cases, the authorisation will not take effect until the Surveillance Commissioner has approved it and given written notification to that effect to the authorising officer (s. 36). The purpose behind this process is to make the system open to independent scrutiny and monitoring, largely in satisfaction of the requirements of the Human Rights Act 1998.

Surveillance Commissioners can quash or revoke authorisations and order the destruction of certain records and materials obtained by intrusive surveillance. Senior authorising officers may appeal against decisions of Surveillance Commissioners to the Chief Surveillance Commissioner.

As in the case of directed surveillance, authorisations last for three months and urgent authorisations granted, for example, by an Assistant Chief Constable last for 72 hours. Authorisations can be renewed before they cease to have effect provided that the criteria for authorisation are still satisfied.

1.5 Entry, Search and Seizure

1.5.1 Introduction

Police powers to enter premises, search them and seize evidence and property are governed mainly by the Police and Criminal Evidence Act 1984 and Code B (**see appendix 2**). The 1984 Act covers entry, search and seizure both with and without a warrant.

1.5.1.1 Officer in Charge

Whenever premises are to be searched under the provisions of Code B, one officer must be appointed to act as the officer in charge of the search (para. 2.10). The duties of this officer (who will normally, but not always, be the most senior officer present—see Note 2F) are set out throughout the Code. Searches carried out by employees designated under the Police Reform Act 2002 are also subject to the provision of Code B (para. 2.11).

1.5.1.2 Persons Searched during Search of Premises

Where a *person* is searched during a search of premises without being arrested, that search should take place in accordance with Code A.

1.5.1.3 Application to Claim Property

Any person claiming property seized by the police generally may make an application to the magistrates' court under the Police Property Act 1897 and should be advised of this procedure (Code B, Note 7A). There are special provisions where the property has been seized under the extended powers of the Criminal Justice and Police Act 2001 (**see para. 1.5.6**).

1.5.2 Powers of Search and Seizure under Warrant

There are many statutes which make provision for a court to issue a search warrant to police officers and other investigators, many of which are covered within this Manual under the relevant headings. Some non-police investigators enjoy specific powers based upon amended versions of the following provisions (see e.g. the Police and Criminal Evidence Act 1984 (Department of Trade and Industry Investigators) Order 2002 (SI 2002/2326)).

The application for and execution of warrants is governed by the 1984 Act, which was amended by the Serious Organised Crime and Police Act 2005, and the Codes of Practice. The amendments made by the 2005 Act related to the issue of warrants to search premises and seize evidence. It also introduced an extension to the specific premises warrant to cover more than one set of premises and provided new safeguards for applications for search warrants. The Codes of Practice do not affect any directions in a search warrant or order requiring seized items to be handed over to the police or other authority (Code B, para. 2.6).

1.5.2.1 Application for Warrant

Section 15 of the Police and Criminal Evidence Act 1984 states:

(1) This section and section 16 below have effect in relation to the issue to constables under any enactment, including an enactment contained in an Act passed after this Act, of warrants to enter and search premises; and an entry on or search of premises under a warrant is unlawful unless it complies with this section and section 16 below.
(2) Where a constable applies for any such warrant, it shall be his duty—
(a) to state—
(i) the ground on which he makes the application;
(ii) the enactment under which the warrant would be issued; and
(iii) if the application is for a warrant authorising entry and search on more than one occasion, the ground on which he applies for such a warrant, and whether he seeks a warrant authorising an unlimited number of entries, or (if not) the maximum number of entries desired;
(b) to specify the matters set out in subsection (2A) below; and
(c) to identify, so far as is practicable, the articles or persons to be sought.
(2A) The matters which must be specified pursuant to subsection (2)(b) above are—
(a) if the application relates to one or more sets of premises specified in the application each set of premises which it is desired to enter and search; and
(b) if the application relates to any premises occupied or controlled by a person specified in the application—
(i) as many sets of premises which it is desired to enter and search as it is reasonably practicable to specify;
(ii) the person who is in occupation or control of those premises and any others which it is desired to enter and search;
(iii) why it is necessary to search more premises than those specified under sub-paragraph (i); and
(iv) why it is not reasonably practicable to specify all the premises which it is desired to enter and search.
(3) An application for such a warrant shall be made ex parte and supported by an information in writing.
(4) The constable shall answer on oath any question that the justice of the peace or judge hearing the application asks him.
(5) A warrant shall authorise an entry on one occasion only unless it specifies that it authorises multiple entries.
(5A) If it specifies that it authorises multiple entries, it must also specify whether the number of entries authorised is unlimited, or limited to a specified maximum.
(6) A warrant—
(a) shall specify—
(i) the name of the person who applies for it;
(ii) the date on which it is issued;
(iii) the enactment under which it is issued;
(iv) each set of premises to be searched, or (in the case of an all premises warrant) the person who is in occupation or control of premises to be searched, together with any premises under his occupation or control which can be specified and which are to be searched; and
(b) shall identify, so far as is practicable, the articles or persons to be sought.
(7) Two copies shall be made of a warrant (see section 8(1A)(a) above) which specifies only one set of premises and does not authorise multiple entries; and as many copies as are reasonably required may be made of any other kind of warrant.
(8) The copies shall be clearly certified as copies.

KEYNOTE

Sections 15 and 16 (see below) apply to *all* warrants to enter and search premises, including those issued to and executed by an Investigating Officer designated under sch. 4 to the Police Reform Act 2002.

'Premises' include any place, and in particular, (a) any vehicle, vessel, aircraft or hovercraft; (b) any offshore installation; (c) any renewable energy installation; (d) any tent or moveable structure (s. 23).

Section 15 has been amended as a result of changes introduced by the Serious Organised Crime and Police Act 2005, and sets out the new safeguards for applications for search warrants. This new s. 15 sets out what must be included in an application for a 'specific premises warrant' or an 'all premises warrant'. In particular, the applicant must set out the grounds on which a multiple entry warrant has been sought.

If the provisions of these sections are not complied with, any entry and search made under a warrant will be unlawful. Although the officers executing the warrant may have some protection from personal liability where there has been a defect in the *procedure* by which the warrant was issued, failure to follow the requirements of ss. 15 and 16 may result in the exclusion of any evidence obtained under the warrant. The details of the extent of the proposed search should be made clear in the application and the officer swearing the warrant out must be prepared to answer *any* questions put to him/her on oath under s. 15(4). Many courts will go into background detail about the particular premises, or part of the premises, and who is likely to be present on the premises at the time the warrant is executed (e.g. children). The action to be taken in relation to the swearing out of a warrant is set out in PACE Code B, para. 3.

Applications for all search warrants must be made with the written authority of an officer of at least the rank of inspector (Code B, para. 3.4). However, in cases of urgency where no such officer is 'readily available', the senior officer on duty may authorise the application.

If an application for a warrant is refused, no further application can be made unless it is supported by additional grounds.

Details of the information needed in applying for a warrant are set out at Code B, para. 3.6. This paragraph makes provision for the warrant to authorise other people to be present during the search (para. 3.6 (f)) but such a person has no authority to force entry, to search for or seize property (Note 3C).

1.5.2.2 Execution of Warrant

Section 16 of the Police and Criminal Evidence Act 1984 states:

(1) A warrant to enter and search premises may be executed by any constable.

(2) Such a warrant may authorise persons to accompany any constable who is executing it.

(2A) A person so authorised has the same powers as the constable whom he accompanies in respect of—

(a) the execution of the warrant, and

(b) the seizure of anything to which the warrant relates.

(2B) But he may exercise those powers only in the company, and under the supervision, of a constable.

(3) Entry and search under a warrant must be within three months from the date of its issue.

(3A) If the warrant is an all premises warrant, no premises which are not specified in it may be entered or searched unless a police officer of at least the rank of inspector has in writing authorised them to be entered.

(3B) No premises may be entered or searched for the second or any subsequent time under a warrant which authorises multiple entries unless a police officer of at least the rank of inspector has in writing authorised that entry to those premises.

(4) Entry and search under a warrant must be at a reasonable hour unless it appears to the constable executing it that the purpose of a search may be frustrated on an entry at a reasonable hour.

(5) Where the occupier of premises which are to be entered and searched is present at the time when a constable seeks to execute a warrant to enter and search them, the constable—

(a) shall identify himself to the occupier and, if not in uniform, shall produce to him documentary evidence that he is a constable;

(b) shall produce the warrant to him; and

(c) shall supply him with a copy of it.

(6) Where—
  (a) the occupier of such premises is not present at the time when a constable seeks to execute such a warrant; but
  (b) some other person who appears to the constable to be in charge of the premises is present, subsection (5) above shall have effect as if any reference to the occupier were a reference to that other person.

(7) If there is no person present who appears to the constable to be in charge of the premises, he shall leave a copy of the warrant in a prominent place on the premises.

(8) A search under a warrant may only be a search to the extent required for the purpose for which the warrant was issued.

(9) A constable executing the warrant shall make an endorsement on it stating—
  (a) whether the articles or persons sought were found; and
  (b) whether any articles were seized, other than articles which were sought; and

unless the warrant is a warrant specifying one set of premises only, he shall do so separately in respect of each set of premises entered and searched, which he shall in each case state in the endorsement.

(10) A warrant shall be returned to the appropriate person mentioned in subsection (10A) below—
  (a) when it has been executed; or
  (b) in the case of a specific premises warrant which has not been executed, or an all premises warrant, or any warrant authorising multiple entries, upon the expiry of the period of three months referred to in subsection (3) above or sooner.

(10A) The appropriate person is—
  (a) if the warrant was issued by a justice of the peace, the designated officer for the local justice area in which the justice was acting when he issued the warrant;
  (b) if it was issued by a judge, the appropriate officer of the court from which he issued it.

KEYNOTE

Although s. 16 allows for other people to be included in the warrant, authorising them to accompany the officer, some warrants *require* the presence of other people when a warrant is executed (e.g. under s. 135 of the Mental Health Act 1983).

Section 16 was amended as a result of the changes made by the Serious Organised Crime and Police Act 2005. Note that under s. 16(3B), where a warrant authorises multiple entries, any subsequent entries must be authorised in writing by an officer of the rank of inspector or above.

Failure to comply with the requirements under s. 16 will make the entry and subsequent seizure of property unlawful. Therefore, where officers failed to provide the occupier of the searched premises with a copy of the warrant (under s. 16(5)(c)), they were obliged to return the property seized during the search (*R* v *Chief Constable of Lancashire, ex parte Parker* [1993] Crim LR 204).

Very minor departures from the letter of the warrant, however, will not render any search unlawful (see *Attorney-General of Jamaica* v *Williams* [1998] AC 351).

If the execution of the warrant is likely to have an adverse effect on community relations, the community liaison officer must be informed unless the case is urgent, in which case that officer must be advised as soon as practicable after the search—see Code B, paras 3–5.

Code B goes on to make further provisions for the execution of the warrant.

If a warrant itself is invalid for some reason, any entry and subsequent seizure made under it are unlawful (*R* v *Central Criminal Court and British Railways Board, ex parte AJD Holdings Ltd* [1992] Crim LR 669). After a warrant has been executed, or if it has not been used within three months (or sooner) from its date of issue, it must be returned to the designated officer for the local justice area in which the justice of the peace issued the warrant, or where it was issued by a judge to the appropriate officer of the court from which it was issued (s. 16 (10) and (10A)).

1.5.2.3 Search Warrants for Indictable Offences

Section 8 of the Police and Criminal Evidence Act 1984 states:

(1) If on an application made by a constable a justice of the peace is satisfied that there are reasonable grounds for believing—
  (a) that an indictable offence has been committed; and
  (b) that there is material on premises mentioned in subsection (1A) below which is likely to be of substantial value (whether by itself or together with other material) to the investigation of the offence; and
  (c) that the material is likely to be relevant evidence; and
  (d) that it does not consist of or include items subject to legal privilege, excluded material or special procedure material; and
  (e) that any of the conditions specified in subsection (3) below applies in relation to each set of premises specified in the application.

he may issue a warrant authorising a constable to enter and search the premises.

(1A) The premises referred to in subsection (1)(b) above are—
  (a) one or more sets of premises specified in the application (in which case the application is for a 'specific premises warrant'); or
  (b) any premises occupied or controlled by a person specified in the application, including such sets of premises as are so specified (in which case the application is for an 'all premises warrant').

(1B) If the application is for an all premises warrant, the justice of the peace must also be satisfied—
  (a) that because of the particulars of the offence referred to in paragraph (a) of subsection (1) above, there are reasonable grounds for believing that it is necessary to search premises occupied or controlled by the person in question which are not specified in the application in order to find the material referred to in paragraph (b) of that subsection; and
  (b) that it is not reasonably practicable to specify in the application all the premises which he occupies or controls and which might need to be searched.

(1C) The warrant may authorise entry to and search of premises on more than one occasion if, on the application, the justice of the peace is satisfied that it is necessary to authorise multiple entries in order to achieve the purpose for which he issues the warrant.

(1D) If it authorises multiple entries, the number of entries authorised may be unlimited, or limited to a maximum.

(2) A constable may seize and retain anything for which a search has been authorised under subsection (1) above.

(3) The conditions mentioned in subsection (1)(e) above are—
  (a) that it is not practicable to communicate with any person entitled to grant entry to the premises;
  (b) that it is practicable to communicate with a person entitled to grant entry to the premises but it is not practicable to communicate with any person entitled to grant access to the evidence;
  (c) that entry to the premises will not be granted unless a warrant is produced;
  (d) that the purpose of a search may be frustrated or seriously prejudiced unless a constable arriving at the premises can secure immediate entry to them.

(4) In this Act 'relevant evidence', in relation to an offence, means anything that would be admissible in evidence at a trial for the offence.

(5) The power to issue a warrant conferred by this section is in addition to any such power otherwise conferred.

KEYNOTE

Section 8 has also been amended by the Serious Organised Crime and Police Act 2005. This section now provides that a constable can apply for two different types of search warrant: a 'specific premises warrant' for the search of one set of premises; and an 'all premises warrant' when it is necessary to search all premises occupied or controlled by an individual, but where it is not reasonably practicable to specify all such premises at the time of applying for the warrant. The warrant allows access to all premises occupied or controlled by that person, both those which are specified on the application, and those which are not. Note that new s. 8 (1C) and (1D) provide that a warrant (either an 'all premises warrant' or a 'specific premises warrant') may authorise access on more than one occasion, and if multiple entries are authorised these may be unlimited or limited to a maximum.

The officer applying for a warrant under s. 8 must have reasonable grounds for believing that material which is *likely to be of substantial value to the investigation of the offence* is on the premises specified. Therefore, when executing such a warrant, the officer must be able to show that any material seized thereunder fell within that description (*R* v *Chief Constable of the Warwickshire Constabulary, ex parte Fitzpatrick* [1998] 1 All ER 65). Possession of a warrant under s. 8 does not authorise police officers to seize all material found on the relevant premises to be taken away and 'sifted' somewhere else (*R* v *Chesterfield Justices, ex parte Bramley* [2000] 2 WLR 409) (this matter is now addressed by s. 50 of the Criminal Justice and Police Act 2001, **see para. 1.5.6**). This means that material which is solely of value for *intelligence* purposes may not be seized under a s. 8 warrant. The limits imposed by this decision on the extent of authority granted by a s. 8 warrant is the reason behind the extended powers of sift and seizure introduced by the Criminal Justice and Police Act 2001 (**see para. 1.5.6**).

The power to apply for and execute a warrant under s. 8 and to carry out the actions under s. 8(2) are among those powers that can be conferred on a person designated as an Investigating Officer under sch. 4 to the Police Reform Act 2002.

The conditions set out under s. 8(1)(e) are part of the *application* process, not part of the general execution process (which is set out at s. 16 above). Therefore the officer swearing out a s. 8 warrant will have to satisfy the court that any of those conditions apply.

Where the search includes information contained in a computer, the provisions of s. 20 apply (**see para. 1.5.4.2**).

1.5.3 Entry, Search and Seizure Powers without Warrant

Apart from a general power of entry to prevent a breach of the peace, all common law police powers of entry were abolished by the Police and Criminal Evidence Act 1984. The Act introduced wide powers of entry, search and seizure particularly when made in connection with an arrest. Note the importance of the general principles and specific content of Code B in relation to these searches (**see appendix 2**).

1.5.3.1 Power to Search after Arrest for Indictable Offence

Section 18 of the Police and Criminal Evidence Act 1984 states:

(1) Subject to the following provisions of this section, a constable may enter and search any premises occupied or controlled by a person who is under arrest for an indictable offence, if he has reasonable grounds for suspecting that there is on the premises evidence, other than items subject to legal privilege, that relates—
  (a) to that offence; or
  (b) to some other indictable offence which is connected with or similar to that offence.

(2) A constable may seize and retain anything for which he may search under subsection (1) above.

(3) The power to search conferred by subsection (1) above is only a power to search to the extent that is reasonably required for the purpose of discovering such evidence.

(4) Subject to subsection (5) below, the powers conferred by this section may not be exercised unless an officer of the rank of inspector or above has authorised them in writing.

(5) A constable may conduct a search under subsection (1)—
  (a) before the person is taken to a police station or released on bail under section 30A; and

(b) without obtaining an authorisation under subsection (4),

if the condition in subsection (5A) is satisfied.

(5A) The condition is that the presence of the person at a place (other than a police station) is necessary for the effective investigation of the offence.

(6) If a constable conducts a search by virtue of subsection (5) above, he shall inform an officer of the rank of inspector or above that he has made the search as soon as practicable after he has made it.

(7) An officer who—

(a) authorises a search; or

(b) is informed of a search under subsection (6) above, shall make a record in writing—

(i) of the grounds for the search; and

(ii) of the nature of the evidence that was sought.

(8) If the person who was in occupation or control of the premises at the time of the search is in police detention at the time the record is to be made, the officer shall make the record as part of his custody record.

KEYNOTE

This power has been amended to apply where the evidence relates to an indictable offence for which the person was arrested or some other indictable offence, as opposed to an 'arrestable' offence, a term repealed by the Serious Organised Crime and Police Act 2005.

For items that relate to legal privilege, **see para. 1.5.5**.

The premises must be occupied or controlled by the arrested person. This expression is not defined but it is a *factual* requirement, i.e. it is not enough that the officer suspects or believes that the premises are occupied or controlled by that person.

The search is limited to evidence relating to the indictable offence for which the person has been arrested or another indictable offence which is similar or connected; it does not authorise a general search for anything that might be of use for other purposes (e.g. for intelligence reports). The extent of the search is limited by s. 18(3). If you are looking for a stolen fridge-freezer, you would not be empowered to search through drawers or small cupboards. You would be able to, however, if you were looking for packaging, receipts or other documents relating to the fridge-freezer.

The search authority must be given in writing and only by an officer of or above the rank of inspector (Code B, para. 4.3). The authorising officer must be satisfied that the necessary grounds exist. If possible he/she should record the authority on the Notice of Powers and Rights given to the occupier, while a record of the grounds for the search and the nature of evidence sought should be made in the custody record (if there is one); otherwise in the officer's pocket book or the search record. That authority is for a search which is lawful *in all other respects*, that is, the other conditions imposed by s. 18 must be met. An inspector cannot make an otherwise unlawful entry and search lawful simply by authorising it (*Krohn* v *DPP* [1997] COD 345).

In addition to the general conditions of Code B above, where officers carry out a search under s. 18 they must, so far as is possible under the circumstances, explain to the occupier(s) the reason for it. If officers attempt to carry out an authorised search under s. 18 without attempting to explain to an occupier the reason, it may mean that the officers are not acting in the execution of their duty and their entry may be lawfully resisted (*Lineham* v *DPP* (1999) *The Independent*, 22 November).

The provision under s. 18(5) relates to cases where the presence of the person *is in fact necessary* for the effective investigation of the offence. This is a more stringent requirement than merely reasonable suspicion or grounds to believe on the part of the officer concerned. If such a search is made, the searching officer must inform an inspector (or above) as soon as practicable after the search.

If the person is in police detention after the arrest, the facts concerning the search must be recorded in the custody record. Where a person is re-arrested under s. 31 for an indictable offence, the powers to search under s. 18 begin again, that is, a new power to search is created in respect of each indictable offence. Where the search includes information contained in a computer, the provisions of s. 20 apply (see para. 1.5.4.2).

1.5.3.2 Powers to Search after Arrest for Other Offences

Where a person is arrested for any other offence, s. 32 of the Police and Criminal Evidence Act 1984 provides a number of general powers of entry, search and seizure.

Section 32 states:

(1) A constable may search an arrested person, in any case where the person to be searched has been arrested at a place other than a police station, if the constable has reasonable grounds for believing that the arrested person may present a danger to himself or others.

(2) Subject to subsections (3) to (5) below, a constable shall also have power in any such case—
  (a) to search the arrested person for anything—
    (i) which he might use to assist him to escape from lawful custody; or
    (ii) which might be evidence relating to an offence; and
  (b) ...

(3) The power to search conferred by subsection (2) above is only a power to search to the extent that is reasonably required for the purpose of discovering any such thing or any such evidence.

(4) The powers conferred by this section to search a person are not to be construed as authorising a constable to require a person to remove any of his clothing in public other than an outer coat, jacket or gloves but they do authorise a search of a person's mouth.

(5) A constable may not search a person in the exercise of the power conferred by subsection (2)(a) above unless he has reasonable grounds for believing that the person to be searched may have concealed on him anything for which a search is permitted under that paragraph.

KEYNOTE

The power to search the arrested person under s. 32(1) is a general one relating to safety.

Section 32(2)(a) then goes on to provide a power to search the person in relation to anything that the arrested person might use to escape from lawful custody and anything that 'might be' evidence relating to *an offence*. There are restrictions placed on the extent and circumstances of the search (s. 32(3) and (4)) and the officer must have reasonable grounds to *believe* (as opposed to mere suspicion) that the person may have such things concealed on him/her (s. 32(5)). Nevertheless, this is still a very wide power. Some years ago the House of Lords confirmed that the police have a common law power to search for and seize property after a lawful arrest (*R* v *Governor of Pentonville Prison, ex parte Osman* [1990] 1 WLR 277). This decision was confirmed recently by the House of Lords in *R (On the Application of Rottman)* v *Commissioner of Police of the Metropolis* [2002] 2 AC 692. In *Rottman* their Lordships held that it was a well-established principle of the common law that an arresting officer had the power to search a room in which a person had been arrested (*per Ghani* v *Jones* [1970] 1 QB 693). This extended power is not limited to purely 'domestic' offences, but also applies to cases involving extradition offences.

Section 32 goes on to state:

(9) A constable searching a person in the exercise of the power conferred by subsection (2)(a) above may seize and retain anything he finds, other than an item subject to legal privilege, if he has reasonable grounds for believing—
  (a) that he might use it to assist him to escape from lawful custody; or
  (b) that it is evidence of an offence or has been obtained in consequence of the commission of an offence.

1.5.3.3 Search of Premises after Arrest

Section 32 also provides that a constable shall have the power in such a case to enter and search any premises in which the person was when arrested or immediately before being arrested for an indictable offence (s. 32(2)(b)). The search may be conducted for the purpose of finding evidence relating to the offence for which the person was arrested.

Section 32 also states:

(6) A constable may not search premises in the exercise of the power conferred by subsection (2)(b) above unless he has reasonable grounds for believing that there is evidence for which a search is permitted under that paragraph on the premises.

(7) In so far as the power of search conferred by subsection (2)(b) above relates to premises consisting of two or more separate dwellings, it is limited to a power to search—

(a) any dwelling in which the arrest took place or in which the person arrested was immediately before his arrest; and

(b) any parts of the premises which the occupier of any such dwelling uses in common with the occupiers of any other dwellings comprised in the premises.

(8) A constable searching a person in the exercise of the power conferred by subsection (1) above may seize and retain anything he finds, if he has reasonable grounds for believing that the person searched might use it to cause physical injury to himself or to any other person.

...

(10) Nothing in this section shall be taken to affect the power conferred by section 43 of the Terrorism Act 2000.

KEYNOTE

Both 'reasonable grounds' and 'immediately' are questions of fact for a court to determine. It has been held that the power under s. 32(2)(b) is one for use at the time of arrest and should not be used to return to the relevant premises some time after the arrest in the way that s. 18 (see above) may be used (*R* v *Badham* [1987] Crim LR 202).

Officers exercising their power to enter and search under s. 32 must have a genuine belief (i.e. more than mere suspicion) that there is evidence on the premises; it is not a licence for a general fishing expedition (*R* v *Beckford* [1991] Crim LR 918).

The Divisional Court has refused to allow s. 32 to be used in a situation where the arrested person had not been in the relevant premises (where he did not live) for a period of over two hours preceding his arrest and where there were no reasonable grounds for believing that he presented a danger to himself or others (*Hewitson* v *Chief Constable of Dorset Police* [2003] EWHC 3296).

Code B sets out the procedure to be followed after searches have been carried out (paras 8 and 9).

1.5.3.4 Other Powers of Entry without Warrant

Just as there are many statutes which provide the police (and others) with powers to apply for warrants, there are as many statutes which provide a power of entry without warrant (an example would be s. 6 of the Scrap Metal Dealers Act 1964 which allows a constable entry at all reasonable times, onto a scrap metal dealer's premises to inspect the register and any scrap metal). Other examples are the power to enter:

- any land other than a dwelling house in order to search for crossbows (under s. 4 of the Crossbows Act 1987);
- *any place* for the purpose of carrying out a search under s. 47 of the Firearms Act 1968;
- school premises in connection with weapons under s. 139B of the Criminal Justice Act 1988; and
- relevant premises in connection with a direction to leave and remove vehicles etc. under s. 62 of the Criminal Justice and Public Order Act 1994.

The Police and Justice Act 2006 amended the Aviation Security Act 1982 and this will give a constable the power to stop and search any person, vehicle or aircraft in any area of an aerodrome for stolen or prohibited articles.

The only common law power of entry without warrant is for dealing with a breach of the peace. This power is preserved by s. 17(6) and only applies where officers have a genuine and reasonable belief that a breach of the peace is happening or is about to happen in the immediate future (*McLeod* v *Commissioner of Police for the Metropolis* [1994] 4 All ER 553).

Where police officers enter premises *lawfully* (including where they are there by invitation), they are on the premises for *all lawful purposes* (see *Foster* v *Attard* [1986] Crim LR 627). This means that they can carry out any lawful functions while on the premises, even if that was not the original purpose for entry. For instance, if officers entered under a lawful power provided by the Misuse of Drugs Act 1971, they may carry out other lawful functions such as enforcing the provisions of the Gaming Act 1968.

If officers are invited onto premises by someone entitled to do so, they are lawfully there unless and until that invitation is withdrawn. Once the invitation is withdrawn, the officers will become trespassers unless they have a power to be there, and the person may remove them by force (*Robson* v *Hallett* [1967] 2 QB 939). If that invitation is terminated, the person needs to communicate that clearly to the officer; it has been held that merely telling officers to 'fuck off' is not necessarily sufficient (*Snook* v *Mannion* [1982] RTR 321).

Once officers are lawfully on premises they may exercise the powers of seizure under s. 19 of the Police and Criminal Evidence Act 1984 (**see para. 1.5.4.1**).

1.5.3.5 Power of Entry: Police and Criminal Evidence Act 1984

Section 17 of the Police and Criminal Evidence Act 1984 states:

> (1) Subject to the following provisions of this section, and without prejudice to any other enactment, a constable may enter and search any premises for the purpose—
> (a) of executing—
> (i) a warrant of arrest issued in connection with or arising out of criminal proceedings; or
> (ii) a warrant of commitment issued under section 76 of the Magistrates' Courts Act 1980;
> (b) of arresting a person for an indictable offence;
> (c) of arresting a person for an offence under—
> (i) section 1 (prohibition of uniforms in connection with political objectives) of the Public Order Act 1936;
> (ii) any enactment contained in sections 6 to 8 or 10 of the Criminal Law Act 1977 (offences relating to entering and remaining on property);
> (iii) section 4 of the Public Order Act 1986 (fear or provocation of violence);
> (iiia) section 4 (driving etc when under influence of drink or drugs) or 163 (failure to stop when required to do so by constable in uniform) of the Road Traffic Act 1988;
> (iiib) section 27 of the Transport and Works Act 1992 (which relates to offences involving drink or drugs);
> (iv) section 76 of the Criminal Justice and Public Order Act 1994 (failure to comply with interim possession order);
> (v) any of sections 4, 5, 6(1) and (2), 7 and 8(1) and (2) of the Animal Welfare Act 2006 (offences relating to the prevention of harm to animals);
> (ca) of arresting, in pursuance of section 32(1A) of the Children and Young Persons Act 1969, any child or young person who has been remanded or committed to local authority accommodation under section 23(1) of that Act;
> (caa) Of arresting a person for an offence to which section 61 of the Animal Health Act 1981 applies;
> (cb) of recapturing any person who is, or is deemed for any purpose to be, unlawfully at large while liable to be detained—

(i) in a prison, remand centre, young offender institution or secure training centre, or
(ii) in pursuance of section 92 of the Powers of Criminal Courts (Sentencing) Act 2000 (dealing with children and young persons guilty of grave crimes), in any other place;

(d) of recapturing any person whatever who is unlawfully at large and whom he is pursuing; or

(e) of saving life or limb or preventing serious damage to property.

(2) Except for the purpose specified in paragraph (e) of subsection (1) above, the powers of entry and search conferred by this section—
(a) are only exercisable if the constable has reasonable grounds for believing that the person whom he is seeking is on the premises; and
(b) are limited, in relation to premises consisting of two or more separate dwellings, to powers to enter and search—
(i) any parts of the premises which the occupiers of any dwelling comprised in the premises use in common with the occupiers of any other such dwelling; and
(ii) any such dwelling in which the constable has reasonable grounds for believing that the person whom he is seeking may be.

(3) The powers of entry and search conferred by this section are only exercisable for the purposes specified in subsection (1)(c)(ii) or (iv) above by a constable in uniform.

(4) The power of search conferred by this section is only a power to search to the extent that is reasonably required for the purpose for which the power of entry is exercised.

(5) Subject to subsection (6) below, all the rules of common law under which a constable has power to enter premises without a warrant are hereby abolished.

(6) Nothing in subsection (5) above affects any power of entry to deal with or prevent a breach of the peace.

KEYNOTE

This section has been amended to apply where the proposed arrest relates to an indictable offence as opposed to an 'arrestable' offence, a term repealed by the Serious Organised Crime and Police Act 2005. The powers have also been extended to include: driving under the influence of drink or drugs (s. 17(1)(c)(iiia)), workers on transport systems being over the prescribed limit (s. 17(1)(c)(iiib)), and provisions relating to the control of rabies (s. 17(1)(caa)).

Section 10 of the Criminal Law Act 1977 contained in s. 17(1)(c)(ii) is not within the scope of the Manuals and relates to the obstruction of court officers executing any process issued by the High Court or county court.

In a case where police had been called to an address by an abandoned 999 call, the officers had to move a man away from the front door in order to gain entry under s. 17. The Queen's Bench Divisional Court held that the officers had the power to use reasonable force in order to do so (*Smith (Peter John)* v *DPP* (2001) 165 JP 432). The source of the power to use force here is s. 117 of the Police and Criminal Evidence Act 1984.

'Unlawfully at large' does not have a particular statutory meaning; it can apply to someone who is subject to an order under the Mental Health Act 1983, or someone who has escaped from custody. The pursuit of the person must be 'fresh', that is, the power will only be available while the officer is actually 'pursuing' the person concerned (*D'Souza* v *DPP* (1993) 96 Cr App 278).

Force may be used in exercising the power of entry where it is necessary to do so. Generally, the officer should first attempt to communicate with the occupier of the premises, explaining by what authority and for what purpose entry is to be made, before making a forcible entry. Clearly though, there will be occasions where such communication is impossible, impracticable or even unnecessary; in those cases there is no need for the officer to enter into such an explanation (*O'Loughlin* v *Chief Constable of Essex* [1998] 1 WLR 374).

The officer must have reasonable grounds to *believe* that the person is on the premises in all cases except saving life and limb at s. 17(1)(e). This expression is narrower than 'reasonable cause to suspect' and you must be able to justify that belief before using this power (although see *Kynaston* v *DPP* (1987) *The Times*, 4 November, where the court accepted reasonable cause to *suspect*).

Note the requirement for an officer to be in uniform for the purposes of s. 17(1)(c)(ii) and (iv), and the restrictions on the power of *search* under s. 17(4) (i.e. that any such search is limited to the extent that is reasonably required *for the purpose for which you entered the premises in the first place*).

Code B regulates the way in which these powers of entry will be executed.

Again this section contains restrictions on the extent of any searches made.

The power to enter and search any premises in the relevant police area for the purpose of saving life or limb or preventing serious damage to property above is among those that can be conferred on a designated person under sch. 4 to the Police Reform Act 2002.

1.5.4 Powers of Seizure under the Police and Criminal Evidence Act 1984

The Police and Criminal Evidence Act 1984 provides many powers for the seizure of property.

1.5.4.1 General Powers of Seizure under the Police and Criminal Evidence Act 1984

Section 19 of the Police and Criminal Evidence Act 1984 states:

(1) The powers conferred by subsections (2), (3) and (4) below are exercisable by a constable who is lawfully on any premises.

(2) The constable may seize anything which is on the premises if he has reasonable grounds for believing—
   (a) that it has been obtained in consequence of the commission of an offence; and
   (b) that it is necessary to seize it in order to prevent it being concealed, lost, damaged, altered or destroyed.

(3) The constable may seize anything which is on the premises if he has reasonable grounds for believing—
   (a) that it is evidence in relation to an offence which he is investigating or any other offence; and
   (b) that it is necessary to seize it in order to prevent the evidence being concealed, lost, altered or destroyed.

(4) The constable may require any information which is stored in any electronic form and is accessible from the premises to be produced in a form in which it can be taken away and in which it is visible and legible or from which it can readily be produced in a visible and legible form if he has reasonable grounds for believing—
   (a) that—
      (i) it is evidence in relation to an offence which he is investigating or any other offence; or
      (ii) it has been obtained in consequence of the commission of an offence; and
   (b) that it is necessary to do so in order to prevent it being concealed, lost, or destroyed.

(5) The powers conferred by this section are in addition to any power otherwise conferred.

(6) No power of seizure conferred on a constable under any enactment (including an enactment contained in an Act passed after this Act) is to be taken to authorise the seizure of an item which the constable exercising the power has reasonable grounds for believing to be subject to legal privilege.

KEYNOTE

For this very wide power to apply, the officer concerned must be on the premises lawfully (**see para. 1.5.3** and also PACE Code B). If the officers are on the premises only with the consent of the occupier, they become trespassers once that consent has been withdrawn (**see para. 1.5.3.4**). Once the officers are told to leave, they are no longer 'lawfully' on the premises—even though they must be given a reasonable opportunity to leave—and cannot then seize any property that they may find. For this reason, it is far safer to exercise a power where one exists, albeit that the *co-operation* of the relevant person should be sought.

The power of seizure only applies where the officer has 'reasonable grounds for believing' that:

- the property has been obtained in consequence of the commission of an offence, or
- the property is *evidence* in relation to an offence, *and*

in each case, that its seizure is *necessary* to prevent the property being concealed, lost or destroyed.

Where the 'premises' searched is a vehicle (see s. 23), the vehicle can itself be seized (*Cowan* v *Commissioner of Police for the Metropolis* [2000] 1 WLR 254). In *Cowan* it was argued that the powers given by ss. 18 (as to which, **see para. 1.5.3**) and 19 authorise the seizure of anything in or on the premises but not the *premises* themselves. The Court of Appeal disagreed, holding that the power to seize 'premises', where it was appropriate and practical to do so, was embodied in both ss. 18 and 19 and also at common law and the defendant's claim for damages following the seizure of his vehicle after his arrest for serious sexual offences was dismissed. This decision is now acknowledged in Code B, Note 7B.

Unless the elements above are satisfied, the power under s. 19 will not apply. Therefore, the power does not authorise the seizure of property purely for intelligence purposes (**see also para. 1.5.2**).

Section 19(5) expressly preserves any common law power of search and seizure; however, in *R (on the application of Rottman)* v *Commissioner of Police for the Metropolis* [2002] 2 All ER 865, the House of Lords held that s. 19 was confined to 'domestic' offences (e.g. and did not extend to extradition offences). The same applies to powers under s. 18 of the Police and Criminal Evidence Act 1984 (**see para. 1.5.3**).

If the warrant under which entry or seizure was made is invalid, the officers will not be on the premises lawfully (**see para. 1.5.2**).

The power of seizure under s. 19(1), along with the power to require information stored in any electronic form to be made accessible under s. 19(4), are among those that can be conferred on an Investigating Officer designated under sch. 4 to the Police Reform Act 2002. The safeguards provided by s. 19(6) in relation to privileged material also apply to the exercise of these powers by designated Investigating Officers.

1.5.4.2 Powers of Seizure and Information in Electronic Form

Section 20 states:

(1) Every power of seizure which is conferred by an enactment to which this section applies on a constable who has entered premises in the exercise of a power conferred by an enactment shall be construed as including a power to require any information stored in any electronic form and accessible from the premises to be produced in a form in which it can be taken away and in which it is visible and legible or from which it can readily be produced in a visible and legible form.

(2) This section applies—
  (a) to any enactment contained in an Act passed before this Act;
  (b) to sections 8 and 18 above;
  (c) to paragraph 13 of Schedule 1 to this Act; and
  (d) to any enactment contained in an Act passed after this Act.

KEYNOTE

This provision applies to:

- powers conferred under pre-PACE statutes;
- powers exercised under a s. 8 warrant (for 'indictable offences');

- powers exercised under s. 18 (following arrest for an indictable offence);
- powers under sch. 1 ('excluded' or 'special procedure material');
- powers exercised under s. 19 (officers lawfully on premises);
- powers of seizure exercised by Investigating Officers designated under sch. 4 to the Police Reform Act 2002.

See also PACE Code B, para. 7.6 which reinforces the power to require electronically stored information to be produced in a visible and legible form that can be taken away or reproduced (**appendix 2**).

The increased use of electronic media to facilitate criminal activity has meant that more conventional police powers of search and seizure have not been adequate for the needs of the police and other investigatory agencies. This is particularly true where data or information that may be of evidential value in a criminal enquiry has been 'encrypted'—that is, where some form of code or password has been used to prevent access to it. Part III of the Regulation of Investigatory Powers Act 2000 addresses these problems by providing a power to serve written notices requiring the holders of 'protected information' to disclose either the information in an intelligible format or, if relevant, the 'key' to it. Protected information in this context is generally electronic data that cannot be accessed readily or put into an intelligible form without a key (s. 56). The power to serve a notice (given by s. 49) generally applies to protected information that has been obtained or seized by some lawful means, for example where a computer has been taken under the authority of a warrant or voluntarily handed in to the police or the Serious Organised Crime Agency. At the time of writing, this part of the Act had not been brought into force.

Which person will have appropriate permission under the 2000 Act to issue the relevant s. 49 notice will depend largely on how the protected information was come by. Broadly, sch. 2 to the Act lists the people who may issue such notices and, just as importantly, appropriate circumstances under which they may do so. A circuit judge in England and Wales will have appropriate permission to grant police applications in all cases. Others included in the schedule are the Secretary of State and chief officers of police (under the appropriate circumstances). As with other areas of the 2000 Act, the power to issue s. 49 notices will be restricted to occasions where its use is both necessary and proportionate to the interests of national security, the prevention or detection of crime and the economic well-being of the United Kingdom. In addition, a s. 49 notice cannot be issued unless it is not reasonably practicable for the person with appropriate permission to obtain the protected information in an intelligible form in any other way. Part III of the Act imposes certain requirements for reporting the use of the s. 49 powers to the Chief Surveillance Commissioner and creates safeguards for the storage and use of any keys and data obtained thereby. Knowingly failing to comply with a s. 49 notice will be, under appropriate circumstances, an offence triable either way and attracting an unlimited fine in the Crown Court (s. 53). There is also to be a more serious offence of 'tipping off' another person where a s. 49 notice has been authorised and that notice contains an express requirement for secrecy (s. 54).

This discussion is merely a summary of the key aspects of this power. To find the full extent of the powers and duties under this Part of the 2000 Act, the statutory text should be used along with the relevant code of practice in force at the time.

1.5.4.3 Supply of Copies of Seized Material

Section 21 of the 1984 Act makes provision for the supplying of copies of records of seizure to certain people after property has been seized. If requested by the person who had custody or control of the seized property immediately before it was seized, the officer in charge of the investigation must allow that person access to it under police supervision. The officer must also make provisions to allow for the property be to photographed or copied by that person or to supply the person with photographs/copies of it within a reasonable time. Such a request need not be complied with if there are reasonable grounds to believe that to do so would prejudice any related investigation or criminal proceedings (s. 21(8)).

1.5.4.4 Retention of Seized Material

The provisions for accessing and copying of seized material as set out in ss. 21 and 22 of the Police and Criminal Evidence Act 1984 also apply to powers of seizure exercised by Investigating Officers designated under sch. 4 to the Police Reform Act 2002.

Section 22 of the 1984 Act makes provision for the retention of seized property. Section 22(1) provides that anything seized may be retained for as long as necessary in all the circumstances. However, s. 22(2) allows for property to be retained for use as evidence in a trial, forensic examination or further investigation *unless a photograph or copy would suffice*. This is reinforced generally by PACE Code B, para. 7.5. Seized property may be retained in order to establish its lawful owner (s. 22(2)(b)). Once this power to retain property is exhausted, a person claiming it can rely on his/her right to possession at the time the property was seized as giving sufficient title to recover the property from the police. This situation was confirmed by the Court of Appeal in a case where the purchaser of a stolen car was allowed to rely upon his possession of the car at the time it was seized. As it could not be established that anyone else was entitled to the vehicle, the Court allowed the claimant's action for return of the car to him (*Costello* v *Chief Constable of Derbyshire Constabulary* [2001] 1 WLR 1437). Clearly any claim based on previous possession where it would be unlawful for the police to return the property (e.g. a controlled drug) could not be enforced. Provisions amending this area of legislation are now contained in the Criminal Justice and Police Act 2001. There is no specific provision under s. 22 for the retention of property for purely intelligence purposes.

The importance of police officers being able to point clearly to the need for retaining property either in order to establish its owner or as a necessary part of the investigative or law enforcement process when relying on the above powers, was highlighted by the Court of Appeal in *Gough* v *Chief Constable of the West Midlands Police* (2004) *The Times*, 4 March. In that case it was clear that neither of these purposes was being served and therefore the officers could not rely on the statutory power for retaining the property.

Property seized simply to prevent an arrested person from using it to escape or to cause injury, damage etc. cannot be retained for those purposes once the person has been released (s. 22(3)). This includes car keys belonging to someone who is released from police detention having been detained under the relevant drink driving legislation.

1.5.4.5 Prohibitions on Reuse of Information Seized

Information gained as a result of a lawful search may be passed on to other individuals and organisations for purposes of investigation and prosecution. It must not be used for private purposes (*Marcel* v *Commissioner of Police for the Metropolis* [1992] Ch 225).

1.5.4.6 Disposal of Property in Police Possession

For the provisions regarding the disposal of property in police possession, see the Police (Property) Act 1897.

1.5.5 Protected Material

Some material cannot be seized, either under the Police and Criminal Evidence Act 1984 or any other enactment; certain other material can only be seized under special circumstances set out in the Act (and the extended 'seize and sift' powers under the Criminal Justice and Police Act 2001—**see para. 1.5.6**).

1.5.5.1 Legally Privileged Material

Material which falls within the definition in s. 10 of the 1984 Act is subject to legal privilege which means that it cannot be searched for or seized.

Section 10 states:

(1) Subject to subsection (2) below, in this Act 'items subject to legal privilege' means—
 (a) communications between a professional legal adviser and his client or any person representing his client made in connection with the giving of legal advice to the client;
 (b) communications between a professional legal adviser and his client or any person representing his client or between such an adviser or his client or any such representative and any other person made in connection with or in contemplation of legal proceedings and for the purposes of such proceedings; and
 (c) items enclosed with or referred to in such communications and made—
  (i) in connection with the giving of legal advice; or
  (ii) in connection with or in contemplation of legal proceedings and for the purposes of such proceedings,
 when they are in the possession of a person who is entitled to possession of them.

KEYNOTE

Items held with the intention of furthering a criminal purpose are no longer subject to this privilege (s. 10(2)). However, when making an application for a warrant to search for and seize such material the procedure under sch. 1 should be used. Occasions where this will happen are very rare and would include instances where a solicitor's firm is the subject of a criminal investigation (see *R* v *Leeds Crown Court, ex parte Switalski* [1991] Crim LR 559). However, it may be possible during a search to ascertain which material is subject to legal privilege and which might be lawfully seized under the warrant being executed. Therefore, although a warrant cannot authorise a search for legally privileged material, the fact that such material is inadvertently seized in the course of a search authorised by a proper warrant does not render the search unlawful (*HM Customs & Excise, ex parte Popely* [2000] Crim LR 388).

1.5.5.2 Excluded Material

Access to 'excluded material' can generally only be gained by applying to a judge for a production order under the procedure set out in s. 9 of, and sch. 1 to the 1984 Act and PACE Code B. That strict statutory procedure also applies to the application for and execution of warrants by Investigating Officers designated under sch. 4 to the Police Reform Act 2002.

Section 11 of the 1984 Act states:

(1) Subject to the following provisions of this section, in this Act 'excluded material' means—
 (a) personal records which a person has acquired or created in the course of any trade, business, profession or other occupation or for the purposes of any paid or unpaid office and which he holds in confidence;
 (b) human tissue or tissue fluid which has been taken for the purposes of diagnosis or medical treatment and which a person holds in confidence;
 (c) journalistic material which a person holds in confidence and which consists—
  (i) of documents; or
  (ii) of records other than documents.
(2) A person holds material other than journalistic material in confidence for the purposes of this section if he holds it subject—
 (a) to an express or implied undertaking to hold it in confidence; or

(b) to a restriction on disclosure or an obligation of secrecy contained in any enactment, including an enactment contained in an Act passed after this Act.

(3) A person holds journalistic material in confidence for the purposes of this section if—
(a) he holds it subject to such an undertaking, restriction or obligation; and
(b) it has been continuously held (by one or more persons) subject to such an undertaking, restriction or obligation since it was first acquired or created for the purposes of journalism.

KEYNOTE

Medical records and dental records would fall into this category, as might records made by priests or religious advisers.

'Personal records' are defined under s. 12 of the 1984 Act and include records relating to the physical or mental health, counselling or assistance given to an individual who can be identified by those records.

'Journalistic material' is defined under s. 13 as material acquired or created for the purposes of journalism.

1.5.5.3 Special Procedure Material

Special procedure material can be gained by applying for a search warrant or a production order under sch. 1 to the 1984 Act.

Section 14 of the 1984 Act states:

(1) In this Act 'special procedure material' means—
(a) material to which subsection (2) below applies; and
(b) journalistic material, other than excluded material.

(2) Subject to the following provisions of this section, this subsection applies to material, other than items subject to legal privilege and excluded material, in the possession of a person who—
(a) acquired or created it in the course of any trade, business, profession or other occupation or for the purpose of any paid or unpaid office; and
(b) holds it subject—
(i) to an express or implied undertaking to hold it in confidence; or
(ii) to a restriction or obligation such as is mentioned in section 11(2)(b) above.

KEYNOTE

For items subject to 'legal privilege' and 'excluded material', see the Keynotes above.

The person believed to be in possession of the material must have come by it under the circumstances set out at s. 14(2)(a) *and* must hold it under the undertakings or obligations set out at s. 14(2)(b).

1.5.6 Seize and Sift Powers

One of the practical problems faced by operational officers when seizing certain types of material is that of sorting the 'wheat from the chaff'—sifting out those documents or computer-stored data that are pertinent to the case from the general mass of material within which they are found. Part 2 of the Criminal Justice and Police Act 2001 now provides the police with specific powers to 'seize and sift' under strict conditions and subject to a number of rigid procedural safeguards. One such safeguard is the specific application of Code B of the Police and Criminal Evidence Act 1984 Codes of Practice (**see appendix 2**).

1.5.6.1 Extended Powers

The first point to note about these seize and sift powers is that they will be rarely used and, even then, those using them will have to be able to show that it was *essential* (rather than simply convenient or preferable) to do so (Code B, para. 7.7). The second thing to note about these powers is that they only extend the scope of *some other existing power*. In other words, they do not provide free-standing powers to seize property—rather they supplement other powers of search and seizure where the relevant conditions and circumstances apply. The full list of these powers is set out in sch. 1 to the Act and includes all the relevant powers under the Police and Criminal Evidence Act 1984, along with those under other key statutes such as the Firearms Act 1968 and the Misuse of Drugs Act 1971. If there is no existing power of seizure other than the Criminal Justice and Police Act 2001, then there is no power.

The Criminal Justice and Police Act 2001 powers allow officers to remove materials from the premises being searched where there are real practical difficulties in not doing so—e.g. because there will be insufficient time to examine all the material properly, where special equipment is needed to examine it or where the material is stored on a computer.

In summary, s. 50 of the Act provides the extended powers to seize material where it is not reasonably practicable to sort through it at the scene of the search. The factors that can be taken into account in considering whether or not it is reasonably practicable for something to be determined, or for relevant material to be separated from other materials, are set out in s. 50(3); these include the length of time and number of people that would be required to carry out the determination or separation on those premises within a reasonable period, whether that would involve damage to property, any apparatus or equipment that would be needed and (in the case of separation of materials) whether the separation would be likely to prejudice the use of some or all of the separated seizable property. Section 50 also allows for the seizure of material that is reasonably believed to be legally privileged (**see para. 1.5.5**) where it is not reasonably practicable to separate it. In some cases, the power to 'seize' will be read as a power to take copies (see s. 63).

Section 51 provides for extended seizure of materials in the same vein as above but where the material is found on people who are being lawfully searched.

One of the main purposes behind this legislative framework is to balance the competing needs of the criminal justice system with the individual rights of the person owning the property (see Code B, paras 7.7 and 7.8). Seizing large volumes of material and removing them from the owner's premises can have considerable consequences, particularly where they are taken from business premises. Therefore there are many strict requirements imposed on the police, not only in seizing the property in the first place, but also after the property has been lawfully seized by virtue of the powers. The first of these is the duty to carry out an initial examination.

1.5.6.2 Initial Examination

Where any property has been seized under ss. 50 or 51, the officer in possession of it is under a duty to make sure that a number of things are done (s. 53). These include ensuring that an initial examination of the property is carried out *as soon as reasonably practicable* after the seizure. In determining the earliest practicable time to carry out an initial examination of the seized property, due regard must be had to the desirability of allowing the person from whom it was seized (or a person with an interest in it) an opportunity of being present, or of being represented, at the examination (s. 53(4)).

The officer must also ensure that any such examination is confined to whatever is *necessary* for determining how much of the property:

- is property for which the person seizing it had power to search when making the seizure but is not property that has to be returned (by s. 54—see below);
- is property authorised to be retained (by s. 56—see below); or

- is something which, in all the circumstances, it will not be reasonably practicable, following the examination, to separate from the property above (see generally s. 53(3)).

The officer must ensure that anything found not to fall within the categories above is separated from the rest of the seized property and *is returned as soon as reasonably practicable* after the examination of all the seized property. That officer is also under a duty to ensure that, until the initial examination of all the seized property has been completed and anything which does not fall within the categories above has been returned, the seized property is kept separate from anything seized under any other power. There are special provisions where the property is inextricably linked to relevant material (e.g. where the 'innocent' material is completely mixed up with or inseparable from the material that is properly the subject of the investigation). However, those provisions place very strict limits on what use can be made of this inextricably linked material (see s. 62).

While there are great sensitivities over the use of widespread powers of seizure such as these in any event, those sensitivities are increased even further where legally privileged or special procedure material is involved (as to which **see para. 1.5.5**). Accordingly the Act imposes specific duties on the police in relation to these materials.

1.5.6.3 Protected Material

If, at any time, after a seizure of anything has been made in exercise of *any statutory power of seizure*, it appears that the property is subject to legal privilege (or it has such an item comprised in it), s. 54 imposes a general duty on the officer in possession of the property to ensure that the item is returned as soon as reasonably practicable after the seizure. This general duty is subject to some exceptions (e.g. where in all the circumstances it is not reasonably practicable for that item to be separated from the rest of that property without prejudicing the use of the rest of that property—see s. 54(2)) but is otherwise very wide-ranging and absolutely clear. A similar duty is generally imposed in relation to property that appears to be excluded material or special procedure material (as to which **see para. 1.5.5**)—s. 55.

1.5.6.4 Retention of Property

The Act authorises the retention of certain seized property by the police. In order to be retained, the property must have been seized on any premises by a constable who was lawfully on the premises, by a person authorised under a relevant statute (see s. 56(5)) who was on the premises accompanied by a constable, or by a constable carrying out a lawful search of any person (s. 56). Generally property so seized will fall within these categories if there are reasonable grounds for believing:

- that it is property obtained in consequence of the commission of an offence; or
- that it is evidence in relation to any offence; *and* (in either case)
- that it is necessary for it to be retained in order to prevent its being concealed, lost, altered or destroyed

(for full details see s. 56(2) and (3)). Note, so far as s. 56(2) is concerned, property may be retained if it is necessary to prevent its being 'damaged', in addition to the other factors listed.

These are fairly wide provisions and, if the property fits the above description, it may be retained even if it was not being searched for. Section 57 goes on to make certain provisions for the retention of property under other statutes including s. 22 of the Theft Act 1968 and s. 5(4) of the Knives Act 1997. Further guidance on retention of property is set out in Code B, paras. 7.14–7.15.

1.5.6.5 Notice

Where a person exercises a power of seizure conferred by ss. 50 or 51, that person will be under a duty, on doing so, to give the occupier or person from whom property is seized a written notice (s. 52). That notice will specify:

- what has been seized and the grounds on which the powers have been exercised;
- the effect of the safeguards and rights to apply to a judicial authority for the return of the property (see below);
- the name and address of the person to whom notice of an application to a judge and an application to be allowed to attend the initial examination should be sent.

Where it appears to the officer exercising a power of seizure under s. 50 that the occupier of the premises is not present at the time of the exercise of the power, but there is some other person present who is in charge of the premises, the officer may give the notice to that other person (s. 52(2)). Where it appears that there is no one present on the premises to whom a notice can be given, the officer must, before leaving the premises, attach a notice in a prominent place to the premises (s. 53(3)).

1.5.6.6 Return of Property Seized

There are specific obligations on the police to return property seized under these powers—particularly where the property includes legally privileged, excluded or special procedure material. The general rule is that any extraneous property initially seized under these provisions must be returned—usually—to the person from whom it was seized unless the investigating officer considers that someone else has a better claim to it (see ss. 53–58).

Any person with a relevant interest in the seized property may apply to the appropriate judicial authority, on one or more of the grounds in s. 59(3), for the return of the whole or a part of the seized property. Generally those grounds are that there was no power to make the seizure or that the seized property did not fall into one of the permitted categories (see s. 59). Where a person makes such an application, the police must secure the property in accordance with s. 61 (e.g. in a way that prevents investigators from looking at or copying it until the matter has been considered by a judge). There are other occasions where protected material is involved that will give rise to the duty to secure the property under s. 61 too. What will amount to 'securing' will vary depending on the type of property and the circumstances and may involve 'bagging up' property and controlling access to it in many cases (see Code B, Note 7F). The 'judicial authority' (at least a Crown Court judge) will be able to make a number of wide-ranging orders in relation to the treatment of the seized property, including its return or examination by a third party. Failure to comply with any such order will amount to a contempt of court (s. 59(9)).

For further details on the extent and use of these powers, see Home Office Circular 19/2003.

1.6 PACE Codes of Practice

1.6.1 Introduction

The powers to detain people who have been arrested and the manner in which they must be dealt with are primarily contained in the Police and Criminal Evidence Act 1984 and the PACE Codes of Practice, whose creation and status come from s. 66 of the Act. The 1984 Act provides directions as to how detained persons should be treated. The main responsibility for detained persons lies with the custody officer, however it is important that all staff, including supervisors involved in investigations or those dealing with detained persons, are aware of the provisions of the Act and the Codes. Failure to follow the requirements of the law could lead to prosecutions failing because evidence is excluded, civil claims against forces, bad publicity, and the possibility of disciplinary action or even criminal proceedings against officers.

It should be noted that the amended Codes of Practice which took effect on 1 February 2008 introduced Welsh language versions of cautions and warnings that should be used when appropriate.

1.6.1.1 The Human Rights Act 1998

The Human Rights Act 1998 makes it even more important to comply with the 1984 Act and its associated Codes of Practice. This can be seen from the case of *R* v *Chief Constable of Kent Constabulary, ex parte Kent Police Federation Joint Branch Board* [2000] 2 Cr App R 196, where it was held that while article 5 of the European Convention on Human Rights was not then part of the domestic law of England and Wales, the article embodied important and basic rights which English law recognised and protected, and any deprivation of liberty must be in accordance with the law. The court went on to say that the 1984 Act and the Codes of Practice represented the balance between the important duty of the police to investigate crime and apprehend criminals and the rights of the private citizen. A breach of Code C is fundamental in affecting the fairness of the evidence (*R* v *Aspinall* [1999] 2 Cr App R 115).

The Human Rights Act 1998 incorporates the European Convention into UK legislation and as such domestic legislation still applies, but will be interpreted so as to incorporate the articles of the Convention and the relevant case law. Where there is a conflict between domestic law and the Convention, it will be for Parliament to change domestic legislation to come into line with the Convention. The main articles which need to be considered for the custody officer and others involved in the detention of a person include articles 3, 5, 6 and 8.

1.6.2 General Requirements

The custody officer carries the main responsibility towards prisoners who are brought to the police station. Initially it must be decided whether the person should be detained as a prisoner at the police station. If there are grounds to detain him/her, the detention period must be *for those reasons only*. Once a decision to detain a person has been made, the manner in which he/she must be treated while in detention is set out in the PACE Codes (**see appendices**). These Codes are intended to protect the basic rights of detained people. If these Codes are followed it is more likely that evidence obtained while people are in custody will be admissible. The provisions of the 1984 Act give guidance in numerous areas including:

- length of time in detention;
- information about the detained person's arrest;
- searching;
- taking of samples;
- interviewing of suspects;
- identification methods;
- charging; and
- bail.

The PACE Codes set out the minimum standard of treatment that a detained person can expect. These requirements may be extended with the incorporation of the European

Convention on Human Rights and its associated case law. The maximum length of detention is also prescribed by the 1984 Act, as are the requirements for charging, bailing and appearances at court.

The following chapter outlines some of the requirements of the legislation and the powers police have in relation to detained people. The chapter is aimed at providing guidance when using the legislation and it is intended to point the reader to the correct sections of the 1984 Act and the PACE Codes of Practice when dealing with detained people and investigations.

Whilst it is common practice for custody officers to have gaolers to assist in managing detained people, it is still the custody officer's responsibility to ensure that PACE is complied with. However, the Police Reform Act 2002 allows the role of support staff to be expanded in this regard (see below).

1.6.3 Designated Support Staff

Sections 38 and 39 of the Police Reform Act 2002 allow persons employed by the police authority or persons employed by a contractor of the police authority (in relation to detention and escort officers) to be designated as investigating officers, detention officers and escort officers.

Designated officers are given powers to carry out certain functions that would up to this time have been carried out by police officers only. Before a person can be given the powers of a designated officer, the chief officer of police must be satisfied that the person is a suitable person to carry out the functions for which he/she is designated, is capable of effectively carrying out those functions, and has received adequate training in the carrying out of those functions and in the exercise and performance of the powers and duties of a designated officer. It should be noted that not all designated officers will be designated with the same range of powers and it will be important to know what powers a particular designated officer has been given and therefore what his/her role will be. Schedule 4 to the Police Reform Act 2002 outlines these powers, some of which are set out below.

1.6.3.1 Investigating Officers

- To act as the supervisor of any access to seized material to which a person is entitled, to supervise the taking of a photograph of seized material, or to photograph it him/herself.
- To arrest a detainee for a further offence if it appears to him/her that the detainee would be liable to arrest for that further offence if released from their initial arrest.
- Power for the custody officer to transfer to a designated civilian investigating officer responsibility for a detainee. This power includes a duty for the person investigating the offence, once the detainee is returned to the custody of the custody officer, to report back to the custody officer on how the Codes were complied with.
- To question an arrested person under ss. 36 and 37 of the Criminal Justice and Public Order Act 1994 about facts which may be attributable to the person's participation in an offence. The designated person may also give the suspect the necessary warning about the capacity of a court to draw inferences from a failure to give a satisfactory account in response to questioning.

1.6.3.2 Detention Officers

- Powers to search detained persons, to take fingerprints and certain samples without consent and to take photographs.

- To require certain defined categories of persons who have been convicted, cautioned, reprimanded or warned in relation to recordable offences to attend a police station to have their fingerprints taken.
- To carry out non-intimate searches of persons detained at police stations or elsewhere and to seize items found during such searches.
- To carry out searches and examinations in order to determine the identity of persons detained at police stations. Identifying marks found during such processes may be photographed.
- To carry out intimate searches in the same very limited circumstances that are applicable to constables.
- To take fingerprints without consent in the same circumstances that a constable can.
- To take non-intimate samples without consent and to inform the person from whom the sample is to be taken of any necessary authorisation by a senior officer and of the grounds for that authorisation.
- To require certain defined categories of persons who have been charged with or convicted of recordable offences to attend a police station to have a sample taken.
- To inform a person that intimate samples taken from him/her may be the subject of a speculative search (i.e. this will satisfy the requirement that the person must be informed that the sample will be the subject of a speculative search).
- To photograph detained persons in the same way that constables can.

1.6.3.3 Escort Officers

- To transport arrested persons to police stations and escort detained persons from one police station to another or between police stations and other locations specified by the custody officer.
- To carry out the duty of taking a person arrested by a constable to a police station as soon as practicable.
- With the authority of the custody officer, to escort detainees between police stations or between police stations and other specified locations.
- To conduct non-intimate searches of the detainee; and to seize or retain, or cause to be seized or retained, anything found on such a search (restrictions on power to seize personal effects are the same as for police officers, as is the requirement that the search be carried out by a member of the same sex).

Where any of the powers allow for the use of reasonable force when exercised by a police constable, a designated person has the same entitlement to use reasonable force as a constable.

The Police Reform Act 2002 creates offences of assaulting, obstructing or impersonating designated persons which mirror offences in ss. 89 and 90 of the Police Act 1996 for such offences against police officers.

Guidance is provided within the various PACE Codes of Practice and in detail in Code C, paras 1.13 to 1.17. It should be noted that the guidance makes it clear that any reference to a police officer includes a designated person acting in the exercise or performance of the powers and duties conferred or imposed on them by their designation.

It is important to note that not all support staff will be designated for the purposes of the Police Reform Act 2002 and non-designated staff will not have the additional powers as outlined above. Code C, para. 1.15 provides that nothing in the Code prevents the custody officer, or other officer given custody of the detainee, from allowing police staff who are not designated persons to carry out individual procedures or tasks at the police station if the law allows. Where staff are used in this way to support the custody officer, the officer remains responsible for making sure that the procedures and tasks are carried out correctly in accordance with the Codes of Practice. Designated persons and other police staff must have regard to any relevant provisions of the Codes (Code C, para. 1.16).

1.6.4 Designated Police Stations

Section 30 of the Police and Criminal Evidence Act 1984 requires that a person who has been arrested must be taken to a police station *as soon as practicable* after arrest, unless the arrested person has been bailed prior to arrival at the police station. Section 30A of the 1984 Act allows a constable to release on bail a person who is under arrest. However, not all police stations have charge rooms or facilities for dealing with prisoners, so the 1984 Act requires that prisoners who will be detained (or who are likely to be detained) for more than six hours must go to a 'designated' police station. A designated police station is one that has enough facilities for the purpose of detaining arrested people. Section 35 requires the Chief Officer of Police to designate sufficient police stations to deal with prisoners. It is for the Chief Officer to decide which stations are to be designated stations and these details are then published. Police stations can be designated permanently or for any specified periods provided that they are not designated for part of a day.

1.6.5 Custody Officers

Custody officers are responsible for the reception and treatment of prisoners detained at the police station.

The role of the custody officer is to act independently of those conducting the investigation, thereby ensuring the welfare and rights of the detained person. This requirement is contained in s. 36(5) of the 1984 Act. PACE Code C, para. 3.4 also supports this point in that it makes it clear that the custody officer must not ask a detained person any questions regarding his/her involvement in any offence. The custody officer should not make any comment which may be seen as placing a value judgement on what the person is alleged to have done, nor should he/she make any other comment which in any way casts doubt on his/her impartiality.

Section 36 requires that one or more custody officers must be appointed for each designated police station. However, in *Vince* v *Chief Constable of Dorset* [1993] 1 WLR 415, it was held that a chief constable was under a duty to appoint one custody officer for each designated police station and had a discretionary power to appoint more than one but this duty did not go so far as to require a sufficient number to ensure that the functions of custody officer were always performed by them. The provision of the facility of a custody officer must be reasonable. Section 36(3) states that a custody officer must be an officer of at least the rank of sergeant. However, s. 36(4) allows officers of any rank to perform the functions of custody officer at a designated police station if a sergeant is not readily available to perform them. The effect of s. 36(3) and (4) is that the practice of allowing officers of any other rank to perform the role of custody officer where a sergeant (*who has no other role to perform*) is in the police station must therefore be unlawful. Should a decision be made to use acting sergeants or untrained custody officers, this may lead to a claim in negligence by the officer or the detained person where there is a breach of the Codes or someone is injured as a result of the failure to manage the custody suite effectively. It could also lead to a prosecution under health and safety legislation.

For cases where arrested people are taken to a non-designated police station, s. 36(7) states that an officer of any rank not involved in the investigation should perform the role of custody officer. If no such person is at the station, the arresting officer (or any other officer involved in the investigation) or the officer that granted him/her bail under s. 30A of the 1984 Act (bail prior to being taken to a police station) should perform the role. In these cases, an officer of at least the rank of inspector at a designated police station must be informed. It is suggested that once informed, that officer should consider the circumstances of the detained person. Code C, para. 2.1A requires a person under arrest or attending the police station to be brought before a custody officer as soon as is practicable after their arrival at the police station. 'At a police station' is now defined as within the boundary of any building or enclosed yard that forms part of that police station.

The role of the custody officer is crucial to the effective and fair operation of the criminal justice system. In addition to protecting the rights of detained people the role, if performed properly, should also prevent evidence being declared inadmissible because of a violation of the rules. In order to provide as full a record as possible about the detention of a person, the custody officer is required to open a custody record for each detained person (Code C, para. 2.1) and entries should be recorded *as soon as practicable*. Guidance on the completion of custody records is given in Code C, paras 2.1 to 2.7. Custody officers must become very familiar with this guidance, as they are responsible for the accuracy and completeness of the custody record (Code C, para. 2.3). It is important that all entries (subject to Code C, para. 2.6A) in the custody record are timed and signed by the maker (Code C, para. 2.6). If a person is requested to sign an entry in accordance with the Codes and refuses, this too should be recorded as should the time the detained person refused (Code C, para. 2.7).

It is also recognised that the role of custody officer is very demanding and, on occasions, the time restraints created by the legislation can become unrealistic. For this reason Code C, para. 1.1A states that a custody officer will not be in breach of the Codes if delay in taking some action was justifiable and reasonable steps had been taken to prevent the unnecessary delay.

However, if that delay was not 'justified', it could lead to actions for unlawful detention and false imprisonment and any evidence obtained as a result may be held to be inadmissible (*Roberts* v *Chief Constable of Cheshire Constabulary* [1999] 1 WLR 662).

Where a custody officer feels that he/she is unable to comply with the minimum standards of detention as required by PACE, it is suggested that he/she should draw this to the attention of the line manager and/or the superintendent responsible for the custody suite. Custody officers should be mindful of article 5 of the European Convention on Human Rights in considering whether they are able to manage the number of detained persons in their custody to ensure that their detention is not any longer than needed.

1.6.6 Police Detention and the Treatment of Detained Persons

Depriving a person of his/her liberty is a serious step. The legislation and the PACE Codes of Practice are intended to ensure that where a person's liberty is taken it is for no longer than is necessary. There is a growing trend towards civil claims against the police for unlawful detention and false imprisonment, some of which is as a result of a failure to follow the guidelines. There are strict limits on a person's detention period and the best defence to such cases is to ensure that the 1984 Act and its Codes of Practice are followed.

1.6.6.1 Meaning of Police Detention

Police detention is defined by s. 118 of the Police and Criminal Evidence Act 1984 which states:

> (2) Subject to subsection (2A) a person is in police detention for the purposes of this Act if—
> (a) he has been taken to a police station after being arrested for an offence or after being arrested under section 41 of the Terrorism Act 2000, or

(b) he is arrested at a police station after attending voluntarily at the station or accompanying a constable to it,

and is detained there or is detained elsewhere in the charge of a constable, except that a person who is at a court after being charged is not in police detention for those purposes.

(2A) Where a person is in another's lawful custody by virtue of paragraph 22, 34(1) or 35(3) of Schedule 4 to the Police Reform Act 2002, he shall be treated as in police detention.

Paragraph 22 of sch. 4 to the Police Reform Act 2002 refers to the power to transfer persons into the custody of investigating officers, para. 34(1) relates to designated escort officers taking an arrested person to a police station, and para. 35(3) deals with a designated escort officer transferring a detainee from one police station to another.

PACE Code of Practice C also states:

1.10 ... Section 15 applies solely to people in police detention, e.g. those brought to a police station under arrest or arrested at a police station for an offence after going there voluntarily.

1.11 People detained under the Terrorism Act 2000, Schedule 8 and section 41 and other provisions of that Act are not subject to any part of this Code. Such persons are subject to the Code of Practice for detention, treatment and questioning of persons by police officers detained under that Act.

1.12 This Code's provisions do not apply to people in custody:

(i) arrested on warrants issued in Scotland by officers under the Criminal Justice and Public Order Act 1994, section 136(2), or arrested or detained without warrant by officers from a police force in Scotland under section 137(2). In these cases, police powers and duties and the person's rights and entitlements whilst at a police station in England or Wales are the same as those in Scotland;

(ii) arrested under the Immigration and Asylum Act 1999, section 142(3) in order to have their fingerprints taken;

(iii) whose detention is authorised by an immigration officer under the Immigration Act 1971;

(iv) who are convicted or remanded prisoners held in police cells on behalf of the Prison Service under the Imprisonment (Temporary Provisions) Act 1980;

(v) not used

(vi) detained for searches under stop and search powers except as required by Code A.

The provisions on conditions of detention and treatment in sections 8 and 9 must be considered as the minimum standards of treatment for such detainees.

KEYNOTE

The last two lines of Code C, para. 1.12 above, make it clear that the way such prisoners are treated should be of no lower standard than that for other detained people. If in doubt as to whether a person falls within the definition of a detained person, it is suggested that he/she should be afforded all the rights and privileges outlined in the Codes of Practice. A similar approach should be adopted when it comes to reviewing a detainee's detention (**see para. 1.6.7.6**).

With the exception of those groups listed in Code C, para. 1.12, Code C applies to people in custody at police stations in England and Wales, whether or not they have been arrested, and to those removed to a police station as a place of safety under the Mental Health Act 1983, ss. 135 and 136.

1.6.6.2 Right to Have Someone Informed

Section 56 of the Police and Criminal Evidence Act 1984 provides that a person arrested and held in custody at a police station or other premises may, on request, have one friend or relative or person known to him/her or who is likely to take an interest in his/her welfare, informed at public expense of his/her whereabouts as soon as practicable (Code C, para. 5.1). (If the detainee's first choice cannot be contacted, see Code C, para. 5.1 and Notes 5C and 5D.) This fundamental human right is known as the right not to be held *incommunicado* and guidance on this right is contained in Code C, paras 5.1 to 5.7A. If a person transfers to another police station, the same right applies at the next police station (Code C, para. 5.3), even if they have already had someone informed at the previous places of detention.

This right can only be delayed if the offence is 'an indictable offence' and an officer of the rank of inspector or above (whether or not connected to the investigation) authorises the delay (see Code C, Annex B) (**see para. 1.6.6.7**). Where a person has to be given information under the Code but is not in a fit state to understand it, it is to be given to him/her as soon as practicable but only when he/she is in a fit state to understand it (see Code C, para. 1.8 for what might amount to not being in a fit state). The delay can only be for a maximum of 36 hours (48 hours in cases involving terrorism), and the 36-hour period is calculated from the 'relevant time' (**see para. 1.6.6.8**). In the case of a juvenile, the power to authorise the delay does not apply to the person responsible for their welfare, but only to any other person the juvenile wishes to have informed (Code C, para. 3.13).

There may be occasions where officers wish to conduct a search under s. 18 of the 1984 Act and the detained person has requested to have someone informed. Clearly if that person is informed before the search is conducted, vital evidence or property may be lost. Often the custody officer has two methods by which he/she can inform the person requested about the detained person's detention; either in person or on the phone. Contacting the person by telephone is likely to be the quickest, however, there is no requirement to use the quickest method in order to pass on this information. While there is no case law on this point, Code C, Note 5D, supports the view that, where the s. 18 search is to be conducted relatively quickly after the request is made by the detained person, it would be permissible to inform that person at the time the s. 18 search is conducted. Where the search is not to be conducted straight away, it is suggested that consideration would have to be given to obtaining the authority of an officer of at least the rank of inspector to delay the notification as outlined in **para. 1.6.6.7**. A lengthy delay may be seen as a breach of this right which may lead to a stay of proceedings or a claim for damages as a breach of the detained person's human rights.

Detained people may also be allowed to speak to one person on the telephone for a reasonable time or send letters. If a person has an interpreter, he/she can do this on the detained person's behalf. This right can be denied or delayed in the case of indictable offences or where a person is detained under s. 41 or sch. 7 to the Terrorism Act 2000 by an officer of the rank of inspector or above (Code C, para. 5.6 and for terrorism cases Code H, para. 5.6). The grounds are the same as those regulating the holding of people *incommunicado* (**see para. 1.6.6.7**). Where a person is allowed to make a telephone call or send a letter, the procedure in Code C, para. 5.7 should be followed. Should there be any delay in complying with a request by a detained person to have someone informed of his/her detention or to communicate with someone, the detained person should be informed of this and told the reason for it and a record kept (s. 56(6) of the 1984 Act). The custody officer also has a discretion to allow visits to the detained person at the police station (Code C, para. 5.4 and Note 5B). It is suggested that with the Codes of Practice outlining the limited rights for the detained person to make telephone calls and the right to restrict these calls, that if the person has a mobile telephone it can be seized for the period of their detention. There is no case law on this point and any force policy should be followed.

1.6.6.3 Right to Have Someone Informed: Juveniles

In the case of juveniles, where practicable, a person who is responsible for a juvenile's welfare must be informed of his/her arrest. This person may be the appropriate adult (see

Code C, para. 1.7(a)) but if not, arrangements must be made for an adult to attend the police station to look after the interests of the juvenile. This action must be undertaken regardless of whether the juvenile wishes to have someone informed or has requested that some other person other than the appropriate adult be informed.

Code C, para. 3.13 states:

> If the detainee is a juvenile, the custody officer must, if it is practicable, ascertain the identity of a person responsible for their welfare. That person:
> - may be:
>   - the parent or guardian;
>   - if the juvenile is in local authority or voluntary organisation care, or is otherwise being looked after under the Children Act 1989, a person appointed by that authority or organisation to have responsibility for the juvenile's welfare;
>   - any other person who has, for the time being, assumed responsibility for the juvenile's welfare.
> - must be informed as soon as practicable that the juvenile has been arrested, why they have been arrested and where they are detained. This right is in addition to the juvenile's right in s. 5 not to be held incommunicado. See Code C, Note 3C.

If a juvenile is known to be subject to a court order under which a person or organisation is given any degree of statutory responsibility to supervise or otherwise monitor them, reasonable steps must also be taken to notify that person or organisation (the 'responsible officer'). The responsible officer will normally be a member of a youth offending team, except for a curfew order which involves electronic monitoring when the contractor providing the monitoring will normally be the responsible officer (Code C, para. 3.14).

1.6.6.4 Right to Have Someone Informed: Special Groups

If the detainee appears to be deaf or there is doubt about his/her hearing or speaking ability or ability to understand English, and the custody officer cannot establish effective communication, the custody officer must, as soon as practicable, call an interpreter for assistance to go through the detainee's rights under Code C, paras 3.1 to 3.5 (Code C, para. 3.12).

If the detainee is a mentally disordered or otherwise mentally vulnerable, the custody officer must, as soon as practicable, inform the appropriate adult of the grounds for their detention and their whereabouts. The appropriate adult should also be asked to come to the police station to see the detainee (Code C, para. 3.15). In managing mentally disordered or otherwise mentally vulnerable persons detained under the Mental Health Act 1983, s. 136, the custody officer must be mindful that it is imperative that the detainee is assessed as soon as possible (Code C, para. 3.16).

Code C, para. 13.1 requires chief officers to make arrangements for suitably qualified interpreters for the deaf and those who do not understand English. The interpreters should be registered with the National Register of Public Service Interpreters or the Council for the Advancement of Communication with Deaf People (CACDP) Directory of British Sign Language/English Interpreters.

1.6.6.5 Right to Have Someone Informed: Detained People from Other Countries

Citizens of independent commonwealth countries or foreign nationals may communicate with their High Commission, Embassy or Consulate as soon as practicable (Code C, para. 7.1). If the country is included on the list at Annex F to Code C, the High Commission, Embassy or Consulate must be informed of their arrest and detention as soon as practicable unless the detained person is a political refugee or is seeking political asylum (para. 7.4).

Where a person who is a friend, relative or a person with an interest in the detained person's welfare, makes inquiries about that person, the detained person should be asked whether he/she agrees to the person being informed prior to any information being given (Code C, para. 5.5). The information must not be given if a delay has been authorised.

1.6.6.6 Right to Legal Advice

Section 58 of the Police and Criminal Evidence Act 1984 provides an almost inalienable right for a person arrested and held in custody at a police station or other premises to consult privately with a solicitor free of charge at any time if he/she requests it (or the appropriate adult makes the request (Code C, para. 3.19)). This provision is very similar to that of s. 56 of the 1984 Act: the right to have a person informed of the arrest. This right to consult a solicitor is considered to be so important that a detained person must be informed of the right when he/she first arrives at the police station and asked for reasons if he/she declines to exercise this right. Detainees are also reminded of this right at other times, e.g. prior to interview and when detention is being reviewed. In *R* v *Alladice* (1988) 87 Cr App R 380 the Court of Appeal made it clear that:

> no matter how strongly and however justifiably the police may feel that their investigation and detection of crime is being hindered by the presence of a solicitor ... they are nevertheless confined to the narrow limits imposed by section 58.

In *R* v *Aspinall* [1999] 2 Cr App R 115 the court stated that the right to access to legal advice was a fundamental right under article 6 of the European Convention on Human Rights and even greater importance had to be attached to advice for a vulnerable person. While the appropriate adult of a juvenile can request legal advice from a solicitor, the detained juvenile cannot be forced to see the solicitor (Code C, para. 6.5A).

Once a person has requested a solicitor this must be provided without delay; what will be considered to be without delay will be a question of fact in each case (*Whitley* v *DPP* [2004] Crim LR 585). It will be important to justify any delay as even short delays in calling a solicitor might be considered to be a breach of the Codes and be challenged by the defence. This was the case in *Kirkup* v *DPP* [2004] Crim LR 230, which involved a seven minute delay from requesting to calling a solicitor. The court held that the delay only just gave rise to a breach of s. 58 of the 1984 Act and the Codes of Practice but that it was so short a period that it did not lead to the exclusion of any evidence under s. 78.

Code C, Annex B provides an exception to this right to legal advice: cases where an officer of the rank of superintendent or above (whether or not connected to the investigation) authorises the exercise of the right to be delayed. This only applies if the offence is an indictable offence and Code C, Annex B applies.

The same exception also apples where the person is held under prevention of terrorism legislation (Terrorism Act 2000, s. 41 or sch. 8) and the conditions in Code H, Annex B apply. In addition, a uniformed officer of at least the rank of inspector not connected with the case may be present if authorised by an Assistant Chief Constable of Commander (Terrorism Act 2000, sch. 8, para. 9 and Code H, paras 6.4, 6.5).

The delay can only be for a maximum of 36 hours (48 hours from the time of arrest in terrorism cases) or until the time the person will first appear at court, whichever is the sooner (see below). The 36-hour period is calculated from the 'relevant time' (**see para. 1.6.6.8**). The authorisation can initially be made orally either in person or by telephone but must be recorded in writing as soon as practicable. Where a delay is authorised then this restricts the drawing of adverse inferences from silence (see Code C, para. 6.6).

The consultation with a solicitor can be either on the telephone, in person or in writing and it must be in private (Code C, para. 6.1). This right to have a private consultation is a good example of where a person's rights under the European Convention need to be considered. In many custody suites this is difficult to comply with (see Code C, Note 6J) but could lead to adverse comment, particularly if officers act on what they heard the detained person say while consulting with their legal representative. Code C, Note 6J gives clear indication that the normal expectation should be that facilities will be available for the detainee to speak in private to a solicitor. This right to have a private consultation also apples to juveniles who, should they wish to have a private consultation without the appropriate adult being present, must be permitted to do so (Code C, Note 1E). This point was considered in *R (On the Application of M (A Child))* v *Commissioner of the Police of the Metropolis* [2002] Crim LR 215, where the court said that ideally there ought be a consultation room at every police station and facilities for private telephone calls to be made for legal consultations. However, there was no breach of article 6(3) of the European Convention where it could not be shown that a detainee had been denied adequate facilities for the preparation of his defence.

Once a person has indicated a wish to have a solicitor, and has not yet been advised by a solicitor, he/she can only be interviewed in limited circumstances as set out in Code C, para. 6.6, but it is not necessary to delay taking breath, blood or urine samples from a motorist until a solicitor arrives or to delay searching the detainee or the taking of non-intimate samples, fingerprints or footwear impressions without consent for evidential purposes (Code C, Note 3D). Of particular note is Code C, para. 6.6(b). This allows an officer of the rank of superintendent or above to allow an interview to take place or continue without a solicitor being present, if he/she has reasonable grounds for believing that:

(i) the consequent delay might:
- lead to interference with, or harm to, evidence connected with an offence;
- lead to interference with, or physical harm to, other people;
- lead to serious loss of, or damage to, property;
- lead to alerting other people suspected of having committed an offence but not yet arrested for it;
- hinder the recovery of property obtained in consequence of the commission of an offence.

(ii) when a solicitor, including a duty solicitor, has been contacted and has agreed to attend, awaiting their arrival would cause unreasonable delay to the process of investigation.

Another exception is in relation to the drink drive procedure for s. 7 of the Road Traffic Act 1988. In *DPP* v *Noe* [2000] RTR 351 a request to see a solicitor or alternatively to consult a law book to verify the legality of the police request for a specimen of breath was not a reasonable excuse under s. 7. This decision has not been affected by the enactment of the Human Rights Act 1998. This is confirmed by *Campbell* v *DPP* [2003] Crim LR 118 who held that it was entirely proportionate to allow a police officer to require a member of the community to provide a specimen albeit that legal advice had not been obtained.

Where Code C, para. 6.6 is used it will have to be justified at court if the interview is to be admissible. This power might prove useful in circumstances where there are 'delaying tactics' by legal representatives, particularly where they are aware that the detained person's relevant time is due to expire within a short period.

Code C, para. 6.6 provides two further occasions where the interview may go ahead without a solicitor being present provided the consent of an officer of inspector rank or above has been obtained. Paragraph 6.6(c) deals with the situation where the solicitor the detainee has nominated or selected from a list cannot be contacted, has previously indicated they do not wish to be contacted, or having been contacted, has declined to attend; and the detainee has been advised of the Duty Solicitor Scheme but has declined to ask for the duty solicitor. Paragraph 6.6(d) deals with the situation where the detainee changes his/her mind, about wanting legal advice. In these circumstances the interview may be started or continued provided that the detainee agrees to do so, in writing or on tape. In this case the officer of inspector rank or above must inquire about the detainee's reasons for their change of mind and must give authority for the interview to proceed. Paragraph 6.6(d) outlines what information must be recorded in the written interview record or the audio or visual interview record.

Where an interview has started without the solicitor being present and access has not been refused under Code C, Annex B, the solicitor must be allowed to be present when he/she arrives at the station unless Code C, para. 6.6(b) applies or he/she has been excluded because of his/her conduct (Code C, para. 6.10).

In considering whether to conduct an interview in these circumstances, guidance is given in Code C, Note 6A.

A solicitor for these purposes means a solicitor who holds a current practising certificate, or an accredited or probationary representative included on the register of representatives maintained by the Legal Services Commission (Code C, para. 6.12). An accredited or probationary representative may also attend and give advice unless an officer of the rank of inspector or above considers that such a visit will hinder the investigation of crime and directs otherwise and once admitted he/she should be treated as any other legal adviser (Code C, para. 6.12A).

In deciding whether to admit an accredited or probationary representative, the officer should take into account in particular whether the identity and status of the accredited or probationary representative have been satisfactorily established; whether he/she is of suitable character to provide legal advice (a person with a criminal record is unlikely to be suitable unless the conviction was for a minor offence and is not of recent date); and any other matters in any written letter of authorisation provided by the solicitor on whose behalf the person is attending the police station (Code C, para. 6.13). The Law Society has advised solicitors that if an accredited or probationary representative is refused admission, a written reason for the decision should be requested. If access is refused or a decision is taken that such a person should not be permitted to remain at an interview, the inspector must forthwith notify a solicitor on whose behalf the accredited or probationary representative was to have acted or was acting, and give him/her an opportunity to make alternative arrangements. The detained person must also be informed and the custody record noted (Code C, para. 6.14 and Note 6F).

1.6.6.7 Authority to Delay Rights under s. 56 or 58 (Code C, Annex B)

An officer of the rank of superintendent or above for s. 58 of the Police and Criminal Evidence Act 1984 and inspector or above for s. 56 of the 1984 Act can only authorise a delay if he/she has reasonable grounds for believing that exercising the s. 56 and s. 58 rights will:

- lead to interference with or cause harm to evidence connected with an indictable offence or lead to interference with or cause physical injury to other people; or
- lead to alerting other people suspected of having committed an indictable offence but not yet arrested for it; or
- hinder the recovery of property obtained as a consequence of the commission of such an offence.

The delay may also be authorised under s. 56 and/or s. 58 where the officer has reasonable grounds for believing that the person detained for an indictable offence has benefited from his/her criminal conduct and the recovery of the value of the property constituting the benefit will be hindered by telling the named person of the arrest or his/her right of access to legal advice.

For these purposes whether a person has benefited from his/her criminal conduct is to be decided in accordance with s. 76(1) and (4) of the Proceeds of Crime Act 2002. Briefly, criminal conduct is conduct which constitutes an offence in England and Wales, or would constitute such an offence if it occurred in England and Wales. A person benefits from conduct if he/she obtains property as a result of or in connection with the conduct.

In cases where the person is detained under the Terrorism Act 2000 an officer of the rank of superintendent or above may delay the exercise of either right or both if he/she has reasonable grounds for believing that the exercise of the right will lead to any of the consequences of:

- interference with, or harm to, evidence connected with an indictable offence;
- interference with, or physical harm to, other people;
- the alerting of other people suspected of having committed an indictable offence but not yet arrested for it;
- hinder the recovery of property obtained as a result of an indictable offence or in respect of which a forfeiture order could be made;
- interference with the gathering of information about the commission, preparation or instigation of acts of terrorism;
- the alerting of any person, making it more difficult to prevent an act of terrorism;
- by alerting any person, making it more difficult to prevent an act of terrorism or secure the apprehension, prosecution or conviction of any person in connection with the commission, preparation or instigation of an act of terrorism;
- the detained person has benefited from his/her criminal conduct, and the recovery of the value of the property constituting the benefit will be hindered by informing the named person of the detained person's detention or access to legal advice. For these purposes whether a person has benefited from his/her criminal conduct is to be decided in accordance with part 2 of the Proceeds of Crime Act 2002. Briefly, criminal conduct is conduct which constitutes an offence in England and Wales, or would constitute such an offence if it occurred in England and Wales. A person benefits from conduct if he/she obtains property as a result of or in connection with the conduct (Code H, Annex B, para. 2).

If the delay is authorised the detained person must be given the reason for the delay which must correspond to one of the above grounds and an entry must be made in the custody record.

Once the reason for authorising the delay has ceased, the detained person must be allowed to exercise his/her rights. Once this point has been reached, the detained person must as soon as practicable be asked if he/she wishes to exercise the right (or rights), the custody record must be noted accordingly, and the relevant action taken (Code C, Annex B, para. 6).

The fact that the grounds for delaying notification of arrest may be satisfied does not automatically mean that the grounds for delaying access to legal advice will also be satisfied (Code C, Annex B, para. 5).

When considering whether to deny access to a solicitor the fact that he/she might advise the person not to answer any questions or that the solicitor was initially asked to attend the police station by someone else, provided that the person himself/herself then wishes to see the solicitor, is not a reason for delaying access to a solicitor (Code C, Annex B, para. 4). When considering the delay of access to a solicitor the authorising officer must bear in mind that access to a solicitor is 'a fundamental right of a citizen' (*R* v *Samuel* [1988] 2 WLR 920). The authorising officer must actually believe that by allowing access to the solicitor he/she will intentionally or inadvertently alert other suspects. There must also be objective reasons upon which the officer authorising the delay can base his/her beliefs. If the reason for authorising the delay of access to a solicitor is because there are concerns with the particular solicitor who has been requested or is offering his/her services to the detained person the officer should offer the detained person access to a solicitor (who is not the specific solicitor referred to above) on the Duty Solicitor Scheme (Code C, Annex B, para. 3). Annex B, Note B3 suggests that occasions where this delay will be authorised in such circumstances will be rare and only when it can be shown that the suspect is capable of misleading that particular solicitor and there is more than a substantial risk that the suspect will succeed in causing information to be conveyed which will lead to one or more of the specified consequences. In deciding whether such an interview will be admissible the court will consider how reliable it is and will consider how the refusal to allow that particular detained person access to a solicitor affected their decision to make a confession. One such case where the confession was excluded is *R* v *Sanusi* [1992] Crim LR 43, where a person from another country was denied access to a solicitor and the court held that his right to advice was particularly significant due to his lack of familiarity with police procedures.

In terrorism cases a direction may be given by an officer of at least the rank of Commander or Assistant Chief Constable which may provide that a detained person who wishes to exercise the right to consult a solicitor may do so only in the sight and hearing of a qualified officer, this person being a uniformed officer of at least the rank of inspector not connected with the investigation from the authorising officer's force.

1.6.6.8 Relevant Time

As discussed above, there are limits on how long a person can be detained. The Police and Criminal Evidence Act 1984 and the Codes of Practice talk of the 'relevant time'. This is the time from which the limits of detention are calculated. The relevant time of a person's detention starts in accordance with s. 41(2) to (5) of the 1984 Act. Section 41 states:

(2) The time from which the period of detention of a person is to be calculated (in this Act referred to as 'the relevant time')—
- (a) in the case of a person to whom this paragraph applies, shall be—
  - (i) the time at which that person arrives at the relevant police station; or
  - (ii) the time 24 hours after the time of that person's arrest,

  whichever is the earlier;
- (b) in the case of a person arrested outside England and Wales, shall be—
  - (i) the time at which that person arrives at the first police station to which he is taken in the police area in England or Wales in which the offence for which he was arrested is being investigated; or
  - (ii) the time 24 hours after the time of that person's entry into England and Wales,

  whichever is the earlier,
- (c) in the case of a person who—
  - (i) attends voluntarily at a police station; or
  - (ii) accompanies a constable to a police station without having been arrested,

  and is arrested at the police station, the time of his arrest;
- (ca) in the case of a person who attends a police station to answer to bail granted under section 30A, the time he arrives at the police station;
- (d) in any other case, except where subsection (5) below applies, shall be the time at which the person arrested arrives at the first police station to which he is taken after his arrest.

(3) Subsection (2)(a) above applies to a person if—
- (a) his arrest is sought in one police area in England and Wales;
- (b) he is arrested in another police area, and
- (c) he is not questioned in the area in which he is arrested in order to obtain evidence in relation to an offence for which he is arrested;

and in sub-paragraph (i) of that paragraph 'the relevant police station' means the first police station to which he is taken in the police area in which his arrest was sought.

(4) Subsection (2) above shall have effect in relation to a person arrested under section 31 above as if every reference in it to his arrest or his being arrested were a reference to his arrest or his being arrested for the offence for which he was originally arrested.

(5) If—

(a) a person is in police detention in a police area in England and Wales ('the first area'); and

(b) his arrest for an offence is sought in some other police area in England and Wales ('the second area'); and

(c) he is taken to the second area for the purposes of investigating that offence, without being questioned in the first area in order to obtain evidence in relation to it,

the relevant time shall be—

(i) the time 24 hours after he leaves the place where he is detained in the first area; or

(ii) the time at which he arrives at the first police station to which he is taken in the second area,

whichever is the earlier.

KEYNOTE

Note that under s. 41(5) the relevant time may vary depending on whether the detainee is interviewed in relation to the offence while still in the first police area.

For those detained under the Terrorism Act 2000 (**see para. 1.9.11**) the detention clock starts from the time the person is arrested, not the time he/she arrives at the police station.

The Criminal Justice Act 2003 inserted s. 41(2)(ca) into the Police and Criminal Evidence Act 1984. This allows for a person who has been arrested to be bailed before being taken to a police station. When the person attends the police station to which he/she has been bailed the relevant time starts when he/she arrives at the police station.

Some situations occur where a person is arrested at one police station and has been circulated as wanted by another police station in the same force area. In these cases, where the person is not wanted on warrant, the detention clock for the second offence starts at the same time as for the original offence for which they were arrested. Consideration will need to be given as to how to protect the detention period for the second offence while officers are dealing with the first matter. Options that might be considered would include bailing the person for one of the offences or conducting both investigations at the same station. Here there may be a risk of 'confusing' the suspect, which may allow him/her to retract or qualify any confession he/she might make.

In *Henderson* v *Chief Constable of Cleveland* [2001] 1 WLR 1103 the court considered the policy of not executing a court warrant until after other matters for which the person had been detained were completed. The court held that, once a warrant was executed, there was a requirement to follow the directions of the warrant. The police however had a discretion as to *when* to execute the warrant. This may be relevant where a person has been arrested for one offence and it is discovered that he/she is also wanted for another offence or where there are warrants in existence for that person at more than one court. In such cases, if the warrant is executed immediately, the direction on the warrant tells officers to take the person before the next available court, an action which could interfere with the investigation. If *Henderson* is followed there is no requirement to execute the warrant straight away and the other matters can be dealt with before the requirement to produce the person at court under the warrant applies.

1.6.6.9 Detention of People under Arrest

Section 37 of the 1984 Act states:

(1) Where—

(a) a person is arrested for an offence—

(i) without a warrant; or

(ii) under a warrant not endorsed for bail,

(b) repealed,

the custody officer at each police station where he is detained after his arrest shall determine whether he has before him sufficient evidence to charge that person with the offence for which he was arrested and may detain him at the police station for such period as is necessary to enable him to do so.

(2) If the custody officer determines that he does not have such evidence before him, the person arrested shall be released either on bail or without bail, unless the custody officer has reasonable grounds for believing that his detention without being charged is necessary to secure or preserve evidence relating to an offence for which he is under arrest or to obtain such evidence by questioning him.

(3) If the custody officer has reasonable grounds for so believing, he may authorise the person arrested to be kept in police detention.

(4) Where a custody officer authorises a person who has not been charged to be kept in police detention, he shall, as soon as is practicable, make a written record of the grounds for the detention.

(5) Subject to subsection (6) below, the written record shall be made in the presence of the person arrested who shall at that time be informed by the custody officer of the grounds for his detention.

People who have been arrested, returned on bail, or have voluntarily given themselves up at a police station, which includes a person who has attended the police station after having been given street bail (**see para. 1.10.2.1**), will be brought before a custody officer who must decide whether the person should be detained at the police station or released. People who attend police stations voluntarily to assist the police with their investigations are not subject to this procedure; their treatment is dealt with by s. 29 of the 1984 Act and PACE Code C, paras 3.21 and 3.22. However if an officer forms a view that the person should be arrested at the police station for the purpose of interview and informs the custody officer of this view, the custody officer can authorise detention for the interview and is entitled to assume the arrest by the officer is lawful (*Fayed* v *Metropolitan Police Commissioner* [2004] EWCA Civ 1579).

The arresting officer must inform the custody officer of the reasons for arrest; these grounds can be given remotely, e.g. by telephone or by a third party (Code C, para. 3.4). This will include *what* offence the person was arrested for and brief details of the *grounds* for the arrest, e.g. the arrest is for robbery and the accused was seen to punch the victim in the face and steal her holdall. As this information must be given to the person on arrest—in most cases—the details given to the custody officer should be fresh in the mind of the arresting officer; they should also accord with the reasons and grounds given to the person on arrest. If the grounds were not given at the time of arrest (on justifiable grounds) the custody officer should consider whether the arrested person is now in a position to be given the grounds for the arrest (as being the first practicable opportunity (s. 28(3) of the 1984 Act)). If the grounds for arrest were not given when they should have been, the arrest is unlawful regardless of what information is given later (*Wilson* v *Chief Constable of Lancashire* (2000) unreported).

Having heard the details of and grounds for the arrest, the custody officer must decide whether or not there are reasons which justify authorising that person's detention (s. 37 of the Police and Criminal Evidence Act 1984 deals with the procedures to be followed before a person is charged). Some commentators have suggested that it is also the role of the custody officer to establish that the arrest itself was lawful. While this would seem to be good practice, the custody officer's duty is confined to acting in accordance with the requirements set out in s. 37 of the 1984 Act. These duties do not appear to include considering whether the arrest was lawful unless this is relevant to the main question of whether there is sufficient evidence to charge the suspect. The view is supported by the decision of the

Divisional Court in *DPP* v *L* [1999] Crim LR 752, where the court held that there was no express or implied requirement imposing a duty on a custody officer to inquire into the legality of an arrest and in that case the custody officer was therefore entitled to assume that it was lawful. A subsequent finding that the arrest was unlawful did not invalidate the decision of the custody officer to hold the person in custody. However, where the custody officer is aware that the arrest is unlawful, he/she will need to consider whether continued detention is justifiable, particularly in light of the Human Rights Act 1998.

If the person is arrested on a warrant, any directions given by the court in the warrant must be followed. Consideration can always be given to contacting the court to get a variation on the conditions of the warrant. (If the warrant was issued for the arrest of a person who has not yet been charged or summonsed for an offence, he/she should be dealt with as any other person arrested for an offence without warrant unless there are any additional directions on the warrant that must be followed.)

Where a person who has been bailed under s. 37(7)(a) in order that the Director of Public Prosecutions can make a case disposal decision answers his/her bail or is arrested for failing to return on bail, detention can only be authorised to allow him/her to be further bailed under s. 37D of the 1984 Act or in order that he/she can be charged or cautioned for offences connected with the original bail. If the person is not in a fit state to be dealt with he/she may be kept in police detention until he/she is (s. 37D of the Police and Criminal Evidence Act 1984).

1.6.6.10 Authorising a Person's Detention

A custody officer can authorise the detention of a person when there is sufficient evidence to charge and, more commonly, when there is *not* sufficient evidence to charge the suspect. If there is insufficient evidence to charge, the custody officer must decide if the detention is necessary to secure or preserve evidence relating to an offence for which the person is under arrest or to obtain such evidence by questioning him/her.

If a person representing the detained person does not feel the detention is lawful he/she can apply to the court for the detainee's release (*habeas corpus*). A detainee may also be able to make an application for release or damages following the incorporation of the European Convention on Human Rights. Article 5(4) states:

> Everyone who is deprived of his liberty by arrest or detention shall be entitled to take proceedings by which the lawfulness of his detention shall be decided speedily by a court and his release ordered if the detention is not lawful.

1.6.6.11 Sufficient Evidence to Charge

Here the custody officer is looking at the evidence in order to satisfy him/herself that no further investigation is needed before the person can be charged. If this is the case, detention may be authorised for the purpose of charging the detained person.

Where a custody officer decides that there is sufficient evidence to charge a suspect who is in police detention, he/she is to have regard to any guidance issued by the DPP in determining whether the suspect should be released without charge but on bail, released without charge and without bail, or charged. Where a case is referred to the CPS to determine whether proceedings should be instituted (and if so on which charge), it was the case that if the decision to charge was not made at the time, the detained person had to be released on police bail with or without conditions. However, the Police and Justice Act 2006 has amended s. 37 of PACE and the person can now be kept in police detention pending the decision (subject to the normal time limits for detention applying). Once the CPS has made a decision the suspect is then to be charged, cautioned, or informed in writing that he/she is not to be prosecuted. For a discussion as to when a detained person should be charged or bailed when there is sufficient evidence, **see para. 1.6.9.**

Where there is sufficient evidence to charge, a delay in bringing charges may be seen to be unreasonable under article 6 of the European Convention on Human Rights (*D* v *HM Advocate* (2000) *The Times*, 14 April). In deciding whether there is sufficient evidence to charge for the purposes of authorising detention or when a person's detention is reviewed; where there is a conflict between the detained person's account and victims' or witnesses' accounts it is reasonable to be in possession of at least one witness statement in the English language before preferring charges (*R* v *Chief Constable of Hertfordshire, ex parte Wiles* [2002] EWHC Admin 387). There is no breach of the Police and Criminal Evidence Act 1984 in keeping the detained person in police detention while a statement is translated. It is suggested that the translation needs to be completed expeditiously.

Under s. 37(9) release can be delayed if the person is not in a fit state to be released (e.g. he/she is drunk), until he/she is fit. Where a person is detained for charge, the custody officer should record the grounds for detention in the custody record in the presence of the detained person if practicable (Code C, para. 3.23).

1.6.6.12 Insufficient Evidence to Charge

This creates two separate criteria for detention, that is to say, where detention is necessary to:

- secure and preserve evidence relating to an offence for which the person is arrested; or
- obtain such evidence by questioning the detained person.

If the custody officer has determined that there is not sufficient evidence to charge the person, the person must be released unless the custody officer has *reasonable grounds* for believing that the person's detention is necessary to preserve or to obtain such evidence by questioning the person. 'Reasonable grounds for believing' requires a greater amount of evidence than 'reasonable cause to suspect' and the custody officer must be able to justify any decision not to release a person from detention.

When deciding if detention should be authorised in order to obtain evidence by questioning, the case of *R* v *McGuinness* [1999] Crim LR 318 should be considered. There the court held that the words 'sufficient evidence to prosecute' and 'sufficient evidence for a prosecution to succeed', in Code C, para. 16.1 (this was the wording under the previous PACE Code of Practice), had to involve some consideration of any explanation, or lack of one, from the suspect. While an interview may not be needed in all cases, questioning of detained people before they are charged may be necessary, particularly where intention or dishonesty is involved or where there may be a defence. It may also be important to put questions to the person about the offence or his/her explanation, as this may be important to negate any defence the person raised at court (see s. 34 of the Criminal Justice and Public Order Act 1994).

Where initial suspicion rests on several people, it may be appropriate to hold all suspects until they all are interviewed before deciding whether there is enough evidence to warrant a charge against any of them. Detention for questioning where there are reasonable grounds for suspecting that an offence has been committed is lawful so long as the suspicion has not been dispelled in the interim and the questioning is not unnecessarily delayed (*Clarke* v *Chief Constable of North Wales* (2000) *The Independent*, 22 May).

The custody officer can detain the person for such period as is necessary in order to make this decision (s. 37(1) of the 1984 Act). Clearly any such period must be 'reasonable' in all the circumstances. For instance, where there are several prisoners waiting to be dealt with it may be reasonable that the last prisoner is not dealt with for 30 minutes because the custody officer is busy with the other prisoners (Code C, para. 1.1A and Note 1H). For the custody officer to be able to make this decision, the arresting officer needs to give sufficient detail about the offence. The account given by the arresting officer should be made in the presence of the arrested person and any comment made by that person in response should be recorded in the custody record (Code C, para. 3.4) (unless the person is violent or it is impractical to do so for some other reason, in which case this fact should also be recorded). If the arresting officer is not available, his/her account must be made either remotely or by a third party.

The mere fact that a person needs to be interviewed about the offence is not of itself justification for authorising detention. The question that has to be asked is whether the person can be bailed prior to the interview or even bailed before being taken to the police station (s. 30A of the 1984 Act). Factors which might be relevant in making this decision include:

- whether the person may interfere with witnesses;
- whether he/she is likely to return if bailed;
- where there is more than one suspect,
- that they would have an opportunity to confer before their interviews;
- whether there is outstanding property;
- whether the person's name and address are verified.

The fact that the officers and any legal representative will be ready to start the interview shortly may also be relevant when making this decision.

Section 37(4) and (5) of the 1984 Act require the custody officer to make a written record of the grounds of detention and to make that record in the presence of the detained person, informing him/her at the same time of the grounds of his/her detention (unless s. 37(6) applies). It is suggested that the custody officer record all the reasons for authorising the person's detention. For example: 'To obtain statements from the victim and witnesses as this information will be needed before interview to fully put the allegation to the suspect and then to allow the suspect to be interviewed about the allegation. If bailed prior to interview he/she may interfere with the witnesses, who are known to the suspect.' It is suggested that detail of at least this minimal level should be included, as it may be necessary in any criminal or civil proceedings. Indeed, it will be difficult for the custody officer to explain his/her decision without such information.

Section 37(6) states:

> Subsection (5) above shall not apply where the person arrested is, at the time when the written record is made—
> (a) incapable of understanding what is said to him;
> (b) violent or likely to become violent; or
> (c) in urgent need of medical attention.

1.6.6.13 Additional Action to be Taken by the Custody Officer

The action to be taken by the custody officer when receiving detained people is set out in Code C, paras 3.1 to 3.11.

Paragraph 3.1 sets out the information the detained person is entitled to. These are *continuing* entitlements and can be requested at any time during the person's detention. See Code C, Note 3B for choice of language and audio versions of these rights.

Paragraph 3.2 deals with written notices which must be given to the detained person in relation to his/her rights. (Code C, para. 1.2 requires that a copy of the Codes of Practice must also be readily available to detained persons should they request it.) There should be versions of these rights in languages other than English available in the custody suite.

Paragraph 3.5 requires the custody officer to establish whether the detained person wishes to have a solicitor at this stage. If he/she declines, the custody officer should ask the person the reason why and, if any reasons are given, these should be recorded in the custody record (Code C, para. 6.5). The detained person must still be asked if they require a solicitor even if they are to be held *incommunicado*.

1.6.7 Limits on Detention and Review

Once detention has been authorised this does not mean that a person can be detained indefinitely. Section 34 of the Police and Criminal Evidence Act 1984 requires the custody officer to release a person if he/she becomes aware that the grounds for detention no longer apply and that no other grounds exist for the continuing detention (unless the person appears to be unlawfully at large when they were arrested). Failure to comply with this could also lead to a breach of article 5 of the European Convention on Human Rights. If there are additional grounds, these should be recorded in the custody record and the person informed of these additional grounds in the same way as when a person is first detained. For example, this could be for new offences or it could be that it becomes necessary to preserve evidence by questioning the detained person.

It is only the custody officer who can authorise the release of a detained person (s. 34(3)). In addition to the requirement to release a person should the grounds for detention no longer exist, there are also maximum time limits for which a person can be detained without charge (**see para. 1.6.7.1**). Once this limit has been reached, it will be necessary to proceed by summons or by warrant.

1.6.7.1 Time Limits: Without Charge

While a person is in police detention there is a requirement that his/her continuing detention is reviewed. There are minimum time requirements for when these reviews must be conducted, with the timing of the first review being calculated from the time detention is authorised. This time can be considered as the 'review time'. The question of whether a person should be kept in custody is a continuous one and the review process is intended as an added protection to the detained person.

The maximum period that a person can be detained without charge is 96 hours (with the exception of suspected acts of terrorism, in which case it is 28 days). The necessity for the continued detention of the person must be reviewed throughout this time. The period of detention is calculated from the 'relevant time' (**see para. 1.6.6.8**) which can be calculated from Table A, below (**see also para. 1.6.7.3**). (*Do not confuse the relevant time with the time from which reviews are due.*) The relevant time 'clock' will always start before, or at the same time as, the review 'clock'. This is because the review clock does not start until detention has been authorised which clearly cannot happen until the person is brought before the custody officer which, as can be seen from the chart below, is at the very latest, the time the prisoner walks into the custody suite (*with the exception of where the person has been under arrest for 24 hours but has not yet been taken to a police station*).

This relevant time period (that is, the maximum period a person can be detained for) relates to the actual time spent in custody and not a 24-hour period in time. This means that every time the person is bailed the clock stops and usually continues from the time that the person returns to custody for the offence(s) for which he/she was bailed.

Where a person has been released and re-arrested for an offence, it is possible that the relevant time will start again. This is covered by s. 47 of the 1984 Act:

(7) Where a person who was released on bail under this Part subject to a duty to attend at a police station is re-arrested, the provisions of this Part of this Act shall apply to him as they apply to a

person arrested for the first time but this subsection does not apply to a person who is arrested under section 46A above or has attended a police station in accordance with the grant of bail (and who accordingly is deemed by section 34(7) above to have been arrested for an offence).

KEYNOTE

In cases where this subsection applies, the relevant time starts again and a fresh clock starts. This will apply where the person has been re-arrested for the same offence because of some new evidence (except at such time as when he/she is returning on bail at the appointed time) under s. 30C(4), 41(9) or 47(2).

Section 41 states:

(9) A person released under subsection (7) [i.e. where his/her relevant time period had expired] above shall not be re-arrested without a warrant for the offence for which he was previously arrested unless new evidence justifying a further arrest has come to light since his release; but this subsection does not prevent an arrest under section 46A below.

Section 47 states:

(2) Nothing in the Bail Act 1976 shall prevent the re-arrest without warrant of a person released on bail subject to a duty to attend at a police station if new evidence justifying a further arrest has come to light since his release.

Section 30C states:

(4) Nothing in section 30A or 30B or in this section prevents the re-arrest without warrant of a person released on bail under section 30A (bail by a constable elsewhere than a police station) if new evidence justifying a further arrest has come to light since his release.

KEYNOTE

The issue will be whether new evidence has come to light since the grant of bail and it will be a question of fact as to what the new evidence is. It is suggested that this must be evidence which was not available at the time the person was last in detention or which would not have been available even if all reasonable inquiries had been conducted.

It will always be important to check how much time is left on the person's 'relevant time' and when his/her next review is due.

1.6.7.2 The Three Stages of Pre-charge Detention

After the custody officer has authorised detention but before a person has been charged there are three distinct stages of detention. These are distinguished by the level at which authorisation for continuing detention is required.

The three stages of detention under the 1984 Act are:

- The basic period of detention, which is the period of detention up to 24 hours, as first authorised by the custody officer.
- Those authorised by an officer of the rank of superintendent or above (s. 42) up to 36 hours (**see para. 1.6.7.4**) (indictable offences only).
- Those authorised by a magistrates' court (ss. 43 and 44) up to a maximum of 96 hours (**see para. 1.6.7.5**).

Each of these is examined in detail below. For offences under s. 41 of the Terrorism Act 2000, **see para. 1.6.7.5**.

1.6.7.3 The Basic Period of Detention

The majority of people detained by the police are detained for less than six hours; most other cases are dealt with within 24 hours. If a person's continued detention is not authorised beyond 24 hours and the person is not charged with an offence, he/she *must* be released (with or without bail) and cannot be re-arrested for the offence unless new evidence comes to light (s. 41(7) and (9) of the 1984 Act). New evidence is not defined by the 1984 Act but it is suggested that it covers evidence which was not available at the time the person was detained, or which would not have been available if the investigating officers had conducted reasonable inquiries.

During this period of detention the custody officer has a responsibility to monitor whether the grounds for detention still exist. An officer of at least the rank of inspector not involved in the investigation (s. 40(1)(b)) must review the person's detention *at least once in the first six hours* and then, after the first review, *within nine hours of that review*. Further reviews must then be conducted *no later than nine hours after the last review* was conducted, until the person is either charged or released. The detention of persons in police custody not subject to the statutory review requirement in Code C, para. 15.1 should still be reviewed periodically as a matter of good practice; these reviews can be carried out by an officer of the rank of sergeant or above (Code C, Note 15B); **see also para. 1.6.7.6.**

If a detained person is taken to hospital for medical treatment, the time at hospital and the period spent travelling to and from the hospital does not count towards the relevant time unless the person is asked questions for the purpose of obtaining evidence about an offence. Where questioning takes place, this period would count towards the relevant time and therefore the custody officer must be informed of it (s. 41(6)).

1.6.7.4 Detention Authorised by an Officer of the Rank of Superintendent or above

Under s. 42(1) of the Police and Criminal Evidence Act 1984, detention can only be authorised beyond 24 hours and up to a maximum of 36 hours from the relevant time if:

- an offence being investigated is an 'indictable offence' (see s. 116 of the 1984 Act); *and*
- an officer of the rank of superintendent or above who is responsible for the station at which the person is detained (referred to here as the authorising officer); *and*
- that that senior officer is satisfied that:
  - there is not sufficient evidence to charge; *and*
  - the investigation is being conducted diligently and expeditiously; *and*
  - that the person's detention is necessary to secure or preserve evidence relating to the offence or to obtain such evidence by questioning that person.

Where a person has been arrested under s. 41 of the Terrorism Act 2000 he/she can be kept in police detection (in this case this is generally from the time of their arrest) up to 48 hours without the court authorising an extension of time (for the grounds, **see para. 1.6.7.7**). If the authorising officer considers that there is sufficient evidence to charge, he/she cannot authorise further detention beyond 24 hours unless the detained person is in custody for another indictable offence for which further detention can be authorised (*R* v *Samuel* [1988] QB 615 and Code H, para. 14.3).

The grounds for this continuing detention are the same as those when the custody officer made the initial decision to detain, with the additional requirements that the case has been conducted diligently and expeditiously. It is suggested that article 5 of the European Convention requires this to be a consideration at all times of detention as a person's right to freedom is one of his/her human rights and any unnecessary periods of detention might be considered actionable. To be able to satisfy the senior officer of this, it will be necessary for the custody record to be available for inspection and details of what inquiries have been made and evidence that the investigation has been moving at a pace that will satisfy the senior officer that the inquiries should not already have been completed. Code C, para. 15.2A outlines issues to be considered before extending the period of detention of juveniles and mentally vulnerable persons.

The authorising officer (which here must be an officer of the rank of superintendent or above who is responsible for the station at which the person is detained) can authorise detention up to a maximum of 36 hours from the 'relevant time' of detention. The period can be shorter than this and can then be further authorised by that officer or any other officer of the rank of superintendent or above who is responsible for the station at which the person is detained to allow the period to be further extended up to the maximum 36-hour period (s. 42(2)). Code C, Note 15E gives guidance as to which officers this would include.

The extension of a person's detention by a superintendent or above must be made within 24 hours of the relevant time and cannot be made before at least two reviews have been carried out by a review officer under s. 40 of the 1984 Act (i.e. those normally carried out by an inspector) (s. 42(4)) (Code C, para. 15.2).

If an extension to the period of detention is authorised, a record must be made and shall state the number of hours and minutes by which the detention period is extended or further extended (Code C, para. 15.16).

Section 42(5) to (8) mirrors the responsibility on the authorising officer at this stage with those of the review officer during the 'general period' of detention with regard to allowing representations, informing the detained person of the decision to authorise further detention and the need to record the decision. The main difference here is that the authorising officer must look into how the case is being investigated and whether this is being done diligently and expeditiously. Consequently, the authorising officer must also consider any representations on these points and these points should also be covered in any record as to whether detention should continue. When considering whether to authorise further detention the authorising officer must check whether the detained person has exercised his/her right to have someone informed and to consult with a legal representative. If these options have not been taken, s. 42(9) requires the authorising officer to inform the detained person of these rights and also whether he/she will be allowed to exercise these rights if it is an indictable offence and the right has so far been delayed as per Code C, Annex B. The authorising officer should record the detainee's decision in the custody record and the grounds for denying the person those rights where appropriate.

If it is proposed to transfer a detained person from one police area to another for the purpose of investigating the offences for which he/she is detained, the authorising officer may take into consideration the period it will take to get to the other police area when deciding whether detention can go beyond 24 hours (s. 42(3)).

1.6.7.5 Detention Authorised by a Magistrates' Court

Once the 36-hour limit has been reached, a person's detention can only continue with the authority of the courts through the issuing of a warrant of further detention and this power only applies to indictable offences. If a person's continued detention is not authorised beyond 36 hours by a court and the person is not charged with an offence, he/she must be released with or without bail and cannot be re-arrested for the offence unless new evidence comes to light (as to new evidence, **see para. 1.6.7.1**).

Warrants of Further Detention

Applications for warrants of further detention are made at the magistrates' court. Initially, the magistrates can issue a warrant for further detention for a period of up to 36 hours. This can be extended by the courts on further applications by police up to a maximum total period of detention of 96 hours. The warrant will specify what period of further detention the court has authorised. If detention of the person is required for any longer period, further applications can be made to the court up to a maximum of 96 hours' detention. The grounds on which the court must decide whether to grant a warrant authorising further detention are the same as those that must be considered by a 'superintendent's review' (**see para. 1.6.7.4**).

Should it be necessary to apply for a warrant it is important that the time restraints are kept in mind at all times and the application procedure followed closely.

Procedure

The application is made in the magistrates' court and both the detained person and the police must be in attendance (s. 43(1) and (2) of the Police and Criminal Evidence Act 1984). The application is made by laying an information before the court. The officer making the application does so on oath and is subject to cross-examination. Under s. 43(14) the information must set out:

- the nature of the offence (this must be an indictable offence);
- the general nature of the evidence on which the person was arrested;
- what inquiries have been made;
- what further inquiries are proposed; and
- the reasons for believing that continuing detention is necessary for the such further inquiries.

It will be important to be able to demonstrate why the person needs to remain in detention while additional inquiries are made, for instance, that further facts need to be verified before further questioning of the suspect can continue and that this cannot be done effectively if the person is released. The detained person must be provided with a copy of the information before the matter can be heard (s. 43(2)). He/she is also entitled to be legally represented. If the person is not legally represented but then requests legal representation at court, the case must be adjourned to allow representation (s. 43(3)). In cases where the person is not represented it may be prudent to remind the person of his/her right to legal representation prior to the court hearing and to make a record of this in the custody record. Should the detained person choose to be legally represented at court, and thereby try to delay the police investigation, s. 43(3)(b) allows the person to be taken back into police detention during the adjournment.

Timing of the application

If it appears likely that the investigation of the indictable offence requires the person's detention to go beyond 36 hours, then thought must be given as to when to make the application to the magistrates' court. Section 43(5) allows the application to be made before the expiry of the 36-hour period (calculated from the relevant time) or, where it has not been practicable for the court to sit within the 36-hour period, the application can be made within the next six hours. There are dangers in applying outside the 36-hour period in that if the court feels that it would have been reasonable to make the application within the 36-hour period then it must refuse the application for the warrant regardless of the merits of the case (s. 43(7)). If the court is not satisfied that there are reasonable grounds for believing that further detention is justified, the court may either refuse the application or adjourn the hearing until such time as it specifies up to the end of the 36-hour period of detention (s. 43(8)). If the application is refused, the person must be charged or released with or without bail at the expiry of the current permissible period of detention (s. 43(15)).

The application for the warrant can be made at any time, *even before a superintendent's review has been carried out*. If the application is made within the 36-hour period and it is refused, it does not mean the person must be released straight away. Section 43(16) allows the person to be detained until the end of the current detention period (24 hours or 36 hours). The benefit of an early application has to be set against the risk that, once the court has refused an application, it is not allowed to hear any further applications for a warrant of further detention unless new evidence has come to light since the application was refused (s. 43(17)). Code C, Note 15D gives guidance on when an application should be made to the court. Note 15D states:

> An application to a magistrates' court under PACE, sections 43 or 44 for a warrant of further detention or its extension should be made between 10 am and 9 pm, and if possible during normal court hours. It will not usually be practicable to arrange for a court to sit specially outside the hours of 10 am to 9 pm. If it appears a special sitting may be needed outside normal court hours but between 10 am and 9 pm, the clerk to the justices should be given notice and informed of this possibility, while the court is sitting if possible.

In *R* v *Slough Justices, ex parte Stirling* [1987] Crim LR 576, the 36-hour period expired at 12.53 pm. The case was not heard by the justices until 2.45 pm. The Divisional Court held that the police should have made their application between 10.30 am and 11.30 am, even though this was before the 36-hour time limit had been reached.

In monitoring a person's detention, officers should be mindful of whether a warrant for further detention may be required and, if it is, consider whether a court will be available to hear the application. If a court will not be available then consideration should be given to making an earlier application. The process the magistrates go through in deciding the merits of the application also provides some safeguards in that the person's continued detention has been considered by the courts and therefore may reduce the likelihood of the defence suggesting that detention was not justified. If a warrant for further detention, or extension, is granted under s. 43 or 44, a record shall be made stating the detention period authorised by the warrant and the date and time it was granted (Code C, para. 15.16).

Applying to Extend Warrants of Further Detention

Under s. 44 of the 1984 Act, the process for applying to extend the warrant follows the same procedure as for the initial warrant, with the exception that the application *must be* made before the expiry of the extension given in the previous warrant. Once the period of detention that has been authorised has expired, and no other applications have been made, the detained person must be charged or released with or without bail.

Terrorism Cases

The court can extend the period of detention of a person up to a total of 28 days. In the case of those arrested under s. 41 this starts at the time of arrest or, if the person was being detained under sch. 7 when he was arrested under s. 41, with the time when his/her examination under that schedule began (Terrorism Act 2000, sch. 8, para. 36(3)).

A person detained in these circumstances may only be held for a maximum of 48 hours without charge before an application must be made to a court to issue or extend a warrant of further detention. At the end of that period, the detained person must either be released or an application to a court for a warrant for an extension to that detention must have

Table A Maximum Periods of Detention for Non Terrorism Act Offences

Arrest	Relevant time starts	Review clock relevant time	24 hours from detention	24 to 36 hours' detention	36 to 42 hours' detention	42 to 78 hours' detention	Up to 96 hours'
Arrested locally.	24 hours from arrest or arrival at police station whichever earliest.		All offences other than indictable offences.	Only indictable offences.	Only indictable offences.	Only indictable offences.	Only indictable offences.
Arrested outside England and Wales.	Time first arrives at police station in police area where matter being investigated or 24 hours after first entered England or Wales, whichever earliest.	Time custody officer authorises detention.	Release unless s. 41(1) applies.	Detention authorised by superintendent or above (s. 42).	Where delay in applying for warrant of further detention is reasonable (s. 43(5)).	First warrant for further detention issued by magistrates' court (s. 42).	Further warrants of detention issued by magistrates' court (s. 43).
Arrested for an offence in one police area in England or Wales then transferred to another police area for separate offence in that second police area which is also in England or Wales.	24 hours from time he/she leaves the police station in the first police area or the time he/she arrives at the first police station in second police area where the crime is being investigated provided not interviewed about the offence while detained in the first police area, whichever is the earliest.	This timing applies where the person was in detention for an offence in the first police area (s. 41(5)).			**See para. 1.6.7.5** for the dangers of not applying within the 36-hour period.	Remember the warrant can be applied for at any stage of detention.	
Arrested and bailed at a place other than a police station.	Time of arrival at the police station to which the notice of bail states he/she must attend.						

Arrest	Relevant time starts	Review clock relevant time	24 hours from detention	24 to 36 hours' detention	36 to 42 hours' detention	42 to 78 hours' detention	Up to 96 hours'
Voluntarily attends police station or accompanies constable to station but not under arrest.	Time of arrest.						
Arrested in one police area in England or Wales for an offence in another police area in England or Wales, there being no 'local' offence(s) for which he/she has been arrested.	From time the suspect arrives at the first police station in the area he/she is being sought or from 24 hours after the time he/she is arrested or if questioned about the offence while in the first police area the relevant time starts from the time he/she first arrived at a police station in the first police area, whichever is the earliest.						

been made and granted prior to the expiry of the initial 48-hour period. Extensions by the court will normally be for a seven day period unless the application for a warrant of further detention requests a shorter period or the court is satisfied that it would be inappropriate for the period to be as long as seven days. If detention is required beyond the first seven days, further applications are required to be made to the court as it is not possible for the court to issue a warrant authorising the full 28 days' detention on the first occasion that a warrant for detention is sought. For the grounds on which a warrant of further detention can be authorised see the review officer's grounds at **para. 1.6.7.7** (Code H, Note 14B).

The application to the court must be made by a superintendent or a crown prosecutor. Usually applications that cover a period of detention that does not extend beyond 14 days are heard by a District Judge in the magistrates' court (unless an application in that case has already been considered by a High Court Judge) and those that cover the period beyond 14 days are heard by a High Court Judge. Paragraph 37 of sch. 8 to the Terrorism Act 2000 states that if at any time the police officer or person in charge of the case considers that the grounds on which the warrant of further detention authorised by the court no longer apply the detained person must be released. Paragraph 33 of sch. 8 to the Terrorism Act 2000 allows for these applications to be conducted by live television links. The person who makes the application may also apply to the court for an order that specified information upon which he/she intends to rely should be withheld from the person to whom the application relates and anyone representing him/her. The order to withhold information can only be made if one of the following applies:

- evidence of an offence under any of the provisions mentioned in s. 40(1)(a) of the Terrorism Act 2000 (**see para. 1.9.11**) would be interfered with or harmed;
- the recovery of property obtained as a result of an offence under any of those provisions would be hindered;
- the recovery of property in respect of which a forfeiture order could be made under s. 23 of the Terrorism Act 2000 would be hindered;
- the apprehension, prosecution or conviction of a person who is suspected of committing offences under the Terrorism Act 2000 would be made more difficult as a result of his/her being alerted;
- the prevention of an act of terrorism would be made more difficult as a result of the person being alerted;
- the gathering of information about the commission, preparation or instigation of an act of terrorism would be interfered with; or
- a person would be interfered with or physically injured;
- the detained person has benefited from his criminal conduct and the recovery of the value of the property constituting the benefit would be hindered if the information were disclosed (sch. 8, part III to the Terrorism Act 2000).

Where a warrant is issued which authorises detention beyond a period of 14 days from the time of arrest the detainee must be transferred from detention in a police station to detention in a designated prison as soon as it is practicable, unless:

(a) the detainee specifically requests to remain in detention at a police station and that request can be accommodated, or
(b) there are reasonable grounds to believe that transferring a person to a prison would:
    (i) significantly hinder a terrorism investigation;
    (ii) delay charging of the detainee or his release from custody, or

(iii) otherwise prevent the investigation from being conducted diligently and expeditiously.

If any of the grounds in (b)(i) to (iii) are relied upon, these must be presented to the judicial authority as part of the application for the warrant that would extend detention beyond a period of 14 days from the time of arrest. After grounds (b)(i) to (iii) cease to apply the person must be transferred to a prison as soon as practicable.

1.6.7.6 The Review

While a person is in police detention (**see para. 1.6.6.1**) before charge, his/her detention must be reviewed by an officer of the rank of inspector or above (inspector reviews). This review acts as another safeguard to protect the detained person's right to be detained for only such periods as are necessary to allow for the investigation of an offence. Reviews of police detention are covered by s. 40 of the Police and Criminal Evidence Act 1984.

Section 40 sets out the times when reviews must be conducted:

(3) Subject to subsection (4) ...
   (a) the first review shall be not later than six hours after the detention was first authorised;
   (b) the second review shall be not later than nine hours after the first;
   (c) subsequent reviews shall be at intervals of not more than nine hours.

KEYNOTE

The periods set out in s. 40(3) are the *maximum* periods that a review can be left; should the review officer wish to review before this time for operational reasons etc., the review could be brought forward. The first review must be made within six hours of the custody officer authorising detention (this, it must be remembered, is not the time from which the 24-hour clock starts, i.e. the time the detainee came into the station, but the time at which the custody officer authorised detention). Thereafter, each review must be made within nine hours of the last review.

Section 40(4)(b) does allow reviews to be delayed if it is not practicable to carry out the review. Conducting late reviews should be avoided where at all possible (see *Roberts* v *Chief Constable of Cheshire Constabulary* [1999] 1 WLR 662). If delayed, the grounds for and extent of any delay must be recorded (Code C, para. 15.13).

Review officer for the purposes of ss. 40 and 40A of the 1984 Act means, in the case of a person arrested but not charged, an officer of at least inspector rank not directly involved in the investigation and, if a person has been arrested and charged, the custody officer. In cases under the Terrorism Act 2000, the review officer means an officer not directly involved in the investigation connected with the detention and of at least inspector rank, for reviews within 24 hours of the detainee's arrest or a superintendent for all other reviews.

It is suggested that even where a detainee is not in police detention as defined by s. 118 of the 1984 Act, consideration should be given to reviewing his/her detention; this can be conducted by the custody officer. A case that supports this view is *Chief Constable of Cleveland Police* v *McGrogan* [2002] 1 FLR 707 which involved a person detained at a police station overnight after having been arrested for breach of the peace. The Court of Appeal held that the need regularly to review the person's detention was required even though breach of the peace was not an 'offence' for the purpose of s. 118.

Section 40(4) provides two other occasions where it may be justified to delay the review if at that time:

- the person in detention is being questioned by a police officer and the review officer is satisfied that an interruption of the questioning for the purpose of carrying out the review would prejudice the investigation in connection with which he/she is being questioned (s. 40(4)(b)(i));
- no review officer is readily available (s. 40(4)(b)(ii)).

It is suggested that it will be necessary to justify why no review officer was available and that where it is known that a review may fall during an interview, the review is conducted prior to the interview where appropriate. It is suggested that with the ability to undertake reviews by telephone or video link, a delay to a review is likely to need greater justification.

In *Roberts*, the defendant had his first review conducted 8 hours, 20 minutes after his detention had been authorised. The Court of Appeal held that under s. 40(1)(b) of the 1984 Act a review of his detention should have been carried out by an officer of the rank of inspector or above 6 hours after detention was first authorised. Section 34(1) was mandatory and provided that a person must not be kept in police detention except in accordance with the relevant provisions of the Act. Therefore, the respondent's detention had been unlawful unless some event occurred to have made it lawful.

The court made it clear that the 1984 Act existed in order to ensure members of the public were not detained except in certain defined circumstances. In the absence of a review, the time spent in detention between 5.25 am, and 7.45 am meant that for that period the defendant's detention was unlawful and amounted to a false imprisonment.

Subject to the passing of regulations, s. 45A of the 1984 Act allows for pre-charge reviews to be conducted by a review officer who is not present in that police station if they have access to the use of video-conferencing facilities that enable him/her to communicate with persons in that station. Provision for video conferencing is included within Code C, however there are currently no regulations allowing such remote reviews.

Where a review is due under s. 40 and the detainee has not been charged, the review may be carried out by means of a discussion, conducted by telephone, with one or more persons at the police station where the arrested person is held. Code C, para. 15.3C provides guidance as to the style of review in terms of telephone, video-conferencing or in-person reviews. Review conducted by telephone or video-conferencing can be terminated by the review officer and then conducted in person.

Where this review is done by telephone, an officer at the station holding the detainee must fulfil the reviewing officer's obligations under the Police and Criminal Evidence Act 1984 (see Code C, para. 15.10). Code C, para. 15.11 identifies the methods that can be used to ensure that the rights of the detainee, appropriate adult and solicitor to make representations to the reviewing officer under Code C, para. 15.3 are satisfied: for example by fax, email message or orally by telephone. The use of telephones to conduct reviews does not include reviews to extend the period of detention beyond the 24-hour clock. Where the review is conducted by telephone, a record must be made of the following: the reason the review officer did not attend the station holding the detainee; the place the review officer was; and the method by which representations were made to the review officer (Code C, para. 15.14). Telephone reviews do not apply to reviews of detention after charge by the custody officer or to reviews under the Terrorism Act 2000, sch. 8, part II in terrorism cases (Code C, Note 15F). If the review is delayed then it must still be conducted as soon as practicable and the reason for the delay must be recorded in the custody record by the review officer. In these circumstances the nine-hour period until the next review is calculated from the latest time the review should have been carried out and not from the time it was actually carried out. For instance, if the review was due at 3.15 pm and was delayed until 4 pm, the next review would have to be conducted no later than 12.15 am and not 1 am. When the review is conducted the review officer does not have to authorise detention for the full nine-hour period; he/she could decide that the case should be reviewed again within a shorter period and the review decision would reflect this.

When reviewing the detention of a person the review officer goes through the same process as the custody officer did when detention was first authorised (ss. 40(8) and 37(1)–(6)), namely by asking:

- Is there sufficient evidence to charge? If 'yes', charge or release the person with or without bail. If 'no', then:
- Is detention necessary in order to secure or preserve evidence or is it necessary to detain the person in order to obtain such evidence by questioning him/her? If 'yes', authorise continued detention. If 'no', release the person with or without bail.

It is suggested that in order to consider whether there is sufficient evidence to charge, the review officer should have consideration for the Code for Crown Prosecutors and the Threshold Test, **see para. 1.6.9**. The situation may arise where the review officer considers that there is sufficient evidence to charge and only authorises continued detention to charge even though the custody officer disagrees. In this case it is suggested that the custody officer must either charge or release the person with or without bail in line with s. 37B of the Police and Criminal Evidence Act 1984. Where bailed this may be in order to submit papers to the CPS in order for a decision to be made as to whether to charge and for what offence. There may also be situations where the custody officer has concluded that there is sufficient evidence to charge but the review officer disagrees; in these cases the review officer cannot overrule the custody officer's decision under s. 37(7). In any case where the decision has been made that there is sufficient evidence to charge, the review officer should confirm that the referral has been made, note the custody record to this effect and, thereafter, check to ensure that the decision is made within a *reasonable time*.

It is suggested that the reviewing officer (or any other officer other than a superintendent or above) cannot tell the custody officer what he/she must do. The reviewing officer may wish to give advice but it will be for the custody officer to decide whether to take that advice. Clearly failure to do so could lead to internal criticism but legally there is no requirement to follow that advice.

If there is not sufficient evidence to charge, the review officer may want to consider the question: 'If this person is bailed, what evidence will be lost'? If the answer is none, continued detention would seem unlawful. As stated above, it is suggested that article 5 of the European Convention on Human Rights requires that an investigation must be conducted diligently and expeditiously in order to minimise the time a person is deprived of his/her liberty (particularly where the case does not lead to a prosecution). In order to monitor the effectiveness of the investigation and the time spent in custody, the reviewing officer should consider the period of detention since the last review to ensure that any defect in the person's treatment is corrected, and where necessary, take steps to speed up the investigation.

In cases where it has been decided that a person should be charged but he/she has been detained because he/she is not in a fit state to be charged (s. 37(9)), the review officer must determine whether the person is yet in a fit state. If the detainee is in a fit state, the custody officer should be informed that the person should be charged or released. If the detainee is not in a fit state, detention can be authorised for a further period (s. 40(9)). In such cases, if the person is still unfit, it may be prudent to consider the welfare of the detained person.

During the process of reviewing a person's detention, the review officer must give the detained person (unless he/she is asleep) or any solicitor representing the detained person who is available at the time of the review, an opportunity to make representations about his/her continued detention (s. 40(12)). If the detained person is likely to be asleep at the time the review is to be carried out, the review should be brought forward to allow the detained person to be present at the time of the review (Code C, Note 15C). If the detainee is asleep when the reviewing officer authorises his/her continued detention, the detainee must be informed of the decision when he/she wakes (Code C, para. 15.7) and the details of the officer who informed the detainee of the decision should also be recorded (Code C, para. 15.16). It may be prudent for the review officer specifically to inform the custody officer of the need for this and record this fact, and details of the custody officer informed, in the custody record. If the detainee makes a comment it may be necessary to inform the reviewing officer (or his/her replacement) of the comment (Code C, para. 15.5). The review officer must also ensure that the detained person is reminded of his/her right to free legal advice and that this reminder is recorded in the custody record (Code C, para. 15.4). In the case of juveniles, the appropriate adult should also be allowed to make representations and the review officer has the discretion to allow other people having an interest in the welfare of the detained person to make representations (Code C, paras 15.3 and 15.3A). These representations may be in writing or oral (s. 40(13)). Where the review is conducted by telephone or video-conferencing, the written representations may be forwarded to the reviewing officer by fax, email or any other medium that ensures they are received. If made in writing, the document should be retained (Code C, para. 15.15). The review officer can refuse to hear oral representations from the detained person if the review officer considers that the person is unfit to make such representations, either because of his/her condition or behaviour (e.g. drunk or violent) (Code C, para. 15.3B). A detainee who is not asleep during the review must be present when the grounds for his/her continued detention are recorded and must at the same time be informed of those grounds unless the review officer considers the person is incapable of understanding what is said, is violent or likely to become violent or is in urgent need of medical attention (Code C, Note 15C); any comment made by the detainee should be recorded (Code C, para. 15.5). However, the review officer must not put any questions to the person about his/her comments (Code C, para. 15.6). Also, as the role of review officer is intended to be independent of the investigation, he/she should not put any questions to the person about his/her involvement in any offence; this mirrors the instruction to custody officers (Code C, para. 15.6).

If at any stage an officer of a rank higher than the review officer gives directions which are at variance with a decision made or action taken by the review officer, or which would have been made by the review officer but for the directions by the more senior officer, then s. 40(11) requires the matter to be referred *at once* to an officer of the rank of superintendent or above who is *responsible for the police station.*

It is important to understand the difference between the action of authorising an extension to the 'detention clock' and the role of the review officer. These are two distinct roles and both need to be carried out. When an officer of the rank of superintendent or above extends the 'relevant time' period, this is not automatically a review (although there is nothing to stop that officer from conducting the review). This means that the 'reviewing' officer may still have to conduct a review even though the relevant time has only recently been extended, unless the officer of the rank of superintendent or above extending the relevant time has shown the review as having been conducted in the custody record.

1.6.7.7 Terrorism Act Reviews

In cases where the person has been detained under the Terrorism Act 2000 the first review should be conducted as soon as reasonably practicable after his/her arrest and then at least every 12 hours; after 24 hours it must be conducted by an officer of the rank of superintendent or above. Once a warrant of further detention has been obtained there is no requirement to conduct further reviews. If an officer of higher rank than the review officer gives directions relating to the detained person, and those directions are at variance with the performance by the review officer of a duty imposed on him/her then he/she must refer the matter at once to an officer of at least the rank of superintendent.

A review officer may only authorise a person's continued detention if he/she is satisfied that it is necessary:

- in order to obtain relevant evidence whether by questioning the person or otherwise;
- to preserve relevant evidence;
- pending a decision whether to apply to the Secretary of State for a deportation notice to be served on the detained person;
- pending the making of an application to the Secretary of State for a deportation notice to be served on the detained person;
- pending consideration by the Secretary of State whether to serve a deportation notice on the detained person; or
- pending a decision whether the detained person should be charged with an offence;
- pending the result of an examination or analysis of any relevant evidence or an examination or analysis of anything that may result in relevant evidence being obtained. An examination or analysis would include a DNA test.

Section 14 of Code H provides guidance on terrorism reviews and extensions of detention. In all cases the review officer must be satisfied that the matter is being dealt with diligently and expeditiously. Where the detained person's rights to a solicitor have been withheld or he/she is being held *incommunicado* at the time of the review, the review officer must consider whether the reason or reasons for which the delay was authorised continue to exist. If in his/her opinion the reason or reasons no longer exist, he/she must inform the officer who authorised the delay of his/her opinion. When recording the grounds for the review the officer must also include his/her conclusion on whether there is a continuing need to withhold the detained person's rights.

In cases where the person is detained under the Terrorism Act 2000 and the review officer does not authorise continued detention, the person does not have to be released if an application for a warrant for further detention is going to be applied for or if an application has been made and the result is pending (s. 41 and sch. 8).

The Prevention of Terrorism Act 2005 allows a control order to be served against an individual that imposes obligations on him/her for purposes connected with protecting members of the public from a risk of terrorism. Section 5 of the 2005 Act allows a constable to arrest a person to ensure that the order can be served on that person. Section 5(2) requires the constable who has arrested an individual to take him/her to the designated place (which are the same as the Terrorism Act 2000) that the constable considers most appropriate as soon as practicable after the arrest.

An individual taken to a designated place under this section may be detained there until the end of 48 hours from the time of his arrest unless:

- he/she has become bound by a derogating control order made against him/her on the Secretary of State's application; or
- the court has dismissed the application.

If the court considers that it is necessary to do so to ensure that the individual in question is available to be given notice of any derogating control order that is made against him, it may, during the 48 hours following his arrest, extend the period for which the individual may be detained under this section by a period of no more than 48 hours (s. 5 of the Prevention of Terrorism Act 2005).

1.6.8 Cautioning, Reprimands and Final Warnings, and Conditional Cautioning

1.6.8.1 Police Caution

There are occasions where a person for whom there is sufficient evidence to charge may be cautioned as an alternative method of disposing with the case. *R* v *Chief Constable of Lancashire Constabulary, ex parte Atkinson* (1998) 162 JP 275 is a case which considered the level of evidence required before a caution can be considered. There the court said that, provided it was clear that there had been an admission of guilt, it was not necessary, for the purposes of administering a caution, to show that the admission had been obtained in circumstances which satisfied the Codes of Practice. That was not to say that police authorities would not be well advised to take precautions which would satisfy the Code, but it did not follow that in every case there had to be a formal interview. However, police officers would be well advised to take precautions that would satisfy Code C. It would be both fairer and more reliable for a formal interview to take place.

Before making a case disposal decision it is essential that the matter has been fully investigated in order to reach an informed decision. In *Omar* v *Chief Constable of Bedfordshire Constabulary* [2002] EWHC 3060, the Divisional Court quashed a caution that had been administered in order to allow a prosecution to be pursued. The court held that a number of reasonable lines of inquiry had not been made, for instance, the police had failed to take a statement from the victim's friend or obtained CCTV footage that was available or fully investigated the victim's injuries. Further, that the length of time in custody (17 hours) should not have been a relevant consideration and that the suspect's admission was ambiguous. Therefore it was in the public interest that a decision to caution rather than to charge should not prevent the subsequent pursuit of the prosecution of the offender.

While there is no general obligation on the police to disclose material prior to charge, there may be a need to make some disclosure to a suspect's legal representative in order that he/she can advise on whether a caution should be accepted (*DPP* v *Ara* [2001] 4 All ER 559). In *Ara*, the suspect had been interviewed without a legal representative being present but the officers refused to disclose the terms of the interview.

Guidance as to the use of cautioning is provided by Home Office Circular 16/2008, *Simple Cautioning of Adult Offenders*. The guidelines should be considered carefully in all cases as any decision can be challenged by judicial review.

In cases where the case has been referred to the Crown Prosecution Service (CPS) under s. 37B of the 1984 Act and a decision has been made that the suspect should receive a caution, an officer involved in the investigation of the offence will be informed in writing. The notification will include the offence in respect of which a caution should be administered. If it is not possible to give the suspect such a caution then they must be charged with the offence (s. 37B(7)).

1.6.8.2 Reprimands and Warnings

Sections 65 and 66 of the Crime and Disorder Act 1998 made provisions for reprimands and warnings for children and young persons which the custody officer must take into account as alternatives to prosecution.

It should be noted that while the *Final Warning Scheme: Guidance for the Police and Youth Offending Teams* indicates when a final warning should be given, the case of *R (On the Application of A)* v *(1) South Yorkshire Police (2) Crown Prosecution Service* [2007] EWHC 1261 acknowledges that where there are aggravating factors, in exceptional circumstances it may justify the person being charged.

There is only one exception to the rule that reprimands and warnings replace cautions, and that is in respect of prostitutes' cautions. This approach to dealing with child prostitutes recognises that they are victims of abuse, and do not consent freely to prostitution. Joint guidance issued by the Home Office and the Department of Health sets out the appropriate way to deal with children in prostitution. That treatment aims to divert children away from prostitution, rather than to prosecute them.

1.6.8.3 Conditional Cautioning

Sections 22 to 27 of the Criminal Justice Act 2003 introduced conditional cautioning, its aim being to deal with offenders without the involvement of the usual court processes.

Section 24A of the Criminal Justice Act 2003 allows a constable to arrest without warrant any person that the officer has reasonable grounds for believing has failed, without reasonable excuse, to comply with any of the conditions attached to the conditional caution. Certain provisions of the Police and Criminal Evidence Act 1984 relating to detention, reviews, searches, and searches and examinations to ascertain identity apply, with modifications, to a person arrested under s. 24A of the Criminal Justice Act 2003.

1.6.9 Charging

1.6.9.1 The Decision to Charge or Not

Section 37 of the Police and Criminal Evidence Act 1984 states:

(1) Where—
 (a) a person is arrested for an offence—
  (i) without a warrant; or
  (ii) under a warrant not endorsed for bail, or
 (b) repealed,
 the custody officer at each police station where he is detained after his arrest shall determine whether he has before him sufficient evidence to charge that person with the offence for which he was arrested and may detain him at the police station for such period as is necessary to enable him to do so.

(2) If the custody officer determines that he does not have such evidence before him, the person arrested shall be released either on bail or without bail, unless the custody officer has reasonable grounds for believing that his detention without being charged is necessary to secure or preserve evidence relating to an offence for which he is under arrest or to obtain such evidence by questioning him.

...

(7) Subject to section 41(7) below [expiry of 24 hours after the relevant time], if the custody officer determines that he has before him sufficient evidence to charge the person arrested with the offence for which he was arrested, the person arrested—
 (a) shall be—
  (i) released without charge and on bail, or
  (ii) kept in police detention,
  for the purpose of enabling the Director of Public Prosecutions to make a decision under section 37B below,
 (b) shall be released without charge and on bail but not for that purpose,
 (c) shall be released without charge and without bail, or
 (d) shall be charged.

(7A) The decision as to how a person is to be dealt with under subsection (7) above shall be that of the custody officer.

(7B) Where a person is released under subsection (7)(a) above, it shall be the duty of the custody officer to inform him that he is being released or (as the case may be) detained, to enable the Director of Public Prosecutions to make a decision under section 37B below.

(8) Where—
 (a) a person is released under subsection (7)(b) or (c) above; and

(b) at the time of his release a decision whether he should be prosecuted for the offence for which he was arrested has not been taken,

it shall be the duty of the custody officer so to inform him.

Section 37A of the Police and Criminal Evidence Act 1984 states:

(1) The Director of Public Prosecutions may issue guidance—
  (a) for the purpose of enabling custody officers to decide how persons should be dealt with under section 37(7) above or 37(C) or 37CA(2) below, and
  (b) as to the information to be sent to the Director of Public Prosecutions under section 37B(1) below.

...

(3) Custody officers are to have regard to guidance under this section in deciding how persons should be dealt with under section 37(7) above or 37CA(2) below.

The custody officer must decide whether there is sufficient evidence to charge a person when he/she is first brought to the police station (s. 37(1) of the 1984 Act) and when an officer in charge of the investigation informs the custody officer that he/she considers there is sufficient evidence to provide a realistic prospect of the detainee's conviction (Code C, para. 16.1). Unless officers are still investigating other offences for which the person is in police detention, s. 37(7) requires the custody officer to review the evidence in order to determine whether there is sufficient evidence to charge the detained person. When a person is arrested under the provisions of the Criminal Justice Act 2003 which allow a person to be retried after being acquitted of a serious offence (**see appendix 3**), provided a further prosecution has not been precluded by the Court of Appeal, an officer of the rank of superintendent or above who has not been directly involved in the investigation is responsible for determining whether the evidence is sufficient to charge (Code C, Note 16AA). If the custody officer decides that there is sufficient evidence to charge the detained person that person must be charged or, if not charged, released in relation to that matter, in any of the following ways:

- without charge on bail for the purpose of enabling the DPP to make a decision under s. 37B (in this case the custody officer must inform the person that he/she is being released to enable the DPP to make a decision as to case disposal);
- without charge on bail but not for the case to be referred to the DPP; or
- without charge and without bail (in either of these last two bullet points if at the time of their release a decision whether they should be prosecuted has not been made it shall be the duty of the custody officer to inform the detained person of this).

Once the custody officer has determined that there is sufficient evidence to charge the detained person (this decision may be taken in consultation with the CPS), he/she can detain that detainee for no longer than is reasonably necessary to decide how that person is to be dealt with, otherwise it is likely that further detention will be unlawful. The detained person must then be released within a reasonable time (Code C, Note 16AB) unless the person is to be charged and bail refused (or they are wanted for another offence).

A detained person should not be kept in custody just for the sole purpose of seeking advice from the CPS as to what offences the offender should be charged with *(R (On the Application of G)* v *Chief Constable of West Yorkshire Police & DPP* [2008] EWCA Civ 28).

Under s. 37A(1) guidance has been issued to enable custody officers to decide whether there is sufficient evidence to charge, this Guidance is contained in the Code for Crown Prosecutors. Custody officers must comply with the Guidance of the DPP in deciding how a person should be dealt with under s. 37(7) as amended. The DPP has set out a list of those offences that require consultation with the CPS before charge, these are listed in Table B, below. Therefore those cases where there is a possibility that the person will be charged and kept in custody for court must be referred to the CPS prosecutor as soon as reasonably practicable; an out-of-hours CPS advice service will be available through the 'CPS Direct' telephone service.

Charging decisions in cases will be made following a review of evidence and in accordance with the Code for Crown Prosecutors. This requires that the custody officer or Crown Prosecutor making the decision is satisfied that there is enough evidence for there to be a realistic prospect of conviction and that it is in the public interest to prosecute (Full Code Test). In order to allow the matter to have full consideration, often the time needed to consider the matter will require the detained person to be bailed. However, there will clearly be occasions where it will not be desirable to bail the detained person but the evidence required to permit the Full Code Test to be applied is not available. In such a case the Threshold Test should be applied, which requires there to be reasonable suspicion that the suspect has committed an offence and it is in the public interest to charge that suspect. The evidential considerations include:

- the evidence available at the time;
- the likelihood and nature of further evidence being obtained;
- the reasonableness for believing that evidence will become available;
- the time it will take to gather that evidence and the steps being taken to do so;
- the impact the expected evidence will have on the case;
- the charges that the evidence will support.

The Code of Practice for Crown Prosecutors, para. 5.9 sets out the public interest factors to be considered. These are:

(a) a conviction is likely to result in a significant sentence;
(b) a conviction is likely to result in a confiscation or any other order;
(c) a weapon was used or violence was threatened during the commission of the offence;
(d) the offence was committed against a person serving the public (for example, a police or prison officer, or a nurse);
(e) the defendant was in a position of authority or trust;
(f) the evidence shows that the defendant was a ringleader or an organiser of the offence;
(g) there is evidence that the offence was premeditated;
(h) there is evidence that the offence was carried out by a group;
(i) the victim of the offence was vulnerable, has been put in considerable fear, or suffered personal attack, damage or disturbance;
(j) the offence was committed in the presence of, or in close proximity to, a child;
(k) the offence was motivated by any form of discrimination against the victim's ethnic or national origin, disability, sex, religious beliefs, political views or sexual orientation, or the suspect demonstrated hostility towards the victim based on any of those characteristics;
(l) there is a marked difference between the actual or mental ages of the defendant and the victim, or if there is any element of corruption;
(m) the defendant's previous convictions or cautions are relevant to the present offence;
(n) the defendant is alleged to have committed the offence while under an order of the court;
(o) there are grounds for believing that the offence is likely to be continued or repeated, for example, by a history of recurring conduct;
(p) the offence, although not serious in itself, is widespread in the area where it was committed; or
(q) a prosecution would have a significant positive impact on maintaining community confidence.

Paragraph 5.10 of the Code of Practice for Crown Prosecutors goes on to consider the public interest factors against prosecution.

Where a decision is made to charge this will need to be reviewed when further evidence is available using the Full Code test.

Table B

<table>
<tr><th>Column A
Police may decide on charge:</th><th>Column B
Prosecutors must decide on charge:</th></tr>
<tr><td>
All cases suitable for early disposal as a guilty plea in the magistrates' court. But not:
<ul>
<li>wounding or GBH—s. 20 of the Offences Against the Person Act 1861;</li>
<li>assault—s. 47 of the Offences Against the Person Act 1861 (ABH);</li>
<li>violent disorder—s. 2 of the Public Order Act 1986;</li>
<li>affray—s. 3 of the Public Order Act 1986;</li>
<li>handling stolen goods—s. 22 of the Theft Act 1968.</li>
</ul>
The police may also charge (whether an early guilty plea case or not):
<ul>
<li>offences contrary to the Bail Act 1976;</li>
<li>offences contrary to s. 5 of the Public Order Act 1986;</li>
<li>Town Police Clauses Act 1847;</li>
<li>Metropolitan Police Act 1839;</li>
<li>Vagrancy Act 1824;</li>
<li>Street Offences Act 1959;</li>
<li>s. 91 of the Criminal Justice Act 1967;</li>
<li>s. 12 of the Licensing Act 1872;</li>
<li>any offence under any bye-law or any summary offence punishable on conviction with a term of imprisonment of three months or less.</li>
</ul>
All motoring cases EXCEPT:
<ul>
<li>cases involving a death;</li>
<li>allegations of dangerous driving;</li>
<li>allegations of driving while disqualified where there has been no admission in a PACE interview to both driving and the disqualification;</li>
<li>offences of being in charge of a motor vehicle while unfit where the statutory defence may be raised;</li>
<li>allegations of the unlawful taking or aggravated taking of a motor vehicle (unless suitable for early disposal as a guilty plea in the magistrates' court).</li>
</ul>
</td><td>
<ul>
<li>Any offence requiring the consent of the Attorney-General, Solicitor-General or Director of Public Prosecutions.</li>
<li>All offences triable on indictment only.</li>
<li>Any either way offence triable only on indictment due to the surrounding circumstances of the commission of the offence or the previous convictions of the person.</li>
<li>Offences under the Terrorism Act 2000 or Prevention of Terrorism Act 2005.</li>
<li>Offences under the Anti-terrorism, Crime and Security Act 2001.</li>
<li>Offences under the Explosive Substances Act 1883.</li>
<li>Offences under any of the Official Secrets Acts.</li>
<li>Any other offence linked with terrorist activity.</li>
<li>Any offence involving any racial, religious or homophobic aggravation.</li>
<li>Any offence classified as domestic violence.</li>
<li>Any offences under the Sexual Offences Act 2003 committed by or upon any person under the age of 18.</li>
<li>Offences involving persistent young offenders, unless chargeable by the police under para. 3.3.</li>
<li>Offences arising directly or indirectly out of activities associated with hunting wild mammals, whether constituting an offence under the Hunting Act 2004 or any other legislation.</li>
<li>Any either way offence not suitable for early disposal in the magistrates' court as a guilty plea (i.e. all contested Crown Court and magistrates' court cases initially listed for an early administrative hearing).</li>
<li>Those cases suitable for early disposal as a guilty plea in the magistrates' court but excluded from police charging.</li>
<li>Those motoring cases excluded from police charging.</li>
<li>Any summary offence not referred to under column A.</li>
</ul>
</td></tr>
</table>

It is the custody officer's responsibility to ensure that there is sufficient evidence to charge the person, albeit directions may be given as to case disposal by the CPS.

Where a detained person is not in a fit state to be charged or released in accordance with s. 34(7) (for instance because he/she is drunk), he/she may be kept in custody until fit (but medical care may have to be considered).

1.6.9.2 Cases where the Detained Person is Bailed to Allow Consultation with the CPS

Section 37B of the Police and Criminal Evidence Act 1984 states:

(1) Where a person is dealt with under section 37(7)(a) above, an officer involved in the investigation of the offence shall, as soon as is practicable, send to the Director of Public Prosecutions such information as may be specified in guidance under section 37A above.
(2) The Director of Public Prosecutions shall decide whether there is sufficient evidence to charge the person with an offence.
(3) If he decides that there is sufficient evidence to charge the person with an offence, he shall decide—
 (a) whether or not the person should be charged and, if so, the offence with which he should be charged, and
 (b) whether or not the person should be given a caution and, if so, the offence in respect of which he should be given a caution.
(4) The Director of Public Prosecutions shall give notice of his decision to an officer involved in the investigation of the offence.
(4A) Notice under subsection (4) above shall be in writing, but in the case of a person kept in police detention under section 37(7)(a) above it may be given orally in the first instance and confirmed in writing subsequently.
(5) If his decision is—
 (a) that there is not sufficient evidence to charge the person with an offence, or
 (b) that there is sufficient evidence to charge the person with an offence but that the person should not be charged with an offence or given a caution in respect of an offence,
 a custody officer shall give the person notice in writing that he is not to be prosecuted.

Where a person has been bailed under s. 37(7)(a) with or without bail conditions, the CPS must be consulted in order to determine what case disposal decision will be made (this may itself require further inquiries to gather further evidence). This referral should be made using forms MG3 (Report to Crown Prosecutor for a Charging Decision), and MG3A (Further Report to Crown Prosecutor for a Charging Decision). The pre-charge advice file can be a pre-charge expedited report (straight forward and guilty plea cases) or a pre-charge evidential report (contested/Crown Court cases) and must also include other relevant information including:

Pre-charge Expedited Report

- MG3
- MG11(s)—Witness statement or Index notes (if offence is witnessed by more than one officer and up to four, use the statement of one officer and summarise the others)
- MG15—Record of interview
- Phoenix print of suspect(s)' previous convictions/cautions/reprimands/final warnings. If there is any other information that may be relevant, include it on form MG6—Case File Information.

Pre-charge Evidential Report

- MG3
- MG5—Case summary (unless the statements cover all elements of the case)
- MG6—Case file information
- MG11—Key witness statement(s), or Index notes (if offence is witnessed by police use the statement of one officer and summarise the others)

- MG12—Exhibit list
- MG15—Interview record
- Crime Report and Incident Log
- Unused material likely to undermine the case
- Copies of key documentary exhibits
- Phoenix print of suspect(s) pre-cons/cautions/reprimands/final warnings.

The Prosecutor will decide whether there is sufficient evidence to charge or caution the person and shall give written notice of the decision to an officer involved in the investigation of the details of the offence. This decision must be followed (s. 37B(6)) if the decision was for the person to be cautioned (this includes conditional cautions) and if the person refuses or for some other reason a caution cannot be given they must be charged with the offence (s. 37B(7)).

In cases where the prosecutor decides that there is not sufficient evidence to charge the person with an offence, or that there is sufficient evidence to charge the person with an offence but that the person should not be charged with an offence or given a caution in respect of an offence, the custody officer must inform the person in writing of the decision. Similarly the person must be informed of those cases where there is insufficient evidence to charge them but if further evidence or information comes to light in the future the case may be reconsidered under the Code for Crown Prosecutors.

In cases where further time is needed to obtain evidence or for the prosecutor to make a case disposal decision, the person can be further bailed. In these cases the custody officer must give the person notice in writing. This does not affect any bail conditions that were included when the detained person was bailed (s. 37D(1) to (3)).

1.6.9.3 Bail to Allow Referral to the CPS

Section 47 of the Police and Criminal Evidence Act 1984 states:

> (1A) The normal powers to impose conditions of bail shall be available to him where a custody officer releases a person on bail under section 37 above or section 38(1) above (including that subsection as applied by section 40(10) above) but not in any other cases.
> In this subsection, 'the normal powers to impose conditions of bail' has the meaning given in section 3(6) of the Bail Act 1976.

Where the person is bailed after charge or bailed without charge and on bail for the purpose of enabling the CPS to make a decision regarding case disposal, the custody officer may impose conditions on that bail (**see para. 1.10.7**) In cases where a person is bailed without being charged under s. 37(7)(b) or (c), the custody officer cannot impose conditions on that bail (s. 47(1A)).

1.6.9.4 Charging the Detained Person

If a decision is taken to charge the detained person, Code C, para. 16 sets out the procedures to be followed by the custody officer. When a detained person is charged with or informed that he/she may be prosecuted for an offence, para. 16.2 requires him/her to be cautioned. The caution varies slightly from that when arrested or interviewed and is as follows:

> You do not have to say anything. But it may harm your defence if you do not mention now something which you later rely on in court. Anything you do say may be given in evidence.

The above caution should not be used in circumstances where the detained person has been denied access to a solicitor (**see para. 1.7.4**) in which case the following cautions should be used:

You do not have to say anything, but anything you do say may be given in evidence.

At the time a person is charged, he/she shall be given a written notice as set out in Code C, para. 16.3 and a record shall be made of anything the person says when charged (para. 16.8). Where the person being charged is a juvenile or is mentally disordered or mentally vulnerable, the appropriate adult should be present and the notice given to him/her (paras 16.3 and 16.6).

Once the person has been charged with or informed that he/she may be prosecuted for an offence, fingerprints can be taken if it is a recordable offence and he/she has not had his/her fingerprints taken during the course of the investigation (s. 61(3) unless the fingerprints previously taken do not constitute a complete set or they are not of sufficient quality to allow satisfactory analysis, comparison or matching (s. 61(3A)). Photographs may also be taken and in some cases DNA samples may be taken (**see para. 1.9.6**).

If fingerprints are taken, the person must be informed of the reason why and that those prints may be used for a speculative search concerning other crimes (**see para. 1.9.3**). The reasons should also be recorded in the custody record, along with confirmation that the detained person has been given the required information. If the person's photograph is taken, this should also be recorded in the custody record.

Once a person has been charged or informed that he/she may be prosecuted for an offence (which does not include the service of the Notice of Intended Prosecution under ss. 1 and 2 of the Road Traffic Offenders Act 1988), generally the person cannot be questioned or spoken to about the matter. Code C, paras 16.4 and 16.5 set out occasions where further investigation involving the person may be allowed and para. 16.9 sets out the procedure to be adopted. It should only be in these circumstances that the custody officer allows any further inquiries involving the detained person to be made. Paragraphs 16.4 and 16.5 deal with:

- written statements made by other people which the investigating officers may wish to show to another person charged;
- questions necessary for the purpose of preventing or minimising harm or loss to some other person or to the public or for clearing up an ambiguity in a previous answer or statement;
- where it is in the interests of justice that the person should have put to him/her—and have an opportunity to comment on—information concerning the offence which has come to light since he/she was charged or informed that he/she might be prosecuted.

1.6.10 Bail After Charge

If the person is charged then the custody officer has to decide whether the person is going to be bailed to appear at court or whether bail will be refused and the person kept in custody until the next available court. This is a review of the person's detention and therefore the person or his/her solicitor should be given an opportunity to make representations to the custody officer. The review should be conducted with regard to Code C, paras 15.1, 15.3 to 15.7.

Where bail has been refused this decision must be reviewed by the custody officer within nine hours of the last review (the first being the post-charge review). These reviews must continue until the person is taken to court in the same manner required by a review officer.

In addition to the grounds for refusing bail covered in **chapter 1.10**, the custody officer may also detain the person after charge if he/she has reasonable grounds for believing that the detention of the person is necessary to enable a sample to be taken from him/her under

s. 63B of the Police and Criminal Evidence Act 1984. The custody officer may authorise a person to be kept in police detention for a period not exceeding six hours beginning when the person was charged with the offence.

For occasions where the custody officer refuses bail of a juvenile after charge, see Code C, para. 16.7.

For a full discussion of bail, **see chapter 1.10**.

In *Williamson* v *Chief Constable of West Midlands* [2004] 1 WLR 14, the Court of Appeal clarified the point that breach of the peace is not a criminal offence. Consequently, as there is no power in the Bail Act 1976 to grant bail except in criminal proceedings, no power exists to grant bail for breach of the peace. This means that if the person is bailed, there is no power to arrest the person or obtain a warrant for his/her failure to appear at court under the Bail Act 1976.

1.6.11 Special Groups and Appropriate Adults

In cases where the detained person is a juvenile or a person who is mentally vulnerable or appears to be suffering from mental disorder, the custody officer must inform an appropriate adult as soon as practicable (this must be done in the case of a juvenile regardless of whether he/she is held *incommunicado* (Code C, para. 3.15). In the case of a juvenile who is the subject of a supervision order, the person supervising the juvenile should also be informed. If the custody officer has any doubt as to the mental state or capacity of a person detained, an appropriate adult should be called (Code C, Note 1G).

A juvenile for the purpose of the 1984 Act is any person who is under the age of 17 or who appears to be under the age of 17 until it is established that he/she is 17 or over (Code C, para. 1.5).

Code C, Note 1G defines 'mentally vulnerable' as applying to any detainee who, because of their mental state or capacity, may not understand the significance of what is said, of questions or of their replies. 'Mental disorder' is defined in the Mental Health Act 1983, s. 1(2) as 'mental illness, arrested or incomplete development of mind, psychopathic disorder and any other disorder or disability of mind'. Code C, para. 1.4 also states:

> If an officer has any suspicion, or is told in good faith, that a person of any age may be mentally disordered or otherwise mentally vulnerable, in the absence of clear evidence to dispel that suspicion, the person shall be treated as such for the purposes of this Code. See Note 1G.

An appropriate adult is defined by Code C, para. 1.7. Paragraph 1.7 states:

> 'The appropriate adult' means, in the case of a:
> (a) juvenile:
>   (i) the parent, guardian or, if the juvenile is in local authority or voluntary organisation care, or is otherwise being looked after under the Children Act 1989, a person representing that authority or organisation;
>   (ii) a social worker of a local authority;
>   (iii) failing these, some other responsible adult aged 18 or over who is not a police officer or employed by the police.
> (b) person who is mentally disordered or mentally vulnerable: See Note 1D:
>   (i) a relative, guardian or other person responsible for their care or custody;
>   (ii) someone experienced in dealing with mentally disordered or mentally vulnerable people but who is not a police officer or employed by the police;
>   (iii) failing these, some other responsible adult aged 18 or over who is not a police officer or employed by the police.

KEYNOTE

The role of the appropriate adult is to assist and advise the detained person. Care should be taken when considering the suitability of an appropriate adult in relation to mentally disordered or mentally vulnerable persons. Code C, Note 1D gives guidance for choosing the appropriate adult. Evidence obtained while a person is in custody where the person called as an appropriate adult does not have that person's best interests in mind or is not capable of assisting them could be excluded.

An appropriate adult is not required for a 17 year old (*R* v *Stratford Youth Court, ex parte Harding* [2001] EWHC 615 (Admin)).

In *R* v *Aspinall* [1999] 2 Cr App R 115, the Court of Appeal emphasised the importance of appropriate adults. There it was held that an appropriate adult played a significant role in respect of a vulnerable person whose condition rendered him/her liable to provide information which was unreliable, misleading or self-incriminating.

It is also important to consider the welfare of the appropriate adult. This is demonstrated by the case of *Leach* v *Chief Constable of Gloucestershire Constabulary* [1999] 1 All ER 215. Here L was asked by a police officer to attend police interviews of a murder suspect who was also thought to be mentally disordered, as an 'appropriate adult' per the requirement of the Codes. She was told only that the suspect was a 52-year-old male, and was not informed of the nature of the case. The suspect was in fact Frederick West, who was being questioned in connection with murders committed in particularly harrowing and traumatic circumstances. For many weeks L acted as an appropriate adult, accompanying the officer and suspect to murder scenes and on many occasions being left alone in a locked cell with the suspect. She claimed to be suffering from post-traumatic stress and psychological injury as well as a stroke as a result of her experiences. The Court of Appeal said that the Fred West case was notorious among modern crimes and it was forseeable that psychiatric harm might arise. While there was no requirement to pre-select or warn appropriate adults as to the nature of the case, however in some cases, counselling or trained help should be offered.

1.7 Interviews

1.7.1 Introduction

The PACE Codes of Practice C, E and F are intended to provide some protection to people being interviewed by the police and lay down guidelines as to how interviews should be conducted. These rules can be found throughout Codes C and E of the PACE Codes of Practice; failure to follow these rules may lead to evidence being excluded and/or disciplinary charges and ultimately could lead to civil claims for compensation. There is an additional section within Code E for the recording of interviews by secure digital network; it should be noted that this section only applies to a pilot by Lancashire Constabulary.

1.7.2 What is an Interview?

Not all discussions between the police and members of the public will be protected or governed by the PACE Codes of Practice. Code C, para. 11.1A defines an interview as follows:

> An interview is the questioning of a person regarding their involvement or suspected involvement in a criminal offence or offences which, under paragraph 10.1, must be carried out under caution. Whenever a person is interviewed they must be informed of the nature of the offence, or further offence. Procedures under the Road Traffic Act 1988, section 7 or the Transport and Works Act 1992, section 31 do not constitute interviewing for the purpose of this Code.

KEYNOTE

Whether an interaction between a police officer and a member of the public is defined as an interview by the court can be crucial as to whether it will be admissible in evidence. It is therefore essential to understand the definition of an interview for the purposes of PACE and when a caution must be given and which caution must be given (for cautions, **see para. 1.7.4**).

If a person is asked questions for reasons *other than obtaining evidence about his/her involvement or suspected involvement in an offence*, this is not an interview (and a caution need not be given). (For the use of cautions, **see para. 1.7.4.**) This point is confirmed in the case of *R* v *McGuinness* [1999] Crim LR 318, where the court confirmed that it was only when a person was suspected of an offence that the caution must be administered before questioning. Consequently, in *R* v *Miller* [1998] Crim LR 209 the court held that asking a person the single question, 'Are these ecstasy tablets?' criminally implicated the person and therefore the conversation was an interview (i.e. it would not be necessary to ask such a question if there were no suspicion that the tablets were a controlled substance).

Guidance on when questions do not amount to an interview is given by Code C, para. 10.1:

> ... A person need not be cautioned if questions are for other necessary purposes, e.g.:
> (a) solely to establish their identity or ownership of any vehicle;
> (b) to obtain information in accordance with any relevant statutory requirement ...;
> (c) in furtherance of the proper and effective conduct of a search, e.g. to determine the need to search in the exercise of powers of stop and search or to seek co-operation while carrying out a search;
> (d) to seek verification of a written record as in paragraph 11.13;
> (e) not used.

KEYNOTE

Code C, para. 10.1 is not an exhaustive list and officers may have other valid reasons to speak to a person before it becomes an interview.

Before a person can be interviewed about their involvement in an offence, that person must be cautioned. So it might be said that an interview is any questioning of a person after such time as a caution has been or should have been administered. Where a person is arrested for an offence, he/she must also be cautioned, as any questioning will amount to an interview.

Where the questions go beyond issues raised by Code C, para. 10.1 and go to the question of guilt, this is likely to be an interview for the purposes of the Police and Criminal Evidence Act 1984. In *CPS* v *O'Shea* (1998) 11 May, unreported, police were called to a road traffic accident. O'Shea, the owner of the vehicle, was near the car, exhibiting signs of drunkenness and there was no one else in the vicinity who might have been driving the vehicle. The officer said to O'Shea the words, 'An accident has just happened that is alleged was your fault'. The court held that it was clear that when the officer had asked O'Shea whether he was driving his vehicle at the time of the accident, the officer had known that he was the owner of the vehicle and therefore the question was not solely to establish whether he was the owner. Accordingly, the thrust of the question was whether he had committed an offence. The defendant's subsequent answer was held to be inadmissible as the PACE Codes of Practice had not been complied with. *O'Shea* can be contrasted with *R* v *Maguire* [1989] Crim LR 815 where the court held that Code C does not prevent a police officer from asking questions at or near the scene of the crime to elicit an explanation which, if true or accepted, would clear the suspect.

Where a suspect makes any comment which is outside the context of an interview but which might be relevant to the offence, a written record must be made of these (Code C, para. 11.13).

1.7.3 When a Caution must be Given

Code C, para. 10.1 states:

> A person whom there are grounds to suspect of an offence, see Note 10A, must be cautioned before any questions about an offence, or further questions if the answers provide the grounds for suspicion, are put to them if either the suspect's answers or silence, (i.e. failure or refusal to answer or answer satisfactorily) may be given in evidence to a court in a prosecution....

KEYNOTE

A caution is required to be given to a person who has been arrested or before asking any further questions of a person where there are grounds to suspect that he/she has committed an offence. The courts have given some guidance as to when a caution should be administered. There must be real grounds for suspicion; a mere hunch is not sufficient. The grounds have to be such as to lead to suspicion that an offence has been committed by that person. This view is confirmed in *Batley* v *DPP* (1998) *The Times*, 5 March, where the court accepted that, in general terms, where police officers had nothing more than a hunch that an offence was being committed, there would not be enough to activate the Code. However, it was necessary to caution a person before asking questions which went to the very heart of the issue as to whether he/she might be committing an offence, especially since the suspect was being invited to incriminate him/herself.

In *Fox* v *United Kingdom* (1990) 13 EHRR 157, the court stated that reasonable suspicion arises from facts or information which would satisfy an objective observer that the person concerned may have committed the offence. Clearly there will be a need to record this information in detail to inform the court of the facts as known at the time of the decision to caution or not to caution.

Further guidance was provided in *R* v *Smith* [2001] 1 WLR 1031 where the court held that establishing a reasonable suspicion was an objective test and an honest belief by a police officer was not required. Suspicion could take into account evidence that could not be adduced, such as hearsay. Except where evidence had been obtained in blatant breach of a statute, improperly obtained information could still be relied on. A case where the court held that a caution was not necessary is *Ridehalgh* v *DPP* [2005] EWHC 1100 (Admin). Here the defendant was a police officer who had been called to a police station to deal with a detained person. Police officers at the station noticed a smell of alcohol on the defendant and the other officers asked if he had been drinking, and whether he had driven to the station. As a result of his answer he was breath tested and then arrested, cautioned and charged. The court held that a necessary precondition for the administration of a caution was that there had to be grounds for the suspicion of a criminal offence. All that the police officers had prior to the questions posed was a smell of alcohol on the defendant's breath; they had no indication as to how much alcohol R had consumed or whether he had driven.

Once a person has been cautioned, consideration of further cautions must be given. The need for additional cautions is provided for by the PACE Codes of Practice. In addition, in *R* v *Miller* [1998] Crim LR 209, the court said that one caution was not necessarily enough, and before other questions are asked of a suspect at a later stage, a further caution may be necessary.

In addition to the duty to caution a suspect, there will be occasions where a person arrested for an offence will have to be given a 'special warning' in interview. Special warnings are concerned with a person's right to silence (see ss. 34 to 37 of the Criminal Justice and Public Order Act 1994). As mentioned above, this will only apply where the detainee has had the opportunity to seek legal advice.

1.7.4 The Caution

Until 2003 there was effectively only one caution that police officers gave to a suspect before the suspect was interviewed or arrested. This caution had itself been amended by the Criminal Justice and Public Order Act 1994 which allowed for inferences to be drawn at court from a suspect's silence to questions put by the interviewing officer. The amended caution following the 1994 Act, along with the special warnings required by ss. 36 and 37 of that Act, were intended to provide the suspect with sufficient warning concerning his/her choice to remain silent. However this position was changed by the case of *Murray* v *United Kingdom* (1996) 22 EHRR 29 and there is now a requirement to consider which of two cautions is required and at what stage of the investigation.

In *Murray* it was held that adverse inferences may not be drawn from the silence of a person who wants legal advice if they have not been allowed an opportunity to receive it. As a result of this decision Code C, Annex C sets out the restriction on drawing adverse inferences from silence and the terms of the caution when the restriction applies. Adverse inferences from silence are restricted in some cases where the detainee has not had legal advice. In these cases the caution that must be given to the person has been amended in order to remove the infringement on the person's right to remain silent.

1.7.4.1 Which Caution Should be Given?

In all cases other than those where the restriction on drawing adverse inferences apply, the caution to be given is set out in Code C, para. 10.5:

> You do not have to say anything. But it may harm your defence if you do not mention when questioned something which you later rely on in Court. Anything you do say may be given in evidence.

Where the use of the Welsh Language is appropriate, a constable may provide the caution directly in Welsh in the following terms:

> *Does dim rhaid i chi ddweud dim byd. Ond gall niweidio eich amddiffyniad os na fyddwch chi'n sôn, wrth gael eich holi, am rywbeth y byddwch chi'n dibynnu arno nes ymlaen yn y Llys. Gall unrhyw beth yr ydych yn ei ddweud gael ei roi fel tystiolaeth.*

The occasions where the alternative caution is required are set out in Code C, Annex C, para. 1, that is occasions where the restriction on drawing an adverse inference apply.

This restriction applies:

- to any detainee at a police station who has asked for legal advice and not been allowed an opportunity to consult a solicitor and has not changed their mind;
- to any detainee at a police station who has had their right to consult a solicitor suspended by an officer of the rank of superintendent or above (Code C, Annex B);
- where an officer of superintendent rank or above has authorised an interview without waiting for the detainee to consult with a solicitor as set out in Code C, para. 6.6(b)(ii);
- where the interview goes ahead without a solicitor, including a duty solicitor, because awaiting their arrival would cause unreasonable delay to the process of the investigation and the person has not changed their mind about wanting a solicitor (Code C, para. 6.6(b)(ii));
- where a person has been charged with, or informed they may be prosecuted for, an offence and:
  - has had brought to their notice a written statement made by another person or the content of an interview with another person which relates to that offence,
  - is interviewed about that offence, or
  - makes a written statement about that offence.

Annex C, para. 2 sets out the alternative terms of the caution to be used when the restriction on drawing adverse inferences from silence applies:

> You do not have to say anything, but anything you do say may be given in evidence.

The situation is likely to occur during a detainee's detention where it will be necessary to administer both of these cautions at various times during his/her detention. As there is a significant difference between them in relation to the right to silence, it will be important to make it clear which caution applies to the detainee during any interview or charge procedure. Guidance as to what the detainee should be told, is provided by Code C, Annex C, Note C2, this paragraph gives sample explanations that need to be explained to the detainee before the change in caution is given.

Full caution already given(in most cases given when arrested)	➔ Detainee's access to legal advice restricted as per Code C, Annex C, para. 1. Need to give alternative caution	➔ Explain change in caution as set out at Code C, Annex C Note C2(a)(i)	➔ Give caution as set out at Annex C, para. 2
Full caution already given	➔ Detainee has been charged but is further interviewed (Code C, Annex C, para. 1). Need to give alternative caution	➔ Explain change in caution as set out at Code C, Annex C, Note C2(a)(ii)	➔ Give caution as set out at Annex C, para. 2
Caution as set out at Annex C, para. 2, given	➔ Detainee has now had access to a solicitor or changed their mind. Need to give alternative caution	➔ Explain change in caution as set out at Code C, Annex C, Note C2(b)	➔ Give caution Code C, para. 10.5

Where Code C, Annex C, para. 1 applies (i.e. the detainee has not been given access to a solicitor) and the detainee is charged with an offence or informed they may be prosecuted, the caution at Annex C, para. 2 should be used, on all other occasions the caution at Code C, para. 16.2 should be used:

> You do not have to say anything. But it may harm your defence if you do not mention now something which you later rely on in court. Anything you do say may be given in evidence.

Where the use of the Welsh Language is appropriate, a constable may provide the caution directly in Welsh in the following terms:

> *Does dim rhaid i chi ddweud dim byd. Ond gall niweidio eich amddiffyniad os na fyddwch chi'n sôn, yn awr, am rywbeth y byddwch chi'n dibynnu arno nes ymlaen yn y llys. Gall unrhyw beth yr ydych yn ei ddweud gael ei roi fel tystiolaeth.*

1.7.4.2 Consequences of Not Giving a Caution

If a person is questioned without being cautioned when a caution should have been given, any admissions made by that person are likely to be inadmissible in evidence. One of the main reasons for this is that a person has a right to remain silent and if the caution has not been given, the suspect has not been warned of this right or of the risks of self-incrimination. Conversely, if a caution is not required and one is given, the person may not make admissions which he/she might otherwise have made. Consequently, it is important to be aware of when to administer a caution and, in cases of doubt, to err on the side of caution. Should an interview be excluded, this may have implications on other evidence obtained as a consequence of the confession.

1.7.4.3 Unsolicited Comments

There will be occasions where suspects make unsolicited comments implicating them in an offence before they are suspected of any involvement and therefore before they are cautioned (or further cautioned if already suspected). Such statements are likely to be admissible provided the PACE Codes of Practice are complied with. Code C, paras 11.13 and 11.14 state:

> 11.13 A written record shall be made of any comments made by a suspect, including unsolicited comments, which are outside the context of an interview but which might be relevant to the offence. Any such record must be timed and signed by the maker. When practicable the suspect shall be given the opportunity to read that record and to sign it as correct or to indicate how they consider it inaccurate. See Note 11E
>
> 11.14 Any refusal by a person to sign an interview record when asked in accordance with this Code must itself be recorded.

Note 11E states:

> When a suspect agrees to read records of interviews and other comments and sign them as correct, they should be asked to endorse the record with, e.g. 'I agree that this is a correct record of what was said' and add their signature. If the suspect does not agree with the record, the interviewer should record the details of any disagreement and ask the suspect to read these details and sign them to the effect that they accurately reflect their disagreement. Any refusal to sign should be recorded.

KEYNOTE

It is particularly important to record the comment and give the person an opportunity to see what has been recorded and to comment/endorse it. Where the person has had this opportunity and signs the record then it will strengthen the evidence and if he/she declines to sign it, this may assist in establishing what the defence case may be.

In *R* v *Miller* [1998] Crim LR 209 the court held that Code C, para. 11.13 requires a written record, timed and signed by the suspect as correct or an opportunity for the suspect to indicate which parts were inaccurate.

While it is suggested that this should be done at an early opportunity, in *Batley* v *DPP* (1998) *The Times*, 5 March, where it was held that as the Code did not require an *immediate* endorsement and no time factor was laid down, there was nothing to constrain the police from returning the next day to get their endorsement.

1.7.5 Interview of Person not Under Arrest

If a person has not been arrested then he/she can be interviewed almost anywhere (but an officer intending to interview a person on private property must consider whether he/she is trespassing. If the interview with a person not under arrest takes place in a police station, Code C, para. 3.21 and Note 1A must be followed.

If the interview is to be with a juvenile, Code C, para. 11.16, gives guidance as to when interviews should take place at a juvenile's place of education. This should only be in exceptional circumstances and with the agreement of the principal or the principal's nominee. The juvenile's parent(s) or person(s) responsible for his/her welfare and the appropriate adult (if a different person) should be notified of the interview and be afforded reasonable time in which to attend. Code C, Note 1B outlines occasions when a person should not act as an appropriate adult). The principal or nominee can act as the appropriate adult where waiting for an appropriate adult would cause unreasonable delay. This is not the case where the juvenile is suspected of an offence against his/her educational establishment (Code C, para. 11.15). Where a juvenile is at a police station Code C, paras

11.18 to 11.20 and Note 11C outline the limited circumstances when a juvenile may be interviewed without an appropriate adult being present.

In cases where the person is not under arrest, certain information must be given to him/her. This is covered by Code C, para. 10.2 which states:

> Whenever a person not under arrest is initially cautioned, or reminded they are under caution, that person must at the same time be told they are not under arrest and are free to leave if they want to. See Note 10C

For the situation where a person is at a police station voluntarily and not under arrest, see Code C, para. 3.21.

When carrying out an interview, officers should be mindful of how they treat the person, this it is suggested also applies to witnesses as well as suspects. For instance in *L* v *Reading Borough Council* [2001] 1 WLR 1575, the court stated that it was arguable that when interviewing a young child victim there was an assumption of responsibility and a special relationship was created. Part of the responsibility was to protect the child from future harm that could ensue from the manner of the investigation. Following this line, failure to protect the victims/witnesses could lead to a claim for damages if they suffer harm. If a child is a witness or victim he/she should be interviewed via visual recording in line with current procedures.

1.7.6 Interview of Person Under Arrest

Any interview of a person who is under arrest must take place at a police station (Code C, para. 11.1) or other authorised place of detention unless waiting until the interview can be conducted at such a place is likely to:

- lead to interference with or harm to evidence connected with an offence or interference with or physical harm to other people or serious loss of, or damage to property; or
- lead to the alerting of other people suspected of having committed an offence but not yet arrested for it; or
- hinder the recovery of property obtained in consequence of the commission of an offence.

Code C requires that interviewing in any of these circumstances shall cease once the relevant risk has been averted or the necessary questions have been put in order to attempt to avert that risk (para. 11.1). There is a danger in these cases of continuing the interview past the point where the risk has been averted, this could lead to the whole interview being excluded.

The courts have recognised that there may be times when a person who is under arrest will be asked questions other than when at the police station. One such example is where the arrested person is present while officers search his/her address. In *R* v *Hanchard* (1999) 6 December, unreported, the court recognised that searches of premises could not be conducted in complete silence. The court stated that it would be unfair and unreasonable not to put any questions to owners of premises undergoing a search; however, what questions can be asked will be a matter of fact and degree in each individual case. Where questions go beyond that needed for the immediate investigation it would be a breach of the Codes. In *Hanchard*, the questions which were admissible included whether cannabis at the address belonged to the suspect and where a large quantity of money had come from.

If a person has been arrested by one police force on behalf of another and the lawful period of detention in respect of that offence has not yet begun (in accordance with s. 41 of the Police and Criminal Evidence Act 1984 (**see para. 1.6.6.8**)), no questions may be put to him/her about the offence while he/she is in transit between the forces except in order to clarify any voluntary statement made by him/her (Code C, para. 14.1).

If a person is in police detention at a hospital, he/she may not be questioned without the agreement of a responsible doctor (Code C, para. 14.2). If an interview does take place, the interviewing officer must inform the custody officer as the period will count to the total time spent in custody (Note 14A).

If questioning does take place in any of these circumstances it will affect the suspect's 'detention clock'. The custody officer must be informed of such an interview as it may affect the lawfulness of the suspect's detention (**see para. 1.6.7.1**).

It is essential to comply with the rules on interviewing after arrest, as a failure could jeopardise any future admissions made in interview. In *R* v *Webster* (2000) 12 December, unreported, the police evidence was that during the search of his house the defendant, having been arrested but not cautioned, had made admissions as to where the drugs were located in his house and as to the amount of drugs that he possessed. No contemporaneous note was taken of the search. The defendant was then interviewed on the same basis as his answers to the questions which had been asked during the search. The court held that the later interview at the police station did not cure the breaches of the Codes of Practice which had occurred during the search and both interviews were excluded.

1.7.7 Person Charged with an Offence

Once a person has been charged with an offence generally he/she cannot be interviewed about the offence unless it is necessary:

- to prevent or minimise harm or loss to some other person or to the public; or
- to clear up an ambiguity in a previous answer or statement; or
- in the interest of justice that the person should have questions put to him/her and have an opportunity to comment on information concerning the offence which has come to light since he/she was charged or informed that he/she might be prosecuted.

It should be noted that the service of the Notice of Intended Prosecution under ss. 1 and 2 of the Road Traffic Offenders Act 1988, does not amount to informing a person that he/she may be prosecuted for an offence and so does not preclude further questioning in relation to that offence (Code C, Note 16B).

If a person is interviewed for any other reason, the interview is likely to be inadmissible in evidence.

Where a person is interviewed after charge, Code C, para. 16.5 states:

> ... Before any such interview, the interviewer shall:
> (a) caution the detainee, 'You do not have to say anything, but anything you do say may be given in evidence.';
> Where the use of the Welsh Language is appropriate, the interviewer shall caution the detainee, *'Does dim rhaid i chi ddweud dim byd, ond gall unrhyw beth yr ydych yn ei ddweud gael ei roi fel tystiolaeth.'*
> (b) remind the detainee about their right to legal advice.
>
> See Note 16B

This caution does not restrict the right to silence. It is not unusual for a person who has been charged with offences (and therefore his/her detention is for other reasons, e.g. because bail has been refused) to be paid a 'social visit' or to be spoken to for debrief intelligence purposes. Clearly there is a risk that the person may provide additional evidence about the offences for which he/she has been detained on other matters. *R* v *Williams* (1992) *The Times*, 6 February, recognised that this practice did occur but gave some guidance. The court held that investigating officers should avoid paying 'social visits' to people in custody whose conduct was under investigation. If, after being charged with an offence, a suspect of his/her own volition said that he/she wished to make a statement admitting or giving details of the offence, after properly cautioning the person and complying with the rest of the Codes of Practice, investigating officers were not debarred from recording what he/she had to say. Prior to a person being visited in his/her cell, the custody officer must give his/her authority and the visit must be recorded in the detained person's custody record.

1.7.8 When must an Interview be Held?

Code C, para. 16.1 states:

> When the officer in charge of the investigation reasonably believes there is sufficient evidence to provide a realistic prospect of the detainee's conviction, see paragraph 11.6, they shall without delay, and subject to the following qualification, inform the custody officer who will be responsible for considering whether the detainee should be charged ...

KEYNOTE

It is suggested that, in a case where a suspect has not been interviewed about an offence, Code C, para. 16.1, requires that person to be asked if he/she has anything further to say about the matter, in which case this will be an interview.

This view is supported by the case of *R* v *Pointer* [1997] Crim LR 676 which held that giving a suspect the opportunity to say something more when the officer already has enough evidence to charge is an interview within the definition of Code C, para. 11.1A, and, therefore, an event which attracts the protection of a caution, legal representation and tape recording.

Interviews in these circumstances are conducted to allow the suspect to make any additional comments and for the interviewing officers to follow up on those responses. If the interview is held for any other reason it is likely to be inadmissible. This was the case in *Pointer* where the court held that there was sufficient evidence to charge prior to the interview and consequently Code C, para. 16.1 had not been complied with. Such an interview may assist the investigating officer to make reasonable lines of inquiry which support the defence.

1.7.9 Conducting and Recording Interviews

The conduct of officers and the proper treatment of the suspect during an interview are essential if an interview is to be admissible in evidence. If an interview is not conducted properly, confessions made during the interview may be excluded. The PACE Codes of Practice are there to afford suspects proper protection from false confessions and treatment which may lead a court to the conclusion that the confession may not be reliable. It is essential, therefore, that officers are fully aware of the relevant Codes and comply with them. For evidential purposes interviews need to be recorded contemporaneously. An accurate record must be made of each interview with a person suspected of an offence, whether or not the interview takes place at a police station (Code C, para. 11.7).

Interviews currently fall into two main groups:

- those that are audibly or visually recorded; and
- those where the only record will be made in writing.

While there is no statutory requirement on police officers to visually record interviews, the contents of Code F should be considered if an interviewing officer decides to make a visual recording, with sound, of an interview with a suspect.

Code F3.1 provides guidance to interviewing officers as to the occasion when it may be appropriate to visually record an interview; it is important to note that the Terrorism Act 2000 has a separate code of practice for the visual recording of interviews in a police station for those detained under sch. 7 or s. 41 of the Act. See Note 3E for those occasions when it only becomes clear during the course of an interview that is being visually recorded that the interviewee may have committed an offence under the Terrorism Act 2000. Code F, para. F3.1 is not intended to preclude visual recordings of interviews at police stations with people cautioned in respect of other offences, or responses made by interviewees after they have been charged with, or informed they may be prosecuted for, an offence. Even a person who is voluntarily attending the police station should be visually interviewed.

While it is at the discretion of the interviewing officers as to when an interview should be visually recorded, a decision not to visually record an interview for any reason may be the subject of comment in court. The authorising officer should therefore be prepared to justify his/her decision in each case. The custody officer may authorise the interviewing officer not to record the interview visually in the circumstances laid out in Code F, para. 3.3.

The Criminal Justice and Police Act 2001 inserted s. 60A into the Police and Criminal Evidence Act 1984. This allows the Secretary of State to issue a code of practice for the visual recording of interviews held by police officers at police stations, and to make an order requiring the use of visual recording of interviews. An order issued by the Secretary of State may specify what offences or police stations or both the order applies to; currently there are no such requirements in place, although a code of practice has been issued (this is Code F of the PACE Codes of Practice, **see appendix 6**).

If a suspect makes unsolicited comments which are outside the context of an interview but which might be relevant to the offence, those comments should be recorded and Code C, para. 11.13 should be followed. Code C, Note 11E gives guidance as to what must be included in the record and when the record should be made. As the relevance of the comment may not be obvious at the time it is made, it is suggested that all comments are recorded.

1.7.9.1 When Interviews must be Audio Recorded

The interviewing of suspects is governed by PACE Code of Practice E. Code E, paras 3.1 and 3.5 set out which interviews at a police station must be audio recorded. The most noticeable absence from this list is for interviews about matters which can only be tried summarily. These requirements do not *preclude* other interviews being audio recorded. Investigators may well be advised to audio record interviews concerning summary only offences as it may be more difficult for the defence to suggest any confession was fabricated. If these interviews are recorded, they must follow the requirements of audio recorded interviews (see Code E, Note 3A).

The whole of each interview shall be recorded, including the taking and reading back of any statement (Code E, para. 3.5).

All interviews listed in Code E, para. 3.1 conducted at a police station must be audio recorded *unless* the custody officer authorises the interviewing officer not to audio record the interview. If the custody officer authorises the interview to go ahead without being audio recorded, the interview must be recorded in writing. A custody officer authorising this may have to justify the decision at court and the reasons for his/her decision should be recorded.

Code E, para. 3.3 allows the custody officer to make this decision where:

- it is not reasonably practicable to audio record the interview because of:
  - failure of the equipment; or
  - the non-availability of a suitable interview room or recorder; and

  - ♦ the custody officer considers on reasonable grounds that the interview should not be delayed until the failure has been rectified or a suitable room or recorder becomes available; or
- it is clear from the outset that no prosecution will ensue
- the custody officer has authorised that the detainee can be interviewed in his/her cell (Code E, para. 3.4).

Further, Code E, para. 3.1 does not apply to:

- certain interviews involving terrorism (Code E, para. 3.2).

For cases where a person objects to the interview being audio recorded, see Code E, para. 4.8.

1.7.9.2 Preparation before Interview at Police Station

Preparation is essential before any interview (indeed it is the first step in the PEACE interviewing model). This preparation should include the following points:

- Decide where the interview will be conducted. Consider the availability of a room and the timing of the interview.
- The location must have a seat for the person being interviewed (Code C, para. 12.6) and should be adequately lit, heated and ventilated (Code C, para. 12.4). The detained person must also have clothing of a reasonable standard of comfort and cleanliness (Code C, para. 8.5). (It will be a question of fact as to what amounts to adequate clothing and it is suggested that if the clothing is such as to degrade the detained person or make him/her uncomfortable, it may lead to the confession being held to be unreliable.)
- If the interview is being audio recorded, ensure that there are sufficient recording media for the anticipated length of the interview (or at least until the first break period). If the interview is being recorded in writing, ensure there are enough forms.
- If the interview is being audio recorded, ensure the notice as set out in Code E, para. 4.19 is available to be given at the end of the interview.
- In deciding the timing of the interview, consideration must be given to the detainee's rest period, which should not be interrupted or delayed unless Code C, para. 12.2 applies. Where the interview goes ahead during the rest period under Code C, para. 12.2(a), a fresh rest period must be allowed. Before a detainee is interviewed, the custody officer, in consultation with the officer in charge of the investigation and appropriate health care professionals as necessary, shall assess whether the detainee is fit enough to be interviewed (Code C, para. 12.3 and Annex G).
- If legal advice has been requested you must arrange for the legal representative to be present at the interview unless Code C, para. 6.6 applies.
- If a person has asked for legal advice and an interview is initiated in the absence of a legal adviser (e.g. where the person has agreed to be interviewed without his/her legal adviser being present or because of the urgent need to interview under Code C, para. 11.1), a record must be made in the interview record (Code C, para. 6.17).
- If an appropriate adult should be present, arrange for his/her attendance. (For the definition of appropriate adult, see Code C, para. 1.7.)
- If an interpreter is needed for the interview, arrange for his/her attendance.

It is also important to draw up an interview plan and to include any relevant areas that may provide a general or specific defence.

- Look at the evidence available and identify any significant statement or silence by the suspect in order that it can be put to him/her in interview (Code C, para. 11.4).

1.7.9.3 Starting Interviews

In order to interview a detained person, the interviewing officer must obtain permission from the custody officer. An entry must be made in the custody record to record that the interviewing officer accepts responsibility for the detained person. If the request to hand over the detained person is declined, the custody officer must record this fact and the reasons why on the custody record (Code C, para. 12.10). The responsibility for the detained person at this stage rests with the officer to whom the transfer is made and remains with this person until the detained person is returned to the custody officer (s. 39(2) of the Police and Criminal Evidence Act 1984). Section 39 of the 1984 Act states:

> (2) If this custody officer, in accordance with any code of practice issued under this Act, transfers or permits the transfer of a person in police detention—
> (a) to the custody of a police officer investigating an offence for which that person is in police detention; or
> (b) to the custody of an officer who has charge of that person outside the police station,
> the custody officer shall cease in relation to that person to be subject to the duty imposed on him by subsection (1)(a) above; and it shall be the duty of the officer to whom the transfer is made to ensure that he is treated in accordance with the provisions of this Act and of any such codes of practice as are mentioned in subsection (1) above.

Before allowing a detainee to be interviewed the custody officer shall undertake a risk assessment in order to ensure that conducting the interview will not significantly harm the detainee's physical or mental state or that their physical or mental state might result in the them saying something in the interview about their involvement or suspected involvement in the offence being considered unreliable in subsequent court proceedings (Code C, Annex G, paras 1 and 2). The risk assessment should be done, where necessary, in consultation with the officer in charge of the investigation and appropriate health care professionals. Annex G, para. 3 sets out a number of factors that must be considered when conducting this risk assessment. Where risks are identified, the custody officer must determine what safeguards are needed to minimise those risks in order to allow the interview to take place. It should be remembered that vulnerable suspects listed at Code C, para. 11.18 must always be treated as if being at some risk during an interview and therefore may not be interviewed except in accordance with Code C, paras 11.18 to 11.20 (Code C, para. 12.3). Code C, Annex G provides guidance to help police officers and health care professionals assess whether a detainee might be at risk in an interview.

The risk assessment can be very important in terms of ensuring that any confession in an interview is admissible. In *R* v *Utip* [2003] EWCA Crim 1256, the court held that the law required that where there were grounds to suspect mental illness, a defendant should be examined by a doctor to establish whether he/she was fit for interview. Where a defendant had been assessed as fit to be interviewed by a psychiatrist and had his/her interests protected by an appropriate adult and solicitor, there was no unfairness in allowing evidence of the interview to go before the jury.

1.7.9.4 Preliminary Issues for Interviews not being Audio Recorded

Before an interview begins the following points must be dealt with:

- Immediately before the commencement of the interview remind the suspect of his/her right to legal advice (Code C, para. 11.2) and make a note of this reminder and any response in the interview record.
- For the interview record, identify all officers present in the interview as required by Code C, para. 12.7.

- If an appropriate adult is present, inform that person of his/her role (Code C, para. 11.17).
- Administer the relevant caution (Code C, para. 10.1) (and re-administer where appropriate, **see para. 1.7.4**).

1.7.9.5 Preliminary Issues for Interviews being Audio Recorded

Before an interview commences the following points must be dealt with:

- The recording media must be unwrapped or opened in the suspect's presence (Code E, para. 4.3).
- In the suspect's sight, load the recorder with new recording media and set it to record (Code E, para. 4.3).
- Inform the suspect about the recording process in accordance with Code E, para. 4.4.
- Verbally identify all persons present at the interview (Code E, para. 4.4).
- Administer the relevant caution (Code E, para. 4.5) (and re-administer where appropriate, **see para. 1.7.4**).
- Remind the suspect of his/her right to free legal advice (Code E, para. 4.5 and Code C, paras 6.1 and 6.5) and ensure that the response is recorded (for instance a nod of the head would not be picked up by the recording).

1.7.9.6 Additional Preliminary Issues for Interviews being Visually Recorded

- Estimate the likely length of the interview and ensure that an appropriate quantity of certified recording media and labels with which to seal the master copies are available in the interview room.
- If not fixed, camera(s) should be placed in the interview room so as to ensure coverage of as much of the room as is practicably possible while the interviews are taking place.
- When the camera is brought into the interview in sight of the suspect, load the recording equipment and set it to record. The recording media must be unwrapped or otherwise opened in the presence of the suspect (Code F, para. 4.3).
- Inform the suspect formally about the visual recording as set out in Code F, para. 4.4.
- The interviewer must caution the suspect, which should follow that set out in Code C (Code F, para. 4.5).
- Remind the suspect of his/her entitlement to free and independent legal advice and that he/she can speak to a solicitor on the telephone (Code F, para. 4.5).

1.7.9.7 What should be Disclosed to the Solicitor

It is important not to confuse the duty of disclosure to a person once charged with the need to disclose evidence to a suspect before interviewing them. After a person has been charged, and before trial, the rules of disclosure are clear and almost all material must be disclosed to the defence.

However, this is not necessarily the case at the interview stage of the investigation. There is no specific provision within the Police and Criminal Evidence Act 1984 for the disclosure of any information by the police at the police station, with the exception of the custody record and, in identification cases, the initial description given by the witnesses. Further, there is nothing within the Criminal Justice and Public Order Act 1994 that states that information must be disclosed before an inference from silence can be made. Indeed, in *R* v *Imran* [1997] Crim LR 754 the court held that it is totally wrong to submit that a defendant should be prevented from lying by being presented with the whole of the evidence against him/her prior to the interview.

In *R* v *Argent* [1997] Crim LR 346 the court dismissed the argument that an inference could not be drawn under s. 34 of the Criminal Justice and Public Order Act 1994 because there had not been full disclosure at the interview. However, the court did recognise that it may be a factor to take into account, but it would be for the jury to decide whether the failure to answer questions was reasonable.

In *R* v *Roble* [1997] Crim LR 449, the court suggested that an inference would not be drawn where a solicitor gave advice to remain silent where, for example, the interviewing officer had disclosed too little of the case for the solicitor usefully to advise his/her client, or where the nature of the offence, or the material in the hands of the police, was so complex or related to matters so long ago that no sensible immediate response was feasible.

It was not uncommon in the past for solicitors to advise on no comment interviews and this has been relied on by defendants to avoid adverse inferences being drawn from their silence. The courts and legal advisers are now very aware of the consequences of advising a suspect to offer no comment. In *R* v *Morgan* [2001] EWCA Crim 445, the Court of Appeal stated that a court was entitled to assume that a solicitor would advise his/her client about the adverse inferences rule. In *R* v *Ali* [2001] EWCA Crim 683, the court stated that the question was not whether the advice to remain silent was good advice but whether it provided an adequate reason for failing to answer questions.

In *R* v *Hoare* [2004] EWCA Crim 784 the Court of Appeal held that the purpose of s. 34 was to qualify a defendant's right to silence rather than to exclude a jury from drawing an adverse inference against a defendant merely because he/she had been advised by their solicitor to remain silent, whether or not he/she genuinely or reasonably relied on that advice. Where a defendant had an explanation to give that was consistent with his/her innocence it was not 'reasonable', within the meaning of s. 34(1), for him/her to fail to give that explanation in interview even where he/she had been advised by his/her solicitor to remain silent. Legal advice by itself could not preclude the drawing of an adverse inference.

There is a balance to be struck between providing the solicitor with enough information to understand the nature of the case against his/her client and keeping back material which, if disclosed, may allow the suspect the opportunity to avoid implicating him/herself. For instance in *R* v *Thirlwell* [2002] EWCA Crim 286, the Court of Appeal agreed that the solicitor had not been entitled to provisional medical evidence as to possible causes of death in a murder case. The disclosure of material may well be a factor which the defendant relies on in showing that the failure to mention possible defences was reasonable. If the officers are not hoping to draw inferences from silence then tactically they may decide not to disclose as much information—it will be a question of fact in each case.

1.7.9.8 Conduct During Interview

- Code C, para. 11.5 reiterates the fact that officers must not act oppressively.
- If a complaint is made by the suspect concerning the provisions of the codes the interviewing officer must inform the custody officer and follow Code C, para. 12.9. If the complaint is not concerning the codes, Code E, Note 4F applies.
- Officers should only indicate the possible effect of refusing to answer questions or of answering questions if he/she is asked about those possible effects by the suspect *unless this is done as part of a special warning* (see Code C, paras 10.10, 10.11 and 11.15).
- Code E, para. 4.8 provides guidance where the person objects to the interview being audio recorded.
- Code C, Note 11C reminds officers of the risks associated with the reliability of interviewing juveniles or people who are mentally disordered or otherwise mentally vulnerable.

At the start of the interview the investigating officer should put to the suspect any significant statement or silence which occurred before his/her arrival at the police station and ask the suspect whether he/she confirms the earlier statement or silence and whether he/she wishes to add anything. Code C, para. 11.4A defines a 'significant' statement or silence. This aspect of the interview is very important in terms of establishing whether the facts are disputed. If they are not disputed at this stage, it is unlikely that they will be challenged at any later court hearing and, if challenged, the defence will have to explain why this was not done at the time of the interview. The courts may also view this failure to put the statement to the suspect in a more sinister light. In *R* v *Allen* (2001) 10 July, unreported, the court were concerned that the police failed to put the admission to the suspect in interview, despite thorough questioning, which they felt clearly placed a question mark over its reliability. If the suspect remains silent in relation to a 'significant silence', that silence may give rise to an adverse inference being drawn under s. 34 of the Criminal Justice and Public Order Act 1994 if the person raises it in his/her defence at court. (As this is a very important issue, it may be necessary to delay the interview until the arrest notes are completed or the officers witnessing the offence/arrest have been consulted to ensure that all matters are put to the suspect at this stage.) Consideration should be given to putting questions to a suspect who makes no comment, or even where the legal representative has stated that the suspect will make no comment, as this may allow the court to draw inferences against a defence that the suspect raises at court (**see para. 1.8.5**). The interviewer may wish to go through any significant statement or silence again if during earlier interviews adverse inferences could not be drawn.

1.7.9.9 Issues Specific to Audio Recorded Interviews

- If the equipment fails, rectify the fault quickly if possible. If this is not possible, look for an alternative recording machine or room. If none available, seek the authority of the custody officer to continue without the interview being audio recorded (see Code E, para. 4.15).
- If *the media or the recording equipment fails*, follow Code E, Note 4H.
- When recording media is removed from the recorder it must be retained (see Code E, para. 4.16) and the procedure at para. 4.18 followed.
- If you need to change recording media during interview, for instance when the recorder shows the recording media only has a short time left, follow Code E, para. 4.11.
- If a suspect objects to the interview being audio recorded at any stage of the interview, the procedure in Code E, para. 4.8 must be followed and Note 4D should be taken into account in deciding whether to continue to audio record the interview.
- If a suspect indicates that he/she wishes to tell the police about matters not connected with the offence(s) being investigated but does not wish this information to be audio recorded, Code E, para. 4.10 requires this to be dealt with at the conclusion of the formal interview. Any comment by the suspect would still need to be recorded in writing.

1.7.9.10 Issues Specific to Visually Recorded Interview

- If the equipment fails, rectify the fault if possible and follow the guidance set out in Code F, para. 4.12 (breaks in interviews) and para. 4.15. If, however, it is not possible to continue recording on that particular recorder and no alternative equipment is readily available, the interview may continue without being recorded visually.
- If a suspect raises objections to the interview being visually recorded at any stage, the procedures in Code F, para. 4.8 must be followed.

- If in the course of an interview a complaint is made by the person being questioned, or on their behalf, concerning the provisions of Code F or of Code C, then the interviewer shall act in accordance with Code C, record it in the interview record and inform the custody officer (Code F, para. 4.9 and Notes 4B and 4C).
- If a suspect indicates that he/she wishes to tell the interviewer about matters not directly connected with the offence(s) of which they are suspected and that they are unwilling for these matters to be recorded, Code F, para. 4.10 requires this to be dealt with at the conclusion of the formal interview.
- If the interviewer needs to change the recording media during the interview, follow Code F, para. 4.11.
- When the recording medium is removed from the recording machine it must be retained (see Code F, para. 4.16) and the procedure at para. 4.18 followed.
- In cases as set out in Code F, para. 2.5 where an officer's identity should not be disclosed, the officer will have their back to the camera and shall use their warrant or other identification number and the name of the police station to which they are attached. Such instances and the reasons for them shall be recorded in the custody record.

1.7.9.11 Breaks

Breaks from interviewing must be made at recognised meal times or at other times that take account of when the person last had a meal (Code C, para. 12.8). Short breaks for refreshment must also be provided at intervals of approximately two hours. Code C, Note 12B gives guidance on how long breaks should be. Code C, para. 12.8 sets out the exceptions to the requirement to provide breaks. These exceptions exist where to break the interview would:

- involve a risk of harm to people or serious loss of, or damage to property;
- delay unnecessarily the person's release from custody; or
- otherwise prejudice the outcome of the investigation.

Any decision to delay a break during an interview must be recorded, with grounds, in the interview record (either on the written record or on the recording media) (Code C, para. 12.12).

1.7.9.12 Breaks—Additional Issues for Visually Recorded Interviews

Whether the recording equipment will be left to run during a break will depend on the circumstances such as length of time of the break and whether the interview room will be vacated; guidance is provided by Code F, paras 4.12 to 4.14. On the re-commencement of an interview, the officer should consider summarising on the record the reason for the break and confirming this with the suspect (Code F, Note 4E).

1.7.9.13 Solicitors and Legal Advice

A 'solicitor' for the purposes of the Codes of Practice means:

- a solicitor holding a current practising certificate;
- a trainee solicitor;
- a duty solicitor representative or an accredited or probationary representative included on the register of representatives maintained by the Legal Services Commission (Code C, para. 6.12).

Where a solicitor is available at the time the interview begins or while it is in progress, the solicitor must be allowed to be present while the person in interviewed (Code C, para. 6.8).

(This applies unless the suspect states that he/she does not want the solicitor to be present or where access is denied under s. 58 of the 1984 Act, see Code C, Annex B.)

If a solicitor arrives at the station to see a suspect, the suspect must be asked whether he/she would like to see the solicitor *regardless of what legal advice has already been received*. The solicitor's attendance and the suspect's decision must be recorded in the custody record (Code C, para. 6.15).

If the investigating officer considers that a solicitor is acting in such a way that he/she is unable properly to put questions to the suspect, he/she will stop the interview and consult an officer not below the rank of superintendent, if one is readily available, otherwise an officer not below the rank of inspector who is not connected with the investigation to decide whether that solicitor should be excluded from the interview. The interview may also have to be stopped in order to allow another solicitor to be instructed (Code C, para. 6.10). For the proper role of the legal representatives, see Code C, Note 6D. Code C, para. 6.6 sets out those occasions where a person can be interviewed without a solicitor being present even though he/she has requested a solicitor (**see para. 1.6.6.6**). Any authority to exclude a solicitor will need to be justified to the court if necessary (Code C, Note 6E).

With regard to the exclusion of probationer solicitor this has to be considered in relation to the specific investigation and whether that person is likely to interfere with the investigation. The decision can take into account the character of the person. Internal advice could also provide guidance as to what the decision should be but the decision has to be made in relation to each individual case. It is not permissible to have blanket bans on such persons (*R* v *Chief Constable of the Northumbria Constabulary, ex parte Thompson* [2001] 1 WLR 1342).

If a request for legal advice is made during an interview, the interviewing officer must stop the interview straightaway and arrange for legal advice to be provided. If the suspect changes his/her mind again, the interview can continue provided Code C, para. 6.6 is complied with.

It is important to remember that Code C, para. 6.4 reminds officers that they should *not* try to dissuade the detained person from obtaining legal advice. If an appropriate adult requests legal advice but the detained juvenile does not wish to consult with the solicitor, he/she cannot be forced to speak to the solicitor (Code C, para. 6.5A).

1.7.9.14 When must the Interview be Concluded?

Guidance is provided by Code C, para. 11.6 as to when an interview should be concluded. Paragraph 11.6 states that the interview shall cease if the investigating officer considers that:

- all the questions relevant to obtaining accurate and reliable information about the offence have been put to the suspect, this includes allowing the suspect an opportunity to give an innocent explanation and asking questions to test if the explanation is accurate and reliable;
- has taken account of any other available evidence; and
- there is sufficient evidence to provide a realistic prospect of conviction for that offence if the person was prosecuted for it.

The investigating officer shall then bring the detained person before the custody officer for charge.

The interview may continue until the above conditions are satisfied with regard to other offences being investigated (Code C, para. 16.1).

It is important to remember that the interview should not be concluded at the point when there is sufficient evidence to prosecute but when there is sufficient evidence to provide a realistic prospect of conviction. (In *Prouse* v *DPP* [1999] All ER (D) 748 the question was said to be not how much evidence there is but the quality of it.) Once there is enough evidence to prosecute, it may still be necessary to cover those other points in the interview that may be relevant to the defence case. If these points are not covered in the interview, the defence may surprise the prosecution case with matters that the prosecution have not covered or with issues that may result in the loss of an inference being drawn from the suspect's silence. This was considered in *R* v *McGuinness* [1999] Crim LR 318 where the court held that the words 'sufficient evidence to prosecute' and 'sufficient evidence for a prosecution to succeed' in Code C, para. 11.6 must involve some consideration of any explanation, or lack of one, from the suspect. It would depend on the facts of a case whether the stage where a suspect ought to be charged has been reached. As a word of caution, the court also said that under Code C, paras 16.1 and 11.6 it was not open for a suspect to be questioned beyond the point when he/she ought to have been charged. If the suspect was questioned beyond that point, then the interview was liable to be ruled inadmissible and the content would not be available to support the prosecution case.

Paragraph 3.4 of the Code of Practice to the Criminal Procedure and Investigations Act 1996 says that in conducting an investigation, the investigator should pursue all reasonable lines of inquiry, whether these point towards or away from the suspect. What is reasonable will depend on the particular circumstances. Interviewers should keep this in mind when deciding what questions to ask in an interview.

1.7.9.15 Special Groups

As a confession can be very damning evidence against a defendant, it is important to provide safeguards that give all suspects the same level of protection. The PACE Codes of Practice recognise certain groups as being in need of additional protection. These groups include juveniles, people who do not speak English, those suffering from a mental impairment and those who are deaf. Such suspects must not be interviewed without the relevant person being present.

For juveniles and those suffering from a mental impairment (or who appear to be such), an appropriate adult must be present (Code C, para. 11.15).

Under Code C, para. 13.2, a person capable of acting as interpreter is required where:

- the suspect has difficulty in understanding English;
- the interviewing officer cannot speak the person's own language; and
- the suspect wishes an interpreter to be present.

If the suspect appears to be deaf or there is any doubt about his/her hearing or speaking ability, an interpreter should be found (unless he/she agrees *in writing* to proceed without an interpreter) (Code C, para. 13.5). This requirement also applies in the case of the appropriate adult who appears to be deaf or there is doubt about his/her hearing or speaking ability (Code C, para. 13.6).

There are limited circumstances where an interview may be conducted without an interpreter or appropriate adult being present. These are set out in Code C, paras 11.1 and 11.15. Once those conditions no longer apply, the interview must be suspended until the appropriate person is present. For it to be an 'interview' a police officer or a designated investigating officer must be present (Code C, para. 13.4).

Where interpreters are required, Code C, paras 13.3 to 13.11 are to be followed.

If an interpreter who can translate straight from the detained person's language to English cannot be found then more than one interpreter should be used to bridge the language gap. It is the *interviewer* who is responsible for ensuring that the detained person can understand and be understood (*R* v *West London Youth Court, ex parte J* [2000] 1 All ER 823).

Audio Recorded Interviews and Special Groups

If the suspect is deaf or there is doubt about his/her hearing ability, a contemporaneous written record should be made as well as the audio recording. This record should be the same as where there is no audio record of the interview (Code E, para. 4.7).

1.7.9.16 Special Warnings

Now that inferences can be drawn from a suspect's silence (albeit in limited circumstances), it is necessary to warn the person of the dangers of remaining silent. For this reason the 'special warning' was introduced (**see para. 1.8.7**) where there is potentially incriminating evidence relating to objects, marks or substances; or relating to the accused's presence at a particular place. If the special warning is not given, inferences from silence will not be allowed to boost the prosecution case but the potentially incriminating evidence may still be admissible. Code C, paras 10.10 to 10.11 must be followed if any questions are to be put to the arrested suspect about:

- any object, marks or substances found on the him/her, or
- in or on his/her clothing or footwear, or
- otherwise in his/her possession, or
- in the place where he/she was arrested

(see s. 36 of the Criminal Justice and Public Order Act 1994).

These provisions also apply to any questions about why the suspect was at any place, at or about the time the offence for which he/she was arrested was committed, and has failed to or refuses to account for their presence at that place (see s. 37 of the Criminal Justice and Public Order Act 1994).

It must be made clear to the suspect what matters he/she is being asked to answer and the consequences of remaining silent on each occasion.

See para. 1.7.4 and Code C, Annex C for occasions when special warnings and adverse inferences do not apply.

1.7.9.17 Conclusion of Interview

Written Interviews

- The person interviewed (and the appropriate adult or the suspect's solicitor if present during the interview (Code C, para. 11.12)) must be given an opportunity to read the interview record and to sign it as correct or to indicate the respects in which he/she considers it inaccurate (Code C, para. 11.11). If the person concerned cannot read or refuses to read the record or to sign it, the senior police officer present shall read it to him/her (Code C, para. 11.11). If there is any delay in recording the interview, if practicable, the suspect should still be given an opportunity to read the statement.
- Any refusal to sign the record must be recorded (Code C, para. 11.14).
- If an interpreter has been present at the interview, he/she should be given an opportunity to read the record and certify its accuracy (Code C, para. 13.7).
- If the person is in police detention, return him/her to the custody officer, informing that officer whether the Codes have been complied with, if any incidents occurred and whether there were any breaches of the Codes (s. 39(3) of the Police and Criminal Evidence Act 1984).

1.7.9.18 Audio Recorded Interviews

- The person interviewed must be offered the opportunity to clarify anything he/she has said during the interview and to add anything he/she may wish (Code E, para. 4.17). This may be important when the case comes to court and the defence try to explain why certain things were said during the interview.
- Turn off the recording medium and seal it with a master recording label (Code E, para. 4.18). If the seal on the master recording needs to be broken for any reason, follow Code E, para. 6.2 or, if decision has been made not to institute criminal proceedings, follow Code E, para. 6.3.
- Sign the label and ask the suspect and any third party present to sign it also. If the suspect or third party refuses to sign it, an inspector, or if not available a custody officer, shall be called into the interview room and asked to sign it (Code E, para. 4.18).
- Hand the suspect the notice which explains the use which will be made of the audio recording and the arrangement for access to it (Code E, para. 4.19).
- Make a personal pocket book entry about the interview as required by Code E, para. 5.1 (see Code E, para. 1.10).
- Follow force standing orders or local procedures in relation to master recording security whether or not the person is charged (Code E, paras 6.1 and 5.2).

1.7.9.19 Conclusion of Interview—Additional Issues for Visually Recorded Interviews

- The person interviewed must be offered the opportunity to clarify anything he/she has said during the interview and to add anything he/she may wish (Code F, para. 4.17). This may be important when the case comes to court and the defence try to explain why certain things were said during the interview.
- Turn off the recording equipment and seal the master record with a master copy label and treat as an exhibit in accordance with the force standing orders (Code F, para. 4.18). In addition to the master copy, a second copy will be used as a working copy. If the seal on the master record needs to be broken for any reason, follow Code E, para. 6.2 or, if a decision has been made not to institute criminal proceedings, follow Code E, para. 6.3.
- Sign the label and ask the suspect and any third party present to sign it also. If the suspect or third party refuses to sign it, an inspector, or if not available a custody officer, must be called into the interview room and asked to sign it (Code F, para. 4.18).
- Hand the suspect the notice which explains the use which will be made of the recording and the arrangement for access to it (Code F, para. 4.19).
- Make a personal pocket book entry about the interview as required by Code F, para. 5.1.
- Follow force standing orders or local procedures in relation to master recording security whether or not the person is charged (Code F, para. 6.1).
- Once the master copy of the interview has been sealed it should only be broken in the circumstances set out in Code F, paras 6.2 to 6.7.

1.7.10 Statements from Suspects

Statements under caution, particularly of a detained person, are less common than interviews. If a person has been interviewed and it has been audio or visually recorded or an interview has been recorded contemporaneously in writing, a statement under caution should normally be conducted only at the person's express wish (Code C, Note 12A). A statement must not be elicited by the use of oppression (Code C, para. 11.5) and, if written at the police station, the statement must be on the correct forms (Code C, para. 12.12). Code C, Annex D sets out how the statement should be taken and matters that must be included in the statement whether it is written by the suspect or a police officer. See Code C, Annex C for restrictions on drawing inferences and Annex D for the variable declarations the person must include in his/her statements.

When completing the statement, the person must always be invited to write down what he/she wants to say and should be allowed to do so without any prompting, except that a police officer may indicate which matters are material or question any ambiguity in the statement. In the case of a person making a statement in a language other than English, Code C, para. 13.4 states:

(a) the interpreter shall record the statement in the language it is made;
(b) the person shall be invited to sign it;
(c) an official English translation shall be made in due course

(in these cases, para. 13.4 means that the person will not be invited to write the statement him/herself which is an exception to the guidance in Annex D).

A juvenile or a person who is mentally disordered or mentally vulnerable, *whether suspected or not*, must not be asked to provide or sign a written statement in the absence of the appropriate adult unless Code C, paras 11.1, 11.18 to 11.20 or Annex C applies (Code C, para. 11.15). Statements made by an accused under caution to the police are confidential. It is clearly implicit in the relationship between the police and the accused that the information, before being used in open court, is used only for the purposes for which it is provided and not for extraneous purposes, such as the media. However, the obligation of confidentiality (which is now included in the Police Code of Conduct) in respect of such a statement will be brought to an end where the contents of the statement are already in the public domain (*Bann* v *British Broadcasting Corporation* (1998) 148 NLJ 979).

1.7.11 Statements from Defence Witnesses

The Criminal Justice Act 2003 introduces a code of practice for police officers interviewing a witness notified by the accused. Although this is still at the consultation stages it is likely to be introduced within the next year.

1.8 Criminal Justice and Public Order Act 1994, Sections 34–37

Evidence can be described as information that may be presented to a court so that it may decide on the probability of some facts asserted before it, that is information by which facts are open to proof—or disproof—and these are discussed below.

1.8.1 Weight and Admissibility of Evidence

The two questions that need to be applied to any evidence are:

- admissibility; and
- weight.

The question of admissibility, to be decided by the judge in all cases, is whether the evidence is relevant to a fact in issue. All evidence of facts in issue and all evidence which is sufficiently relevant to prove (or disprove) facts in issue are potentially admissible.

The admissibility of evidence is very important to the outcome of any trial as it is from this that a person's guilt is decided. When collecting evidence in a case it should always be a consideration whether the evidence being collected is the best available and whether it will be admissible.

Once it is established that the evidence is admissible, it is put before the court to determine what weight it will attach to the evidence; that is, how much effect does it have on proving or disproving the case.

1.8.1.1 Evidence Gathering

The word evidence must not be confused with information. In relation to preparing an offence file, the investigation of the offence will result in the collection of information. What is and what is not evidence can be decided at a later stage with the help of the Crown Prosecution Service. The importance of this distinction is that rules of evidence should not restrict the initial collection of information, otherwise a fact vital to the outcome of the case may be disregarded as irrelevant and/or inadmissible.

1.8.1.2 Reasons for Excluding Admissible Evidence

Even though evidence may be admissible in criminal cases, at common law, the trial judge has a general discretion to exclude legally admissible evidence tendered by the prosecution. This can be seen in *R* v *Sang* [1980] AC 402, where it was held that:

- A trial judge, as part of his/her duty to ensure that an accused receives a fair trial, always has a discretion to exclude evidence tendered by the prosecution if in his/her opinion its prejudicial effect outweighs its probative value. In deciding if the evidence should be admitted, the question the judge asks himself/herself is whether it is fair to allow the evidence, not whether it is obtained fairly or by unfair means.
- With the exception of admissions and confessions (here s. 76 of the Police and Criminal Evidence Act 1984 applies) and generally with regard to evidence obtained from the accused after the commission of the offence, the judge generally has no discretion whether to exclude relevant admissible evidence on the ground that this was obtained by improper or unfair means.

If the evidence is relevant to the matters in issue then it is admissible and the court is not concerned with how the evidence was obtained (*Kuruma, Son of Kaniu* v *The Queen* [1955] AC 197). This proposition was upheld in *Jeffrey* v *Black* [1978] QB 490 where evidence was admissible concerning the unlawful search of premises.

Evidence may also be excluded for the following reasons:

- the incompetence of the witness;
- it relates to previous convictions, the character or disposition of the accused;
- it falls under hearsay;
- it is non-expert opinion evidence;
- it is privileged information;
- it is withheld as a matter of public policy.

There are also powers to exclude evidence under ss. 76 and 78 of the Police and Criminal Evidence Act 1984.

1.8.2 Facts in Issue

In a criminal case, facts in issue are those facts which must be proved by the prosecution in order to establish the defendant's guilt, or in exceptional cases those facts which are the essential elements of a defence, where the burden of proof is on the defendant to prove the defence.

Such facts will include:

- the identity of the defendant;
- the *actus reus*;
- the *mens rea*.

The relevant criminal conduct (*actus reus*) and state of mind (*mens rea*) will always be facts in issue, and it is therefore essential that these features are understood, both as general concepts and also in relation to the particular offence being investigated.

1.8.3 Burden of Proof

The facts in issue fall into two distinct categories:

- the facts that the *prosecution* bear the burden of proving or disproving in order to establish the defendant's guilt;
- the facts which, in exceptional circumstances, the *defence* need to prove to show that the defendant is not guilty.

1.8.3.1 Duty of the Prosecution

'Throughout the web of the English criminal law one golden thread is always to be seen; that is the duty of the prosecution to prove the prisoner's guilt.' This famous passage is taken from the House of Lords' decision in *Woolmington* v *DPP* [1935] AC 462. The underlying principle was perhaps best explained by Geoffrey Lawrence QC in an address to the jury in a murder trial:

> The possibility of guilt is not enough, suspicion is not enough, probability is not enough, likelihood is not. A criminal matter is not a question of balancing probabilities and deciding in favour of probability.
>
> If the accusation is not proved beyond reasonable doubt against the man accused in the dock, then by the law he is entitled to be acquitted, because that is the way our rules work. It is no concession to give him the benefit of the doubt. He is entitled by law to a verdict of not guilty.

(See Brian Harris, *The Literature of the Law*, Blackstone Press, 1998.)

Therefore the general rule is that the prosecution have the legal (or persuasive) burden of proving all the elements of the offence in order to prove guilt.

In *Evans* v *DPP* (2001) *The Times*, 9 July, it was held that the justices had wrongly applied *the balance of probabilities* in finding the defendant guilty rather than the full criminal standard of proof.

Where the defendant enters a plea of not guilty to the charge, the onus is on the prosecution to prove the whole of their case. This includes 'the identity of the accused, the nature of the act and the existence of any necessary knowledge or intent' (*R* v *Sims* [1946] KB 531).

Generally the onus is on the prosecution in the first instance to establish particular facts to prove the accused's guilt beyond all reasonable doubt. However, once a prima facie case is made out, the defence has to establish particular facts in order to rebut the prosecution evidence. Here there is a shift of the onus to establish particular facts.

1.8.3.2 Duty of the Defence

Exceptionally, the defence may have the burden of proof. In such circumstances the standard of proof for the defence is less rigorous than for the prosecution when establishing guilt (beyond all reasonable doubt). The defence will succeed if the court or jury are satisfied that the defence evidence is more probably true than false. This standard of proof is referred to as *the balance of probabilities*, the same standard of proof that operates in a civil trial.

Generally the prosecution bear the duty of proving or disproving certain facts and, if they fail to do so, the defence need say nothing; the prosecution fails and the defendant is acquitted.

Exceptionally, the common law (e.g. the defence of insanity), or a statute (e.g. diminished responsibility (s. 2 of the Homicide Act 1957)), may impose a burden on the defence to prove the defence.

The law relating to the carrying of weapons is a good illustration of where the defence may have a burden of proof. Once the prosecution have proved (beyond a reasonable doubt) that a defendant was carrying an offensive weapon, the burden then shifts to the defence to prove (on the balance of probabilities) that the defendant had lawful authority or reasonable excuse.

There will also be occasions where the defence has what is called an *evidential burden* in relation to certain specific defences they intend to rely on. Common examples of defences that only place an evidential burden on the defence are defences relating to alibis, self-defence, accident and provocation. In contrast to the evidential burden borne by the prosecution (to show that there is a case to answer by the end of the prosecution evidence), the defence's evidential burden arises somewhat differently. Unlike those defences that place a full legal burden of proof on the defence, the defence does not have to satisfy the judge of anything as such. All that the defence has to do is to ensure that there is enough evidence relating to the defence that is to be raised to enable the judge to direct the jury upon that defence as a live issue.

Section 101 of the Magistrates' Courts Act 1980 places a legal burden of proof on the accused either expressly or by implication. The section provides that where the accused relies for his/her defence on any *exemption*, *proviso*, *excuse* or *qualification*, the burden of proving this is on the accused.

KEYNOTE

An example of a summary offence where the burden of proof is on the defence is driving without insurance where the accused is required to prove he/she is insured (*Williams* v *Russell* (1933) 149 LT 190). An example of an indictable offence is where the accused was convicted on indictment of selling intoxicating liquor without a licence and the Court of Appeal held that it was for the accused to prove that he was the holder of a licence (*R* v *Edwards* [1975] QB 27).

1.8.4 Inferences from Silence

At common law, when being questioned about involvement in a criminal offence, a suspect is under no obligation to answer any of the questions. This is another key feature of the criminal justice system in England and Wales and is the reason behind the cautioning of suspects required by the Police and Criminal Evidence Act 1984. However, ss. 34 to 38 of the Criminal Justice and Public Order Act 1994 have a potentially important impact on the law in relation to the accused's silence.

Sections 34 to 37 permit the court to draw 'such inferences as appear proper' against the accused in the circumstances contained within the sections.

1.8.5 Inferences from Silence when Questioned or Charged

Section 34 of the Criminal Justice and Public Order Act 1994 provides that inferences can be drawn if, when questioned by the police under caution, charged or officially informed that he/she may be prosecuted, the accused fails to mention a fact on which he/she later relies in his/her defence, and which he/she could reasonably have been expected to mention at the time.

Section 34 states:

(1) Where, in any proceedings against a person for an offence, evidence is given that the accused—
   (a) at any time before he was charged with the offence, on being questioned under caution by a constable trying to discover whether or by whom the offence had been committed, failed to mention any fact relied on in his defence in those proceedings; or
   (b) on being charged with the offence or officially informed that he might be prosecuted for it, failed to mention any such fact,

   being a fact which in the circumstances existing at the time the accused could reasonably have been expected to mention when so questioned, charged or informed, as the case may be, subsection (2) below applies.

(2) Where this subsection applies—
   (a) a magistrates' court inquiring into an offence as examining justices in deciding whether to grant an application for dismissal made by the accused under section 6 of the Magistrates' Courts Act 1980 (application for dismissal of charge in course of proceedings with a view to transfer for trial);
   (b) a judge, in deciding whether to grant an application made by the accused under—
      (i) section 6 of the Criminal Justice Act 1987 (application for dismissal of charge of serious fraud in respect of which notice of transfer has been given under section 4 of that Act); or
      (ii) paragraph 5 of schedule 6 to the Criminal Justice Act 1991 (application for dismissal of charge of violent or sexual offence involving child in respect of which notice of transfer has been given under section 53 of that Act);
   (c) the court, in determining whether there is a case to answer; and
   (d) the court or jury, in determining whether the accused is guilty of the offence charged,

   may draw such inferences from the failure as appear proper.

(2A) Where the accused was at an authorised place of detention at the time of the failure, subsections (1) and (2) above do not apply if he had not been allowed an opportunity to consult a solicitor prior to being questioned, charged or informed as mentioned in subsection (1) above.

(3) Subject to any directions by the court, evidence tending to establish the failure may be given before or after evidence tending to establish the fact which the accused is alleged to have failed to mention.

(4) This section applies in relation to questioning by persons (other than constables) charged with the duty of investigating offences or charging offenders as it applies in relation to questioning by constables; and in subsection (1) above 'officially informed' means informed by a constable or any such person.

(5) This section does not—
   (a) prejudice the admissibility in evidence of the silence or other reaction of the accused in the face of anything said in his presence relating to the conduct in respect of which he is charged, in so far as evidence thereof would be admissible apart from this section; or
   (b) preclude the drawing of any inference from any such silence or other reaction of the accused which could properly be drawn apart from this section.

KEYNOTE

Although judges have discretion in individual cases it has been recommended that in relation to s. 34 they should closely follow the Judicial Studies Board specimen direction. This direction was followed in *Beckles v United Kingdom (Chenia)* [2003] 2 Cr App R 83 and accepted by the European Court of Human Rights. However, failure to give proper direction does not necessarily involve a breach of article 6 (right to a fair trial).

Section 34 deals with the 'failure to mention any fact' and the word 'fact' is given its normal dictionary definition of 'something that is actually the case' (*R* v *Milford* [2001] Crim LR 330). Where an accused alleges that they did mention the relevant fact when being questioned it is for the prosecution to prove the contrary before any adverse inference can be drawn.

There have been numerous domestic and European case decisions about failure to advance facts following legal advice to remain silent, and more recent cases have attempted to unravel the difficulties experienced in this area. These cases have accepted that a genuine reliance by a defendant on his/her solicitor's advice to remain silent is not in itself enough to preclude adverse comment. The real question to be answered is whether the defendant remained silent, not because of legal advice, but because there was no satisfactory explanation to give (*R* v *Beckles* [2005] EWCA Crim 2766, *R* v *Bresa* [2005] EWCA Crim 1414, and *R* v *Loizou* [2006] EWCA Crim 1719).

In relation to s. 34, the accused cannot be convicted solely on an inference drawn from silence. In *Condron* v *United Kingdom* (2001) 31 EHRR 1, the European Court of Human Rights, although accepting that there are cases which clearly call for an accused to provide an explanation, the court is required to apply 'particular caution' before invoking the accused's silence against him.

In *R* v *Argent* [1997] 2 Cr App R 27, the court stated that personal factors which might be relevant to an assessment of what an individual could reasonably have been expected to mention were age, experience, mental capacity, state of health, sobriety, tiredness and personality.

In *R* v *Flynn* [2001] EWCA Crim 1633, the court held that the police are entitled to conduct a second interview with a suspect, having obtained evidence from their witnesses which was not available in the first interview, and adverse inference could be drawn from the suspect's silence.

Where an accused, following legal advice, fails to answer questions during interview but presents a prepared statement, no adverse inference can be drawn where the accused's defence does not rely on any facts not mentioned in the interview (*R* v *Campbell* [2005] EWCA Crim 1249). However, this would not be the case when evidence of facts relied on during the trial was not contained within the pre-prepared statement (*R* v *Turner* [2003] EWCA Crim 3108).

Section 34 differs from the other 'inference' sections in that the questioning need not occur at a police station and therefore the presence of a legal representative is not required. However, it appears clear that, should the prosecution seek to draw any inferences of an accused's silence where such questioning has occurred, the questions would need to be asked of the suspect again once he/she had access to legal advice.

A requirement to caution the person is contained in s. 34(1)(a) to make it clear of the risks connected with a failure to mention facts which later form part of the defence.

The National Centre for Policing Excellence produces a practice advice document, 'Right to Silence', which outlines the legislation, provides practical advice for investigators and considers the special warnings under the provisions of ss. 34, 36 and 37.

When the provisions of the Criminal Justice Act 2003 are in force s. 34(2)(a) and (2)(b)(i) and (ii) will be repealed and replaced by sch. 3, para. 2 to the Crime and Disorder Act 1998. In relation to cases sent for trial under s. 51 or 51A(3)(d), this is in force, but for all other purposes the date in force is yet to be appointed. Section 6 of the Magistrates' Courts Act 1980 will also be repealed by the 2003 Act.

1.8.6 Where Access to Legal Advice is Delayed

Guidance has been provided by the government (Home Office Circular 53/1998). This requires that where access to legal advice has been delayed in accordance with Annex B of PACE Code C, the procedures for conducting the interview at the police station should be as follows:

- the interviewing officer should conduct any interview with the suspect at the police station in accordance with PACE Code C.

- the interviewing officer should make a written note of those questions which the suspect has failed or refused to answer;
- once the suspect has had the opportunity of access to legal advice, the interviewing officer should put these questions to the suspect again; and ask the suspect whether he/she wishes to say/add anything further.

(For a full discussion on delaying access to legal advice, **see para. 1.6.6.7**).

1.8.7 Inferences from Silence: Failure to Account for Objects, Substances and Marks

Section 36 of the Criminal Justice and Public Order Act 1994 provides that inferences can be drawn from an accused's failure to give evidence or refusal to answer any question about any object, substance or mark which may be attributable to the accused in the commission of an offence.

Section 36 states:

(1) Where—
  (a) a person is arrested by a constable, and there is—
    (i) on his person; or
    (ii) in or on his clothing or footwear; or
    (iii) otherwise in his possession; or
    (iv) in any place in which he is at the time of his arrest,
  any object, substance or mark, or there is any mark on any such object; and
  (b) that or another constable investigating the case reasonably believes that the presence of the object, substance or mark may be attributable to the participation of the person arrested in the commission of an offence specified by the constable; and
  (c) the constable informs the person arrested that he so believes, and requests him to account for the presence of the object, substance or mark; and
  (d) the person fails or refuses to do so,
then if, in any proceedings against the person for the offence so specified, evidence of those matters is given, subsection (2) below applies.

(2) Where this subsection applies—
  (a) a magistrates' court inquiring into an offence as examining justices in deciding whether to grant an application for dismissal made by the accused under section 6 of the Magistrates' Courts Act 1980 (application for dismissal of charge in course of proceedings with a view to transfer for trial);
  (b) a judge, in deciding whether to grant an application made by the accused under—
    (i) section 6 of the Criminal Justice Act 1987 (application for dismissal of charge of serious fraud in respect of which notice of transfer has been given under section 4 of that Act); or
    (ii) paragraph 5 of schedule 6 to the Criminal Justice Act 1991 (application for dismissal of charge of violent or sexual offence involving child in respect of which notice of transfer has been given under section 53 of that Act);
  (c) the court, in determining whether there is a case to answer; and
  (d) the court or jury, in determining whether the accused is guilty of the offence charged,
  may draw such inferences from the failure or refusal as appear proper.

(3) Subsections (1) and (2) above apply to the condition of clothing or footwear as they apply to a substance or mark thereon.

(4) Subsections (1) and (2) above do not apply unless the accused was told in ordinary language by the constable when making the request mentioned in subsection (1)(c) above what the effect of this section would be if he failed or refused to comply with the request.

(4A) Where the accused was at an authorised place of detention at the time of the failure or refusal, subsections (1) and (2) do not apply if he had not been allowed an opportunity to consult a solicitor prior to the request being made.

(5) This section applies in relation to officers of customs and excise as it applies in relation to constables.

(6) This section does not preclude the drawing of any inference from a failure or refusal of the accused to account for the presence of an object, substance or mark or from the condition of clothing or footwear which could properly be drawn apart from this section.

KEYNOTE

As with s. 37 below, an inference may only be drawn where four conditions are satisfied:

- the accused has been arrested;
- a constable reasonably believes that the object, substance or mark (or the presence of the accused (s. 37)) may be attributable to the accused's participation in a crime (s. 36 (an offence 'specified by the constable') or s. 37 (the offence for which he/she was arrested));
- the constable informs the accused of his/her belief and requests an explanation (by giving a special warning (see below));
- the constable tells the suspect (in ordinary language) the effect of a failure or refusal to comply with the request.

It is considered that the request for information under both s. 36 and s. 37 is a form of questioning and should be undertaken during the interview at the police station. The request for such information prior to this would be an exception to the rule.

The interviewing officer is required to give the accused a 'special warning' for an inference to be drawn from a suspect's failure or refusal to answer a question about one of these matters or to answer it satisfactorily. This 'special warning' is provided by PACE Code C, para. 10.11 which states that the interviewing officer must first tell the suspect *in ordinary language*:

- what offence is being investigated;
- what fact the suspect is being asked to account for;
- that the interviewing officer believes this fact may be due to the suspect's taking part in the commission of the offence in question;
- that a court may draw a proper inference if the suspect fails or refuses to account for the fact about which he/she is being questioned;
- that a record is being made of the interview and that it may be given in evidence at any subsequent trial.

As with s. 34, in relation to s. 36 the accused cannot be convicted solely on an inference drawn from a failure or refusal (s. 38(3)) **(see para. 1.8.10)**.

When the provisions of the Criminal Justice Act 2003 are in force s. 36(2)(a) and (2)(b)(i) and (ii) will be repealed and replaced by sch. 3, para. 2 to the Crime and Disorder Act 1998.

1.8.8 Inferences from Silence: Failure to Account for Presence

Section 37 of the Criminal Justice and Public Order Act 1994 provides that inferences can be drawn from an accused's failure to give evidence or refusal to answer any question about his/her presence at a place or time when the offence for which he/she was arrested was committed.

Section 37 states:

(1) Where—

(a) a person arrested by a constable was found by him at a place at or about the time the offence for which he was arrested is alleged to have been committed; and

(b) that or another constable investigating the offence reasonably believes that the presence of the person at that place and at that time may be attributable to his participation in the commission of the offence; and

(c) the constable informs the person that he so believes, and requests him to account for that presence; and

(d) the person fails or refuses to do so,

then if, in any proceedings against the person for the offence, evidence of those matters is given, subsection (2) below applies.

(2) Where this subsection applies—

(a) a magistrates' court inquiring into an offence as examining justices in deciding whether to grant an application for dismissal made by the accused under section 6 of the Magistrates' Courts Act 1980 (application for dismissal of charge in course of proceedings with a view to transfer for trial);

(b) a judge, in deciding whether to grant an application made by the accused under—

(i) section 6 of the Criminal Justice Act 1987 (application for dismissal of charge of serious fraud in respect of which notice of transfer has been given under section 4 of that Act); or

(ii) paragraph 5 of schedule 6 to the Criminal Justice Act 1991 (application for dismissal of charge of violent or sexual offence involving child in respect of which notice of transfer has been given under section 53 of that Act);

(c) the court, in determining whether there is a case to answer; and

(d) the court or jury, in determining whether the accused is guilty of the offence charged,

may draw such inferences from the failure or refusal as appear proper.

(3) Subsections (1) and (2) do not apply unless the accused was told in ordinary language by the constable when making the request mentioned in subsection (1)(c) above what the effect of this section would be if he failed or refused to comply with the request.

(3A) Where the accused was at an authorised place of detention at the time of the failure or refusal, subsections (1) and (2) do not apply if he had not been allowed an opportunity to consult a solicitor prior to the request being made.

(4) This section applies in relation to officers of customs and excise as it applies in relation to constables.

(5) This section does not preclude the drawing of any inference from a failure or refusal of the accused to account for his presence at a place which could properly be drawn apart from this section.

KEYNOTE

Section 37 appears somewhat restrictive in that it is only concerned with the suspect's location at the time of arrest and applies only when he/she was found at that location at or about the time of the offence.

PACE Code C also applies to s. 37 in relation to the 'special warning' required to be given by the interviewing officer.

Unlike s. 36, here the officer that sees the person at or near the scene of the alleged offence must be the arresting officer.

As with ss. 34 and 36, in relation to s. 37 the accused cannot be convicted solely on an inference drawn from a failure or refusal (s. 38(3)) **(see para. 1.8.10)**.

When the provisions of the Criminal Justice Act 2003 are in force s. 37(2)(a) and (2)(b)(i) and (ii) will be repealed and replaced by sch. 3, para. 2 to the Crime and Disorder Act 1998.

1.8.9 Inferences from Silence at Trial

Section 35 of the Criminal Justice and Public Order Act 1994 provides that inferences can be drawn from an accused's failure to give evidence or refusal to answer any question, without good cause, where the person has been sworn. Section 35 states:

(1) At the trial of any person for an offence, subsections (2) and (3) below apply unless—

(a) the accused's guilt is not in issue; or

(b) it appears to the court that the physical or mental condition of the accused makes it undesirable for him to give evidence;

but subsection (2) below does not apply if, at the conclusion of the evidence for the prosecution, his legal representative informs the court that the accused will give evidence or, where he is unrepresented, the court ascertains from him that he will give evidence.

(2) Where this subsection applies, the court shall, at the conclusion of the evidence for the prosecution, satisfy itself (in the case of proceedings on indictment with a jury, in the presence of the jury) that the accused is aware that the stage has been reached at which evidence can be given for the defence and that he can, if he wishes, give evidence and that, if he chooses not to give evidence, or having been sworn, without good cause refuses to answer any question, it will be permissible for the court or jury to draw such inferences as appear proper from his failure to give evidence or his refusal, without good cause, to answer any question.

(3) Where this subsection applies, the court or jury, in determining whether the accused is guilty of the offence charged, may draw such inferences as appear proper from the failure of the accused to give evidence or his refusal, without good cause, to answer any question.

(4) This section does not render the accused compellable to give evidence on his own behalf, and he shall accordingly not be guilty of contempt of court by reason of a failure to do so.

(5) For the purposes of this section a person who, having been sworn, refuses to answer any question shall be taken to do so without good cause unless—

(a) he is entitled to refuse to answer the question by virtue of any enactment, whenever passed or made, or on the ground of privilege; or

(b) the court in the exercise of its general discretion excuses him from answering it.

(6) [repealed]

KEYNOTE

In *R* v *Friend* [1997] 1 WLR 1433 (in considering s. 35(1)(b) of the Act), the accused was aged 15 with a mental age of nine and an IQ of 63. It was held that the accused's mental condition did not make it 'undesirable' for him to give evidence and it was right that inferences be drawn under s. 35(3).

As with s. 34, in relation to s. 35 the accused cannot be convicted solely on an inference drawn from a failure or refusal (s. 38(3)) **(see para. 1.8.10)**.

It must be made clear to the accused that when the prosecution case has finished he/she may give evidence if he/she so wishes. The court must inform the accused that if he/she fails to give evidence or, being sworn, refuses to answer any question without good cause, then the jury may infer such inferences that appear proper from such a failure to give evidence or a refusal to answer any question (*Practice Direction (Criminal Proceedings: Consolidation)* [2002] 1 WLR 2870, para. 44, defendant's right to give or not to give evidence). In *R* v *Gough* [2002] 2 Cr App R 121, it was held that it is mandatory for the court to inform the accused of his/her right to give or not to give evidence even where the accused has absconded.

1.8.10 Inferences from Silence: No Conviction on Silence Alone

Section 38 of the Criminal Justice and Public Order Act 1994 applies to all of the four provisions relating to inferences from silence (ss. 34, 35, 36 and 37) and provides that an inference cannot be the sole basis for a finding of a case to answer, issue or dismissal of a notice to transfer, or for a finding of guilt. Nothing in s. 38 prejudices the court's general powers to exclude evidence.

In *Murray* v *United Kingdom* [1996] 22 EHRR 29 it was held that it would be incompatible with the rights of an accused to base a conviction 'solely or mainly' on their silence, or on their refusal to answer questions or give evidence in person. The Court of Appeal also held that in cases involving directions under s. 34, the burden of proof remained on the Crown despite the fact that the accused chose to make no comment (*R* v *Gowland-Wynn* [2001] EWCA Crim 2715).

1.9 Identification

1.9.1 Introduction

A critical issue in the investigation and prosecution of offences is the identification of the offender and this, like all other facts in issue, must be proved beyond a reasonable doubt. Many different methods of identification exist but the main feature which must be considered in relation to each is its *reliability*. Identification evidence is governed by Code D of the PACE Codes of Practice (**see appendix 4**). These Codes were amended on 31 January 2008 and have effect in relation to any identification procedure carried out after midnight on 31 January 2008.

Generally, the methods of identification covered by Code D can be divided into two:

- occasions where the identity of the suspect is known; and
- occasions where the identity of the suspect is not known.

Where the identity of the suspect is known this can be further divided into those cases where the suspect is available and those where he/she is not available.

Although a breach of Code D (or any of the other Codes of Practice) will not automatically result in the evidence being excluded (*R* v *Khan* [1997] Crim LR 584), the judge or magistrate(s) will consider the effects of any breach on the fairness of any subsequent proceedings. The Codes are intended to provide protection to suspects and, if it is felt that the breach of Code D has resulted in unfairness or other prejudicial effect on the defendant, the court may exclude the related evidence under s. 78 of the Police and Criminal Evidence Act 1984.

The Police Reform Act 2002 has introduced designated support staff who have some of the powers that police officers have.

1.9.2 Methods of Identification

1.9.2.1 Visual

The visual identification of suspects by witnesses is one of the most common forms of identification; it is also one of the most unreliable. Even under research conditions, the recall of eye witnesses is inconsistent; where the witness sees or experiences the spontaneous commission of a crime, that reliability is reduced even further.

It was for these reasons that the *Turnbull* guidelines were set out, together with the provisions of Code D. If there is no identification evidence, the *Turnbull* guidelines will not apply. It should be remembered that a witness who does not identify the suspect may still be able to provide other valuable evidence to the case, for instance a description of the person who committed the offence, or a description of what they were wearing. Again it is not uncommon for witnesses to qualify their identification of the suspect by indicating that they 'cannot be quite certain'. While a defendant cannot be convicted on such a qualified identification alone, it may be admissible to support the case where other evidence is also available (*R* v *George* [2003] Crim LR 282).

Problems of reliability in identification can arise even where the person accused is known to the witness. See, for example, *R* v *Conway* (1990) 91 Cr App R 143 (**see para. 1.9.2.4**).

A lot will depend on the individual circumstances of each case but it is essential that these issues are covered in any interview or other evidence gathering process.

'Dock identifications', where the witness's first identification of the accused involves pointing out the person in the dock, are often dramatised by film makers but, in practice, are generally disallowed as being unreliable and unfair.

The rules for identification differ between cases where the suspect *is known* and those where suspect is *not known*. Code D, para. 3.4 defines the terms as:

> ... a suspect being 'known' mean there is sufficient information known to the police to justify the arrest of a particular person for suspected involvement in the offence. A suspect being 'available' means they are immediately available or will be within a reasonably short time and willing to take an effective part in at least one of the following which it is practicable to arrange;
> - video identification;
> - identification parade; or
> - group identification.

Code D requires that a first description provided of a person suspected of a crime (regardless of the time it was given) must be recorded (para. 3.1) and that a copy of the record should, where practicable, be given to the defence before certain procedures such as identification parades are carried out. This record must be made and kept in a form which enables details of that description to be accurately produced from it, in a visible and legible form (Code D, para. 3.1), which can be given to the suspect or the suspect's solicitor. Such a record could be made electronically or be paper based. The Code also makes provision for the disclosure of materials previously released to the media in relation to an inquiry and for witnesses to be asked if they saw such material before they took part in any identification procedure.

1.9.2.2 Identification where there is a Known Suspect

Where the suspect is known, there are four possible methods of identification provided for in Code D (paras 3.4 to 3.24). These are:

- video identification;
- identification parades;
- group identification; and
- confrontation (this is only of limited use and value).

The emphasis is placed on video identification with moving images or, if necessary, still images. Code D, paras 3.5 to 3.10 define the four types of identification procedure.

The Code draws a distinction between situations where the known suspect is available and where they are unavailable. The Code suggests that video identification, identification parades and group identification are appropriate where the suspect is known and available and that confrontation may be an added appropriate identification procedure where the suspect is known and unavailable.

It is crucial that once the person becomes a known suspect, any witnesses, *including police officers*, who might be used at an identification parade, are kept apart from the suspect, as any contact could jeopardise a conviction. In *R* v *Lennon* (1999) 28 June, unreported, a suspect was arrested for public order offences after his description was circulated by the police officers that witnessed the offence. The suspect was placed in a van and the officers accidentally went in the van and identified the suspect. The court held that the person was a known suspect and the identification evidence should have been excluded. Paragraph 3.4 gives guidance as to when a suspect will become 'known' or 'available'. Code D, Note 3D gives guidance where a person deliberately makes him/herself unavailable.

The Code also makes provision for the disclosure of materials previously released to the media in relation to an inquiry and for witnesses to be asked if they saw such material before taking part in any identification procedure. When a witness has previously been shown photographs or computerised or artist's composite or similar likeness, the suspect and their solicitor must be informed of this fact before the identification procedure takes place. It is the responsibility of the officer in charge of the investigation to make the identification officer aware that this is the case (Code D, Annex E, para. 9).

The Codes recognise that the showing of films or photographs to the public through the national or local media, or to police officers for the purposes of recognition and tracing suspects, may be necessary. However, Code D, para. 3.28, provides that when such material is shown to potential witnesses, including police officers, to obtain identification evidence, it shall be shown on an individual basis to avoid any possibility of collusion, and, as far as possible, the showing shall follow the principles for video identification if the suspect is known, or identification by photographs if the suspect is not known (see Code D, paras 3.4 and 3.3.).

When a broadcast or publication is made, a copy of the relevant material released to the media for the purposes of recognising or tracing the suspect shall be kept. The suspect or their solicitor shall be allowed to view such material before any identification procedure is carried out provided that it is practicable and would not unreasonably delay the investigation. After they have taken part each witness involved in the procedure shall be asked whether they have seen any broadcast or published films or photographs relating to the offence or any description of the suspect and their replies shall be recorded. This paragraph does not affect any separate requirement under the Criminal Procedure and Investigations Act 1996 to retain material in connection with criminal investigations (Code D, para. 3.29).

Where it has been decided that an identification procedure is to be held (see Code D, para. 3.12), the identification officer and the officer in charge of the investigation must consult each other to determine which procedure is to be offered (Code D, para. 3.14). The suspect shall initially be offered a video identification unless:

- a video identification is not practicable; or
- an identification parade is both practicable and more suitable than a video identification; or
- the officer in charge of the investigation considers a group identification is more suitable than a video identification or an identification parade and the identification officer considers it practicable to arrange (Code D, para. 3.16).

A video identification would normally be more suitable if it could be arranged and completed sooner than an identification parade.

If a suspect refuses the identification procedure first offered, the suspect shall be asked to state their reason for refusing and may get advice from their solicitor and/or if present, their appropriate adult. The suspect, solicitor and/or appropriate adult shall be allowed to make representations about why another procedure should be used. A record should be made of the reasons for refusal and any representations made. After considering any reasons given, and representations made, the identification officer shall, if appropriate, arrange for the suspect to be offered an alternative which the officer considers suitable and practicable. If the officer decides it is not suitable and practicable to offer an alternative identification procedure, the reasons for that decision must be recorded (Code D, para. 3.15).

Where a suspect is identified by witnesses, other evidence should still be sought to strengthen the case (or to prove the person's innocence) as identification evidence is often challenged at court. Such supporting evidence may include admissions by the suspect that links him/her to the identification evidence; for example, that he/she owns the vehicle that was driven at the time of the offence (*R* v *Ward* [2001] Crim LR 316).

The photographing of a suspect is covered in Code D, paras 5.1 to 5.24. Such photographs might prove useful for an identification procedure process.

1.9.2.3 When Must an Identification Procedure be Held?

Identification procedures should be held for the benefit of the defence as well as the prosecution (*R* v *Wait* [1998] Crim LR 68). The Codes give guidance on when an identification parade shall be held. Code D, paras 3.12 and 3.13 state:

3.12 Whenever:

(i) a witness has identified a suspect or purported to have identified them prior to any identification procedure set out in paragraphs 3.5 to 3.10 having been held; or

(ii) there is a witness available, who expresses an ability to identify the suspect, or where there is a reasonable chance of the witness being able to do so, and they have not been given an opportunity to identify the suspect in any of the procedures set out in paragraphs 3.5 to 3.10,

and the suspect disputes being the person the witness claims to have seen, an identification procedure shall be held unless it is not practicable or it would serve no useful purpose in proving or disproving whether the suspect was involved in committing the offence. For example, when it is not disputed that the suspect is already well known to the witness who claims to have seen them commit the crime.

3.13 Such a procedure may also be held if the officer in charge of the investigation considers it would be useful.

KEYNOTE

Code D, para. 3.12(ii) provides that there is no need to go through any of the identification procedures where it is not practicable or it would serve no useful purpose in proving or disproving whether the suspect was involved in committing the offence. This view is supported by the Court of Appeal decision *R* v *Chen* (2001) *The Times*, 17 April. The defence in that case was one of duress but the appeal was based on the failure of the police to hold identification parades. The Court of Appeal stated that this was not a case about identification as none of the defendants denied their presence at the scene. What they denied was their criminal participation in the activities that took place. It followed, therefore, that Code D did not apply. Other examples would be where it is not in dispute that the suspect is already well known to the witness who claims to have seen the suspect commit the crime or where there is no reasonable possibility that a witness would be able to make an identification.

There have been a number of Court of Appeal cases concerning the requirement to hold identification parades. It is suggested that these should be applied to the revised Code regardless of which form of identification procedure is used. The leading case is *R* v *Forbes* [2001] 2 WLR 1, which was based on earlier versions of the Code of Practice. The House of Lords held that if the police are in possession of sufficient evidence to justify the arrest of a suspect, and that suspect's identification depends on eye-witness identification evidence, even in part, then if the identification is disputed, the Code requires that an identification parade should be held with the suspect's consent, unless one of the exceptions applies. The exceptions are set out in Code D, para. 3.12. This is particularly so where the suspect disputes identification.

The House of Lords went on to say that this mandatory obligation to hold an identification parade ('parade' at the time of judgment was right but this applies equally to any identification procedure) applies even if there has been a 'fully satisfactory', 'actual and complete' or 'unequivocal' identification of the suspect.

Despite the wording of Code D, it has been held that a suspect's right to have an identification [procedure] is not confined to cases where a dispute over identity has already arisen; that right also applies where such a dispute might reasonably be anticipated (*R* v *Rutherford and Palmer* (1994) 98 Cr App R 191). Similarly, a suspect's failure to request an identification [procedure] does not mean that the police may proceed without one (*R* v *Graham* [1994] Crim LR 212).

It is important to consider the distinction between identification of a suspect and the suspect's clothing or other features. In *D* v *DPP* (1998) *The Times*, 7 August, a witness had observed two youths for a continuous period of five to six minutes and then informed the police of what he had seen, describing the age of the youths and the clothes that they were wearing. The court held that there had not been an identification within the terms of the Codes of Practice because the witness had at no stage identified the defendant or the co-accused. He had described only their clothing and their approximate ages, and the police, acting on that information, had made the arrests. An identification parade could have served no useful purpose since the clothing would have been changed and those persons used for the parade would have been the same approximate age. This point was further supported in *R* v *Haynes* (2004) *The Times*, 27 February, where the Court of Appeal held that as a practical point the identification parade, whether or not the suspect was regarded as a known or unknown suspect, was of little value where the witness identified the suspect by clothing and not by recognition of the suspect's features. An identification parade would have provided little assistance.

The *key factor* to consider when deciding whether to hold an identification parade is whether *a failure to hold a parade could be a matter of genuine potential prejudice to the suspect*. If it is decided to hold an identification procedure, it should be held as soon as practicable (Code D, para. 3.11).

The question for the court will be whether it is fair to admit the identification evidence. When looking at this issue the court will consider how reliable that identification evidence is.

Any decision to proceed without an identification parade must be capable of justification later to the relevant court. The courts have taken different approaches to justification based on practical difficulties. In an early case, the submissions of the identification officer that it was impracticable to find enough people who sufficiently resembled the defendant were treated fairly dismissively by the trial judge (*R* v *Gaynor* [1988] Crim LR 242). In later cases, however, the courts have been more lenient, accepting that the timescales involved in arranging identification parades may render them 'impracticable' (see *R* v *Jamel* [1993] Crim LR 52 where the court refused an objection by the defence to a group identification). A group identification was used in *Jamel* because a parade using mixed-race volunteers would have taken too long to arrange. All reasonable steps must be taken to investigate the possibility of one identification option before moving on to an alternative, and an offer from a suspect's solicitor to find volunteers to stand on a parade is such a 'reasonable' step (*R* v *Britton and Richards* [1989] Crim LR 144).

1.9.2.4 Recognition Cases

Recognition cases, that is to say, those cases where the witness states that they know the person who committed the offence as opposed to only being able to give a description, need to be carefully considered. In *R* v *Ridley* (1999) *The Times*, 13 October, the Court of Appeal stated that there has never been a rule that an identification parade had to be held in all recognition cases and that it will be a question of fact in each case whether or not there is a need to do so. The view that an identification procedure is not required in these cases is supported by para. 3.12(ii).

The facts in *Ridley*, which it is suggested are not uncommon among patrolling officers, were that two police officers in a marked police vehicle noticed a car, which had been stolen earlier that day, drive past them. Both officers said that they recognised the defendant driving the car. The officers gave chase and gave evidence that the car was speeding and being driven dangerously. They decided that it was unsafe to continue pursuit, but arrested the suspect six days later. One of the officers claimed to have recognised the suspect because she had interviewed him for some 20 minutes five months previously and had seen him about town. She gave evidence that she had a view of the suspect in the car for about nine seconds. The other officer said that he recognised the suspect from a photograph but could not say when he had seen that photograph. He said that he had seen the suspect in the car for about two seconds. The Court found that the female police officer's identification had been complete and there was no requirement for her to have further identified the suspect.

Ridley can be contrasted with *R* v *Conway* (1990) 91 Cr App R 143, where the witnesses' evidence was not as strong. There the witnesses stated that they recognised the accused simply because they knew him. The defence argument was that the witnesses did not actually know the accused and so could not have recognised him at the time of the offence. His conviction was quashed because of the prejudice caused by the absence of a parade. In *R* v *Davies* [2004] EWHC 2242 a witness identified a masked attacker from his voice and eyes. The court in this case held that this identification evidence coupled with other circumstantial evidence was sufficient for a conviction.

A case can still amount to one of recognition even where the witness does not know the name of the suspect but later obtained those details from a third party, for example where the witness and the suspect went to the same school and the witness became aware of the suspect's full names from other pupils at the school (*R* v *C*; *R* v *B* (2003) 4 March 2003).

In *H* v *DPP* (2003) 24 January, the court accepted that it was reasonable for the police not to undertake an identification procedure. In the circumstances of the case the police had every reason to believe that the claimant and the victim were well known to each other. The claimant had accepted that the victim knew her. There was no question of doubt as to the victim's ability to recognise the claimant and as such this was a case of pure recognition where it was futile to hold an identification parade.

Care must be taken in cases where it is believed that the case is one of recognition not requiring an identification procedure. In *R* v *Harris* [2002] EWCA Crim 174 the witness stated that he recognised the suspect as being someone he went to school with. The suspect gave a prepared statement in which he disputed the suggestion that he was well known to the witness. Here the court held that an identification procedure should have been undertaken, as the circumstances of the case did not fall within the general exception of the Code, that it would serve no useful purpose in proving or disproving whether the suspect had been involved in committing the offence.

When a suspect is filmed committing an offence, it is admissible to give evidence of identification by way of recognition from a witness not present at the scene but who knew the defendant and who, having seen the film, identified the suspect as being the defendant (*Attorney-General's Reference (No. 2 of 2002)* [2003] Crim LR 192).

1.9.2.5 Identification of Disqualified Drivers

Another common identification problem is that of disqualified drivers and being able to satisfy the court that the person charged with disqualified driving is the same person who was disqualified by the court. This is because s. 73 of the Police and Criminal Evidence Act 1984 requires proof that the person named in a certificate of conviction as having been convicted is the person whose conviction is to be proved. There has been some guidance from the courts as to how this can be achieved. In *R* v *Derwentside Justices, ex parte Heaviside* [1996] RTR 384, the court stated that this could be done by:

- fingerprints under s. 39 of the Criminal Justice Act 1948;
- the evidence of a person who was present in court when the disqualification order was made;
- admission of the defendant (preferably in interview) (*DPP* v *Mooney* (1997) RTR 434);
- requiring the suspect's solicitor who was present when he/she was disqualified on the earlier occasion to give evidence (such a summons is a last resort when there was no other means of identifying whether an individual had been disqualified from driving) (*R (On the Application of Howe) and Law Society (Interested Party)* v *South Durham Magistrates' Court and CPS (Interested Party)* [2004] EWHC 362).

The methods outlined in *Ex parte Heaviside* are not exhaustive, but just suggested methods (*DPP* v *Mansfield* [1997] RTR 96).

1.9.2.6 Control of the Identification Process

The arrangements for and conduct of identification procedures is the responsibility of an officer not below the rank of inspector who is not involved with the investigation ('the identification officer'). However, except where the Codes expressly state otherwise, the identification officer may allow another officer or police staff to make arrangements for, and to conduct, any of the identification procedures in paras 3.11, 3.19 (serving the notice of the identification process on the detained person) and 2.21. When the identification officer delegates these procedures, he/she must be able to supervise effectively and either intervene or be available to be contacted for advice.

It is important to note that no officer or any other person involved with the investigation of the case against the suspect, may take any part in these procedures or act as the identification officer. However, the identification officer may consult the officer in charge of the investigation in order to determine which procedure to use.

If the identification officer considers that it is not practicable to hold a video identification or identification parade, the reasons shall be recorded and explained to the suspect (para. 3.26). Should the suspect fail or refuse to co-operate in a video identification, identification parade or group identification, a record should be made including any reasons (paras 3.15 and 3.27).

Just because a suspect has an unusual physical feature it does not mean that a video identification procedure is impracticable. Code D, Annex A, paras 2A to 2C give guidance as to how to manage such situations which includes concealment of the unusual physical feature or replicating the feature on other people. Before a video identification, an identification parade or group identification is arranged, para. 3.17 outlines a number of matters that must be explained to the suspect and must be recorded in a written notice and handed to the suspect. Paragraph 3.17 must be completed by the identification officer or if it is proposed to hold an identification procedure at a later date and an inspector is not available to act as the identification officer, it can be performed by the custody officer before the suspect leaves the station. When dealing with a witness who is or appears to be mentally disordered, otherwise mentally vulnerable or a juvenile, the procedure should take place in the presence of a pre-trial support person. However, the support person must not be allowed to prompt any identification of a suspect by a witness (Code D, para. 2.15A). (See also guidance at Code D, Note 2A as to how the appropriate adult should be dealt with.) Code D, Note 2AB explains the role of *a pre-trial support person.*

1.9.2.7 Which Identification Procedure should be Used?

Initially the choice should be that of a video identification or an identification parade (para. 3.14). However, a group identification could be used where the officer in charge of the investigation considers that in the particular circumstances it is more suitable and practicable to arrange (para. 3.16). The identification officer and the officer in charge of the investigation shall consult each other to determine which of these two options is the most suitable and practicable in the particular case. Paragraphs 3.14 to 3.16 give guidance as to factors to consider.

While the choice of procedure is for the police, the suspect, solicitor and/or appropriate adult shall be allowed to make representations as to why another procedure should be used (para. 3.15). If a suspect refuses the identification procedure which is first offered, he/she must be asked to state his/her reasons for refusing and may obtain advice from his/her solicitor and appropriate adult if present (para. 3.15).

Even where a person refuses to take part in an identification procedure, it is still possible to use covert video identification, covert group identification or confrontation (paras 3.21 to 3.24). If the identification officer and the officer in charge of the investigation have reasonable grounds to suspect that the person will take steps to avoid being seen by a witness in any identification procedure, the identification officer has a discretion to arrange for images of him/her to be obtained for use in a video identification procedure. If images of the suspect are obtained in these circumstances, the suspect may, for the purposes of a video identification procedure, co-operate in providing suitable images which shall be used in place of those previously taken (para. 3.20).

Section 64A of the Police and Criminal Evidence Act 1984 provides powers to take photographs and images of detained suspects and allows the photographs and images so taken to be used to assist with arranging the identification process. After being so used or disclosed, they may be retained but may not be used or disclosed for any purpose other than that related to the prevention or detection of crime, the investigation of offences or the conduct of prosecutions by, or on behalf of, police or other law enforcement and prosecuting authorities inside and outside the United Kingdom or the enforcement of a sentence. After being so used or disclosed, they may be retained but can be used or disclosed only for the same purposes (Code D, para. 3.30).

Code D, paras 3.31 to 3.33 provide further guidance on the destruction and retention of photographs taken for the purpose of or in connection with identification procedures.

Where a known suspect is not available (or has ceased to be available for any reason), the identification officer has a discretion to make arrangements for a video identification to be conducted. This must be done in accordance with the provisions applicable to covert video identification (para. 3.21 and Note 3D).

If necessary, the identification officer may follow the video identification procedures but using still images. Any suitable moving or still images may be used and these may be obtained covertly if necessary. Any covert activity should be strictly limited to that necessary to test the ability of the witness to identify the suspect. Alternatively, the identification officer may make arrangements for a group identification. These provisions may be applied to juveniles where the consent of their parent or guardian is either refused or reasonable efforts to obtain that consent have failed (Code D, paras 3.21 and 3.22).

It is only if none of the other options are practicable that the identification officer may arrange for the suspect to be confronted by the witness. A confrontation does not require the suspect's consent. In *R* v *McCullock* (1999) 6 May, unreported, the Court of Appeal made it clear that confrontations between suspects and witnesses should only be carried out if no other procedure is practicable (see below).

1.9.2.8 Conduct of Identification Parades

Identification evidence can be crucial to the success of a prosecution. There are clear guidelines that must be followed. Where such guidelines are not followed it is likely that the defence will strongly attempt to have the identification evidence excluded. In *R* v *Jones* (1999) *The Times*, 21 April, identification evidence was excluded as the officers told the suspect that if he did not comply with the procedure, force would be used against him.

Annexes A to F of Code D set out in detail the procedures and requirements which must be followed in conducting identification procedures. There is also guidance concerning documentation and retention of material. Identification procedures must be conducted as soon as practicable (Code D, para. 3.11).

Although the courts are aware of the many practical difficulties involved in organising and running identification procedures (see e.g. *R* v *Jamel* [1993] Crim LR 52), any flaws in the procedure will be considered in the light of their potential impact on the defendant's trial. Serious or deliberate breaches (such as the showing of photographs to witnesses before the parade), will invariably lead to any evidence so gained being excluded (*R* v *Finley* [1993] Crim LR 50). The key question for the court will be whether the breach of the Codes is likely to have made the identification less reliable. Officers must therefore fully understand and follow the Codes of Practice and relevant Annex for the procedure being used.

Breaches which appear to impact on the safeguards imposed by Annexes A to F to separate the functions of investigation and identification (e.g. where the investigating officer becomes involved with the running of the parade in a way which allows him/her to talk to the witnesses (*R* v *Gall* (1989) 90 Cr App R 64)) will also be treated seriously by the court.

The case of *R* v *Marrin* (2002) *The Times*, 5 March, provides some guidance as to methods that could be used to get a suitable pool of participants for an ID parade. The court held that there was nothing inherently unfair or objectionable in some colouring or dye being used on the facial stubble of some volunteers to make them look more like the suspect. However, care needed to be taken with such measures because the procedure would be undermined if it was obvious to the witness that make-up had been used. Another point raised was that it may sometimes be appropriate for those on parade to wear hats, but if possible the wearing of hats should be avoided if hats had not been worn during the offence because this would make it more difficult for a witness to make an identification. However, there could be circumstances where the wearing of hats could help to achieve a resemblance and might be desirable to minimise differences. Finally an identification of a suspect was not invalidated by the witness's request for the removal of a hat. There was nothing unfair in that taking place and there was no breach of any Code either. Under para. 18 of Annex B, a witness could ask for any parade member to adopt any specified posture or that he/she should move.

It is important to follow the guidance in the Codes regardless of what agreement is obtained from the suspect or his/her solicitor. In *R* v *Hutton* [1999] Crim LR 74, at the suggestion of the suspect's solicitor, all the participants in the identification parade wore back to front baseball caps and had the lower part of their faces obscured by material. That identification was the only evidence against the defendant on that count. The court excluded the evidence and did not accept the fact that the decision had been agreed by the defence.

It will be essential that any photographs, photofits or other such material is stored securely in a manner that restricts access so as to be able to demonstrate to the court that the material cannot have been viewed by any of the witnesses and that copies have not been made that have not been accounted for.

1.9.2.9 Identification where there is No Suspect

Where the police have no suspect, Code D provides for witnesses (including police officers) to be shown photographs (Annex E) or taken to a place where the suspect might be (paras 3.2 and 3.3).

If photographs are to be shown, the procedure set out at Annex E must be followed. Once a witness has made a positive identification from the photographs, computerised or artist's composite, no further witnesses should be shown photographs (para. 3.3) (unless the person identified is eliminated from the inquiry (Annex E, para. 6)).

Using photographs from police criminal records can affect the judgment of a jury and nothing should be done to draw their attention to the fact that the defendant's photograph was already held by the police (*R* v *Lamb* (1979) 71 Cr App R 198). This rule does not apply if the jury are already aware of the defendant's previous convictions (*R* v *Allen* [1996] Crim LR 426).

The showing of a CCTV film used for security purposes is addressed at para. 3.28 of Code D.

If a film which has been shown to a witness is later lost or unavailable, the witness may give evidence of what he/she saw on that film but the court will have to consider all the relevant circumstances in deciding whether to admit that evidence *and* what weight to attach to it. (For a discussion of those circumstances, see *Taylor* v *Chief Constable of Cheshire* [1986] 1 WLR 1479.) This is particularly so as the Codes require that the film is retained (Annex A, para. 15 and para. 3.29).

Videos or photographs can be shown to the public at large through the national or local media, or to police officers for the purposes of recognition and tracing suspects. However, when such material is shown to potential witnesses (including police officers) it should be shown on an individual basis so as to avoid any possibility of collusion, and the showing shall, as far as possible, follow the principles for video identification if the suspect is known (paras 3.28, 3.29 and Annex A) or identification by photographs if the suspect is not known (see paras 3.4, 3.3 and Annex E).

1.9.2.10 Identification at the Scene

There are occasions where the identification is made immediately after the alleged offence. This usually happens when the witness is taken round a particular area to try and find the suspect (in which case Code D, para. 3.2 must be complied with). The need for 'scene identifications' was recognised by Lord Lane CJ in *R* v *Oscar* [1991] Crim LR 778 and by the Court of Appeal in *R* v *Rogers* [1993] Crim LR 386.

In *Oscar*, the court held that there had been no requirement for an identity parade in that case and Lord Lane pointed out that, in any case, a later parade where the suspect was dressed differently would be of no value at all. In *Rogers*, the suspect was found near a crime scene and was confronted by a witness who positively identified him. The court held that the identification in that case was necessary for an arrest to be made, although the court felt a later parade could have been carried out.

In such cases, where the meeting of the suspect and the witness takes place soon after the event, wherever possible the officers should comply with para. 3.2. Matters to consider before doing a 'scene identification' include:

- where practicable, a record shall be made of any description of the suspect given by the witness as in para. 3.1(a);
- care must be taken not to direct the witness's attention to any individual unless, taking into account all the circumstances, this cannot be avoided;
- if there is more than one witness, try to keep them separate;

- once there is sufficient information to justify the arrest of a suspect, a formal identification procedure must be adopted;
- the officer or police staff accompanying the witness must make a record in his/her pocket book of the action taken as soon as practicable and in as much detail as possible.

The admissibility of identification evidence obtained when carrying out a 'scene identification' may be compromised if before a person is identified, the witness's attention is specifically drawn to that person.

Careful consideration must be given before a decision to identify a suspect in this manner is used. If there is sufficient evidence to arrest the suspect without using a witnesses identification, then it is likely the courts will find that an identification method outlined at **para. 1.9.2.2** should have been used and the evidence may be excluded. Confrontations between witnesses and suspects on the street can be useful at times, but where this takes place it defeats the formal identification process and needs to be carefully considered. The reason for this is that, even if the suspect is picked out on the identification parade by that witness, the defence will be able to argue that the identification was from the confrontation after the incident and not at the time of the commission of the offence. If there is more than one witness available and a decision is taken to use a witness to try to identify a suspect at the scene, other witnesses should be moved away, so as to reduce the possibility of a chance encounter with the suspect. Where possible, these witnesses should be kept apart until the identification parade and ideally should not discuss the matter between themselves.

An example where a street identification was appropriate is *R* v *El-Hannachi* [1998] 2 Cr App R 226. Here an affray took place in the car park of a public house. A witness had seen the man earlier in the pub and she had had an unobstructed view in good light before the attack. The witness described the attacker's clothing to the police and then identified a group of men who had been stopped by other officers a short distance away. The court accepted that this was the correct approach. The defendants were not known suspects when they were stopped by the police prior to the witness's identification. The court also accepted that it had not been practicable for a record to have been made of the witness's description, as required by Code D, para. 3.1, prior to the identification. Where a record has been made prior to the identification this may support the identification itself. It should be remembered, however, that the description does not now have to be recorded in writing and could be recorded by some quicker method (e.g. tape recording) (para. 3.1).

A not uncommon situation is where police officers chase a suspect who is arrested by other officers on the description circulated by the chasing officer, who then attends the scene to confirm the person's identity. The case of *R* v *Nunes* [2001] EWCA Crim 2283, covers this point and points out the dangers of this practice. The facts of the case were that a police officer saw a man inside a house and circulated a description on his radio. A person fitting the description was seen and arrested. The first officer arrived on the scene and identified the arrested person as the man he had earlier seen in the house. The Court of Appeal held that on the particular facts of this case the identification amounted to a breach of the Code. By the time of the identification, the man had been arrested for suspected involvement in the offence and, on his arrest, the identity of the suspect was known to the police. Therefore, by the time the witnessing officer arrived on the scene, the case involved 'disputed identification evidence' because the suspect had said that he had not done anything while the police had told him he matched the description of a suspected burglar. That said, the court did go on to hold that the judge had the discretion to allow the identification evidence to be adduced notwithstanding the breach of the Codes but a full and careful direction regarding the breaches, together with a warning about the shortcomings in the procedure, would have been necessary.

1.9.2.11 Photographs, Image and Sound Reproduction Generally

The use of photographic and computer-generated images (such as E-Fit) to identify suspects has increased considerably over the last few years. Although the courts will exercise considerable caution when admitting such evidence (see *R* v *Blenkinsop* [1995] 1 Cr App R 7), these methods of identification are particularly useful. Expert evidence may be admitted to interpret images on film (see e.g. *R* v *Stockwell* (1993) 97 Cr App R 260) and police officers who are very familiar with a particular film clip (e.g. of crowd violence at a football match) may be allowed to assist the court in interpreting and explaining events shown within it (see *R* v *Clare* (1995) 159 JP 412).

Logically E-Fit and other witness-generated images would be treated as 'visual statements', in that they represent the witness's recollection of what he/she saw. However, the Court of Appeal has decided that they are not to be so treated (*R* v *Cook* (1987) 1 All ER 1049) and therefore the restrictions imposed by the rule against hearsay will not apply (see also *R* v *Constantinou* (1990) 91 Cr App R 74 where this ruling was followed in relation to a photofit image).

1.9.2.12 Voice Identification

Voice identification from what a suspect on an identification parade says, is dealt with under para. 18 of Annex B to Code D. The Codes do not preclude the police making use of aural identification procedures such as a 'voice identification parade', where they judge that appropriate.

Generally, a witness may give evidence identifying the defendant's voice (*R* v *Robb* (1991) 93 Cr App R 161), while expert testimony may be admitted in relation to tape recordings of a voice which is alleged to belong to the defendant. In the latter case, the jury should be allowed to hear the recording(s) so that they can draw their own conclusions (*R* v *Bentum* (1989) 153 JP 538). In *R* v *Flyn*: *R* v *St John* [2008] EWCA Crim 970 the Court of Appeal held that where the voice identification is from a recording, a prerequisite for making a speaker identification was that there should be a sample of an adequate size from the disputed recording that could confidently be attributed to a single speaker. The court also recognised that expert evidence showed that lay listeners with considerable familiarity with a voice and listening to a clear recording could still make mistakes. It is therefore suggested that other supporting evidence will be needed for a conviction to succeed.

Home Office Circular 57/2003, *Advice on the Use of Voice Identification Parades*, provides guidance on the use of voice identification parades which is based on procedures devised by DS McFarlane of the Metropolitan Police in the case of *R* v *Khan & Bains*.

1.9.3 Fingerprints

Identification by fingerprints applies when a person's fingerprints are taken to compare with fingerprints found at the scene of a crime, check and prove convictions, or help to ascertain a person's identitiy (Code D, para. 1.3).

A fingerprint is defined by Code D, para. 4.1 and s. 65(1) of the Police and Criminal Evidence Act 1984 as any record, produced by any method, of the skin pattern and other physical characteristics or features of a person's fingers or palms. Fingerprints can be taken electronically provided that they are taken using such devices as the Secretary of State has approved for the purposes of electronic fingerprinting (s. 61(8A) of the 1984 Act). Where a person's fingerprints are to be taken without their consent, under the powers set out in Code D, paras 4.3 and 4.4, reasonable force may be used if necessary.

Expert evidence on fingerprints is admissible from suitably qualified individuals who have at least five years' experience in that field.

Whether fingerprint evidence is admissible as evidence tending to prove guilt, depends on:

- the experience and expertise of the witness,
- the number of similar ridge characteristics (if there are fewer than eight ridge characteristics matching the fingerprints of the accused with those found by the police, it is unlikely that a judge would exercise his/her discretion to admit such evidence),
- whether there are dissimilar characteristics,
- the size of print relied on, and
- the quality and clarity of print relied on.

The jury should be warned that expert evidence is not conclusive in itself and that guilt has to be proved in the light of all evidence (*R* v *Buckley* (1999) 163 JP 403).

1.9.3.1 Before Conviction

The power to take fingerprints has been amended by the Criminal Justice Act 2003 which has amended s. 61 of the Police and Criminal Evidence Act 1984. This amendment to s. 61 of the 1984 Act is intended to prevent persons who come into police custody and who may be wanted on a warrant or for questioning on other matters, from avoiding detection by giving the police a false name and address. Using Livescan technology, which enables the police to take fingerprints electronically and which is linked to the national fingerprint database (NAFIS), the police will be able to confirm a person's identity while still in police detention if the person's fingerprints have been taken previously. It will also assist in enabling vulnerable or violent people to be identified more quickly and dealt with more effectively. The taking of finger and palm prints is governed by s. 61 of the Police and Criminal Evidence Act 1984.

Section 61 states:

(1) Except as provided by this section no person's fingerprints may be taken without the appropriate consent.

(2) Consent to the taking of a person's fingerprints must be in writing if it is given at a time when he is at a police station.

(3) The fingerprints of a person detained at a police station may be taken without the appropriate consent if—
 (a) he is detained in consequence of his arrest for a recordable offence; and
 (b) he has not had his fingerprints taken in the course of the investigation of the offence by the police.

(3A) Where a person mentioned in paragraph (a) of subsection (3) or (4) has already had his fingerprints taken in the course of the investigation of the offence by the police, that fact shall be disregarded for the purposes of that subsection if—
 (a) the fingerprints taken on the previous occasion do not constitute a complete set of his fingerprints; or
 (b) some or all of the fingerprints taken on the previous occasion are not of sufficient quality to allow satisfactory analysis, comparison or matching (whether in the case in question or generally).

(4) The fingerprints of a person detained at a police station may be taken without the appropriate consent if—
 (a) he has been charged with a recordable offence or informed that he will be reported for such an offence; and

(b) he has not had his fingerprints taken in the course of the investigation of the offence by the police.

(4A) The fingerprints of a person who has answered to bail at a court or police station may be taken without the appropriate consent at the court or station if—

(a) the court, or

(b) an officer of at least the rank of inspector,

authorises them to be taken.

KEYNOTE

Where fingerprints have been taken and they do not constitute a complete set of that person's fingerprints; or some or all of the fingerprints taken on the previous occasion are not of sufficient quality to allow satisfactory analysis, comparison or matching further fingerprints can be taken (Code D, para. 4.3(a), (b)).

An officer of at least the rank of inspector (or the court) may authorise the taking of a person's fingerprints who has answered to bail at a court or police station if the person who has answered to bail has answered to it for a person whose fingerprints were taken on a previous occasion and there are reasonable grounds for believing that he/she is not the same person or the person claims to be a different person from a person whose fingerprints were taken on a previous occasion (s. 61(4A) and (4B)). This authority may be given orally or in writing but, if he/she gives it orally, he/she shall confirm it in writing as soon as is practicable (s. 61(5) of the 1984 Act).

Where a person has been arrested on suspicion of being involved in a recordable offence or has been charged with such an offence or has been informed that he/she will be reported for such an offence, fingerprints taken from the person may be checked against:

(a) other fingerprints or samples to which the person seeking to check has access and which are held by or on behalf of any one or more relevant law enforcement authorities or which are held in connection with or as a result of an investigation of an offence. This speculative search of the fingerprint crime scene database may reveal if the person has been involved in other crimes.

(b) information derived from other samples if the information is contained in records to which the person seeking to check has access and which are held as mentioned in paragraph (a) above (s. 63A of the 1984 Act).

Before any fingerprints are taken the person must be informed of the reason their fingerprints are to be taken, if Code D, para. 4.3(c) applies the grounds on which the relevant authority has been given, that their fingerprints may be retained and may be the subject of a speculative search (unless destruction of the fingerprints is required in accordance with Annex F, Part (a)), and that if their fingerprints are required to be destroyed, they may witness their destruction as provided for in Annex F, Part (a) (Code D, para. 4.7).

A record must be made when a person has been informed of the possibility that their fingerprints may be the subject of a speculative search (Code D, para. 4.9). A record must also be made, as soon as possible, of the reason for taking a person's fingerprints without consent and, if force is used, the circumstances and those present (Code D, para. 4.8). Where the person is detained at a police station these records must be made in their custody record.

Where the suspect does consent to their fingerprints being the subject of such a speculative search, the consent must be in writing. Note 6E provides an example of a basic form of words. Once the suspect has given consent for the sample to be retained and used, he/she cannot withdraw this consent. **See para. 1.9.10** and Code D, Annex F regarding the retention and use of fingerprints and samples taken with consent for elimination purposes. Note 4B explains what a speculative search means. Code D, paras 4.10 to 4.15 deal with the taking of fingerprints in connection with immigration inquiries and Annex F, para. 5 deals with their retention and destruction.

1.9.3.2 After Conviction, Reprimand or Caution

Fingerprints may be taken with the appropriate consent, where a person refuses to give that consent, fingerprints can only be taken if s. 61(6) of the 1984 Act applies, i.e. from a person who has been:

- convicted of a recordable offence;
- given a caution in respect of a recordable offence which, at the time of the caution, the person admitted; or
- warned or reprimanded under s. 65 of the Crime and Disorder Act 1998 for a recordable offence.

For the purposes of taking fingerprints, the meaning of appropriate consent is in relation to:

- a person 17 or over, his/her consent;
- a person 14 to 17, the consent of that person and his/her parent or guardian;
- a person under 14, the consent of his/her parent or guardian.

Section 27 of the 1984 Act provides that a person may be required to attend a police station to have his/her fingerprints taken if he/she:

- has been convicted of a recordable offence; given a caution in respect of a recordable offence which, at the time of the caution, the person admitted; or warned or reprimanded under s. 65 of the Crime and Disorder Act 1998, for a recordable offence; and
- the fingerprints taken on the previous occasion do not constitute a complete set of his/her fingerprints; or some or all of the fingerprints taken on the previous occasion are not of sufficient quality to allow satisfactory analysis, comparison or matching; or
- where a person has been convicted of a recordable offence and has already had his/her fingerprints taken but the fingerprints taken on the previous occasion did not constitute a complete set of his/her fingerprints or some or all of the fingerprints taken on the previous occasion are not of sufficient quality to allow satisfactory analysis, comparison or matching (s. 27(1A)).

The requirement must be made within one month of the date the person is convicted, cautioned, warned or reprimanded and the person must be given a period of at least seven days within which to attend. This seven-day period need not fall during the month allowed for making the requirement. If a person fails to comply with the requirement, he/she can be arrested without warrant (Code D, para. 4.4).

Before any fingerprints are taken with or without consent as above, the person must be informed of the reason his/her fingerprints are to be taken. Before any fingerprints are taken at the police station, the person must also be informed that his/her fingerprints may be retained and may be the subject of a speculative search against other fingerprints. Code D, Note 4B explains what a speculative search means (Code D, para. 4.7). A record must be made when a person has been informed of the possibility that his/her fingerprints may be the subject of a speculative search (Code D, para. 4.9). A record must also be made, as soon as possible, of the reason for taking a person's fingerprints without consent and, if force is used, a record must be made of the circumstances and those present (Code D, para. 4.8).

1.9.3.3 Retention of Fingerprints

In terms of the disposal of the case, cautioning a person for an offence is the equivalent of a conviction at court. Therefore if the person has been in police detention and has not had his/her fingerprints taken prior to the caution, there is no power to take that person's fingerprints under the 1984 Act (**see para. 1.9.3.1**). This is also the case where a person is released and subsequently summonsed.

It should be noted that s. 64 of the 1984 Act, as amended by the Criminal Justice and Police Act 2001, has removed the requirement to destroy fingerprints of suspects who are not convicted and custody officers should no longer inform detained persons of the right to destruction (see Code D, Annex F). The Act removes this obligation in relation to fingerprints and samples where the person is cleared of the offence for which they were taken or a decision is made not to prosecute (**see para. 1.9.10**). The obligation to destroy is replaced by a rule to the effect that any fingerprints or samples retained can only be used for the purposes related to the prevention and detection of crime, the investigation of any offence or the conduct of any prosecution. This means that if a match is established at a subsequent crime scene with an individual who has been cleared of an earlier offence, the police are able to use this information in the investigation of the crime. The system of retaining DNA samples and fingerprint evidence after a suspect had been cleared of the offence that gave rise to the collection of those items of evidence is compatible with both article 8 and article 14 of the European Convention on Human Rights (*R* v *Chief Constable of South Yorkshire, ex parte Marper* (2002) *The Times*, 4 April).

Fingerprints and samples taken from a person suspected of committing a recordable offence but not arrested, charged or informed they will be reported for it, may be subject to a speculative search only if the person consents in writing. Code D, Note 4B gives an example of the wording to be used for the consent. Once taken, the sample or fingerprints will be retained and used for purposes related to the prevention and detection of a crime, the investigation of an offence or the conduct of a prosecution either nationally or internationally. Once the person gives consent for the sample to be retained, it cannot be withdrawn.

Where a person, who is not a suspect, provides a sample or fingerprints voluntarily, e.g. for the purposes of elimination, there is no obligation for him/her to allow the samples or fingerprints to be retained or used other than for the purpose for which they were taken. Where consent is not given the fingerprints or samples must be destroyed and the information derived from them cannot be used in evidence against the person concerned or for the purposes of investigation of any offence. When seeking consent from a person for elimination samples and fingerprints the consents should be obtained separately and whether the person is consenting to their use and retention needs to be fully explained. Code D, Annex F, Note F1 should be followed when consent is being requested.

1.9.3.4 Criminal Record and Conviction Certificates

Under s. 118 of the Police Act 1997, in certain circumstances the Secretary of State issues certificates concerning an individual's previous convictions. In some cases the Secretary of State will not do this until he/she has been able to verify the person's identity, which can be done through the taking of their fingerprints. Where this is the case, the Secretary of State may require the police officer in charge of the specified police station, or any other police station he/she reasonably determines, to take the applicant's fingerprints at the specified station at such reasonable time as the officer may direct and notify to the applicant.

If fingerprints are taken in these circumstances they must be destroyed as soon as is practicable after the identity of the applicant is established to the satisfaction of the Secretary of State. The destruction can be witnessed by the person giving the fingerprints if he/she requests and/or the person can ask for a certificate stating the fingerprints have been destroyed. The certificate must be issued within three months of the request.

In the case of an individual under the age of 18 years the consent of the applicant's parent or guardian to the taking of the applicant's fingerprints is also required.

1.9.3.5 Footwear Impressions

The Serious Organised Crime and Police Act 2005 inserted a new s. 61A into the Police and Criminal Evidence Act 1984. The section provides power for a police officer to take a person's footwear impressions in connection with the investigation of an offence without consent from any person over the age of ten years who is detained at a police station (reasonable force may be used if necessary) and any other persons with their consent (if at a police station this must be in writing). Where the person does not consent he/she must be in police detention in consequence of being arrested for a recordable offence or must have been charged with a recordable offence, or informed that he/she will be reported for such an offence.

Such an impression cannot be taken from a detained person without his/her consent unless he/she has not had an impression of his/her footwear taken in the course of the investigation of the offence or the previously taken impression is not complete or is not of sufficient quality to allow satisfactory analysis, comparison or matching (Code D, paras 4.16 to 4.18). Code C, para. 4.19 sets out what the person must be told before the impression is taken and Code D, paras 4.20 and 4.21 set out what documentation is required.

1.9.4 Other Body Prints

Whilst the more established and convincing body marks are fingerprints, it is possible for other body prints to be used as evidence to identify a suspect. In *R* v *Kempster* [2008] EWCA Crim 975 the police recovered an ear print from the fixed window pane to the side of the window that had been forced in order to gain entry to the property. In this case the conviction was not successful, however it was recognised that an ear print comparison was capable of providing information that could identify a person who had left an ear print on a surface. This would only be achieved with certainty where the minutiae of the ear structure could be identified and matched.

1.9.5 Body Samples and Impressions

The taking of samples and impressions is governed by ss. 62 to 63A of the Police and Criminal Evidence Act 1984, together with Code D (paras 6.1 to 6.12) (**see appendix 4**).

Inferences from a defendant's refusal to consent to the taking of certain samples may be drawn by a court.

1.9.5.1 DNA Profiles

DNA stands for deoxyribo-nucleic acid. It is the chemical which is found in virtually every cell in our bodies and which carries genetic information from one generation to the next and determines our physical characteristics such as hair and eye colour. A number of techniques have been used to identify DNA:

- **SGM**—Second Generation Multiplex is a DNA profiling system which looks at seven areas (six areas plus a sex indicator area) to give a DNA profile. The average discrimination potential for an SGM profile is one in 50 million.
- **SGM Plus®**—The current technique, used since June 1999, for profiling DNA samples on the NDNAD. It looks at 11 areas (10 areas plus a sex indicator area) to give a DNA profile. The average discrimination potential for an SGM Plus is one in a billion.
- **DNA LCN**—DNA Low Copy Number is an extension of the SGM Plus profiling technique. It is more sensitive and enables scientists to produce DNA profiles from samples containing very few cells even if they are too small to be visible to the naked eye.

The purpose behind the taking of many samples is to enable the process of DNA profiling. Very basically, this involves an analysis of the sample taken from the suspect (the first sample), an analysis of samples taken from the crime scene or victim (the second sample) and then a comparison of the two. Both the process and the conclusions which might be drawn from the results are set out by Lord Taylor CJ in *R* v *Deen* (1994) *The Times*, 10 January.

The matching process involves creating 'bands' from each sample and then comparing the number of those bands which the two samples share. The more 'matches' that exist between the first and second samples, the less probability there is of that happening by pure chance. A 'good match' between the two samples does not of itself prove that the second sample came from the defendant. In using such samples to prove identification the prosecution will give evidence of:

- the *probability* of such a match happening by chance; and
- the *likelihood* that the person responsible was in fact the defendant.

While DNA evidence is often portrayed in the media as conclusive evidence of guilt, the question for the courts remains 'how reliable is this piece of evidence in proving or disproving the person's involvement in the offence?' The jury's task was set out by Phillips LJ in *R* v *Doheny* [1997] 1 Cr App R 369. In that case, involving a semen sample, his Lordship said:

> If you accept the scientific evidence called by the Crown, that indicates there are probably only four or five white males in the United Kingdom from whom that semen stain could have come. The defendant is one of them. The decision you have to reach, on all the evidence, is whether you are sure that it was the defendant who left that stain or whether it is possible that it is one of that other small group of men who share the same DNA characteristics.

(**See also Blackstone's Criminal Practice 2008, para. F18.31.**)

In most cases there will be other evidence against the defendant, evidence which clearly increases the likelihood of his/her having committed the offence.

It will be for the prosecution to produce other facts to the court which reduces the 'chance' of the DNA sample belonging to someone other than the defendant. This may require further inquiries linking the suspect to the area or circumstances of the crime or may come from questions put to the suspect during interview. In *R* v *Lashley* (2000) 25 February, unreported, the sole evidence against the defendant for a robbery was DNA evidence from a half-smoked cigarette found behind the counter of the post office. The DNA matched a sample obtained from the suspect and would have matched the profile of seven to ten other males in the United Kingdom. The court held that the significance of DNA evidence depended critically upon what else was known about the suspect. Had there been evidence that the suspect was in the area, or normally lived there, or had connections there, at the material time, then the jury could have found that the case was compelling. This, the court said, would be because it may have been almost incredible that two out of seven men in the United Kingdom were in the vicinity at the relevant time. The courts are willing to allow the jury to consider partial or incomplete DNA profiles in some circumstances. In *R* v *Bates* [2006] EWCA Crim 1395, DNA evidence at the scene produced a partial profile that was interpreted as providing a 1 in 610,000 probability that Bates was the killer. The Court of Appeal held that there was no reason why partial profile DNA evidence should not be admissible provided that the jury are made aware of its inherent limitations and are given a sufficient explanation to enable them to evaluate it.

It is also important to ensure that there is no cross-contamination of DNA evidence between crime scenes, victims and suspects as was seen in the infamous American case of

OJ Simpson's murder trial. It will be important to ensure that any allegations that officers may have contaminated evidence through handling/being present at several crime scenes can be successfully challenged. It is suggested that the best evidence here will be through records of crime scene logs and, where suspects have are being held in custody, records of who visited the custody suite. It will also be important that suspects and victims are kept apart. The integrity and continuity of DNA samples will be important evidence and likely to be challenged by the defence if not managed properly.

The Criminal Justice Act 2003 contains provisions that extend the circumstances in which a non-intimate sample may be taken without consent from a person in police detention. These provisions were implemented on 5 April 2005.

As a result, s. 23 of Home Office Circular 16/1995, *National DNA Database* which provides guidance regarding charging where DNA identification is involved, has been amended by Home Office Circular 58/2004, *Charges on Basis of Speculative Search Match on the National DNA Database*, and it states:

> Speculative searches may be carried out of the National DNA Database and a suspect may now be charged on the basis of a match between a profile from DNA from the scene of the crime and a profile on the National DNA Database from an individual, *so long as there is further supporting evidence.*

It should also be noted that the databases can also now be used for the purpose of identifying a deceased person or a person from whom a body part came (Serious Organised Crime and Police Act 2005, s. 117(7) amending s. 64 of the 1984 Act).

However, there is a significant chance that matches involving partial DNA profiles (including SGM profiles) will not match if the profiles are upgraded to SGM Plus. Therefore, where any match is on the basis of a partial or SGM profile:

(a) strong consideration should be given to upgrading the partial or SGM profile to SGM Plus to ensure there is still a match before the matter comes to trial;
(b) if there is a decision to charge on the basis of such a match, the supporting evidence needs to be all the stronger. The amount of supporting evidence required will depend on the value of the DNA evidence in the context of the case. A scientist should be consulted where the value of the DNA evidence requires clarification.

1.9.6 Intimate and Non-Intimate Samples

The analysis of intimate and non-intimate samples may provide essential evidence in showing or refuting a person's involvement in an offence. However, the courts have made it clear that DNA evidence alone will not be sufficient for a conviction and that there needs to be supporting evidence to link the suspect to the crime. Such evidence may include confessions, or may show that the suspect was near the crime scene at the time of the offence or that the suspect lived in the locality or had connections in the area.

The police powers to obtain intimate and non-intimate samples are provided by the Police and Criminal Evidence Act 1984 and were extended by amendments made by the Criminal Justice and Public Order Act 1994. Further guidance as to the exercise of these powers is contained within Code D of the PACE Codes of Practice.

1.9.6.1 Intimate and Non-intimate Samples Defined

Code D, para. 6 1 provides the definition of intimate and non-intimate samples:

> (a) an 'intimate sample' means, a dental impression or sample of blood, semen or any other tissue fluid, urine, or pubic hair, or a swab taken from any part of a person's genitals or from a person's body orifice other than the mouth;

(b) a 'non-intimate sample' means:

(i) a sample of hair, other than pubic hair, which includes hair plucked with the root, see Note 6A;

(ii) a sample taken from a nail or from under a nail;

(iii) a swab taken from any part of a person's body other than a part from which a swab taken would be an intimate sample;

(iv) saliva;

(v) a skin impression which means any record, other than a fingerprint, which is a record, in any form and produced by any method, of the skin pattern and other physical characteristics or features of the whole, or any part of, a person's foot or of any other part of their body.

Code D, Note 6A sets out advice for taking non-intimate hair samples and states:

> When hair samples are taken for the purpose of DNA analysis (rather than for other purposes such as making a visual match), the suspect should be permitted a reasonable choice as to what part of the body the hairs are taken from. When hairs are plucked, they should be plucked individually, unless the suspect prefers otherwise and no more should be plucked than the person taking them reasonably considers necessary for a sufficient sample.

1.9.7 Intimate Samples

Section 62 of the Police and Criminal Evidence Act 1984 sets out police powers to take intimate samples. Code D of the PACE Codes of Practice provides additional guidance as to the exercise of the powers. The provisions of s. 62 together with Code D describe the circumstances and manner in which intimate samples can be taken. These can be understood by considering a number of key issues.

1.9.7.1 Consent

Before an intimate sample can be taken from a person in police detention, the consent of an officer of at least the rank of inspector is necessary, *together with the written consent of the person*. Without the consent of *both*, such a sample cannot be taken (Code D, para. 6.2).

Taking a sample without the relevant authority may amount to inhuman or degrading treatment under article 3 of the European Convention on Human Rights. It may also amount to a criminal offence of assault and give rise to liability at civil law.

Where a person (who is a suspect) is not in police detention, an intimate sample may be taken where that person has already provided two (or more) non-intimate samples in the course of the investigation of the offence, which have proved insufficient for *the same means of analysis*. Should this pre-condition apply then the consent of both a police officer of at least the rank of inspector and the person concerned is necessary, as in the case of a person in police detention (Code D, para. 6.2).

Note 6C of Code D recognises that a sample may be taken from a person not in police detention, for the purposes of elimination, providing his/her consent is given.

In all cases where an intimate sample is to be taken from a young person aged over 14 but under 17, the consent of his/her parents or guardian is also necessary. If the person is a child under 14, the consent of his/her parents or guardian is necessary only.

1.9.7.2 Grounds for Authorisation

Regardless of whether the person is in police detention or not, a inspector may only give his/her authorisation if he/she has reasonable grounds:

- for suspecting the involvement of the person from whom the sample is to be taken in a recordable offence; *and*

- for believing that the sample will tend to confirm or disprove the person's involvement in the offence.

1.9.7.3 Information to be Given to the Suspect

Where an authorisation has been given and it is proposed to take a sample, an officer shall inform the suspect that the authorisation has been given *and* of the grounds for its being given. If the person has been arrested on suspicion of being involved in a recordable offence, charged or reported for a recordable offence then, in addition to the above, an officer must also inform the person, before the sample is taken, that the sample may be subject to a 'speculative search' (Code D, para. 6.8, Note 6E).

(A speculative search is a check made against other samples and information derived from other samples contained in records or held by or on behalf of the police or held in connection with or as a result of an investigation of an offence.)

Paragraph 6.3 of Code D also requires that, before the sample is given, the suspect must be warned that if he/she refuses without good cause, that refusal may harm his/her case if it comes to trial. Where the suspect is in police detention, or is at the police station voluntarily, the officer shall also explain the entitlement to legal advice.

1.9.7.4 Recording the Authorisation

An inspector's authorisation may be given orally but, if so given, it must be confirmed in writing as soon as practicable. The consent from the suspect must be given in writing (s. 62(3) and (4) of the 1984 Act).

1.9.7.5 Other Information to be Recorded

Where an intimate sample is taken, certain information must be recorded. This information includes:

- the reasons for taking a sample or impression and if applicable, of its destruction must be made as soon as practicable;
- that the person gave written consent (and where that record can be found);
- if they are a suspect that they have been warned that if they refuse without good cause, their refusal may harm their case if it comes to trial (see para. 6.3);
- if they are in police detention or voluntarily at the police station that they have been reminded of their right to legal advice;
- that the person has been informed as in para. 6.8(c) that samples may be subject to a speculative search.

This information shall be recorded as soon as practicable after the sample has been taken. Where a suspect is in police detention the information shall be recorded in the custody record.

1.9.7.6 Refusal of a Suspect to Give Consent

Where a suspect refuses, without good cause, to provide an intimate sample, then, in proceedings against that person for an offence, the court may draw such inferences as appear proper. The court may use such an inference for the purposes of determining:

- guilt;
- whether there is a case to answer;
- whether to commit for trial;

- whether an application to dismiss charges should be granted (where a notice of transfer from a magistrates' court to a Crown Court for an indictable only offence and any other linked offences has been given earlier) (s. 62(10)).

1.9.7.7 Taking an Intimate Sample

Dental impressions may only be taken by a registered dentist. Intimate samples, other than urine, may only be taken by a registered medical practitioner or a registered nurse or a registered paramedic (Code D, para. 6.4).

Paragraph 6.9 of Code D sets out the provisions to be followed where clothing needs to removed in circumstances likely to cause embarrassment. These are:

- no person of the opposite sex may be present (other than a registered medical practitioner or registered health care professional);
- only people whose presence is necessary for the taking of the sample should in fact be present;
- in the case of a juvenile or mentally disordered or mentally vulnerable person, an appropriate adult of the opposite sex may be present *if specifically requested by the person and the person is readily available*;
- in the case of a juvenile, clothing may only be removed in the absence of an appropriate adult if the person signifies (in the presence of the appropriate adult) that he/she prefers his/her absence and the appropriate adult agrees.
- Clearly, as consent is needed to take a sample, the use of force would be inappropriate.

1.9.8 Non-Intimate Samples

The taking by police of non-intimate samples is governed by s. 63 of the Police and Criminal Evidence Act 1984. Additional guidance in the exercise of the powers is provided by Code D. The key requirements of these provisions are:

1.9.8.1 Consent

A person may consent to the taking of a non-intimate sample. If he/she does so, the consent must be given in writing.

Code D, para. 6.6 sets out those occasions when non-intimate samples can be taken without consent; these circumstances vary as to whether the person is in police detention or not.

In police detention

A non-intimate sample may be taken from a person without the appropriate consent if the person is in police detention in consequence of his arrest for a recordable offence and he/she either:

- has not had a non-intimate sample of the same type and from the same part of the body taken in the course of the investigation of the offence by police; or
- he/she has had such a sample taken but it proved insufficient (s. 63(2A) to (2C)).

If the person is being held in custody by the police on the authority of a court an officer of at least the rank of inspector may authorise the taking of a non-intimate sample without the appropriate consent if he/she has reasonable grounds for believing the person's involvement in a recordable offence and believes that the sample will tend to confirm or disprove his/her involvement. Such an authority must not be given for a non-intimate sample consisting of a skin impression if a skin impression of the same part of the body has already been taken from that person in the course of the investigation of the offence and the impression previously taken is not one that has proved insufficient (s. 63(3), (4) and (5A)).

Whether or not in police detention

A non-intimate sample may be taken from a person (whether or not he/she is in police detention or is being held in custody by the police on the authority of a court) without the appropriate consent if he/she has been:

- charged with a recordable offence or informed that he/she will be reported for such an offence; and either he/she has not had a non-intimate sample taken from him/her in the course of the investigation of the offence by the police or he/she has had a non-intimate sample taken from him/her but either it was not suitable for the same means of analysis or, though so suitable, the sample proved insufficient (Code D, para. 6.6(b));
- detained following acquittal on grounds of insanity or finding of unfitness to plead;
- convicted of a recordable offence (s. 63(3A) to (3C)).

'Recordable offences' in relation to the PACE Codes relate to those offences for which convictions, cautions, reprimands or warnings may be recorded in national police records (see Code D, Note 4A). In order to close a gap in the legislation, the Criminal Evidence (Amendment) Act 1997 was passed, allowing the taking of non-intimate samples without consent in the case of people serving sentences for certain sexual, violent or other specified offences. The effect of ss. 1 and 2 of the 1997 Act is to allow the taking of such samples from people serving a sentence of imprisonment or being detained under a hospital order (under the Mental Health Act 1983) if they were convicted of a recordable offence listed at sch. 1 before 10 April 1995. The provisions also extend to people who were not convicted by reason of their insanity or their unfitness to plead but who were detained at the relevant time under the Mental Health Act 1983.

1.9.8.2 Information to be Given to the Suspect

Where an authorisation has been given by an officer of at least the rank of inspector and it is proposed to take a sample, an officer shall inform the suspect that the authorisation has been given *and* of the grounds for it being given (including the nature of the offence the person is suspected of committing).

Where a non-intimate sample is taken as a result of the suspect being charged, informed he/she is to be reported, following conviction for a recordable offence or while in police detention following his/her arrest for a recordable offence, he/she must be told of the reason why the sample is to be taken and the reason shall be recorded as soon as practicable after the sample is taken.

The person must be informed—before the sample is taken—that the sample may be subject to a 'speculative search' (Code D, para. 6.8) (**see para. 1.9.7**).

1.9.8.3 Recording the Authorisation

Where an authorisation is required from an officer of at least the rank of inspector this may be given orally, but if so given, must be confirmed in writing as soon as practicable. The consent from the suspect must be given in writing (Code D, para. 6.10).

1.9.8.4 Other Information to be Recorded

Where a non-intimate sample is taken as a result of an officer of at least the rank of inspector's authority, the following information should be recorded:

- the *authorisation* by virtue of which the sample was taken;
- the *grounds* for the authorisation;
- the fact that the person has been informed that the sample may be subject to a *speculative search*.

This information must be recorded *as soon as practicable* after the sample has been taken.

In other cases where a sample is taken without the person's consent, the reason shall be recorded as soon as practicable after the sample is taken.

Where a suspect is in police detention, the information shall be recorded in the custody record (s. 63(9) of the 1984 Act).

1.9.8.5 Use of Force

Paragraph 6.7 of Code D provides that reasonable force may be used if necessary to obtain non-intimate samples in the circumstances described. Where force is used, a record should be made of the circumstances and those present at the time.

1.9.8.6 Taking a Non-intimate Sample

Where clothing needs to be removed in order to take a non-intimate sample, para. 6.9 of Code D should be applied to prevent embarrassment.

Where a non-intimate sample consisting of a skin impression is taken electronically from a person, it must be taken only in such manner, and using such devices, as the Secretary of State has approved for the purpose of the electronic taking of such an impression (s. 63(9A)). No such devices are currently approved.

1.9.9 Power to Require Persons to Attend a Police Station to Provide Samples

In addition to the powers outlined, s. 63A of the Police and Criminal Evidence Act 1984 also provides for a constable to require a person to attend a police station for samples to be taken. The circumstances under which this requirement can be made are summarised as follows.

1.9.9.1 When Can the Requirement be Made?

A constable may make the requirement:

- where a person has been charged with a recordable offence or informed that he/she will be reported, or
- where the person has been convicted of a recordable offence,

and, in either case, the person has not had a sample taken in the course of the investigation into the offence, or he/she has had a sample taken but it proved either unsuitable for the same means of analysis or the sample was insufficient.

1.9.9.2 The Period during which a Constable may Make the Requirement

The requirement to attend a police station must be made:

- within one month of the date of charge or of conviction or within one month of the date of reporting; or
- within one month of the appropriate officer being informed that the sample is not suitable or has proved insufficient for analysis.

In making the requirement the officer:

- shall give the person at least seven days within which the person must attend; and
- may direct the person to attend at a specified time of day or between specified times of day.

1.9.9.3 Failure to Comply with the Requirement

Should a person fail to comply with the requirement, a constable may arrest the person without a warrant.

An appropriate officer is:

- the officer investigating the offence in the case of a person charged or told he/she will be reported;
- the officer in charge of the police station from which the investigation was conducted in the case of a person convicted.

For the corresponding power to take finger and palm prints, **see para. 1.9.3**.

1.9.10 Destruction of Samples

Code D, Annex F deals with the destruction and the speculative searches of fingerprints and samples and speculative searches of footwear impressions. It is important that the Annex is followed particularly in relation to obtaining consent and explaining to volunteers what they are consenting to. Annex F, Note F1 provides suggested wordings that can be used when obtaining a person's consent to provide fingerprints or footwear impressions or DNA samples for elimination purposes. It is important to use the correct wording depending on what the person has volunteered to, for example whether it is just to allow the fingerprint or sample to be used only for the purposes of a specific investigation; or for that investigation *and* retained by the police for future use. Such future use is limited to purposes related to the prevention or detection of crime, the investigation of an offence or the conduct of a prosecution in, as well as outside, the United Kingdom and may also be subject to a speculative search. This includes checking fingerprints and samples against other fingerprints or footwear impressions and DNA records held by, or on behalf of, the police and other law enforcement authorities in, as well as outside, the United Kingdom.

When fingerprints or footwear impressions or DNA samples are taken from a person in connection with an investigation and the person is not suspected of having committed the offence, the fingerprints or footwear impressions and/or sample must be destroyed as soon as they have fulfilled the purpose for which they were taken unless:

- they were taken for the purposes of an investigation of an offence for which a person has been convicted; and
- fingerprints or footwear impressions or samples were also taken from the convicted person for the purposes of that investigation.

The reason why fingerprints or footwear impressions and samples are retained is to allow for all fingerprints or footwear impressions and samples in a case to be available for any subsequent miscarriage of justice investigation. They may not be used in the investigation of any offence or in evidence against the person who is, or would be, entitled to the destruction of the fingerprints or footwear impressions and samples unless the person gives their written consent for their fingerprints or footwear impressions or sample to be retained and used after they have fulfilled the purpose for which they were taken.

Annex F, para. 3 details what must be done when a person's fingerprints or footwear impressions or sample are to be destroyed; this includes all copies of the fingerprints or footwear impressions.

Annex F, para. 5 deals with the retention and destruction of fingerprints or footwear impressions taken in connection with Immigration Service inquiries.

1.9.11 Terrorism Offences

There are additional powers and procedures for those suspects arrested in connection with terrorism which are contained in the Terrorism Act 2000.

With the exception of fingerprints, non-intimate samples or intimate samples, a constable may take any steps which are reasonably necessary for:

- photographing the detained person;
- measuring him/her, or identifying him/her (sch. 8, para. 2 to the 2000 Act).

1.9.11.1 Fingerprints and Non-intimate Samples

Fingerprints and non-intimate samples may be taken from a person detained under s. 41 of or sch. 7 to the Terrorism Act 2000 only if they are taken by a constable either:

- with the consent of the detained person given in writing; or
- where he/she is detained at a police station and does not give constant, a police officer of at least the rank of superintendent authorises the fingerprints or sample to be taken; or
- where the person has been convicted of a recordable offence and does not give consent, where a non-intimate sample is to be taken, he/she was convicted of the offence on or after 10 April 1995 (sch. 8, para. 10(1) to (4) to the 2000 Act).

1.9.11.2 Intimate Samples

An intimate sample may be taken from a detained person only if:

- he/she is detained at a police station;
- the appropriate consent is given in writing;
- a police officer of at least the rank of superintendent authorises the sample to be taken (sch. 8, para. 10(5) to the 2000 Act).

The sample must be taken by a constable but an intimate sample, other than a sample of urine or a dental impression, may be taken only by a registered medical practitioner acting on the authority of a constable. An intimate sample which is a dental impression may be taken only by a registered dentist acting on the authority of a constable.

The grounds for which an authorisation may be given under the Terrorism Act 2000 are:

- the officer reasonably suspects that the person has been involved in an offence under any of the provisions mentioned in s. 40(1)(a) of the Terrorism Act 2000 and the officer reasonably believes that the fingerprints or sample will tend to confirm or disprove his/her involvement; or
- the officer is satisfied that the taking of the fingerprints or sample from the person is necessary in order to assist in determining whether he/she is or has been concerned in the commission, preparation or instigation of acts of terrorism (s. 40(1)(b) of the Terrorism Act 2000); or
- the officer is satisfied that the taking of fingerprints of the detained person will facilitate the ascertainment of that person's identity (or showing that he/she is not a particular

person): and that person has refused to identify him/herself or the officer has reasonable grounds for suspecting that that person is not who he/she claims to be.

Section 40(1)(a) of the Terrorism Act 2000 refers to offences of:

- membership to a proscribed organisation;
- arranging, managing or assisting in arranging or managing a meeting to support a proscribed organisation or to further the activities of a proscribed organisation;
- addressing a meeting for the purpose of encouraging support for a proscribed organisation or to further its activities;
- fund-raising for the purposes of terrorism;
- using and possessing money or other property for the purposes of terrorism or making arrangements for its use;
- money laundering;
- providing instruction or training in the making or use of weapons;
- directing terrorist organisation;
- possession of articles for terrorist purposes;
- collection or possession of information of a kind likely to be useful to a person committing or preparing an act of terrorism;
- inciting terrorism overseas;
- funding arrangements.

Before fingerprints or a sample are taken from a person he/she must be informed that the authorisation has been given, the grounds upon which it has been given and, where relevant, of the nature of the offence in which it is suspected that he/she has been involved.

Where appropriate written consent to the taking of an intimate sample from a person is refused without good cause, in any proceedings against that person for an offence, the court, in determining whether to commit him/her for trial or whether there is a case to answer, may draw such inferences from the refusal as appear proper, and the court or jury, in determining whether that person is guilty of the offence charged, may draw such inferences from the refusal as appear proper.

It should be noted that s. 63A, as amended by the Criminal Justice and Police Act 2001 and the Serious Organised Crime and Police Act 2005, widens the extent to which fingerprints, footwear impressions and DNA profiles can be cross-searched against those held by another UK or Island force. This has been extended to other police forces (for example, foreign police forces, the Ministry of Defence and the Armed Forces police forces) on the same basis that already exists between UK and Island forces. This also applies to fingerprints and samples obtained under the Terrorism Act 2000. Section 118 of the Serious Organised Crime and Police Act 2005 makes a number of consequential amendments to ss. 63A and 64 of the Police and Criminal Evidence Act 1984 to allow footwear impressions to be retained and searched against the National Footwear Reference Collection and speculatively searched against the Mark Intelligence Index.

Where a sample proves to be insufficient there are provisions for obtaining further samples; this must be authorised by an officer of the rank of superintendent or above.

1.10 Bail

1.10.1 Introduction

The Bail Act 1976 is the primary source of legislation in relation to bail in criminal proceedings granted by the police and courts. Other legislation also impacts upon bail, in particular the Police and Criminal Evidence Act 1984 and the Criminal Justice and Public Order Act 1994.

The meaning of 'bail in criminal proceedings' is contained in s. 1 of the Bail Act 1976 which states:

> (1) In this Act 'bail in criminal proceedings' means—
> (a) bail grantable in or in connection with proceedings for an offence to a person who is accused or convicted of the offence, or
> (b) bail grantable in connection with an offence to a person who is under arrest for the offence or for whose arrest for the offence a warrant (endorsed for bail) is being issued, or
> (c) bail grantable in connection with extradition proceedings in respect of an offence.

KEYNOTE

This section provides that bail can be granted immaterial of whether the offence was committed in 'England or Wales or elsewhere', and immaterial as to which country's law the offence relates (s. 1(5)).

1.10.2 Police Bail

Bail can either be granted by a custody officer at a police station or by a constable elsewhere than at a police station (known as 'street bail').

1.10.2.1 Street Bail

The Police and Criminal Evidence Act 1984, s. 30A provides for persons arrested elsewhere than at a police station to be released on bail without being required to attend a police station.

The Police and Justice Act 2006 has amended s. 30A of the 1984 Act to provide that bail provisions already available in relation to people at the charging stage of the process are now available to officers granting bail elsewhere than at a police station.

1.10.2.2 Release on Bail

Section 30A(1) A constable may release on bail a person who is arrested or taken into custody in the circumstances mentioned in s. 30(1).

Section 30A(2) A person may be released on bail under subs. (1) at any time before he arrives at a police station.

Section 30A(3) A person released on bail under subs. (1) must be required to attend a police station.

Section 30A(3A) Where a constable releases a person on bail under subs. (1)—

(a) no recognisance for the person's surrender to custody shall be taken from the person,

(b) no security for the person's surrender to custody shall be taken from the person or from anyone else on the person's behalf,

(c) the person shall not be required to provide a surety or sureties for his surrender to custody, and

(d) no requirement to reside in a bail hostel may be imposed as a condition of bail.

Section 30A(3B) Subject to s. 30A(3A), where a constable releases a person on bail under s. 30A(1) the constable may impose, as conditions of the bail, such requirements as appear to the constable to be necessary—

(a) to secure that the person surrenders to custody,
(b) to secure that the person does not commit an offence while on bail,
(c) to secure that the person does not interfere with witnesses or otherwise obstruct the course of justice, whether in relation to himself or any other person, or
(d) for the person's own protection or, if the person is under the age of 17, for the person's own welfare or in the person's own interests.

Section 30A(4) Where a person is released on bail under s. 30A(1), a requirement may be imposed on the person as a condition of bail only under the preceding provisions of this section.

Section 30A(5) The police station which the person is required to attend may be any police station.

KEYNOTE

Section 30A(3B) enables the officer granting bail to consider attaching conditions relevant and proportionate to the suspect and the offence. The conditions that may be considered are the same as those available to a custody officer as contained in s. 3A(5) of the 1976 Act (**see para. 1.10.7.2**), except for those specified in s. 30A(3A) above.

Guidance on street bail is contained in Home Office Circular 61/2003, *Bail Elsewhere than at a Police Station.* Although there is no limit on the time for which 'street' bail may be granted, the Circular suggests a normal maximum time of six weeks.

1.10.2.3 Notice in Writing

Section 30B(1) Where a constable grants bail to a person under s. 30A, he must give that person a notice in writing before he is released.

Section 30B(2) The notice must state:
(a) the offence for which he was arrested, and
(b) the grounds on which he was arrested.

Section 30B(3) The notice must inform him that he is required to attend a police station.

Section 30B(4) It may also specify the police station which he is required to attend and the time when he is required to attend.

Section 30B(4A) If the person is granted bail subject to conditions under s. 30A(3B), the notice also—
(a) must specify the requirements imposed by those conditions,
(b) must explain the opportunities under ss. 30CA(1) and 30CB(1) for variation of those conditions, and
(c) if it does not specify the police station at which the person is required to attend, must specify a police station at which the person may make a request under s. 30CA(1)(b).

Section 30B(5) If the notice does not include the information mentioned in s. 30B(4), the person must subsequently be given a further notice in writing which contains that information.

Section 30B(6) The person may be required to attend a different police station from that specified in the notice under s. 30B(1) or (5) or to attend at a different time.

Section 30B(7) He must be given notice in writing of any such change as is mentioned in s. 30B(6) but more than one such notice may be given to him.

KEYNOTE

This section requires that the person bailed be given a written notice identifying the offence and grounds for arrest, informing him/her that he/she is required to attend a police station. It may also specify the police station which he/she is required to attend and the time when he/she is required to attend or a further notice containing this information must be sent. Section 30B(4A), inserted by the Police and Justice Act 2006, requires the notice to include how the bailed person may apply for variation to any bail conditions. It also states that the notice must (a) specify the requirements imposed by those conditions and (b) if it does not specify the police station at which the person is required to attend, must specify a police station at which the person may make a request under s. 30CA(1)(b).

1.10.2.4 Release, Attendance and Re-arrest

Section 30C(1) A person who has been required to attend a police station is not required to do so if he is given notice in writing that his attendance is no longer required.

Section 30C(2) If a person is required to attend a police station which is not a designated police station he must be:

(a) released, or

(b) taken to a designated police station,

not more than six hours after his arrival.

Section 30C(3) Nothing in the Bail Act 1976 applies in relation to bail under s. 30A.

Section 30C(4) Nothing in s. 30A or 30B or in this section prevents the re-arrest without warrant of a person released on bail under s. 30A if new evidence justifying a further arrest has come to light since his release.

1.10.2.5 Variation of Bail Conditions: Police

Section 30CA(1) Where a person released on bail under s. 30A(1) is on bail subject to conditions—

(a) a relevant officer at the police station at which the person is required to attend, or

(b) where no notice under s. 30B specifying that police station has been given to the person, a relevant officer at the police station specified under s. 30B(4A)(c),

may, at the request of the person but subject to subs. (2), vary the conditions.

Section 30CA(2) On any subsequent request made in respect of the same grant of bail, s. 30CA(1) confers power to vary the conditions of the bail only if the request is based on information that, in the case of the previous request or each previous request, was not available to the relevant officer considering that previous request when he/she was considering it.

Section 30CA(3) Where conditions of bail granted to a person under s. 30A(1) are varied under s. 30CA(1)—

(a) paragraphs (a) to (d) of s. 30A(3A) apply,

(b) requirements imposed by the conditions as so varied must be requirements that appear to the relevant officer varying the conditions to be necessary for any of the purposes mentioned in paragraphs (a) to (d) of s. 30A(3B), and

(c) the relevant officer who varies the conditions must give the person notice in writing of the variation.

Section 30CA(4) Power under s. 30CA(1) to vary conditions is, subject to s. 30CA(3)(a) and (b), power—

(a) to vary or rescind any of the conditions, and

(b) to impose further conditions.

KEYNOTE

The 'relevant officer' (s. 30CA(3)(c)) means a custody officer in relation to a designated police station, or a constable or person designated as a staff custody officer in any other police station. A constable involved in the investigation should not deal with the request unless no other constable or officer is available (s. 30CA(5)).

1.10.2.6 Variation of Bail Conditions: Court

Section 30CB(1) Where a person released on bail under s. 30A(1) is on bail subject to conditions, a magistrates' court may, on an application by or on behalf of the person, vary the conditions if—

(a) the conditions have been varied under s. 30CA(1) since being imposed under s. 30A(3B),

(b) a request for variation under s. 30CA(1) of the conditions has been made and refused, or

(c) a request for variation under s. 30CA(1) of the conditions has been made and the period of 48 hours beginning with the day when the request was made has expired without the request having been withdrawn or the conditions having been varied in response to the request.

KEYNOTE

Where the court vary the conditions they must be seen as necessary for any of the purposes mentioned in s. 30A(3B)(a) to (d), and bail continues subject to the varied conditions (s. 30CB(3)(b) and (c)).

1.10.2.7 Power of Arrest for Non-attendance and Breach of Bail Conditions

Section 30D(1) A constable may arrest without warrant a person who:

(a) has been released on bail under s. 30A subject to a requirement to attend a specified police station, but

(c) fails to attend the police station at the specified time.

Section 30D(2)	A person arrested under s. 30D(1) must be taken to a police station (which may be the specified police station or any other police station) as soon as practicable after the arrest.
Section 30D(2A)	A person who has been released on bail under s. 30A may be arrested without a warrant by a constable if the constable has reasonable grounds for suspecting that the person has broken any of the conditions of bail.
Section 30D(2B)	A person arrested under s. 30D(2A) must be taken to a police station (which may be the specified police station mentioned in s. 30D(1) or any other police station) as soon as practicable after the arrest.
Section 30D(3)	In subs. (1), 'specified' means specified in a notice under s. 30D(1) or (5) of s. 30B or, if notice of change has been given under s. 30D(7) of that section, in that notice.

KEYNOTE

Sections 30D(1) and 30D(2) relate to a person's failure to answer their bail at the specified time and place. Sections 30D(2A) and 30D(2B) were inserted by the Police and Justice Act 2006 to provide a power of arrest where a constable has reasonable grounds to suspect that a person has broken any of the conditions of bail.

1.10.3 Bail Without Charge

The Police and Criminal Evidence Act 1984 provides that where one of the following conditions applies then the custody officer must release a detained person either unconditionally or on bail:

- there is insufficient evidence to charge and the officer is not willing to authorise detention for questioning, etc. (s. 37(2)).
- there is sufficient evidence to charge for the purpose of enabling the Director of Public Prosecutions to make a decision under s. 37B (s. 37(7)(a));
- there is sufficient evidence to charge but not for the purpose outlined in s. 37(7)(a) above (this would usually be where further inquiries are to be made) (s. 37(7)(b));
- the officer conducting the review concludes the detention without charge can no longer be justified (s. 40(8));
- at the end of 24 hours' detention without charge unless the detained person is suspected of an indictable offence and continued detention up to 36 hours is authorised by a superintendent (s. 41(7)).

Section 37B above relates to the decision by the CPS as to whether the person will be charged, cautioned or informed in writing that they are not to be prosecuted. Section 37(7)(a) allows the custody officer to either release the person without charge and on bail, or keep them in police detention pending the prosecutor's decision as to whether or not to bring a charge. It is a matter for the custody officer to determine on an individual basis whether the person should be detained or granted bail whilst awaiting the outcome of the statutory charging process. Where a person is released under this section their bail conditions may be varied by the custody officer by notice in writing (s. 37D(1) and (2)). (**See para. 1.6.9** for a full discussion on charging and bail.)

In relation to s. 41(7) above, where continued detention is authorised for up to 36 hours, the detained person must be released with or without bail at or before the expiry of this time. Alternatively, for indictable offences an application can be made to a magistrates' court for a warrant of further detention (s. 42(10) of the 1984 Act).

There is no time limit for which bail may be granted under the 1984 Act and it has been held that courts would only intervene in exceptional circumstances (*R (On the Application of C)* v *Chief Constable of A* [2006] EWHC 2352).

1.10.4 Bail After Charge

Where a person is charged at the police station (otherwise than on a warrant backed for bail), the custody officer must make a decision:

- to keep the person in custody until he/she can be brought before a magistrates' court, or to release the person; and
- to release the person either unconditionally or on bail (s. 38(1) of the 1984 Act).

This is a review of the person's detention and therefore the person and his/her legal representative should be given an opportunity to make representations to the custody officer. The review should be conducted with regard to PACE Code of Practice, Code C, paras 15.1 to 15.16. Where the detained person is a juvenile, an opportunity to make representations should also be given to the 'appropriate adult'.

Where the decision is made to release a person who has been charged, it would be usual for the person to be released on bail being required to attend at the magistrates' court on a specified day and time.

With the exception of the circumstances set out below in s. 25 of the Criminal Justice and Public Order Act 1994, a person charged with an offence will be given bail unless certain conditions (contained in s. 38 of the 1984 Act) exist allowing the custody officer to refuse bail.

1.10.5 Bail Restrictions

The decision to deny any unconvicted person bail is a significant one, both personally and constitutionally. Every person has a general right not to be subject to unnecessarily onerous bail conditions, a right which has existed since the Magna Carta in the thirteenth century.

However, the Criminal Justice and Public Order Act 1994 provides for those occasions when bail may only be granted in exceptional circumstances where a person is charged with certain specified offences. Section 25 of the 1994 Act states:

(1) A person who in any proceedings has been charged with or convicted of an offence to which this section applies in circumstances to which it applies shall be granted bail in those proceedings only if the court or, as the case may be, the constable considering the grant of bail is satisfied that there are exceptional circumstances which justify it.

(2) This section applies, subject to subsection (3) below, to the following offences, that is to say—
- (a) murder;
- (b) attempted murder;
- (c) manslaughter;
- (d) rape under the law of Scotland or Northern Ireland;
- (e) an offence under section 1 of the Sexual Offences Act 1956 (rape);
- (f) an offence under section 1 of the Sexual Offences Act 2003 (rape);
- (g) an offence under section 2 of that Act (assault by penetration);
- (h) an offence under section 4 of that Act (causing a person to engage in sexual activity without consent) where the activity caused involved penetration within subsection (4)(a) to (d) of that section;

(i) an offence under section 5 of that Act (rape of a child under 13);
(j) an offence under section 6 of that Act (assault of a child under 13 by penetration);
(k) an offence under section 8 of that Act (causing or inciting a child under 13 to engage in sexual activity), where an activity involving penetration within subsection (3)(a) to (d) of that section was caused;
(l) an offence under section 30 of that Act (sexual activity with a person with a mental disorder impeding choice), where the touching involved penetration within subsection (3)(a) to (d) of that section;
(m) an offence under section 31 of that Act (causing or inciting a person, with a mental disorder impeding choice, to engage in sexual activity), where an activity involving penetration within subsection (3)(a) to (d) of that section was caused;
(n) an attempt to commit an offence within any of paragraphs (d) to (m).

(3) This section applies to a person charged with or convicted of any such offence only if he has been previously convicted by or before a court in any part of the United Kingdom of any such offence or of culpable homicide and, in the case of a previous conviction of manslaughter or of culpable homicide, if he was then sentenced to imprisonment or, if he was then a child or young person, to long-term detention under any of the relevant enactments.
(4) This section applies whether or not an appeal is pending against conviction or sentence.
(5) In this section—
'conviction' includes—
(a) a finding that a person is not guilty by reason of insanity;
(b) a finding under section 4A(3) of the Criminal Procedure (Insanity) Act 1964 (cases of unfitness to plead) that a person did the act or made the omission charged against him; and
(c) a conviction of an offence for which an order is made discharging the offender absolutely or conditionally;

and 'convicted' shall be construed accordingly; and
'the relevant enactments' means—
(a) as respects England and Wales, section 91 of the Powers of Criminal Courts (Sentencing) Act 2000;
(b) as respects Scotland, sections 205(1) to (3) and 208 of the Criminal Procedure (Scotland) Act 1995;
(c) as respects Northern Ireland, section 73(2) of the Children and Young Persons Act (Northern Ireland) 1968.

KEYNOTE

Section 25 provides that bail may not be granted where a person is charged with murder, attempted murder, manslaughter, rape or attempted rape if they have been convicted of any of these offences *unless* there are exceptional circumstances.

In *R (On the Application of O)* v *Crown Court at Harrow* [2006] UKHL 42 it was held that s. 25 was compatible with the European Convention on Human Rights 1950, Art. 5(3)—presumption of an individual's right to liberty. Even where a person's custody time limit had expired s. 25 could still be applied and the evidential burden was on the defence to demonstrate that exceptional circumstances existed. Also, in the case of *Hurnam* v *State of Mauritius* [2005] UKPC 49, the Privy Council stated that the seriousness of the offence is not a conclusive reason for refusing bail and the court must consider whether or not the accused is likely to abscond if released on bail.

In all other cases the custody officer must consider the issue of bail and s. 38(1) of the 1984 Act sets out the occasions where bail can be refused (**see para. 1.10.6**). Where bail is refused, the custody officer must inform the detained person of the reasons why and make an entry as to these reasons in the custody record (s. 38(3) and (4)).

1.10.5.1 Condition of Detained Person and Communication of Refused Bail

A detained person should be informed of the bail decision as soon as it is made. This can be delayed if the conditions set out in Code C, para. 1.8 apply, in which case the detainee should be informed as soon as practicable. The conditions are that the detained person:

- is incapable of understanding what is said;
- is violent, or likely to become violent; or
- is in urgent need of medical attention.

In reaching a decision as to whether a person should be refused bail the custody officer should consider whether the same objective can be achieved by imposing conditions to the bail, that is, for the person to appear at an appointed place at an appointed time. If conditions attached to a person's bail are likely to achieve the same objective as keeping the person in detention, bail must be given.

In *Gizzonio* v *Chief Constable of Derbyshire* (1998) *The Times*, 29 April, Gizzonio had been remanded in custody in respect of certain charges which had not ultimately been pursued. Damages (for the wrongful exercise of lawful authority) were sought on the basis that the police had wrongly opposed the grant of bail. It was held that the decision regarding bail is part of the process of investigation of crime with a view to prosecution and so the police enjoyed immunity in that respect.

1.10.6 Grounds for Refusing Bail

Section 38(1) of the Police and Criminal Evidence Act 1984 provides that a custody officer need not grant bail to an unconvicted accused who is charged with an offence if one or more of the following grounds apply.

1.10.6.1 Name and Address cannot be Ascertained

If there are reasonable grounds for doubting whether the accused's name and address is correct, these doubts would have to be recorded, along with the decision to refuse bail, on the custody record. If the person refuses to give his/her name, this does not automatically satisfy the requirements of s. 38. The actual wording of the section is that the name *or* address *cannot be ascertained* or that which is given is doubted.

1.10.6.2 Risk of Absconding

If there are reasonable grounds for believing that the accused will fail to appear at court if bailed, there are certain factors which the custody officer should consider when taking a decision to refuse bail under this section. These factors include:

- the nature and seriousness of the offence;
- the character, antecedents, associations and community ties of the accused;
- the accused's 'record' for having answered bail in the past;
- the strength of the evidence against the accused.

1.10.6.3 Interference with Administration of Justice

There may be reasonable grounds for believing that detention is necessary to prevent the detained person from interfering with the administration of justice or with the investigation of offences or a particular offence.

This ground would not apply for the purpose of the police making further inquiries or where other suspects are still to be arrested. It is generally intended to protect witnesses, keeping them free from fear of intimidation or bribery and enabling other evidence to be properly obtained.

1.10.6.4 Commission of Further Offences (Imprisonable Offences Only)

If there are reasonable grounds for believing that bail should be refused to prevent the accused committing other offence(s) the custody officer should give due weight to whether the accused had committed offences when previously on bail and also the 'factors' outlined under **para. 1.10.6.2** above.

1.10.6.5 Risk of Injury to Another, etc. (Non-imprisonable Offences Only)

There may be reasonable grounds for believing that detention is necessary to prevent the accused causing physical injury to another or causing loss or damage to property.

1.10.6.6 Own Protection

There may also be reasonable grounds for believing that detention is necessary for the accused's own protection. 'Own protection' can relate to protection from themselves, such as people who are suicidal, alcoholic, drug addicted or mentally unstable, or protection from others, such as in child abuse cases where there is a lot of public anger directed at the suspect.

1.10.6.7 Juvenile: Welfare

Reasonable grounds for believing that detention is necessary for the juvenile's own welfare provide another reason whereby bail may be denied.

The expression 'welfare' has a wider meaning than just 'protection' and could apply to juveniles who, if released, might be homeless or become involved in prostitution or vagrancy.

In respect of the above conditions, the custody officer must have regard to the same considerations that a court has to consider in taking the corresponding decisions under sch. 1, part I, para. 2 to the Bail Act 1976 (s. 38(2A) of the Police and Criminal Evidence Act 1984). This relates to imprisonable offences where a court need not grant bail if it is satisfied there are *substantial* grounds for believing the accused would:

- fail to surrender to custody;
- commit an offence; or
- interfere with witnesses or otherwise obstruct the course of justice, whether in relation to him/herself or any other person.

1.10.7 Bail Consideration by the Custody Officer

The granting of bail in criminal proceedings is provided by s. 3 of the Bail Act 1976 and this section examines the general provisions in relation to bail granted by a custody officer, the conditions that may be attached and applications to vary or remove those conditions.

1.10.7.1 General Provisions

The general provisions as to bail in criminal proceedings are provided by s. 3 of the 1976 Act, but this is modified by s. 3A which relates specifically to a custody officer. Section 3 states:

> (1) A person granted bail in criminal proceedings shall be under a duty to surrender to custody, and that duty is enforceable in accordance with section 6 of this Act.
> (2) No recognisance for his surrender to custody shall be taken from him.
> (3) Except as provided by this section—
> (a) no security for his surrender to custody shall be taken from him,

(b) he shall not be required to provide a surety or sureties for his surrender to custody, and
(c) no other requirement shall be imposed on him as a condition of bail.

(4) He may be required, before release on bail, to provide a surety or sureties to secure his surrender to custody.

(5) He may be required, before release on bail, to give security for his surrender to custody. The security may be given by him or on his behalf.

(6) He may be required to comply, before release on bail or later, with such requirements as appear to the court to be necessary—
(a) to secure that he surrenders to custody,
(b) to secure that he does not commit an offence while on bail,
(c) to secure that he does not interfere with witnesses or otherwise obstruct the course of justice whether in relation to himself or any other person,
(ca) for his own protection or, if he is a child or young person, for his own welfare or in his own interests,

(7) If a parent or guardian of a child or young person consents to be surety for the child or young person for the purposes of this subsection, the parent or guardian may be required to secure that the child or young person complies with any requirement imposed on him by virtue of subsection (6), (6ZAA) or (6A) above but—
(a) no requirement shall be imposed on the parent or the guardian of a young person by virtue of this subsection where it appears that the young person will attain the age of 17 before the time to be appointed for him to surrender to custody; and
(b) the parent or guardian shall not be required to secure compliance with any requirement to which his consent does not extend and shall not, in respect of those requirements to which his consent does extend, be bound in a sum greater than £50.

KEYNOTE

Guidance to courts, applicable also to a custody officer, when approaching the decision to grant bail was given in *R* v *Mansfield Justices, ex parte Sharkey* [1985] 1 All ER 193, where it was held that any relevant risk, for example, absconding, must be a 'real' risk, not just a fanciful one.

Where a custody officer grants bail there is a requirement for a record to be made of the decision in the prescribed manner and containing the prescribed particulars. If requested, a copy of the record of the decision must, as soon as practicable, be given to the person in relation to whom the decision was taken (s. 5(1)).

Further details on sureties and security are provided in **paras 1.10.7.4 and 1.10.7.5**, respectively.

1.10.7.2 Bail Conditions

The power of a custody officer to impose bail conditions is provided by s. 3A of the 1976 Act, which states:

(5) Where a constable grants bail to a person no conditions shall be imposed under subsections (4), (5), (6) or (7) of section 3 of this Act unless it appears to the constable that it is necessary to do so—
(a) for the purpose of preventing that person from failing to surrender to custody, or
(b) for the purpose of preventing that person from committing an offence while on bail, or
(c) for the purpose of preventing that person from interfering with witnesses or otherwise obstructing the course of justice, whether in relation to himself or any other person, or
(d) for that person's own protection, or if he is a child or young person, for his own welfare or in his own interests.

Where a custody officer decides to grant bail and considers one or more of the requirements in s. 3A(5)(a) to (d) apply, one or more of the following conditions can be imposed:

- the accused is to live and sleep at a specified address;
- the accused is to notify any changes of address;

- the accused is to report periodically (daily, weekly or at other intervals) to his/her local police station;
- the accused is restricted from entering a certain area or building or to go within a specified distance of a specified address;
- the accused is not to contact (whether directly or indirectly) the victim of the alleged offence and/or any other probable prosecution witness;
- the accused is to surrender his/her passport;
- the accused's movements are restricted by an imposed curfew between set times (i.e. when it is thought the accused might commit offences or come into contact with witnesses);
- the accused is required to provide a surety or security.

In *McDonald* v *Procurator Fiscal, Elgin* (2003) *The Times*, 17 April, it was held that a condition for an accused to remain in his dwelling at all times except between 10am and 12 noon did not amount to detention or deprivation of his liberty and did not constitute an infringement of his right to liberty under the European Convention on Human Rights, article 5.

In relation to non-imprisonable offences it has been held that a hunt protester who was arrested for an offence under s. 5 of the Public Order Act 1986 was rightly required as a condition of his bail not to attend another hunt meeting before his next court appearance (*R* v *Bournemouth Magistrates' Court, ex parte Cross* [1989] Crim LR 207).

KEYNOTE

The conditions outlined in this section can also be imposed by a constable granting bail elsewhere than at a police station under s. 30A(3B) of the Police and Criminal Evidence Act 1984 (**see para. 1.10.2.2**).

1.10.7.3 Applications to Vary or Remove Bail Conditions

The power to vary or remove conditions is provided by s. 3A of the Bail Act 1976. Section 3A(4) substitutes s. 3(8) and states:

> Where a custody officer has granted bail in criminal proceedings he or another custody officer serving at the same police station may, at the request of the person to whom it was granted, vary the conditions of bail and in doing so he may impose conditions or more onerous conditions.

KEYNOTE

Section 3A(5) above also applies on any request to a custody officer to vary or remove conditions of bail (**see para. 1.10.7.2**).

There is a requirement that a custody officer either imposing or varying the conditions of bail must include a note of the reasons in the custody record and give a copy of that note to the person in relation to whom the decision was taken (s. 5A(3)).

An accused may also apply to the magistrates' court under s. 43B(1) of the Magistrates' Courts Act 1980, to vary conditions of police bail. Details of the procedure to be followed are contained in r. 19(1) of the Criminal Procedure Rules 2005 (**see Blackstone's Criminal Practice 2008, Appendix 1**).

1.10.7.4 Sureties

Section 3(4) of the Bail Act 1976 provides that before a person is granted bail he/she may be required to provide one or more sureties to secure his/her surrender to custody. A custody officer is entitled (as a court) to require such sureties.

The question of whether or not sureties are necessary is at the discretion of the custody officer (or court) but this condition can be applied only where it is believed the accused may abscond, commit further offences, interfere with witnesses, etc. (sch. 1, part I). It should be noted that sureties have no responsibilities (liability) in relation to an accused committing further offences or interfering with witnesses etc. while on bail.

The suitability of sureties is provided by s. 8 of the 1976 Act and provides for the following considerations as to a surety's suitability:

- financial resources
- character and previous convictions
- relationship to the accused.

The decision as to the suitability of individual sureties is a matter for the custody officer.

The normal consequence for a surety if the accused does not answer bail is that the surety is required to forfeit the entire sum in which he/she stood surety. The power to forfeit recognisances is a matter for the court and is contained in s. 120(1) to (3) of the Magistrates' Courts Act 1980 and rr. 21 and 21A of the Crown Court Rules 1982.

It is not necessary to prove that the surety had any involvement in the accused's non-appearance (*R* v *Warwick Crown Court, ex parte Smalley* [1987] 1 WLR 237). However, where a surety has taken all reasonable steps to ensure the appearance of an accused it was held that the recognisance ought not to be forfeited (*R* v *York Crown Court, ex parte Coleman* (1987) 86 Cr App R 151). In *R* v *Stipendiary Magistrate for Leicester, ex parte Kaur* (2000) 164 JP 127, it was held that the means of the surety *at the time of enforcement* must be taken into account when the court decides whether or not to remit the whole or part of the forfeited recognisance. Section 7(3)(c) of the Bail Act 1976 provides for a surety to notify a constable *in writing* that the accused is unlikely to surrender to custody and that for that reason the surety wishes to be relieved of his/her obligations as a surety. Such an action may well be determined to be 'reasonable steps'.

1.10.7.5 Security

Section 3(5) of the Bail Act 1976 provides that, before a person is granted bail, he/she may be required to give security for his/her surrender to custody. As with sureties, a custody officer is entitled (as a court) to require such security, as far as s. 3(6)(a) to (c) (surrender to custody, not commit an offence on bail, interfere with witnesses, etc.) applies. The security required may be a sum of money or other valuable item and may be given either by the accused or someone on his/her behalf. A third party may make an asset available to an accused for the purpose of providing a security and where the security is forfeited there is no requirement for the third party to be informed (*R (On the Application of Stevens)* v *Truro Magistrates' Court* [2002] 1 WLR 144).

As with sureties, where an accused absconds this would result in forfeiture of the security. This would not be the case if there appears reasonable cause for the (accused's) failure to surrender to custody (s. 5(7) to (9) of the 1976 Act).

1.10.7.6 The Human Rights Act 1998

Generally, the approach of European Court and Commission is that an accused person should be released unconditionally unless factors that would otherwise lead to a refusal of bail can be met by imposing bail conditions.

Against this background the Court has accepted:

- use of sureties (*Schertenlieb* v *Switzerland* (1980) 23 DR 137)
- surrender of a passport (*Stögmüller* v *Austria* (1969) 1 EHRR 155)
- restrictions on movement (*Schmid* v *Austria* (1985) 44 DR 195).

In the case of *Neumeister* v *Austria* (1968) 1 EHRR 91, the Court considered that it would be a violation of the Convention where the amount of a surety was set by reference to the losses allegedly caused by the person charged.

1.10.8 Juveniles Refused Bail

Under s. 38(6) of the Police and Criminal Evidence Act 1984, where a juvenile has been refused bail, the custody officer must try and make arrangements for the detained juvenile to be taken into the care of a local authority in order that he/she can be detained pending appearance in court.

Two exceptions are provided:

- where the custody officer certifies that it is impracticable to do so, or
- in the case of a juvenile of at least 12 years of age, where no secure accommodation is available and there is a risk to the public of serious harm from that juvenile which cannot be adequately protected by placing the juvenile in other local authority accommodation.

The certificate signed by the custody officer must be produced when the juvenile first appears at court (s. 38(7)).

PACE Code C, Note 16D makes it clear that the availability of secure accommodation is only a factor in relation to a juvenile aged 12 or over, when the local authority accommodation would not be adequate to protect the public from serious harm from the juvenile.

The obligation to transfer a juvenile to local authority accommodation applies equally to a juvenile charged during the daytime as it does to a juvenile to be held overnight, subject to a requirement to bring the juvenile before a court in accordance with s. 46 of the 1984 Act (see below).

1.10.9 Offence of Absconding

Section 6 of the Bail Act 1976 creates an offence of absconding and states:

> (1) If a person who has been released on bail in criminal proceedings fails without reasonable cause to surrender to custody he shall be guilty of an offence.
> (2) If a person who—
> (a) has been released on bail in criminal proceedings, and
> (b) having reasonable cause therefor, has failed to surrender to custody,
> fails to surrender to custody at the appointed place as soon after the appointed time as is reasonably practicable he shall be guilty of an offence.

KEYNOTE

The burden of proof in relation to showing 'reasonable cause' (s. 6(1)) is a matter for the accused (s. 6(3)).

A person who has 'reasonable cause' still commits the offence if he/she falls to surrender 'as soon after the appointed time as is reasonably practicable'. In *Laidlaw* v *Atkinson* (1986) *The Times*, 2 August, it was held that being mistaken about the day on which one should have appeared was not a reasonable excuse. Also, there is no requirement on the court to inquire as to whether a person arrested for failing to comply with bail conditions had any reasonable excuse for breaching bail (*R* (*On the Application of Vickers*) v *West London Magistrates' Court* (2003) 167 JP 473).

However, in *R* v *Ashley* [2004] 1 WLR 2057 the accused had been bailed on condition that he surrender his passport and not leave the country. He both failed to surrender his passport and left the country but in fact returned for the trial on the appointed day. He was convicted of contempt of court but on appeal this was overturned as although he had breached bail conditions he had returned for his trial and s. 7 of the Bail Act 1976 does not itself create any offence.

Section 6(4) also states:

> A failure to give to a person granted bail in criminal proceedings a copy of the record of the decision shall not constitute reasonable cause for that person's failure to surrender to custody.

The procedure for prosecuting offences under s. 6 is provided by *Practice Direction (Bail: Failure to Surrender and Trials in Absence)* [2004] 1 Cr App R 402. In relation to a person who has been bailed by the police to attend at a magistrates' court or a police station and fails to attend, proceedings should be initiated by charging the accused or by the laying of an information. For a person granted bail by a magistrates' court, the court initiates proceedings for failure to appear by its own motion where there has been an express invitation to do so by the prosecutor.

A magistrates' court may only try an offence of absconding, where a person was bailed by a constable, if an information is laid for the relevant offence within six months from the time of the commission of the relevant offence and/or if an information is laid for the relevant offence no later than three months from the time of the occurrence of the first of the events to occur after the commission of the relevant offence. Those events are:

- the person surrenders to custody at the appointed place;
- the person is arrested, or attends at a police station, in connection with the relevant offence or the offence for which he was granted bail;
- the person appears or is brought before a court in connection with the relevant offence or the offence for which he was granted bail (s. 6(10)–(14)).

The Crown Court can deal with a breach of bail as a criminal contempt of court but is required to decide whether an offence under s. 6(1) (failure to surrender without reasonable cause), has been committed (*R* v *Hourigan* [2003] EWCA Crim 2306).

1.10.9.1 Failure to Comply with Police Bail

There are occasions where a person who has been bailed to return to a police station at a later date or to appear at court may be arrested without warrant. These occasions are dealt with by s. 46A of the Police and Criminal Evidence Act 1984 and s. 7 of the Bail Act 1976.

Section 46A of the Police and Criminal Evidence Act 1984 states:

> (1) A constable may arrest without a warrant any person who, having been released on bail under this Part of this Act subject to a duty to attend at a police station, fails to attend at that police station at the time appointed for him to do so.
> (1A) A person who has been released on bail under section 37, 37C(2)(b) or 37CA(2)(b) above may be arrested without warrant by a constable if the constable has reasonable grounds for suspecting that the person has broken any of the conditions of bail.
> (2) A person who is arrested under this section shall be taken to the police station appointed as the place at which he is to surrender to custody as soon as practicable after the arrest.
> (3) For the purposes of—
> (a) section 30 above (subject to the obligation in subsection (2) above), and
> (b) section 31 above,
> an arrest under this section shall be treated as an arrest for an offence.

KEYNOTE

The offence for which the person is arrested under subsection (1) above is the offence for which he/she was originally arrested (s. 34(7) of the 1984 Act). This power of arrest applies only where the person *has failed* to attend the police station at the appointed time; it does not extend to situations where there is a 'reasonable suspicion' that the person has failed to attend.

This should be contrasted with s. 46A(1A) where the arresting officer only has to have reasonable grounds for suspecting that the person has broken any of the conditions of bail.

1.10.9.2 Failure to Appear at Court (or Expected Not to Appear)

Section 7 of the Bail Act 1976 states:

(1) If a person who has been released on bail in criminal proceedings and is under a duty to surrender into the custody of a court fails to surrender to custody at the time appointed for him to do so the court may issue a warrant for his arrest.

(1A) Subsection (1B) applies if—
- (a) a person has been released on bail in connection with extradition proceedings,
- (b) the person is under a duty to surrender into the custody of a constable, and
- (c) the person fails to surrender to custody at the time appointed for him to do so.

(1B) A magistrates' court may issue a warrant for the person's arrest.

(2) If a person who has been released on bail in criminal proceedings absents himself from the court at any time after he has surrendered into the custody of the court and before the court is ready to begin or to resume the hearing of the proceedings, the court may issue a warrant for his arrest but no warrant shall be issued under this subsection where that person is absent in accordance with leave given to him by or on behalf of the court.

(3) A person who has been released on bail in criminal proceedings and is under a duty to surrender into the custody of a court may be arrested without warrant by a constable—
- (a) if the constable has reasonable grounds for believing that person is not likely to surrender to custody;
- (b) if the constable has reasonable grounds for believing that person is likely to break any of the conditions of his bail or has reasonable grounds for suspecting that that person has broken any of those conditions; or
- (c) in a case where that person was released on bail with one or more surety or sureties, if a surety notifies a constable in writing that that person is unlikely to surrender to custody and that for that reason the surety wishes to be relieved of his obligations as a surety.

KEYNOTE

Section 7 therefore provides a power of arrest without warrant if the constable:

- has reasonable grounds for believing that the person is not likely to surrender to custody;
- has reasonable grounds for believing that the person is likely to break, or reasonable grounds for suspecting that the person has broken, any conditions of bail; or
- is notified by a surety in writing that the person is unlikely to surrender to custody and for that reason the surety wishes to be relieved of his/her obligations as a surety.

Where a person is arrested under s. 7 he/she shall be brought before a magistrate as soon as practicable and in any event within 24 hours (s. 7(4)(a)).

This section requires that a detainee not merely be brought to the court precincts or cells but actually be dealt with by a justice within 24 hours of being arrested (*R (On the Application of Culley)* v *Crown Court sitting at Dorchester* [2007] EWHC 109 (Admin)).

Where a person is arrested within 24 hours of the time appointed for him/her to surrender to custody he/she must be brought before the court at which he/she was to have so surrendered (s. 7(4)(b)). In reckoning the 24-hour period no account is to be taken of Christmas Day, Good Friday or any Sunday (s. 7(7)).

In dealing with a person brought before the court under subsection (4), if the magistrate is of the opinion that the person is not likely to surrender to custody or has broken or is likely to break any bail conditions he/she may:

- remand or commit the person to custody;
- grant bail subject to the same or different conditions.

Where the justice is not of such an opinion, he/she shall grant bail with the same conditions (if any) as were originally imposed (s. 7(5)).

Where the person being dealt with is a child or young person and the justice does not grant bail, he/she should remand such person to the care of the local authority (s. 7(6)).

1.10.10 Remands in Police Custody

Where a person is remanded in custody it normally means detention in prison. However, s. 128 of the Magistrates' Courts Act 1980 provides that a magistrates' court may remand a person to police custody:

- for a period not exceeding three days (24 hours for persons under 17—s. 23(14) of the Children and Young Persons Act 1969) (s. 128(7));
- for the purpose of inquiries into offences (other than the offence for which he/she appears before the court) (s. 128(8)(a));
- as soon as the need ceases he/she must be brought back before the magistrates (s. 128 (8)(b));
- the conditions of detention and periodic review apply as if the person was arrested without warrant on suspicion of having committed an offence (s. 128(8)(c) and (d)).

This option is colloquially referred to as a 'three day lie down'.

1.10.11 Human Rights Act 1998

Custody officers need to be aware and give consideration to the rights and freedoms guaranteed under the European Convention on Human Rights when reaching a decision as to bail.

Article 5 of the Convention relates to the right to liberty and security. Article 5(3) provides that a person arrested under article 5(1)(c) is entitled to 'trial within a reasonable time or to release pending trial'. Article 5(1)(c) states:

> ... the lawful arrest or detention of a person effected for the purpose of bringing him before the competent legal authority on reasonable suspicion of having committed an offence or when it is reasonably considered necessary to prevent his committing an offence or fleeing after having done so ...

It should be noted that 'trial within a reasonable time' and 'release pending trial' have been held not to be alternatives (*Wemhoff* v *Germany* (1968) 1 EHRR 55).

The Convention requires that every arrested person be brought 'promptly' before a judge or other judicial officer. The meaning of 'promptly' is not specified but in *Brincat* v *Italy* (1992) 16 EHRR 591, the European Court held that a person who had been detained for four days on blackmail charges before being brought before a court was not treated in accordance with the article. However it is likely that the periods of detention provided by the Police and Criminal Evidence Act 1984 would be acceptable for most purposes of the Convention.

Article 5(3) provides the right to be released pending trial where a person's continuing detention ceases to be reasonable (*Neumeister* v *Austria* (1968) 1 EHRR 91). Bail should only be refused where there are 'relevant' and 'sufficient' reasons and in all cases these reasons should be provided (*Wemhoff* v *Germany*, above; *Tomasi* v *France* (1992) 15 EHRR 1). In *Yagci and Sargin* v *Turkey* (1995) 20 EHRR 505, the European Court was sceptical about what it referred to as 'stereotyped' reasons for refusing bail and it is likely that our domestic courts will take a similar view to anything other than a genuine consideration of each person's individual circumstances.

In *R (On the Application of DPP)* v *Havering Magistrates' Court* [2001] 1 WLR 805, no oral evidence was available to prove the breach of bail conditions. It was held that such a hearing does not equate to facing a criminal charge and therefore article 6 (right to a fair trial) does not apply. Also article 5 would not necessarily be breached as evidence could be considered which was not admissible in the strict sense and the case did not need to be proved beyond reasonable doubt.

The European Court has identified four grounds where the refusal of bail may be justified under the Convention:

- fear of absconding
- interference with the course of justice
- the prevention of crime
- the preservation of public order.

These will be considered in turn.

1.10.11.1 Fear of Absconding

The seriousness of the offence alone has been deemed not to be a sufficient reason to suppose a person will necessarily abscond (*Yagci and Sargin* v *Turkey* (1995) 20 EHRR 505). Regard must be taken of other factors including the character of the detained person, their background, financial status, etc. (*W* v *Switzerland* (1993) 17 EHRR 60).

1.10.11.2 Interference with the Course of Justice

As with s. 38(1) of the Police and Criminal Evidence Act 1984 (**see para. 1.10.6**), this would apply where there are reasonable grounds for believing that detention is necessary to prevent the interference with the administration of justice or with the investigation of offences or a particular offence.

The approach in some European cases has been that where further evidence is obtained and statements taken, the risk of interference diminishes and further detention under this ground is difficult to justify (*W* v *Switzerland*, above). Also, if the detained person has previously been bailed and there was no evidence of interference with the course of justice, using this ground would be very difficult to justify (*Ringeisen* v *Austria* (1971) 1 EHRR 455).

1.10.11.3 The Prevention of Crime

Again, this is similar to the condition contained in s. 38(1) of the Police and Criminal Evidence Act 1984, where the custody officer has reasonable grounds for believing that the detained person will commit other offence(s) if bailed. It was held in *Matznetter* v *Austria*

(1979–80) 1 EHRR 198 and *Toth* v *Austria* (1991) 14 EHRR 551 that a reasonable risk of the person committing further offences while on bail was a valid reason for refusal.

In considering a person's previous convictions, the European Court has held that, where these were not comparable either in nature or in seriousness with the offence(s) charged, their use as grounds for refusing bail would not be acceptable for the purposes of article 5 (*Clooth* v *Belgium* (1991) 14 EHRR 717).

1.10.11.4 The Preservation of Public Order

This provides for the temporary detention of a person where the particular gravity of the offence(s) and the likely public reaction are such that the release may give rise to public disorder (*Letellier* v *France* (1991) 14 EHRR 83). This may be difficult to reconcile with the approach of the Court in *Redmond-Bate* v *DPP* (1999) 163 JP 789, where the predicted unlawful acts of others were held not to be a reason for arresting and detaining the individual whose lawful behaviour was antagonising them.

1.11 Disclosure of Evidence

1.11.1 Introduction

The need for the prosecution to provide the defence with material relating to the charge(s) in a case has been recognised by the courts and the government to be crucial in ensuring that defendants get a fair trial. This point is further enforced with the introduction of the Human Rights Act 1998 which incorporates the European Convention on Human Rights and in this area brings in article 6, the right to a fair trial including disclosure of evidence.

The requirement to provide the defence with material can be divided between that required prior to the person pleading, which is known as advanced information and that which is required once the defendant has pleaded not guilty in the magistrates' court or is committed/transferred to the Crown Court. The second stage assumes that the defence has been provided with the prosecution case and therefore any evidence that is left is unused material and that it will remain unused by the prosecution. This is usually referred to as 'disclosure'. These two stages are considered below.

Within this chapter reference will be made to the Criminal Procedure and Investigations Act 1996 (as amended by the Criminal Justice Act 2003), the Code of Practice for the 1996 Act (the Code), the 2005 Attorney-General's Guidelines: Disclosure of Information in Criminal Proceedings (which provides further guidance/interpretation to the Act and Codes) and the Prosecution Team Disclosure Manual, that replace the Joint CPS/Police Project JOPI Guidelines which set out in detail actions required to meet the disclosure requirements of the 1996 Act. The Criminal Justice Act 2003 made changes to the 1996 Act, some of which came into force on 4 April 2005 and therefore applies to cases from that date. These changes are discussed against the existing legislation contained in earlier editions of this book. It will be important to note when an investigation started as this will determine whether the changes introduced on 4 April 2005 apply or the previous disclosure rules. Further guidance has also been given by the Court of Appeal in Disclosure: A protocol for the Control and Management of Unused Material in the Crown Court. In this document the Court of Appeal stated that, for the Criminal Procedure and Investigations Act 1996 to work properly, investigators and disclosure officers responsible for the gathering, inspection, retention and recording of relevant unused prosecution material must perform their tasks thoroughly, scrupulously and fairly. In this, they must adhere to the appropriate provisions of the CPIA Code of Practice.

1.11.2 Advanced Information

Advance information refers to the material that the defence are entitled to have in order to consider whether to plead guilty or not guilty. In some cases it is not a question of whether the defendant committed the crime but whether the prosecution are in a position to prove the offence and, in order to consider this, the defence are unlikely to agree to plead or decide on the mode of trial without knowing the strength of the prosecution case. It is clearly in the public interest that guilty pleas are entered or indicated as soon as possible (*R* v *Calderdale Magistrates' Court, ex parte Donahue* [2001] Crim LR 141) and often this cannot be achieved unless advanced information has been provided. The need to know as early as possible whether a defendant is going to plead not guilty can be particularly important as there are time limits by which the courts have to set trials and committals. Often these can be delayed because the prosecution have not complied with their disclosure duties.

Ensuring that all defendants receive copies of any advanced information (or any later disclosure) is also important. In *R* v *Tompkins* [2005] EWCA Crim 3035 the court held that where there has been non-disclosure at the time a plea had been entered, a defendant who had pleaded guilty should not in any way be in a worse position than those who had pleaded not guilty.

1.11.2.1 Obligations on Prosecution Regarding Advanced Information

The prosecution is required, on request, to supply the defence with a summary of the prosecution case and/or copies of the statements of the proposed prosecution witnesses. In indictable and either way offences this is covered by parts 21 to 26 of the Criminal Procedure Rules 2005 and in summary only cases by the Attorney-General's Guidelines: Disclosure of Information in Criminal Proceedings. In *R* v *K* [2006] EWCA Crim 724, the court held that criminal trials are dependent on and subject to the Criminal Procedure Rules 2005 which imposed duties and burdens on all the participants in a criminal trial. Whereas the rules state that advanced information is only required when requested by the defence, in practice this should, where possible, be made available to the CPS at the first hearing.

It is suggested that article 6 of the European Convention supports the need to provide advanced information to the defence and that this should be done as soon as possible:

Article 6(3)(a) states that a person is:

> ... to be informed promptly ... and in detail, of the nature and cause of the accusation against him;

Article 6(3)(b), states that an accused is entitled to:

> ... have adequate time ... for the preparation of his defence.

The point concerning advanced information in summary cases was considered in *R* v *Stratford Justices, ex parte Imbert* [1999] 2 Cr App R 276 where the court gave their opinion that article 6 does not give an absolute right to pre-trial disclosure, it will be a question of whether the defendant can have a fair trial. Clearly it will be easier to satisfy this test where advanced information as been provided to the defence.

Rule 21.3 of the 2005 Rules provides that the prosecutor, when requested, must provide the accused or a person representing the accused who requests the prosecutor to furnish him/her with advance information:

- a copy of those parts of every written statement which contain information as to the facts and matters of which the prosecutor proposes to adduce evidence in the proceedings; or

- a summary of the facts and matters of which the prosecutor proposes to adduce evidence in the proceedings.

Advanced information might also include the following and so consideration should be had to providing this material to the prosecutor so that he/she can forward it to the defence where appropriate (ensuring the addresses and other details of witnesses and victims are protected):

- copy of the custody record;
- copies of any interview tape(s);
- copy of any first descriptions where relevant;
- significant information that might affect a bail decision or that might enable the defence to contest the committal proceedings (A-G's Guidelines, para. 55);
- any material which is relevant to sentence (e.g. information which might mitigate the seriousness of the offence or assist the accused to lay blame in whole or in part upon a co-accused or another person) (A-G's Guidelines, para. 58);
- statements and/or a summary of the prosecution cases;
- copy of any video evidence.

Where a person has made several statements but all the relevant evidence for the prosecution case is contained in one statement, it is only that one statement which needs to be disclosed. In order to comply with advanced information the defence needs to be either given a copy of the document or allowed to inspect the document (or a copy of it).

However, where the OIC considers that providing advanced information might lead to a witness being intimidated or some other interference with the course of justice he/she should consult with the CPS as the rules allow the prosecutor to limit disclosure of some or all of the prosecution case (2005 Rules, r. 21.4).

1.11.3 Disclosure and the Criminal Procedure and Investigations Act 1996

As stated above this stage assumes that the defence has already been informed of the details of the prosecution case. In most investigations there will be material that has come to the attention of the police which will not be used as evidence to prove the prosecution case but which might be useful to the defence. It is through the disclosure rules that this information will be provided to the defendant. The rules of disclosure are governed by the Criminal Procedure and Investigations Act 1996. The 1996 Act puts the prosecution duty to disclose information to the defence on a statutory footing, and also introduced a new concept in criminal law where the defence have a duty to advise the prosecution of certain matters relating to their case. This is also supported by the 1996 Act Code of Practice, the Attorney-General's Guidelines on Disclosure and the Disclosure Manual.

The 1996 Act is further recognition of the need to disclose material to each side to allow the case to be dealt with fairly. This point as well as the need for timely disclosure of material, is further reinforced by article 6(3) of the European Convention on Human Rights.

In *Jasper* v *United Kingdom* (2000) 30 EHRR 441 the court expressed the importance of equality of arms being a fundamental aspect of a fair trial; both the defence and the prosecution must be given the opportunity to have knowledge of and comment on filed observations and evidence adduced by the other party. The court did recognise that the entitlement to disclosure of relevant evidence was not an absolute right but could be restricted as was strictly necessary (**see para. 1.11.20**).

1.11.3.1 The Criminal Procedure and Investigations Act 1996

The Criminal Procedure and Investigations Act 1996 is made up of seven parts. It is the first two parts which are of interest to the police:

- Part I sets out the procedures for disclosure and the effects of failing to comply with the Act; and
- Part II sets out the duties of police officers in relation to the disclosure provisions.

1.11.3.2 Aims of the 1996 Act

The aim of the disclosure rules within the Criminal Procedure and Investigations Act 1996 is to make sure that a defendant gets a fair trial and speeds up the whole trial process. This was confirmed by *R* v *Stratford Justices, ex parte Imbert* [1999] 2 Cr App R 276, where the court said that the legislation was to try to ensure that nothing which might assist the defence was kept from the accused.

Paragraph 3 of A-G's Guidelines states that:

> The scheme set out in the Criminal Procedure and Investigations Act 1996 (as amended by the Criminal Justice Act 2003) (the Act) is designed to ensure that there is fair disclosure of material which may be relevant to an investigation and which does not form part of the prosecution case. Disclosure under the Act should assist the accused in the timely preparation and presentation of their case and assist the court to focus on all the relevant issues in the trial. Disclosure which does not meet these objectives risks preventing a fair trial taking place.

The Act originally placed a responsibility on the prosecution to make *primary* disclosure of material to the defence; a responsibility for the defence—under certain conditions—to disclose their case to the prosecution with a further responsibility on the prosecution to make a *secondary* disclosure to the defence. As a 'catch all' the prosecution also have a continuing duty to review the material they have disclosed.

From 4 April 2005, this distinction between primary and secondary disclosure has now changed. The changes introduced by the Criminal Justice Act 2003 provide for an initial duty to disclose with a continuing duty to disclose until the accused is acquitted or convicted or the prosecutor decides not to proceed with the case. One of the effects of this change is that under the pre April 2005 position the prosecution only had to provide disclosure of material that was relevant to the prosecution case. Now disclosure from the start has to consider any material that might undermine the prosecution case or assist the defence. It is submitted that this requires the prosecution to consider in more detail the types of defence that might be used at trial.

This now places a duty on the prosecutor to disclose to the defence material which may prove helpful to the defendant's case. This has to be balanced against the risk of disclosing so much material under their duty to disclose that the defence collapses under the sheer volume of paperwork. Alternatively, allowing the defence relentless requests for material which may be of no real value ('fishing expeditions') could lead to situations where a guilty person is acquitted.

While the duty of disclosure is placed on the prosecutor, the police have a responsibility to assist in this process. It is therefore vital that police officers understand, not only the statutory requirements made of them, but also the extent of their role within the whole disclosure process. This view is supported by the 2005 A-G's Guidelines. Paragraph 23 states:

> Investigators and disclosure officers must be fair and objective and must work together with prosecutors to ensure that disclosure obligations are met. . . .

1.11.3.3 Jurisdiction of the 1996 Act

The Criminal Procedure and Investigations Act 1996 is primarily concerned with the disclosure of material which does not form part of the prosecution case resulting from a criminal investigation (i.e. 'unused material'). A criminal investigation is defined by s. 1(4) of the 1996 Act and para. 2.1 of the Code of Practice. In order to satisfy the disclosure requirements police officers should consider recording and retaining material in the early stages of an investigation. This will include:

- investigations into crimes that have been committed;
- investigations whose purpose is to ascertain whether a crime has been committed, with a view to the possible institution of criminal proceedings; and
- investigations which begin in the belief that a crime may be committed,

for example when the police keep premises or individuals under observation for a period of time, with a view to the possible institution of criminal proceedings.

In these cases the investigation may well have started some time before the defendant became a suspect. In such cases all the material from the investigation/operation would have to be considered to see if it was relevant to the defence case. In cases where there is a surveillance operation or observation point, it may be that the details of the observation point and the surveillance techniques would not be revealed but it would be necessary to retain material generating from it (**see para. 1.11.20**).

It will be important to know when an investigation commenced as to whether the changes introduced on 4 April 2005 or the earlier rules should still be used, the MG6 must state when the investigation started (Disclosure Manual, para. 6.7).

1.11.3.4 Failure to Comply

Compliance with the rules of disclosure, by both the defence and prosecution, is essential if the 1996 Act is to have any real value. First, in cases where the defence are obliged to make disclosure to the prosecution, failure to do so may lead to the court or jury drawing such inferences as appear proper in deciding the guilt or innocence of the accused (s. 11(5)). Should the prosecution fail to comply with their obligations then an accused does not have to make defence disclosure and no such inference can be made. Secondly, failure by the prosecution to comply with the rules could lead to the court staying the proceedings on the grounds that there has been an abuse of process (s. 10). It could also lead to an action for damages or such other relief as the court sees fit under the Human Rights Act 1998, particularly in relation to article 6 of the European Convention and the right to a fair trial.

Additionally, where the prosecution have not made disclosure on time or fully, a stay on the proceedings or a further adjournment is possible. It is suggested that the more adjournments in a case, the more likely that witnesses will get fed up with the delays and will fail to attend on the next occasion and the case could therefore be lost!

Even if there has been a failure to comply with disclosure the case will not automatically be stayed and therefore any failings should be brought to the attention of the CPS so that the matter can be considered. In *R (On the Application of Ebrahim)* v *Feltham Magistrates' Court* [2001] 1 WLR 1293 the court stated that:

> It must be remembered that it is a commonplace in criminal trial for the defendant to rely on holes in the prosecution case. If in such a case, there is sufficient credible evidence, apart from the missing evidence, which, if believed, would justify safe conviction then the trial should proceed, leaving the defendant to seek to persuade the jury or magistrates not to convict because evidence might otherwise have been available was not before the court through no fault of the defendant.

Further guidance was provided in *R* v *Brooks* (2004) 13 August, CA, unreported, a case where the prosecution failed to comply with the disclosure requirements. The Court of Appeal held that if the court was satisfied that the prosecution had deliberately withheld evidence from the court or frustrated the defence, the court did have the power to stay the prosecution. If the court was not so satisfied it would consider whether, despite all that had gone wrong, a fair trial was possible.

Failure to disclose may result in convictions being overturned, for instance in *R* v *Poole* (2003) *The Times*, 26 June, the Court of Appeal allowed appeals against convictions for murder because the non-disclosure of prosecution evidence influenced the jury's assessment of the reliability of the evidence of a key eye-witness. In this case the witness gave an account that was false in a material particular. However, the police did not follow up those inconsistencies and they failed to inform the CPS that his evidence was unreliable. The level of disclosure that is required will be a question of fact in each case. In *Filmer* v *DPP* [2006] EWHC 3450 (Admin) the court held that the extent of disclosure required from the prosecution depends on the evidence and issue in a particular case. The prosecution are required to provide sufficient disclosure to enable a defendant to present their case. The court went on to say that this has to be the approach otherwise the prosecution would have to second guess every question the defence may want to ask (this is where the defence disclosure becomes relevant, see **para. 1.11.7**).

1.11.4 Part I of the 1996 Act: Rules of Disclosure

1.11.4.1 Application of the Disclosure Provisions

Section 1 of the Criminal Procedure and Investigations Act 1996 defines in which type of cases the disclosure provisions apply. In reality this applies to all cases other than those where the defendant pleads guilty at the magistrates' court. These rules only apply where no criminal investigation into the alleged offence took place before 1 April 1997. If an investigation began before 1 April 1997, then it will be necessary to refer to the common law rules, however ACPO have stated that the 1996 Act should be followed in all cases when considering disclosure. For those investigations that started after 4 April 2005, the amendments introduced by the Criminal Justice Act 2003 will apply.

Some guidance is given by the case of *R* v *Uxbridge Magistrates' Court, ex parte Patel* (2000) 164 JP 209, as to the time an investigation begins. There it was said that the phrase 'criminal investigation' in s. 1(3) of the 1996 Act means that a criminal investigation could begin into an offence before it was committed. This could be so in a surveillance case or where a series of cases was committed, some before and some after the appointed day. Whether in any given case that was the correct view would be a question of fact for the court to determine.

Section 1 also defines a criminal investigation and states:

> (4) For the purposes of this section a criminal investigation is an investigation which police officers or other persons have a duty to conduct with a view to it being ascertained—
> (a) whether a person should be charged with an offence, or
> (b) whether a person charged with an offence is guilty of it.

Consequently, this part of the Act also applies to other people, besides the police, who carry out investigations where they have a duty to ascertain whether criminal offences have been committed (e.g. HM Revenue and Customs; Benefits Agency investigators). It does not apply to those whose primary responsibility does not relate to criminal offences (e.g. local authorities and schools). It also includes the situation where an investigation is started before any offence has been committed, for instance where a surveillance operation is being conducted with a view to gathering prosecution evidence. In this case it is only the information obtained and not the surveillance operation that is disclosable.

1.11.5 Primary or Initial Disclosure by Prosecutor

This is covered by s. 3 of the Criminal Procedure and Investigations Act 1996. This section talks about material which '*might undermine the prosecution case against the accused*'. The courts are likely to consider this to include material which has an adverse effect on the strength of the prosecution case. Section 3 was amended by the Criminal Justice Act 2003, so for cases where the investigation commenced after 4 April 2005 the requirement is wider in that it covers material that might reasonably be considered capable of undermining the case for the prosecution against the accused, or of assisting the case for the accused. This introduces a more objective test and in effect incorporates the previous secondary disclosure test at this earlier stage. Clearly there is a need to guess what the defence case may be in considering what should be disclosed but this can be further reviewed after the defence disclosure.

Under the 1996 Act, while a schedule of all relevant material must be provided, only material that undermines the prosecution case must be disclosed at the primary or initial disclosure stage. There is only limited case law in this area but it is likely that such material will consist mainly of material which raises question marks over the strength of the prosecution case, the value of evidence given by witnesses and issues relating to identification. If officers feel that the material is not relevant to the prosecution case but may be useful to the defence in cross-examination, it may well come within the category of material which undermines the prosecution case. Disclosure of previous convictions and other matters that might affect the credibility of a witness may 'undermine the prosecution case' as it may limit the value of the witness's testimony. This factor may not be apparent at the time but may come to light after the initial disclosure, such as where it becomes known that the witness has a grudge against the defendant. This is one reason why the 1996 Act requires the decision as to whether material undermines the prosecution case to be continuously monitored throughout the case.

The Code of Practice at para. 3.5 states that:

> In conducting an investigation, the investigator should pursue all reasonable lines of inquiry, whether these point towards or away from the suspect. What is reasonable in each case will depend on the particular circumstances.

In *R (On the Application of Ebrahim)* v *Feltham Magistrates' Court* [2001] 1 WLR 1293 the court stated that the extent of the investigation should be proportionate to the seriousness of the matter being investigated. What is reasonable in a case may well depend on such factors as the staff and resources available, the seriousness of the case, the strength of evidence against the suspect and the nature of the line of inquiry to be pursued. If in doubt it is suggested the CPS are contacted for guidance.

Paragraph 5.16 of the Disclosure Manual makes important observations concerning negative results: when making inquiries 'negative results can sometimes be as significant to an investigation as positive ones'. It is impossible to define precisely when a negative result may be significant, as every case is different. However, it will include the result of any inquiry that differs from what might be expected, given the prevailing circumstances. Not only must material or information which points towards a fact or an individual be retained, but also that which casts doubt on the suspect's guilt, or implicates another person. Examples of negative information include:

- a CCTV camera that did not record the crime/location/suspect in a manner which is consistent with the prosecution case. (The fact that a CCTV camera did not function or have videotape loaded will not usually be considered relevant negative information);
- where a number of people present at a particular location at the particular time that an offence is alleged to have taken place state they saw nothing unusual;
- where a finger-mark from a crime scene cannot be identified as belonging to a known suspect;
- any other failure to match a crime scene sample with one taken from the accused.

The prosecution only have to disclose material relevant to the prosecution in question. For instance, surveillance logs concerning another matter would not need to be disclosed (*R* v *Dennis* (2000) 13 April, unreported). It is up to the prosecutor to decide on the format in which material is disclosed to the accused. If material is to be copied, s. 3(3) leaves open the question of whether this should be done by the prosecutor or by the police. The prosecutor must also provide the defence with a schedule of all non-sensitive material (s. 4(2)). This includes all other information in police possession, or material that has been examined by the police other than 'sensitive material' (this is disclosed to the prosecutor separately). 'Sensitive material' is material which it is not in the public interest to disclose. At this stage the defence is not entitled to inspect items on the schedule that have not been disclosed (s. 3(6) and (7)).

Material must not be disclosed to the extent that the court concludes it is not in the public interest to disclose it and orders accordingly or it is material whose disclosure is prohibited by s. 17 of the Regulation of Investigatory Powers Act 2000 unless it falls within the exception provided by s. 18 of the Act.

1.11.6 Time Period for Primary/Initial Disclosure

While there are provisions to set specific time periods by which primary initial disclosure must be met, none currently exist. Until such times primary initial disclosure must be made as soon as practicable after the duty arises. Where disclosure is not made within a reasonable period it could lead to the case being lost. In *R* v *Bourimech* [2002] EWCA Crim 2089 the defendant sought disclosure following the service of his defence statement of a previous crime report made by the victim. One day before the trial was scheduled to begin the crime report relating to that incident was served among other papers on the defence. This report escaped the notice of the defence until the final day of the trial. The court held that the defect in disclosure amounted to unfairness in the proceedings and the court could not be confident that if the victim had been cross-examined in relation to the previous allegation the jury might have been influenced by the credit and credibility of the witness.

The 1996 Act in effect only applies once the defendant has been committed/transferred to the Crown Court or is proceeding to trial in the magistrates'/youth court. In most cases prosecution disclosure can wait until after this time without jeopardising the defendant's right to a fair trial. However, the prosecutor must always be alive to the need to make advance disclosure of material that should be disclosed at an earlier stage (*R* v *DPP, ex parte Lee* [1999] 2 All ER 737). Examples include:

- previous convictions of a complainant or a deceased if that information could reasonably be expected to assist the defence when applying for bail;
- material that might enable a defendant to make a pre-committal application to stay the proceedings as an abuse of process;
- material that might enable a defendant to submit that he/she should only be committed for trial on a lesser charge, or perhaps that he/she should not be committed for trial at all;

- depending on what the defendant chooses to reveal about his/her case at this early stage, material that would enable the defendant and his/her legal advisers to make preparations for trial that would be significantly less effective if disclosure were delayed; for example, names of eye-witnesses whom the prosecution did not intend to use.

It should be noted that any disclosure by the prosecution prior to committal would not normally exceed the initial disclosure which, after committal, would be required by s. 3 of the 1996 Act.

1.11.7 Disclosure by the Defence

The duty on the defence to make disclosure only arises *after* the prosecution has made the initial disclosure (s. 5(1)). This duty falls into two categories:

- compulsory
- voluntary.

The disclosure required by the defence is limited to material that they intend to use at trial.

There may be occasions where the defence statement is allowed to be used in cross-examination when it is alleged that the defendant has changed his defence or in re-examination to rebut a suggestion of recent invention (*R* v *Lowe* [2003] EWCA Crim 3182).

1.11.7.1 Compulsory Disclosure by Defence (s. 5)

The duty for the defence to make disclosure does not apply to cases being tried summarily. The duty on the defence, whether the accused is represented or not, is to provide a defence statement to the court and the prosecutor within 14 days of the prosecution making primary disclosure (this period can be extended by the courts). From 4 April 2005, where there are other accused in the proceedings and the court so orders, the accused must also give a defence statement to each of the other accused specified by the court, and a request for a copy of the defence statement may be made by any co-accused. The court will set the time for disclosure to be given where a defence statement is to be given to a co-accused (s. 5(5A) to (5D)).

The defence statement should outline the defence case in general terms, including any particular defences on which he/she intends to rely. In addition, those issues, relevant to the case, which the accused disputes with the prosecution must be set out with reasons. Additionally, from 4 April 2005 the defence statement must indicate any point of law (including any point as to the admissibility of evidence or an abuse of process) which he/she wishes to take, and any authority on which he/she intends to rely for that purpose (s. 6A of the 1996 Act). This requirement to give reasons is intended to stop the defence going on a 'fishing expedition' to speculatively look at material in order to find some kind of defence.

Where the defence case involves an alibi, the statement must give details of the alibi, including the name and address of any alibi witness. In cases where there are co-accused, there is no duty to disclose this information to the other defendants, although this could be done voluntarily.

It should be noted that the changes added since 4 April 2005 define an alibi for the purposes of the defence statement as evidence tending to show that by reason of the presence of the accused at a particular place or in a particular area at a particular time, he/she was not, or was unlikely to have been, at the place where the offence is alleged to have been committed at the time of its alleged commission. Where this applies, the defence must provide details including the name, address and date of birth of any witness the accused believes is able to give evidence in support of the alibi, or as many of those details as are known to the accused when the statement is given. Where such details are not known, the statement must include any information in the accused's possession which might be of material assistance in identifying or finding any such witness (s. 6A(2) of the 1996 Act).

1.11.7.2 Voluntary Disclosure by Defence (s. 6)

The purpose of s. 6 of the 1996 Act is to allow the defence, in cases where the case is being tried summarily as a not guilty plea, to obtain further disclosure from the prosecution after the primary disclosure. This is only likely to happen where:

- the defence are not satisfied with the material disclosed at the primary disclosure stage or where they wish to examine items listed in the schedule of non-sensitive material;
- the defence wish to show the strength of their case in order to persuade the prosecution not to proceed.

If the defence decide to make a defence statement they must comply with the same conditions imposed on compulsory defence disclosure.

1.11.7.3 Effect of Failure in Defence Disclosure

If the defence fail to give a defence statement under s. 5 or, where a defence statement is provided, they:

- are outside the time limits;
- set out inconsistent defences in a defence statement or at trial put forward a different defence; or
- at trial adduce evidence in support of an alibi without having given particulars of the alibi in a defence statement, or call a witness in support of an alibi without providing details of the witness or information that might help trace the witness;

then the following sanctions may apply:

- the court or, with the leave of the court, any other party may make such comment as appears appropriate;
- the court or jury may draw such inferences as appear proper in deciding whether the accused is guilty of the offence concerned (but there must also be other evidence to convict the defendant).
- Even if the defence serve the defence statement outside the 14 days the prosecution must still consider the impact of the statement in terms of the need for any further disclosure (*Murphy* v *DPP* [2006] EWHC 1753).

1.11.8 Secondary Disclosure by Prosecutor (s. 7)/Further Disclosure

For investigations commencing after 4 April 2005, s. 7 is repealed. Once a defence statement has been provided, the prosecutor must disclose to the accused any prosecution material which has not previously been disclosed to the accused and which might be reasonably expected to assist the accused's defence as disclosed by the defence statement. However, if after reviewing the defence material he/she considers that there is no further material to disclose, he/she must give the accused a written statement that there is no such material. The discussion below still applies.

Once a defence statement has been provided (whether compulsorily or voluntarily), the prosecution must disclose any prosecution material that:

- might be reasonably expected to assist the accused's defence; and
- has not already been disclosed.

It will be a question of fact whether material in police possession might be reasonably expected to assist the defence case. If the court feels that material that was not disclosed would to any reasonable person have been expected to help the defence case, the case may fail. The test for secondary disclosure (i.e. pre 4 April 2005 investigations) is wider than primary disclosure in that this test is objective in that it requires disclosure where any reasonable person would expect the material to assist the defence whereas primary disclosure talks of 'the prosecutor's opinion'.

If there is no additional material to be disclosed then the prosecutor must give a written statement to this effect. It is not the responsibility of the prosecutor or the police to examine material held by third parties which the defence have stated they wish to examine (the defence can request this from the third party or apply for a witness summons). However, there may be occasions where matters disclosed in the defence statement lead investigators to look at material held by third parties as it might impact on the prosecution case. This stage of the disclosure process may require further inquiries prompted by the defence statement. The result of those inquiries may then have to be disclosed because it either undermines the prosecution case or it assists the accused's defence.

Material must not be disclosed to the extent that the court concludes it is not in the public interest to disclose it and orders accordingly or it is material whose disclosure is prohibited by s. 17 of the Regulation of Investigatory Powers Act 2000.

1.11.9 Continuing Duty of Prosecutor to Disclose (s. 9)

For investigations commencing after 4 April 2005, s. 9 is repealed and replaced by s. 7A, which places a continuing duty on the prosecutor at any time between the initial disclosure and the accused being acquitted or convicted or the prosecutor deciding not to proceed with the case concerned, to keep under review the question of further disclosure. In considering the need for further disclosure the prosecutor must consider whether material might reasonably be considered capable of undermining the case for the prosecution against the accused or of assisting the case for the accused. If there is any such material it must be disclosed to the accused as soon as is reasonably practicable. Consideration of what might need to be disclosed could change depending on the state of affairs at that time (including the case for the prosecution as it then stands) and so should be reviewed on a continuing basis (s. 7A(4)).

There is a duty on the prosecution to continue to review the disclosure of prosecution material right up until the case is completed (acquittal, conviction or discontinuance of the case).

For investigations that commenced before 4 April 2005, this duty to review is in two stages:

- after primary disclosure the prosecutor must review material not disclosed in terms of whether it might undermine the prosecution case (s. 9); and
- after secondary prosecution disclosure (s. 7).

The review of the material must also be in terms of whether material might be reasonably expected to assist the accused's defence as disclosed by the defence statement. This responsibility is mirrored in the Code of Practice. This is a continuous duty even after secondary disclosure has been made, failure to review could lead to an acquittal, abuse of process or even acquittal at a later appeal.

If the defence is not satisfied that the prosecution have disclosed all they should have, s. 8 of the 1996 Act allows for the defence to apply to the court for further disclosure.

1.11.10 Roles and Responsibilities under the 1996 Act

The Code of Practice identifies certain roles within the disclosure process:

- prosecutor
- officer in charge of the case (OIC)
- disclosure officer
- investigator
- supervisor of OIC and disclosure officer.

In addition, it is the responsibility of the chief officer of police of each force to put arrangements in place to ensure that the identity of the OIC and disclosure officer is recorded for each criminal investigation (Code of Practice, para. 3.3). Force policy should be followed in recording this information.

The MG6 series should be used when complying with disclosure to the CPS.

The roles described within the 1996 Act are independent of each other but all must be completed for the disclosure provisions to work (para. 3.1). All police officers involved in an investigation are likely to have to comply with the role of investigator.

Some investigations may involve a large quantity of material, both used and unused. Examples of cases where this may occur include substantial frauds; large-scale conspiracies; drug related offences involving manufacture, importation or supply; homicide or other major inquiries. These are often large or complex cases and additional guidance for these cases is provided in the CPS/Police Joint Operational Instructions (JOPI) Guidelines (2003), paras 2.113 to 2.117.

Although the police roles are independent they may be combined, the OIC may also be an investigator and, depending on the complexity of the case, may also be the disclosure officer. Whether there is one officer involved in the case or several, each role can be considered separately and must be completed fully in order that the right information can be given to the prosecutor who, ultimately, is responsible for the disclosure of material to the defence. It is important that all officers consult fully in order that the disclosure officer can complete his/her task properly. Each role is considered below as if undertaken by a different person.

1.11.11 Prosecutor

This role is defined by s. 2(3) of the 1996 Act as being 'any person acting as prosecutor whether an individual or a body'. In other words, the person who will be taking the case to court. On most occasions this will be the CPS. It would also apply to the Serious Fraud Office or the Data Protection Registrar. In the case of private prosecutions, the prosecutor is obliged to comply with the disclosure provisions of the 1996 Act but does not have to comply with the Code of Practice. The prosecutor is responsible for ensuring that primary initial disclosure is made to the defence and, where appropriate, secondary disclosure. The prosecutor should also be available to advise the OIC, disclosure officer and investigators on matters relating to the relevance of material recorded and retained by police, sensitive material and on any other disclosure issues that might arise.

Should there need to be an application to the court to withhold material because of public interest (**see para. 1.11.20**), this will be done through the prosecutor.

A more detailed explanation of the roles and responsibilities of the prosecutor are set out in the CPS/Police Joint Operational Instructions (JOPI) Guidelines (2003).

1.11.12 Officer in Charge of the Case (OIC)

This role may be performed by a person directly involved in the investigation or by a person who has been given the role of overseeing the investigation (Disclosure Code, paras 3.1 and 3.4). Whoever has this role is both responsible and accountable for the investigation (para. 3.4). (See also Disclosure Manual, para. 3.5.)

The A-G's Guidelines state that an individual must not be appointed as disclosure officer, or continue in that role, if that is likely to result in a conflict of interest, for instance, if the disclosure officer is the victim of the alleged crime which is the subject of criminal proceedings. It is suggested that the same approach should also be taken when identifying the OIC. This is an important consideration as it should be remembered that the officer is a victim and may be in need of support.

The OIC is responsible for ensuring that proper procedures are in place for the recording of information and that records and materials are retained for the required period (**see para. 1.11.19**). Paragraph 4.1 of the Code requires that the material is recorded in a durable and retrievable form and that, where possible, the record is made contemporaneously. If not, the record must be made as soon as practicable. These requirements to record information should be paramount in the mind of all investigators, as well as the OIC.

The need for contemporaneous records is also required under the Police and Criminal Evidence Act 1984 and if not complied with could affect the admissibility of important evidence (see s. 78 of the 1984 Act). Note that, under para. 4.3, relevant material to be recorded includes *negative* material. Such material might include the fact that several people at the scene of a crime were spoken to and claimed to have seen nothing, or that they saw several other people at the scene as well. This last point reiterates the position at common law; that police officers have a duty to get to the truth and allow a suspect a fair trial, a duty which includes recording and retaining material which helps the defence (this also assists in complying with article 6 of the European Convention).

Having made sure that material is recorded and retained by the investigators in the case, the OIC must make the material available to the disclosure officer (Code, para. 3.4). Where the function of disclosure officer is carried out by the OIC, there is little problem as the OIC should have a full understanding of the case and the implication of all the material collected, in terms of it being adverse to the case or being of a sensitive nature. In cases where the roles are performed by different people, it is important that the OIC and the disclosure officer consult fully about the material in order that the disclosure officer has as full an understanding of the case as he/she can in order to carry out his/her functions properly (para. 3.1 of the Disclosure Manual). This must be done in order that the disclosure officer can complete the certification stage (paras 3.1 and 9.1). These responsibilities can be delegated to other police officers or non-police staff but it remains the responsibility of the OIC to ensure that the tasks are completed (para. 3.4). It may be necessary to demonstrate to the court that these powers have been carried out.

As with all people involved in the disclosure process, s. 9 of the 1996 Act (from 4 April 2005, s. 7A) places a duty on the OIC to review material in the case. This duty is emphasised by para. 5.3 of the Code so that, where the OIC becomes aware that previously examined material which has not been disclosed has since become relevant to the case, he/she must take steps to ensure that the material is retained and inform the prosecutor so that disclosure can be made to the defence. At this stage it will be for the OIC to decide in which format that material should be retained (para. 4.1) considering the need to be able to produce it for inspection by the court.

1.11.13 Disclosure Officer

The disclosure officer creates the link between the investigation team and the prosecutor (CPS) and is therefore very important to the disclosure process. For investigations carried out by the police, generally speaking there is no restriction on who performs this role however they must be suitably trained and experienced. It could be the OIC or, equally, it could be performed by police support staff (Code, paras 2.1 and 3.4), or the disclosure officer who is responsible for providing information and material to the prosecutor at the primary disclosure stage (para. 7.1) and, where necessary, carrying out any additional work requested by the prosecutor before the primary disclosure is made (para. 7.4). The role and responsibility of the disclosure officer is set out in the Disclosure Manual at para. 3.9. It is important that the disclosure officer does not have a conflict of interest, this is set out in the A-G's Guidelines at para. 25:

> An individual must not be appointed as disclosure officer, or continue in that role, if that is likely to result in a conflict of interest, for instance, if the disclosure officer is the victim of the alleged crime which is the subject of criminal proceedings. The advice of a more senior officer must always be sought if there is doubt as to whether a conflict of interest precludes an individual acting as the disclosure officer. If thereafter the doubt remains, the advice of a prosecutor should be sought.

In some cases it will be desirable to appoint a disclosure officer at the outset of the investigation. In making this decision, the OIC should have regard to the nature and seriousness of the case, the volume of material which may be obtained or created, and the likelihood of a committal or a not guilty plea. If not appointed at the start of an investigation, a disclosure officer must be appointed in sufficient time to be able to prepare the unused material schedules for inclusion in the full file submitted to CPS (Disclosure Manual, para. 3.11).

The disclosure officer is responsible for examining all material retained by the police during the investigation (Code, para. 2.1). The first step is to establish that all material which has been retained in relation to the case has been recorded and made available for examination. The disclosure officer should verify with the OIC that all material has been made available to him/her.

There is now a recognition that the disclosure officer may need to have deputy disclosure officers, this is particularly so in investigations where there is material of a sensitive nature. There may be a number of disclosure officers, especially in large and complex cases. However, there must be a lead disclosure officer who is the focus for inquiries and whose responsibility it is to ensure that the investigator's disclosure obligations are complied with.

Disclosure officers, or their deputies, must inspect, view or listen to all relevant material that has been retained by the investigator, and the disclosure officer must provide a personal declaration to the effect that this task has been done.

There will occasionally be cases where the police investigation has been intelligence led, there may be a deputy disclosure officer appointed just to deal with intelligence material which, by its very nature, is likely to be sensitive (**see para. 1.11.20**). In cases where more than one disclosure officer has been appointed to deal with different aspects of the case, a lead disclosure officer should be identified as the single point of contact for the prosecutor. Where an officer other than the lead disclosure officer submits a disclosure schedule to the prosecutor, that officer should inform the lead disclosure officer (2005 A-G's Guidelines, para. 26).

Should the disclosure officer fail to provide information to the prosecutor within a reasonable time or to comply with any requests made by the prosecutor for additional material, this could lead to the defence not having to provide a defence statement or adverse remarks being made in court. At worse it could lead to a stay of proceedings for an abuse of process (s. 10 of the 1996 Act).

1.11.14 Duties of Investigators

Under s. 3 of the 1996 Act all previously undisclosed material that might undermine the prosecution case must be disclosed to the defence (for the position of cases since 4 April 2005, **see para. 1.11.5**). If there is no such material, then the accused must be given a written statement to that effect. This applies to all material in possession of the police or that has been inspected under the provisions of the Disclosure Code of Practice. This therefore requires the disclosure officer to know what material exists and what material has already been made available to the defence.

Where disclosure is required, the first task is to create a schedule of all *non-sensitive material*, which has been retained by the police and which does not form part of the prosecution case, which may be relevant to the investigation (Code, para. 6.3). If in doubt, the prosecutor should be consulted so that he/she can advise on the relevance of material (para. 6.1). This schedule must be endorsed by the disclosure officer to the effect that, to his/her best belief, it does not contain any sensitive material.

Initially, these schedules only have to be produced where the person is charged with an indictable offence, where the offence is triable either way or where the defendant will be tried summarily and is likely to plead not guilty. If the offence is witnessed by a police officer, or the person has admitted an either way or summary offence, then a schedule is not required unless the person then pleads not guilty. This provision has been added to avoid preparing material which will never be needed. If the person then pleads not guilty the schedule must be prepared as soon as practicable (Code, para. 6.8). However, some forces may require the schedule to be prepared in all cases.

The next step is to create a separate schedule of all sensitive material, which must include the reasons why the disclosure officer believes the material is of a sensitive nature (para. 6.4). Paragraph 6.12 gives examples of the type of material that would be classed as sensitive. If all material has been disclosed and there is no sensitive material, then a statement to that effect should be included on a schedule of sensitive material. The schedule(s) should include all material, excluding that which forms part of the prosecution case (para. 6.2).

There may be cases where material is so sensitive that the disclosure officer or other investigators consider that it should not even appear on the schedule (**see para. 1.11.20**). In these cases the prosecutor should be informed of these separately (para. 6.4). It is the responsibility of the investigator who knows the details of the sensitive material to inform the prosecutor.

Once the schedules have been completed, the disclosure officer must decide what material, if any (whether listed on the schedules or not), might undermine the prosecution case. There will be a great reliance placed on the opinion of the disclosure officer as to what material might undermine the prosecution case, and for those investigations that started after the 4 April 2005, material that might be capable of assisting the case for the accused. It is only material that falls into this category that the defence can inspect at this stage. The disclosure officer should draw the attention of the prosecutor to any material an investigator has retained which may satisfy the test for prosecution disclosure in the Act, and should explain why he/she has come to this view (para. 7.2) (depending on when the investigation started this may or may not include material that assists the prosecution case). This creates a catch-all provision and presumably requires the disclosure officer to make inquiries of the other officers in the case to ensure all material is included.

The A-G's Guidelines give guidance as to what material might potentially undermine the prosecution case. Paragraph 10 states that:

> Generally, material which can reasonably be considered capable of undermining the prosecution case against the accused or assisting the defence case will include anything that tends to show a fact inconsistent with the elements of the case that must be proved by the prosecution. Material

can fulfil the disclosure test:
(a) by the use to be made of it in cross-examination; or
(b) by its capacity to support submissions that could lead to
  (i) the exclusion of evidence; or
  (ii) a stay of proceedings; or
  (iii) a court or tribunal finding that any public authority had acted incompatibly with the accused's rights under the ECHR, or
(c) by its capacity to suggest an explanation or partial explanation of the accused's actions.

This would include any material individually or when viewed with other factors. Examples are material which:

- casts doubt upon the accuracy of any prosecution evidence;
- may point to another person, whether charged or not (including a co-accused) having involvement in the commission of the offence;
- casts doubt upon the reliability of a confession;
- might go to the credibility of a prosecution witness;
- might support a defence that is either raised by the defence or apparent from the prosecution papers;
- which may have a bearing on the admissibility of any prosecution evidence;
- relates to the defendant's mental or physical health, his/her intellectual capacity;
- relates to any ill-treatment which the defendant may have suffered when in the investigator's custody (A-G's Guidelines, paras 12 and 14).

However, what needs to be disclosed should be balanced by A-G's Guidelines, para. 3.

The case of *R* v *Hadley* [2006] EWCA Crim 2544, it is suggested, shows that the courts will err on the side of caution when deciding if material should be disclosed as possibly undermining the prosecution case and that this approach should be considered prior to trial to avoid later appeals. In this case the court held that, given the importance of disclosure in ensuring a fair trial, the court is likely to be slow to accept that the safety of a conviction is unaffected if it was satisfied that a substantial volume of disclosable material is wrongly withheld from the acccused, unless the court could be satisfied that the evidence tending to establish guilt is so strong that the undisclosed material could have made no difference to the outcome of the case.

1.11.14.1 Completing the Schedules

It is important that the schedules themselves are completed fully. Guidance is given by paras 6.9 to 6.11 of the Code and in detail in the Disclosure Manual, chs 6 to 8. The schedule should have each item numbered consecutively with a description of the item in sufficient detail to allow the prosecutor, when examining the schedule to make an informed decision about the importance of the item, and whether it needs to be disclosed to the defence, in addition to the items suggested by the disclosure officer, as undermining the prosecution case or assisting the defence (A-G's Guidelines, para. 29). While items should be listed separately, there may be occasions where items are similar or the same, in which case these may be listed together (Disclosure Manual, para. 7.4). This also applies to sensitive schedules, in so far as is possible without compromising the confidentiality of the information (see also the Disclosure Manual, para. 7.4). Paragraph 9 of the A-G's Guidelines also allow in some circumstances, because of the large volumes of material, not to examine all the material. If such material is not examined by the investigator or disclosure officer, and it is not intended to examine it, its existence should be made known to the accused in general terms.

The schedules and copies of any material which is considered to undermine the prosecution case should be given to the prosecutor (Code, paras 7.1 to 7.3). The disclosure officer should include an explanation as to why they consider that the material should be disclosed (para. 7.2). As it is unlikely that the prosecutor will have a chance to examine all the material, it is important that the disclosure officer gives clear reasons in his/her report. For the type of material which might undermine the prosecution case, **see para. 1.11.8**.

In addition to the schedules and copies of material which undermine the prosecution case or, where appropriate, assists the accused, para. 7.3 requires the disclosure officer to provide a copy of any material which falls into the following categories:

- information provided by an accused person which indicates an explanation for the offence with which he/she has been charged;
- any material casting doubt on the reliability of a confession;
- any material casting doubt on the reliability of a prosecution witness;
- any other material which the investigator believes may satisfy the test for prosecution disclosure in the Act.

The following items should also be considered when deciding on initial disclosure in cases where the disclosure is in the public interest (that is where they are not '*sensitive material*'). The material is (A-G's Guidelines, para. 12) (see also Disclosure Manual, para. 10.1):

- Any material casting doubt upon the accuracy of any prosecution evidence.
- Any material which may point to another person, whether charged or not (including a co-accused) having involvement in the commission of the offence.
- Any material which may cast doubt upon the reliability of a confession.
- Any material that might go to the credibility of a prosecution witness.
- Any material that might support a defence that is either raised by the defence or apparent from the prosecution papers.
- Any material which may have a bearing on the admissibility of any prosecution evidence.

The disclosure officer must certify that, to the best of his/her knowledge, all material which has been retained by police and made available to them has been revealed to the prosecutor in accordance with the para. 9.1 of the Code. While the disclosure officer may not always be able to know if all material has been made available to him/her, he/she should consult with the OIC to verify as far as possible that it has been (para. 3.1). The disclosure officer should be mindful of the need to demonstrate that he/she has taken all reasonable steps should it transpire that full disclosure had not been made.

Often the police may not possess all the material that could become relevant in a case. It may be that this material has been inspected and a decision made that the material is not relevant to the case at this stage, or that it was not necessary to inspect the material. To cover the risk of material being lost, the disclosure officer should inform third parties of the investigation and invite them to retain material. The disclosure officer should inform the prosecutor that third parties may have such material (para. 3.1). (**See para. 1.11.21** for third party material.)

Under para. 8.1 of the Code, information provided by the disclosure officer may be accepted by the prosecutor or might be returned with requests for additional information or for amendments to be made to the schedule or items to be disclosed to the defence. The disclosure officer should comply with any instructions given by the prosecutor and any request for the inspection or copying of material should be met (para. 7.4). If the disclosure officer and OIC consider that material is so sensitive it should not be copied, the disclosure officer should inform the prosecutor and make arrangements for the prosecutor to inspect the material instead (para. 7.4). If copies of materials which are not in writing are requested, the disclosure officer and prosecutor must agree on the format of how it will be provided to the prosecutor (para. 7.5).

It should be remembered that the prosecutor is required to advise the disclosure officer of any omissions or amendments or where there are insufficient or unclear descriptions, or where there has been a failure to provide schedules at all. The disclosure officer must then take all necessary remedial action and provide properly completed schedules to the prosecutor. Failure to do so may result in the matter being raised with a senior officer. There may also be occasions where schedules need to be edited; this is covered in the Disclosure Manual at paras 7.7 and 7.8.

Once this stage is complete, the prosecutor is able to make initial disclosure to the defence. It will be the responsibility of the disclosure officer to disclose material to the defence if requested to do so by the prosecutor (Code, para. 10.1).

The defence do not have to provide a defence statement until such times as initial disclosure has been made, they then (subject to an extension from the court) have 14 days in which to serve their defence statement. Clearly the sooner initial disclosure is made the more time, in theory, the disclosure officer will have to complete his/her responsibilities under secondary disclosure before the next effective court date.

1.11.14.2 Duties of the Disclosure Officer: Secondary Disclosure/Ongoing Disclosure

For investigations that commenced before 4 April 2005 this stage of the disclosure process involved a review of the unused material to see whether it undermined the prosecution case or assisted the defence case. Since 4 April 2005, consideration of the unused material in terms of its assisting the accused is made from the start of the disclosure process and therefore this will be just a review which is further informed by knowing what the defence statement contains.

Once initial disclosure has been made, the defence may provide a defence statement setting out their case, together with reasons why they wish to inspect additional items on the schedule which have not been disclosed. Under para. 8.3 of the Code, once the defence statement has been provided, the disclosure officer must:

- review the material which is contained on the schedules; and
- inform the prosecutor of any material which might reasonably be expected to assist the defence case.

This role will often be performed in conjunction with the prosecutor and, at times, may even be undertaken by the prosecutor. However, the Code of Practice does require the disclosure officer to carry out this function and as such there is a duty to review this material even if it is also done by the prosecutor. This responsibility remains with the disclosure officer and must be complied with. It should be remembered that the review of disclosure is based on the defence statement, not a full investigation.

After the material has been reviewed, further disclosure can be made to the defence. As with the initial disclosure stage, the disclosure officer must certify that, to the best of his/her knowledge, all material which has been retained by the police and made available to them has been revealed to the prosecutor in accordance with para. 9.1 of the Code. Again, while the disclosure officer may not always know if all material has been made available to him/her, he/she should consult with the OIC to verify as far as possible that it has been (Code, para. 3.1). Guidance on continuing duty to review is provided in chapter 14 of the Disclosure Manual.

Where the defence statement points the prosecution to other lines of inquiry, e.g. the investigation of an alibi, or where forensic expert evidence is involved, the disclosure officer should inform the officer in charge of the investigation and copy the defence statement to him/her, together with any CPS advice provided if appropriate (Disclosure Manual, para. 15.17).

1.11.14.3 Continuing Duty of Disclosure Officer

The disclosure officer has a continuing duty to review material for items that should be disclosed to the defence as undermining the prosecution case or which might assist the defence case (Code, para. 8.3).

In *R* v *Tyrell* [2004] EWCA Crim 3279 this responsibility was clearly outlined. The court held that there was an obligation to consider whether there was any material in the hands of the prosecution which might undermine the case against the applicants or might reasonably be expected to assist the disclosed defences. In addition, the Crown had to consider whether there was any material which might be relevant to an issue which might feature in the trial; this clearly required a continuing duty. In this case the court found that disclosure had been considered many times as the case progressed in relation to a variety of issues as they arose and ensured a fair trial.

1.11.14.4 Disclosing Material to the Defence

The disclosure officer may also be involved in the actual disclosure of material to the defence which is covered in para. 10 of the Code of Practice.

The court can also order disclosure of material which the prosecution contend is sensitive. In such cases it may be appropriate to seek guidance on whether to disclose the material or offer no evidence thereby protecting the sensitive material or the source of that material (e.g. where informants or surveillance techniques are involved).

The disclosure officer can make disclosure to the defence by either:

- providing copies of the material; or
- allowing the defence to inspect the material (para. 10.3 of the Codes).

Where a request is made for copies, the material must be provided unless it is not practicable or desirable to do so. Examples of such occasions are given in para. 10.3 of the Code. In cases where the material is not recorded in a written format (for instance an audio or video tape) then the disclosure officer has a discretion whether to provide a copy of the item or transcript of what is contained on the tape. This must be certified as a true copy of the tape (para. 10.4). For further guidance, see the Disclosure Manual, paras 10.16, 10.17 and 12.25. Forces may have instructions as to providing further copies when requested by the defence in relation to procedures and costs. It is suggested that where copies are provided, some proof of delivery should be obtained.

1.11.14.5 Duties of Investigators

The roles of investigator may involve just one officer or several officers. An 'investigation' may be completed in a very short time, e.g. from stopping a car, discovering it was stolen, arresting the suspect, obtaining a victim statement and charging the suspect. Alternatively, the case may involve a long, protracted inquiry with several officers, various witnesses and numerous suspects, arrests and interviews.

An officer who is classed as an investigator must pursue all reasonable lines of inquiry (Code, para. 3.5) and having done so retain all material which is relevant to the case (**see para. 1.11.19**), whether or not it is helpful to the prosecution (Code, para. 5.1). Failure to do so could lead to a miscarriage of justice. In *R* v *Poole* (2003) 1 WLR 2931 Y provided a statement to police in a murder case. It transpired that N had been with Y at the relevant time and this cast doubt over Y's evidence. The police did not follow up the inconsistencies. The Court of Appeal held that the failure to disclose N's evidence was a material irregularity which in part led to a successful appeal by the defendant. The investigator also has a responsibility to identify material that could be sensitive and bring this to the attention of the CPS (**see para. 1.11.20**). Where material is identified steps must be taken to record and retain the material. For information recorded on computers, see the JOPI Guidelines from para. 2.29 onwards.

The issue of sensitive material is discussed below (**see para. 1.11.20**). Often it is only the investigator who obtained the evidence who will be fully aware of the sensitive nature of the material. In order to balance the need to protect sensitive material yet give the prosecutor full details of why the material is sensitive, para. 6.14 of the Code places the responsibility of informing the prosecutor of details of sensitive material on the investigator. The investigator must take steps to ensure the prosecutor can inspect the material. This does not mean that the disclosure officer or any other officer cannot carry out this function; simply that the investigator must ensure that it is carried out.

When completing the disclosure schedules the investigating officer must be mindful that there may be cases where material is so sensitive that he/she or other investigators consider that it should not even appear on the schedule (such as where disclosure would be likely to lead directly to the loss of life or directly threaten national security (para. 6.13)). It is the responsibility of the investigator who knows the details of the sensitive material to inform the prosecutor.

1.11.14.6 Continuing Duty of Investigators

The continuing duty of disclosure imposed by ss. 7 and 9 of the 1996 Act (for cases since 4 April 2005, both s. 7 and s. 9 have been replaced by s. 7A of the 1996 Act) means that investigators have a corresponding duty to keep under review the revelation of material which meets the test for disclosure. It is therefore important that investigators are aware of which material might undermine the prosecution case and which might assist the defence case. It is also important therefore that investigators are aware of the content of defence statements provided after primary disclosure. This will therefore require consultation between OICs, disclosure officers and investigators. If investigators do not carry out their function properly, this has an impact on all the others involved in the disclosure process and may lead to disclosure on the defence being defective, which in turn could lead to a miscarriage of justice or stay of proceedings.

1.11.15 Supervisor of OIC and Disclosure Officer

In all cases there must be an OIC and a disclosure officer. If for any reason, either the OIC or the disclosure officer can no longer perform their respective tasks, para. 3.7 of the Code places a responsibility on that person's supervisor or the police officer in charge of investigations within the police force concerned to assign another person to take over that role. It is suggested, that this requires a supervisor to know what cases their staff are involved in and who the OIC and disclosure officer is in each of those cases.

1.11.16 Definitions

Paragraph 2.1 of the Code provides definitions to be used when considering the Code and some additional guidance is provided below.

1.11.17 Relevant Material

The 1996 Act is concerned with the disclosure of material which is obtained during the course of a criminal investigation and which may be relevant to the investigation. Material can be in any form and should be widely interpreted. This applies to any material coming to the knowledge of officers involved in the case at any stage of the investigation or even after a suspect has been charged. This is material which the investigator, OIC or disclosure officer considers has some bearing on any offence being investigated or any people being investigated for those offences or any of the surrounding circumstances.

The material will be *relevant* whether it is beneficial to the prosecution case, weakens the prosecution case or assists the defence case. It is not only material that will become 'evidence' in the case that should be considered, any information, record or thing which may have a bearing on the case can be material for the purposes of disclosure. The way in which evidence has been obtained may in itself be relevant.

What is relevant to the offence is once again a question of fact and will not include everything. In *DPP* v *Metten* (1999) 22 January, unreported, it was claimed that the constables who had arrested the defendant had known the identities of potential witnesses to the arrest and these had not been disclosed. The court said that this was not relevant to the case as it did not fall within the definition of an investigation in s. 2(1) of the Criminal Proceedings and Investigations Act 1996 in that it concerned the time of arrest not what happened at the time the *offence* was committed. Paragraphs 5.4 and 5.5 of the Code give guidance on items that might be considered to be relevant material in a case. They include:

- crime reports (including crime report forms, relevant parts of incident report books or police officer's notebooks);
- custody records;
- records which are derived from tapes of telephone messages (for example, 999 calls) containing descriptions of an alleged offence or offender;
- final versions of witness statements (and draft versions where their content differs from the final version), including any exhibits mentioned (unless these have been returned to their owner on the understanding that they will be produced in court if required);
- interview records (written records, or audio or video tapes, of interviews with actual or potential witnesses or suspects);
- communications between the police and experts such as forensic scientists, reports of work carried out by experts, and schedules of scientific material prepared by the expert for the investigator, for the purposes of criminal proceedings;
- records of the first description of a suspect by each potential witness who purports to identify or describe the suspect, whether or not the description differs from that of subsequent descriptions by that or other witnesses;
- any material casting doubt on the reliability of a witness;
- information provided by an accused person which indicates an explanation for the offence with which he/she has been charged;
- any material casting doubt on the reliability of a confession;
- any material casting doubt on the reliability of a prosecution witness.

Relevant material may relate to the credibility of witnesses such as previous convictions, the fact that they have a grudge against the defendant or even the weather conditions for the day if relevant to the issue of identification. It may include information that house to house inquiries were made and that no one witnessed anything.

It should be noted that where material is available to police from a particular source, e.g. local authority records, a decision that some of the material is relevant does not mean that it all has to be disclosed. This point is reinforced by the case of *R* v *Abbott* where the Court of Appeal held that the defendant was not entitled to blanket disclosure of all the files. He was certainly not entitled to documents which were not relevant to the case.

1.11.18 Material that Undermines the Prosecution Case

There is only limited case law in this area but it is likely that such material will consist mainly of material which raises question marks over the strength of the prosecution case, the value of evidence given by witnesses and issues relating to identification. If officers feel that the material is not relevant to the prosecution case but may be useful to the defence in cross-examination, it may well come within the category of material which undermines the prosecution case.

Disclosure of previous convictions and other matters that might affect the credibility of a witness may 'undermine the prosecution case' as it may limit the value of the witness's testimony. This factor may not be apparent at the time but may come to light after primary disclosure, such as where it becomes known that the witness has a grudge against the defendant. This is one reason why the 1996 Act requires the decision as to whether material undermines the prosecution case to be continually monitored throughout the case. If in doubt advice should be sought from the CPS.

The amendment to s. 3 of the 1996 Act which adds **might reasonably be considered capable** of undermining the case for the prosecution against the accused, introduces a more objective test as to what needs to be disclosed.

1.11.19 Retention of Material

Clearly in order to disclose material to the defence there is a need first to find it and secondly retain it. Retention of material applies to documents and other evidence, including videos. Failure to retain material could lead to the prosecution losing the case, particularly where the court feel its absence will lead to the defendant not being able to receive a fair trial (article 6 of the European Convention). In *Mouat* v *DPP* [2001] 1 WLR 1293 the defendant had been charged with speeding. Police officers had recorded a video of the defendant driving at speed and had showed the video to the defendant prior to charge but had later recorded over it. The defendant contended that he had been intimidated by the unmarked police car being driven only inches from his rear bumper. The policy of the force was to keep videos for 28 days, unless they recorded an offence, in which case they were kept for 12 months. The court held that the police were under a duty to retain the video tapes at least until the end of the suspended enforcement period, during which time the defendant was entitled to consider whether he wished to contest his liability in court.

In considering what material should be retained in an investigation consideration should be given to any force orders, what powers there are to seize and retain the said material, as well as the Disclosure Code and the A-G's Guidelines. Where an investigator discovers material that is relevant to the case, he/she must record that information or retain the material (Code, para. 4.1). Once again, this duty to record and retain material relevant to the case includes material that would be regarded as negative to the prosecution case (Code, para. 4.3). This does not just mean witness statements and evidence from inquiries but would include arrest notes, custody records, forensic reports, records of interview and all other material the investigator is aware of that might be relevant to the investigation. To this end, para. 5.1 of the Code places a duty on the investigator to retain all relevant material. Paragraph 5.1 of the Code states that:

> The investigator must retain material obtained in a criminal investigation which may be relevant to the investigation. Material may be photographed, video-recorded, captured digitally or otherwise retained in the form of a copy rather than the original at any time, if the original is perishable; the original was supplied to the investigator rather than generated by him and is to be returned to its owner; or the retention of a copy rather than the original is reasonable in all the circumstances.

Often, particularly at the early stages of an investigation (sometimes not until the defence statement is provided outlining the defence case), it will not be possible to know whether material is relevant. If in doubt it should be recorded and placed on the schedule of undisclosed material. Throughout the case, investigators and all others involved should continually review the material in the light of the investigation. Any material which becomes relevant and which has not been disclosed should be disclosed and, where it has not been retained, the OIC should be informed in order that he/she can decide what action to take (Code, para. 5.3).

When deciding if the material should be retained the A-G's Guidelines provide that: 'investigators should always err on the side of recording and retaining material where they have any doubt as to whether it may be relevant' (A-G's Guidelines, para. 24).

It is important to note that the material itself does not have to be admissible in court for it to undermine the prosecution case. This point was made in *R* v *Preston* (1994) 98 Cr App R 405, where it was said that:

> In the first place, the fact that an item of information cannot be put in evidence by a party does not mean that it is worthless. Often, the train of inquiry which leads to the discovery of evidence which is admissible at a trial may include an item which is not admissible, and this may apply, although less frequently, to the defence as well as the prosecution.

In cases where officers are in doubt as to whether material should be recorded and retained, the prosecutor should be consulted. If this cannot be done, the material should be retained and recorded. If the material is not in a format that can be retained (ofor instance because it was said orally), it should be recorded in a durable and retrievable form (Code, paras 4.1 and 4.2).

If during the lifetime of a case, the OIC becomes aware that material which has been examined during the course of an investigation, but not retained, becomes relevant as a result of new developments, para. 5.3 of the Code will apply. That officer should take steps to recover the material wherever practicable, or ensure that it is preserved by the person in possession of it (Disclosure Manual, para. 5.25).

1.11.19.1 CCTV

CCTV is becoming more prevalent in towns and cities, both from 'in store' cameras and those run through local authorities. The likelihood of an incident being caught on CCTV can be quite strong, which raises the question as to the responsibility of the police to investigate the possibility of there being a tape and retaining the tape. This point was considered in *R (On the Application of Ebrahim)* v *Feltham Magistrates' Court* [2001] 1 WLR 1293. These cases related to the obliteration of video evidence. In coming to their judgment, the court considered a number of previous decisions where the police were not required to retain CCTV evidence. The general question for the court was whether the prosecution had been under a duty to obtain or retain video evidence. If there was no such duty, the prosecution could not have abused the process of the court simply because the material was no longer available, i.e. it was a reasonable line of inquiry (as to whether they were under a duty to obtain the evidence, **see para. 1.11.14.5**). *Ebrahim* shows that CCTV footage does not necessarily have to be retained in all cases. *R* v *Dobson* [2001] All ER (D) 109 (Jul) followed *Ebrahim*. Dobson had been convicted of arson with intent to endanger life, his defence being that he was elsewhere at the time. There had been a strong possibility that the route that Dobson claimed to have taken would have been covered by CCTV but it would have depended on which side of the road he had been using and which way the cameras were pointing at the time. Dobson's solicitors had not asked for the tapes to be preserved at interview and the police confirmed that the possibility of investigating the tapes had been overlooked. The tapes had been overwritten after 31 days. In following the principles set down in *Ebrahim*, the police, by their own admissions, had failed in their duty to obtain and retain the relevant footage. While there was plainly a degree of prejudice in Dobson being deprived of the opportunity of checking the footage in the hope that it supported his case, that prejudice was held not to have seriously prejudiced his case given the uncertainty of the likelihood that it would assist and the fact that Dobson had equally been in a position to appreciate the possible existence and significance of the tapes. The fact that there was no suggestion of malice or intentional omission by the police was also an important consideration for the court.

1.11.19.2 Complaints Against Police Officers Involved in a Case

Not only might the credibility of witnesses undermine the prosecution case, but so too might complaints against officers involved in the case, together with any occasions where officers have not been believed in court in the past. In these cases, it will be necessary to decide whether this information should be disclosed to the defence and, if disclosed, in how much detail. This question is probably best answered by the following extract from advice given to prosecutors by the DPP:

> It is, of course, necessary in the first instance for the police to bring such matters to the notice of the prosecutor, but it is submitted that the prosecutor should have a greater element of discretion than with the disclosure of previous convictions. With convictions against prosecution witnesses, disclosure normally follows, whereas in relation to disciplinary findings regard should be had to the nature of the finding and its likely relevance to the matters in issue. Findings which involve some element of dishonesty should invariably be disclosed, while matters such as disobedience to orders, neglect of duty and discreditable conduct will often have no relevance to the officer's veracity or the guilt or otherwise of a defendant. Certainly, there should be no duty on the prosecution to disclose details of unsubstantiated complaints even though this is a popular type of inquiry from some defence representatives. The imposition of such a duty would only encourage the making of false complaints in the hope that they might be used to discredit an officer in the future.

Detailed guidance is provided in chapter 18 of the Disclosure Manual.

The prosecutor should be informed if officers involved in a case have discipline matters on their record. This may well appear on the schedule in order that the prosecutor can consider the matter and amend the schedule if necessary. It is suggested that advice should be sought from the prosecutor as to what information is included on the schedule and if disclosure is to be made, advice on what information to be included should also be sought.

Some guidance is given by the courts. In *R* v *Edwards* [1991] 2 All ER 266 the court held that a disciplinary finding and reprimand of a DCI for countersigning interview notes which had been wrongly re-written in another case should have been disclosed to the defence. *R* v *Guney* [1998] Cr App R 242 followed *Edwards*, in *Guney* six police officers went to the defendant's home with a warrant to search for drugs. Three of the officers had formerly been members of a squad which had been subject to 'considerable internal police interest'. The court held that the defence was not entitled to be informed of every occasion when any officer had given evidence 'unsuccessfully' or whenever allegations were made against him/her. In this case the information should have been disclosed. The court went on to say that the records available to the CPS should include transcripts of any decisions of the Court of Appeal Criminal Division where convictions were quashed because of the misconduct or lack of veracity of identified police officers as well as cases stopped by the trial judge or discontinued on the same basis. The systematic collection of such material was preferable to the existing haphazard arrangement.

Once again, if in doubt advice should be sought from the CPS.

Disclosure of Statements in Cases of Complaints against the Police

Statements made by witnesses during an investigation of a complaint against a police officer are disclosable, however the timing of the disclosure may be controlled. In *R* v *Police Complaints Authority, ex parte Green* [2002] EWCA Civ 389, the Court of Appeal stated that there is no requirement to disclose witness statements to eyewitness complainants during the course of an investigation. The evidence of such complainants could be contaminated and, therefore, disclosure would risk hindering or frustrating the very purpose of the investigation. A complainant's legitimate interests were appropriately and adequately safeguarded by his/her right to a thorough and independent investigation, to contribute to the evidence, to be kept informed of the progress of the investigation and to be given reasoned conclusions on completion of the investigation. However, a complainant had no right to participate in the investigation as though he/she were supervising it. The general rule was that complainants, whether victims or next of kin, were not entitled to the disclosure of witness statements used in the course of a police investigation until its conclusion at the earliest.

Police complaints and disciplinary files may also fall within sensitive material that does not have to be disclosed (*Halford* v *Sharples* [1992] 1 WLR 736). However this would not apply to written complaints against the police prompting investigations or the actual statements obtained during the investigations, although immunity may be claimed in the case of a particular document by reason of its contents (*Chief Constable of the West Midlands Police, ex parte Wiley* [1995] 1 AC 274). However, the working papers and reports prepared by the investigating officers do form a class which is entitled to immunity, and therefore production of such material should be ordered only where the public interest in disclosure of their contents outweighs the public interest in preserving confidentiality (*Taylor* v *Anderton* [1995] 1 WLR 447).

1.11.20 Sensitive Material

This is material which the investigator believes is not in the public interest to disclose. While the general principle that governs the 1996 Act and article 6 of the European Convention is that material should not be withheld from the defence, sensitive material is an exception to this. In *Van Mechden* v *Netherlands* (1997) 25 EHRR 647, the court stated that in some cases it may be necessary to withhold certain evidence from the defence so as to preserve the fundamental rights of another individual or to safeguard an important public interest. However, only such measures restricting the rights of the defence which are strictly necessary are permissible under article 6. It should be noted that the court did recognise that the entitlement of disclosure of relevant evidence was not an absolute right but could only be restricted as was strictly necessary. In *R* v *Keane* [1994] WLR 746 Lord Taylor CJ stated that 'the judge should carry out a balancing exercise, having regard both to the weight of the public interest in non-disclosure and to the importance of the documents to the issues of interest, present and potential, to the defence, and if the disputed material might prove a defendant's innocence or avoid a miscarriage of justice, the balance came down resoundingly in favour of disclosure'.

Decisions as to what should be withheld from the defence are a matter for the court and where necessary an application to withhold the material must be made to the court (*R* v *Ward* [1993] 1 WLR 619). The application of public interest immunity was considered by the House of Lords in *R* v *H* [2004] 2 AC 134. In this case the defendants were charged with conspiracy to supply a class A drug following a covert police investigation, and sought disclosure of material held by the prosecution relating to the investigation. The prosecution resisted the disclosure on grounds of public interest immunity. The court held that if the material did not weaken the prosecution case or strengthen the defence, there would be no requirement to disclose it. Only in truly borderline cases should the prosecution seek a judicial ruling on the disclosability of material in its hands. In considering any disclosure issue the trial judge had constantly to bear in mind the overriding principle that deorgation from the principle of full disclosure had always to be the minimum necessary to protect the public interest in question and must never imperil the overall fairness of the trial. Such applications will usually be made at the primary or secondary disclosure stages. Once material is considered to be sensitive then it should be disclosed only if the public interest application fails (unless abandoning the case is considered more appropriate) or with the express written approval of the Treasury Solicitor. Such material is not as wide as it seems, for instance it does not mean evidence which might harm the prosecution case. This category is quite limited and the Code of Practice, at para. 6.12, gives a number of examples of such material. It will be for the disclosure officer to decide what material, if any, falls into this category. Guidance is provided in chapters 13 and 18 of the Disclosure Manual.

Paragraph 6.12 states that depending on the circumstances, examples of such material may include the following among others:

- material relating to national security;
- material received from the intelligence and security agencies;
- material relating to intelligence from foreign sources which reveals sensitive intelligence gathering methods;
- material given in confidence;
- material relating to the identity or activities of informants, or undercover police officers, or witnesses, or other persons supplying information to the police who may be in danger if their identities are revealed;
- material revealing the location of any premises or other place used for police surveillance, or the identity of any person allowing a police officer to use them for surveillance;
- material revealing, either directly or indirectly, techniques and methods relied upon by a police officer in the course of a criminal investigation, for example covert surveillance techniques, or other methods of detecting crime;
- material whose disclosure might facilitate the commission of other offences or hinder the prevention and detection of crime;
- material upon the strength of which search warrants were obtained;
- material containing details of persons taking part in identification parades;
- material supplied to an investigator during a criminal investigation which has been generated by an official of a body concerned with the regulation or supervision of bodies corporate or of persons engaged in financial activities, or which has been generated by a person retained by such a body;
- material supplied to an investigator during a criminal investigation which relates to a child or young person and which has been generated by a local authority social services department, an Area Child Protection Committee or other party contacted by an investigator during the investigation;
- material relating to the private life of a witness.

Many of these items are included within the common law principles of public interest immunity. The case law in this area will still apply to decisions regarding the disclosure of such material. These groups are not exclusive and the areas most likely to apply will be those concerning the protection of intelligence and intelligence methods. In any consideration as to what should be withheld the provisions of part II of the Regulation of Investigatory Powers Act 2000 should be referred to. Part II of the Act will make provision, not only for the gathering and recording of intelligence, but also disclosure of any material gained and methods used. Claims to withhold material may be made by parties other than the prosecutor (who would do so on behalf of the police). In some cases, the relevant minister or the Attorney-General may intervene to claim immunity. Alternatively, the claim to immunity may be made by the party seeking to withhold the evidence, either on its own initiative or at the request of the relevant government department.

Guidance is also provided in paras 20 to 22 of the A-G's Guidelines, even where an application is made to the court to withhold material a prosecutor should aim to disclose as much of the material as he/she properly can (by giving the defence redacted or edited copies of summaries). *R* v *Davis* (1993) unreported, sets out further guidance when applying for immunity from disclosure. The court said that the procedure to be adopted in such cases depended upon the sensitivity of the material for which public interest immunity was claimed. In most cases where the prosecution sought to avoid disclosure the matter could be resolved by an *inter partes* hearing but in ultra sensitive cases the prosecution should notify the defence of an *ex parte* application which it would make. Where, however, disclosure of the category of material for which immunity was to be claimed would 'let the cat out of the bag' the prosecution might apply to the court without putting the defence on notice. Where the court ruled for non-disclosure before the hearing, the decision was not necessarily final as the situation might change and issues might emerge so that the public interest in non-disclosure was eclipsed by the need to secure fairness for the defendant. The court would therefore have to continually monitor the issue and it was desirable that the same judge who made the ruling should hear the whole case or, if that was impossible, the court must continually keep in mind the ruling which had been made. If there was such a change the prosecution must be told so that it could decide whether to disclose or offer no further evidence.

In deciding whether material attracts public interest immunity the court will have to be satisfied that the material in no way helps the defence or undermines the prosecution case. Where the material related to secret or confidential systems they should not be revealed as this would aid serious criminal enterprise in the future (*R* v *Templair* (2003) unreported).

Where police consider that material should not be disclosed due to their sensitive nature the Disclosure Manual should be followed. These are covered at paras 8.5 to 8.27. Some of the key points from these paragraphs include:

- Consultation should take place at a senior level, and a senior officer (who may be independent of the investigation) should be involved.
- The consultation should cover:
  - the reasons why the material is said to be sensitive;
  - the degree of sensitivity said to attach to the material, i.e. why it is considered that disclosure will create a real risk of serious prejudice to an important public interest;
  - the consequences of revealing to the defence:
    - the material itself,
    - the category of the material,
    - the fact that an application is being made;
  - the apparent significance of the material to the issues in the trial;
  - the involvement of any third parties in bringing the material to the attention of the police;
  - where the material is likely to be the subject of an order for disclosure, what police views are regarding continuance of the prosecution.
- Any submission that is to be made to the court will be signed by the prosecutor, and by the senior officer, who will state that to the best of his/her knowledge and belief the assertions of fact on which the submission is based are correct. In applications for public interest immunity the CPS has an obligation to ensure that all such material is in their possession and the police have a duty to pass the material on (*R* v *Menga* [1998] Crim LR 58).
- whether it is possible to disclose the material without compromising its sensitivity.

Care must be taken to safeguard material that is sensitive and keep it separate from other material because if the material subject to a public interest immunity order for non-disclosure is inadvertently disclosed by the prosecution to lawyers for the defendants, those lawyers cannot be ordered not to further disseminate that material to any third party, including their own clients (*R* v *G* [2004] 1 WLR 2932).

1.11.20.1 Informants

The courts recognise the need to protect the identity of informants to ensure that the supply of information about criminal activities does not dry up and for their own safety. However, there may be occasions where if the case is to continue the identity of the informant will have to be disclosed.

> . . . if the judge should be of opinion that the disclosure of the name of the informant is necessary or right in order to show the prisoner's innocence, then one public policy is in conflict with another public policy, and that which says that an innocent man is not to be condemned when his innocence can be proved is the policy that must prevail.
>
> (*Marks* v *Beyfus* (1890) 25 QBD 494, per Lord Esher MR at p. 498)

This is particularly so where there is a suggestion that an informant has participated in the events constituting, surrounding or following the crime, the judge must consider whether this role so impinges on an issue of interest to the defence, present or potential, as to make disclosure necessary (*R* v *Turner* [1995] 1 WLR 264).

In *R* v *Agar* [1990] 2 All ER 442 the court held that if a defence was manifestly frivolous and doomed to failure, a trial judge might conclude that it must be sacrificed to the general public interest in the protection of informers. But if there was a tenable defence the rule of public policy protecting informants was outweighed by the stronger public interest in allowing a defendant to put forward a case. In this case the defendant alleged that the police had arranged with an informer to ask the accused to go to the informer's house, where drugs allegedly found on him had been planted by the police and the court ruled that the disclosure of the informant should have been made.

The need to disclose details of informants has been considered by the Court of Appeal in two recent cases. The first case, *R* v *Denton* [2002] EWCA Crim 72, concerned a defendant who was a police informer. The defendant was charged with murder and alleged that he had been told by his police handlers not to tell his lawyers about his status. The Court held that there was no duty for the Crown to disclose to the defence, or to seek a ruling from the judge, as to any information regarding an accused being a police informer. On any common sense view the material had already been disclosed to the defendant and the Crown had no duty to supply the defendant with information with which he was already familiar. This last point may also be relevant to other situations. The second case, *R* v *Dervish* [2002] 2 Cr App R 105 concerned an undercover operation that was commenced after an informant gave information. The court held in this case that the public interest in protecting the identification of an informant had to be balanced against the right of the defendant to a fair trial, if there was material that might assist the defence, the necessity for the defendant to have a fair trial would outweigh the other interests in the case and the material would have to be disclosed or the prosecution discontinued. There had been no such material in this case.

Where an informant who has participated in the crime is called to give evidence at the trial there would have to be very strong reasons for this fact not to be disclosed (*R* v *Patel* [2002] Crim LR 304).

1.11.20.2 Observation Points and the *Johnson* Ruling

R v *Rankine* [1986] 2 WLR 1075 considering previous cases stated that it was the rule that police officers should not be required to disclose sources of their information, whether those sources were paid informers or public spirited citizens, subject to a discretion to admit to avoid a miscarriage of justice and that observation posts were in this rule.

In *R* v *Johnson* [1988] 1 WLR 1377, the appellant was convicted of supplying drugs. The only evidence against him was given by police officers, who testified that, while stationed in private premises in a known drug-dealing locality, they had observed him selling drugs. The defence applied to cross-examine the officers on the exact location of the observation posts, in order to test what they could see, having regard to the layout of the street and the objects in it. In the jury's absence the prosecution called evidence as to the difficulty of obtaining assistance from the public, and the desire of the occupiers, who were also occupiers at the time of the offence, that their names and addresses should not be disclosed because they feared for their safety.

The judge ruled that the exact location of the premises need not be revealed. The appeal was dismissed; although the conduct of the defence was to some extent affected by the restraints placed on it, this led to no injustice. The jury were well aware of the restraints, and were most carefully directed about the very special care they had to give to any disadvantage they may have brought to the defence. *Johnson* was applied and approved in *R* v *Hewitt* (1992) 95 Cr App R 81 (see also *R* v *Grimes* [1994] Crim LR 213).

In *Johnson*, Watkins LJ at pp. 1385–6 gave the following guidance as to the minimum evidential requirements needed if disclosure is to be protected:

(a) The police officer in charge of the observations to be conducted, no one of lower rank than a sergeant should usually be acceptable for this purpose, must be able to testify that beforehand he visited all observation places to be used and ascertained the attitude of occupiers of premises, not only to the use to be made of them, but to the possible disclosure thereafter of the use made and facts which could lead to the identification of the premises thereafter and of the occupiers. He may of course in addition inform the court of difficulties, if any, usually encountered in the particular locality of obtaining assistance from the public.

(b) A police officer of no lower rank than a chief inspector must be able to testify that immediately prior to the trial he visited the places used for observations, the results of which it is proposed to give in evidence, and ascertained whether the occupiers are the same as when the observations took place and whether they are or are not, what the attitude of those occupiers is to the possible disclosure of the use previously made of the premises and of facts which could lead at the trial to identification of premises and occupiers.

Such evidence will of course be given in the absence of the jury when the application to exclude the material evidence is made. The judge should explain to the jury, as this judge did, when summing up or at some appropriate time before that, the effect of his ruling to exclude, if he so rules.

The guidelines in *Johnson* do not require a threat of violence before protection can be afforded to the occupier of an observation post; it suffices if the occupier is in fear of harassment (*Blake* v *DPP* (1993) 97 Cr App R 169).

This extended the rules established in *R* v *Rankine* [1986] QB 861 and is based on the protection of the owner or occupier of the premises, and not on the identity of the observation post. Thus, where officers have witnessed the commission of an offence as part of a surveillance operation conducted from an unmarked police vehicle, information relating to the surveillance and the colour, make and model of the vehicle should not be withheld (*R* v *Brown and Daley* (1987) 87 Cr App R 52). Hodgson J said in *Brown*:

> We do not rule out the possibility that with the advent of sophisticated methods of criminal investigation, there may be cases where the public interest immunity may be successfully invoked in criminal proceedings to justify the exclusion of evidence as to police techniques and methods. But if and when such an argument is to be raised, it must, in the judgment of this court, be done properly. ... It would seem clear that if such a contention is put forward the judge must be given as much information as possible and the application will have to be supported, not by the instructions of the junior officer in charge of the case, but by the independent evidence of senior officers.

1.11.21 Third Party Material

Third party material can be considered in two categories:

(a) that which is or has been in the possession of the police or which has been inspected by the police;
(b) all other material not falling under (a).

Material that falls into the first category is covered by the same rules of disclosure as any other material the police have. Where police do not have material that they believe may be relevant to the case, para. 3.6 of the Code provides that:

> If the officer in charge of an investigation believes that other persons may be in possession of material that may be relevant to the investigation, and if this has not been obtained under paragraph 3.5 above, he should ask the disclosure officer to inform them of the existence of the investigation and to invite them to retain the material in case they receive a request for its disclosure. The disclosure officer should inform the prosecutor that they may have such material. However, the officer in charge of an investigation is not required to make speculative enquiries of other persons: there must be some reason to believe that they may have relevant material. That reason may come from information provided to the police by the accused or from other inquiries made or from some other source.

In the vast majority of cases the third party will make the material available to the investigating officer. However there may be occasions where the third party refuses to hand over the material and/or allow it to be examined.

If the OIC, the investigator or the disclosure officer believes that a third party holds material that may be relevant to the investigation, that person or body should be told of the investigation. They should be alerted to the need to preserve relevant material. Consideration should be given as to whether it is appropriate to seek access to the material, and if so, steps should be taken to obtain such material. It will be important to do so if the material or information is likely to undermine the prosecution case, or to assist a known defence. A letter should be sent to the third party together with the explanatory leaflet, specimens of which are provided in the Disclosure Manual at Annex B.

Where access to the material is declined or refused by the third party and it is believed that it is reasonable to seek production of the material before a suspect is charged, the investigator should consider making an application under sch. 1 to the Police and Criminal Evidence Act 1984 (special procedure material).

Where the suspect has been charged and the third party refuses to produce the material, application will have to be made to the court for a witness summons. In the magistrates' court this is covered by s. 97 of the Magistrates' Courts Act 1980 and in the Crown Court it is covered by ss. 2(2) and 2A–2D of the Criminal Procedure (Attendance of Witnesses) Act 1965. The third party may still wish to resist the requirement to produce the material and the point was considered in *R* v *Brushett* [2001] Crim LR 471 (this was a case that concerned Social Services Department files relating to a children's home). The court considered a number of earlier cases and established some central principles as follows:

- To be material evidence documents must be not only relevant to the issues arising in the criminal proceedings, but also documents admissible as such in evidence.
- Documents which are desired merely for the purpose of possible cross-examination are not admissible in evidence and, thus, are not material for the purposes of s. 97.
- Whoever seeks production of documents must satisfy the justices with some material that the documents are 'likely to be material' in the sense indicated, likelihood for this purpose involving a real possibility, although not necessarily a probability.
- It is not sufficient that the applicant merely wants to find out whether or not the third party has such material documents. This procedure must not be used as a disguised attempt to obtain discovery.

- Where social services documents are supplied to the prosecution, the prosecution should retain control of such material as part of the disclosure regime. That is envisaged by the rules. It cannot be acceptable to return material to social services to avoid the obligations arising under the rules. In any event, the obligation would arise in relation to the notes taken and retained.
- The obligation laid on the prosecution by statute and rules cannot be avoided by a third party making an agreement with the prosecution that the prosecution will abrogate any duties laid upon it by either common law or statute.
- If circumstances arise where it would be unjust not to allow disclosure of certain other material, so a defendant would not receive a fair trial, in the sense that he/she could not establish his innocence where he/she might otherwise do so, then that material must be disclosed.
- The fact that the prosecution have knowledge of the third party material may be a relevant factor to allow the defence access.
- Material concerning false allegations in the past may be relevant material (*R* v *Bourimech* [2002] EWCA Crim 2089).
- If the disputed material might prove the defendant's innocence or avoid a miscarriage of justice, the weight came down resoundingly in favour of disclosing it (*R* v *Reading Justices, ex parte Berkshire County Council* (1996) 1 Cr App R 239).

In *R* v *Alibhai* [2004] EWCA Crim 681 the Court of Appeal held that under the Criminal Procedure and Investigations Act 1996 the prosecutor was only under a duty to disclose material in the hands of third parties if that material had come into the prosecutor's hands and the prosecutor was of the opinion that such material undermined the case. However, the A-G's Guidelines went further by requiring a prosecutor to take steps pursuing third party disclosure if there was a suspicion that documents would be detrimental to the prosecution or of assistance to the defence. However, in such circumstances, the prosecutor enjoyed a margin of consideration as to what steps were appropriate. The provisions for disclosure are not intended to create duties for third parties to follow. The disclosure duties under the 1996 Act were created in respect of material that the prosecution or the police had and which the prosecution had inspected. Material was not prosecution material unless it was held by the investigator or by the disclosure officer (*DPP* v *Wood and McGillicuddy* [2006] EWHC 32).

The A-G's Guidelines also deal with materials held by third parties (including government agencies) in paras 47 to 54. Paragraphs 47 to 50 deal with material held by government departments or other Crown bodies and suggests that reasonable steps should be taken to identify and consider material that may be relevant to an issue in the case. Paragraph 51 examines the circumstances in which the prosecution should take steps to obtain access to material or information in the possession of other third parties. In such cases consideration should be given to take steps to obtain such material or information. It will be important to do so if the material or information is likely to undermine the prosecution case, or assist a known defence. Paragraph 52 deals with the situation where the police or prosecutor meet with a refusal by the third party to supply such material or information. If, despite the reasons put forward for refusal by the third party, it still appears reasonable to seek its production, a witness summons requiring the third party to produce the material should be applied for (such an application can also be made by the defence). The third party can then argue at court that it is not material, or that it should not be disclosed on grounds of public interest immunity.

1.11.22 Confidentiality

The defence may only use material disclosed to them under the 1996 Act for purposes related to the defence case; any other use will be a contempt of court. Once evidence has been given in open court, however, the material is available for other purposes.

1.11.23 Retention Periods

Material must be retained in all cases until a decision is taken whether to institute proceedings against a person for an offence. Where a decision is taken to institute proceedings material must then be retained until the case has been dealt with. The Code gives specific guidance in cases where a person is convicted as to how long material must be retained for. Paragraphs 5.7 to 5.10 set out the retention periods where a person has been convicted. All material which may be relevant must be retained at least until:

- the person is released from custody or discharged from hospital in cases where the court imposes a custodial sentence or hospital order;
- in all other cases, for six months from the date of conviction.

If the person is released from the custodial sentence or discharged from hospital earlier than six months from the date of conviction, the material must be retained for at least six months from the date of conviction. If an appeal is in progress at the end of one of these periods, or an application is being considered by the Criminal Cases Review Commission, the period is extended until:

- the appeal is determined; or
- the Commission decide not to refer the application to the Court of Appeal; or
- the Court of Appeal determines the appeal resulting from the reference.

Where material has been seized under the powers provided by the Police and Criminal Evidence Act 1984, para. 5.2 confirms that retention of the material should reflect the provisions of s. 22 of the 1984 Act.

1.12 Presumptions in Law

Facts in issue and relevant facts must generally be proved before a court by admissible evidence before they can be accepted by the court as being true. There are occasions, however, when the courts will allow the proof of a fact or number of facts which lead it to presume the existence of a further fact, without any evidence of that fact being given in evidence. That is, from the facts that have been given in evidence, the court will then presume another fact for which no direct evidence has been given. A presumption is normally a conclusion which can be drawn until, where permissible, the contrary is proved.

There are three types of these 'presumptions':

- irrebuttable presumptions of law;
- rebuttable presumptions of law;
- presumptions of fact.

1.12.1 Irrebuttable Presumptions of Law

This is also known as a conclusive presumption. In these cases, where the courts accept the existence of certain basic fact(s) then they must also assume the existence of another fact and the other party to the proceedings cannot produce evidence questioning its existence.

For instance, s. 50 of the Children and Young Persons Act 1933 states:

It shall be conclusively presumed that no child under the age of ten years can be guilty of any offence.

1.12.2 Rebuttable Presumptions of Law

In these cases, once one party has satisfied the court of the basic fact from which a presumption about other facts must be made, it is for the other party to prove that the presumed fact does not exist. That is, the other party can *rebut* the presumption but, if he/she is unable to do so, the court will draw the appropriate inference from it.

There are a number of rebuttable presumptions but the most likely to apply to criminal cases are 'presumptions of regularity'.

A typical example is on a charge of assaulting a police officer in the course of his/her duty. Evidence that the police officer acted in that capacity is sufficient proof of his/her due appointment (*R* v *Gordon* (1789) 1 Leach 515; and see *Cooper* v *Rowlands* [1971] RTR 291).

There is also a presumption that mechanical and other instruments were in working order at the time of their use. For example, automatic traffic signals are presumed to be in proper working order unless the contrary is proved (*Tingle Jacobs & Co.* v *Kennedy* [1964] 1 WLR 638).

1.12.3 Presumptions of Fact

The court may, after evidence is given about certain facts, presume (in the absence of sufficient evidence to the contrary), that another fact exists. This differs from rebuttable presumptions of law in that here the court *may* presume the fact exists from other facts presented to the court. With rebuttable presumptions of fact the court *must* presume the fact exists unless it is proved to the contrary. In reality this is just another way of showing that the courts use circumstantial evidence to infer that a fact is true.

Cases where the courts regularly infer the existence of facts from other circumstantial evidence are labelled 'presumptions of fact'.

An example is the 'presumption of life': where evidence that a person was alive on a certain date is given to the court, it may be presumed that he/she was still alive on some subsequent date (*Mac Darmaid* v *Attorney-General* [1950] P 218; *Re Peete* [1952] 2 All ER 599). Of course, where additional evidence is provided showing that the person was in good health and spirits, the chances of such an inference being made will be greater.

1.13 Admissibility of Written Statements

1.13.1 Admissibility of Written Statements in Summary Proceedings

Section 9 of the Criminal Justice Act 1967 states:

(1) In any criminal proceedings, other than committal proceedings, a written statement by any person shall, if such of the conditions mentioned in the next following subsection as are applicable are satisfied, be admissible as evidence to the like extent as oral evidence to the like effect by that person.

(2) The said conditions are—
   - (a) the statement purports to be signed by the person who made it;
   - (b) the statement contains a declaration by the person to the effect that it is true to the best of his knowledge and belief and that he made the statement knowing that, if it were tendered in evidence, he would be liable to prosecution if he wilfully stated in it anything which he knew to be false or did not believe to be true;

(c) before the hearing at which the statement is tendered in evidence, a copy of the statement is served, by or on behalf of the party proposing to tender it, on each of the other parties to the proceedings; and
(d) none of the other parties or their solicitors, within seven days from the service of the copy of the statement, serves a notice on the party so proposing objecting to the statement being tendered in evidence under this section:

Provided that the conditions mentioned in paragraphs (c) and (d) of this subsection shall not apply if the parties agree before or during the hearing that the statement shall be so tendered.

KEYNOTE

The statement must be signed by the person making it but the declaration outlined at s. 9(2)(b) need not be separately signed.

The procedure for serving a statement under s. 9 is set out in r. 27.1 of the Criminal Procedure Rules 2005 (SI 2005/384) which provides for a notice to be sent to the defendant, or if legally represented, their solicitor. The notice informs the defendant of the effect of the procedure and requires them, within seven days, to inform the prosecutor if they wish the witness to attend court. Failure to inform the prosecutor will deprive the defendant of his/her right to insist on the witness's attendance.

Statements that are admitted under s. 9 are either read out in full to the court or parts of it may be summarised at the court's discretion; however, the court may still require a witness to attend and give oral evidence even where there has been no objection from the other parties (s. 9(4)(b)).

1.13.2 Victim Personal Statements

The victim personal statements scheme provides victims of crime with an opportunity to provide a statement saying how the crime has affected them and enables the court to take such statements into account when determining sentence. Guidance on the relevance of victim personal statements is provided by *Practice Direction* (*Criminal Proceedings: Consolidation*) [2002] 1 WLR 2870, para. 28, personal statements of victims, and the decision of the Court of Appeal in *R* v *Perks* [2001] 1 Cr App R (S) 66.

When taking a statement from a victim a police officer is required to inform the victim of the scheme. The decision as to whether to make such a statement is entirely a matter for the victim. A victim personal statement may be made or updated at any time prior to the disposal of the case.

The Domestic Violence, Crime and Victims Act 2004 has introduced a Victims' Code and a code of practice setting out the services to be provided to victims of criminal conduct or any aspect of the criminal justice system (s. 32(1)). The Code may include a provision requiring or permitting the services that are to be provided to a victim to be provided to one or more others. This might include a relative of a deceased victim or the parent/guardian of a juvenile to make a victim personal statement. A person can be a 'victim' even where no person has been charged with or convicted of an offence in respect of criminal conduct (s. 32(6)).

Where a person is convicted of a sexual or violent offence, and a relevant sentence has been imposed, victims may make representations, through the local probation board, as to any licence conditions or supervision requirements in the event of an offender's release from custody (s. 35). The local probation board is also required to keep victims informed of any such conditions or requirements (s. 35).

From April 2006 a pilot scheme, introduced by the Lord Chancellor, allowed murder and manslaughter victims' relatives to make a statement in court about the effect the crime has had on them. The statement can be given either by a relative or a third party, such as a lawyer, and will be given at the sentencing stage after a defendant has been found guilty.

1.14 Offences Against the Administration of Justice and Public Interest

1.14.1 Perjury

OFFENCE: **Perjury in Judicial Proceeding—*Perjury Act 1911, s. 1***

• Triable on indictment • Seven years' imprisonment

The Perjury Act 1911, s. 1 states:

(1) If any person lawfully sworn as a witness or as an interpreter in a judicial proceeding wilfully makes a statement material in that proceeding, which he knows to be false or does not believe to be true, he shall be guilty of perjury...

(2) The expression 'judicial proceeding' includes a proceeding before any court, tribunal, or person having by law power to hear, receive, and examine evidence on oath.

(3) Where a statement made for the purposes of a judicial proceeding is not made before the tribunal itself, but is made on oath before a person authorised by law to administer an oath to the person who makes the statement, and to record or authenticate the statement, it shall, for the purposes of this section, be treated as having been made in a judicial proceeding.

KEYNOTE

To commit this offence a defendant must have been *lawfully sworn* (see the Evidence Act 1851, s. 16). The statement made in 'judicial proceeding' can be one given orally before the court or tribunal, or it can be given in the form of an affidavit (sworn statement). If a witness tenders a false statement (MG 11) used under s. 89 of the Criminal Justice Act 1967, he/she commits a separate, lesser offence.

'Wilful' in this case means deliberate as opposed to accidental.

A 'statement material in that proceeding' means that the content of the evidence tendered in that case must have some importance to it and not just be of passing relevance. Whether something is material to a case is a question of law for a judge to decide. Whether a motorist had taken a drink between the time of his/her having a road traffic accident and being breathalysed would be such a material issue, and to get a witness to provide false evidence about that matter would be a 'statement material in that proceeding' (*R* v *Lewins* (1979) 1 Cr App R (S) 246).

To prove perjury you must also show that the defendant *knew* the statement to be false or *did not believe it to be true.*

Evidence of an opinion provided by a witness who does not genuinely hold such an opinion may also be perjury.

Perjury may be proved by using a court transcript or the evidence of others who were present at the proceeding in question (see Perjury Act 1911, s. 14).

Corroboration is required in cases of perjury (see Perjury Act 1911, s. 13. The requirement for corroboration is solely in relation to the *falsity* of the defendant's statement. There is no requirement under s. 13 for corroboration of the fact that the defendant *actually made* the alleged statement, nor that he/she knew or believed it to be untrue. However, as that corroboration can be documentary and may even come from the defendant's earlier conduct (*R* v *Threlfall* (1914) 10 Cr App R 112) this requirement does not appear to present much of a hurdle to the prosecution.

Evidence given by live TV link under the provisions of the Criminal Justice Act 1988, s. 32 is also subject to the offence of perjury.

1.14.1.1 Aiding and Abetting

OFFENCE: **Aiding and Abetting Perjury—*Perjury Act 1911, s. 7***

• If principal offence is contrary to s.1 triable on indictment • Seven years' imprisonment • Otherwise either way • Two years' imprisonment on indictment • Six months' imprisonment and/or a fine summarily

The Perjury Act 1911, s. 7 states:

(1) Every person who aids, abets, counsels, procures, or suborns another person to commit an offence against this Act shall be liable to be proceeded against, indicted, tried and punished as if he were a principal offender.
(2) Every person who incites... another person to commit an offence against this Act shall be guilty of a misdemeanour.

KEYNOTE

'Subornation' is the same as procuring. This specific section does not appear to add anything to the general offences of aiding and abetting principal offenders.

1.14.2 Perverting the Course of Justice

OFFENCE: **Perverting the Course of Justice—*Common Law***

- Triable on indictment • Life imprisonment and/or a fine

It is an offence at common law to do an act tending and intended to pervert the course of public justice.

KEYNOTE

'The course of public justice' includes the process of criminal investigation (see *R* v *Rowell* (1977) 65 Cr App R 174).

Although traditionally referred to—and charged—as 'attempting' to pervert the course of justice, it is recognised that behaviour which is *aimed* at perverting the course of public justice does just that and the substantive offence should be charged (see *R* v *Williams* (1991) 92 Cr App R 158).

One way in which this offence is commonly committed is where a prisoner uses a false identity when he/she is arrested. Although the offence of perverting the course of justice may be made out in these—or similar—circumstances in connection with a number of other substantive offences, the Court of Appeal has held that, in many cases, the addition of such a charge is unnecessary and only serves to complicate the sentencing process (*R* v *Sookoo* (2002) *The Times*, 10 April). Where, as in *Sookoo*, a defendant makes an unsophisticated attempt to hide their identity and fails, the Court felt that a specific separate count of perverting the course of justice should not be laid. If it was shown that there were serious aggravating features, for instance where a lot of police time and resources had been involved or innocent members of the public had been arrested as a result, a specific charge may be appropriate and could be justified.

Perverting the course of justice requires positive acts by the defendant, not merely standing by and allowing an injustice to take place. The offence will include cases where evidence is deliberately destroyed, concealed or falsified as well as cases where witnesses and jurors are intimidated (**see para. 1.14.3**).

Admitting to a crime to enable the true offender to avoid prosecution would fall under this offence (*R* v *Devito* [1975] Crim LR 175), as would abusing your authority as a police officer to excuse someone of a criminal charge (*R* v *Coxhead* [1986] RTR 411). Other examples include:

- making a false allegation of an offence (*R* v *Goodwin* (1989) 11 Cr App R (S) 194 (rape));
- giving another person's personal details when being reported for an offence (*R* v *Hurst* (1990) 12 Cr App R (S) 373);
- destroying and concealing evidence of a crime (*R* v *Kiffin* [1994] Crim LR 449).

It is important that the requisite intention is proved in every case as that intention cannot be implied, even from admitted facts (*R* v *Lalani* [1999] 1 Cr App R 481).

Where a person makes a false allegation to the police justifying a criminal investigation with the possible consequences of detention, arrest, charge or prosecution and that person intends that the allegation be taken seriously, the offence of perverting the course of justice is *prima facie* made out—whether or not the allegation is capable of identifying specific individuals. This is clear from *R* v *Cotter* [2002] 2 Cr App R 29, a case involving the boyfriend of a well-known black Olympic athlete who claimed to have been attacked as part of a racist campaign.

1.14.3 Considerations Affecting Witnesses, Jurors and Others

Great care is needed by police officers in handling witnesses. Any behaviour that is seen as interfering with witnesses (or potential witnesses) by promises of favours and rewards or by threats will be a contempt of court (see *R* v *Kellett* [1975] 3 All ER 468). However, there is no 'property' in a witness. Protecting witnesses is one thing but trying to restrict the way in which defendants and/or their legal advisers obtain evidence for their defence—e.g. by properly approaching witnesses—can also amount to a contempt of court (see *Connolly* v *Dale* [1996] 1 All ER 224).

So far as the police are concerned there are several significant areas of common and statute law to consider when considering witnesses, including the legislative framework involved where it is felt that the witness (who may be a police officer or other person engaged in policing) requires some specific form of protection. The full detail of witness protection arrangements is beyond the scope of this Manual. However the main legislative provisions are set out below.

The Serious Organised Crime and Police Act 2005 sets out specific provisions relating to witness protection arrangements. In fact these arrangements stretch beyond witnesses and extend to a series of people involved in the criminal justice process, including people who are *or have been*:

- constables
- employees accredited under the Police Reform Act 2002
- jurors
- magistrates (or their equivalent outside the United Kingdom)
- holders of judicial office (whether in the United Kingdom or elsewhere)
- the DPP, criminal prosecutors and staff of the Crown Prosecution Service

(see the Serious Organised Crime and Police Act 2005, sch. 5).

Chapter 4 of the Act allows for the making of arrangements to protect these and other relevant people ordinarily resident in the United Kingdom where the 'protection provider' (usually the Chief Officer of Police or the Director General of the Serious Organised Crime Agency) considers that the person's safety is at risk by virtue of their being a witness, constable, juror etc. (s. 82(1)). A protection provider may vary or cancel any arrangements made by him/her under subs. (1) if he/she considers it appropriate to do so. Joint arrangements (e.g. between police forces) can be made where appropriate, and public authorities (other than courts and tribunals or parliament) are under a duty to take reasonable steps to assist protection providers where requested to do so (see ss. 83 and 85).

1.14.3.1 Witnesses or Jurors in Investigation or Proceedings for an Offence

The first measure can be found in the Criminal Justice and Public Order Act 1994.

OFFENCE: **Intimidating Witnesses and Jurors—*Criminal Justice and Public Order Act 1994, s. 51***

- Triable either way • Five years' imprisonment and/or a fine on indictment
- Six months' imprisonment and/or a fine summarily

The Criminal Justice and Public Order Act 1994, s. 51 states:

(1) A person commits an offence if—
  (a) he does an act which intimidates, and is intended to intimidate, another person ('the victim'),
  (b) he does the act knowing or believing that the victim is assisting in the investigation of an offence or is a witness or potential witness or a juror or potential juror in proceedings for an offence, and
  (c) he does it intending thereby to cause the investigation or the course of justice to be obstructed, perverted or interfered with.

(2) A person commits an offence if—
  (a) he does an act which harms, and is intended to harm, another person or, intending to cause another person to fear harm, he threatens to do an act which would harm that other person,
  (b) he does or threatens to do the act knowing or believing that the person harmed or threatened to be harmed ('the victim'), or some other person, has assisted in an investigation into an offence or has given evidence or particular evidence in proceedings for an offence, or has acted as a juror or concurred in a particular verdict in proceedings for an offence, and
  (c) he does or threatens to do it because of that knowledge or belief.

(3) For the purposes of subsections (1) and (2) it is immaterial that the act is or would be done, or that the threat is made—
  (a) otherwise than in the presence of the victim, or
  (b) to a person other than the victim.

(4) The harm that may be done or threatened may be financial as well as physical (whether to the person or a person's property) and similarly as respects an intimidatory act which consists of threats.

(5) The intention required by subsection (1)(c) and the motive required by subsection (2)(c) above need not be the only or the predominating intention or motive with which the act is done or, in the case of subsection (2), threatened.

KEYNOTE

As discussed above, this section is aimed at protecting people involved in the investigation or trial of criminal offences.

These offences are designed to exist alongside the common-law offence of perverting the course of justice (**see para. 1.14.2**) and there will be circumstances which may fall under both the statutory and the common-law offences. Such behaviour may also be punishable as a contempt of court, **see Blackstone's Criminal Practice 2008, section B14.69**.

This is an offence of 'specific intent' or perhaps even multiple intent as it must be shown that the act was done with the intentions set out in s. 51(1)(a) and (c). It must also be shown that the defendant knew or believed the other person to be assisting in the investigation of an offence or that he/she was going to testify/appear on the jury in proceedings for an offence.

For 'knowing or believing' in this context the prosecution must present evidence that an investigation was in fact being carried out at the time of the alleged offence (*R* v *Singh* [2000] 1 Cr App R 31). In a decision that appears to contradict the specific wording of the statute, the Court of Appeal has confirmed that 'an act which intimidates' does not have to result in the victim *actually* being intimidated. In *R* v *Patrascu* [2004] 4 All ER 1066 the court held that a person did an act which intimidated another within the meaning of s. 51(1) if he/she put that other person in fear, or sought by threat or violence to deter him or her from some relevant action such as giving evidence. However mere pressure which did not put the victim in fear or contained no element of threat or violence was insufficient. Therefore, if a defendant seeks to deter the victim from giving evidence, the offence could be made out even if the victim was not in fear. While slightly odd in the light of the words of the Act above, this reasoning is in line with the law relating to assault (as to which **see para. 3.2.4**).

'Harm' for the purposes of s. 51(2) means physical harm and not simply an assault or battery. Therefore spitting at a person does not amount to 'harm' for these purposes (even though it would amount to other public order or assault offences) (*R* v *Normanton* [1998] Crim LR 220).

Section 51(2) provides a similar offence for acts done or threatened in the knowledge or belief that the person, *or another person*, has so assisted or taken part in proceedings. Doing acts to third parties in order to intimidate or harm the relevant person is also covered by this offence (s. 51(3)). Making threats by telephone will amount to 'doing an act to another' (*DPP* v *Mills* [1997] QB 300).

Section 51(8) creates a statutory presumption under certain circumstances that the defendant had the required motive at the time of his/her actions or threats.

Making a *threat* via a third person knowing it will be passed on and that the ultimate recipient would be intimidated by it amounts to an offence under s. 51(1) (*Attorney-General's Reference (No. 1 of 1999)* [1999] 3 WLR 769).

The intention to obstruct, pervert or interfere with the course of justice need not be the only or even the main intention (s. 51(5)).

1.14.3.2 Intimidation of Witnesses in Other Proceedings

In addition to the measures aimed at protecting those involved in the investigation and trial of criminal offences, there are further statutory measures designed to protect witnesses and others who are (or may become) involved in other proceedings.

OFFENCE: **Intimidation of Witnesses—*Criminal Justice and Police Act 2001, s. 39***

• Triable either way • Five years' imprisonment on indictment • Six months' imprisonment and/or fine summarily

The Criminal Justice and Police Act 2001, s. 39 states:

(1) A person commits an offence if—
  (a) he does an act which intimidates, and is intended to intimidate, another person ('the victim');
  (b) he does the act—
    (i) knowing or believing that the victim is or may be a witness in any relevant proceedings; and
    (ii) intending, by his act, to cause the course of justice to be obstructed, perverted or interfered with;
  and
  (c) the act is done after the commencement of those proceedings.

KEYNOTE

This offence has some similarities to the Criminal Justice and Public Order Act 1994 offence in the earlier paragraph. References to doing an act include threats—against a person and/or their property—and the making of any other statement (s. 39(6)). The key difference is that this offence is concerned with protecting people who are in some way connected with 'relevant proceedings' which are '*any proceedings in or before the Court of Appeal, the High Court, the Crown Court or any county or magistrates' court which are not proceedings for an offence*' (s. 41(1)). This means that the offence will be relevant if the proceedings involved are civil proceedings in the higher courts or the county court or if they are non-offence proceedings in the Crown Court or magistrates' court. Examples of the latter would be a hearing to deal with a breach of a community order or an application for an anti-social behaviour order. You must show that the relevant proceedings had already commenced by the time of the offence.

Note that some proceedings, such as inquests or police conduct hearings, will not be covered by the s. 41 definition and therefore the offences above.

As with the Criminal Justice and Public Order Act offence, this requires proof of 'multiple' intent in that, as well as showing the intimidatory act, it must also be shown that the elements set out at s. 39(1)(a)–(c) are present. However, if you can prove that the defendant:

- did any act that intimidated, and was intended to intimidate, another person, and
- that he/she did that act knowing or believing that that other person was or might be a 'witness' in any relevant proceedings that had already commenced,

there will be a presumption that the defendant did the act with the intention of causing the course of justice to be obstructed, perverted or interfered with (s. 39(3)). This presumption is, however, rebuttable. 'Witness' here is a very wide expression and extends to anyone who provides, or is able to provide, any information, document or other thing which might be used in evidence in those proceedings (see s. 39(5)).

In proving the offence it is immaterial whether the act:

- is done in the presence of the victim
- is done to the victim himself/herself or to another person

or whether or not the intention to obstruct, pervert or interfere with the course of justice is the main intention of the person doing it (s. 39(2)).

This offence is intended to exist alongside the common law offence of perverting the course of justice (as to which, **see para. 1.14.2**) and came into force on 1 August 2001.

For the specific measures involving witness protection programmes **see para. 1.14.3**.

1.14.4 Harming Witnesses

OFFENCE: **Harming Witnesses—*Criminal Justice and Police Act 2001, s. 40***

- Triable either way • Five years' imprisonment on indictment • Six months' imprisonment and/or fine summarily

The Criminal Justice and Police Act 2001, s. 40 states:

(1) A person commits an offence if in circumstances falling within subsection (2)—
  (a) he does an act which harms, and is intended to harm, another person; or
  (b) intending to cause another person to fear harm, he threatens to do an act which would harm that other person.
(2) The circumstances fall within this subsection if—
  (a) the person doing or threatening to do the act does so knowing or believing that some person (whether or not the person harmed or threatened or the person against whom harm is threatened) has been a witness in relevant proceedings; and
  (b) he does or threatens to do that act because of that knowledge or belief.

KEYNOTE

A distinction between this and the s. 39 offence is that the offence above refers to someone who *has been* (or is believed to have been) a witness in relevant proceedings. Again, 'witness' is very wide and extends to anyone who has provided any information, document, etc. which was (or might have been) used in evidence in those proceedings (see s. 40(7)). For 'relevant proceedings' see the s. 39 offence. This offence is aimed at the general protection of people who have been involved in relevant proceedings. Therefore there is no requirement here for any intention to pervert or interfere with the course of justice. The harm caused or threatened does not have to be directed towards the witness themselves; the key element is the motivation of the defendant. In relation to that motivation, the Act creates a presumption as follows. If you can prove that, between the start of the proceedings and one year after they are concluded, the defendant:

- did an act which harmed, and was intended to harm, another person, or
- threatened to do an act which would harm another person intending to cause that person to fear harm

with the knowledge or belief required by s. 40(2)(a) above, he/she will be presumed to have acted because of that knowledge or belief (s. 40(3)). Again, this is rebuttable. It is immaterial whether the act or threat is made (or would be carried out) in the presence of the person who is or would be harmed, or of the person threatened or whether the motive mentioned in s. 40(2)(b) is the main motive. The harm done or threatened can be physical or financial and can be made to a person or property (s. 40(4)). This offence came into force on 1 August 2001.

For the specific measures involving witness protection programmes **see para. 1.14.3.**

1.14.5 Assisting Offenders

OFFENCE: **Assisting Offenders—*Criminal Law Act 1967, s. 4***

• Triable on indictment; either way if original offence is either way • Where sentence for original offence is fixed by law, ten years' imprisonment and/or a fine on indictment; six months' imprisonment and/or a fine summarily • Where sentence for original offence is 14 years' imprisonment, seven years' imprisonment and/or a fine on indictment; six months' imprisonment and/or a fine summarily • Where sentence for original offence is ten years imprisonment, five years' imprisonment and/or a fine on indictment; six months' imprisonment and/or a fine summarily • Otherwise three years' imprisonment and/or a fine on indictment; six months' imprisonment and/or a fine summarily

The Criminal Law Act 1967, s. 4 states:

(1) Where a person has committed a relevant offence, any other person who, knowing or believing him to be guilty of the offence or of some other relevant offence, does without lawful authority or reasonable excuse any act with intent to impede his apprehension or prosecution shall be guilty of an offence.

(1A) In this section and section 5 below, 'relevant offence' means—

(a) an offence for which the sentence is fixed by law,

(b) an offence for which a person of 18 years or over (not previously convicted) may be sentenced to imprisonment for a term of five years (or might be so sentenced but for the restrictions imposed by section 33 of the Magistrates' Courts Act 1980).

KEYNOTE

This offence must involve some positive act by the defendant; simply doing or saying nothing will not suffice.

Although there is no duty on people to assist the police in their investigations generally (though, **see para. 3.2.14**), this offence and the one below create a negative duty not to interfere with investigations after an offence has taken place.

For there to be an offence under s. 4 or 5 (para. 1.14.6) there must first have been a relevant offence committed by someone. That relevant offence must, in the case of the above offence, have been committed by the 'assisted' person.

The defendant can commit the offence before the person he/she has assisted is convicted of committing the relevant offence.

It must be shown that the defendant knew or believed the person to be guilty of that, *or some other* relevant offence. Therefore, if the defendant believed that the 'assisted' person had committed a robbery when in fact he/she had committed a theft, that mistaken part of the defendant's belief will not prevent a conviction for this offence.

By analogy with the requirements for handling stolen goods mere *suspicion*, however strong, that the 'assisted' person had committed a relevant offence will not be enough.

This offence requires the consent of the DPP before a prosecution is brought (s. 4(4)).

This offence cannot be 'attempted' (Criminal Attempts Act 1981, s. 1(4)).

1.14.6 Concealing Relevant Offences

OFFENCE: **Concealing Relevant Offences—*Criminal Law Act 1967, s. 5***

• Triable on indictment; either way if original offence is triable either way • Two years' imprisonment on indictment • Six months' imprisonment and/or a fine summarily

The Criminal Law Act 1967, s. 5 states:

(1) Where a person has committed a relevant offence, any other person who, knowing or believing that the offence or some other relevant offence has been committed, and that he has information which might be of material assistance in securing the prosecution or conviction of an offender for it, accepts or agrees to accept for not disclosing that information any consideration other than the making good of loss or injury caused by the offence, or the making of reasonable compensation for that loss or injury, shall be liable...

KEYNOTE

This offence also requires the consent of the DPP before a prosecution can be brought (s. 5(3)).

It is also excluded from the provisions of the Criminal Attempts Act 1981 (s. 1(4)).

Again, someone must have committed a relevant offence before this particular offence can be committed.

The main focus of this offence is:

- the acceptance of, or agreement to accept 'consideration' (i.e. anything of value)
- beyond reasonable compensation for loss/injury *caused by the relevant offence*
- in exchange for not disclosing material information.

'Disclosure' does not appear to be confined to information passed to the police. It would probably extend to other agencies with a duty to investigate offences but is perhaps even wider than that.

This offence requires proof, not only of the defendant's knowledge or belief that a relevant offence had been committed, but also that he/she has information that might be of material assistance in securing the *prosecution or conviction* of *an offender* for it. Given this very broad wording, the possession of information that might provide useful intelligence in an investigation into relevant offences may meet the requirements of s. 5, although *proving* that the defendant had the required knowledge or belief presents considerable practical problems.

PART TWO

Property Offences

2.1 Theft

2.1.1 Theft

OFFENCE: **Theft—*Theft Act 1968, s. 1***

• Triable either way • Seven years' imprisonment on indictment • Six months' imprisonment and/or a fine summarily

The Theft Act 1968, s. 1 states:

(1) A person is guilty of theft if he dishonestly appropriates property belonging to another with the intention of permanently depriving the other of it; and 'thief' and 'steal' shall be construed accordingly.

KEYNOTE

It is important to understand each element of this offence. The Theft Act 1968 provides some detailed guidance as to parts of the above definition, while our common law has clarified some of the others.

In order for an offence of theft to exist, each element of the definition must be proved and those elements are considered in detail below.

While some thefts or acts of shoplifting can cause harassment, alarm or distress and so fall within the provisions of the Crime and Disorder Act 1998, not all thefts and acts of shoplifting fall within those criteria. Therefore it is necessary to consider the individual facts of each case, and Anti-Social Behaviour Orders cannot be made automatically simply on the basis that the theft could potentially have caused harassment, alarm or distress—*R (On the Application of Mills)* v *Birmingham Magistrates' Court* [2005] EWHC 2732.

The component parts of theft are considered more closely below.

Note that offences of theft from businesses involving values not exceeding £200 can be dealt with by way of fixed penalty notice.

As described above, there are five key elements to the offence of theft. These are:

- dishonesty
- appropriation
- property
- belonging to another
- intention of permanently depriving.

2.1.2 Dishonestly

If a person cannot be shown to have acted 'dishonestly', he/she is not guilty of theft. The decision as to whether or not a defendant was in fact dishonest is one for the jury or magistrate(s). Perhaps surprisingly given its central importance in the offence, there is no statutory definition of this term. Instead the 1968 Act sets out a number of specific circumstances where the relevant person will *not* be treated as dishonest and one circumstance where a person *may* be dishonest.

The Theft Act 1968, s. 2 states:

(1) A person's appropriation of property belonging to another is not to be regarded as dishonest—
  (a) if he appropriates the property in the belief that he has in law the right to deprive the other of it, on behalf of himself or of a third person; or
  (b) if he appropriates the property in the belief that he would have the other's consent if the other knew of the appropriation and the circumstances of it; or

(c) (except where the property came to him as trustee or personal representative) if he appropriates the property in the belief that the person to whom the property belongs cannot be discovered by taking reasonable steps.

(2) A person's appropriation of property belonging to another may be dishonest notwithstanding that he is willing to pay for the property.

KEYNOTE

In all three instances it is the person's *belief* that is important.

Right

- Under s. 2(1)(a) if a person in dispute with a bookmaker believes he/she has a legal contractual *right* to take something of a value equal to his/her unpaid winnings from the bookmaker's stand, that person will not be regarded as dishonest—even though gambling debts are not legally enforceable. His/her belief need not even be reasonable, only honestly held, and could be based on a 'mistake' (contrast the general defence of mistake.

Consent

- Under s. 2(1)(b) the person appropriating the property must believe both elements, i.e. that the other person would have *consented* had he/she known of the appropriation *and the circumstances of it.* For example, a person is about to run out of time on a street parking meter and needs £2 to park for the next hour otherwise he/she will incur a £20 fine. Believing that his/her work colleague would consent in this situation, the person takes £2 belonging to the work colleague from a change jar on the work colleague's desk. Although the person need not have given his/her consent to the appropriation, the presence of such consent may be very relevant in establishing the honest existence of the defendant's belief.

Lost

- Under s. 2(1)(c), the belief has to be in relation to the likelihood of *discovering* the 'owner' by taking reasonable steps. Both the nature and value of the property, together with the attendant circumstances, will be relevant. The chances of finding the owner of a valuable, monogrammed engagement ring found after a theatre performance would be considerably greater than those of discovering the owner of a can of beer found outside Twickenham stadium following a Six Nations match between Wales and England. Again, it is the defendant's *belief* at the time of the appropriation that is important here, not that the defendant went on to take reasonable steps to discover the person to whom the property belongs.

Under s. 2(2), if a person appropriates another's property, leaving money or details of where he/she can be contacted to make restitution will not *of itself* negate dishonesty (see *Boggeln* v *Williams* [1978] 1 WLR 873). The wording of s. 2(2) gives latitude to a court where the defendant was willing to pay for the property. The subsection says that such an appropriation *may* be dishonest, not that it *will always* be dishonest.

2.1.3 Dishonesty: The Ruling in *Ghosh*

Section 2 will not cater for every circumstance and indeed ss. 2 to 6 only affect the interpretation of the basic elements of theft as set out in s. 1 unless the Act says otherwise (s. 1(3)). Since the case of *R* v *Ghosh* [1982] QB 1053 there has been a requirement for juries to be given some form of direction where the issue of dishonesty is raised and s. 2 is of no assistance. As well as clarifying that the defendant's dishonesty is a matter for a jury to decide, the Court of Appeal in *Ghosh* also identified two aspects which the jury should consider when so deciding. If s. 2 is not applicable or helpful then a jury must decide:

- whether, according to the ordinary standards of reasonable and honest people, what was done was 'dishonest'; *and*, if it was
- whether 'the defendant himself must have realised that what was done was dishonest' *by those standards*.

This test against the standards of reasonable and honest people means that a defendant who has a purely *subjective* belief that he/she is doing what is morally right (e.g. an anti-vivisectionist taking animals from a laboratory) can still be 'dishonest'. The *Ghosh* test is probably the source of the questions so loved by some interviewing officers: 'But what would an *honest* person have done?' or 'What would have been the *honest* thing to do?'

2.1.4 Appropriates

The Theft Act 1968, s. 3 states:

> (1) Any assumption by a person of the rights of an owner amounts to an appropriation, and this includes, where he has come by the property (innocently or not) without stealing it, any later assumption of a right to it by keeping or dealing with it as owner.

KEYNOTE

It is important to note that there can be an 'appropriation' without any criminal liability and appropriation itself does not amount to an offence; it describes one of the elements of the criminal conduct that must exist before a charge of theft can be made out. An appropriation requires no mental state on the part of the appropriator. It is an objective act.

Where an appropriation takes place and is accompanied by the required dishonesty and intention to deprive permanently, there will be a theft.

Appropriation under s. 3(1) envisages a *physical* act—*Biggs* v *R* (2003) 12 December, unreported.

When and where the particular act amounting to an appropriation took place is therefore of critical importance when bringing a charge of theft; it is also vital when establishing other offences such as robbery (see para. 2.4), aggravated burglary (see para. 2.3) and handling stolen goods (see para. 2.7).

Appropriation and Consent: *R* v *Gomez*

The decision of the House of Lords in *R* v *Gomez* [1993] AC 442 is significant in the development of the meaning of 'appropriation'. Gomez worked in a shop in London. He was approached by a friend who asked him to accept two building society cheques in exchange for some expensive electrical goods from the shop. Knowing the cheques to be stolen, Gomez took them to his store manager asking him to authorise the supply of goods. Gomez assured the manager that the cheques had been confirmed and that they were 'as good as cash'. With this reassurance the manager authorised the supply of the goods. Gomez paid the cheques into the store's account and the large quantity of electrical goods was dispatched to Gomez's friend. Some time later, the cheques were returned with a 'not to pay' order on them as they had been reported stolen.

Gomez was arrested for theft of the electrical goods, together with his friend, and sent for trial. There, counsel for Gomez submitted that there was no case to answer in respect of the theft because the store manager had authorised their supply and therefore there had been no 'appropriation' under s. 3(1) of the Theft Act 1968. The submission was rejected by the trial judge but was upheld on appeal on the grounds that, when Gomez's friend took possession of the electrical goods, he was entitled to do so under the terms of the contract of sale entered into by the store manager. The court went on to say that, although the contract of sale may have been 'voidable' (that is, the other parties to it could have it set aside because they had been duped into it), nevertheless the goods were transferred to Gomez's friend with the express authority of the 'owner' (the store manager) who had consented to the transaction.

On the appeal by the DPP to the House of Lords, Lord Keith followed an earlier case (*Lawrence* v *Metropolitan Police Commissioner* [1972] AC 626). His Lordship disagreed with the argument that an act expressly or impliedly authorised by the owner can never amount to an 'appropriation' and pointed out that the decision in *Lawrence* was a direct contradiction of that proposition. The House of Lords upheld the men's convictions for theft and accepted that there are occasions where property can be 'appropriated' for the purposes of the Theft Act 1968, *even though the owner has given his/her consent or authority.*

A number of issues come from this decision:

- *Taking or depriving.* First, it is not necessary that the property be 'taken' in order for there to be an appropriation (contrast this with the offence under s. 12 of taking a conveyance) neither need the owner be 'deprived' of the property. Similarly, there is no need for the defendant to 'gain' anything by an appropriation which can also be caused by damaging or destroying property (*R* v *Graham* [1997] 1 Cr App R 395).
- *Consent.* Secondly, it is irrelevant to the issue of appropriation whether or not the owner consented to that appropriation (again, contrast the offence under s. 12). This is well illustrated in *Lawrence*, the decision followed by the House of Lords in *Gomez*. In *Lawrence* a tourist gave his wallet full of unfamiliar English currency to a taxi driver for the latter to remove the correct fare. The driver in fact helped himself to ('appropriated') far more than the amount owed. It has held that the fact that the wallet and its contents were handed over freely (with consent) by the owner did not prevent the taxi driver's actions from amounting to an 'appropriation' of it. The Court of Appeal appears—at least on one occasion—to have interpreted *Gomez* as deciding that consent *obtained by fraud* is irrelevant to the issue of appropriation (see *R* v *Mazo* [1997] 2 Cr App R 518). However, there is no such restriction placed on the decision in *Gomez* and it seems safe to assume that consent given by the owner will not prevent an 'appropriation' of property for the purposes of the Theft Act 1968.
- *Interfering with goods.* Our higher courts were greatly concerned for a number of years by the swapping of price labels on goods displayed for sale in shops and whether or not such behaviour amounted to an appropriation. A third point that is now clear from the decision in *Gomez* is that simply swapping the price labels on items displayed for sale in a shop *would* amount to an 'appropriation'. This is because to do so, irrespective of any further intention, involves an assumption of one of the owner's rights in relation to the property. If that appropriation were accompanied by the required circumstances of dishonesty and intention to deprive, then there would be a *prima facie* case of theft.
- *More than one appropriation.* A fourth point apparent from *Gomez* is that there may be an appropriation of the same property on more than one occasion. However, once property has been *stolen* (as opposed to merely appropriated), that same property cannot be stolen again by the same thief (*R* v *Atakpu* [1994] QB 69). Appropriation can also be a continuing act, that is, it can include the whole episode of entering and ransacking a house and the subsequent removal of property (*R* v *Hale* (1978) 68 Cr App R 415). Therefore identifying the exact point at which property was appropriated with the requisite intention and accompanying dishonesty can cause practical difficulties.

Summary

In *R* v *Hinks* [2000] UKHL 53, the House of Lords was asked to rule on whether a person could 'appropriate' property belonging to another where the other person made her an absolute gift of property, retaining no proprietary interest in the property or any right to resume or recover it. In that case the defendant had befriended a middle aged man of limited intelligence who had given her some £60,000 over a period of time. The defendant was charged with five counts of theft and, after conviction, eventually appealed to the House of Lords. Their Lordships held that:

- in a prosecution for theft it was unnecessary to prove that the taking was without the owner's consent (as in *Lawrence* above);

- it was immaterial whether the act of appropriation was done with the owner's consent or authority (as in *Gomez*); and
- *Gomez* therefore gave effect to s. 3(1) by treating 'appropriation' as a neutral word covering 'any assumption by a person of the rights of an owner'.

Although consistent with earlier cases, this approach creates a few problems. If acceptance of the gift were treated as an 'appropriation', the defendant would seem to have had a belief that she had a right to deprive the donor of the property (**see para. 2.1.2**) and therefore she was not 'dishonest'. Further, under s. 5 of the 1968 Act (**see para. 2.1.7**) the prosecution has to prove that, at the time of the alleged appropriation, the relevant property belonged to another. In *Hinks* the defendant had been validly given the property, therefore it is difficult to see how the money still belonged to the donor at the time of appropriation.

These and other concerns were raised by Lord Hobhouse who pointed out that ss. 1 to 6 should be read as a whole and that attempts to 'compartmentalise' each element only lead to contradictions. However, he was in a minority and the case decision stands, compartments and all.

If a person, having come by property—innocently or not—without stealing it, later assumes any rights to it by keeping it or treating it as his/her own, then he/she 'appropriates' that property (s. 3(1)).

An exception to these circumstances is provided by s. 3 which states:

(2) Where property or a right or interest in property is or purports to be transferred for value to a person acting in good faith, no later assumption by him of rights which he believed himself to be acquiring shall, by reason of any defect in the transferor's title, amount to theft of the property.

KEYNOTE

If a person buys a car in good faith and gives value for it (i.e. a reasonable price) but then discovers it has been stolen, his/her refusal to return it to the vendor will not, without more, *attract liability for theft.* Without s. 3(2) the retention of the vehicle would be caught by s. 3(1). This narrow exemption does not mean however that the innocent purchaser gets good title to the car (see *National Employers' Mutual Insurance Association Ltd* v *Jones* [1990] 1 AC 24), nor would it provide a defence if the stolen goods are a gift and the 'donee' (recipient) subsequently discovers that they had been stolen.

2.1.5 Property

The Theft Act 1968, s. 4 states:

(1) 'Property' includes money and all other property, real or personal, including things in action and other intangible property.

(2) A person cannot steal land, or things forming part of land and severed from it by him or by his directions, except in the following cases, that is to say—

(a) when he is a trustee or personal representative, or is authorised by power of attorney, or as liquidator of a company, or otherwise, to sell or dispose of land belonging to another, and he appropriates the land or anything forming part of it by dealing with it in breach of the confidence reposed in him; or

(b) when he is not in possession of the land and appropriates anything forming part of the land by severing it or causing it to be severed, or after it has been severed; or

(c) when, being in possession of the land under a tenancy, he appropriates the whole or part of any fixture or structure let to be used with the land.

For purposes of this subsection 'land' does not include incorporeal hereditaments; 'tenancy' means a tenancy for years or any less period and includes an agreement for such a tenancy, but a person who after the end of a tenancy remains in possession as statutory tenant or otherwise is to be treated as having possession under the tenancy, and 'let' shall be construed accordingly.

(3) A person who picks mushrooms growing wild on any land, or who picks flowers, fruit or foliage from a plant growing wild on any land, does not (although not in possession of the land) steal what he picks unless he does it for reward or for sale or other commercial purpose. For purposes of this subsection 'mushroom' includes any fungus, and 'plant' includes any shrub or tree.

(4) Wild creatures, tamed or untamed, shall be regarded as property; but a person cannot steal a wild creature not tamed nor ordinarily kept in captivity, or the carcase of any such creature, unless either it has been reduced into possession by or on behalf of another person and possession of it has not since been lost or abandoned, or another person is in course of reducing it into possession.

KEYNOTE

Specific Types of Property

Under s. 4(1) 'things in action' would include patents and trademarks and other things which can only be enforced by legal action as opposed to physical possession. (See also the Copyright etc. and Trade Marks (Offences and Enforcement) Act 2002.) Other intangible property would include software programs and perhaps credits accumulated on 'smart cards'. Confidential information—such as the contents of an examination paper—is not intangible property *per se* (see *Oxford* v *Moss* (1978) 68 Cr App R 183). However, the document itself would be property. It has been accepted by the Court of Appeal that contractual rights obtained by buying a ticket for the London Underground may amount to a 'thing in action' (see *R* v *Marshall* [1998] 2 Cr App R 282), though this view is extremely contentious.

Although an area of criminal activity causing increasing concern (and cost) is that of so-called 'identity theft', this is something of a misnomer. Adopting another person's characteristics and using their administrative data (such as national insurance number) is not theft as this information is not 'property' for these purposes, however confidential it might be.

Cheques

Cheques will be property as they are pieces of paper (albeit of very little intrinsic value). The contents of a bank or building society account, however, are also a 'thing in action' that can be stolen *provided the account is in credit or within the limits of an agreed overdraft facility* (*R* v *Kohn* (1979) 69 Cr App R 395). Therefore reducing the credit balance in one account, and transferring a like sum into your own account amounts to an 'appropriation' of property within the meaning of s. 1. This principle (set out in *Kohn*) was reaffirmed in *R* v *Williams (Roy)* [2001] 1 Cr App R 362 by the Court of Appeal.

Land

Under s. 4(2) you cannot generally steal land even though it is 'property' for the purposes of criminal damage. An exception to this general rule is that if you are a trustee or personal representative or someone in a position of trust to dispose of land belonging to another, you can be guilty of stealing it if, in such circumstances, you dishonestly dispose of it.

If you are in possession of land under a tenancy then things forming part of that land to be used with it are 'property' capable of being stolen. Such fittings and fixtures (including fireplaces, fitted kitchens, etc.) would be particularly relevant to agricultural tenants or those occupying council property.

Section 4(3) obliquely includes mushrooms, flowers, fruit and foliage in the ambit of 'property' unless they are growing wild on any land. If they are so growing, then the person picking them must be shown to have done so for reward, sale or other commercial purpose in order to be guilty of theft. It is arguable that, if the person does not have such a *purpose at the time of the picking*, any later intention to sell the fruit, etc. may not bring it within the provisions of s. 4(3).

Animals

Section 4(4) acknowledges that all wild creatures are 'property' but goes on to qualify the occasions when they will be capable of being the subject matter of a charge of theft. Once a person has reduced it into possession (say, by trapping, capturing or shooting it), a wild animal can be 'stolen', by another, but not the person reducing it into possession. This is why poaching is not generally theft. If the animal is lost or abandoned after it has been reduced into possession or killed then it cannot be 'stolen'.

These provisos appear to relate more to the concept of 'belonging to another' (see below) than 'property'.

Pets and animals that are tamed or ordinarily kept in captivity are always property for the purposes of theft.

2.1.6 What is not Property?

Human bodies are not property (*Doodeward* v *Spence* (1908) 6 CLR 406) although a driver has been convicted of stealing a specimen of his own urine (*R* v *Welsh* [1974] RTR 478). This principle was upheld by the Court of Appeal in *R* v *Kelly* [1999] QB 621, after the conviction of two people involved in the theft of body parts from the Royal College of Surgeons. The court upheld the convictions for theft on the grounds that the process of *alteration* (amputation, dissection and preservation) which the body parts had undergone did make them 'property' for the purposes of the 1968 Act. The common law rule was that there is no property in a corpse and any change to that rule would have to be made by Parliament.

2.1.7 Belonging to Another

The Theft Act 1968, s. 5 states:

(1) Property shall be regarded as belonging to any person having possession or control of it, or having in it any proprietary right or interest (not being an equitable interest arising only from an agreement to transfer or grant an interest).

(2) Where property is subject to a trust, the persons to whom it belongs shall be regarded as including any person having a right to enforce the trust, and an intention to defeat the trust shall be regarded accordingly as an intention to deprive of the property any person having that right.

KEYNOTE

Property can be 'stolen' from any person who has possession or control or a right or interest in that property. In one case where the defendant sneaked into a garage to recover his own recently-repaired car, he was convicted of stealing the car which at the time 'belonged to' the garage proprietor who had possession and control of it (*R* v *Turner (No. 2)* [1971] 1 WLR 901). In determining whether or not a person had 'possession' of property for the purposes of s. 5(1), the period of possession can be finite (i.e. for a given number of hours, days, etc.) or infinite (*R* v *Kelly* [1998] 3 All ER 741).

It is not necessary to show who does own the property—only that it 'belongs to' someone other than the defendant. (For rights of the Crown under the Treasure Act 1996 and other statutes, **see Blackstone's Criminal Practice 2008, section B4.18.**)

A good example of how this principle operates can be seen in a case before the Court of Appeal where the two defendants went diving in a lake on a golf course, recovering sacks of 'lost' balls which it was believed they were going to sell. Although the defendants argued that the balls had been abandoned by their owners, the Crown had shown that they were 'property belonging to another' and therefore the convictions were safe (*R* v *Rostron*; *R* v *Collinson* [2003] EWCA Crim 2206).

Where money is given by members of the public to charity collectors it becomes the property of the relevant charitable trustees at the moment it goes into the collecting tin (*R* v *Dyke* [2002] Crim LR 153). This will be important when framing the relevant charge or indictment. If in doubt as to the 'ownership' of property that is the subject of a theft, the advice of the CPS should be sought.

When a cheque is written, that will create a 'thing in action'. That thing in action belongs only to the payee. Therefore a payee of a cheque cannot 'steal' the thing in action which it creates (*R* v *Davis* (1988) 88 Cr App R 347). The piece of paper on which a cheque is printed will also be property—however low in value (**see para. 2.1.5**).

In proving theft, you must show that the property belonged to another *at the time of the appropriation*. This requirement has caused some difficulty where a defendant's decision not to pay for goods has been made *after* property passed to him/her. In such cases (e.g. people refusing to pay for meals after they have eaten or deciding to drive off having filled their car with petrol), the proper charge (historically) was deception but would now be covered by the Fraud Act 2006 or making off without payment. But it should be remembered that the appropriation can be an extended and continuing act (*R* v *Atakpu* [1994] QB 69). The House of Lords' ruling in *Gomez* raises some questions over such cases (**see para. 2.1.4**). As the consent of the owner is irrelevant to the issue of 'appropriation', the key element in such cases is whether the property 'belonged to another' at the time of the act of appropriation. If ownership of the property had passed to the defendant *before* he/she appropriated it (e.g. by virtue of the Sale of Goods Act 1979; see *Edwards* v *Ddin* [1976] 1 WLR 942) then this element of theft would not be made out and an alternative charge should be considered.

2.1.8 Obligations Regarding Another's Property

The Theft Act 1968, s. 5 states:

(3) Where a person receives property from or on account of another, and is under an obligation to the other to retain and deal with that property or its proceeds in a particular way, the property or proceeds shall be regarded (as against him) as belonging to the other.

KEYNOTE

'Obligation' means a legal obligation, not simply a moral one (*R* v *Hall* [1973] QB 126). Whether or not such an obligation exists is a matter of law for a trial judge to decide (*R* v *Dubar* [1994] 1 WLR 1484).

Instances under s. 5(3) most commonly involve receiving money from others to retain and use in a certain way (e.g. travel agents taking deposits; solicitors holding funds for mortgagees; or pension fund managers collecting contributions (*R* v *Clowes (No. 2)* [1994] 2 All ER 316)). The Court of Appeal has held that one effect of s. 5(3) is that property can be regarded as belonging to another even where it does not 'belong' to them on a strict interpretation of civil law (*R* v *Klineberg* [1999] 1 Cr App R 427). In that case the defendants collected money from customers in their timeshare business.

Although the customers were told that their deposits would be placed with an independent trustee, the defendants paid the sums into their company account, thereby breaching the 'obligation' under s. 5(3) to deal with the money in a particular way. Section 5(3) would also include, say, the owners of shopping malls where coins thrown into a fountain are to be donated to charity; if the owners did not deal with those coins in the way intended, the provisions of s. 5(3) may well apply.

2.1.9 Obligation to Restore Another's Property

The Theft Act 1968, s. 5 states:

(4) Where a person gets property by another's mistake, and is under an obligation to make restoration (in whole or in part) of the property or its proceeds or of the value thereof, then to the extent of that obligation the property or proceeds shall be regarded (as against him) as belonging to the person entitled to restoration, and an intention not to make restoration shall be regarded accordingly as an intention to deprive that person of the property or proceeds.

KEYNOTE

Before s. 5(4) was enacted, an employee who was mistakenly credited with extra money in his/her bank account could not be prosecuted for larceny (the predecessor of theft) (*Moynes* v *Cooper* [1956] 1 QB 439). In such circumstances under s. 5(4) the employee will be liable for stealing the extra money if he/she keeps it (see *Attorney-General's Reference (No. 1 of 1983)* [1985] QB 182 where a police officer's account was credited with money representing overtime which she had not actually worked).

Section 5(4) only applies where someone *other than the defendant* has made a mistake. It is clear that such a mistake can be a mistake as to a material fact; whether or not a mistake as to *law* would be covered is unclear.

Again, the obligation to make restoration is a *legal* one and, as with s. 5(3), an unenforceable or moral obligation will not be covered by s. 5(4). (See *R* v *Gilks* [1972] 1 WLR 1341 where a betting shop mistakenly paid out winnings against the wrong horse. As gambling debts are not legally enforceable the defendant was not under 'an obligation' to restore the money and therefore s. 5(4) did not apply.)

2.1.10 Intention of Permanently Depriving

If you cannot prove an intention permanently to deprive you cannot prove theft (see *R* v *Warner* (1970) 55 Cr App R 93).

If there is such an intention at the time of the appropriation, giving the property back later will not alter the fact and the charge will be made out (*R* v *McHugh* (1993) 97 Cr App R 335).

In certain circumstances s. 6 may help in determining the presence or absence of such an intention.

The Theft Act 1968, s. 6 states:

(1) A person appropriating property belonging to another without meaning the other permanently to lose the thing itself is nevertheless to be regarded as having the intention of permanently depriving the other of it if his intention is to treat the thing as his own to dispose of regardless of the other's rights; and a borrowing or lending of it may amount to so treating it if, but only if, the borrowing or lending is for a period and in circumstances making it equivalent to an outright taking or disposal.

KEYNOTE

The key feature of s. 6(1) is the intention to treat 'the thing' as one's own to dispose of regardless of the other's rights. An example of such a case would be where property is 'held to ransom' (*R* v *Coffey* [1987] Crim LR 498). The borrowing or lending of another's property is specifically caught within s. 6(1). If a person takes property from his/her employer (e.g. carpet tiles) and uses it in a way which makes restoration unlikely or impossible (e.g. by laying them in his/her living room), then s. 6(1) will apply (see *R* v *Velumyl* [1989] Crim LR 299).

Similarly, if a person borrowed a season ticket causing the owner to miss a match, s. 6(1) would help prove the required intention because the circumstances of the borrowing make it equivalent to an outright taking.

In a case involving robbery (see below), the defendants took the victim's personal stereo headphones from him and broke them in two, rendering them useless before returning them to him. The Administrative Court held that a person who took something and dealt with it for the purpose of rendering it useless in this way demonstrated the intention of treating that article as his/her own to dispose of. The court did not accept the argument that the property had to be totally exhausted before s. 6 applied (see also *R* v *Fernandes* [1996] 1 Cr App R 175) and held that the magistrates had been wrong to accept the submission of no case to answer on this point (*DPP* v *J* (2002) LTL 20 February).

The Theft Act 1968, s. 6 states:

(2) Without prejudice to the generality of subsection (1) above, where a person, having possession or control (lawfully or not) of property belonging to another, parts with the property under a condition as to its return which he may not be able to perform, this (if done for purposes of his own and without the other's authority) amounts to treating the property as his own to dispose of regardless of the other's rights.

KEYNOTE

Section 6(2) deals with occasions such as pawning another's property. If there is a likelihood that the defendant will be unable to meet the conditions under which he/she parted with another person's property, s. 6(2) would help in proving an intention permanently to deprive.

2.2 Burglary

The main offence of burglary is split into two—s. 9(1)(a) and s. 9(1)(b). These are discussed below.

2.2.1 Section 9(1)(a)

OFFENCE: **Burglary—*Theft Act 1968, s. 9***

• Triable on indictment if 'ulterior offence' is so triable, or if committed in dwelling and violence used; otherwise triable either way • Fourteen years' imprisonment if building/part of building is dwelling • Otherwise ten years' imprisonment on indictment • Six months' imprisonment and/or a fine summarily

The Theft Act 1968, s. 9 states:

(1) A person is guilty of burglary if—
 (a) he enters any building or part of a building as a trespasser and with intent to commit any such offence as is mentioned in subsection (2) below; or ...
(2) The offences referred to in subsection (1)(a) above are offences of stealing anything in the building or part of a building in question, of inflicting on any person therein any grievous bodily harm and of doing unlawful damage to the building or anything therein.

KEYNOTE

Enters

What action on the part of the defendant constitutes 'entry' into a building or part of a building? The Theft Act 1968 does not define the term 'entry' and so we are left to resolve the meaning of this term by reference to case law and the decisions of the courts. The common law rule was that the insertion of any part of the body, *however small*, was sufficient to be considered an 'entry'. So where D pushed in a window pane and the forepart of his finger was observed in the building that was enough (*R* v *Davis* (1823) Russ & Ry 499). This approach was narrowed considerably in *R* v *Collins* [1973] QB 100, where it was said that entry needed to be 'effective and substantial'. The ruling in *Collins* was rejected by the Court of Appeal in *R* v *Brown* [1985] Crim LR 212, CA, where it was stated that the 'substantial' element was surplus to requirements and that entry need only be 'effective'. Whether an entry was 'effective' or not was for the jury to decide. So the decision of the court in *Brown* appears to be the current accepted approach to defining the term; entry must therefore be 'effective'.

An 'effective' entry does not mean that the defendant has to enter a building or part of a building to such a degree that the ulterior offence, which he is entering with the intention to commit (the theft, GBH or criminal damage), can be committed (*R* v *Ryan* [1996] Crim LR 320, CA). Nor does it mean that the defendant must get his whole body into the building. In *Brown*, the defendant had his feet on the ground outside the building with the upper half inside the building as he searched for goods to steal; this was held to be an entry. In *Ryan*, the defendant, who had become trapped by his neck with only his head and right arm inside the window, was held to have 'entered' the building. In *Brown*, the Court of Appeal stated that it would be astounding if a smash-and-grab raider, who inserted his hand through a shop window to grab goods, was not considered to have 'entered' the building.

At common law, the insertion of an instrument would constitute entry as long as the instrument was inserted to enable the ulterior offence to take place, e.g. a hook inserted into premises to steal property or the muzzle of a gun pushed through a letterbox with a view to cause GBH. Insertion of an instrument merely to facilitate entry, e.g. using a coat hanger to open a window lock, *would not* be entry. Although there is no recent authority on the issue, it is likely that this line of reasoning in relation to the use of instruments in burglary is still acceptable.

Entry must be deliberate and not accidental.

Ultimately, whether the defendant has entered a building or not will be a question of fact for the jury or magistrate(s).

Trespasser

For a person to be guilty of the offence of burglary he must know that he is entering as a trespasser (i.e. he must know he is entering without a right by law or permission to do so) or be reckless as to that fact. Sometimes a defendant may have a general permission to enter premises from which he then steals. In such circumstances the exceeding of the granted permission places the defendant in a position of being a trespasser from the outset. In *R* v *Jones and Smith* [1976] 1 WLR 672, the defendant was convicted of burglary when he took two televisions from his father's home. He had a key to the premises and was free to come and go as he liked but when he entered his father's house (using the key) accompanied by a friend at 3am and stole the television sets, he committed burglary as it was his intention to steal—such an intent voids the general permission to enter.

2.2.2 Building

The Theft Act 1968 s. 9 states:

(4) References in subsections (1) and (2) above to a building, . . . and the reference in subsection (3), above,to a building which is a dwelling, shall apply also to an inhabited vehicle or vessel,

and shall apply to any such vehicle or vessel at times when the person having a habitation in it is not there as well as at times when he is.

KEYNOTE

Building

A building is generally considered to be a structure of a permanent nature (*Norfolk Constabulary* v *Seekings and Gould* [1986] Crim LR 167), although a substantial portable structure with most of the attributes of a building can be a 'building' for the purposes of burglary. For example, in *B & S* v *Leathley* [1979] Crim LR 314, Crown Ct, a portable container measuring 25ft by 7ft by 7ft and weighing three tons, which had occupied the same position for three years, was connected to mains electricity and which was due to remain in the same position for the foreseeable future, was considered to be a building for the purposes of burglary. An unfinished house can be a building for the purposes of burglary (*R* v *Manning* (1871) LR 1 CCR 338). Tents and marquees are considered to fall outside the term, even if the tent is someone's home (the Criminal Law Revision Committee intended tents to be outside the protection of burglary).

The effect of s. 9(4) is to include house boats and vehicles used as potential dwellings within the term. This does depend on whether the vehicle or vessel is 'inhabited'; a canal boat used as a permanent home is capable of being burgled.

Part of a Building

A person may commit burglary when, although he is in one part of a building with legitimate access, he enters another part of it as a trespasser.

- A tenant of a block of flats has a pass-key that provides access to a communal foyer of the block of flats. He uses the pass-key to enter the foyer (*entering a building and plainly not a trespasser at this stage*) Instead of entering his own flat he forces entry to a neighbour's flat by breaking down the neighbour's door that can be accessed via the communal foyer (*moving from one part of a building to another in the process and certainly a trespasser at this stage*).

Part of a building does not mean that there has to be a physical separation of one room from another. In *R* v *Walkington* [1979] 2 All ER 716, the defendant walked behind a moveable counter in a shop with the intention to steal and was found guilty of burglary as this was held to be 'part of a building'. A 'no entry' or a rope could mark off one part of a building from another.

2.2.3 Intentions at the Time of Entry

The intentions must be as follows:

- Stealing—this means an intention to commit theft under s. 1 (**see para. 2.1.1**). It will not include abstracting electricity because abstracting under s. 13 is not stealing (*Low* v *Blease* [1975] Crim LR 513), neither will it include taking a conveyance. The property which the defendant intends to steal must be in a building or part of a building.
- Inflicting grievous bodily harm—if grievous bodily harm is inflicted, then the second offence under s. 9(1)(b) below would apply. In proving an intention to commit grievious bodily harm under s. 9(1)(a), it is not necessary to prove that an assault was actually committed (*Metropolitan Police Commissioner* v *Wilson* [1984] AC 242). The offence in question in respect of a burglary under s. 9(1)(a) is of grievous bodily harm contrary to s. 18 of the Offences Against the Person Act 1861.
- Causing unlawful damage—this includes damage, not only to the building but to anything in it.

2.2.4 Conditional Intent

Provided the required intention can be proved, it is immaterial whether or not there is anything 'worth stealing' within the building (*R* v *Walkington* [1979] 1 WLR 1169). The same will be true if the person whom the defendant intends to cause serious harm is not in the building or part of the building at the time.

2.2.5 Section 9(1)(b)

OFFENCE: **Burglary—*Theft Act 1968, s. 9***
(see para. 1.11.4.1)

The Theft Act 1968, s. 9 states:

(1) A person is guilty of burglary if—

...

(b) having entered any building or part of a building as a trespasser he steals or attempts to steal anything in the building or that part of it or inflicts or attempts to inflict on any person therein any grievous bodily harm.

KEYNOTE

The second type of burglary involves a defendant's behaviour *after* entering a building or part of a building.

The defendant must have entered the building or part of a building as a trespasser; it is not enough that he/she subsequently became a trespasser by exceeding a condition of entry (e.g. hiding in the public area of a shop during open hours until the shop closes). However, where a person has entered a particular building (such as a shop or a pub) lawfully and without trespassing, if he/she later moves to *another part* of the building as a trespasser, this element of the offence will be made out.

EXAMPLE

D enters a public house near closing time with a friend who buys him a drink from the bar. D's entry onto that part of the premises has been authorised by the implied licence extended to members of the adult public by the publican and therefore D is not a trespasser. D then goes into the lavatories to use them as such. At this point he has entered another part of a building but again his entry is made under the implied licence to customers wishing to use the lavatories. While inside the lavatory area, D decides to hide until closing time in order to avoid buying his friend a drink. He hides inside one of the cubicles. At this point, although D's intention in hiding may be considered a little mean-spirited, he has none of the required intentions for the purposes of s. 9(1)(a) (**see para. 2.2.1**).

Once the publican has shut the pub for the night, D leaves the lavatory and walks into the bar area. Now D has entered *a part of a building as a trespasser* because the licence extended to members of the public by the publican certainly does not cover wandering around in the bar after it has been closed. Having no particular intention at this point, however, D has still not committed an offence of burglary.

On seeing the gaming machines in the public bar, D decides to break into them and steal the money inside. At this point, although he has *two* of the required intentions for s. 9(1)(a) (an intention to steal and an intention to cause unlawful damage), those intentions were formed *after* his entry. Therefore, D has not committed burglary under s. 9(1)(a). Because he has not stolen/attempted to steal or inflicted/attempted to inflict grievous bodily harm on any person therein, D has not committed burglary under s. 9(1)(b) either.

D then breaks open a gaming machine. At this point he commits burglary under s. 9(1)(b). This is because, having entered a part of a building (the public bar area) as a trespasser (because the pub is closed and D knows that to be the case), he *attempts to steal*. If he simply damaged the machine without an intention of stealing the contents, D would not commit this offence because causing unlawful damage is only relevant to the offence under s. 9(1)(a).

Unlike s. 9(1)(a), there are only two further elements to the offence under s. 9(1)(b)—the subsequent theft/attempted theft of anything in the building or part of it, and the subsequent inflicting/attempted inflicting of grievous bodily harm to any person therein. The offence in question in respect of a burglary under s. 9(1)(b) is of grievous bodily harm contrary to s. 18 or s. 20 of the Offences Against the Person Act 1861.

2.3 Aggravated Burglary

OFFENCE: **Aggravated Burglary—*Theft Act 1968, s. 10***

- Triable on indictment
- Life imprisonment

The Theft Act 1968, s. 10 states:

(1) A person is guilty of aggravated burglary if he commits any burglary and at the time has with him any firearm or imitation firearm, any weapon of offence, or any explosive;...

KEYNOTE

An aggravated burglary is committed when a person commits an offence of burglary (either a s. 9(1)(a) or a s. 9(1)(b)) and at the time he has with him his **WIFE**.

W –Weapon of offence

I –Imitation firearm

F –Firearm

E –Explosive

Two points in the definition merit further discussion: (i) *at the time* and (ii) *has with him.*

At the time

These words require consideration of the type of burglary the defendant is charged with. The moment at which a burglary under s. 9(1)(a) is committed is at the point of entry, therefore it is essential that the defendant has the WIFE with him/her when entering a building or part of a building with the intention of committing one of the trigger offences under s. 9(1)(a). If that is the case, the defendant commits aggravated burglary. The moment at which a burglary under s. 9(1)(b) is committed is when the defendant steals, inflicts grievous bodily harm on any person or attempts to do either. If the defendant has the WIFE with him/her when committing or attempting to commit either offence, an aggravated burglary is committed.

EXAMPLE

A person (X) enters the kitchen of a house as a trespasser intending to steal the contents. At the point of entry X does not have any WIFE item with him, so at this point in time X has committed a s. 9(1)(a) burglary. While X is in the kitchen the occupier of the house enters the kitchen and disturbs him. X picks up a carving knife and threatens the occupier with it. This is not an aggravated burglary as X has not committed or attempted to commit theft or to inflict GBH. The occupier rushes towards X who stabs the occupier, inflicting GBH in the process. This is a s. 9(1)(b) burglary and at the time of its commission X has a WIFE item with him, as a result this becomes an aggravated burglary.

Has with him

'Has with him' is more restrictive than the term 'possession'. It will require the defendant to have some degree of *immediate control* of the item (*R* v *Pawlicki* [1992] 1 WLR 827) and will normally be the same as 'carrying' (*R* v *Klass* [1998] 1 Cr App R 453) although the defendant need not actually have the WIFE item *on his/her person* to be in *immediate control* of it. It is also essential that the individual has knowledge of the presence of the WIFE item. So if a burglary is committed by a single offender who knows he/she has a bayonet in his coat pocket when the offence is committed the issue of aggravated burglary is clear. However, what of the situation where two offenders commit such a burglary? Liability depends on knowledge.

EXAMPLE

X and Y decide to commit a burglary together. X is concerned about being disturbed during the burglary and decides to take a flick-knife along with him when the burglary takes place; he does not tell Y about the flick-knife. When X and Y enter the building they intend to burgle, both commit a s. 9(1)(a) burglary. As X has a flick-knife with him at the time, X commits an aggravated burglary. However, Y does not commit the aggravated offence because he has no knowledge of the existence of the WIFE item. If X had told Y about the flick-knife then Y would have the required knowledge and would be deemed to have it with him so both would be guilty under s. 10 (*R* v *Jones* [1979] CLY 411).

Therefore, if the defendant has no knowledge of the WIFE item he/she does not commit the aggravated offence. If several people are charged with the offence of aggravated burglary, it must be shown that one of the defendants who actually entered the building or part of a building had the weapon with him/her (*R* v *Klass* [1998] 1 Cr App R 453).

It is important to note that the aggravated offence is committed due to the presence of the WIFE when the s. 9(1)(a) or s. 9(1)(b) burglary is carried out. It is irrelevant that the defendant had the item with him/her for some other purpose unconnected with the burglary offence. The thought process underpinning this point is that if a burglar has the WIFE item with him/her during the course of a domestic burglary and is confronted by the householder, there would be a strong temptation to make use of it regardless of why the burglar had the WIFE with him/her in the first place.

Instant Arming

Ordinary items can, instantaneously, change into weapons of offence; it is the intention of the person to use an item in a particular way that allows this to take place. A good illustration of this concept is the case of *R* v *Kelly* (1992) 97 Cr App R 245. The defendant entered a building using a screwdriver to facilitate entry. When he was confronted he prodded the person confronting him in the stomach with the screwdriver. At that moment the screwdriver instantly became a weapon of offence and the defendant was later convicted of aggravated burglary.

2.3.1 Firearm/Weapon of Offence/Explosive

The Theft Act 1968, s. 10 goes on to state:

(1) ... and for this purpose—

(a) 'firearm' includes an airgun or pistol, and 'imitation firearm' means anything which has the appearance of being a firearm, whether capable of being discharged or not, and

(b) 'weapon of offence' means any article made or adapted for use for causing injury to or incapacitating a person, or intended by the person having it with him for such use; and
(c) 'explosive' means any article manufactured for the purpose of producing a practical effect by explosion, or intended by the person having it with him for that purpose.

Weapon of Offence

This is a wider definition than that under the Prevention of Crime Act 1953. It includes:

- Items *made* for causing injury, e.g. a bayonet or a flick-knife (as above).
- Items *adapted* for causing injury, e.g. a screwdriver that has been sharpened at the tip.
- Items *intended* for causing injury, e.g. an ordinary cutlery knife. The cutlery knife is certainly inoffensive in everyday use but if the defendant *intends* to use it to injure, it will fall into this category.
- Items *made, adapted or intended* to incapacitate a person, e.g. handcuffs, rope, CS spray and chloroform.

The defendant must not only know of the presence of the weapon but also that it is a weapon of offence.

Imitation Firearm

This includes anything which has the appearance of being a firearm, whether capable of being discharged or not (but note that this will not include the defendant's fingers pointed at someone under a coat to resemble a firearm (*R* v *Bentham* [2005] UKHL 18)).

Firearm

This does not relate to the definition under the Firearms Act 1968. Indeed, the term is not defined other than to include airguns and air pistols.

Explosive

This would cover explosives such as TNT and items such as grenades—both manufactured to produce a practical effect by explosion. It also covers an item intended by the person having it with him/her for such a purpose, potentially bringing home-made devices or substances into the equation. The issue in relation to fireworks has yet to be firmly resolved by the courts, although they may well be excluded from the definition as fireworks are, by and large, manufactured to produce a pyrotechnic rather than practical effect by explosion and have been described as 'things that are made for amusement' (*Bliss* v *Lilley* (1862) 32 LJMC 3)).

2.4 Robbery

OFFENCE: **Robbery—*Theft Act 1968, s. 8***
- Triable on indictment • Life imprisonment

The Theft Act 1968, s. 8 states:

(1) A person is guilty of robbery if he steals, and immediately before or at the time of doing so, and in order to do so, he uses force on any person or puts or seeks to put any person in fear of being then and there subjected to force.

KEYNOTE

The Theft Element of the Offence

For there to be a robbery, there must be a theft; so if there is no theft, then there can be no robbery. The word 'steal' in the offence relates to the offence under s. 1 of the Theft Act 1968 and, therefore, if any element of theft cannot be proved the offence of robbery will not be made out. For example, in *R* v *Robinson* [1977] Crim LR 173, D, who was owed £7 by P's wife, approached P, brandishing a knife. A fight followed, during which P dropped a £5 note. D picked it up and demanded the remaining £2 owed to him. Allowing D's appeal against a conviction for robbery, the Court of Appeal held that the prosecution had to prove that D was guilty of theft, and that he would not be (under the Theft Act 1968, s. 2(1)(a)) if he believed that he had a right in law to deprive P of the money, even though he knew that he was not entitled to use the knife to get it.

The Robbery Time Frame

Section 8(1) requires that the force must be used or the threat made 'immediately before or at the time' of the theft. There is no guidance as to what 'immediately before' means. Clearly, if the force used or threatened is *after* the offence of theft has taken place, there will be no robbery; however theft can be a continuing offence. This was decided in *R* v *Hale* (1978) 68 Cr App Rep 415, where the Court of Appeal stated that appropriation is a continuing act and whether it has finished or not is a matter for the jury to decide. From the robbery perspective, *Hale* decides that where D had assumed ownership of goods in a house, the 'time' of stealing is a continuing process. It does not end as soon as the property is picked up by the defendant and can be a continuing act so long as he is in the course of removing it from the premises. So, if D uses or threatens force to get away with the property (whilst still in the house for example), a robbery is committed. This would probably not be the case if the defendant used force outside the house as there must come a time when the appropriation ends. The issue may be resolved by asking the question, 'Was D still on the job?' (*R* v *Atakpu* [1994] QB 69).

In Order to Do So

The use or threat of force must be 'in order' to carry out the theft. Force used in any other context means the offence is not committed, for example:

- Two men have an argument outside a pub and begin fighting each other. One man punches the other in the face and the force of the blow knocks the man out. As the injured man falls the floor, his wallet drops out of his jacket pocket and onto the pavement. His opponent decides that he will steal the wallet. *No robbery is committed in these circumstances because the force is used for a purpose other than to steal.*

The question to ask in such circumstances is 'Why has the force been used and/or threatened?' If the answer is anything other than 'To enable the defendant to commit theft' then there is no offence of robbery.

Force

The slightest use of force to accomplish a theft changes that theft into a robbery. An illustration can be found in the case of *R* v *Dawson* (1976) 64 Cr App R 170, where the defendant and two others surrounded their victim. One of the attackers 'nudged' the victim and while he was unbalanced another stole his wallet. In *Dawson*, the court declined to define 'force' any further than to say that juries would understand it readily enough. In line with general principles of *actus reus* (criminal conduct), the force used by the defendant must be used voluntarily. Therefore, the accidental use of force such as when a pickpocket, in the process of stealing a wallet from his victim on a train, is pushed into his victim by the train jolting on the railway line would not be a robbery.

On Any Person

The force used to accomplish a robbery need not be used against the owner or possessor of the property. For example, a gang of armed criminals use force against a security guard in order to overpower him and steal cash from the safe he is standing outside and guarding.

Force does not actually have to be used 'on' the *person* i.e. on the actual body of the victim. It may be used on something that the victim is carrying as in the case of *R* v *Clouden* [1987] Crim LR 65, where the Court of Appeal dismissed an appeal against a conviction for robbery when the defendant had wrenched the victim's shopping basket from her hand and ran off with it.

The Fear of Force

Where only the *threat* of force is involved the intention must be to put a person in fear for *himself*; an intention to put someone in fear for another is not enough (*R* v *Taylor* [1996] 10 Archbold News 2, CA). This may seem at odds with the approach to the actual *use* of force in the offence of robbery (in that force *can* be used against a third party who is unconnected with the property subject to the theft). For example:

- A man enters a betting shop and approaches the cashier. Without saying a word he passes a note to the cashier that simply says, 'Look to your left'. The cashier looks to her left and sees the man's accomplice standing several feet away and pointing a knife at the back of one of the betting shop customers. The customer is oblivious to the actions of the man's accomplice. The man passes a second note to the cashier that says, 'Give me the money in the till or else he gets it!' *At this stage there is no robbery committed as the cashier cannot fear force for the betting shop customer. However, whilst there is no robbery there would be an offence of blackmail* (Theft Act 1968, s. 21). The cashier shakes her head and refuses to hand over any money. At this point, the man signals to his accomplice who pulls the customer's head backwards and drags the knife across the side of the customer's throat causing a small cut. The customer screams in terror and at this point the cashier concedes to the man's demand and hands over the till contents. *At this point in time a robbery is committed as force is actually being used (albeit on a third party).*

General Points

Any threats to use force at some time in the future (even by a matter of minutes) would constitute an offence of blackmail. Threats to use force at some place other than the location of the offence fall into the same category. This effectively excludes threats made via the telephone in all but the most improbable of situations.

2.5 Blackmail

GAIN FOR SELF/OTHER LOSS TO ANOTHER UNWARRANTED DEMAND WITH MENACES

OFFENCE: **Blackmail—*Theft Act 1968, s. 21***

- Triable on indictment • 14 years' imprisonment

The Theft Act 1968, s. 21 states:

(1) A person is guilty of blackmail if, with a view to gain for himself or another or with intent to cause loss to another, he makes any unwarranted demand with menaces; and for this purpose a demand with menaces is unwarranted unless the person making it does so in the belief—

(a) that he has reasonable grounds for making the demand; and

(b) that the use of the menaces is a proper means of reinforcing the demand.

(2) The nature of the act or omission demanded is immaterial, and it is also immaterial whether the menaces relate to action to be taken by the person making the demand.

KEYNOTE

In proving this offence you must show that a defendant acted either with a view to gain for himself/herself or another or with intent to cause loss to another. The distinction here is important. The phrase 'with a view to' has been held (albeit under a different criminal statute) by the Court of Appeal to be less than 'with intent to' (*R* v *Zaman* [2003] FSR 13). In *Zaman*, the court accepted that a lesser degree of *mens rea* was required to prove that a defendant acted 'with a view to' something and that this phrase meant simply that the defendant had something in his/her contemplation as *something that realistically might occur*, not that he/she necessarily intended or even wanted it to happen. Clearly this is a very different test from 'intent'. The alternative is an 'intent' to cause loss—a harder element to prove.

There is no requirement for dishonesty, deception or theft and the offence is aimed at the making of the demands rather than the consequences of them.

2.5.1 Meaning of Gain and Loss

Section 34 of the 1968 Act states:

(2) For the purposes of this Act—
- (a) 'gain' and 'loss' are to be construed as extending only to gain or loss in money or other property, but as extending to any such gain or loss whether temporary or permanent; and—
  - (i) 'gain' includes a gain by keeping what one has, as well as a gain by getting what one has not; and
  - (ii) 'loss' includes a loss by not getting what one might get, as well as a loss by parting with what one has;

KEYNOTE

Keeping what you already have can amount to a 'gain'. Similarly, not getting something that you might expect to get can be a 'loss'.

EXAMPLE

A person makes unwarranted demands with menaces with a view to getting a sports fixture cancelled and thereby to avoid losing money that he has bet on the outcome of that fixture. Here it could be argued that the intention of keeping what the defendant already had (the money at risk on the bet) amounts to 'gain' as defined under s. 34(2). Similarly, the intention of preventing others getting what they might have got (their winnings or the club's earnings) could amount to a 'loss'.

2.5.2 Criminal Conduct

The offence of blackmail is complete when the demand with menaces is made. It does not matter whether the demands bring about the desired consequences or not. If a demand is made by letter, the act of making it is complete when the letter is posted. The letter does not have to be received (*Treacy* v *DPP* [1971] AC 537).

The Court of Appeal has held that words or conduct which would not intimidate or influence anyone to respond to the demand would not be 'menaces'. As such, the term requires threats and conduct of such a nature and extent that a person of normal stability and courage might be influenced or made apprehensive so as to give in to the demands (see *R* v *Clear* [1968] 1 QB 670).

Menaces will therefore include threats but these must be significant *to the victim*. If a threat bears a particular significance for a victim (such as being locked in the boot of a car to someone who is claustrophobic) that will be enough, provided the defendant was aware of that fact. If a victim is particularly timid and the defendant knows it, that timidity may be taken into account when assessing whether or not the defendant's conduct was 'menacing' (*R* v *Garwood* [1987] 1 WLR 319).

2.5.3 Unwarranted?

If a defendant raises the issue that his/her demand was reasonable and proper, you will have to prove that he/she did not believe:

- that he/she had reasonable grounds for making the demand; and
- that the use of the particular menaces employed was not a proper means of reinforcing it.

The defendant's *belief* will be a subjective one and therefore could be entirely unreasonable. However, if the threatened action would itself be unlawful (such as a threat to rape the victim) then it is unlikely that the courts would accept any claim by a defendant that he/she believed such a demand to be 'proper' (see *R* v *Harvey* (1980) 72 Cr App R 139).

2.6 Fraud

2.6.1 Introduction

Until 2007 there was no single, general fraud law in English law; instead there were a number of statutory crimes (under the Theft Acts 1968 and 1978) such as 'obtaining property by deception' and 'obtaining services by deception' that catered for such criminal behaviour. The inadequacy of existing law to deal with activities carried out utilising computer technology, and several loopholes in preceding anti-fraud legislation, provided the impetus for the new Act which has replaced previous legislation with more contemporary offences that the Government say are far more suited to modern fraud. The Act provides for a general offence of fraud with three ways of committing it (by false representation, by failing to disclose information, and by abuse of position) as well as creating new offences of obtaining services dishonestly, and possessing, making, and supplying articles for use in fraud. It also creates offences in relation to fraudulent business activities by sole traders and companies but these are beyond the scope of this manual.

2.6.2 Fraud

OFFENCE: **Fraud—*Fraud Act 2006, s. 1***

- Triable either way • Ten years' imprisonment and/or a fine on indictment
- Twelve months' imprisonment and/or a fine summarily

The Fraud Act 2006, s. 1 states:

(1) A person is guilty of fraud if he is in breach of any of the sections listed in subsection (2) (which provide for different ways of committing the offence).

(2) The sections are—

(a) section 2 (fraud by false representation),

(b) section 3 (fraud by failing to disclose information), and
(c) section 4 (fraud by abuse of position)

KEYNOTE

The heart of all three methods of committing the offence of fraud is in the *conduct and ulterior intent* of the defendant. This differs from previous deception-related offences where the *consequences* of the defendant's actions were important. The effect of this approach is that a defendant's unsuccessful 'attempt' to commit the offence of fraud may amount to the commission of the substantive offence, effectively excluding the possibility of an offence under the Criminal Attempts Act 1981.

2.6.3 Fraud by False Representation

The Fraud Act 2006, s. 2 states:

(1) A person is in breach of this section if he—
  (a) dishonestly makes a false representation, and
  (b) intends, by making the representation—
    (i) to make a gain for himself or another, or
    (ii) to cause loss to another or to expose another to the risk of loss.
(2) A representation is false if—
  (a) it is untrue or misleading, and
  (b) the person making it knows that it is, or might be, untrue or misleading.
(3) 'Representation' means any representation as to fact or law, including a representation as to the state of mind of—
  (a) the person making the representation, or
  (b) any other person.
(4) A representation may be express or implied.
(5) For the purposes of this section a representation may be regarded as made if it (or anything implying it) is submitted in any form to any system or device designed to receive, convey or respond to communications (with or without human intervention).

KEYNOTE

Dishonestly

The 'dishonestly' referred to in s. 2(1)(a) is a reference to the test of dishonesty established in *R* v *Ghosh* [1982] QB 1053. The same test applies to ss. 3 and 4 of the Act.

Gain and Loss

Section 2(1)(b) refers to 'gain' and 'loss' and that the person making the representation must do so with the intention of making a gain or causing a loss or risk of loss to another. *The gain or loss does not actually have to take place* (the terms 'gain' and 'loss' are discussed at **para. 2.6.6**.

Representation

A representation is false if it is untrue or misleading *and* the person making it knows this is or knows this might be the case. Therefore, an untrue statement made in the honest belief that it is in fact true, would not suffice. The words 'or might be' must involve a subjective belief on the part of the person making the representation.

The representation may be express or implied and can be communicated in words or conduct. There is no limitation on the way in which the representation must be expressed, so it could be written, spoken or posted on a website. A representation may also be implied by conduct. For example, a person dishonestly misusing a credit card to pay for items hands the card to a cashier without saying a word. By handing the card to the cashier he is falsely representing that he has authority to use it for that transaction. It is immaterial that the cashier accepting the card for payment is deceived by the representation. The fact that the cashier's state of mind plays no part in the commission of the offence marks a significant departure from the previous law governing this type of activity. Deception offences under the Theft Acts 1968 and 1978 required the 'target' of the deception to be deceived by the words or conduct of the defendant; if this element were not present there would only be an attempted deception. The Fraud Act 2006 removes this requirement so that where a defendant makes a false representation knowing that it is false or might be, the offence of fraud is complete. Any representation made must be one as to fact or law, so a broken promise is not in itself a false representation. However, a statement may be false if it misrepresents the current intentions or state of mind of the person making it or anyone else. For example, D visits V's house and tells V that he needs emergency work carried out on his roof. D states that he is in a position to do the work immediately but only if V pays him £1000 there and then. V gives D the money and D then leaves without carrying out the work; the truth of the matter was that D had never intended to carry out the work. Such a 'promise' by D would amount to an offence as it involved a false representation i.e. he never intended to keep the promise.

The offence is complete the moment the false representation is made (a similar position can be found with the offence of blackmail (**see para. 2.5**)). The representation need never be heard nor communicated to the recipient and if carried out by post, would be complete when the letter is posted (*Treacy* v *DPP* [1971] AC 537).

Phishing

The offence would also be committed by someone who engages in 'phishing'. This is the practice of sending out e-mails in bulk, purporting to represent a well-known brand in the hope of sending victims to a bogus website that tricks them into disclosing bank account details. 'Phishing kits' have long been available on the Internet but it was difficult to prosecute sellers. The offence under s. 2 now covers such activity.

Machines

Under the old law, a machine could not be deceived and any activity carried out that fooled a machine or computer would not amount to deception. Section 2(5) of the Fraud Act enables the offence of fraud to apply in such cases, as necessity for human involvement in any response from the person making the false representation has been dispensed with (for example where a person enters a number into a 'Chip and PIN' machine).

2.6.4 Fraud by Failing to Disclose

The Fraud Act 2006, s. 3 states:

A person is in breach of this section if he—
- (a) dishonestly fails to disclose to another person information which he is under a legal duty to disclose, and
- (b) intends, by failing to disclose the information—
  - (i) to make a gain for himself or another, or
  - (ii) to cause loss to another or to expose another to a risk of loss.

KEYNOTE

Section 3 creates an offence of dishonestly failing to disclose information where there is a legal duty to do so. The term 'legal duty' has not been defined but will include duties under oral contracts as well as written contracts. The Law Commission's *Report on Fraud* dealt with the concept of legal duty and stated that duties might arise:

- from statute
- where the transaction is one of the utmost good faith
- from the express or implied terms of a contract
- from the custom of a particular trade or market, or
- from the existence of a fiduciary relationship between parties.

The legal duty to disclose information will exist if:

- the defendant's actions give the victim a cause in action for damages or
- if the law gives the victim the right to set aside any change in his or her legal position to which he or she may have consented as a result of the non-disclosure.

A fiduciary relationship is one relating to the responsibility of looking after someone else's money in a correct way. Examples of such behaviour would include a solicitor failing to share vital information with a client in the context of their work relationship, in order to carry out a fraud upon that client, or if a person intentionally failed to disclose information relating to a heart condition when making an application for life insurance.

2.6.5 Fraud by Abuse of Position

The Fraud Act 2006, s. 4 states:

(1) A person is in breach of this section if he—
  (a) occupies a position in which he is expected to safeguard, or not to act against, the financial interests of another person,
  (b) dishonestly abuses that position, and
  (c) intends, by means of the abuse of that position—
    (i) to make a gain for himself or another, or
    (ii) to cause loss to another or to expose another to a risk of loss.

(2) A person may be regarded as having abused his position even though his conduct consisted of an omission rather than an act.

KEYNOTE

The crux of this offence is the financial and dishonest abuse of a privileged position of trust. An offence under s. 4 may be committed in a variety of ways as the 'position' that the defendant occupies may be the result of an assortment of relationships. The Law Commission explained the meaning of 'position' at paragraph 7.38:

> The necessary relationship will be present between trustee and beneficiary, director and company, professional person and client, agent and principle, employee and employer, or between partners. It may arise otherwise, for example within a family, or in the context of voluntary work, or in any context where the parties are not at arm's length.

The term 'abuse' is not defined by the Act.

Liability for the offence could develop from a wide range of conduct, for example:

- An employee of a software company uses his position to clone software products with the intention of selling the products on.
- An estate agent values a house belonging to an elderly person at an artificially low price and then arranges for his brother to purchase the house.

- A person who is employed to care for a disabled person and has access to that person's bank account, abuses his position by transferring funds to invest in a high-risk business venture of his own.

The offence can also be committed by omission, for example:

- An employee fails to take up the chance of a crucial contract in order that an associate or rival company can take it up instead of and at the expense of the employer.

2.6.6 Gain and Loss

The Fraud Act 2006, s. 5 states:

(1) The references to gain and loss in sections 2 to 4 are to be read in accordance with this section.
(2) 'Gain' and 'loss'—
(a) extend only to gain and loss in money or other property;
(b) include any such gain or loss whether temporary or permanent;
and 'property' means any property whether real or personal (including things in action and other intangible property).
(3) 'Gain' includes a gain by keeping what one has, as well as getting what one does not have.
(4) 'Loss' includes a loss by not getting what one might get, as well as a loss by parting with what one has.

KEYNOTE

The definition of 'gain' and 'loss' is very similar to that of the 'gain' and 'loss' in blackmail (**see para. 2.5.1**). It is important to note that the 'gain' and 'loss' relates only to *money and other property*. The definition of property covers all forms of property including intellectual property and is based on the definition of 'property' contained in s. 4(1) of the Theft Act 1968 (**see para. 2.1.5**).

2.6.7 Possession or Control of Articles for Use in Frauds

OFFENCE: **Possession or Control of Articles for Use in Frauds—*Fraud Act 2006, s. 6***

- Triable either way • Five years' imprisonment and/or fine on indictment • Twelve months' imprisonment and/or fine summarily

The Fraud Act 2006, s. 6 states:

(1) A person is guilty of an offence if he has in his possession or under his control any article for use in the course of or in connection with any fraud.

KEYNOTE

This offence replaces the 'cheat' element of the offence of 'going equipped' under s. 25 of the Theft Act 1968. It has far more scope than its predecessor, as the limitation of the 'going equipped' offence to circumstances when the defendant was 'not at his place of abode' has been excluded. This means that the offence under s. 6 can be committed *anywhere at all*. It also widens times that the defendant may commit the offence as not only is it committed when the defendant has articles in his possession but also when he has them in his control—a term that indicates that the defendant may be some distance away from the articles and yet still commit the offence. Further, the 'cheat' element of 'going equipped' only applied to the offence of 'obtaining property by deception'; the offence under s. 6 applies to *all fraud offences* under the 2006 Act. However, much like the offence of 'going equipped' the offence is only committed in respect of *future* offences and not offences that have already taken place. The offence can be committed if possession, or control is to enable *another* to commit an offence of fraud. The definition of the term 'article' is discussed at para. 2.6.9.

2.6.8 Making or Supplying Articles for Use in Frauds

OFFENCE: **Making or Supplying Articles for Use in Frauds—*Fraud Act 2006, s.7***

• Triable either way • Ten years' imprisonment on indictment and/or fine • Twelve months' imprisonment and/or fine summarily

The Fraud Act 2006, s. 7 states:

(1) A person is guilty of an offence if he makes, adapts, supplies or offers to supply any article—
 (a) knowing that it is designed or adapted for use in the course of or in connection with fraud, or
 (b) intending it to be used to commit, or assist in the commission of, fraud.

KEYNOTE

The broad terms of the offence ensure that any activity in respect of the making, supplying etc. of any 'article' for use in fraud offences is an offence. Making an 'offer to supply' would not require the defendant to be in possession of the 'article' (a similar situation to offering to supply a controlled drug, see para. 3.8.5.3). Examples of such behaviour include:

- A person makes a viewing card for a satellite TV system, enabling him to view all satellite channels for free.
- The same person then offers to sell similar cards to work colleagues although he has only made the one prototype card and does not actually have further cards to sell.
- A number of the person's work colleagues express an interest in buying the cards, so the person makes a dozen more cards and then actually supplies them to his work colleagues.

2.6.9 'Article'

The Fraud Act 2006, s. 8 states:

(1) For the purposes of—
 (a) sections 6 and 7, and
 (b) the provisions listed in subsection (2), so far as they relate to articles for use in the course of or in connection with fraud,
 'article' includes any program or data held in electronic form.
(2) The provisions are—
 (a) section 1(7)(b) of the Police and Criminal Evidence Act 1984 (c 60),
 (b) ...
 (c) ...

Section 8 extends the meaning of 'article' for the purposes of ss. 6 and 7 of the Act to include any program or data held in electronic form. Examples of cases where electronic programs or data could be used in fraud are:

- a computer program that generates credit card numbers
- a computer template that can be used for producing blank utility bills
- a computer file that contains lists of other people's credit card details.

2.6.10 Obtaining Services Dishonestly

OFFENCE: **Obtaining Services Dishonestly—*Fraud Act 2006, s. 11***

• Triable either way • Five years' imprisonment and/or fine on indictment • Twelve months' imprisonment and/or fine summarily

The Fraud Act 2006, s. 11 states:

(1) A person is guilty of an offence under this section if he obtains services for himself or another—
 (a) by a dishonest act, and
 (b) in breach of subsection (2).
(2) A person obtains services in breach of this subsection if—
 (a) they are made available on the basis that payment has been, is being or will be made for or in respect of them,
 (b) he obtains them without any payment having been made for in respect of them or without payment having been made in full, and
 (c) when he obtains them, he knows—
  (i) that they are being made available on the basis described in paragraph (a), or
  (ii) that they might be,
 but intends that payment will not be made, or will not be made in full.

KEYNOTE

The offence under s. 11 of the Fraud Act 2006 replaces the offence of 'obtaining services by deception' under s. 1 of the Theft Act 1978. It is important to note that unlike the other offences created as a consequence of the Fraud Act 2006, the offence under s. 11 is not a conduct crime; it is a *result crime* and requires the *actual obtaining* of the service. However, the offence does not require a fraudulent representation or deception. A person would commit this offence if, intending to avoid payment, he slipped into a concert hall to watch a concert without paying for the privilege. The offence can be committed where the defendant intends to avoid payment or payment in full but the defendant must know that the services are made available on the basis that they are chargeable, i.e. services provided for free are not covered by the offence. The terms 'service' and 'obtaining' are not defined by the Act.

2.7 Handling Stolen Goods

OFFENCE: **Handling Stolen Goods—*Theft Act 1968, s. 22***

• Triable either way • Fourteen years' imprisonment on indictment • Six months' imprisonment and/or a fine summarily

The Theft Act 1968, s. 22 states:

(1) A person handles stolen goods if (otherwise than in the course of the stealing) knowing or believing them to be stolen goods he dishonestly receives the goods, or dishonestly undertakes or assists in their retention, removal, disposal or realisation by or for the benefit of another person, or if he arranges to do so.

KEYNOTE

Handling can only be committed *otherwise than in the course of stealing*. Given the extent of theft and the fact that it can be a continuing act (see para. 2.1.1), it is critical to identify at what point the theft of the relevant property ended. It is also useful, in cases of doubt, to include alternative charges.

You must show that the defendant *knew* or *believed* the goods to be stolen. Mere suspicion, however strong, will not be enough (*R* v *Griffiths* (1974) 60 Cr App R 14). Deliberate 'blindness' to the true identity of the goods would suffice but the distinction is a fine one in practice. It can be very difficult to prove knowledge or belief on the part of, say, a second-hand dealer who 'asks no questions'. Because there are practical difficulties in proving the required *mens rea*, s. 27(3) of the 1968 Act makes special provision to allow evidence of the defendant's previous convictions, or previous recent involvement with stolen goods, to be admitted.

Dishonestly retaining goods may amount to theft (**see para. 2.1.1**), in which case that is the relevant charge.

'Goods' will include money and every other description of property except land, and includes things severed from the land by stealing (s. 34(2)(b) of the Act).

2.7.1 Stolen Goods

The Theft Act 1968, s. 24 states:

(1) The provisions of this Act relating to goods which have been stolen shall apply whether the stealing occurred in England or Wales or elsewhere, and whether it occurred before or after the commencement of this Act, provided that the stealing (if not an offence under this Act) amounted to an offence where and at the time when the goods were stolen; and references to stolen goods shall be construed accordingly.

(2) For purposes of those provisions references to stolen goods shall include, in addition to the goods originally stolen and parts of them (whether in their original state or not),—
   (a) any other goods which directly or indirectly represent or have at any time represented the stolen goods in the hands of the thief as being the proceeds of any disposal or realisation of the whole or part of the goods stolen or of goods representing the stolen goods; and
   (b) any other goods which directly or indirectly represent or have at any time represented the stolen goods in the hands of a handler of the stolen goods or any part of them as being the proceeds of any disposal or realisation of the whole or part of the stolen goods handled by him or of goods so representing them.

(3) But no goods shall be regarded as having continued to be stolen goods after they have been restored to the person from whom they were stolen or to other lawful possession or custody, or after that person and any other person claiming through him have otherwise ceased as regards those goods to have any right to restitution in respect of the theft.

(4) For purposes of the provisions of this Act relating to goods which have been stolen (including subsections (1) to (3) above) goods obtained in England or Wales or elsewhere either by blackmail or subject to subsection (5) below, by fraud (within the meaning of the Fraud Act 2006) shall be regarded as stolen; and 'steal', 'theft' and 'thief' shall be construed accordingly.

(5) Subsection (1) above applies in relation to goods obtained by fraud as if—
   (a) the reference to the commencement of this Act were a reference to the commencement of the Fraud Act 2006, and
   (b) the reference to an offence under this Act were a reference to an offence under section 1 of that Act.

The Theft Act 1968, s. 24A states:

(7) Subsection (8) below applies for purposes of provisions of this Act relating to stolen goods (including subsection (4) above).

(8) References to stolen goods include money which is dishonestly withdrawn from an account to which a wrongful credit has been made, but only to the extent that the money derives from the credit.

KEYNOTE

If goods are not stolen there is no handling. Whether they are so stolen is a question of fact for a jury or magistrate(s). There is no need to prove that the thief, blackmailer, etc. has been convicted of the primary offence before prosecuting the alleged handler, neither is it always necessary to *identify* who that person was.

However, care needs to be taken if a defendant is to be accused of handling goods stolen *from a specific person or place*. If that is the case then ownership of the goods will become an integral part of the prosecution case and it will be necessary to provide evidence proving that aspect of the offence (*Iqbal* v *DPP* [2004] EWHC 2567 (Admin).

Goods obtained by fraud and blackmail are included in the definition of 'stolen goods' under s. 24(4) and s. 24(5). The references to fraud are to the general offence of fraud under s. 1 of the Fraud Act 2006. Clearly goods gained through robbery or burglary will, by definition, be 'stolen' as theft is an intrinsic element of both offences.

'Wrongful credits' are included within the meaning of stolen goods under certain circumstances.

2.7.2 Section 24 Explained

Under s. 24(1) a person can still be convicted of handling if the goods were stolen outside England and Wales but only if the goods were taken under circumstances which amounted to an offence in the other country.

Under s. 24(2), goods will be classed as stolen only if they are the property which was originally stolen or if they have at some time represented the *proceeds* of that property in the hands of the thief or a 'handler'.

Therefore if a DVD recorder is stolen, sold to an unsuspecting party who then part-exchanges it for a new one at a high street retailer, the first DVD recorder will be 'stolen' goods, the new one will not. If the first person buying the original DVD recorder *knew* or *believed* that it was stolen, the new DVD recorder will be treated as stolen goods.

Tracing the proceeds of theft, fraud, blackmail, etc. can be complex; proving them to be stolen even more so. There is an overlap between this legislation—which deals with goods that have been stolen—and other legislation such as the Criminal Justice Act 1988 which relates to criminally-obtained property generally or the Drug Trafficking Act 1994. For further guidance, **see Blackstone's Criminal Practice 2008, section B22**.

Under s. 24(3), once goods have been restored to lawful possession they cease to be stolen. This situation formerly caused practical problems when police officers recovered stolen property but waited for it to be collected by a handler (see *Houghton* v *Smith* [1975] AC 476). Since the Criminal Attempts Act 1981 and the common-law rulings on 'impossibility', this has been less problematic. In such cases you may consider:

- Theft—collecting the property will be an 'appropriation'.
- Handling—an *arrangement* to come and collect stolen goods will probably have been made while they were still 'stolen'.
- Criminal attempt—the person collecting the goods has gone beyond merely preparing to handle them.

Section 24(4) widens the occasions on which goods will be deemed to be stolen goods beyond strictly theft-based offences such as burglary and robbery.

2.7.3 Proof that Goods were Stolen

The Theft Act 1968, s. 27 states:

(4) In any proceedings for the theft of anything in the course of transmission (whether by post or otherwise), or for handling stolen goods from such a theft, a statutory declaration made by any

person that he dispatched or received or failed to receive any goods or postal packet, or that any goods or postal packet when dispatched or received by him were in a particular state or condition, shall be admissible as evidence of the facts stated in the declaration, subject to the following conditions:—

(a) a statutory declaration shall only be admissible where and to the extent to which oral evidence to the like effect would have been admissible in the proceedings; and

(b) a statutory declaration shall only be admissible if at least seven days before the hearing or trial a copy of it has been given to the person charged, and he has not, at least three days before the hearing or trial or within such further time as the court may in special circumstances allow, given the prosecutor written notice requiring the attendance at the hearing or trial of the person making the declaration.

KEYNOTE

The above provisions allow for specific evidence to be admitted in proving that goods 'in the course of transmission' have been stolen. These provisions allow for a statutory declaration by the person dispatching or receiving goods or postal packets as to when and where they were dispatched and when or if they arrived and, in each case, their state or condition (e.g. if they had been opened or interfered with). Such a statutory declaration will only be admissible in circumstances where an oral statement would have been admissible *and* if a copy has been served on the defendant at least seven days before the hearing and he/she has not—within three days of the hearing—served written notice on the prosecutor requiring the attendance of the person making the declaration.

This section is to be construed in accordance with s. 24 generally (s. 27(5)).

2.7.4 Handling

Despite some views to the contrary, there is only one offence of handling stolen goods (albeit made up of many facets). Therefore to charge a defendant without specifying a particular form of handling is not bad for duplicity (*R* v *Nicklin* [1977] 1 WLR 403). However, the offence can be divided for practical purposes into two parts:

- *receiving/arranging to receive* stolen goods, in which case the defendant acts for his/her own benefit, and
- *assisting/acting for the benefit of another* person, in which case that assistance to another or benefit of another must be proved.

2.7.5 Receiving

Often used as shorthand for handling stolen goods generally, this is a specific part of the overall offence. Receiving does not require the physical reception of goods and can extend to exercising control over them. Things in action—such as bank credits from a stolen cheque—can be 'received'.

'Arranging to receive' would cover circumstances which do not go far enough to constitute an attempt—that is, actions which *are* merely preparatory to the receiving of stolen goods may satisfy the elements under s. 22 even though they would not meet the criteria under the Criminal Attempts Act 1981.

If the goods have yet to be stolen, then s. 22 would not apply and the offence of conspiracy should be considered (see *R* v *Park* (1987) 87 Cr App R 164).

2.7.6 Assisting/Acting for Another's Benefit

Assisting or acting for the benefit of another can be committed by misleading police officers during a search (see *R* v *Kanwar* [1982] 1 WLR 845).

Disposing of the stolen goods or assisting in their disposal or realisation usually involves physically moving them or converting them into a different form (see *R* v *Forsyth* [1997] 2 Cr App R 299).

If the only person 'benefiting' from the defendant's actions is the defendant himself/herself, this element of the offence will not be made out (*R* v *Bloxham* [1983] 1 AC 109).

Similarly, if the only 'other' person to benefit is a co-accused on the same charge, the offence will not be made out (*R* v *Gingell* [2000] 1 Cr App R 88).

2.7.7 Guilty Knowledge in Cases of Handling and Theft

Section 27 of the Theft Act 1968 allows for the admissibility of previous misconduct and states:

> (3) Where a person is being proceeded against for handling stolen goods (but not for any offence other than handling stolen goods), then at any stage of the proceedings, if evidence has been given of his having or arranging to have in his possession the goods the subject of the charge, or of his undertaking or assisting in, or arranging to undertake or assist in, their retention, removal, disposal or realisation, the following evidence shall be admissible for the purpose of proving that he knew or believed the goods to be stolen goods—
> (a) evidence that he has had in his possession, or has undertaken or assisted in the retention, removal, disposal or realisation of, stolen goods from any theft taking place not earlier than 12 months before the offence charged; and
> (b) (provided that seven days' notice in writing has been given to him of the intention to prove the conviction) evidence that he has within the five years preceding the date of the offence charged been convicted of theft or of handling stolen goods.

KEYNOTE

This provision applies to all forms of handling (*R* v *Ball* [1983] 1 WLR 801) and can be used where handling is the only offence involved in the proceedings.

The question as to what constitutes recent possession is a matter of fact and degree dependent on the circumstances of each case. This presumption can be rebutted by the person offering a true explanation for the possession (*R* v *Schama* (1914) 84 LJ KB 396, *R* v *Garth* [1949] 1 All ER 773, *R* v *Aves* [1950] 2 All ER 330 and *R* v *Williams* [1962] Crim LR 54).

The term 'recent possession' is not defined and so is a question of fact in each case. In *R* v *Smythe* (1980) 72 Cr App R 8, the Court of Appeal held that property found in the possession of an accused, stolen two or three months earlier during some robberies and burglaries, did not amount to recent possession for the offence of handling stolen goods generally. (For a full discussion on handling stolen goods, **see** para. 2.7)

2.8 Proceeds of Crime

2.8.1 Proceeds of Crime Act 2002

The offences and powers under the Proceeds of Crime Act 2002 are not just within the purview of specialist financial investigation departments. While 'serious crime' is likely to play a significant part in the use of the powers the Act provides, police officers must remember that the Act is also connected with day to day criminality and therefore involves all police officers whatever rank and role they fulfil. This section will not attempt to provide a detailed analysis of the Act but will provide an overview of the three principal offences relating to 'Money Laundering' created by s. **327** (concealing criminal property), s. **328** (arrangements in relation to criminal property) and s. **329** (acquisition, use and possession of criminal property) of the Act. To begin with, there must be a brief examination of the concepts relating to 'criminal conduct' and 'criminal property'.

2.8.2 Criminal Conduct

The Proceeds of Crime Act 2002, s. 340 states:

(2) Criminal conduct is conduct which—
   (a) constitutes an offence in any part of the United Kingdom, or
   (b) would constitute an offence in any part of the United Kingdom if it occurred there.

KEYNOTE

Section 340(4) states that it is immaterial:

- who carried out the criminal conduct
- who benefited from it
- whether the conduct occurred before or after the passing of the Act.

So criminal conduct not only includes the behaviour of the defendant him/herself but also of any other person. Effectively this states that *any offence*, committed by *any person*, *anywhere* at all and at *any time* is 'criminal conduct'. This represents a significant departure from earlier law which required the prosecution to show that the criminal property existed as a consequence of a specific offence or class of offences. As a consequence of s. 340, a conviction can be obtained under the Proceeds of Crime Act even if the prosecution cannot specify the offence or offences that gave rise to the proceeds or identify the person(s) responsible for the offence(s).

2.8.3 Criminal Property

The Proceeds of Crime Act 2002, s. 340 states:

(3) Property is criminal property if—
   (a) it constitutes a person's benefit from criminal conduct or it represents such a benefit (in whole or in part and whether directly or indirectly) and,
   (b) the alleged offender knows or suspects that it constitutes or represents such a benefit.

KEYNOTE

Although the offences under ss. 327, 328 and 329 are often referred to as 'money laundering', it should be noted that the definition of 'property' is exceptionally wide and *does not just relate to money.* Section 340(9) of the Act defines property as *all* property *wherever* situated and includes:

- money
- all forms of property, real or personal, heritable or movable, and
- things in action and other intangible or incorporeal property.

(Incorporeal property relates to property or an asset that does not have value in material form, such as a right or a patent).

The *mens rea* relating to criminal property and therefore to all three offences is knowing or *suspecting*. Dishonesty is not required. In *R* v *Da Silva* [2006] EWCA Crim 1654, it was said that:

> to suspect something, you have to have a state of mind well short of knowing that the matter you suspect is true. It is an ordinary English word. . . the dictionary definition of 'suspicion' [is] an act of suspecting, the imagining of something without evidence or on slender evidence, inkling, mistrust.

The Court of Appeal upheld the conviction, concluding that the word 'suspect' meant that the defendant had to think that there was a possibility, which was more than fanciful, that the relevant facts existed. A vague feeling of unease would not suffice. The fact the suspicion alone will suffice means that proving such offences is remarkably less burdensome for the prosecution than the potential alternative to such offences, a charge of handling stolen goods (s. 22 of the Theft Act 1968, **see para. 2.7**) where the defendant must be proved to know or believe that goods are stolen goods.

2.8.4 Concealing Criminal Property

OFFENCE: **Concealing Criminal Property—*Proceeds of Crime Act 2002, s. 327***

• Triable either way • 14 years' imprisonment on indictment and/or fine • Six months' imprisonment and/or fine summarily

The Proceeds of Crime Act 2002, s. 327 states:

(1) A person commits an offence if he—
- (a) conceals criminal property;
- (b) disguises criminal property;
- (c) converts criminal property;
- (d) transfers criminal property;
- (e) removes criminal property from England and Wales and Scotland or from Northern Ireland.

(2) But a person does not commit such an offence if—
- (a) he makes an authorised disclosure under section 338 and (if the disclosure is made before he does the act mentioned in subsection (1)) he has the appropriate consent;
- (b) he intended to make such a disclosure but had a reasonable excuse for not doing so:
- (c) the act he does is done in carrying out a function he has relating to the enforcement of any provision of this Act or of any other enactment relating to criminal conduct or benefit from criminal conduct;

(3) Concealing or disguising criminal property includes concealing or disguising its nature, source, location, disposition, movement or ownership or any rights with respect to it.

KEYNOTE

There is a noticeable overlap between the activities relating to concealing criminal property and the offence of handling stolen goods, particularly when considering the list of activities that a defendant may undertake in the commission of both offences. However, whereas handling only occurs 'otherwise than in the course of stealing' and 'by or for the benefit of another', the offence under s. 327 can potentially be committed *during the commission of an offence* and *for the benefit of the thief.* On a literal reading of s. 327, a thief who conceals, disguises or sells property that he has just stolen may thereby commit offences under that section because the definition of criminal property applies to the laundering of an offender's own proceeds of crime as well as those of someone else.

Section 2 creates several defences to charges under s. 327.

2.8.5 Arrangements in relation to Criminal Property

OFFENCE: **Arrangements in relation to Criminal Property—*Proceeds of Crime Act 2002, s. 328***

• Triable either way • 14 years' imprisonment on indictment and/or fine • Six months' imprisonment and/or fine summarily

The Proceeds of Crime Act 2002, s. 328 states:

(1) A person commits an offence if he enters into or becomes concerned in an arrangement which he knows or suspects facilitates (by whatever means) the acquisition, retention, use or control of criminal property by or on behalf of another person.

KEYNOTE

To establish an offence under this section, the prosecutor would need to prove that a person entered into or became concerned in an arrangement which he knew or suspected would make it easier for another person to acquire, retain, use or control criminal property and that the person concerned also knew or suspected that the property constituted or represented benefit from criminal conduct. This offence will often be apt for the prosecution of those who launder on behalf of others. Not only could this catch persons who work in financial or credit institutions, accountants etc, who in the course of their work facilitate money laundering by or on behalf of other persons, but also family members (husband/wife, partner etc.).

Section 328 includes the same defences against committing the offence, as are included in s. 327(2).

2.8.6 Acquisition, Use and Possession of Criminal Property

OFFENCE: **Acquisition, Use and Possession of Criminal Property—*Proceeds of Crime Act 2002, s. 329***

• Triable either way • 14 years' imprisonment on indictment and/or fine • Six months' imprisonment and/or fine summarily

The Proceeds of Crime Act 2002, s. 329 states:

(1) A person commits an offence if he—
  (a) acquires criminal property;
  (b) uses criminal property;
  (c) has possession of criminal property.

KEYNOTE

As with the previous offences, this offence is only committed where a person knows or suspects that the property which is acquired etc constitutes or represents his own or another's benefit from criminal conduct. Again, the same defences against committing the offence apply as in s. 327.

An additional defence exists under s. 329(2)(c) which states that a person will not commit the offence if he acquired or used or had possession of the property for adequate consideration (an example of adequate consideration would be being paid a proper market price of £3000 to fix a roof). The effect of the defence in s. 329(2)(c) is that persons, such as tradesmen, who are paid for ordinary consumable goods and services in money that comes from crime are not under any obligation to question the source of the money. However, the defence is not available to a defendant who provides goods or services knowing or suspecting that those goods or services will help a person *to actually carry out criminal conduct*.

The coincidence between an offence of handling stolen goods and those described from the Proceeds of Crime Act 2002 might provide a dilemma as to which offence to charge. In such a situation, CPS guidance states that if it is possible to charge money laundering or handling stolen goods then money laundering may be more appropriate if 'either a defendant has possessed criminal proceeds in large amounts or in lesser amounts, but repeatedly and where assets are laundered for profit'. However, a money laundering charge should only be considered where proceeds are more than *de minimis* (about minimal things) in any circumstances where the defendant who is charged with the underlying offence has done more than simply consume his proceeds of crime.

2.9 Criminal Damage

2.9.1 Introduction

The chances of any police officer going through their career without dealing in some way with an offence of criminal damage are minuscule. The prevalence of offences of criminal damage is well documented and damage in all forms has harmful effect on the environment, the community and the economy.

2.9.1.1 Types of Offence

The law regulating *criminal* damage is largely contained within one statute, the Criminal Damage Act 1971. This Act deals with occasions where a person:

- actually damages or destroys the property of another (simple damage);
- damages or destroys his/her own property or that of another where there are 'aggravating' factors or circumstances (aggravated damage);
- threatens to damage or destroy property;
- has articles to be used for damaging or destroying property.

In addition, the Crime and Disorder Act 1998 created an offence of racially or religiously aggravated criminal damage.

2.9.2 Simple Damage

OFFENCE: **Simple damage—*Criminal Damage Act 1971, s. 1(1)***

• Triable either way • Ten years' imprisonment on indictment • Six months' imprisonment and/or a fine summarily

OFFENCE: **Racially or Religiously Aggravated—*Crime and Disorder Act 1998, s. 30(1)***

• Triable either way • Fourteen years' imprisonment and/or a fine on indictment • Six months' imprisonment and/or a fine summarily

The Criminal Damage Act 1971, s. 1 states:

(1) A person who without lawful excuse destroys or damages any property belonging to another intending to destroy or damage any such property or being reckless as to whether any such property would be destroyed or damaged shall be guilty of an offence.

KEYNOTE

Although triable either way, if the value of the property destroyed or the damage done is less than £5,000, the offence is to be tried summarily (Magistrates' Courts Act 1980, s. 22). If the damage in such a case was caused by fire (arson) (see para. 2.9.4) then this rule will not apply.

The fact that the substantive offence is, by virtue of the value of the damage caused, triable only summarily does not make simple damage a 'summary offence' for all other purposes. If it did, you could only be found guilty of *attempting* to commit criminal damage if the value of the intended damage was more than £5,000 (because the Criminal Attempts Act 1981 does not extend to summary offences). Therefore, where a defendant tried to damage a bus shelter in a way that would have cost far less than £5,000 to repair, his argument that he had only attempted what was in fact a 'summary offence' was dismissed by the Divisional Court (*R* v *Bristol Magistrates' Court, ex parte E* [1998] 3 All ER 798). Note that offences of damage involving values not exceeding £200 can be dealt with by way of fixed penalty notice.

If the offence involves only the painting or writing on, or the soiling, marking or other defacing of, any property by whatever means, the power to issue a graffiti notice may apply.

The racially or religiously aggravated form of this offence (see below) is triable either way irrespective of the cost of the damage.

2.9.2.1 Racially or Religiously Aggravated Damage

The racially or religiously aggravated circumstances set out at s. 28(1)(a) of the Crime and Disorder Act 1998 deal with situations where the defendant demonstrates hostility:

- at the time of
- or immediately before or after

committing the offence, towards the *victim* and that hostility is *based on the victim's membership or presumed membership of a racial or religious group*. The courts have shown that they are prepared to adopt a wide approach when interpreting this important legislation. This can be seen in two particular cases. In the first, the Divisional Court confirmed that the relevant hostility can be demonstrated even if the victim is no longer present—*DPP* v *Parry* [2004] EWHC 3112. However, the need for any such hostility to be demonstrated *immediately* means that it must be shown to have taken place in the immediate context of the criminal damage offence. In *Parry* the only evidence of the racial hostility towards the victim came in the form of comments made to the officers attending the scene *some 20 minutes after* the defendant had caused the damage (by throwing nail polish at a neighbour's door). The court held that the wording of the statute meant that any hostility had to be demonstrated *immediately* before or *immediately* after the substantive offence and that the courts below had not been entitled to consider the retrospective effect of the comments made later by the defendant.

In another case where a juvenile used the words 'bloody foreigners' immediately before smashing the window of a kebab shop, the Divisional Court held that this was capable of amounting to an expression of hostility based on a person's membership or presumed membership of a racial group for the purposes of s. 28(1)(a) of the Crime and Disorder Act 1998—*DPP* v *M* [2004] 1 WLR 2758. Although the statutory wording used the expression 'a racial group', the court held that a specific and inclusive definition of such a group had to be used by the defendant (e.g. the defendant did not have to single out a specific nationality) and the size of group referred to by a defendant (such as all 'foreigners') was irrelevant. However, in the case of *M* the youth court had inadvertently mixed the two tests of hostility and motivation under s. 28(1)(b) and his appeal was allowed. Therefore, when considering whether an offence was racially motivated under s. 28 of the Crime and Disorder Act 1998, hostility demonstrated to foreign nationals simply because they are 'foreign' can be just as objectionable as hostility based on some more limited racial characteristic. This was clarified by the Court of Appeal in *R* v *Rogers* [2005] EWCA Crim 2863 where the defendant had called three Spanish women 'bloody foreigners' and told them to 'go back to your own country'. The prosecution case was that the defendant had demonstrated hostility based on the women's membership of a racial group. The court's decision clarifies the position that, for an offence to be aggravated under s. 28, the defendant has first to form a view that the victim is a member of a racial group (within the definition in s. 28(4)—**see para. 3.7.4**) and then has to say (or do) something that demonstrates hostility towards the victim based on membership of that group. However, the Court of Appeal noted that the very wide meaning of racial group under s. 28(4) gives rise to a danger of aggravated offences being charged where mere 'vulgar abuse' had included racial epithets that did not truly indicate hostility to the race in question. Consequently, s. 28 should not be used unless the prosecuting authority is satisfied that the facts truly suggest that the offence was aggravated (rather than simply accompanied) by racism.

To clarify such situations in relation to racially or religiously aggravated damage, s. 30(3) provides that the person to whom the property belongs or is treated as belonging, will be treated as the 'victim'.

This provision is helpful where the aggravated offence is one under s. 28(1)(a)—the 'demonstration' type of aggravation—and the property is privately owned.

Where the property is owned by a corporate body (e.g. a bus shelter or tube station) however, there will clearly be problems in proving that the defendant's hostility was based on the *victim's* membership/presumed membership of a racial or religious group. Even though property for these purposes may be treated as belonging to more than one person (**see para. 2.9.2.4**) this means that, where the damage is caused by racist graffiti in publicly-owned places or on property owned by large corporations, the most suitable charge will probably be under s. 28(1)(b) of the Act—by far the harder to prove. Harder still would be the situation where any such graffiti is of a *religious* nature and the hostility was based on the victim's membership of a religious group. The revised wording of s. 28 of the Crime and Disorder Act 1998 (amended after the events of 11 September 2001) now includes 'religious groups'—and these will include groups of people defined not only by their religious belief, but also by their *lack* of any such belief.

The provisions of s. 30 of the Crime and Disorder Act 1998 only apply to the offence of 'simple' damage under s. 1(1) of the 1971 Act; they do not apply to any of the other offences in this chapter.

2.9.2.2 Destroy or Damage

Although a key feature of the 1971 Act, the terms 'destroy' or 'damage' are not defined. The courts have taken a wide view when interpreting these terms. 'Destroying' property would suggest that it has been rendered useless but there is no need to prove that 'damage' to property is in any way permanent or irreparable.

EXAMPLE

A group of youths in a shopping precinct walk up to a grocery display and begin juggling with some apples. They drop several apples, some of which smash on the pavement while others are soiled and bruised.

In the example above, the apples which were smashed were clearly 'destroyed'; those which were soiled, even though they could be washed, would probably be unfit for sale and therefore 'damaged' for the purposes of s. 1(1).

Whether an article has been damaged will be a question of fact for each court to determine on the evidence before it. Situations where courts have accepted that property has been damaged include the defacing of a pavement by an artist using only water-soluble paint (*Hardman* v *Chief Constable of Avon and Somerset* [1986] Crim LR 330). It has also been held by the Divisional Court that graffiti smeared in mud can amount to damage, even though it is easily washed off (*Roe* v *Kingerlee* [1986] Crim LR 735).

A good operational example of the courts' approach can be seen in *R* v *Fiak* [2005] EWCA Crim 2381. In that case the defendant had been arrested and placed in a police cell which he flooded by stuffing a blanket down the cell lavatory and repeatedly flushing. The defendant argued that there was no evidence that the blanket or the cell had been 'damaged'; the water had been clean and both the blanket and the cell could be used again when dry. The Court of Appeal disagreed and held that, while the effect of the defendant's actions in relation to the blanket and the cell was remediable, the reality was that the blanket could not be used until it had been dried and the flooded cell was out of action until the water had been cleared. Therefore both had sustained damage for the purposes of the Act.

It can be seen therefore that putting property temporarily out of use—even for a short time and in circumstances where it will revert to its former state of its own accord—may fall within the definition of 'damage'.

2.9.2.3 Property

Property is defined in the 1971 Act by s. 10 which states:

> (1) In this Act 'property' means property of a tangible nature, whether real or personal, including money and—
> (a) including wild creatures which have been tamed or are ordinarily kept in captivity and any other wild creatures or their carcasses if, but only if, they have been reduced into possession... or are in the course of being reduced into possession; but
> (b) not including mushrooms growing wild on any land or flowers, fruit or foliage of a plant growing wild on any land.
>
> ...

KEYNOTE

This definition has similarities with the definition of 'property' for the purposes of theft but 'real' property (i.e. land and things attached to it) can be damaged even though it cannot be stolen. Trampling flower beds, digging up cricket pitches, chopping down trees in a private garden and even pulling up genetically-modified crops may all amount to criminal damage if accompanied by the required circumstances.

It is important to remember when dealing with disputes involving pets or farm animals that they are property for the purposes of this Act. Cases of horses being mutilated would, in addition to the offence of 'cruelty' itself, amount to criminal damage. There may also be occasions—such as domestic or neighbour disputes—involving harm or cruelty to such animals where it will be more appropriate and effective to consider offences under the 1971 Act.

Note that the destroying or damaging of another's property can amount to treating that property as your own, or otherwise falling within the parameters of s. 6 of the Theft Act.

2.9.2.4 Belonging to Another

Section 10 states:

(2) Property shall be treated for the purposes of this Act as belonging to any person—
  (a) having the custody or control of it;
  (b) having in it any proprietary right or interest (not being an equitable interest arising only from an agreement to transfer or grant an interest); or
  (c) having a charge on it.

KEYNOTE

This extended meaning of 'belonging to another' is similar to that used in the Theft Act 1968. One result is that if a person damages his/her own property, he/she may still commit the offence of simple criminal damage if that property also 'belongs to' someone else.

2.9.2.5 Lawful excuse

Section 5 of the Criminal Damage Act 1971 provides for two occasions where a defendant may have a 'lawful excuse'. These can be remembered as 'permission' (s. 5(2)(a)) and 'protection' (s. 5(2)(b)). Both involve the belief of the defendant. The wording of s. 5 indicates that these particular defences are not the only ones available to a charge of criminal damage and other general defences may apply.

2.9.2.6 Permission

A person shall be treated as having lawful excuse under s. 5(2):

(a) if at the time of the act or acts alleged to constitute the offence he believed that the person or persons whom he believed to be entitled to consent to the destruction of or damage to the property in question had so consented, or would have so consented to it if he or they had known of the destruction or damage and its circumstances ...

KEYNOTE

An example of 'lawful excuse' under s. 5(2)(a) would be if you, as a police officer, were asked by a motorist to help them get into their partner's car after locking the keys inside. If, during that attempt you damaged the rubber window surround, s. 5(2)(a) would provide you with a statutory defence to any later charge of criminal damage by the owner. The key elements here would be:

- the consent of someone whom you believed to be entitled to consent to that damage, and
- the circumstances under which it was caused.

If the driver was not available and your reason for opening the door was to get a better look at some personal documents for intelligence purposes, it is unlikely that the driver or the owner would have consented, either to the damage or the circumstances in which it was caused. Therefore you could not use this particular defence.

2.9.2.7 Protection

A person shall be treated as having lawful excuse under s. 5(2):

(b) if he destroyed or damaged or threatened to destroy or damage the property in question or, in the case of a charge of an offence under section 3 above, intended to use or cause or permit the use of something to destroy or damage it, in order to protect property belonging to himself or another or a right or interest in property which was or which he believed to be vested in himself or another, and at the time of the act or acts alleged to constitute the offence he believed—

(i) that the property, right or interest was in immediate need of protection; and
(ii) that the means of protection adopted or proposed to be adopted were or would be reasonable having regard to all the circumstances.

KEYNOTE

Situations where such a defence can be used involve causing damage to property in order to protect other property. This defence also applies to the offence of having articles for causing damage (**see para. 2.9.6**). Key features of this defence are the immediacy of the need to protect the property and the reasonableness of the means of protection adopted. This defence has attracted the most attention of the courts in cases involving demonstrators claiming to be acting in furtherance of their political beliefs. For instance, in a case involving 'peace campaigners' it was held that the threat presented by a possible nuclear attack in the future did not excuse the carrying of a hacksaw for cutting through the perimeter fence of an airbase (*R* v *Hill* (1989) 89 Cr App R 74).

The 1971 Act goes on to say that it is immaterial whether a 'belief' above was justified as long as it was honestly held (s. 5(3)). This test is problematic because, although it is supposed to be an *objective* one, the evidence will be based largely on what was going through a defendant's mind at the time—or sometimes what was *not* going through their mind! In *Jaggard* v *Dickinson* [1981] QB 527 the defendant had broken a window to get into a house. Being drunk at the time, she had got the wrong house but the court accepted that her belief (that it was the right house and that the owner would have consented) had been honestly held, and that it did not matter whether that belief was brought about by intoxication, stupidity, forgetfulness or inattention. That is not to say, however, that *any* honestly held belief will suffice. An example of someone claiming—though unsuccessfully—a defence under both s. 5(2)(a) and (b) can be seen in *Blake* v *DPP* [1993] Crim LR 586. There the defendant was a vicar who wished to protest against Great Britain's involvement in the Gulf War. In order to mark his disapproval, the defendant wrote a quotation from the Bible in ink on a pillar in front of the Houses of Parliament. He claimed:

- that he was carrying out God's instructions and therefore had a lawful excuse based on his belief that God was the person entitled to consent to such damage and that he had in fact consented or would have done so (s. 5(2)(a)); and
- that he had damaged the property as a reasonable means of protecting other property located in the Gulf from being damaged by warfare (s. 5(2)(b)).

Perhaps unsurprisingly the Divisional Court did not accept either proposition holding that, in the first case a belief in The Almighty's consent was not a 'lawful excuse' and, in the second, that the defendant's conduct was too remote from any immediate need to protect property in the Gulf States. The test in relation to the defendant's belief appears then to be largely subjective (i.e. what was/was not going on in his/her head at the time) but with an objective element in that the judge/magistrate(s) must decide whether, on the facts as believed by the defendant, his/her acts were capable of protecting property.

A similar approach was tried more recently in a case where the defendant was arrested after making 22 cuts in a perimeter fence of a base where nuclear warheads were produced. The defendant claimed that the activity at the base was unlawful in international law and therefore acts to prevent that activity amounted to a lawful excuse under the 1971 Act. The Divisional Court did not accept this argument, nor the argument that the defendant's acts were merely an expression of her opinion under article 10 of the European Convention on Human Rights (*Hutchinson* v *DPP* (2000) *Independent*, 20 November). Taking a different tack, peace campaigners in *R* v *Jones (Margaret)* [2004] EWCA Crim 1981 argued that their fear of the consequences of war in Iraq—which they claimed to be illegal—prompted them to conspire to cause damage at an airbase and that such fear amounted both to duress and lawful excuse under s. 5(2)(b) above. The Court of Appeal held that a jury would be entitled to consider some of the subjective beliefs of the defendants in determining the reasonableness of their actions.

Finally, a demonstrator at the Guildhall Gallery knocked the head off a statue of Baroness Thatcher and claimed that he acted in fear for his son's future which had been placed in jeopardy by the joint actions of the US and UK governments, and for which Baroness Thatcher was partly responsible. His appeal against conviction brought under s. 5(2)(b)—with a few technicalities added on—failed (*R* v *Kelleher* [2003] EWCA Crim 2846).

The Act also states, at s. 5(4), that a right or interest in property includes any right or privilege in or over land, whether created by grant, licence or otherwise.

Section 5(5) allows for other general defences at criminal law to apply in addition to those listed under s. 5.

It is not an offence to damage your own property unless there are aggravating circumstances (**see para. 2.9.3**). Even if the intention in doing so is to carry out some further offence—such as a fraudulent insurance claim—this fact still does not make it an offence under s. 1(1) of the Criminal Damage Act 1971 (*R* v *Denton* [1981] 1 WLR 1446). (It may, however, give rise to other offences of dishonesty.)

2.9.2.8 Recklessness

An offence of criminal damage under s. 1(1) can be proved by showing that the defendant was 'reckless'. The former concept of *objective* or 'Caldwell' recklessness (as set out in *Metropolitan Police Commissioner* v *Caldwell* [1982] AC 341) has now gone and the law has been restored to its former position by *R* v *G* & *R* [2003] 3 WLR 1060. In that case, the House of Lords decided that 'recklessness' in the context of criminal damage did not mean something different from the previous requirement of 'malicious damage'—namely that the defendant had foreseen the risk yet gone on to take it. Their Lordships held that a person acts recklessly for the purposes of s. 1(1) of the Act:

- with respect to a circumstance when he/she is aware of a risk that existed or would exist;
- with respect to a result or consequence when he/she is aware of a risk that it would occur and it is, in the circumstances known to him/her, unreasonable to take the risk.

In the *R* v *G* & *R* case, two children (aged 11 and 12), set fire to some newspapers in the rear yard of a shop premises while camping out. The children put the burning papers under a wheelie bin and left them, expecting the small fire to burn itself out on the concrete floor of the yard. In fact the fire spread causing around £1,000,000 of damage. Under the former law (*Caldwell*), the children were convicted on the basis that the risk of the fire would have been obvious to any reasonable bystander. However, their convictions were quashed by the House of Lords who reinstated the general subjective element described above.

2.9.3 Aggravated Damage

OFFENCE: **Aggravated damage—*Criminal Damage Act 1971, s. 1(2)***
- Triable on indictment • Life imprisonment

The Criminal Damage Act 1971, s. 1 states:

(2) A person who without lawful excuse destroys or damages any property, whether belonging to himself or another—

(a) intending to destroy or damage any property or being reckless as to whether any property would be destroyed or damaged; and

(b) intending by the destruction or damage to endanger the life of another or being reckless as to whether the life of another would be thereby endangered;

shall be guilty of an offence.

KEYNOTE

The aggravating factor in this offence, and the reason why it attracts such a heavy maximum sentence, is the ulterior intention of endangering life or recklessness as to whether life is endangered. As such, evidence of self-induced intoxication may provide a defence to a charge under this section. This form of 'aggravation' should not be confused with the 'racially or religiously aggravated' form of criminal damage.

The reference to 'without lawful excuse' does not refer to the statutory excuses under s. 5 (**see para. 2.9.2.5**) which are not applicable here, but to general excuses such as self-defence or the prevention of crime.

For the relevant test of recklessness **see para. 2.9.2.8.**

You must also show that the defendant either intended or was reckless as to each of the following consequences:

- the damage being caused, and
- the *resultant* danger to life.

It does not matter that the *actual* damage caused by the defendant turned out to be minor. What matters is the *potential* for damage and danger created by the defendant's conduct.

Where a defendant set fire to furniture in a house which was unoccupied at the time, the court nevertheless found him guilty of this offence. The court's reasoning for doing so turned on the fact that, had a reasonable bystander been present, he/she would have seen the possible risk that the fire might cause to the lives of others in the area, even though with hindsight it was shown that there had been no likelihood of the fire spreading to neighbouring properties (*R* v *Sangha* [1988] 1 WLR 519). This decision was taken while the concept of 'objective' or *Caldwell* recklessness was still in place for criminal damage offences. As a result, it will need to be reconsidered and it will probably be necessary to show that there *was* some likelihood of life being endangered. In this case there was clearly recklessness as to the damage caused *and* recklessness as to the danger to life *presented by the damage*. In contrast, where a defendant fired a gun through a window pane he was clearly reckless as to the damage his actions would cause. However, the court felt that, even though two people were standing behind the window and that they were obviously put in some danger, it was the *missile* which endangered their lives and not the result of the damage. Therefore the court held that the defendant was not guilty of this particular offence (*R* v *Steer* [1988] AC 111). This distinction seems to be a fine one, particularly if you are the person behind the window.

If someone were to smash the windscreen of a moving car or to cause a large display window to collapse into a busy street, this would probably be enough to support a charge under s. 1(2) (see *R* v *Webster* [1995] 2 All ER 168).

2.9.4 Arson

OFFENCE: **Arson—*Criminal Damage Act 1971, s. 1(3)***

- Triable either way • Life imprisonment on indictment • Where life is not endangered six months' imprisonment and/or a fine summarily

The Criminal Damage Act 1971, s. 1 states:

(3) An offence committed under this section by destroying or damaging property by fire shall be charged as arson.

KEYNOTE

In any of the above cases of criminal damage, if the destruction or damage is caused by fire, the offence will be charged as 'arson'. Given the potential for extensive damage and danger to life that fire-raising has, the restrictions on the mode of trial for simple damage under s. 1(1) (**see para. 2.9.2**) do not apply to cases of arson.

Again, in light of the potential for serious injury and death, the link between this offence and the various homicide offences often arises. An example of where criminal liability for either gross negligence or unlawful act manslaughter arose from an offence of arson can be seen in *R* v *Willoughby* (2004) *The Times*, 21 December. In that case the defendant enlisted the help of another man in burning down a public house on which the defendant owed money. Having poured petrol around the inside of the building, the defendant set fire to it, killing the other person and injuring himself in the process. The defendant was convicted of both arson and manslaughter. The Court of Appeal held that by convicting the defendant of arson, the jury had showed that they were sure that he (on his own or jointly) had deliberately spread petrol by being reckless or with the intention that the premises would be destroyed. Provided that such conduct had been the cause of the death, the jury were therefore also bound to convict the defendant of manslaughter.

Aggravated damage caused by arson is triable only on indictment and carries a maximum penalty of life imprisonment.

2.9.5 Threats to Destroy or Damage Property

OFFENCE: **Threats to destroy or damage property—*Criminal Damage Act 1971, s. 2***

• Triable either way • Ten years' imprisonment on indictment • Six months' imprisonment and/or a fine summarily

The Criminal Damage Act 1971, s. 2 states:

> A person who without lawful excuse makes to another a threat, intending that that other would fear it would be carried out,—
> (a) to destroy or damage any property belonging to that other or a third person; or
> (b) to destroy or damage his own property in a way which he knows is likely to endanger the life of that other or a third person;
> shall be guilty of an offence.

KEYNOTE

This is an offence of *intention*, that is, the key element is the defendant's intention that the person receiving the threat fears it would be carried out.

The s. 2 offence, which originates from the need to tackle protection racketeers, is very straightforward: there is no need to show that the other person actually feared or even believed that the threat would be carried out. There is no need to show that the defendant intended to carry it out; nor does it matter whether the threat was even capable of being carried out.

EXAMPLE

If a person, enraged by a neighbour's inconsiderate parking, shouts over the garden wall, '*When you've gone to bed I'm going to T-cut that heap with paint stripper!*', the offence will be complete, provided you can show that the person making the threat intended the neighbour to fear it would be carried out.

Where a group of protestors staged a protest in the pods of the London Eye and threatened to set fire to themselves, their conduct was held by the Court of Appeal to be capable of amounting to a threat to damage the property of another contrary to s. 2(a) (*R* v *Cakmak* [2002] 2 Cr App R 10).

In *Cakmak* the court held that the gist of the offence under s. 2(a) was the making of a threat and that any such threat had to be considered objectively.

Whether:

- there has been such a threat to another
- the threat amounted to 'a threat to damage or destroy property'
- the defendant had the necessary state of mind (*mens rea*) at the time

are all questions of fact for the jury to decide (per *Cakmak*).

While not usually enough to amount to the substantive offence under s. 2 above, a person's *conduct* which represents a threat to damage property may be relevant in triggering police action. This can be seen in yet another case involving a political protest against war. In *Clements* v *DPP* [2005] EWHC 1279 several protestors left a public highway, crossed a ditch and approached the perimeter fence of an RAF base. The defendant ignored a police warning to return to the road and the police attempted to restrain the protestors in order to prevent criminal damage to the fence. After a scuffle the defendant was subsequently convicted of assaulting a police constable in the execution of his duty (as to which **see para. 3.2.13**). The key issues at trial were whether the police officer had acted in the course of his duty and the extent to which the officer had reasonable grounds to believe that the defendant would cause criminal damage. The Divisional Court held that the officer had to consider the whole event in context and at the relevant time a political protest was ensuing; the defendant had deliberately left the public highway and refused to return to it; he had no legitimate reason to approach the fence; and it was plainly reasonable for the police officer to believe that he could cause criminal damage to the fence.

2.9.6 Having Articles with Intent to Destroy or Damage Property

OFFENCE: **Having articles with intent to destroy or damage property—*Criminal Damage Act 1971, s. 3***

• Triable either way • Ten years' imprisonment on indictment • Six months' imprisonment and/or a fine summarily

The Criminal Damage Act 1971, s. 3 states:

> A person who has anything in his custody or under his control intending without lawful excuse to use it or cause or permit another to use it—
> (a) to destroy or damage any property belonging to some other person; or
> (b) to destroy or damage his own or the user's property in a way which he knows is likely to endanger the life of some other person;
> shall be guilty of an offence.

KEYNOTE

Often referred to as 'possessing articles' for causing damage, this offence is, in reality, far wider than that. Although it also originates from the need to control organised crime, this offence covers *anything* which a defendant has '*in his custody or under his control*', a deliberately broader term than 'possession'. (Compare this with the narrower expression—'has with him'—used in the law preventing the carrying of weapons, and the Theft Act 1968.)

As a result, this offence applies to graffiti 'artists' carrying aerosols, advertisers with adhesives for sticking illicit posters and neighbours with paint stripper. The key element, once again, is an *intention*. This time the required intention is that the 'thing' be used to cause criminal damage to another's property or to the defendant's own property in a way which he/she knows is likely to endanger the life of another. Such articles are now 'prohibited' articles for the purposes of the power of stop and search under s. 1 of the Police and Criminal Evidence Act 1984.

A conditional intent—that is, an intent to use something to cause criminal damage if the need arises—will be enough (*R* v *Buckingham* (1976) 63 Cr App R 159).

Just as it is not an offence to damage your own property in a way which endangers no one else, neither is it an offence to have something which you intend to use to cause damage under those circumstances.

EXAMPLE

If the owner of a 10 metre high conifer decides to trim the top with a chainsaw and a ladder, putting himself—but no one else—at considerable risk, he commits no offence, either by causing the damage or by having the chainsaw. If he intends to fell the tree in a way which a reasonable bystander would say presents a danger to his neighbours or passers by, then he may commit offences on both counts.

Police Powers

There is a statutory power to apply to a magistrate for a search warrant under s. 6.

PART THREE

Assaults, Drugs, Firearms and Defences

PROVOCATION
SUICIDE PACT } I/V MANSLAUGHTER.
DIM RESP

MANSLAUGHTER

- UNLAWFUL ACT. — RISK OF HARM
  UNLAWFUL ACT
  MENS REA.
- GROSS NEGLIGENCE
- CORP MANSLAUGHTER — A DUTY OF CARE
  B REACHED
  C RIMINAL ACT
  D EATH CAUSED

3.1 Homicide

3.1.1 Introduction

Homicide covers not only the offences of murder and manslaughter, but also other occasions where a person causes, or is involved in, the death of another. The common law which has grown up around the subject of homicide is important, not only because of the gravity of the offences themselves, but also because the cases have defined a number of key issues in criminal law which are applicable to many other offences.

In all cases of homicide the general criminal conduct (*actus reus*) is the same—the killing of another person—but there are often complex arguments over *causation*.

Although offences of homicide are still relatively rare in day-to-day policing, many assaults can turn into homicides simply by the consequent and causally-connected death of the victim. For this reason, it is necessary that police officers have at least a general understanding of the key concepts. One of the most significant changes to homicide legislation comes in the form of the Corporate Manslaughter and Corporate Homicide Act 2007. The Act is discussed later in this chapter.

As a result of several high profile cases involving homicide, a number of technical changes have been made to the availability of alternative verdicts by the Domestic Violence, Crime and Victims Act 2004 (see s. 6). These are more matters for the courts and legal representatives than for police officers and investigators.

3.1.2 Murder

OFFENCE: **Murder—*Common Law***

- Life imprisonment (mandatory)

Murder is committed when a person unlawfully kills another human being under the Queen's Peace, with malice aforethought (**see Blackstone's Criminal Practice 2008, section B1**).

KEYNOTE

A conviction for murder carries a mandatory sentence of life imprisonment (in the case of a defendant who is under 18, 'detention at Her Majesty's pleasure': Powers of Criminal Courts (Sentencing) Act 2000, s. 90).

'Unlawful killing' means actively causing the death of another without justification and includes occasions where someone fails to act after creating a situation of danger.

'Another human being' includes a baby who has been born alive and has an existence independent of its mother. If a person injures a baby while it is in its mother's womb and it subsequently dies from those injuries *after being born*, it may be appropriate to bring a charge of murder.

If the defendant intended only to cause serious injury to the mother, that intention cannot support a charge of *murder* in respect of the baby if it goes on to die after being born alive. It may, however, support a charge of *manslaughter*. This departure from the earlier law is clear from the House of Lords' ruling in *Attorney-General's Reference (No. 3 of 1994)* [1998] AC 245, a ruling that overturned the Court of Appeal's previous decision in the same case. The House of Lords ruled that the doctrine of 'transferred malice' does not fully apply in cases of unborn children (*in utero*). Any liability of the defendant for the subsequent death of a child that he/she injured before it was born alive will depend on the defendant's intentions at the time of causing the injury. Clearly an intention to kill the mother could be sufficient in bringing a charge of murder following the subsequent and connected death of the child.

'Under the Queen's Peace' appears to exclude deaths caused during the legitimate prosecution of warfare (see the War Crimes Act 1991). Under the provisions of the Offences Against the Person Act 1861 any British citizen who commits a murder anywhere in the world may be tried in England or Wales.

It should be noted that the only state of mind or *mens rea* that will support a charge of attempted murder is an *intention to kill*. Nothing less will suffice.

Where a charge of murder is brought there may be specific restrictions on the applicability of a defence that might otherwise be available. For example, a claim of self-defence based on a mistake arising out of voluntary drunkenness will not be allowed in a prosecution for murder (or manslaughter).

3.1.2.1 Malice Aforethought

After the cases of *R* v *Moloney* [1985] AC 905 and *R* v *Hancock* [1986] AC 455, the *mens rea* required for murder is an intention:

- to kill, or
- to cause grievous bodily harm.

Murder is therefore a crime of 'specific intent'.

The term 'malice aforethought' is often associated with some form of premeditation; this is not required.

3.1.2.2 Year and a Day

A rule which no longer applies is the 'year and a day' requirement. Since the Law Reform (Year and a Day Rule) Act 1996 there is no longer a need to show that a victim died within a year and a day of the defendant's actions (s. 1).

If a victim of an alleged murder dies *more than three years after receiving their injury* then the consent of the Attorney-General (or Solicitor-General) is needed before bringing a prosecution (s. 2(2)(b)). That consent is also needed if the defendant has already been convicted of an offence committed under the circumstances connected with the death (s. 2(2)(a)).

3.1.3 Special Defences

As a conviction for murder leaves a judge no discretion in sentencing a defendant, a number of 'special defences' have developed around the offence. These 'defences' are now provided by the Homicide Act 1957 and, rather than securing an acquittal, allow for a conviction of voluntary manslaughter instead of murder. As such these defences fall outside the more common defences that are generally available in respect of criminal offences.

These 'special defences' are:

- diminished responsibility
- provocation
- suicide pact.

3.1.3.1 Diminished Responsibility

The Homicide Act 1957, s. 2 states:

(1) Where a person kills or is party to the killing of another, he shall not be convicted of murder if he was suffering from such abnormality of mind (whether arising from a condition of arrested or retarded development of mind or any inherent causes or induced by disease or injury) as substantially impaired his mental responsibility for his acts or omissions in doing or being a party to the killing.

(2) On a charge of murder, it shall be for the defence to prove that the person charged is by virtue of this section not liable to be convicted of murder.
(3) A person who but for this section would be liable, whether as principal or as accessory, to be convicted of murder shall be liable instead to be convicted of manslaughter.
(4) The fact that one party to a killing is by virtue of this section not liable to be convicted of murder shall not affect the question whether the killing amounted to murder in the case of any other party to it.

KEYNOTE

'Abnormality of mind' has been held to be 'a state of mind so different from that of ordinary human beings that the reasonable man would term it abornmal' (*R* v *Byrne* [1960] 2 QB 396). This includes the mental inability to exert control over one's behaviour and to form rational judgement.

'Impairment of mental responsibility'—this impairment must be 'substantial'. Whether or not that is the case will be a question of fact for the jury to decide. Minor lapses of lucidity will not be enough. There may be any number of causes of the 'abnormality' of the mind. Examples accepted by the courts to date have included pre-menstrual symptoms (*R* v *Reynolds* [1988] Crim LR 679) and 'battered wives' syndrome' (*R* v *Hobson* [1998] 1 Cr App R 31). A further example arose in the case of *R* v *Dietschmann* [2003] 1 AC 1209 where the House of Lords accepted that a mental abnormality caused by a grief reaction to the recent death of an aunt with whom the defendant had had a physical relationship could suffice. In that case their Lordships went on to hold that there is no requirement to show that the 'abnormality of mind' was the *sole* cause of the defendant's acts in committing the killing.

The burden of proving these features lies with the defence and the standard required is one of a balance of probabilities. While this issue of 'reverse onus of proof' has created some inconsistent decisions across different statutory provisions—and in particular its relationship with the European Convention on Human Rights—in *R* v *Lambert* [2001] 2 WLR 211, the Court of Appeal held that this burden of proof did not breach an individual's right to a presumption of innocence or the right to a fair trial under the Convention.

3.1.3.2 Provocation

The Homicide Act 1957, s. 3 states:

> Where on a charge of murder there is evidence on which a jury can find that the person charged was provoked (whether by things done or by things said or by both together) to lose his self-control, the question whether the provocation was enough to make a reasonable man do as he did shall be left to be determined by the jury; and in determining that question the jury shall take into account everything both done and said according to the effect which, in their opinion, it would have on a reasonable man.

KEYNOTE

The question of provocation here is not a general consideration of the ordinary English meaning of the word, but a highly technical pleading that has developed through the common law. The real relevance of this area to police officers will be in the gathering and recording of any evidence that might support or undermine the claim that the defendant was 'provoked'.

The main questions to be considered are:

- Was the defendant actually provoked?
- Might a reasonable person have acted as the defendant did under the same circumstances?

Whether the defendant *was* in fact provoked will be a matter for the jury.

It is clear that words (*DPP* v *Camplin* [1978] AC 705) or even sounds (*R* v *Doughty* [1986] 83 Cr App R 319 (baby crying)) have amounted to 'provocation'. It is also clear that the words or acts need not be directed towards the defendant, nor need they originate from the ultimate victim. Therefore a defendant may be sufficiently provoked by things which X says to Y that he/she kills Z and the 'defence' of provocation could be available. In addition to the 'battered wives' syndrome' mentioned above, where the provocation has been endured by the defendant over a prolonged period (such as the abused wife in *R* v *Ahluwalia* [1992] 4 All ER 889), he/she may be able to show an eventual and sudden lack of self-control brought about by that prolonged behaviour or by a particular event which proved to be 'the last straw' (*R* v *Humphreys* [1995] 4 All ER 1008). If a defendant simply panics or acts out of fear, as opposed to losing control, the defence will not be made out. Unlike the general defence of 'duress', there is no defence of 'provocation by circumstances'; the provocation must come from something done by or to a third person (*R* v *Acott* [1997] 1 WLR 306).

If there is no loss of control by the defendant, then the provocation defence will not be available. See, for example, *R* v *Cocker* [1989] Crim LR 740 where the defendant had endured pleas from his chronically-ill wife to kill her. He had not lost control at the time of the killing—quite the reverse—and the judge had no alternative but to pass a life sentence. Several relatively recent cases (*R* v *James* [2006] EWCA Crim 14 and *Attorney General (Jersey)* v *Holley* [2005] UKPC 23) have led the courts to support the approach to the standard of self-control as laid down in the case of *Luc Thiet Thuan* v *The Queen* [1997] AC 131. Here, the defendant's characteristics could affect the gravity of the provocation to be taken into account (a subjective inquiry for the jury) but the standard of self-control to be expected of the particular individual should be the same as the 'reasonable man' (a second and objective inquiry for the jury).

3.1.3.3 Suicide Pact

The Homicide Act 1957, s. 4 states:

(1) It shall be manslaughter, and shall not be murder, for a person acting in pursuance of a suicide pact between him and another to kill the other or be a party to the other being killed by a third person.

KEYNOTE

The *defendant* must show that:

- a suicide pact had been made, and
- he/she had the intention of dying at the time the killing took place.

'Suicide pact' is defined by the Homicide Act 1957, s. 4(3) as:

a common agreement between two or more persons having for its object the death of all of them, whether or not each is to take his own life, but nothing done by a person who enters into a suicide pact shall be treated as done by him in pursuance of the pact unless it is done while he has the settled intention of dying in pursuance of the pact.

3.1.4 Manslaughter

Traditionally this subject is divided into two classifications—voluntary and involuntary manslaughter.

The three sets of circumstances where 'special defences' may reduce a murder charge to one of manslaughter make up one type or classification of the offence (*voluntary* manslaughter). They have been covered in **paras 3.1.3.1 to 3.1.3.3** above. In that sense, voluntary manslaughter is more a finding by a court than an offence with which someone can be charged. The second classification (*involuntary* manslaughter) occurs where the defendant causes the death of another but is not shown to have had the required *mens rea* for murder.

As with murder (**see para. 3.1.2**) a defendant on a charge of manslaughter cannot rely on a mistake induced by their own voluntary intoxication in claiming self defence—*R* v *Hatton* (2006) 1 Cr App R 16.

OFFENCE: **Manslaughter—*Common Law***

- Triable on indictment • Life imprisonment

KEYNOTE

Manslaughter, like murder is the unlawful killing of another human being. What it does not require is the intention to kill or to cause grievous bodily harm.

The second classification of manslaughter, that is, those cases which do not involve the 'special defences' under the Homicide Act 1957 (**see para. 3.1.3**) can be separated into occasions where a defendant:

- kills another by an *unlawful act* which was *likely to cause bodily harm*, or
- kills another by *gross negligence*.

3.1.4.1 Manslaughter by Unlawful Act

In order to prove manslaughter by an unlawful act (constructive manslaughter), you must prove:

- An unlawful act by the defendant, that is, an act which is *unlawful in itself*, irrespective of the fact that it ultimately results in someone's death. The act must be inherently unlawful. An act that only becomes unlawful by virtue of the way in which it is carried out will not be enough. A good example is 'driving'. Driving is clearly not an inherently unlawful act but becomes so if done inconsiderately on a road or public place. Therefore if someone drives inconsiderately and thereby causes the death of another, the act of driving—albeit carried out in a way that attracts criminal liability—is *not* an 'unlawful act' for the purposes of constructive manslaughter (see *Andrews* v *DPP* [1937] AC 576). This is one reason why there are statutory offences addressing most instances of death that are caused by poor standards of driving. The act need not be directed or aimed at anyone and can include acts committed against or towards property (*R* v *Goodfellow* (1986) 83 Cr App R 23).

  Generally, if the actions of the victim break the chain of causation between the defendant's unlawful act and the cause of death, the defendant will not be responsible for the death of that victim.

  This is why drug dealers who supply controlled drugs cannot generally be held liable for the ultimate deaths of their 'victims' (See *R* v *Dalby* [1982] 1 WLR 621 and *R* v *Armstrong* [1989] Crim LR 149). This view was affirmed in the recent case of *R* v *Kennedy* [2007] UKHL 38. The circumstances of the case were that the defendant had prepared a dose of heroin for the deceased and had given the syringe to the deceased before leaving the room they were both in. The deceased injected the drug and as a result died. The House of Lords ruled that a supplier of a drug is not guilty of manslaughter where the deceased freely and voluntarily self-administered the drug. Thus the greater weight of authorities suggests that a supplier of a drug is unlikely to be convicted of an offence of manslaughter unless he/she has done far more than just supply the drug.

An *omission* to do something will not suffice. Any unlawful killing caused by an omission would either come under the circumstances outlined in **chapter 1.2** or under those required to prove gross negligence (**see para. 3.1.4.2**).

- That the act involved a risk of somebody being harmed. That risk will be judged *objectively*, that is: would the risk be apparent to a reasonable and sober person watching the act? (See *R* v *Church* [1966] 1 QB 59.) Such acts might include dropping a paving stone off a bridge into the path of a train (*DPP* v *Newbury* [1977] AC 500), setting fire to your house (*Goodfellow* above) or firing a gun at police officers and then holding someone else in front of you when the officers return fire (*R* v *Pagett* (1983) 76 Cr App R 279). 'Harm' must be physical; the risk of emotional or psychological harm does not appear to be enough (see *R* v *Dawson* (1985) 81 Cr App R 150). In *R* v *C* [2006] EWCA Crim 17 the deceased—aged 15—had been out walking with friends and had met the defendants who had been drinking alcohol all afternoon. The defendants were verbally abusive and threatening to the deceased and her group. One defendant punched one of the deceased's group and another attacked the deceased herself, pulling her hair back and punching her in the face. Two boys intervened and stopped the attack, at which point the deceased ran off but collapsed and died later that night. The medical evidence showed that, unknown to her doctors or her family, the deceased had a severely diseased heart, and that she might not have died had she not been running.

  On appeal it was held that the manslaughter charge (of which the first defendant was convicted) should have been withdrawn from the jury. Although the attack was unpleasant and accompanied by bullying, any injuries caused had been slight. None of the defendants had intended to cause really serious harm to any of the victims and they did not intend that the deceased should die. The Court of Appeal reiterated the general principle that a person who inflicts a slight injury that unforeseeably leads to the death of the victim nevertheless commits manslaughter (per *R* v *Church* [1966] 1 QB 59). However, to hold the defendants liable for the deceased's death in the circumstances of this case would have involved an 'unwarranted extension of the law'. The court observed that the law of unlawful act manslaughter required the commission of an unlawful act which was recognised, by a sober and reasonable person, as being dangerous and likely to subject the victim to the risk of some physical harm which in turn caused their death. In the instant case the only act committed against the deceased that was 'dangerous' was the assault and the physical harm resulting from it did not cause her death.
- That the defendant had the required *mens rea* for the relevant 'unlawful act' (e.g. for an assault or criminal damage) which led to the death of a victim. If he/she did not have that *mens rea*, the offence of manslaughter will not be made out. See, for example, *R* v *Lamb* [1967] 2 QB 981 where the defendant pretended to fire a revolver at his friend. Although the defendant believed that the weapon would not fire, the chamber containing a bullet moved round to the firing pin and the defendant's friend was killed. As Lamb did not have the *mens rea* required for an assault his conviction for manslaughter was quashed.

There is no logical reason why, if a defendant uses a motor vehicle as a means to commit an 'unlawful act' (e.g. an assault) that he/she cannot be charged with manslaughter as long as the 'act' goes beyond poor driving. The CPS has published a policy document which sets out the way in which it will deal with cases of bad driving. Unlawful act manslaughter will be considered the most appropriate charge when there is evidence to prove that the vehicle was used as an instrument of attack (but where the necessary intent for murder was absent), or to cause fright, and death resulted. There are, however, reasons of policy (see *R* v *Lawrence* [1982] AC 510) why, in all but the most deliberate of cases, the offence under the Road Traffic Act 1988, as amended, should be used.

3.1.4.2 Manslaughter by Gross Negligence

Manslaughter is the only criminal offence at common law capable of being committed by negligence. The degree of that negligence has been the source of considerable debate over the years and particular problems have arisen in trying to distinguish the level of negligence required for manslaughter and that required to prove 'recklessness'.

A charge of manslaughter may be brought where a person, by an instance of *gross negligence*, has brought about the death of another. The ingredients of this offence were reviewed and re-stated by the Court of Appeal and essentially consist of death resulting from a negligent breach of a duty of care owed by the defendant to the victim in circumstances so reprehensible as to amount to gross negligence (*R* v *Misra and Srivastava* [2004] EWCA Crim 2375). The most difficult task in defining the degree of negligence that will qualify as 'gross' falls to the trial judge when he/she addresses the jury. Whether a defendant's conduct will amount to gross negligence is a question of fact for the jury to decide in the light of all the evidence (*R* v *Bateman* (1925) 19 Cr App R 8).

Although the lack of clarity around this offence has resulted in its being challenged under the European Convention on Human Rights, the Court of Appeal has held that its ingredients are sufficiently certain for those purposes (*R* v *Misra and Srivastava*). What is clear from the decided cases is that civil liability, although a starting point for establishing the breach of a duty of care, is not enough to amount to 'gross negligence', neither is objective 'recklessness' (*R* v *Adomako* [1995] 1 AC 171).

The test in *Adomako* as summarised by Lord Mackay seems to provide the leading authority on the area. Lord Mackay put the test for the jury as being:...'whether, having regard to the risk of death involved, the conduct of the defendant was so bad in all the circumstances as to amount in their judgment to a criminal act or omission'.

Note that from 6 April 2008, it is no longer possible to bring proceedings for gross negligence manslaughter against a company or other organisation to which the offence under the Corporate Manslaughter and Corporate Homicide Act 2007 applies (s. 20 of the Corporate Manslaughter and Corporate Homicide Act 2007).

For the practical difficulties and the inconsistencies in the case law on this area generally, **see Blackstone's Criminal Practice 2008, section B1.55.**

3.1.4.3 Corporate Manslaughter and Corporate Homicide Act 2007

Originating from a proposal in a Law Commission Report, the Corporate Manslaughter and Corporate Homicide Act 2007 came into force on 6 April 2008 after nearly ten years of development in Parliament. While most of the Act has been brought into force, it is of particular relevance to police officers (especially custody officers) to note that the provisions contained in the Act in respect of deaths in custody will not be brought into force for some time. At the time of writing the government indicated that this period could be as long as three and possibly five years from the date the Act came into force.

OFFENCE: **Corporate Manslaughter—Corporate Manslaughter and Corporate Homicide Act 2007, s.1**

- Triable on indictment • Unlimited fine

The Corporate Manslaughter and Corporate Homicide Act 2007, s. 1 states:

(1) An organisation to which this section applies is guilty of an offence if the way in which its activities are managed or organised—
   (a) causes a person's death, and
   (b) amounts to a gross breach of a relevant duty of care owed by the organisation to the deceased.

KEYNOTE

The offence is concerned with the way in which an organisation's activities were managed or organised. Under this test, the courts will examine management systems and practices across the organisation, and whether the adequate standard of care was applied to the fatal activity.

The threshold for the offence is gross negligence. The way in which the activities were managed or organised must have fallen far below what could reasonably have been expected.

The failure to manage or organise activities properly must have caused the victim's death.

A duty of care is an obligation that an organisation has to take reasonable steps to protect a person's safety. These duties exist, for example, in respect of the systems of work and equipment used by employees, the condition of worksites and other premises occupied by an organisation and in relation to products or services supplied to customers. The duty must be a *relevant* one. Relevant duties are set out in s. 2 of the Act and include:

- Employer and occupier duties
- Duties connected to:
  - Supplying goods and services
  - Commercial activities
  - Construction and maintenance work
  - Using or keeping plant, vehicles or other things
- Duties relating to holding a person in custody (bearing in mind that this part of the Act is not yet in force)

In relation to policing and law enforcement in the Act, there are some exceptions to the relevant duty of care obligation (s. 5 of the Act), these are in:

- Operations for dealing with terrorism, civil unrest or serious disorder, that involve the carrying on of policing or law-enforcement activities where officers or employees of the public authority in question come under attack, or face the threat of attack or violent resistance, in the course of the operations
- Activities carried out in preparation for, or directly in support of, such operations as above
- Training of a hazardous nature or training carried out in a hazardous way in order to improve or maintain the effectiveness of officers or employees of the public authority with respect to such operations as above

Police services and authorities are still subject to the Act and could be prosecuted in matters where death relates to the organisation's responsibility *as an employer* (or to others working for the organisation) or as *an occupier of premises.*

The Corporate Manslaughter and Corporate Homicide Act 2007, s. 1 states:

(2) The organisations to which this section applies are—
  (a) a corporation;
  (b) a department or other body listed in Schedule 1;
  (c) a police force;
  (d) a partnership or trade union or employers' association, that is an employer.

KEYNOTE

The Act applies to:

- Companies incorporated under companies legislation or overseas
- Other corporations including:

- ♦ Public bodies incorporated by statute such as local authorities, NHS bodies and a wide range of non-departmental public bodies
- ♦ Organisations incorporated by Royal Charter
- ♦ Limited liability partnerships
- All other partnerships, and trade unions and employer's associations, if the organisation concerned is an employer
- Crown bodies such as government departments
- Police forces

Under the Act a corporation would include a police authority.

The offence is concerned with the corporate liability of the organisation itself and *does not apply* to individual directors, senior managers or other individuals. It is not possible to convict an individual of assisting or encouraging this offence (s. 18). This does not change the position that individuals can be prosecuted for the offence of gross negligence manslaughter.

The Corporate Manslaughter and Corporate Homicide Act 2007, s. 1 states:

(3) An organisation is guilty of an offence under this section only if the way in which its activities are managed or organised by its senior management is a substantial element in the breach referred to in subsection (1).

KEYNOTE

The term 'senior management' is defined in s. 1(4) of the Act to mean those persons who play a significant role in the management of the whole or of a substantial part of the organisation's activities. This covers those individuals in the direct chain of management as well as those in, for example, strategic or regulatory compliance roles.

The offence can be prosecuted if the harm resulting in death occurs in the United Kingdom, in the United Kingdom's territorial waters (for example, an incident involving commercial shipping or leisure craft), on a British ship, aircraft or hovercraft or on an oil rig or other offshore installation covered by UK criminal law.

Proceedings for an offence of corporate manslaughter may not be instituted in England and Wales without the consent of the DPP. An organisation that is guilty of the offence is liable on conviction on indictment to a fine (these fines are likely to run into many millions of pounds). The Act also provides for remedial orders (under s. 9) and publicity orders (under s. 10). A remedial order will force an organisation to address the cause of the fatal injury; publicity orders will require an organisation to publicise the fact of its conviction and certain details of the offence in a way specified by the court.

3.1.5 Causing or Allowing the Death of a Child or Vulnerable Adult

In addition to the categories of manslaughter discussed above, there is a specific offence to cater for circumstances where a relevant person causes or allows the death of a child or vulnerable adult. This offence came about as a result of the practical difficulties that arise where a child or other vulnerable person dies as a result of the unlawful act of one of several people but it cannot be shown which of them actually caused the death or allowed it to occur.

OFFENCE: **Causing or Allowing the Death of a Child or Vulnerable Adult—*Domestic Violence, Crime and Victims Act 2004, s. 5***

- Triable on indictment • 14 years' imprisonment

The Domestic Violence, Crime and Victims Act 2004, s. 5 states:

(1) A person ('D') is guilty of an offence if—
  (a) a child or vulnerable adult ('V') dies as a result of the unlawful act of a person who—
    (i) was a member of the same household as V, and
    (ii) had frequent contact with him,
  (b) D was such a person at the time of that act,
  (c) at that time there was a significant risk of serious physical harm being caused to V by the unlawful act of such a person, and
  (d) either D was the person whose act caused V's death or—
    (i) D was, or ought to have been, aware of the risk mentioned in paragraph (c),
    (ii) D failed to take such steps as he could reasonably have been expected to take to protect V from the risk, and
    (iii) the act occurred in circumstances of the kind that D foresaw or ought to have foreseen.

KEYNOTE

This offence has a number of key components that must be proved before it is made out.

First you must show that the victim was a child or vulnerable adult. 'Child' means a person under the age of 16 and 'vulnerable adult' means a person aged 16 or over whose ability to protect themselves from violence, abuse or neglect is significantly impaired through physical or mental disability or illness, through old age or otherwise (s. 5(6)).

It will then be necessary to prove that the victim died *as a result of the unlawful act* of a person who fits a number of criteria. For these purposes 'act' includes 'omissions' and an act or omission will generally only be 'unlawful' if it would have amounted to an offence (see s. 5(5) and (6)). The first criterion that must be shown to apply to the defendant is that, *at the time of the act* they were a member of the same household as the victim *and* had frequent contact with him or her. For these purposes a person will be a member of a particular household if they visit it so often and for such periods of time that it is reasonable to regard them as a member of it—even if they do not actually live there (s. 5(4)(a)). Where, as often happens, the victim lived in different households at different times, the 'same household' criterion will mean the household in which the victim was living at the time of the act that caused their death (s. 5(4)(b)).

Finally it must be shown that, at the time, there was a significant risk of serious physical harm being caused to the victim by the unlawful act of a person meeting these criteria. 'Serious harm' means grievous bodily harm for the purposes of the Offences against the Person Act 1861 (see para. 3.2.20).

Once these elements have been established, the offence is completed in one of two ways: directly (i.e. by the defendant's act causing the victim's death) or indirectly and the prosecution does not have to prove which alternative applies (see s. 5(2)). However, in cases where indirect causation is suspected, three further things must be shown, namely that:

(1) the defendant was (or ought to have been) aware of the risk of grievous bodily harm;
(2) the defendant failed to take such steps as he or she could reasonably have been expected to take to protect the victim from the risk; *and*
(3) the act occurred in the kind of circumstances that the defendant foresaw (or ought to have foreseen).

Unless the defendant is the mother or father of the victim (a) they cannot be charged with an offence under this section if they were under 16 at the time of the act and (b) restrictions will be made on what steps would have been reasonable for a defendant to have taken while under that age (see s. 5(3)).

3.2 Offences Against the Person

3.2.1 Introduction

Non-fatal offences against others cover a wide range of behaviour from a raised fist to a calculated wounding. The importance of this subject lies not only in the number of occasions when officers will need to refer to it, but also because it deals with violence and the fear of violent crime—areas in which victims are particularly traumatised. As courts are being urged to focus on the effects of a defendant's conduct upon their victim, the scope for bringing a charge of assault is widening.

3.2.2 Key Issues

While there are several distinct categories of offence that can be committed against other people, there are some features that are important for both understanding the law and the practical application of it. These key issues are set out below.

3.2.3 Assault and Battery

Assault and battery are, strictly speaking, two separate things. What people generally think of as being an 'assault' (e.g. a punch on the nose) is a 'battery', that is, the infliction of unlawful force on someone else. While it would cover a punch on the nose, an 'assault' in its proper legal sense has a much wider meaning and includes any act whereby the defendant 'intentionally—or recklessly—causes another person to apprehend immediate and unlawful personal violence' (*Fagan* v *Metropolitan Police Commissioner* [1969] 1 QB 439).

3.2.4 Assault or Battery?

Although these terms—assault and battery—have distinct legal meanings they are often referred to as simply 'assaults' or 'common assault'. It is, however, important to separate the two expressions when charging or laying an information against a defendant as to include both may be bad for duplicity (*DPP* v *Taylor* [1992] QB 645).

The term battery, or the application of 'force', creates a misleading impression as a very small degree of physical contact will be enough. That force can be applied directly or indirectly. For example, where a defendant punched a woman causing her to drop and injure a child she was holding, he was convicted of assaulting that child (*Haystead* v *Chief Constable of Derbyshire* [2000] 3 All ER 890). The *actus reus* needed to prove an assault is an act which caused the victim to apprehend the immediate infliction of unlawful force, although 'apprehension' does not mean 'fear' and there is no need to show that the victim was actually in fear. The force or violence apprehended by the victim does not have to be a 'certainty'. Causing a fear of some possible violence can be enough (see *R* v *Ireland* [1998] AC 147) provided that the violence feared is about to happen in the immediate future (see *R* v *Constanza* [1997] 2 Cr App R 492).

There is some academic debate as to whether battery and assault are still common law offences or whether they are now statutory offences. What is clear is that the Criminal Justice Act 1988, s. 39 stipulates that they must be tried summarily and sets out the maximum penalty that may be imposed (**see para. 3.2.11**).

While some offences can be committed by an act or an *omission* (e.g. manslaughter) for a charge of assault to succeed there must be an *act* (*Fagan*).

It also is important to remember that the state of mind of the *victim* in an assault is relevant to the *actus reus*. The victim must apprehend the immediate use of unlawful force. For these reasons, if a defendant threatened someone with an imitation pistol, he/she could still be charged with assault provided the victim *believed* that the pistol was real—the defendant had caused an apprehension of possible immediate force being used (*Logdon* v *DPP* [1976] Crim LR 121).

Words can amount to an assault provided they are accompanied by the required *mens rea*. This was made clear by the decision in *R* v *Ireland* [1998] AC 147 where it was held that telephone calls to a victim, followed by silences, could amount to an assault. In *Ireland*, the House of Lords accepted that '*a thing said is also a thing done*' and rejected the view that words can never amount to an assault. *Ireland* involved the making of threatening telephone calls which led the victims to fear that unlawful force would be used against them. The House of Lords accepted that, in such cases, even *silence* could fulfil the requirements for the *actus reus* of assault if it brought about the desired consequences (e.g. fear of the immediate use of unlawful force).

Where the words threatening immediate unlawful force come in the form of letters, the Court of Appeal has held that an assault may have been committed (see *Constanza* above).

3.2.4.1 Conditional Threats

As well as constituting an assault, words can also *negate* an assault if they make a conditional threat, e.g., where you attend an incident and one person says to another '*If these officers weren't here I'd chin you!*' (*Tuberville* v *Savage* (1669) 1 Mod R3—a very ancient and therefore long-standing authority). In this type of case the defendant is making a *hypothetical* threat and is really saying 'if it weren't for the existence of certain circumstances, I would assault you'. This should be contrasted with occasions where the defendant makes an immediate threat conditional upon some real circumstance, e.g. '*If you don't cross the road, I'll break your neck*'. Such threats have been held, in a civil case, to amount to an assault (*Read* v *Coker* (1853) 13 CB 850).

3.2.4.2 What is 'Immediate'?

Although the force threatened must be immediate, that immediacy is—like most legal interpretation—somewhat elastic. Courts have accepted that, where a person makes a threat from outside a victim's house to the victim who is inside, an assault is still committed even though there will be some time lapse before the defendant can carry out the threat.

In *Ireland* the House of Lords suggested that a threat to cause violence 'in a minute or two' might be enough to qualify as an assault. The victim must be shown to have feared the use of *force*; it will not be enough to show that a person threatened by words—or silence—feared more calls or letters. The fear of force is the key to assault.

3.2.5 Intentionally or Recklessly

The *mens rea* needed to prove common assault is either:

- an intention to cause apprehension of immediate unlawful violence, or
- subjective recklessness (i.e. foresight) as to that consequence.

When considering the *mens rea of* any assault, it is important to separate the assault or battery (**see para. 3.2.4**) from *any further consequences caused by* that assault or battery. The *mens rea* needed for the assault/battery is set out above. If a defendant's behaviour causes another to fear immediate and unlawful personal violence, he/she commits an 'assault' provided it can be shown that, at the time, the defendant *intended* to cause that fear or was *subjectively reckless* as to whether such a fear would result from his/her actions.

So what happens where the defendant's actions cause more than just fear; they cause more serious injury? Unfortunately that appears to depend on the extent of the injury and the wording of the offence charged. Among the more serious offences under the Offences Against the Person Act 1861 (**see para. 3.2.18**) are causing 'actual bodily harm' (s. 47) and 'wounding' or inflicting/causing 'grievous bodily harm' (ss. 18 and 20). The *mens rea* required for an offence under s. 47, causing actual bodily harm, is the same as that required for the basic offence of assault (*R* v *Savage* [1992] 1 AC 699). This is because s. 47 makes no specific requirement for any greater degree of *mens rea* by the defendant and, in effect, the offence of causing actual bodily harm becomes simply an assault or battery with a more serious outcome. From the defendant's point of view this is really pot luck because there is no requirement for him/her to have intended or even foreseen the actual bodily harm. In the case of woundings and grievous bodily harm, the situation is different because ss. 18 and 20 use the word 'maliciously' (**see para. 3.2.20**). This element introduces the element of intention or subjective recklessness *in relation to the injuries suffered by the victim* (*Savage* above), thereby adding a further requirement to the *mens rea*.

EXAMPLE

Take the example of two people in a pub. They are arguing. One person, the defendant, threatens to throw a pint of beer over the other, the victim. At this point the defendant has caused the victim to fear that immediate unlawful personal violence will be used against him—an 'assault'. In order to prove an offence of assault under the Criminal Justice Act 1988, you must show that, at the time of the threat, the defendant either intended to cause the fear of violence or was subjectively reckless in that regard. If such an intention or recklessness cannot be shown, there is no offence of assault.

After the threat, a third person pushes past the defendant, accidentally knocking him into the victim and spilling the beer over him. At this point there has been no 'assault' by the defendant because there has been no *actus reus* by him, irrespective of his intentions.

The defendant continues to argue and then raises his glass and throws the contents over the victim. Clearly there has now been a voluntary application of unlawful force—a 'battery'—which the defendant intended to apply and he commits an offence under the Criminal Justice Act 1988. In the act of throwing the beer, however, the defendant's hand slips and he in fact hits the victim in the face with his beer glass causing a broken tooth. At this point the defendant's actions have gone beyond those intended by him and his victim has suffered injuries which the defendant had neither intended nor considered. Nevertheless, at the time of the assault (and battery) the defendant had the required *mens rea* for the assault/battery and therefore is liable for any actual bodily harm suffered by the victim as a result. Therefore the defendant commits the offence of assault occasioning actual bodily harm under s. 47 of the Offences Against the Person Act 1861, even though he neither intended nor considered the injuries to his victim.

Having a small amount of beer left in the glass, the defendant flicks the 'dregs' from the glass at the victim. The defendant loses his grip on the glass and it flies from his hand, hitting the victim in the eye and breaking on impact. The victim suffers a deep wound to the eye. Although the defendant is still liable for any actual bodily harm, he can only be liable for the more serious offences of wounding and causing/inflicting *grievous* bodily harm if it can be shown that he acted 'maliciously'. Malice for these purposes means that he must have intended to cause the harm or realised that there was a risk of at least some harm being suffered by the victim. If he did realise that the victim was at risk of being harmed by his actions, the defendant may be liable for an offence under s. 20 of the Offences Against the Person Act 1861 (**see para. 3.2.20**). If it can be shown that he intended to bring about *serious* harm, the defendant may be liable for the offence under s. 18 of the 1861 Act (**see para. 3.2.21**).

If the victim goes on to die from the injury, the defendant would be guilty of murder, or manslaughter by unlawful or dangerous act, depending on the level of *mens rea*.

Given the requirements for *mens rea*, together with the respective penalties, it is not surprising that charges of 'actual bodily harm' might be preferred over charges of malicious wounding or inflicting grievous bodily harm.

A further example of the issues arising in the context of an arrest can be seen in *D* v *DPP* [2005] Crim LR 962 (see para. 1.1.4.2).

3.2.6 Consent

A key element in proving an assault is the *unlawfulness* of the force used or threatened. Although the courts have accepted consent as a feature which negatives any offence, they have been reluctant to accept this feature in a number of notable cases.

3.2.7 Consent to Sado-masochistic Injuries

These cases have developed as a question of public policy and were summarised in the House of Lords in the so-called 'spanner trial' (*R* v *Brown* [1994] 1 AC 212).

That case involved members of a sado-masochist group who inflicted varying degrees of injuries on one another for their own gratification. Charged with many offences against the person, the group claimed that they had consented to the injuries and therefore no assault or battery had taken place. Their Lordships followed an earlier policy that *all assaults which result in more than transient harm will be unlawful unless there is good reason for allowing the plea of 'consent'*. Good reason will be determined in the light of a number of considerations:

- the practical consequences of the behaviour
- the dangerousness of the behaviour
- the vulnerability of the 'consenting' person.

Further difficulties in clarifying what will amount to 'true' or effective consent were added by the decision of the Court of Appeal in *R* v *Wilson* [1997] QB 47. In that case the court accepted that a husband might lawfully brand his initials on his wife's buttocks with a hot knife provided she consented (as she appeared to have done). The reasoning behind the judgment seems to be based on the fact that the branding was similar to a form of tattooing (see below), but also on the policy grounds that consensual activity between husband and wife is not a matter for criminal investigation. This causes several problems, not least of which is the fact that sado-masochistic 'branding' was denounced by the House of Lords in *Brown* above. Therefore, if a situation arose where a husband and wife took part in mutual branding in the privacy of their home, their criminal liability would arguably depend on whether they caused the harm for purposes of sado-masochistic pleasure or out of some affectionate wish to be permanently adorned with the mark of their loved one. It is also unclear how far the policy aspect of the decision in *Wilson* would extend and whether or not it would encompass unmarried or homosexual couples.

Sado-masochistic injury may justifiably be made the subject of criminal law on grounds of the 'protection of health'. It was for this reason that the European Court of Human Rights held that there had been no violation of the defendants' right to private life (under article 8) in the *Brown* case above. Although the defendants asserted that the interference by the criminal law in their consensual sexual practices amounted to an unnecessary restriction of their individual rights under article 8, the court held that this was a justifiable intrusion on the grounds set out above (*Laskey, Jaggard and Brown* v *United Kingdom* (1997) 24 EHRR 39).

3.2.8 Legitimate Consent to Risk of Injury

Clearly there are times when a person may consent to even serious harm such as during properly conducted sporting events (see *Attorney-General's Reference (No. 6 of 1980)* [1981] QB 715), tattooing and medical operations. Where the activity falls outside those parameters, such as an off-the-ball incident in a football match (*R* v *Lloyd* (1989) 11 Cr App R (S) 36) or an unauthorised prize fight, the plea of consent will not apply. However, the Court of Appeal has stated that the criminal prosecution of those who inflict injury on another in the course of a sporting event is reserved for those situations where the conduct was sufficiently grave to be properly categorised as criminal—*R* v *Barnes* [2004] EWCA Crim 3246. In that case the defendant appealed against his conviction for inflicting grievous bodily harm (**see para. 3.2.20**) after he caused a serious leg injury by way of a tackle during a football match. The tackle took place after the victim had kicked the ball into the goal but, while accepting that the tackle was hard, the defendant maintained that it had been a fair challenge and that the injury caused was accidental. The court held that where injuries were sustained in the course of contact sports, public policy limited the availability of the defence of consent to situations where there had been implicit consent to what had occurred. Whether conduct reached the required threshold to be treated as 'criminal' would depend on all the circumstances. The fact that the actions of the defendant had been within the rules and practice of the game would be a firm indication that what had occurred was not criminal, although in highly competitive sports even conduct *outside the rules* could be expected to occur in the heat of the moment, and such conduct still might not reach the threshold level required for it to be criminal. The court held that the threshold level was an objective one to be determined by the type of sport, the level at which it was played, the nature of the 'act', the degree of force used, the extent of the risk of injury and the state of mind of the defendant.

Other more straightforward policy considerations would include the implied consent by people getting on to crowded tube trains or moving around at a packed concert venue. In these cases it will be a matter of fact to decide whether the behaviour complained of went beyond what was acceptable in those particular circumstances.

Where a dentist who had been suspended by the General Dental Council continued to operate on patients, her failure to inform those patients of her suspension did not affect their true 'consent' and the dentist's actions were not an 'assault' (*R* v *Richardson* [1999] QB 444). The situation would be very different if the dentist had no formal qualifications at all, or if her actions went beyond the proper professional activities of a dentist (e.g. an indecent touching of patients).

One area where the issue of legitimate consent has raised considerable debate is that of infection with a sexually transmitted disease. Here there are two aspects to the 'consent'—one is consent to the sexual activity itself, the other is consent to the risk of contracting the disease (such as HIV). It is clear from the authorities that consent to the former does not necessarily provide consent to the latter (**see para. 3.2.20**).

3.2.9 Lawful Chastisement

For many years the common and statute law allowed for those acting in *loco parentis* (meaning in place of the parent) of a child to be able to use reasonable force in controlling the behaviour of that child. What was 'reasonable' varied widely and became increasingly difficult to define let alone justify given the breadth and depth of social attitudes and conventions within England and Wales.

In a case involving an allegation of assault by a stepfather on his stepson, the European Court of Human Rights held that the United Kingdom was in breach of its obligation to protect individuals from inhuman or degrading punishment (under article 3 of the European Convention on Human Rights) because the law in this area was not clear enough (*A* v *United Kingdom* (1999) 27 EHRR 611). Additionally, Protocol 1, article 2 (the right to education) of the Convention requires a state to have regard to the religious and philosophical convictions of parents in its schools. This requirement was at the centre of a successful challenge against corporal punishment in a state school (*Campbell* v *United Kingdom* (1982) 4 EHRR 293). The School Standards and Framework Act 1998 outlaws corporal punishment in all British schools, although staff may use reasonable force in restraining violent or disruptive pupils. The Divisional Court has held that this legislation removes entirely the defence of reasonable chastisement from any teacher when they are acting as such (*Williamson* v *Secretary of State for Education and Employment* [2001] EWHC Admin 960, later affirmed by the House of Lords [2005] UKHL 15). The legislation gave effect to a clear parliamentary intention to abolish corporal punishment in all schools, including independent schools, and did not infringe the human rights of any of the claimants.

So far as the general issue of lawful chastisement by parents and carers is concerned, the Children Act 2004 provides that battery of a person under 18 years of age cannot be justified on the ground that it constituted reasonable punishment in relation to an offence under s. 47 of the Offences against the Person Act 1861 (assault occasioning actual bodily harm) or an offence under ss. 18 or 20 (wounding or causing grievous bodily harm)—as to which **see para. 3.2.20** (s. 58).

In addition, the 2004 Act goes on to provide that battery of a person under 18 years of age causing actual bodily harm to the person cannot be justified in any *civil* proceedings on the ground that it constituted reasonable punishment (s. 58(3)). A recent review of the rules under the Children Act 2004 regarding the smacking of children found no evidence that the current rules were not working and at the present time the Government has ruled out a complete ban on smacking.

3.2.10 Offences

Having considered the key common elements in this area, the specific offences are set out below.

3.2.11 Common Assault and Battery

OFFENCE: **Common Assault/Battery—*Criminal Justice Act 1988, s. 39***

- Triable summarily • Six months' imprisonment

OFFENCE: **Racially or Religiously Aggravated—*Crime and Disorder Act 1998, s. 29(1)(c)***

- Triable either way • Two years' imprisonment and/or a fine on indictment
- Six months' imprisonment and/or a fine summarily

KEYNOTE

Common assault was deemed by the legislators to be one of those offences where it was necessary to increase the maximum penalty available to the courts if it was committed under racially or religiously aggravated circumstances (see the Crime and Disorder Act 1998, s. 29(1)(c)). A further effect of the racially or religiously aggravated offence is that it can be tried on indictment without having to be included alongside another indictable offence as is the case with common assaults generally (see the Criminal Justice Act 1988, s. 40).

The Divisional Court has held that the words 'white man's arse licker' and 'brown Englishman' when used to accompany an assault on an Asian victim did not necessarily make the assault 'racially aggravated' and that the prosecution had not done enough to show that the assailants' behaviour fell under the definition set out in s. 28 of the 1998 Act (*DPP* v *Pal* [2000] Crim LR 756).

Under the racially and religiously aggravated public order offences the courts have held that police officers are entitled to the same protection under the legislation as anyone else (see *R* v *Jacobs* [2001] 2 Cr App R (S) 38) and the same principle ought to apply to physical assault.

If an assault upon a police officer is 'racially or religiously aggravated' per the requirements of s. 28 of the Crime and Disorder Act 1998, it may be preferable to consider this offence rather than one of the offences under the Police Act 1996 (as to which, **see para. 3.2.13**).

CPS Charging Standards state that a charge under s. 39 of the Act will be appropriate where injuries amount to no more than the following:

- grazes
- scratches
- abrasions
- minor bruising
- swelling
- reddening of the skin
- superficial cuts
- a 'black eye'

The injury sustained by the victim should always be considered first, and in most cases the degree of injury will determine whether the appropriate charge is an assault under s. 39 of the Act or a more serious assault under s. 47 of the Offences Against the Person Act 1861. There will be borderline cases, such as where an undisplaced broken nose has resulted. Generally, where injuries amount to no more than those described above, common assault will be the appropriate charge.

3.2.12 Assault with Intent to Resist Arrest

OFFENCE: **Assault with Intent to Resist Arrest—*Offences Against the Person Act 1861, s. 38***

- Triable either way • Two years' imprisonment

The Offences Against the Person Act 1861, s. 38 states:

> Whosoever . . . shall assault any person with intent to resist or prevent the lawful apprehension or detainer of himself or of any other person for any offence, shall be guilty of a misdemeanour . . .

KEYNOTE

This is a crime of *specific intent.* It must be shown that the defendant intended to resist or prevent a lawful arrest. It must also be shown that the defendant knew the arrest was lawful. Provided they were acting within their powers, this offence can apply to arrests made, not only by police officers, but also by store detectives, Benefits Agency staff and custody assistants. If the person assaulted was assisting a police officer in the execution of his/her duty, the offence below may also apply.

Once the lawfulness of the arrest is established, the state of mind necessary for the above offence is an intention to resist/prevent that arrest, accompanied by knowledge that the person assaulted was trying to make or help in the arrest. It is irrelevant whether or not the person being arrested had actually committed an offence. These principles were set out recently by the Court of Appeal in a case where the defendant mistakenly believed that the arresting officers had no lawful power to do so. The court held that such a mistaken belief does not provide a defendant with the defence of 'mistake'. Similarly, a belief in one's own innocence, however genuine or honestly held, cannot afford a defence to a charge under s. 38 (*R* v *Lee* [2000] Crim LR 991).

3.2.13 Assaults on Police

There is an offence which deals specifically with assaults on police officers.

OFFENCE: **Assault Police—*Police Act 1996, s. 89***

- Triable summarily • Six months' imprisonment and/or a fine

The Police Act 1996, s. 89 states:

(1) Any person who assaults a constable in the execution of his duty, or a person assisting a constable in the execution of his duty, shall be guilty of an offence...

KEYNOTE

It is critical to this offence that the officer was acting in the execution of his/her duty when assaulted. Given the almost infinite variety of situations that police officers may find themselves in, it is difficult to define the precise boundaries of the execution of their duty. There have been many instances of officers being assaulted after entering premises as technical 'trespassers' or not following statutory or common law requirements when stopping and questioning people. If it is not proved that the constable was in the execution of his/her duty then part of the *actus reus* will be missing. However, a court may infer from all the circumstances that an officer was in fact acting in the execution of his/her duty (*Plowden* v *DPP* [1991] Crim LR 850).

Where the assault is made in reaction to some form of physical act by the officer, it must be shown that the officer's act was not in itself unlawful. Two cases serve as good examples here. In the first, police officers attended a house to investigate a domestic incident. The defendant's female partner and her children told the officers they believed that if the defendant remained at the premises she might be subjected to violence by him. The officers tried to speak with the defendant but he ignored them. Despite warnings from the officers, the defendant refused to leave the premises and he was arrested to prevent a breach of the peace. During a subsequent struggle with the defendant one of the officers was injured. The defendant argued that the officers were wrong to believe that there was a risk of imminent or immediate violence and there was insufficient evidence for that belief. Dismissing the appeal, the Divisional Court held that the officers had to assess whether, by leaving the defendant in the house that night, there was a risk that his partner would be subjected to violence by him. In doing so there were matters that the officers had to consider such as the fact that the defendant had been drinking and it was reasonable for the officers to take into account the partner's fear of violence by him and the statements of her children. The officers were entitled to take into account the fact that the defendant had failed to respond to their requests to address the situation and had attempted to intimidate them. Therefore it had been reasonable in the circumstances of the case for the police to believe that a breach of the peace would be committed in the imminent future if the defendant remained at the premises and consequently his arrest had been lawful (*Wragg* v *DPP* [2005] EWHC 1389).

In the second case, the defendant was convicted of assaulting a police officer in the execution of his duty after the police had gone to her home address to arrest her son. The defendant followed her son into the police vehicle and refused to get out. She was given a warning and was verbally abusive, and only got out of the car when a second one arrived. She started to walk towards her house at which point a police officer took hold of her arms. The defendant bit the police officer on the arm and was prosecuted on the basis that the police officer had arrested her for a breach of the peace and that the assault had occurred in the execution of that duty. Allowing her appeal, the Divisional Court held that the defendant had exhibited nothing more than an aggressive manner and that, while her conduct may have given rise to an imminent threat of violence, there was no evidence to suggest that it involved any violence justifying the conclusion that she had actually committed a breach of the peace in the presence of the police officer. In the circumstances, her arrest had been unlawful and the conviction for assaulting a police officer in the execution of his duty could not stand (*R (On the Application of Hawkes)* v *DPP* [2005] EWHC 3046).

Although the common law complaint of breach of the peace still exists where appropriate the question of the lawfulness of any arrest will become even more important to this offence in light of s. 24 of the Police and Criminal Evidence Act 1984. Other than the powers of arrest and detention, police officers have no general power to take hold of people in order to question them or keep them at a particular place while background enquiries are made about them. Therefore, if an officer does hold someone by the arm in order to question them without arresting them, there may well be a 'battery' by that officer (*Collins* v *Wilcock* [1984] 1 WLR 1172). The courts have accepted, however, that there may be occasions where a police officer is justified in taking hold of a person to attract their attention or to calm them down (*Mepstead* v *DPP* (1996) 160 JP 475).

However, where a prisoner is arrested and brought before a custody officer, that officer is entitled to assume that the arrest has been lawful. Therefore, if the prisoner goes on to assault the custody officer, that assault will nevertheless be an offence under s. 89(1) even if the original arrest turns out to have been unlawful (*DPP* v *L* [1999] Crim LR 752).

There is no need to show that the defendant knew—or suspected—that the person was in fact a police officer or that he/she was acting in the lawful execution of his/her duty (*Blackburn* v *Bowering* [1994] 1 WLR 1324). However, if the defendant claims to have been acting in self-defence under the mistaken and honestly held belief that he/she was being attacked, there may not be sufficient *mens rea* for a charge of assault.

These offences are simply a form of common assault upon someone carrying out a lawful function. There is a further offence which deals with behaviour not amounting to an actual assault.

3.2.14 Obstructing a Police Officer

OFFENCE: **Obstruct Police—*Police Act 1996, s. 89***

- Triable summarily • One month's imprisonment and/or a fine

The Police Act 1996, s. 89 states:

> (2) Any person who resists or wilfully obstructs a constable in the execution of his duty, or a person assisting a constable in the execution of his duty, shall be guilty of an offence...

KEYNOTE

Resistance suggests some form of physical opposition; obstruction does not and may take many forms. For instance, warning other drivers of a speed check operation (*Betts* v *Stevens* [1910] 1KB 1), providing misleading information (*Ledger* v *DPP* [1991] Crim LR 439), or deliberately drinking alcohol before providing breath specimen (*Ingleton* v *Dibble* [1972] 1 QB 480). Obstruction has been interpreted as making it more difficult for a constable to carry out his/her duty (*Hinchcliffe* v *Sheldon* [1955] 1 WLR 1207). Refusing to answer an officer's questions is not obstruction (*Rice* v *Connolly* [1966] 2 QB 414)—unless perhaps the defendant was under some duty to provide information. Any obstruction must be *wilful*, that is the defendant must intend to do it. The obstruction will not be 'wilful' if the defendant was simply trying to help the police, even if that help turned out to be more of a hindrance (*Willmot* v *Atack* [1977] QB 498).

Obstruction can be caused by omission but only where the defendant was already under some duty towards the police or the officer. There is also a common law offence of refusing to go to the aid of a constable when asked to do so in order to prevent or diminish a breach of the peace (*R* v *Waugh* (1986) *The Times*, 1 October).

Tipping off people who were about to commit crime has been held to amount to obstruction (*Green* v *Moore* [1982] QB 1044), and some extreme forms of obstruction may amount to more serious offences such as perverting the course of justice or concealing offences. There are also specific statutory offences of 'tipping off' in relation to money laundering and drug trafficking offences.

3.2.15 Assault/Obstructing Designated or Accredited Persons

OFFENCE: **Assaulting Designated or Accredited Person—*Police Reform Act 2002, s. 46(1)***

- Triable summarily • Six months' imprisonment and/or a fine

The Police Reform Act 2002, s. 46 states:

(1) Any person who assaults—
  (a) a designated person in the execution of his duty,
  (b) an accredited person in the execution of his duty, or
  (bc) an accredited inspector in the execution of his duty, or
  (c) a person assisting a designated or accredited person or an accredited inspector in the execution of his duty

shall be guilty of an offence.

KEYNOTE

This, and the following offence, relates to individuals who are designated or accredited under the provisions of the Police Reform Act 2002.

As with the corresponding offence against police officers (as to which, see para. 3.2.13) issues relating to the person's 'execution of duty' are paramount and particular care will need to be taken to prove that the relevant person had complied with all the applicable requirements as to wearing of uniform, badges and the production of their designation/accreditation. If a person is acting outside his/her powers as specifically designated or accredited, he/she will not have the protection of this offence. Also in common with the police offences, this offence (and the offence of obstruction below) applies to an assault on/wilful obstruction of someone who is helping the relevant officer.

Any acts causing more than minor or superficial injury may be dealt with under the general offences for assaults and woundings in this chapter. The fact that a victim was acting in the capacity of a designated/accredited person (or assisting them) at the time would still be relevant when considering sentence.

OFFENCE: **Obstructing Designated or Accredited Person—*Police Reform Act 2002, s. 46(2)***

- Triable summarily • One month's imprisonment and/or a fine

The Police Reform Act 2002, s. 46 states:

(2) Any person who resists or wilfully obstructs—
(a) a designated person in the execution of his duty,
(b) an accredited person in the execution of his duty, or
(bc) an accredited inspector in the execution of his duty, or
(c) a person assisting a designated or accredited person or an accredited inspector in the execution of his duty

is guilty of an offence.

KEYNOTE

As with the previous offence, the important issue here will be proof that the relevant person was in fact acting in the execution of their duty. For a discussion of the ingredients needed in proving this offence in the context of the corresponding offence against police officers, **see para. 3.2.13.**

Again, if a person is acting outside his/her powers as specifically designated or accredited, he/she will not have the protection of this offence.

3.2.16 Assaults on Providers of Emergency Services

In light of the increase of assaults on emergency workers, the Emergency Workers (Obstruction) Act 2006 was passed. The Act is designed to offer protection to persons outside the police (to members of the Fire Brigade and staff of the NHS, for example) who face an increasing and unacceptable amount of violence simply by carrying out their functions.

3.2.16.1 Obstructing or Hindering Emergency Workers

OFFENCE: **Obstructing or Hindering Certain Emergency Workers Responding to Emergency Circumstances—*Emergency Workers (Obstruction) Act 2006, s. 1***

- Triable summarily • Fine

The Emergency Workers (Obstruction) Act 2006, s. 1 states:

(1) A person who without reasonable excuse obstructs or hinders another while that other person is, in a capacity mentioned in subsection (2) below, responding to emergency circumstances, commits an offence.

(2) The capacity referred to in subsection (1) above is—
(a) that of a person employed by a fire and rescue authority in England and Wales;
(b) in relation to England and Wales, that of a person (other than a person falling within paragraph (a)) whose duties as an employee or as a servant of the Crown involve—
(i) extinguishing fires; or
(ii) protecting life and property in the event of a fire;
(c) that of a person employed by a relevant NHS body in the provision of ambulance services (including air ambulance services), or of a person providing such services pursuant to arrangements made by, or at the request of, a relevant NHS body;
(d) that of a person providing services for the transport of organs, blood, equipment or personnel pursuant to arrangements made by, or at the request of, a relevant NHS body;
(e) that of a member of Her Majesty's Coastguard;

(f) that of a member of the crew of a vessel operated by—
  (i) the Royal National Lifeboat Institution, or
  (ii) any other person or organisation operating a vessel for the purpose of providing a rescue service,

or a person who musters the crew of such a vessel or attends to its launch or recovery.

KEYNOTE

It should be noted that these offences not only cover a wide variety of occupations within the emergency services but also cover those individuals as they respond to 'emergency circumstances' by:

- going anywhere for the purpose of dealing with emergency circumstances occurring there; or
- dealing with emergency circumstances or preparing to do so.

(s. 1(3)(a) and (b) of the Act)

Section 1(4) of the Act defines an 'emergency' circumstance as a present or imminent circumstance likely to cause:

(i) serious injury to or the serious injury (including mental illness) of a person;
(ii) serious harm to the environment (including the life and health of plants and animals);
(iii) serious harm to any building or other property; or
(iv) a worsening of any such injury, illness or harm;

or which is likely to cause the death of a person.

'Relevant NHS body' means (in relation to England and Wales) an NHS foundation trust, NHS trust, Special Health Authority, Primary Care Trust or Local Health Board. In relation to Northern Ireland the same phrase means a Health and Social Services trust or a Health and Social Services Board.

3.2.16.2 Obstructing or Hindering Persons Assisting Emergency Workers

OFFENCE: **Obstructing or Hindering Persons Assisting Emergency Workers—*Emergency Workers (Obstruction) Act 2006, s. 2***

- Triable summarily • Fine

The Emergency Workers (Obstruction) Act 2006, s. 2 states:

(1) A person who without reasonable excuse obstructs or hinders another in the circumstances described in subsection (2) below commits an offence.

(2) Those circumstances are where the person being obstructed or hindered is assisting another while that person is, in a capacity mentioned in section 1(2) of this Act, responding to emergency circumstances.

KEYNOTE

Section 3(1) states that a person may be convicted of an offence under ss. 1 and 2 of the Act notwithstanding that the act is effected by means other than physical means or is effected by action directed only at any vehicle, vessel, apparatus, equipment or other thing or any animal used or to be used by a person referred to in that section.

For the purposes of ss. 1 and 2 of the Act, circumstances to which a person is responding are to be taken to be emergency circumstances if the person believes and has reasonable grounds for believing they are or may be emergency circumstances (s. 3(2)).

3.2.17 Threats to Kill

OFFENCE: **Making a Threat to Kill—*Offences Against the Person Act 1861, s. 16***

- Triable either way • Ten years' imprisonment on indictment
- Six months' imprisonment and/or a fine summarily

The Offences Against the Person Act 1861, s. 16 (amended by Criminal Law Act 1977, s. 65, sch. 12) states:

> A person who without lawful excuse makes to another a threat, intending that that other would fear it would be carried out, to kill that other or a third person shall be guilty of an offence ...

KEYNOTE

The proviso that the threat must be made 'without lawful excuse' means that a person acting in self-defence or in the course of his/her duty in protecting life (e.g. an armed police officer) would not commit this offence (provided that his/her behaviour was 'lawful').

You must show that the threat was made (or implied (*R* v *Solanke* [1969] 3 All ER 1383)) with the intention that the person receiving it would fear that it would be carried out. It is the *intention* of the person who makes the threat which is important in this offence. It does not matter whether the person to whom the threat is made *does* fear that the threat would be carried out. The threat may be to kill another person at some time in the future or it may be an immediate threat, but the threatened action must be directly linked with the defendant. Simply passing on a threat on behalf of a third person would probably be insufficient for this offence.

3.2.18 Offences Involving Significant or Lasting Injury

If an assailant causes any significant or lasting injury then one of the following offences may apply.

These offences—and the injuries they cause—can be committed in many different ways, with or without weapons or implements. In relation to injuries brought about by driving motor vehicles, although there is a specific offence of dangerous driving the Court of Appeal has held that there is nothing wrong in principle in charging a driver with causing grievous bodily harm (**see para. 3.2.20**) as well as dangerous driving in appropriate circumstances (*R* v *Bain* [2005] EWCA Crim 7). It follows that bringing about other forms of significant or lasting injury with a motor vehicle could be dealt with under the offences in this part of the chapter. However, in *Bain* it was held that where a driver was charged with both offences (causing grievous bodily harm and dangerous driving), a court could not impose consecutive terms of imprisonment for both offences arising out of the same incident.

3.2.19 Assault Occasioning Actual Bodily Harm

OFFENCE: **Assault Occasioning Actual Bodily Harm—*Offences Against the Person Act 1861, s. 47***

- Triable either way • Five years' imprisonment on indictment • Six months' imprisonment and/or a fine summarily

OFFENCE: **Racially or Religiously Aggravated—*Crime and Disorder Act 1998, s. 29(1)(b)***

- Triable either way • Seven years' imprisonment and/or a fine on indictment
- Six months' imprisonment and/or a fine summarily

The Offences Against the Person Act 1861, s. 47 states:

> Whosoever shall be convicted ... of any assault occasioning actual bodily harm shall be liable ... to be kept in penal servitude ...

KEYNOTE

It must be shown that 'actual bodily harm' was a consequence, directly or indirectly, of the defendant's actions. Such harm can include shock (*R* v *Miller* [1954] 2 QB 282) and mental 'injury' (*R* v *Chan-Fook* [1994] 1 WLR 689).

So what is 'actual bodily harm'? In *DPP* v *Smith* [1961] AC 290, it was noted that the expression needed 'no explanation' and, in *Chan-Fook*, the court advised that the phrase consisted of 'three words of the English language which require no elaboration and in the ordinary course should not receive any'. While the phrase 'bodily harm' has its ordinary meaning, it has been said to include any hurt calculated to interfere with the health or comfort of the victim: such hurt need not be permanent, but must be more than transient and trifling (*R* v *Donovan* [1934] 25 Cr App Rep 1, CCA).

The Administrative Court has accepted that a momentary loss of consciousness caused by a kick but without any physical injury can be 'actual harm' because it involved an injurious impairment of the victim's sensory abilities which did not fall within the 'trifling' category described in *Donovan* above (see *T* v *DPP* [2003] Crim LR 622).

For a discussion of the relevant *mens rea* for this offence, **see para. 3.2.5**. The state of mind required is the same as that for an assault or battery.

In an interesting decision the Divisional Court accepted that the cutting of a person's hair against their will could amount to actual bodily harm (*DPP* v *Smith (Ross Michael)* [2006] EWHC 94). In *Smith* the defendant cut off his ex-partner's ponytail, deliberately and without her permission. The court held that, even though medically and scientifically speaking, the hair above the surface of the scalp is no more than dead tissue, it remains part of the body and is attached to it. While it is so attached, it falls within the meaning of 'bodily' in the phrase 'actual bodily harm' as it is concerned with the body of the individual victim. Therefore the same would be true of fingernails.

Futher examples of what will amount to 'actual bodily harm' can be found in the CPS Charging Standards and include:

- Loss or breaking of teeth
- Temporary loss of sensory functions, which may include loss of consciousness (*T* v *DPP* [2003] EWHC 266 (Admin))
- Extensive or multiple bruising
- Displaced broken nose
- Minor fractures
- Minor, but not merely superficial, cuts of a sort probably requiring medical treatment (e.g. stitches)
- Psychiatric injury that is more than merely emotions such as fear, distress or panic.

Where psychiatric injury is relied upon as the basis for an allegation of assault occasioning actual bodily harm, and the matter is not admitted by the defence, then expert evidence must be called by the prosecution (*R* v *Chan-Fook* [1994] 1 WLR 689).

As with common assault, this offence was deemed by the legislators to be one where it was necessary to increase the maximum penalty available to the courts if it was committed under racially aggravated circumstances (see Crime and Disorder Act 1998, s. 29(1)(b)).

3.2.20 Wounding or Inflicting Grievous Bodily Harm

OFFENCE: **Wounding or Inflicting Grievous Bodily Harm—*Offences Against the Person Act 1861, s. 20***

- Triable either way • Five years' imprisonment on indictment
- Six months' imprisonment and/or a fine summarily

OFFENCE: **Racially or Religiously Aggravated—*Crime and Disorder Act 1998, s. 29(1)(a)***

- Triable either way • Seven years' imprisonment and/or a fine on indictment
- Six months' imprisonment and/or a fine summarily

The Offences Against the Person Act 1861, s. 20 states:

> Whosoever shall unlawfully and maliciously wound or inflict any grievous bodily harm upon any other person, either with or without any weapon or instrument, shall be guilty of a misdemeanour . . .

KEYNOTE

Wounding means the breaking of the continuity of the whole of the outer skin, or the inner skin within the cheek or lip. A cut which goes right through all the layers of a person's skin, whether caused externally (e.g. a knife wound) or internally (e.g. a punch causing a tooth to puncture the cheek), will amount to a wound. It does not include the rupturing of internal blood vessels.

The definition of wounding may encompass injuries that are relatively minor in nature, for example a small cut or laceration. An assault resulting in such minor injuries should more appropriately be charged contrary to s. 47 of the Act. An assault contrary to s. 20 should be reserved for the type of wounds considered to be serious (thus equating the offence with the infliction of grievous, or serious, bodily harm).

The word 'inflict' has caused problems in the past. However, the House of Lords in *R* v *Ireland* [1998] AC 147 has made it clear that no 'assault' (**see para. 3.2.4**) is needed for this offence and that harm could be 'inflicted' indirectly (in this case by menacing telephone calls inflicting psychiatric harm). Therefore there is now little if any difference between inflicting harm and 'causing' harm (**see para. 3.2.21**). It should be enough to show that the defendant's behaviour brought about the resulting harm to the victim.

There have also been many judicial attempts at defining grievous bodily harm. In *R* v *Saunders* [1985] Crim LR 230 it was held that the expression meant 'serious or really serious harm'. This harm will now include psychiatric harm (*Ireland*). Examples of what will amount to 'grievous bodily harm' can be found in the CPS Charging Standards and include:

- injury resulting in some permanent disability or visible disfigurement
- broken or displaced limbs or bones
- injuries requiring blood transfusion or lengthy treatment.

Following the well-publicised case of Mohammed Dica in 2003, there was an acceptance that the deliberate infection of another with the HIV virus could amount to grievous bodily harm—although there were still significant difficulties with regard to 'consent' if the infection had taken place as a result of consensual sexual activity. This issue was explored further by the Court of Appeal in *R* v *Konzani* [2005] EWCA Crim 706. In that case the defendant appealed against convictions for inflicting grievous bodily harm on three women contrary to s. 20 above. The defendant had unprotected consensual sexual intercourse with the women, but without having disclosed that he was HIV positive. The women subsequently contracted the HIV virus. In hearing the appeals, the Court held that there was a critical distinction between taking a risk as to the various potentially adverse (and possibly problematic) consequences of unprotected consensual intercourse, and the giving of informed consent *to the risk of infection with a fatal disease*. Before consent to the risk of contracting HIV could provide a defence, that consent had to be an *informed* consent in this latter sense (see *R* v *Dica* [2004] EWCA Crim 1103). Therefore, simply having an honestly held belief that the other person was consenting would only help if that consent would itself have provided a defence to the passing of the infection.

This approach was confirmed in *R* v *B* (2006) unreported, where the Court of Appeal stated that, while a defendant's condition (being HIV positive) was immaterial in relation to the consent issue in an offence of rape, the defendant would have no defence to the harm created by the sexual activity merely by virtue of that consent, as the consent related to the sexual activity and not to the disease.

'Maliciously'—although the word maliciously suggests some form of evil premeditation, 'malice' here amounts to subjective recklessness. It means that the defendant must realise that there is a risk of some harm being caused to the victim. The defendant does not need to foresee the degree of harm which is eventually caused, only that his/her behaviour may bring about some harm to the victim.

3.2.21 Wounding or Causing Grievous Bodily Harm with Intent

OFFENCE: **Wounding or Causing Grievous Bodily Harm with Intent—*Offences Against the Person Act 1861, s. 18***

- Triable on indictment only • Life imprisonment

The Offences Against the Person Act 1861, s. 18 states:

> Whosoever shall unlawfully and maliciously by any means whatsoever wound or cause any grievous bodily harm to any person with intent to do some grievous bodily harm to any person, or with intent to resist or prevent the lawful apprehension or detainer of any person, shall be guilty of felony . . .

KEYNOTE

This is a crime of *specific intent.* Although there are similarities with the offence under s. 20 (see above), you must show the appropriate *intent* (e.g. to do grievous bodily harm to *anyone* or to resist/prevent the lawful apprehension/detention of *anyone*); recklessness and foresight are not sufficient. Factors that may indicate such a specific intent include:

- a repeated or planned attack
- deliberate selection of a weapon or adaptation of an article to cause injury, such as breaking a glass before an attack
- making prior threats
- using an offensive weapon against, or kicking a victim's head.

Where the intent was to cause grievous bodily harm, the issue of 'malice' will not arise. However, where the intent was to resist or prevent the lawful arrest of someone, the element of maliciousness as set out above (**see para. 3.2.20**) will need to be proved. The word 'cause', together with the expression 'by any means whatsoever', seems to give this offence a wider meaning than s. 20. However, the increasingly broad interpretation of the s. 20 offence means that there is little difference in the *actus reus* needed for either offence.

The provisions of ss. 28 and 29 of the Crime and Disorder Act 1998 in relation to racially or religiously aggravated assaults do not apply to this offence as it was felt by the legislators that there was nothing to be gained by creating a special offence, given that the maximum sentence available is already life imprisonment. However, the courts must still take notice of any element of racial or religious aggravation when determining sentence (s. 145 of the Criminal Justice Act 2003—increase in sentences for racial or religious aggravation).

3.3 Child Abduction

There is a Convention between the United Kingdom and many other countries which is designed to help with the civil law practicalities of recovering children from other jurisdictions. The full list of such countries can be found in the Child Abduction and Custody (Parties to Conventions) Order 1986 (SI 1986/1159), as amended.

There are two offences of abducting children, one which applies to people 'connected with the child' and the second by others.

3.3.1 Person Connected with Child

OFFENCE: **Child Abduction—Person Connected with Child—*Child Abduction Act 1984, s. 1***

• Triable either way • Seven years' imprisonment on indictment • Six months' imprisonment and/or a fine summarily

The Child Abduction Act 1984, s. 1 states:

(1) Subject to subsections (5) and (8) below, a person connected with a child under the age of 16 commits an offence if he takes or sends the child out of the United Kingdom without the appropriate consent.

'Connected with a Child'

The Child Abduction Act 1984, s. 1 states:

(2) A person is connected with the child for the purposes of this section if—
- (a) he is a parent of a the child; or
- (b) in the case of a child whose parents were not married to each other at the time of his birth, there are reasonable grounds for believing that he is the father of the child; or
- (c) he is a guardian of the child; or
- (ca) he is a special guardian of the child; or
- (d) he is a person in whose favour a residence order is in force with respect to the child; or
- (e) he has custody of the child.

'Appropriate Consent'

The Child Abduction Act 1984, s. 1 states:

(3) In this section 'the appropriate consent' in relation to a child, means—
- (a) the consent of each of the following—
  - (i) the child's mother;
  - (ii) the child's father, if he has parental responsibility for him;
  - (iii) any guardian of the child;
  - (iiia) any special guardian of the child;
  - (iv) any person in whose favour a residence order is in force with respect to the child;
  - (v) any person who has custody of the child; or
- (b) the leave of the court granted under or by virtue of any provision of Part II of the Children Act 1989; or
- (c) if any person has custody of the child, the leave of the court which awarded custody to him.

KEYNOTE

This offence can only be committed by those people listed in s. 1(2). To be guilty they must take or send the child out of the United Kingdom. The taking or sending must be shown to have been done without the consent of *each* of those persons listed in s. 1(3)(a) above.

The consent of the DPP is needed before a charge of child abduction is brought under this section (s. 4(2)): there are also restrictions on charging kidnapping where the offence involves an offence under s. 1 above by a person connected with the child (s. 5).

3.3.2 Defence for Person Connected with a Child

The Child Abduction Act 1984, s. 1 states:

(4) A person does not commit an offence under this section by taking or sending a child out of the United Kingdom without obtaining the appropriate consent if—
(a) he is a person in whose favour there is a residence order in force with respect to the child, and he takes or sends the child out of the United Kingdom for a period of less than one month; or
(b) he is a special guardian of the child and he takes or sends the child out of the United Kingdom for a period of less than three months.

(4A) Subsection (4) above does not apply if the person taking or sending the child out of the United Kingdom does so in breach of an order under Part II of the Children Act 1989.

(5) A person does not commit an offence under this section by doing anything without the consent of another person whose consent is required under the foregoing provisions if—
(a) he does it in the belief that the other person—
(i) has consented; or
(ii) would consent if he was aware of all the relevant circumstances; or
(b) he has taken all reasonable steps to communicate with the other person but has been unable to communicate with him; or
(c) the other person has unreasonably refused to consent.

KEYNOTE

Note the specific defence (at s. 1(5))—if the defendant believes that the appropriate person has consented or would have consented had they known of the circumstances.

A further provision (s. 1(5A)) states that s. 1(5)(c) will not apply if the person who refused to consent is a person:

- in whose favour there is a residence order in force with respect to the child; or
- who has custody of the child; or
- who is a special guardian of the child; or
- is, by taking or sending the child out of the United Kingdom, acting in breach of a court order in the United Kingdom.

3.3.3 Person Not Connected with Child

OFFENCE: **Child Abduction—Person Not Connected with Child—*Child Abduction Act 1984, s. 2***

• Triable either way • Seven years' imprisonment on indictment • Six months' imprisonment and/or a fine summarily

The Child Abduction Act 1984, s. 2 states:

(1) Subject to subsection (3) below, a person other than one mentioned in subsection (2) below, commits an offence if, without lawful authority or reasonable excuse, he takes or detains a child under the age of 16—
   (a) so as to remove him from the lawful control of any person having lawful control of the child: or
   (b) so as to keep him out of the lawful control of any person entitled to lawful control of the child.

(2) The persons are—
   (a) where the father and mother of the child in question were married to each other at the time of his birth, the child's father and mother;
   (b) where the father and mother of the child in question were not married to each other at the time of his birth, the child's mother; and
   (c) any other person mentioned in section 1(2)(c) to (e) above.

KEYNOTE

This offence requires the taking or detaining of a child under 16 years. This will include keeping a child in the place where he/she is found and inducing the child to remain with the defendant or another person. The distinction between s. 2(1) (a) and (b) is important. You must show that the defendant acted without lawful authority or reasonable excuse. Unlike kidnapping, the consent of the victim is irrelevant. The word 'remove' for the purpose of s. 2(1)(a) means effectively a substitution of authority by a defendant for that of the person lawfully having it and physical removal from a particular place is not required (see *Foster* v *DPP* [2004] EWHC 2955).

Section 2(1)(a) requires the child *there and then* to be in the lawful control of someone entitled to it when they are taken or detained, whereas s. 2(1)(b) requires only that the child be kept out of the lawful control of someone entitled to it when taken or detained. Whether or not a person is under the lawful control of another is a question of fact (*R* v *Leather* (1993) *The Times,* 21 January). Proving the absence of reasonable excuse could be difficult. Clearly a defendant could argue, particularly in the case of a very young child, that he/she was acting in the child's best interests, a claim which might be difficult to refute. Note that s. 3 makes further practical provisions in relation to 'taking, sending and detaining'.

3.3.4 Defence for Person Not Connected with a Child

The Child Abduction Act 1984, s. 2 states:

(3) ... it shall be a defence for [the defendant] to prove—
   (a) where the father and mother of the child in question were not married to each other at the time of his birth—
      (i) that he is the child's father; or
      (ii) that, at the time of the alleged offence, he believed, on reasonable grounds, that he was the child's father; or
   (b) that, at the time of the alleged offence, he believed that the child had attained the age of 16.

KEYNOTE

Section 2(3)(b) provides a defence if the accused can show that he/she believed the child to be 16 or over.

3.4 False Imprisonment

OFFENCE: **False Imprisonment—*Common Law***

- Triable on indictment • Unlimited maximum penalty

It is an offence at common law falsely to imprison another person.

KEYNOTE

This offence is the first in an ascending order of aggravated offences against the person and is more usually dealt with under civil law or as kidnapping/abduction (see below).

These offences are particularly relevant to the offence of committing a criminal offence with intent to commit a relevant sexual offence.

The elements required for this offence are the unlawful and intentional/reckless restraint of a person's freedom of movement (*R* v *Rahman* (1985) 81 Cr App R 349). Locking someone in a vehicle or keeping them in a particular place for however short a time may amount to false imprisonment if done unlawfully. An unlawful arrest may amount to such an offence and it is not uncommon for such an allegation to be levelled at police officers against whom a public complaint has been made. On the other hand, a *lawful* arrest will provide a defence to the offence as will reasonable defence of property. In respect of the latter, a person would have a defence to a charge of false imprisonment if he/she detained a person in the genuine belief that a person was a burglar—even if this genuine belief were unreasonable (*R* v *Shwan Faraj* [2007] EWCA Crim 1033). In *Shwan Faraj*, the court stated that there was no reason why a householder should not be entitled to detain someone in his house whom he genuinely believed to be a burglar; he would be acting in defence of his property in doing so. However, a householder would have to honestly believe he needed to detain the suspect and would have to do so in a way that was reasonable.

The state of mind required to prove this offence is 'subjective' recklessness (*R* v *James* (1997) *The Times*, 2 October).

3.5 Kidnapping

OFFENCE: **Kidnapping—*Common Law***

- Triable on indictment • Unlimited maximum penalty

It is an offence at common law to take or carry away another person without the consent of that person and without lawful excuse.

KEYNOTE

The required elements of this offence are the unlawful taking or carrying away of one person by another by force or fraud (*R* v *D* [1984] AC 778). These requirements go beyond those of mere restraint needed for false imprisonment. Parents may be acting without lawful excuse, for instance, if they are acting in breach of a court order in respect of their children.

The taking or carrying away of the victim must be without the consent of the victim. If the victim consents to an initial taking but later withdraws that consent, the offence would be complete. If the consent is obtained by fraud, the defendant cannot rely on that consent and the offence—or attempted offence—will be made out (see *R* v *Cort* [2003] 3 WLR 1300). In *R* v *Hendy-Freegard* [2007] EWCA Crim 1236 the defendant was a confidence trickster who pretended to be an undercover agent working for MI5 or Scotland Yard. He would tell his victims that he was investigating the activities of the IRA and that his investigations had revealed that they were in danger. This allowed him to take control of their lives for a number of years and in doing so to direct them to move about the country from location to location. The defendant was eventually arrested and convicted of kidnapping on the basis of the Crown's case that the offence of kidnapping had occurred as his victims had made journeys around the country which they had been induced to make as a result of the defendant's false story. The defendant successfully appealed against the kidnapping conviction, with the court stating that causing a person to move from place to place *when unaccompanied by the defendant* could not itself constitute either taking or carrying away or deprivation of liberty, which were necessary elements of the offence.

If the victim is a child, the consent will probably be that of the parents but the more appropriate charge in such a case may be one under the Child Abduction Act 1984.

The state of mind required for this offence is the same as that for false imprisonment, indeed the only thing separating the two offences seems to be *actus reus* (*R* v *Hutchins* [1988] Crim LR 379). For *actus reus* generally, **see chapter 1.2**.

3.6 Public Order Act 1986 Offences

Many of the most common offences regulating public disorder and threats to public order were formerly contained in the Public Order Act 1936. This left several key offences, such as riot and affray to the common law. These provisions were felt to be inadequate and the Public Order Act 1986 was passed in an attempt to codify the law in this area.

3.6.1 Violence

Section 8 of the Public Order Act 1986 provides guidance on when conduct will amount to 'violence':

'violence' means any violent conduct, so that—

(a) except in the context of affray, it includes violent conduct towards property as well as violent conduct towards persons, and

(b) it is not restricted to conduct causing or intended to cause injury or damage but includes any other violent conduct (for example, throwing at or towards a person a missile of a kind capable of causing injury which does not hit or falls short).

KEYNOTE

It has been held that the use of the term 'unlawful' in the 1986 Act has been included to allow for the general defences—such as self-defence to be applicable (see *R* v *Rothwell* [1993] Crim LR 626).

3.6.2 Drunkenness

Parliament has specifically catered for self-induced intoxication, not just for the offence of riot, but in relation to other offences under the 1986 Act by s. 6 which states:

(5) For the purposes of this section a person whose awareness is impaired by intoxication shall be taken to be aware of that of which he would be aware if not intoxicated, unless he shows

either that his intoxication was not self-induced or that it was caused solely by the taking or administration of a substance in the course of medical treatment.

(6) In subsection (5) 'intoxication' means any intoxication, whether caused by drink, drugs or other means, or by a combination of means.

3.6.3 Violent Disorder

3+ use/threaten u.v. conduct together cause P.R.F @ scene to fear

OFFENCE: **Violent disorder—*Public Order Act 1986, s. 2***

- Triable either way • Five years' imprisonment and/or a fine on indictment
- Six months' imprisonment and/or a fine summarily

The Public Order Act 1986, s. 2 states:

(1) Where 3 or more persons who are present together use or threaten unlawful violence and the conduct of them (taken together) is such as would cause a person of reasonable firmness present at the scene to fear for his personal safety, each of the persons using or threatening unlawful violence is guilty of violent disorder.

(2) It is immaterial whether or not the 3 or more use or threaten unlawful violence simultaneously.

(3) No person of reasonable firmness need actually be, or be likely to be, present at the scene.

(4) Violent disorder may be committed in private as well as in public places.

KEYNOTE

In order to convict any defendant of this offence, you must show that there were three or more people using or threatening violence. In the case of two of the defendants being acquitted, the remaining defendant can still be convicted (*R* v *Mahroof* (1989) 88 Cr App R 317).

The requirements as to the hypothetical effects on an equally hypothetical person of reasonable firmness are the same as for the offence of riot. However, there is no requirement to prove a common purpose.

Again, a defendant must be shown to have *intended* to use/threaten violence or to have *been aware* that his/her conduct may have been violent (s. 6(2)) and the offence may be committed in private as well as in a public place. 'Violence' for these purposes can include violent conduct towards property (s. 8).

3.6.4 Affray

OFFENCE: **Affray—*Public Order Act 1986, s. 3***

- Triable either way • Three years' imprisonment and/or a fine on indictment
- Six months' imprisonment and/or a fine summarily

The Public Order Act 1986, s. 3 states:

(1) A person is guilty of affray if he uses or threatens unlawful violence towards another and his conduct is such as would cause a person of reasonable firmness present at the scene to fear for his personal safety.

(2) Where 2 or more persons use or threaten the unlawful violence, it is the conduct of them taken together that must be considered for the purposes of subsection (1).

(3) For the purposes of this section a threat cannot be made by the use of words alone.

(4) No person of reasonable firmness need actually be, or be likely to be, present at the scene.

(5) Affray may be committed in private as well as in public places.

KEYNOTE

Formerly an offence requiring more than one person, this offence may now be committed by a single defendant although, if he/she acts with another, the conduct of them taken together will be the relevant factor in determining their criminal conduct (s. 3(2)).

The House of Lords has held that, in order to prove the offence of affray, the threat of unlawful violence has to be towards a person(s) present at the scene (*I* v *DPP* [2002] 1 AC 285). Once this element has been proved, it will be necessary to prove the second element, namely whether the defendant's conduct would have caused a hypothetical person present at the scene to fear for his/her personal safety (*R* v *Sanchez* (1996) 160 JP 321 and *R* v *Carey* [2006] EWCA Crim 17).

The threat cannot be made by words alone (s. 3(3)), therefore there must be some action by the defendant—even if that 'action' consists of utilising something else such as a dog to threaten the violence (*R* v *Dixon* [1993] Crim LR 579).

The effect of s. 3(4) is that it is not necessary to show that the defendant's behaviour either was or could have been seen by someone at the time. Contrast this with the lesser offence under s. 5.

Although violence is 'not restricted to conduct causing or intended to cause injury or damage but includes any other violent conduct' (s. 8), the expression does not include conduct towards property as it does with the offences under ss. 1 and 2.

Once more, a defendant must be shown to have *intended* to use/threaten violence or to have *been aware* that his/her conduct may have been violent (s. 6(2)).

3.7 Racially and Religiously Aggravated Offences

3.7.1 The Offences

Sections 28 to 32 of the Crime and Disorder Act 1998 did not so much create *new* offences, but rather took *existing* offences and set out circumstances under which those offences will be deemed to be 'aggravated'. Those offences are:

- wounding or grievous bodily harm—Offences Against the Person Act 1861, s. 20
- causing actual bodily harm—Offences Against the Person Act 1861, s. 47
- common assault—Criminal Justice Act 1988, s. 39
- 'simple' criminal damage—Criminal Damage Act 1971, s. 1(1)
- causing fear or provocation of violence—Public Order Act 1986, s. 4
- intentional harassment, alarm or distress—Public Order Act 1986, s. 4A
- causing harassment, alarm or distress—Public Order Act 1986, s. 5
- harassment—Protection from Harassment Act 1997, s. 2
- putting people in fear of violence—Protection from Harassment Act 1997, s. 4.

This area of the law was changed once again after the terrorist attacks of 11 September 2001 by the Anti-terrorism, Crime and Security Act 2001. Part 5 of that Act amended the Crime and Disorder Act 1998, extending the provisions of what were 'racially aggravated' offences to include 'racially *or religiously* aggravated' offences (as to which, see below).

In order to prove these offences there must be proof of the relevant, substantive offence (e.g. common assault) together with further proof of the aggravating circumstances.

Once both conditions have been made out, the offences attract greater maximum penalties and powers. For that reason the specific effects of this legislation are dealt with under the relevant chapters in this Manual.

3.7.2 'Racially or Religiously Aggravated'

The test for racial or religious aggravation is set out at s. 28 of the Crime and Disorder Act 1998:

(1) An offence is racially or religiously aggravated for the purposes of sections 29 to 32 . . . if—
   (a) at the time of committing the offence, or immediately before or after doing so, the offender demonstrates towards the victim of the offence hostility based on the victim's membership (or presumed membership) of a racial or religious group; or
   (b) the offence is motivated (wholly or partly) by hostility towards members of a racial or religious group based on their membership of that group.

(2) In subsection (1)(a) above—
   'membership', in relation to a racial or religious group, includes association with members of that group; 'presumed' means presumed by the offender.

(3) It is immaterial for the purposes of paragraph (a) or (b) of subsection (1) above whether or not the offender's hostility is also based, to any extent, on any other factor not mentioned in that paragraph.

(4) In this section 'racial group' means a group of persons defined by reference to race, colour, nationality (including citizenship) or ethnic or national origins.

(5) In this section 'religious group' means a group of persons defined by reference to religious belief or lack of religious belief.

KEYNOTE

The aggravating factors for the purposes of s. 28 can be divided into:

- *demonstration* of hostility by the defendant
- *motivation* by hostility of the defendant.

The second type of situation, where the defendant is *motivated* by racial or religious hostility, is the type at which the government's policies to tackle racism are aimed; it is also by far the harder of the two to prove, even though the relevant offence need only be *partly* motivated by racial or religious hostility.

The revised wording of s. 28 (amended after the events of 11 September 2001) now includes 'religious groups'. These will include groups of people defined, not only by their religious belief, but also their *lack* of any such belief. An example of where this element has been proved is a case where a juvenile used the words 'bloody foreigners' immediately before smashing the window of a kebab shop. The Divisional Court held that this was capable of amounting to an expression of hostility based on a person's membership or presumed membership of a racial group for the purposes of the Crime and Disorder Act 1998, s. 28(1)(a)—*DPP* v *M* [2004] 1 WLR 2758.

In a case involving the abuse and assault of a doorman, the Administrative Court held that a racial insult uttered a few moments before an assault was enough to make the offence racially aggravated for the purposes of s. 29 of the Crime and Disorder Act 1998. The Court also held that the victim's own perception of the words used was irrelevant, as was the fact that he was not personally upset by the situation. Similarly, the fact that the defendant might have been motivated to utter the words merely by frustration rather than racism was also irrelevant (*DPP* v *Woods* [2002] EWHC Admin 85).

3.7.3 Hostility

Common to both factors under s. 28(1)(a) and (b) is the notion of hostility.

Hostility is not defined. However, in comparison to the problematic expression of 'racial hatred' used in the Public Order Act 1986 (**see para. 3.7.9**), hostility may well be much easier to identify and prove. The *Oxford English Dictionary* defines 'hostile' as 'of the nature or disposition of an enemy; unfriendly, antagonistic'. It would seem relatively straightforward to show that someone's behaviour in committing the relevant offences was 'unfriendly or antagonistic'. The difficult bit will come when trying to show that the hostility was *based on* the relevant person's membership of a racial or religious group.

A further difficulty for the courts will be making sure they do not confuse the two tests (see *DPP* v *M* [2004] 1 WLR 2758 where the youth court inadvertently mixed the two tests of hostility and motivation (under s. 28(1)(b)) as a result of which M's appeal against conviction was allowed).

3.7.4 Racial Groups

In each case the hostility must be based on the relevant person's membership of a racial group, i.e. membership of a group of people defined by reference to:

- race
- colour
- nationality (including citizenship)
- ethnic origins
- national origins (s. 28(4)).

This definition is the same as that used in the Public Order Act 1986 (see below). It is also very similar to that used in the Race Relations Act 1976. In determining whether or not a group is defined by *ethnic origins*, the courts will have regard to the judgment in the House of Lords in *Mandla* v *Dowell Lee* [1983] 2 AC 548. In that case their Lordships decided that Sikhs were such a group (for the purposes of the Race Relations Act 1976) after considering whether they as a group had:

- a long shared *history*;
- a *cultural tradition* of their own, including family and social customs and manners, often, but not necessarily, associated with religious observance;
- either a *common geographical origin* or descent from a small number of *common ancestors*;
- a *common language*, not necessarily peculiar to that group;
- a *common literature* peculiar to that group;
- a *common religion* different from that of neighbouring groups or the general community surrounding the group; and
- the characteristic of being a *minority* or an *oppressed* or a *dominant* group within a larger community.

Lord Fraser's dictum suggests that the first two characteristics above are essential in defining an 'ethnic group', while the others are at least relevant. His Lordship also approved a decision from New Zealand to the effect that Jews are a group with common ethnic origins (*Kings-Ansell* v *Police* [1979] 2 NZLR 531).

KEYNOTE

When considering whether an offence was racially motivated under s. 28, hostility demonstrated to people who were foreign nationals simply because they were 'foreign' could be just as objectionable as hostility based on some more limited racial characteristic. This was clarified by the Court of Appeal in *R* v *Rogers* [2006] 1 Cr App R 14 where the defendant had called three Spanish women 'bloody foreigners' and told them to 'go back to your own country'. The prosecution case was that the defendant had demonstrated hostility based on the women's membership of a racial group. The court held that, for an offence to be aggravated under s. 28 the defendant had first to form a view that the victim was a member of a racial group (within the definition in s. 28(4) and then had to say or do something that demonstrated hostility towards the victim based on membership of that group.

3.7.5 Religion

Lord Fraser's sixth point above refers to religion as a possible defining characteristic of an ethnic group. Although this was a notable omission from the ambit of *racial groups* as defined under the original s. 28(4) of the Crime and Disorder Act 1998, religious groups have now been included as a result of the Anti-terrorism, Crime and Security Act 2001. In addition, there are now specific regulations dealing with the area of less favourable treatment by employers on grounds of religious belief. This means that the former case law (mostly arising in an employment context) over whether religious groups could also be regarded as racial groups is largely irrelevant. The change means that a purely religious group such as Rastafarians (who have been held not to be members of an ethnic group *per se* (*Dawkins* v *Crown Suppliers (Property Services Agency)* (1993) *The Times*, 4 February; [1993] ICR 517) are now covered by the aggravated forms of offences. In reality, a number of racial groups will overlap with religious groups in any event—Rastafarians would be a good example. An attack on a Rastafarian might be a racially aggravated offence under s. 28 because it was based on the defendant's hostility towards a *racial group* (e.g. African-Caribbeans) into which many Rastafarians fall. Alternatively, an attack might be made on a white Rastafarian based on the victim's religious beliefs (or lack of religious beliefs), i.e. his 'membership of a religious group'. Muslims have also been held not to be a racial group (*J.H. Walker* v *Hussain* [1996] ICR 291) but Muslims are clearly members of a religious group and, as such, are now covered by the Act.

Note that there is some disparity here between the recognition of religion for these specific purposes and those that appear under article 9 of the European Convention on Human Rights.

3.7.6 Other Racial Groups

Traditional 'gypsies' (as opposed to travellers) are capable of being a racial group on the basis of ethnic origin (*Commission for Racial Equality* v *Dutton* [1989] QB 783). English and Scottish people have been held to constitute groups defined by reference to national origins and thus as members of 'racial groups' in the broad sense as defined and protected from discrimination under the Race Relations Act 1976 (*Northern Joint Police Board* v *Power* [1997] IRLR 610). This decision ought logically to extend to Irish and Welsh people. In *Attorney-General's Reference (No. 4 of 2004), sub nom Attorney-General* v *D* [2005] 1 WLR 2810 the use of the word 'immigrant', in its simple implication that a person was 'non-British', was specific enough to denote membership of a 'racial group' within its meaning in the Crime and Disorder Act 1998, s. 28(4).

3.7.7 Membership

An important extension of 'racial or religious groups' lies in the inclusion of people who associate with members of that group. 'Membership' *for the purposes of s. 28(1)(a)* will include *association* with members of that group (a slightly circular definition) (s. 28(2)). This means that a white man who has a black female partner would potentially fall within the category of a 'member' of her racial group—and *vice versa*. Moreover, people who work within certain racial or religious groups within the community could also be regarded as members of those groups for these purposes.

For the purposes of s. 28(1)(a), 'membership' will also include anyone *presumed by the defendant* to be a member of a racial or religious group. Therefore, if a defendant wrongly presumed that a person was a member of a racial or religious group, say a Pakistani Muslim, and assaulted them as a result, the defendant's *presumption* would be enough to make his/her behaviour 'racially or religiously aggravated', even though the victim was in fact an Indian Hindu.

Such a presumption would not extend to the aggravating factors under s. 28(1)(b). The only apparent reason for this would seem to be that the s. 28(1)(a) offence requires hostility to be demonstrated towards a particular person ('the victim') while the offence under s. 28(1)(b) envisages hostility towards members of a racial or religious group generally and does not require a specific victim.

Section 28(3) goes on to provide that it is immaterial whether the defendant's hostility (in either case under s. 28(1)) is also based to any extent on *any other factor*.

This concession in s. 28(3) only prevents the defendant pointing to another *factor* in order to explain his/her behaviour in committing the relevant offence (assault, criminal damage, etc.). Although it removes the opportunity for a defendant to argue that his/her behaviour was as a result of other factors (e.g. arising out of a domestic dispute), the subsection does not remove the burden on the prosecution to show that the defendant either demonstrated racial or religious hostility or was motivated by it.

3.7.8 Demonstration of Hostility

Under s. 28(1)(a) it must be shown that the defendant *demonstrated* the required hostility:

- at the time of the offence
- immediately before, or
- immediately after committing the offence.

No guidance is given as to how 'immediately' will be interpreted. It is submitted that whether a defendant's demonstration of hostility came immediately before or after the relevant offence will be a question of fact to be decided in light of all the circumstances.

In deciding the issue of immediacy the courts will have to consider the degree of proximity between the defendant's demonstration of racial or religious hostility and the relevant offence itself. It is submitted that the degree of proximity will have to be very high before the defendant's hostility could be shown to have been *immediately* before or after the *actus reus* of the offence. This might cause problems with offences that are said to be 'continuing' or 'ongoing'.

The courts have shown that they are prepared to adopt a wide approach when interpreting this important legislation. In the context of criminal damage, the Divisional Court has confirmed that the relevant hostility can be demonstrated even if the victim is no longer present—*DPP* v *Parry* [2004] EWHC 3112. However, the need for any such hostility to be demonstrated *immediately* means that it must be shown to have taken place in the immediate context of the offence.

In the context of the offence under s. 4 of the Public Order Act 1986 the Divisional Court held that, where a court finds that the defendant has committed an offence under s. 4 and used racist, threatening and abusive words, it is immaterial for the purposes of s. 28(1)(a) of the 1998 Act that the defendant might have had additional reasons for using that language (*DPP* v *McFarlane* [2002] EWHC 485).

It is also necessary, for the purposes of s. 28(1)(a), to show that the defendant demonstrated his/her hostility *towards the victim of the offence*. Again this may be problematic in relation to certain offences, e.g. criminal damage.

Racially or religiously aggravated offences can be committed where the aggravating behaviour is directed at or towards a police officer and police officers are entitled to the protection offered by this offence in the same way as any other person (see *R* v *Jacobs* (2000) *The Times*, 28 December).

3.7.9 Other Offences involving Racial and Religious Hatred

The Racial and Religious Hatred Act 2006 inserts part 3A into the Public Order Act 1986 which provides new offences of stirring up hatred against persons on religious grounds. This section provides a summary of the offences introduced by the 1986 Act aimed at addressing incidents specifically motivated by racial hatred, and the new offences, created by the Racial and Religious Hatred Act 2006, motivated by religious hatred.

For the purposes of the offences contrary to ss. 18 to 23 of the 1986 Act, 'racial hatred' means hatred against a group of persons defined by reference to colour, race, nationality (including citizenship) or ethnic or national origins (s. 17).

For the purposes of the new offences contrary to ss. 29B to 29G of the 2006 Act, 'religious hatred' means hatred against a group of persons defined by reference to religious belief or lack of religious belief (s. 29A).

3.7.10 Use of Words, Behaviour or Display of Written Material

OFFENCE: **Use of words or behaviour or display of written material—*Public Order Act 1986, s. 18***

- Triable either way • Seven years' imprisonment and/or a fine on indictment
- Six months' imprisonment and/or a fine summarily

The Public Order Act 1986, s. 18 states:

(1) A person who uses threatening, abusive or insulting words or behaviour, or displays any written material which is threatening, abusive or insulting, is guilty of an offence if—
   (a) he intends thereby to stir up racial hatred, or
   (b) having regard to all the circumstances racial hatred is likely to be stirred up thereby.

(2) An offence under this section may be committed in a public or a private place, except that no offence is committed where the words or behaviour are used, or the written material is displayed, by a person inside a dwelling and are not heard or seen except by other persons in that or another dwelling.

KEYNOTE

This, and the other offences under this part of the Act, may not be prosecuted without the consent of the Attorney-General (or Solicitor-General).

Generally, in order to prove these offences, you must show that a defendant:

- *intended* to stir up racial hatred; or
- that he/she *intended* the relevant words, behaviour or material to be threatening, abusive or insulting; or
- that he/she *was aware* that the relevant words/behaviour/material might be threatening, abusive or insulting.

This offence does not apply to broadcasts in a programme (but see below) and there are exemptions in the case of fair and accurate reports of parliamentary or court proceedings.

3.7.10.1 Defence

The Public Order Act 1986, s. 18 states:

(4) In proceedings for an offence under this section it is a defence for the accused to prove that he was inside a dwelling and had no reason to believe that the words or behaviour used, or the written material displayed, would be heard or seen by a person outside that or any other dwelling.

3.7.11 Publishing or Distributing Written Material

OFFENCE: **Publishing or distributing written material—*Public Order Act 1986, s. 19***

- Triable either way • Seven years' imprisonment and/or a fine on indictment
- Six months' imprisonment and/or a fine summarily

The Public Order Act 1986, s. 19 states:

(1) A person who publishes or distributes written material which is threatening, abusive or insulting is guilty of an offence if—
  (a) he intends thereby to stir up racial hatred, or
  (b) having regard to all the circumstances racial hatred is likely to be stirred up thereby.

(2) ...

(3) References in this Part to the publication or distribution of written material are to its publication or distribution to the public or a section of the public.

KEYNOTE

The Anti-terrorism, Crime and Security Act 2001 increased the penalty for this offence due to the prominence it was attracting. Prosecution of this offence needs the consent of the Attorney-General (or Solicitor-General).

3.7.11.1 Defence

The Public Order Act 1986, s. 19 states:

(2) In proceedings for an offence under this section it is a defence for an accused who is not shown to have intended to stir up racial hatred to prove that he was not aware of the content of the material and did not suspect, and had no reason to suspect, that it was threatening, abusive or insulting.

3.7.12 Use of Words, Behaviour or Display of Written Material

OFFENCE: **Use of words or behaviour or display of written material—*Public Order Act 1986, s. 29B***

• Triable either way • Not exceeding seven years' imprisonment and/or a fine on indictment • Not exceeding six months' imprisonment and/or a fine summarily

The Public Order Act 1986, s. 29B states:

(1) A person who uses threatening words or behaviour, or displays any written material which is threatening, is guilty of an offence if he intends thereby to stir up religious hatred.

(2) An offence under this section is committed in a public or private place, except that no offence is committed where the words or behaviour are used, or the written material is displayed, by a person inside a dwelling and are not heard or seen except by other persons in that or another dwelling.

KEYNOTE

This differs from the other sections under the 1986 Act which have no specific power of arrest since the provisions of the Serious Organised Crime and Police Act 2005 were introduced.

All of the new offences are similar to that under s. 18 in that they require the consent of the Attorney-General before proceedings can be taken (s. 29L), and the same defences apply to this particular section—no reason to believe the words or behaviour, etc., would be heard or seen outside the dwelling (s. 29B(4)), or where used solely for the purpose of being included in a programming service (s. 29B(5)).

Section 29J of the Act provides that the offences of stirring up religious hatred are not intended to limit or restrict discussion, criticism or expressions of antipathy, dislike, ridicule or insult or abuse of particular religions or belief systems or lack of religion or of the beliefs and practices of those who hold such beliefs or to apply to persons newly converted to a religious faith, evangelism or the seeking to convert people to a particular belief or to cease holding a belief.

3.7.13 Publishing or Distributing Material

OFFENCE: **Publishing or distributing written material—*Public Order Act 1986, s. 29C***

• Triable either way • Not exceeding seven years' imprisonment and/or a fine on indictment • Not exceeding six months' imprisonment and/or a fine summarily

The Public Order Act 1986, s. 29C states:

(1) A person who publishes or distributes written material which is threatening is guilty of an offence if he intends thereby to stir up religious hatred.

(2) References in this Part to the publication or distribution of written material are to its publication or distribution to the public or a section of the public.

3.8 Misuse of Drugs

3.8.1 Classification

Drugs which are subject to the provisions of the Misuse of Drugs Act 1971 are listed in Parts I, II and III of Schedule 2 of the Act.

The divisions are made largely on the basis of each substance's potential effects on both the person taking it and society in general.

Classification is important in determining the sentencing powers of the courts.

- **Class A**—This class includes the most notorious and dangerous drugs such as heroin and morphine, opiates, cocaine, some amphetamines and LSD; it also includes fungus (of any kind) which contains psilocin ('magic mushrooms'). It also includes the drug 'crystal meth' (methylamphetamine).
- **Class B**—This class includes codeine and some amphetamines.
- **Class C**—This class includes some commonly-abused prescription drugs. It includes cannabis resin and ketamine.

There has been much publicity and attention devoted the reclassification of cannabis (which took place in 2004) from a Class B drug to a Class C drug. The fact remains that cannabis is still illegal and possession, production and supply of the drug remain offences; only the penalty for such offences has changed.

If the charge alleges possession of one particular drug then that drug must be identified.

While crystal meth is a Class A drug, the leaves produced by the khat plant (sometimes chewed for a mild stimulant effect) are not controlled drugs for the purposes of the 1971 Act even though the substance produced is banned in some other jurisdictions in Europe and the United States of America.

Note that, although a substance may appear in sch. 2 to the Act, there may be restrictions on the occasions where possession is treated as an offence **(see para. 3.8.5.5)**.

The main practical effect of the classification of controlled drugs is the mode of trial which may affect the available powers and sentence. Difficulties in identifying a plant, pill or powder precisely mean that officers will frequently have to rely on criminal intelligence and/or their 'reasonable suspicions' when dealing with suspected drugs offences.

It is not necessary, when prosecuting an offence, to distinguish between the various chemical forms in which a drug exists (i.e. as a salt, ester or other form) (*R* v *Greensmith* [1983] 1 WLR 1124).

A defendant's admission may, in some cases, be relied upon to prove his/her knowledge as to what a particular substance is (see *R* v *Chatwood* [1980] 1 WLR 874).

3.8.1.1 Cannabis

The Misuse of Drugs Act 1971, s. 37 states:

> 'cannabis' (except in the expression 'cannabis resin') means any plant of the genus *Cannabis* or any part of any such plant (by whatever name designated) except that it does not include cannabis resin or any of the following products after separation from the rest of the plant, namely—
> (a) mature stalk of any such plant,
> (b) fibre produced from mature stalk of any such plant, and
> (c) seed of any such plant,
>
> 'cannabis resin' means the separated resin, whether crude or purified, obtained from any plant of the genus *Cannabis*;

KEYNOTE

There can scarcely have been anyone in England and Wales who failed to notice all the media coverage over the change of class for cannabis from B to C. At the time of writing there is now a debate as to whether the drug should be reclassified as class B once again. Whatever its classification, as cannabis and cannabis resin are both in the same class for the purposes of the 1971 Act there would be no duplicity if a person is charged with possessing either one or the other in the same charge (*R* v *Best* [1980] 70 Cr App R 21).

3.8.1.2 Drug Testing

Section 63B of the Police and Criminal Evidence Act 1984 enables the police to require urine or non-intimate samples to be taken from adults in police detention under certain circumstances. The purpose of such tests is to ascertain whether the person has any specified Class A drug in their body. The power to require such a sample can be activated in a number of ways.

The Powers of Criminal Courts (Sentencing) Act 2000 makes further provision for the courts to impose drug treatment and testing orders.

3.8.2 Possession

Possession is a concept that is relevant to a number of different offences. In respect of drugs offences it is necessary to consider issues relating to physical control and knowledge of possession.

3.8.2.1 Physical Control

A good starting point in understanding 'possession' is to realise that it is a neutral concept, not implying any kind of blame or fault. This is the key feature to understand first before going on to consider specific offences under *any* legislation. In order to be in possession of *anything*, the common law requires physical control of the object plus knowledge of its presence. This requirement is particularly problematic where containers of some sort (whether they be boxes, handbags, cigarette packets or whatever) are involved or where the person claims not to have realised what it was that he/she 'possessed'. In such cases, the common law makes the same requirements; you need to show that the person had physical control of the container together with a knowledge that it contained *something*. Once you have established possession, you then need to show that the substance/object/material possessed was in fact proscribed by the relevant statute.

In *R* v *Forsyth* [2001] EWCA Crim 2926, the defendant argued that there was a distinction between a person carrying something *in* a container and a person carrying *something inside something else* in a container! In that particular case, the defendant was found in possession of a box which contained a safe; inside the safe was a significant quantity of a controlled drug. The defendant argued that this type of possession should be differentiated from the situation where someone simply had possession of a box with drugs in it. The Court of Appeal ruled that there was no difference and the issues of proof were the same.

3.8.2.2 Knowledge of Possession

In relation to controlled drugs, the issue becomes complicated further by the specific defences provided by the 1971 Act. The very reason those defences (**see para. 3.8.4**) have been drafted in this way is to reflect the common law concept of possession and to provide some protection from its effects where drugs are concerned (see *R* v *Bett* [1999] 1 WLR 2109).

So, if a person has a container with him/her and that container is found to have controlled drugs in it, he/she is in possession of those drugs *provided he/she knew that there was something in the container*. That does not mean that, at this point, the person necessarily commits an offence (and he/she may still have a statutory defence); it means that he/she was in 'possession' of the drugs. This merely satisfies one element of a number of possible offences; just as if you were trying to prove that a person was 'driving' a vehicle. (Driving is also a neutral concept and only satisfies one element within a number of possible offences.)

The Misuse of Drugs Act 1971 creates offences under certain circumstances where a person has been shown to have been in 'possession' of a controlled drug. However, the Act also provides a defence which includes a mental element on the part of the defendant. It is true that this situation in relation to possession is impracticable—like many others in our system—and it is not even consistently applied (e.g. in cases of strict liability such as some firearms offences involving 'possession' (see *R* v *Bradish* [1990] 1 QB 981)). Nevertheless, until the concept of 'possession' at common law is changed to include an element of blame or fault, these rules will continue to apply and presumably statutes will continue to contain defences which, like s. 28 of the 1971 Act, are aimed at correcting any unjust results.

Nevertheless it is clear from the House of Lords' decisions in *Warner* v *Metropolitan Police Commissioner* [1969] 2 AC 256 and *R* v *Boyesen* [1982] AC 768, and also the Court of Appeal judgment in *R* v *McNamara* (1988) 87 Cr App R 246 that the basic elements required are that a person 'knows' that he/she is in possession of something which is, in fact, a prohibited or controlled object or substance.

Some of the further practical difficulties that can arise from this view of 'possession' were highlighted in *Adams* v *DPP* [2002] EWHC 438 (Admin). In that case a small quantity of controlled drugs was found in the defendant's home during the execution of a search warrant. There was no proof that the drugs were owned by the defendant, nor that she was specifically aware of their presence but the defendant *did* know that her home was used by various people who were highly likely to bring controlled drugs into it. She was convicted of possession. In hearing her appeal against conviction by way of case stated, the Administrative Court held that, where knowledge of possession of drugs was limited to the fact that a visitor had brought drugs into the defendant's home intending to take them, that was not sufficient evidence from which it was appropriate to infer that she had control over the drugs.

The court also held that giving consent (explicitly or impliedly) for the use of a controlled drug did not of itself constitute possession. Similarly, an inference that the defendant knew whose drugs had been found in her home did not amount to evidence of control over the drug itself—even though she may well have been able to exercise control over what actually took place in her home.

3.8.2.3 Points to Prove

To prove possession of a controlled drug then, you must show that a defendant both:

- *had* a controlled drug in his/her possession; and
- *knew* that he/she had something in his/her possession which was in fact a controlled drug.

EXAMPLE

Consider the following circumstances: After a stop and search, a defendant is found with a knife in his pocket. The knife has traces of brown powder on the blade. Later examination shows the powder to be heroin.

In order to prove 'possession' of the heroin you must show:

- that the defendant actually had the knife
- that the knife had a substance which was a controlled drug on it and that
- the defendant knew *of the existence of the substance* (i.e. the powder).

3.8.2.4 Quality

You would not have to show that he/she knew what the powder was. That is, you do not need to show that the defendant knew the *quality* of what he/she possessed.

If the defendant admits to knowing that the powder was there but thought it was sand, he/she is in possession of it (see *R* v *Marriott* [1971] 1 WLR 187).

Therefore if a defendant had a packet of cigarettes with him/her and admitted to knowing that he/she had them, he/she would be in possession of a controlled drug if one cigarette was shown to have contained cannabis. The fact that the defendant thought they contained tobacco would be irrelevant (*Searle* v *Randolph* [1972] Crim LR 779) (although clearly they may be able to raise the defence under s. 28: see below).

3.8.2.5 Quantity

The *quantity* of a controlled drug, however, may be so small that the defendant could not possibly have known about it; therefore it could not be 'possessed'.

Each case will have to be decided on its merits but the House of Lords have suggested that if something is 'visible, tangible and measurable', that may be sufficient (*Boyesen*). If the amount recovered is too small to support a charge of possession, it might be used to prove earlier possession of the drug (see *R* v *Graham* [1970] 1 WLR 113n and *Hambleton* v *Callinan* [1968] 2 QB 427 (traces of a controlled drug in a urine sample held to be possible evidence of earlier possession of that drug)).

Quantity is not only relevant to the fact of possession; it is also relevant to the intention of the person in whose possession the drug is found. Larger quantities (particularly if they are also divided into smaller amounts) may be indicative of an intention to supply and may be assumed to be proof of that intention in some circumstances (**see para. 3.8.5.6**).

3.8.3 Regulated Possession and Supply of Controlled Drugs

The statutory framework governing controlled drugs does not simply ban substances and their possession outright. People working at various levels within the system need to be able to access, analyse and prescribe substances that are controlled by the 1971 Act. To that end, the framework takes account of the differing legitimate activities that may be relevant to individual people or particular circumstances. The majority of the exceptions and conditions imposed on this lawful possession and use can be found in the Misuse of Drugs Regulations 2001 (SI 2001/3998) as amended and also in the Misuse of Drugs and Misuse of Drugs (Safe Custody) (Amendment) Regulations (SI 2007/2154).

The importance of the 2001 Regulations lies in the fact that they exempt certain drugs and certain people (pharmacists, medical staff and laboratory workers etc.)—including police officers—from the main offences of possession, supply and importation.

Among the key regulations are:

- Regulation 4—which sets out those controlled drugs which will be exempted from the main offences of importation/exportation when they are contained in medicinal products.
- Regulation 5—allowing people holding a licence issued by the Secretary of State to produce, supply, offer to supply or have in their possession a controlled drug—*provided* that their activities (e.g. of supplying etc.) are carried out in accordance with their licence and any conditions attached to it. If the licence holder goes outside the terms of his/her

licence (say by offering to supply a drug that is not covered by it) or fails to comply with any conditions attached to the licence (e.g. by keeping the drugs in a different place from that specified), he/she commits the relevant offence(s) in the ordinary way.

- Regulation 6—this allows anyone who is *lawfully* in possession of a controlled drug to give the drug back to the person from whom he/she obtained it and would cover registered heroin addicts properly returning methadone to a chemist. Regulation 6 also allows others to possess and supply certain controlled drugs under strict conditions. Regulation 6 allows police constables to have any controlled drug in their possession, or to supply such a drug to anyone who is lawfully allowed to have it (reg. 6(5)–(7)). These exemptions only apply where the constable is *acting in the course of his/her duty as such*.

  Other people who are given the same protection are customs and excise officers, postal workers and people engaged in conveying the drug to someone who may lawfully possess it. This last category would include civilian support staff, exhibits officers and others who, although not police constables, are nevertheless properly engaged in conveying controlled drugs to others.

The remainder of the regulations are generally concerned with exemptions for doctors, dentists, vets and others who may need to store or supply controlled drugs; the 2001 Regulations also impose requirements on some such people in relation to record keeping and the provision of information when requested.

The Regulations make provision for medical practitioners and some nurses (extended formulary nurse prescribers) to prescribe controlled drugs under certain circumstances. Where controlled drugs are supplied lawfully by healthcare providers, other regulations (e.g. the Misuse of Drugs (Supply to Addicts) Regulations 1997 (SI 1997/1001)) may also be relevant and should be consulted.

The 2001 Regulations provide that records of activity, authority and prescription may be preserved in computerised form in accordance with specified best practice guidance. The Secretary of State or an authorised person can request that a computerised register form be produced by sending a copy of it to the appropriate person.

3.8.4 Defences

In addition to the generic defences available in criminal law, offences under the Misuse of Drugs Act 1971 may attract specific defences set out in the legislation. So far as the generic defences are concerned, there have been several (unsuccessful) attempts to claim defences such as 'medical necessity' in respect of possession, supply and production of controlled drugs. In addition, the Court of Appeal would not allow a defendant to rely on effectively the same defence by presenting it as a human rights issue (*R* v *Altham* [2006] EWCA Crim 7). In that case the defendant argued that criminalising his use of cannabis to treat his severe medical symptoms was subjecting him to inhuman or degrading treatment, in contravention of article 3 of the European Convention on Human Rights. The court held that the prohibition in article 3 was against subjection to torture or to inhuman or degrading treatment or punishment. The state had not done anything to the defendant to exacerbate his condition or to cause him inhuman or degrading treatment, and its obligation under article 3 did not extend to permitting him (even though he suffered from chronic pain) to smoke cannabis as a form of pain relief.

Before considering the various offences under the Misuse of Drugs Act 1971 it is useful to address the specific statutory defences provided by ss. 5 and 28 of the Act.

3.8.4.1 Section 5 Defence to Unlawful Possession

Section 5 provides a defence to an offence of unlawful *possession*:

(4) In any proceedings for an offence under subsection (2) above in which it is proved that the accused had a controlled drug in his possession, it shall be a defence for him to prove—

(a) that, knowing or suspecting it to be a controlled drug, he took possession of it for the purpose of preventing another from committing or continuing to commit an offence in connection with that drug and that as soon as possible after taking possession of it he took all such steps as were reasonably open to him to destroy the drug or to deliver it into the custody of a person lawfully entitled to take custody of it; or

(b) that, knowing or suspecting it to be a controlled drug, he took possession of it for the purpose of delivering it into the custody of a person lawfully entitled to take custody of it and that as soon as possible after taking possession of it he took all such steps as were reasonably open to him to deliver it into the custody of such a person.

KEYNOTE

This defence envisages two distinct situations. The purpose in taking possession of the controlled drug under s. 5(4)(a) must be to:

- prevent *another*
- from committing (in the future) or
- continuing to commit

an offence in connection with *that* drug.

The first situation might arise where a parent, guardian or carer finds a child in possession of something which appears to be a controlled drug. Provided that that person takes all reasonable steps to destroy the drug or to take it to someone lawfully entitled to possess it (like a general practitioner or police officer), *as soon as possible after taking possession of it*, he/she commits no offence *of unlawful possession*.

The finer technical issues of this defence were examined in *R* v *Murphy* [2003] 1 WLR 422. In that case the defendant found some cannabis in his father's car which was outside a prison at the time. The defendant took the drug and buried it in the hope that it would be destroyed by the forces of nature over time. The Administrative Court held that the trial judge had been right not to leave the s. 5(4)(a) defence to the jury. The defendant had to show that he had taken all steps that were reasonably open to him to destroy the drug directly and relying on the forces of nature did not provide this defence on that occasion.

The second situation (under s. 5(4)(b)) may arise where a person finds what he/she believes to be a controlled drug and he/she takes possession of it *solely for the purpose of delivering it to a person lawfully entitled to take custody of it*. The defendant must prove that this was his/her intention at the time of taking possession (*R* v *Dempsey and Dempsey* [1986] 82 Cr App R 291).

In either case above, s. 5(4) will not provide a defence to any other offence connected with the controlled drug (e.g. supplying or offering to supply).

3.8.4.2 General Defence under Section 28

However, there is a more general defence provided by s. 28 of the Act. Section 28 applies to offences of:

- unlawful production (s. 4(2))
- unlawful supply (s. 4(3))

- unlawful possession (s. 5(2))
- possession with intent to supply (s. 5(3))
- unlawful cultivation of cannabis (s. 6(2))
- offences connected with opium (s. 9).

The defences under s. 28 are *not* available in cases of conspiracy as they are not offences under the 1971 Act (*R* v *McGowan* [1990] Crim LR 399). In *R* v *Lambert* [2001] 3 WLR 206 the House of Lords considered the requirements of the defences under ss. 5(4) and 28 in relation to their effect on the presumption of innocence (imposed at both common law and under article 6). It was argued that the statutory defence shifted the legal burden of proof from the prosecution onto the defendant and, therefore, was incompatible with the Convention. Their Lordships held that the defences could legitimately be read by the courts in a way that moved the *evidential* burden only onto the defendant. Such an approach, they held, was compatible with the Convention and the Human Rights Act 1998.

Section 28 states:

> (2) Subject to subsection (3) below, in any proceedings for an offence to which this section applies it shall be a defence for the accused to prove that he neither knew of nor suspected nor had reason to suspect the existence of some fact alleged by the prosecution which it is necessary for the prosecution to prove if he is to be convicted of the offence charged.
>
> (3) Where in any proceedings for an offence to which this section applies it is necessary, if the accused is to be convicted of the offence charged, for the prosecution to prove that some substance or product involved in the alleged offence was the controlled drug which the prosecution alleges it to have been, and it is proved that the substance or product in question was that controlled drug, the accused—
>
> (a) shall not be acquitted of the offence charged by reason only of proving that he neither knew nor suspected nor had reason to suspect that the substance or product in question was the particular controlled drug alleged; but
>
> (b) shall be acquitted thereof—
>
> (i) if he proves that he neither believed nor suspected nor had reason to suspect that the substance or product in question was a controlled drug; or
>
> (ii) if he proves that he believed the substance or product in question to be a controlled drug, or a controlled drug of a description, such that, if it had in fact been that controlled drug, or a controlled drug of that description, he would not at the material time have been committing any offence to which this section applies.

KEYNOTE

This defence envisages three distinct situations:

- a lack of knowledge by the defendant of some fact which is alleged by the prosecution;
- a general lack of knowledge by the defendant about the drug in question;
- a conditional belief held by the defendant about the drug in question.

These situations are discussed below.

3.8.4.3 Lack of Knowledge of Some Alleged Fact

Section 28(2) allows a defence where the defendant did not *know, suspect* or *have reason to suspect* the existence of some fact which is essential to proving the case.

EXAMPLE

Consider the following example. A youth is stopped in the street by a stranger who asks him to drop off an envelope at a nearby address in exchange for £10. As the youth approaches the address he is arrested for possessing a controlled drug (which had been inside the envelope), with intent to supply.

Section 28(2) would allow the youth to discharge the evidential burden by showing that he neither knew, nor suspected that the envelope contained a controlled drug, and that he neither knew nor suspected that he was supplying it to another. Both of these elements would be facts which the prosecution would have to allege in order to prove the offence.

If the youth knew the person to be a local drug dealer, or the reward for his errand was disproportionately large—say £1000—then he may not be able to discharge this, albeit evidential, burden.

It has been held that the test for 'reason to suspect' is an *objective* one (*R* v *Young* [1984] 1 WLR 654). Consequently, where a 'reason to suspect' was not apparent to a defendant because he/she was too intoxicated to see it, the defence will not apply.

3.8.4.4 General Lack of Knowledge about Drug in Question

The wording of s. 28(3)(a) prevents defendants from claiming a 'defence' when what they thought was one type of controlled drug was in fact another, different controlled drug.

Section 28(3)(b) however, has two strands, one concerned with the defendant's general lack of knowledge about the drug in question and the other (see below) concerning the defendant's conditional belief.

Section 28(3)(b)(i) will allow a defendant to prove that he/she did not believe or suspect the substance in question to be a controlled drug and that he/she had no reason so to suspect.

This clearly overlaps with s. 28(2) and the youth in the above example would also be able to claim this lack of knowledge. If he believed the envelope to contain amphetamine when it turned out to contain heroin, however, this lack of knowledge would not be permitted as a defence under s. 28(3).

3.8.4.5 Conditional Belief about Drug in Question

In contrast to s. 28(3)(a), the second strand of s. 28(3)(b)(ii) allows a defendant to discharge the evidential burden by showing that he/she *did* believe the drug in question to be a particular controlled drug. It is then open to him/her to claim that, had the drug in question actually been the drug which he/she believed it to be, then he/she would not have committed any of the offences in **para. 3.8.4** above.

EXAMPLE

A registered heroin addict may have been prescribed methadone. If she collects her prescription from a chemist but is mistakenly given pethidine instead, she may be able to discharge the evidential burden by showing that she *believed* the drug in question to be methadone *and* that, if it had been, she would not have committed an offence by possessing it.

3.8.5 Offences Involving the Misuse of Controlled Drugs

Clearly there are occasions when the production, supply and possession of controlled drugs will be lawful and most of these occasions are addressed in either the Misuse of Drugs Regulations 2001 (SI 2001/3998) or in s. 28 of the Misuse of Drugs Act 1971 (**see para. 3.8.4**).

In the offences which follow, the aspects which generally make the behaviour 'unlawful' are either the lack of authority under the relevant regulations, or the absence of the circumstances outlined in the defences under s. 28.

3.8.5.1 Production

OFFENCE: **Producing Controlled Drug—*Misuse of Drugs Act 1971, s. 4(2)***

• Triable either way • Class A (life imprisonment and/or fine on indictment; six months' imprisonment and/or prescribed sum summarily) • Class B (14 years' imprisonment and/or fine on indictment; six months' imprisonment and/or prescribed sum summarily) • Class C (five years' imprisonment and/or fine on indictment; three months' imprisonment and/or fine summarily)

The Misuse of Drugs Act 1971, s. 4 states:

> (2) Subject to section 28 of this Act, it is an offence for a person—
> (a) to produce a controlled drug in contravention of subsection (1)...; or
> (b) to be concerned in the production of such a drug in contravention of that subsection by another.

KEYNOTE

'Produce' means producing by manufacture, cultivation or any other method and 'production' has a corresponding meaning (Misuse of Drugs Act 1971, s. 37).

Converting one form of a Class A drug into another has been held to be 'producing' (*R* v *Russell* (1992) 94 Cr App R 351) as has harvesting, cutting and stripping a cannabis plant (*R* v *Harris* [1996] 1 Cr App R 369).

3.8.5.2 Supply

OFFENCE: **Supplying Controlled Drug—*Misuse of Drugs Act 1971, s. 4(3)***

• Triable either way • Class A (life imprisonment and/or fine on indictment; six months' imprisonment and/or prescribed sum summarily) • Class B (14 years' imprisonment and/or fine on indictment; six months' imprisonment and/or prescribed sum summarily) • Class C (14 years' imprisonment and/or fine on indictment; three months' imprisonment and/or fine summarily)

The Misuse of Drugs Act 1971, s. 4 states:

> (3) Subject to section 28 of this Act, it is an offence for a person—
> (a) to supply or offer to supply a controlled drug to another in contravention of subsection (1) above; or
> (b) to be concerned in the supplying of such a drug to another in contravention of that subsection; or
> (c) to be concerned in the making to another in contravention of that subsection of an offer to supply such a drug.

KEYNOTE

The word supply 'connotes more than the mere transfer of physical control of [something] from one person to another' (per Lord Keith in *Holmes* v *Chief Constable of Merseyside Police* [1976] Crim LR 125). The offence of supplying requires a further element, namely that the person receiving the item (the controlled drug) is thereby enabled to apply it to his/her own purposes. Whether or not a person has 'supplied' a controlled drug to another is a question of fact.

'Supplying' includes distributing (s. 37(1)).

This offence most frequently occurs where one person hands over a controlled drug to another, in which case there is little argument about the meaning of supply.

3.8.5.3 Specific Situations

There is a whole spectrum along which the supply of controlled drugs can take place. Ranging from handing someone their own cannabis after holding it for a while to taking orders for class A drugs from schoolchildren, the different prevailing circumstances of the 'supply' must be taken into account. Section 4A of the Misuse of Drugs Act 1971 recognises this and requires courts to treat certain conditions as 'aggravating' factors when considering the seriousness of the offence under s. 4(3) if committed by a person aged 18 or over.

The conditions are either:

1. that the offence was committed on or in the vicinity of school premises at a relevant time. 'Vicinity' is not defined and will be left to each court relying on its local knowledge. Other buildings and premises (e.g. cafes and shopping centres) can fall within this description and courts may decide that a route used to get to or from a school or a place where schoolchildren gather (even if trespassing) may be in the 'vicinity'. School premises are land used for the purposes of a school but *excluding* any land occupied solely as a dwelling *by a person employed at the school* (s. 4A(8)). A 'relevant time' is any time when the school premises are in use by people under the age of 18 (and one hour before the start/after the end of any such time) (s. 4A(5)); or
2. that in connection with the commission of the offence the offender used a 'courier' who, at the time the offence was committed, was under the age of 18. A person uses a courier if he/she causes or permits another person (the courier):
   (a) to deliver a controlled drug to a third person, or
   (b) to deliver a 'drug related consideration' (basically any money, goods etc. obtained or intended to be used in connection with the supply of a controlled drug) to him/herself or a third person (s. 4A(6) and (7)).

Other specific situations involving the supply of controlled drugs (which may or may not also be accompanied by the aggravating factors of s. 4A) are considered below.

The concept of supplying another with a drug generally conjures up something along the lines of a straightforward sale or exchange. It has been held that, where a person holds on to a controlled drug belonging to another for a short while and then hands it back, there is no 'supply' (although there may be unlawful possession) (*R* v *Dempsey and Dempsey* (1986) 82 Cr App R 291, see below). If the person looking after the drugs for another is in some way benefiting from that activity, then the return of those drugs to the depositor *will* amount to 'supplying', and the offences of supplying or possession with intent to supply will be applicable (*R* v *Maginnis* [1987] AC 303, see below). *Dempsey* involved a registered drug addict who was in lawful possession of a controlled drug and who asked his partner to hold on to some of that drug while he went to administer the remainder of it to himself in a gents' toilet. Both the addict and his partner were arrested, the addict being subsequently charged with 'supplying' his partner with the drug. The Court of Appeal held that, if the partner had simply been given the drug for safekeeping until the addict's return, there would be no 'supplying'. If however, she had been given the drug for her own use, then there clearly *would* be a 'supplying' of that drug and the offence under s. 4(3)(a) would be complete.

Leaving Drugs with Another

Other situations where the *initial* possession of the controlled drug is itself unlawful have also raised difficult questions. If a drug trafficker leaves drugs with a third person temporarily, what criminal liability is incurred by the third person when he/she returns the drugs to the trafficker? Will returning the drug to its owner under these circumstances, which are different from those in *Dempsey* (above), amount to 'supplying'? This situation was faced by the House of Lords in *R* v *Maginnis* [1987] AC 303. In that case their Lordships decided that Maginnis would have been 'supplying' the controlled drug had he returned it to the drug trafficker who had left a package of cannabis resin in Maginnis' car. Therefore he was in possession with intent to supply and so committed an offence under s. 5(3) (**see para. 3.8.5.6**). Once again however, the court expressed the view that if the person left with temporary possession of the controlled drug was not benefiting from so possessing it, there would be no 'supplying'. That being the case, it is at least arguable that the third person is *aiding and abetting* the trafficker to possess with intent to supply.

This issue has been further complicated by a decision involving a person who claimed that he had been coerced into holding controlled drugs for unnamed dealers. When found in possession of the drugs, the defendant claimed the defence of duress and said that he had only been an 'involuntary custodian' of them, intending to return them at a later date. The Court of Appeal decided that it was irrelevant whether a person was a voluntary or involuntary custodian of the drugs and that an intention to return them to their depositor amounted to an 'intention to supply' (*R* v *Panton* (2001) *The Times*, 27 March).

If a police informer provides a controlled drug to another in order that the other be arrested, there will still be a 'supplying' of the drug (*R* v *X* [1994] Crim LR 827).

Injecting Others

Injecting another with his/her own controlled drug has been held not to amount to 'supplying' in a case where the defendant assisted in pushing down the plunger of a syringe that the other person was already using. Parker CJ's comments in that case suggest that simply injecting another person with their own drug would not amount to 'supplying' (*R* v *Harris* [1968] 1 WLR 769). It may, however, amount to an offence of 'poisoning' under s. 23 of the Offences Against the Person Act 1861. The key problem with charging the supplier of drugs for self-injection by someone who then dies as a result lies in the issues of causation. While there are some authorities that say a supplier of a drug for self-injection which leads to the death of the recipient *can potentially* amount to unlawful act manslaughter great difficulties have arisen and the general view is that the supplier is unlikely to be held liable for *causing* death in such a case (see *R* v *Dias* [2002] 2 Cr App R 5). Where the defendant carries out the injection as opposed to merely the supply of the drug, liability for causing the death of another in this way can be made out however—even if the drug injected is not a controlled drug (see *R* v *Andrews* [2003] Crim LR 477—injection of insulin with consent; see also *R* v *Rogers* [2003] 1 WLR 1374—applying and holding a tourniquet to the arm of a drug abuser while injecting heroin can amount to the *actus reus* for manslaughter).

Dividing up controlled drugs which have been jointly purchased will amount to 'supplying' (*R* v *Buckley* (1979) 69 Cr App R 371).

The Court of Appeal has held that there is no statutory defence of 'religious use' to the above offence and that, even where it was accepted that the supply was for religious purposes, bringing a prosecution for the offence did not amount to an infringement of the defendant's rights under articles 8 and 9 of the European Convention on Human Rights (*R* v *Taylor* [2002] 1 Cr App R 314).

The offence of offering to supply a controlled drug is complete when the offer is made. It is irrelevant whether or not the defendant actually has the means to meet the offer or even intends to carry it out (see *R* v *Goodard* [1992] Crim LR 588). If the offer is made by conduct alone (i.e. without any words), it may be difficult to prove this offence. If words are used, the defence under s. 28 (**see para. 3.8.4**) does not appear to apply (see *R* v *Mitchell* [1992] Crim LR 723). If the offer is made to an undercover police officer, the offence is still committed and the defendant cannot claim that such an offer was not a 'real' offer (*R* v *Kray* (1998) 10 November, unreported).

In each case it will be a question of fact for the magistrate(s)/jury to decide whether or not the conduct amounted to a supply or offer to supply.

3.8.5.4 Points to Prove

In order to prove the offence of being concerned in the supply/offer to supply a controlled drug, you must show:

- the actual supply of, or making of an offer to supply, a controlled drug
- the participation of the defendant in that enterprise, and
- knowledge by the defendant that the enterprise involved the supply of, or making of an offer to supply, a controlled drug

(per the Court of Appeal in *R* v *Hughes* (1985) 81 Cr App R 344).

If the object of a conspiracy is to supply a controlled drug to a co-conspirator, any subsequent charge must make that clear; stating that the defendants conspired to supply the drug to 'another' implies that the supply was to be made to someone *other than any of the conspirators* (*R* v *Jackson* [2000] 1 Cr App R 97n).

3.8.5.5 Possession

OFFENCE: **Possession of Controlled Drug—*Misuse of Drugs Act 1971, s. 5(2)***

• Triable either way • Class A (seven years' imprisonment and/or fine on indictment; six months' imprisonment and/or prescribed sum summarily) • Class B (five years' imprisonment and/or fine on indictment; three months' imprisonment and/or fine summarily) • Class C (two years' imprisonment and/or fine on indictment; three months' imprisonment and/or fine summarily)

The Misuse of Drugs Act 1971, s. 5 states:

> (2) Subject to section 28 of this Act and to subsection (4) below, it is an offence for a person to have a controlled drug in his possession in contravention of subsection (1) . . .

KEYNOTE

See para. 3.8.2 above for meaning of 'possession'.

In 2004, the Home Secretary consulted the Advisory Council on the Misuse of Drugs (ACMD) for advice on changing the classification of cannabis. The Advisory Council was clear that cannabis is a harmful drug and should remain illegal; however the toxicity and harmfulness of cannabis is not comparable either with Class A drugs, such as crack, heroin or ecstasy, or with substances such as amphetamines, which are Class B (under the Misuse of Drugs Act 1971). The Council therefore recommended that cannabis and all cannabis preparations, including cannabis resin, should be reclassified to Class C. The government accepted the recommendation and cannabis was re-classified as a Class C drug. The fact that cannabis has been re-classified does not mean that possession is no longer a crime, as the then Home Secretary stated, 'all controlled drugs are harmful, all will remain illegal'.

Where the controlled drug involved is a fungus containing psilocin (a class A drug) or an ester of psilocin (commonly known as magic mushrooms) possession will not be unlawful in certain circumstances. In summary, those circumstances are generally where the fungus is growing *uncultivated* and it:

- is picked by a person already in *lawful possession* of it (for example the landowner on whose land the mushrooms are growing) for the purpose of delivering it (as soon as is reasonably practicable) into the custody of a person lawfully entitled to take custody of it and it remains in that person's possession for (and in accordance with) that purpose; or

- it is picked by anyone either for the purpose of delivering it (as soon as reasonably practicable) into the custody of a person lawfully entitled to take custody of it or destroying it (as soon as is reasonably practicable) and it is held for that purpose.

Note that there is no defence of medical necessity to the offence of possession of a controlled drug and the courts will not condone any form of self-prescription where controlled drugs are involved.

3.8.5.6 Possession with Intent to Supply

OFFENCE: **Possession with Intent to Supply—*Misuse of Drugs Act 1971, s. 5(3)***

• Triable either way • Class A (life imprisonment and/or fine on indictment; six months' imprisonment and/or prescribed sum summarily) • Class B (14 years' imprisonment and/or fine on indictment; six months' imprisonment and/or prescribed sum summarily) • Class C (14 years' imprisonment and/or fine on indictment; three months' imprisonment and/or fine summarily)

The Misuse of Drugs Act 1971, s. 5 states:

> (3) Subject to section 28 of this Act, it is an offence for a person to have a controlled drug in his possession, whether lawfully or not, with intent to supply it to another in contravention of section 4(1) of this Act.

KEYNOTE

This is a crime of *specific* intent.

It is important to note that the lawfulness or otherwise of the *possession* is irrelevant; what matters here is the lawfulness of the intended supply. If a vet or a police officer or some other person is in lawful possession of a controlled drug but they intend to supply it unlawfully to another, this offence will be made out.

You must show that the intention was that *the person in possession of the controlled drug* (rather than some third party) would supply it at some point in the future (*R* v *Greenfield* [1984] 78 Cr App R 179).

If more than one person has possession of the relevant controlled drug, you must show an individual intention to supply it by each person charged; it is not enough to show a joint venture whereby one or more parties simply knew of another's intent (*R* v *Downes* [1984] Crim LR 552). Given the decision of the Court of Appeal in *Kray* (**see para. 3.8.5.3**), possession with intent to supply a controlled drug to a person who is in fact an undercover police officer would appear to amount to an offence under this section.

All that is necessary in proving the offence under s. 5(3) is to show that the defendant had a controlled drug in his/her possession and intended to supply that substance to another. If the substance in the defendant's possession is a Class A drug and he/she intended to supply it to another person, the fact that he/she thought the drug was some other type of drug does not matter (*R* v *Leeson* [2000] 1 Cr App R 233).

While the possession by a defendant of drugs paraphernalia (e.g. clingfilm, paper, scales, contact details, etc.) will be relevant evidence to show that he/she was an active dealer in drugs generally, it does not prove the intention to supply and the trial judge will give a jury very careful directions as to the probative value of such items found in the defendant's possession (see *R* v *Haye* [2003] Crim LR 287).

Where a Rastafarian was prosecuted for possessing cannabis with intent to supply others as part of their religious worship, he claimed that his rights under articles 8 and 9 of the European Convention had been unnecessarily and disproportionately interfered with. The Court of Appeal, while reducing the sentence, held that such a prosecution had been properly brought (*R* v *Taylor* [2002] Crim LR 314).

In proving an intention to supply you may be able to adduce evidence of the defendant's unexplained wealth (*R* v *Smith (Ivor)* [1995] Crim LR 940) or the presence of large sums of money with the drugs seized (see *R* v *Wright* [1994] Crim LR 55).

For the meaning of 'supply', **see para. 3.8.5.2**. Note that the Drugs Act 2005 introduces a statutory presumption that, where a person has a certain quantity of drugs in their possession, their intention was to supply others. At the time of writing, this provision has not been brought into force.

3.8.5.7 Cultivation of Cannabis

OFFENCE: **Cultivation of Cannabis—*Misuse of Drugs Act 1971, s. 6***

- Triable either way • 14 years' imprisonment and/or a fine on indictment • Six months' imprisonment and/or prescribed sum summarily

The Misuse of Drugs Act 1971, s. 6 states:

(1) Subject to any regulations under section 7 of this Act for the time being in force, it shall not be lawful for a person to cultivate any plant of the genus *Cannabis*.

(2) Subject to section 28 of this Act, it is an offence to cultivate any such plant in contravention of subsection (1) above.

KEYNOTE

'Cultivate' is not defined but it appears that you would have to show some element of attention (such as watering or feeding) to the plant by the defendant in order to prove this offence. This offence does not permit police officers to tend plants which have been seized as evidence in order to preserve them as exhibits for court.

In proving the offence, you need only show that the plant is of the genus *Cannabis* and that the defendant cultivated it; you need not show that the defendant knew it to be a cannabis plant (*R* v *Champ* [1981] 73 Cr App R 367).

A person may be licensed to cultivate cannabis plants by the Secretary of State (under reg. 12 of the Misuse of Drugs Regulations 2001).

3.8.5.8 Supply of Articles

OFFENCE: **Supplying Articles for Administering or Preparing Controlled Drugs—*Misuse of Drugs Act 1971, s. 9A***

- Triable summarily • Six months' imprisonment and/or fine

The Misuse of Drugs Act 1971, s. 9A states:

(1) A person who supplies or offers to supply any article which may be used or adapted to be used (whether by itself or in combination with another article or other articles) in the administration by any person of a controlled drug to himself or another, believing that the article (or the article as adapted) is to be so used in circumstances where the administration is unlawful, is guilty of an offence.

(2) ...

(3) A person who supplies or offers to supply any article which may be used to prepare a controlled drug for administration by any person to himself or another believing that the article is to be so used in circumstances where the administration is unlawful is guilty of an offence.

KEYNOTE

This offence is designed to address the provision of drug 'kits'.

'Supply' for these purposes is likely to be interpreted in the same way as for the earlier sections in the 1971 Act.

Hypodermic syringes, or parts of them, are not covered by this offence (s. 9A(2)).

The administration for which the articles are intended must be 'unlawful'. Section 9A states:

> (4) For the purposes of this section, any administration of a controlled drug is unlawful except—
> (a) the administration by any person of a controlled drug to another in circumstances where the administration of the drug is not unlawful under section 4(1) of this Act, or
> (b) the administration by any person of a controlled drug to himself in circumstances where having the controlled drug in his possession is not unlawful under section 5(1) of this Act.
> (5) In this section, references to administration by any person of a controlled drug to himself include a reference to his administering it to himself with the assistance of another.

3.8.5.9 Occupiers, etc.

OFFENCE: **Occupier or Manager of Premises Permitting Drug Misuse—*Misuse of Drugs Act 1971, s. 8***

• Triable either way • Class A or B (14 years' imprisonment and/or fine on indictment; six months' imprisonment and/or prescribed sum summarily) • Class C (14 years' imprisonment and/or a fine on indictment; three months' imprisonment and/or fine summarily)

The Misuse of Drugs Act 1971, s. 8 states:

> A person commits an offence if, being the occupier or concerned in the management of any premises, he knowingly permits or suffers any of the following activities to take place on those premises, that is to say—
> (a) producing or attempting to produce a controlled drug in contravention of section 4(1) of this Act;
> (b) supplying or attempting to supply a controlled drug to another in contravention of section 4(1) of this Act, or offering to supply a controlled drug to another in contravention of section 4(1);
> (c) preparing opium for smoking;
> (d) smoking cannabis, cannabis resin or prepared opium.

KEYNOTE

The courts have adopted a 'common sense' approach to the interpretation of whether someone is an 'occupier' or not (see *R* v *Tao* [1977] QB 141). You will not need to prove that a defendant falls within some narrow legal meaning of an occupier. What is important in proving this offence is showing that the defendant had enough control over the premises to prevent the sort of activity listed above (see *R* v *Coid* [1998] Crim LR 199).

If a person cannot be shown to be an occupier in this sense, it may be that he/she can be shown to be involved in the planning, organising and actual use of the premises by taking part in more than just menial tasks. If so, this level of involvement may amount to 'management' of the premises (see *R* v *Josephs* (1977) 65 Cr App R 253).

'Premises' is not defined and has not been clarified at common law but the meaning has been given a wide definition elsewhere (such as in the Police and Criminal Evidence Act 1984.

The permitting or suffering of these activities requires a degree of *mens rea Sweet* v *Parsley* [1970] AC 132—even if that degree is little more than wilful blindness (see *R* v *Thomas* (1976) 63 Cr App R 65). For the purposes of s. 8(b)—and therefore presumably s. 8(a)—it is not necessary to show that the defendant knew exactly which drugs were being produced, supplied etc.; only that they were 'controlled drugs' (*R* v *Bett* [1999] 1 All ER 600).

However, the precise activities that are described under s. 8 will need to be proved. So, for instance, if the offence charged is one of knowingly permitting the smoking of cannabis (under s. 8 (d)), it must be shown that this actually took place; it is not enough that the owner/occupier had given permission for this to happen (see *R* v *Auguste* (2003) *The Times,* 15 December).

An occupier who permits the growing of cannabis plants also commits this offence (*Taylor* v *Chief Constable of Kent* [1981] 1 WLR 606).

An occupier will not commit the above offence *in relation to the smoking of cannabis or cannabis resin* if the premises are covered by a research licence from the Secretary of State (see reg. 13 of the Misuse of Drugs Regulations 2001).

3.8.5.10 Closure Notices

Section 1 of the Anti-social Behaviour Act 2003 states:

(1) This section applies to premises if a police officer not below the rank of superintendent (the authorising officer) has reasonable grounds for believing—
  (a) that at any time during the relevant period the premises have been used in connection with the unlawful use, production or supply of a Class A controlled drug, and
  (b) that the use of the premises is associated with the occurrence of disorder or serious nuisance to members of the public.

KEYNOTE

This provision is primarily designed to allow the police to close so-called 'crack houses'. If the above conditions are met the authorising officer may authorise the issuing of a closure notice.

The 'relevant period' referred to means the period of three months ending with the day on which the authorising officer considers whether to authorise the issue of a closure notice in respect of the premises (s. 1(10)).

'Premises' are defined as including any land or other place (whether enclosed or not) and any outbuildings which are or are used as part of the premises (s. 11).

The authorising officer may authorise the issue of a closure notice in respect of premises to which this section applies if he/she is satisfied:

(a) that the local authority for the area in which the premises are situated has been consulted;
(b) that reasonable steps have been taken to establish the identity of any person who lives on the premises or who has control of or responsibility for or an interest in the premises.

An authorisation may be given orally or in writing, but if it is given orally the authorising officer must confirm it in writing as soon as is practicable (s. 1(3)).

Note that it is immaterial whether any person has been convicted of an offence relating to the use, production or supply of a controlled drug (though clearly it will help in showing relevant grounds to support a closure notice and a closure order (see below) if someone has been convicted in connection with the use of the premises). The Secretary of State may make regulations specifying premises or descriptions of premises to which this power does not apply (s. 1(9)).

There is also a general power for local authorities to make a closure order in relation to noise and nuisance being caused in connection with the use of premises under s. 40 of the Act.

3.8.5.11 The Notice

The notice, which must be served by a police officer, must also:

- give notice that an application will be made under s. 2 for the closure of the premises
- state that access to the premises by any person (other than a person who habitually resides in the premises or the owner of the premises) is prohibited
- specify the date and time when and the place at which the application will be heard
- explain the effects of a closure order
- state that failure to comply with the notice amounts to an offence
- give information about the names of and means of contacting people and organisations in the area that provide advice about housing and legal matters.

Service of the notice will be effected by fixing a copy of the notice to:

- at least one prominent place on the premises
- each normal means of access to the premises
- any outbuildings which appear to the constable to be used with or as part of the premises; and

by giving a copy of the notice to at least one person who appears to the constable to have control of or responsibility for the premises and also to any person who lives on the premises or who has control of or responsibility for or an interest in the premises (see s. 1(6)).

For the purpose of effecting service of the notice a constable may enter any premises to which the section applies, using reasonable force if necessary (s. 1(7A)).

3.8.5.12 The Closure Order

If a closure notice has been issued under s. 1 a police officer must apply to a magistrates' court for the making of a closure order and that application must be heard by the court not later than 48 hours after the notice has been served (s. 2).

However, the court may adjourn the hearing of the application for a period of not more than 14 days to enable the occupier or another person with control of, responsibility for or an interest in the premises to show why an order should not be made (s. 2(6)).

The magistrates' court cannot use a power under other enactments relating to adjournments to adjourn any hearing of that application for more than 14 days (see *Commissioner of Police for the Metropolis* v *Hooper* [2005] EWHC 199 (Admin)).

The magistrates' court may make a closure order only if it is satisfied that:

- the premises in respect of which the closure notice was issued have been used in connection with the unlawful use, production or supply of a Class A controlled drug
- the use of the premises is associated with the occurrence of disorder or serious nuisance to members of the public, and
- the making of the order is necessary to prevent the occurrence of such disorder or serious nuisance for the period specified in the order.

(s. 2(3))

A closure order is an order that all or any part of the premises are closed to all people for such period (not exceeding three months) as the court decides (s. 2(4)). The police can apply for an order to be extended at any time before it expires but that application must be authorised by an officer not below the rank of superintendent after consultation with the local authority (see s. 5). An order cannot be extended beyond a total of six months

(s. 5(5)). Further specific provisions are made by the Act in relation to the discharge of closure notices and the bringing of appeals.

3.8.5.13 Enforcement

A police officer or an authorised person may enter the premises in respect of which the order is made and/or do anything reasonably necessary to secure the premises against entry by any person and may use reasonable force to do so (see s. 3).

A police officer or authorised person may also enter the premises at any time while the order is in force for the purpose of carrying out essential maintenance of or repairs to the premises (s. 3(5)).

A police officer or authorised person seeking to enter the premises for these purposes must, if required to do so by or on behalf of the owner, occupier or other person in charge of the premises, produce evidence of his/her identity and authority before entering the premises (s. 3(4)).

3.8.5.14 Obstructing or Breaching Closure Order

OFFENCE: **Obstruction and Breaching Closure Order—*Anti-social Behaviour Act 2003, s. 4***

- Triable summarily • Six months' imprisonment and/or fine

The Anti-social Behaviour Act 2003, s. 4 states:

(1) A person commits an offence if he remains on or enters premises in contravention of a closure notice.

(2) A person commits an offence if—
(a) he obstructs a constable or an authorised person acting under section 1(6) or 3(2),
(b) he remains on premises in respect of which a closure order has been made, or
(c) he enters the premises.

KEYNOTE

A person does not commit an offence under s. 4(1) or s. 4(2)(b) or (c) if he/she has a reasonable excuse for entering or being on the premises (as the case may be) (s. 4(4)).

Any person who occupies or owns any part of a building or structure in which closed premises are situated and in respect of which the closure order does not have effect may apply to the court for an order allowing access to any part of the premises.

3.8.5.15 Importation of Controlled Drugs

It is an offence under s. 3 of the Misuse of Drugs Act 1971 to import or export a controlled drug unless authorised by the regulations made under the Act. The relevant offences and their respective penalties are contained in the Customs and Excise Management Act 1979. Schedule 1 to the 1979 Act provides for the following penalties for the improper importation or exportation of controlled drugs:

- **Class A**—life imprisonment
- **Class B**—14 years' imprisonment
- **Class C**—14 years' imprisonment.

3.8.5.16 **Assisting or Inducing Offence Outside United Kingdom**

OFFENCE: **Assisting or Inducing Misuse of Drugs Offence Outside UK—*Misuse of Drugs Act 1971, s. 20***

- Triable either way • 14 years' imprisonment and/or a fine on indictment
- Six months' imprisonment and/or fine summarily

The Misuse of Drugs Act 1971, s. 20 states:

> A person commits an offence if in the United Kingdom he assists in or induces the commission in any place outside the United Kingdom of an offence punishable under the provisions of a corresponding law in force in that place.

KEYNOTE

In order to prove this offence, you must show that the offence outside the United Kingdom actually took place. The circumstances where this offence is likely to be committed will clearly overlap with the offences of importation/exportation (see para. 3.8.5.15).

'Assisting' has been held to include taking containers to another country in the knowledge that they would later be filled with a controlled drug and sent on to a third country (*R* v *Evans* (1977) 64 Cr App R 237). For an offence to amount to one under 'corresponding law' for these purposes, a certificate relating to the domestic law concerned with the misuse of drugs must be obtained from the government of the relevant country (s. 36).

3.8.5.17 **Incitement**

OFFENCE: **Incitement—*Misuse of Drugs Act 1971, s. 19***

- Triable and punishable as for substantive offence incited

The Misuse of Drugs Act 1971, s. 19 states:

> It is an offence for a person to incite another to commit such an offence.

KEYNOTE

Although the offence of incitement exists for most other offences generally, the Act makes a specific offence of inciting another to commit an offence under its provisions. On the arguments in *DPP* v *Armstrong* [2000] Crim LR 379, it would seem that a person inciting an undercover police officer may commit an offence under s. 19 even though there was no possibility of the officer actually being induced to commit the offence.

3.8.6 Enforcement

In addition to the general policing powers available for offences, the 1971 Act provides a number of specific enforcement powers.

3.8.6.1 **Powers of Entry, Search and Seizure**

The Misuse of Drugs Act 1971, s. 23 states:

> (1) A constable or other person authorised in that behalf by a general or special order of the Secretary of State (or in Northern Ireland either of the Secretary of State or the Ministry of Home Affairs for Northern Ireland) shall, for the purposes of the execution of this Act, have power to enter the premises of a person carrrying on business as a producer or supplier of any controlled drugs and to demand the production of, and to inspect, any books or documents relating to dealings in any such drugs and to inspect any stocks of any such drugs.

(2) If a constable has reasonable grounds to suspect that any person is in possession of a controlled drug in contravention of this Act or of any regulations made thereunder, the constable may—
   (a) search that person, and detain him for the purpose of searching him;
   (b) search any vehicle or vessel in which the constable suspects that the drug may be found, and for that purpose require the person in control of the vehicle or vessel to stop it;
   (c) seize and detain, for the purposes of proceedings under this Act, anything found in the course of the search which appears to the constable to be evidence of an offence under this Act.

In this subsection 'vessel' includes a hovercraft within the meaning of the Hovercraft Act 1968; and nothing in this subsection shall prejudice any power of search or any power to seize or detain property which is exercisable by a constable apart from this subsection.

(3) If a justice of the peace (or in Scotland a justice of the peace, a magistrate or a sheriff) is satisfied by information on oath that there is reasonable ground for suspecting—
   (a) that any controlled drugs are, in contravention of this Act or of any regulations made thereunder, in the possession of a person on any premises; or
   (b) that a document directly or indirectly relating to, or connected with, a transaction or dealing which was, or an intended transaction or dealing which would if carried out be, an offence under this Act, or in the case of a transaction or dealing carried out or intended to be carried out in a place outside the United Kingdom, an offence against the provisions of a corresponding law in force in that place, is in the possession of a person on any premises,

he may grant a warrant authorising any constable acting for the police area in which the premises are situated at any time or times within one month from the date of the warrant, to enter, if need be by force, the premises named in the warrant, and to search the premises and any persons found therein and, if there is reasonable ground for suspecting that an offence under this Act has been committed in relation to any controlled drugs found on the premises or in the possession of any such persons, or that a document so found is such a document as is mentioned in paragraph (b) above, to seize and detain those drugs or that document, as the case may be.

KEYNOTE

This is a very wide statutory provision granting authority for a broad range of enforcement measures in connection with controlled drugs.

Particular care will need to be taken when drafting the application for a warrant under s. 23. Where police officers are on premises under the authority of such a warrant it will be important to have established the precise *extent* of the warrant. If such a warrant authorises the search of *premises only*, that in itself will not give the officers authority to search *people* found on those premises unless the officer can point to some other power authorising the search (see e.g. *Chief Constable of Thames Valley Police* v *Hepburn* (2002) *The Times*, 19 December).

However, where the warrant authorises the search of premises *and* people, the Divisional Court has held that it is reasonable to restrict the movement of people within the premises to allow the search to be conducted properly (see *DPP* v *Meaden* (2004) *The Times*, 2 January).

PACE Code A, applies to the exercise of any power to search people for controlled drugs specifically included in a warrant issued under s. 23.

The Serious Organised Crime and Police Act 2005 has not changed the duration of a warrant issued under s. 23 of the Misuse of Drugs Act 1971. A warrant issued under s. 23 of the Act lasts for a period of one month from the date of issue.

3.8.6.2 Obstruction

OFFENCE: **Obstruction—*Misuse of Drugs Act 1971, s. 23(4)***

- Triable either way • Two years' imprisonment and/or a fine on indictment • Six months' imprisonment and/or fine summarily

The Misuse of Drugs Act 1971, s. 23 states:

(4) A person commits an offence if he—
(a) intentionally obstructs a person in the exercise of his powers under this section; or
(b) conceals from a person acting in the exercise of his powers under subsection (1) above any such books, documents, stocks or drugs as are mentioned in that subsection; or
(c) without reasonable excuse (proof of which shall lie on him) fails to produce any such books or documents as are so mentioned where their production is demanded by a person in the exercise of his powers under that subsection.

KEYNOTE

The offence of obstructing a person in the exercise of his/her powers is only committed if the obstruction was intentional (*R* v *Forde* (1985) 81 Cr App R 19).

3.8.6.3 Travel Restriction Orders

The Criminal Justice and Police Act 2001 makes provision for courts to impose travel restrictions on offenders convicted of drug trafficking offences. Travel restriction orders prohibit the offender from leaving the United Kingdom at any time during the period beginning from his/her release from custody (other than on bail or temporary release for a fixed period) and up to the end of the order. The minimum period for such an order is two years (s. 33(3)).

Where a court

- has convicted a person of a drug trafficking offence
- and it has determined that a sentence of four years or more is appropriate

it is under a *duty* to consider whether or not a travel restriction order would be appropriate (s. 33). If the court decides not to impose an order, it must give its reasons for not doing so.

An offender may also be required to surrender his/her UK passport as part of the order.

The offences which are covered by travel restriction orders include the production and supply of controlled drugs (**see paras 3.8.5.1 and 3.8.5.2**), the importation/exportation offences described at **para. 3.8.5.15** along with attempting, or inciting—either at common law or under the Misuse of Drugs Act 1971, s. 19 (**see para. 3.8.5.17**).

The Secretary of State may add to this list (see s. 34(2)).

An offender may apply to the court that made a restriction order to have it revoked or suspended (s. 35) and the court must consider the strict criteria set out in s. 35 when considering any such suspension or revocation. If an order is suspended, the offender has a legal obligation to be back in the United Kingdom when the period of suspension ends (s. 35(5)(a)).

The general importance of all this to police officers is in the offence below.

OFFENCE: **Contravening a Travel Restriction Order—*Criminal Justice and Police Act 2001, s. 36***

- Triable either way • Five years' imprisonment and/or a fine on indictment
- Six months' imprisonment and/or fine summarily

The Criminal Justice and Police Act 2001, s. 36 states:

(1) A person who leaves the United Kingdom at a time when he is prohibited from leaving it by a travel restriction order is guilty of an offence . . .

(2) A person who is not in the United Kingdom at the end of a period during which a prohibition imposed on him by a travel restriction order has been suspended shall be guilty of an offence . . .

KEYNOTE

These offences make no specific requirement for a particular state of mind. The first offence simply requires proof of two things—that there was an order in existence in respect of the offender and that he/she left the United Kingdom during the time it was in force. There is no requirement that the person leave the United Kingdom *voluntarily* in order to be guilty (although they would have a pretty good argument if they were taken out of the jurisdiction against their will or without their knowledge).

However, travel restriction orders do not prevent the proper exercise of any prescribed power to remove a person from the United Kingdom (see s. 37—the relevant powers are set out in the Travel Restriction Order (Prescribed Removal Powers) Order 2002 (SI 2002/313)). For instance, if the Secretary of State deports someone who is under a travel restriction order, that person would not commit the above offence.

The second offence requires proof that there was a suspended order in existence in respect of the offender and that, at the end of the suspension period, the offender was not in the United Kingdom.

Failing to deliver up a UK passport when required by an order will be a summary offence carrying six months' imprisonment and/or a fine (s. 36(3)).

3.9 Firearms and Gun Crime

3.9.1 Firearms Generally

Section 57 of the Firearms Act 1968 states:

(1) In this Act, the expression 'firearm' means a lethal barrelled weapon of any description from which any shot, bullet or other missile can be discharged, and includes—
  (a) any prohibited weapon, whether it is such a lethal weapon as aforesaid or not; and
  (b) any component part of such a lethal or prohibited weapon; and
  (c) any accessory to any such weapon designed or adapted to diminish the noise or flash caused by firing the weapon.

KEYNOTE

'Lethal barrelled weapon' is not defined under the 1968 Act.

The way in which the courts have determined whether or not something amounts to such a weapon is by asking:

- Can any shot, bullet or other missile be discharged from the weapon, or
- Could the weapon be adapted so that any shot, bullet or other missile can be discharged?
- If so, is the weapon a 'lethal barrelled' weapon?

(See *Grace* v *DPP* [1989] COD 374.)

A weapon is a lethal barrelled weapon if it is capable of causing injury, irrespective of the intentions of its maker (*Read* v *Donovan* [1947] KB 326). In determining whether a firearm is in fact a lethal barrelled weapon from which missiles can be discharged a court need not consider any specific evidence of someone who has seen the effects of it being fired. Therefore, where magistrates had heard evidence from a gun shop assistant that an air rifle was in working order, they were entitled to conclude that it fell within the definition even though no evidence was given as to the actual effects of the gun being fired (*Castle* v *DPP* (1998) *The Times*, 3 April).

Air pistols (*R* v *Thorpe* [1987] 1 WLR 383), imitation revolvers (*Cafferata* v *Wilson* [1936] 3 All ER 149) and signalling pistols (*Read* v *Donovan*, above) have all been held to be lethal barrelled weapons. That is not to say, however, that they will always be so and each case must be determined in the light of the evidence available.

Although ordinary air weapons not classified as being specially dangerous may not be capable of firing a lethal shot, possession of such a weapon was held, under the former legislation, still to be capable of amounting to an offence under s. 19 (see *Street* v *DPP* (2004) *The Times*, 23 January). In the context of the specific offence under s. 19, this decision has been overtaken in any event by the legislation but it is still of interest in defining the term 'firearm'.

Component parts, such as triggers or barrels, are also included in the definition, as are silencers and accessories to hide the muzzle flash of a weapon. If a defendant is found in possession of a silencer which has been manufactured for a weapon that is also in the defendant's possession, that will be enough to bring it under s. 57(1). If, however, the silencer is made for a different weapon, it may still come under the s. 57 definition but the prosecution will have to show that it could be used with the defendant's weapon and that he/she had it for that purpose. This slightly odd situtation is the result of the Court of Appeal's decision in *R* v *Buckfield* [1998] Crim LR 673. Following that reasoning, a silencer or accessory on its own does not appear to be a firearm for the purposes of s. 57(1). Section 57(1) does not include telescopic sights.

3.9.1.1 Deactivation of Firearms

A weapon may cease to be a firearm if it is deactivated in line with the provisions of the Firearms (Amendment) Act 1988, s. 8 which states:

> For the purposes of the principal Act and this Act it shall be presumed, unless the contrary is shown, that a firearm has been rendered incapable of discharging any shot, bullet or other missile, and has consequently ceased to be a firearm within the meaning of those Acts, if—
> (a) it bears a mark which has been approved by the Secretary of State for denoting that fact and which has been made either by one of the two companies mentioned in section 58(1) of the principal Act or by such other person as may be approved by the Secretary of State for the purposes of this section; and
> (b) that company or person has certified in writing that work has been carried out on the firearm in a manner approved by the Secretary of State for rendering it incapable of discharging any shot, bullet or other missile.

KEYNOTE

A deactivated weapon must remain in its complete state. Where it is disassembled the parts that are then made available are capable of being reassembled into a working weapon and are therefore component parts of a firearm (*R* v *Ashton* [2007] EWCA Crim 234).

The 'two companies' referred to in s. 8(a) above are the Society of the Mystery of Gunmakers of the City of London and the Birmingham Proof House.

3.9.2 Definitions

The law regulating firearms classifies weapons into several categories, each of which is specifically defined. As with offences under road traffic legislation, it is critical that the relevant definition is considered before deciding upon a particular charge or offence.

3.9.2.1 Prohibited Weapon

A prohibited weapon is defined under the Firearms Act 1968, s. 5. The definition formerly covered the more powerful or potentially destructive firearms—and their ammunition—such as automatic weapons and specialist ammunition.

Since the Firearms (Amendment) Acts of 1997, however, s. 5 also covers many small firearms which were formerly covered by other parts of the 1968 Act.

The test as to whether a weapon is a 'prohibited' weapon is a purely objective one and is not affected by the intentions of the defendant. Therefore, where a firearm was capable of successively discharging two or more missiles without repeated pressure on the trigger, that weapon was 'prohibited' irrespective of the intentions of the firearms dealer who was in possession of it (*R* v *Law* [1999] Crim LR 837).

Whereas a firearms certificate is usually needed in order to possess, buy or acquire firearms and ammunition, the authority of the Secretary of State is needed if the firearm or ammunition is a 'prohibited weapon'.

3.9.2.2 List of Prohibited Weapons and Ammunition

The full list of prohibited weapons and ammunition is contained in s. 5(1) and (1A) of the Firearms Act 1968 (**see Blackstone's Criminal Practice 2008, para. B12.50**). This list includes:

- automatic weapons
- most self-loading or pump-action weapons
- any firearm which either has a barrel less than 30 cm in length or is less than 60 cm in length overall, other than an air weapon, a muzzle-loading gun or a firearm designed as signalling apparatus
- most smooth bore revolvers
- any weapon, of whatever description, designed or adapted for the discharge of any noxious liquid, gas or other thing
- any air rifle, air gun or air pistol which uses, or is designed or adapted for use with, a self-contained gas cartridge system
- military weapons and ammunition including grenades and mortars.

KEYNOTE

In relation to weapons designed or adapted for the discharge of any noxious liquid, gas or other thing, taking empty washing-up bottles and filling them with a noxious fluid such as hydrochloric acid does not amount to adapting them, neither is such a thing a 'weapon' for the purposes of s. 5 (*R* v *Formosa, R* v *Upton* [1991] 2 QB 1).

An electric 'stun gun' has been held to be a prohibited weapon as it discharges an electric current (*Flack* v *Baldry* [1988] 1 WLR 393) and it continues to be such even if it is not working (*Brown* v *DPP* (1992) *The Times*, 27 March).

Note that s. 5A of the Firearms Act 1968 creates exemptions under the European Council Directive 91/477/EEC on control of the acquisition and possession of weapons [1991] OJ L256/51 which allows people from Member States to possess some prohibited weapons under certain circumstances.

3.9.2.3 Shotguns

A shotgun is defined under s. 1(3)(a) of the Firearms Act 1968. Section 1 (amended by Firearms (Amendment) Act 1988 s. 2) states:

(3) ...

(a) a shotgun within the meaning of this Act, that is to say a smooth-bore gun (not being an airgun) which—

(i) has a barrel not less than 24 inches in length and does not have any barrel with a bore exceeding 2 inches in diameter;

(ii) either has no magazine or has a non-detachable magazine incapable of holding more than two cartridges; and

(iii) is not a revolver gun...

(3A) A gun which has been adapted to have such a magazine as is mentioned in subsection (3)(a)(ii) above shall not be regarded as falling within that provision unless the magazine bears a mark approved by the Secretary of State for denoting that fact and that mark has been made, and the adaptation has been certified in writing as having been carried out in a manner approved by him, either by one of the two companies mentioned in section 58(1) of this Act or by such other person as may be approved by him for that purpose.

KEYNOTE

A barrel's length is measured from the muzzle to the point at which the charge is exploded on firing the weapon (s. 57(6)(a) of the 1968 Act).

For the 'two companies' referred to in s. 1(3A) above **see para. 3.9.1.1**.

3.9.2.4 Air Weapons

Air weapons are defined under s. 1(3)(b) of the Firearms Act 1968. In summary these are air rifles, air guns or air pistols which do not fall within s. 5(1) (**see para. 3.9.2.2**) and which are not of a type declared to be specially dangerous. Any air rifle, air gun or air pistol that uses or is designed or adapted for use with a self-contained gas cartridge system *does* fall within the definition of a prohibited weapon at s. 5(1).

Some air weapons are deemed to be specially dangerous and therefore subject to stricter control than conventional air weapons. Those which are subject to this stricter control are those declared to be so by the Secretary of State. Listed in r. 2 of the Firearms (Dangerous Air Weapons) Rules 1969, as amended, they include:

(1) [any] air rifle, air gun or air pistol—

(a) which is capable of discharging a missile so that the missile has, on being discharged from the muzzle of the weapon, kinetic energy in excess, in the case of an air pistol, of 6ft lb or, in the case of an air weapon other than an air pistol, of 12ft lb, or

(b) which is disguised as another object.

Note that this does not include a weapon falling within para. (1)(a) above and which is designed for use only when submerged in water (r. 2(2)).

The Violent Crime Reduction Act 2006 amended the Firearms Act 1968 and made it an offence for a person, other than a registered firearms dealer, to sell or transfer an air weapon, or expose such a weapon for sale or transfer, or have possession of such a weapon for sale or transfer (s. 3(1)(c) of the 1968 Act). The 2006 Act increased the age from 17 to 18 for the acquisition or possession of air weapons, and removed the age restriction for firing an air weapon beyond premises.

Section 32 of the 2006 Act also imposed a 'face to face' requirement on trade transactions by persons selling air weapons.

OFFENCE: **Sales of air weapons by way of trade or business to be face to face—*Violent Crime Reduction Act 2006, s. 32***

- Triable summarily • 51 weeks' imprisonment and/or a fine

The Violent Crime Reduction Act 2006, s. 32 states:

(1) This section applies where a person sells an air weapon by way of trade or business to an individual in Great Britain who is not registered as a firearms dealer.

(2) A person is guilty of an offence if, for the purposes of the sale, he transfers possession of the air weapon to the buyer otherwise than at a time when both—

(a) the buyer, and

(b) either the seller or a representative of his,

are present in person.

KEYNOTE

A representative of the seller is a reference to a person who is employed by the seller in his/her business as a registered firearms dealer; a registered firearms dealer who has been authorised by the seller to act on his/her behalf in relation to the sale; or a person who is employed by a person falling within s. 32(3)(b) in his/her business as a registered firearms dealer. This allows an air weapon to be sent from one registered firearms dealer to another to make the final transfer in person to the buyer. It also enables someone to buy an air weapon from a dealer in a distant part of the country without one or other party to the transaction having to make a long journey, while still preserving the safeguards of a face-to-face handover.

3.9.2.5 Section 1 Firearm

There is a group of firearms which, although not a category defined in the 1968 Act, are subject to a number of offences including s. 1 (see below). Firearms which fall into this group are often referred to as 'section 1 firearms' and include all firearms except shotguns (**see para. 3.9.2.3**) and conventional air weapons (**see para. 3.9.2.4**). However, shotguns which have been 'sawn off' (i.e. had their barrels shortened) are section 1 firearms, as are air weapons declared to be 'specially dangerous'.

Section 1 ammunition includes any ammunition for a firearm except:

- cartridges containing five or more shot, none of which is bigger than 0.36 inches in diameter;
- ammunition for an airgun, air rifle or air pistol; and
- blank cartridges not more than one inch in diameter (s. 1(4)).

3.9.2.6 Conversion

Some weapons which began their life as section 1 firearms or prohibited weapons will remain so even after their conversion to a shotgun, air weapon or other type of firearm (see s. 7 of the Firearms (Amendment) Act 1988).

3.9.2.7 Imitation Firearms

Some, though not all, offences which regulate the use of firearms will also apply to *imitation* firearms. Whether they do so can be found either in the specific wording of the offence, or by virtue of the Firearms Act 1982.

Put simply there are two types of imitation firearms:

- general imitations—those which have the appearance of firearms (which are covered by s. 57 of the Firearms Act 1968); and
- imitations of section 1 firearms—those which both have the appearance of a *section 1 firearm* and which can be readily converted into such a firearm (which are covered by ss. 1 and 2 of the Firearms Act 1982).

Where 'imitation firearms' are referred to *in the wording of the offence*, that offence will apply to the first category above, that is, 'anything which has the appearance of being a firearm'. The House of Lords has held that the definition in s. 57 requires the defendant to be carrying a 'thing' which is separate and distinct from him/herself and therefore capable of being possessed (*R* v *Bentham* [2005] 1 WLR 1057). Holding your fingers under your coat and pretending that this is a firearm—as happened in *Bentham*—will not therefore amount to an imitation firearm for the relevant offences. Their Lordships held that an unsevered hand or finger was part of oneself and therefore could not be 'possessed' in the way envisaged by the Act. The 'imitation' must have the appearance of a firearm and it is not necessary for any object to have been constructed, adapted or altered so as to resemble a firearm (*R* v *Williams* [2006] EWCA Crim 1650). In *K* v *DPP* [2006] EWHC 2183 it was held that in some circumstances a realistic toy gun, in this case a plastic ball bearing gun, could become an imitation firearm. Note that this category does not include anything which resembles a prohibited weapon *under s. 5(1)(b)*. Prohibited weapons under s. 5(1)(b) are those which are designed or adapted to discharge noxious liquid etc. (**see para. 3.9.2.2**).

In some other offences, *the definition of the 1982 Act is applicable*. These offences are all offences which involve section 1 firearms, except those under ss. 4(3) and (4), 16 to 20 and 47 of the 1968 Act.

If an offence does not come within either of the circumstances above, it will not apply to an imitation firearm.

Whether or not something has the appearance of being a firearm will be a question of fact for the jury/magistrate(s) to decide in each case.

The Violent Crime Reduction Act 2006, ss. 36 to 41, introduced measures to deal with the misuse of firearms. These sections created the three specific summary offences detailed below.

Section 36 makes it an offence to manufacture, import or sell realistic imitation firearms as defined in s. 38.

Section 39 makes it an offence to manufacture, modify or import an imitation firearm that does not conform to specifications set out in regulations to be made by the Secretary of State.

Section 40 inserted a new s. 24A into the 1968 Act and makes it an offence to sell an imitation firearm to a person under 18. It also makes it an offence for a person under 18 to purchase an imitation firearm (**see para. 3.9.7.2**).

KEYNOTE

For the purposes of the 2006 Act, an 'imitation firearm' is defined as that used in the Firearms Act 1968. A 'realistic imitation firearm' is defined as an imitation firearm which has an appearance that is so realistic as to make it indistinguishable, for all practical purposes, from a real firearm and is neither a deactivated firearm nor itself an antique (s. 38(1)). An imitation firearm will be regarded as distinguishable if its size, shape or principal colour is unrealistic for a real firearm (s. 38(3)). The Violent Crime Reduction Act 2006 (Realistic Imitation Firearms) Regulations 2007 (SI 2007/2606) provide defences for an offence under s. 36, and make provision in connection with the definition of 'realistic imitation firearm' in s. 38, specifying the sizes and colours which are to be regarded as unrealistic for a real firearm.

3.9.3 Possessing etc. Firearm or Ammunition without Certificate

OFFENCE: **Possessing etc. firearm or ammunition without certificate—*Firearms Act, 1968 s. 1***

- Triable either way • Five years' imprisonment and/or a fine on indictment
- Six months' imprisonment and/or a fine summarily

The Firearms Act 1968, s. 1 states:

(1) Subject to any exemption under this Act, it is an offence for a person—

(a) to have in his possession, or to purchase or acquire, a firearm to which this section applies without holding a firearm certificate in force at the time, or otherwise than as authorised by such a certificate;

(b) to have in his possession, or to purchase or acquire, any ammunition to which this section applies without holding a firearm certificate in force at the time, or otherwise than as authorised by such a certificate, or in quantities in excess of those so authorised.

KEYNOTE

This offence relates to those firearms described above as section 1 firearms.

If the firearm involved is a sawn-off shotgun, the offence becomes 'aggravated' (under s. 4(4)) and attracts a maximum penalty of seven years' imprisonment.

The Firearms Act 1982 applies to this section and therefore the second definition of 'imitation firearms' at para. 3.9.2.7 above applies here.

The certificate referred to is issued by the chief officer of police under s. 26A. Such certificates may carry significant restrictions on the types of firearms which the holder is allowed, together with the circumstances under which he/she may have them (see s. 44(1) of the Firearms (Amendment) Act 1997).

The purpose of the legislation regulating the licensing of firearms is to provide certainty and consistency in the effective control of such weapons. Therefore the issue of whether a certificate covers a particular category of weapon is a matter of law for the judge to decide and cannot be affected by the intentions or misunderstanding of the defendant (*R* v *Paul* (1998) 95(32) LSG 30).

For the forms to be used in relation to the grant of certificates and permits, see the Firearms Rules 1998 (SI 1998/1941 made under Firearms Act 1968).

A person may hold a European firearms pass or similar document, in which case he/she will be governed by the provision of ss. 32A to 32C of the Firearms Act 1968.

If a person has such a certificate which allows the possession etc. of the firearm in question and under the particular circumstances encountered, no offence is committed.

The Violent Crime Reduction Act 2006 has created a summary offence that restricts the purchase and sale of primers to persons who hold a relevant firearms certificate or who otherwise have lawful authority for having them (s. 35). This relates to the cap-type primers designed for use in metallic ammunition for a firearm, containing a chemical compound that detonates on impact.

3.9.3.1 Possession

As in other areas of criminal law, the meaning of possession is wider here than actual physical custody of the firearm in question. A person can remain in possession of a firearm even if someone else has custody of it (*Sullivan* v *Earl of Caithness* [1976] QB 966).

Possession for the purposes of this offence does not require any specific knowledge on the part of the defendant. For example, if X knows he is in possession of *something* (e.g. a box), then X is in possession of its contents, *even though X does not know what those contents are* (*R* v *Hussain* [1981] 1 WLR 416).

Therefore there is no need to prove that the defendant knew the nature of the thing which he/she possessed in order to prove this offence (and the offence under s. 19, **see para. 3.9.6.7**). If a defendant is carrying a rucksack and that rucksack turns out to contain ammunition for a section 1 firearm, the defendant is 'in possession' of that ammunition irrespective of his/her knowledge—or ignorance—of its presence in the rucksack (see *R* v *Waller* [1991] Crim LR 381 and *R* v *Cremin* [2007] EWCA Crim 666).

3.9.3.2 Acquire

Acquire will include hiring, accepting as a gift and borrowing (s. 57(4) of the Firearms Act 1968).

3.9.3.3 Exemptions

The offence specifies that it is subject to any exemptions under the 1968 Act. There are three main categories of exemption under the firearms legislation:

- General exemptions—listed below.
- European exemptions—these are made under s. 5A to reflect the European Weapons Directive (**see para. 3.9.5.1**).
- Special exemptions—which apply to the provisions affecting prohibited weapons under s. 5 (**see para. 3.9.5.1**).

Many of the exemptions overlap as they follow a fairly common sense approach to the necessary possession and use of firearms/ammunition in the course of work and leisure.

3.9.3.4 General Exemptions

The general exemptions, which apply to the provisions of ss. 1 to 5 of the Firearms Act 1968 are mainly concerned with the various occupations of people whom you might expect to be in contact with firearms in one form or another. They include:

Police permit holders

Under s. 7(1) of the 1968 Act, the chief officer of police may grant a permit authorising the possession of firearms or ammunition under the conditions specified in the permit.

Clubs, athletics and sporting purposes

Section 11 of the 1968 Act provides exemptions for a person:

- borrowing the firearm/ammunition from a certificate holder *for sporting purposes only* (s. 11(1));
- possessing a firearm at an athletic meeting for the purposes of starting races (s. 11(2));
- in charge of a miniature rifle range buying, acquiring or possessing miniature rifles and ammunition, and using them at such a rifle range (s. 11(4));
- who is a member of an approved rifle club, miniature rifle club or pistol club to possess a firearm or ammunition *when engaged as a club member in target practice* (s. 15(1) of the Firearms (Amendment) Act 1988);
- borrowing a shotgun from the occupier of private premises and using it on those premises in the occupier's presence (s. 11(5) of the 1968 Act);
- using a shotgun at a time and place approved by the chief officer of police for shooting at artificial targets (s. 11(6)).

Borrowed rifle on private premises

Section 16 of the Firearms (Amendment) Act 1988 allows a person to borrow a rifle from the occupier of private premises, provided the person is on those premises and in the presence of the occupier (or his/her servant), as long as the occupier holds a certificate and that the borrowing of the rifle complies with that certificate. The person borrowing the rifle may buy or acquire ammunition for it in accordance with the certificate's conditions.

Visitors' permits

Section 17 of the Firearms (Amendment) Act 1988 provides for the issuing of a visitors' permit by a chief officer of police and for the possession of firearms and ammunition by the holder of such a permit.

Visitors' permits will not be issued to anyone without a European firearms pass. It is a summary offence (punishable with six months' imprisonment) to make a false statement in order to get a visitors' permit, and it is a similar offence to fail to comply with any conditions within such a permit (see s. 17(10)).

Antiques as ornaments or curiosities

Section 58(2) of the 1968 Act allows for the sale, buying, transfer, acquisition or possession of antique firearms *as curiosities or ornaments*. Whether a firearm is such an antique will be a question of fact to be determined by the court in each case. Mere belief in the fact that a firearm is an antique will not be enough (*R* v *Howells* [1977] QB 614).

Authorised firearms dealers

Section 8(1) of the 1968 Act provides for registered firearms dealers (or their employees) to possess, acquire or buy firearms or ammunition in the ordinary course of their business without a certificate. If the possession etc. is not in the ordinary course of their business, the exemption will not apply.

KEYNOTE

In addition to the above, other occupations of people exempt include: auctioneers, carriers and warehouse staff; licensed slaughterers; theatrical performers; ships, aircraft or aerodrome equipment; Crown servants; proof houses; and holders of a museums licence.

3.9.4 Shotgun Offences

OFFENCE: **Possessing shotgun without certificate—*Firearms Act 1968, s. 2(1)***

- Triable either way • Five years' imprisonment and/or a fine on indictment
- Six months' imprisonment and/or a fine summarily

The Firearms Act 1968, s. 2 states:

(1) Subject to any exemption under this Act, it is an offence for a person to have in his possession, or to purchase or acquire, a shotgun without holding a certificate under this Act authorising him to possess shot guns.

KEYNOTE

For the definition of 'shotgun', see para. 3.9.2.3.

The relevant exemptions above will also apply to shotguns.

A shotgun certificate is granted by a chief officer of police under s. 26B of the 1968 Act and will have certain conditions attached to it. A person failing to comply with those conditions commits the following offence:

OFFENCE: **Failing to comply with conditions of shot gun certificate—*Firearms Act 1968, s. 2(2)***

- Triable summarily • Six months' imprisonment and/or a fine

The Firearms Act 1968, s. 2 states:

(2) It is an offence for a person to fail to comply with a condition subject to which a shot gun certificate is held by him.

The conditions and forms used in relation to the grant of shotgun certificates are contained in the Firearms Rules 1998 (SI 1998/1941) and the Firearms (Amendment) Rules 2005 (SI 2005/3344).

3.9.5 Possessing or Distributing Prohibited Weapons or Ammunition

OFFENCE: **Possessing or distributing prohibited weapons or ammunition—*Firearms Act 1968, s. 5***

- Triable either way • Ten years' imprisonment and/or a fine on indictment
- Six months' imprisonment and/or a fine summarily

The Firearms Act 1968, s. 5 states:

(1) A person commits an offence if, without the authority of the Secretary of State or the Scottish Ministers, he has in his possession, or purchases, or acquires, or manufactures, sells or transfers [a prohibited weapon or ammunition] . . .

KEYNOTE

See para. 3.9.2.1 for prohibited weapons. For 'possession', see para. 3.9.3.1.

'Self-loading' and 'pump-action' mean designed or adapted so that the weapon is either automatically reloaded, or is reloaded by manual operation of the fore-end or forestock (s. 57 of the 1968 Act).

Section 5(7) and (8) provides guidance in determining whether certain arms and ammunition will fall within the descriptions in s. 5, including the fact that any folding or detachable butt-stock of a firearm will not count when measuring the weapon's overall length.

3.9.5.1 Exemptions

The first set of exemptions were discussed in relation to the offence under s. 1 (**see para. 3.9.3.3**); the second and third set are relevant to the offences under s. 5. Those remaining exemptions are:

- European exemptions—exemptions to conform with the European Weapons Directive.
- Special exemptions.

European Weapons Directive

The European Weapons Directive (91/477/EEC) was brought into effect in order to adjust our domestic legislation in line with the expansion of the European internal market. Its effect is to create certain additional savings and exemptions in relation to the possession of, or some transactions in, specified firearms and ammunition by people who have the relevant certificates or who are recognised as collectors under the law of another country.

To this end, s. 5A of the Firearms Act 1968 provides for a number of occasions where the authority of the Secretary of State will not be required to possess or deal with certain weapons under certain conditions.

The main areas covered by s. 5A are:

- authorised collectors and firearms dealers possessing or being involved in transactions of weapons and ammunition;
- authorised people being involved in transactions of particular ammunition used for lawful shooting and slaughtering of animals, the management of an estate or the protection of other animals and humans.

Section 57(4A) of the Firearms Act 1968 makes other provisions in relation to the European directive as an authority for certain uses of firearms.

Special exemptions

The list of special exemptions to the offences involving firearms under s. 5(1)(aba) focuses largely on people in jobs where they will need to come into contact with firearms mainly in connection with animals or leisure activities.

The exemptions include:

- **Slaughterers**—A slaughterer, if entitled under s. 10 of the 1968 Act (**see para. 3.9.3.4**), may possess a slaughtering instrument. In addition, persons authorised by certificate to possess, buy, acquire, sell or transfer slaughtering instruments are exempt from the provisions of s. 5 (s. 2 of the Firearms (Amendment) Act 1997). This is the most common exemption.
- **Humane killing of animals**—A person authorised by certificate to possess, buy or acquire a firearm solely for use in connection with the humane killing of animals may possess, buy, acquire, sell or transfer such a firearm (s. 3 of the Firearms (Amendment) Act 1997). When determining whether a firearm falls within the meaning of a 'humane killer', the definition of a 'slaughtering instrument' under s. 57(4) may be referred to (*R* v *Paul (Benjamin)* (1998) 95(32) LSG 30).

- **Shot pistols for vermin**—A person authorised by certificate to possess, buy or acquire a 'shot pistol' solely for the shooting of vermin, may possess, buy, acquire, sell or transfer such a pistol (s. 4(1) of the Firearms (Amendment) Act 1997). A 'shot pistol' is a smooth-bored gun chambered for .410 cartridges or 9mm rim-fire cartridges (s. 4(2)).
- **Treatment of animals**—A person authorised by certificate to possess, buy or acquire a firearm for use in connection with the treatment of animals may possess, buy, acquire, sell or transfer any firearm or ammunition designed or adapted for the purpose of tranquillising or treating any animal (s. 8 of the Firearms (Amendment) Act 1997). This exemption also applies to offences involving firearms under s. 5(1)(b) and (c) (**see para. 3.9.2.2**).
- **Races at athletic meetings**—A person may possess a firearm at an athletic meeting for the purpose of starting races at that meeting (s. 5(a) of the Firearms (Amendment) Act 1997). Similarly, a person authorised by certificate to possess, buy or acquire a firearm solely for the purposes of starting such races may possess, buy, acquire, sell or transfer a firearm for such a purpose (s. 5(b)).
- **Trophies of war**—A person authorised by certificate to do so may possess a firearm which was acquired as a trophy before 1 January 1946 (s. 6 of the Firearms (Amendment) Act 1997).
- **Firearms of historic interest**—Some firearms are felt to be of particular historical, aesthetic or technical interest. Section 7(4) of the Firearms (Amendment) Act 1997 makes detailed provision for the exemption of such firearms, exemptions which exist in addition to the general exemptions under s. 58 of the Firearms Act 1968 (**see para. 3.9.3.4**). These provisions are set out in the Firearms (Amendment) Act 1997 (Firearms of Historic Interest) Order 1997 (SI 1997/1537) and the Firearms (Amendment) Act 1997 (Transitional Provisions and Savings) Regulations 1997 (SI 1997/1538).
- **Air weapons**—In relation to air weapons with self-contained gas cartridges, owned before 20 January 2004, the owner, if he/she applied for a firearms certificate before 1 April 2004, may retain his/her weapons.

3.9.6 Further Offences

Further to the more straightforward possession offences discussed above, there are a number of important offences where the purpose of the person with the firearm, or the circumstances in which he/she has it, are aggravating factors. These offences are discussed below.

3.9.6.1 Possession with Intent to Endanger Life

OFFENCE: **Possession with intent to endanger life—*Firearms Act 1968, s. 16***

- Triable on indictment • Life imprisonment and/or a fine

The Firearms Act 1968, s. 16 states:

> It is an offence for a person to have in his possession any firearm or ammunition with intent by means thereof to endanger life or to enable another person by means thereof to endanger life, whether any injury has been caused or not.

KEYNOTE

There is no reference to imitation firearms in the wording of the offence, neither does the 1982 Act apply, therefore this offence cannot be committed by possessing an imitation firearm (**see para. 3.9.2.7**).

The offence involves 'possession' (see para. 3.9.3.1); there is no need for the firearm to be produced or shown to another.

This is a crime of 'specific intent'. You will have to show an intention by the defendant to behave in a way that he/she knows will in fact endanger the life of another (*R* v *Brown and Ciarla* [1995] Crim LR 327).

That intent does not have to be an immediate one and it may be conditional (e.g. an intent to shoot someone if they do not do as they are asked) (*R* v *Bentham* [1973] QB 357).

The life endangered must be the life of 'another', not the defendant's (*R* v *Norton* [1977] Crim LR 478) but that other person may be outside the UK (*R* v *El-Hakkoui* [1975] 1 WLR 396).

The firearm must provide the means by which life is endangered; it is not enough to have a firearm at the time when life is endangered by some other means (e.g. by dangerous driving).

There may be occasions where self-defence can be raised in answer to a charge under s. 16 of the 1968 Act but these circumstances will be very unusual (see *R* v *Georgiades* [1989] 1 WLR 759). This defence could apply where the defendant is carrying a weapon for his own defence anticipating an imminent attack (*R* v *Salih* [2007] EWCA Crim 2750).

3.9.6.2 Possession with Intent to Cause Fear of Violence

OFFENCE: **Possession with intent to cause fear of violence—*Firearms Act 1968, s. 16A***

- Triable on indictment • Ten years' imprisonment and/or a fine

The Firearms Act 1968, s. 16A (added by Firearms (Amendment) Act 1994, s. 1) states:

It is an offence for a person to have in his possession any firearm or imitation firearm with intent—
(a) by means thereof to cause, or
(b) to enable another person by means thereof to cause,

any person to believe that unlawful violence will be used against him or another person.

KEYNOTE

This offence includes imitation firearms in the general sense (see para. 3.9.2.7).

This is a crime of 'specific intent'.

Section 16A is committed by possession, accompanied by an intention to cause fear of violence at or immediately before the defendant's actions which are designed to cause such fear (*R* v *Goluchowski* [2006] EWCA Crim 1972). There is no need for a firearm/imitation firearm to be produced or shown to anyone, though it must provide the 'means' of the threat. Possession of a firearm/imitation firearm while making a general threat to someone who does not know of its presence is unlikely to fall within this section.

3.9.6.3 Using Firearm to Resist Arrest

OFFENCE: **Using firearm to resist arrest—*Firearms Act 1968, s. 17(1)***

- Triable on indictment • Life imprisonment and/or a fine

The Firearms Act 1968, s. 17 states:

(1) It is an offence for a person to make or attempt to make any use whatsoever of a firearm or imitation firearm with intent to resist or prevent the lawful arrest or detention of himself or another person.

KEYNOTE

If the defendant has the firearm or imitation firearm with them at the time of resisting or preventing an arrest, they commit the offence under s. 18 (**see para. 3.9.6.6**).

The 'firearm' to which s. 17 refers is that defined at **para. 3.9.1**, *except* component parts and silencers/flash diminishers (s. 17(4)).

This offence includes imitation firearms in the general sense (**see para. 3.9.2.7**) but not imitation component parts, etc.

This is a crime of 'specific intent'. It requires proof, not of possession, but of evidence that the defendant made some actual use of the firearm and did so intending to resist/prevent the arrest of themselves or someone else. Any arrest which the defendant intended to prevent/resist must have been 'lawful'.

3.9.6.4 Possessing Firearm while Committing a Schedule 1 Offence

OFFENCE: **Possessing firearm while committing or being arrested for sch. 1 offence —*Firearms Act 1968, s. 17(2)***

- Triable on indictment
- Life imprisonment and/or a fine

The Firearms Act 1968, s. 17 states:

(2) If a person, at the time of his committing or being arrested for an offence specified in schedule 1 to this Act, has in his possession a firearm or imitation firearm, he shall be guilty of an offence under this subsection unless he shows that he had it in his possession for a lawful object.

KEYNOTE

This offence may be committed in two ways; either by being in possession of the weapon at the time of committing the sch. 1 offence or by being in possession of it *at the time of being arrested* for such an offence. Clearly in the second case, there may be some time between actually committing the sch. 1 offence and being arrested for it.

Nevertheless, if the defendant is in possession of the firearm at the time of his/her arrest, the offence is committed (unless he/she can show that it was for a lawful purpose).

For this offence, you need to prove that the person *was in possession* of the firearm but not that they actually *had it with them*. This fine but important distinction was reviewed by the Court of Appeal where it was reiterated that the two expressions have different meanings throughout the Act, with possession being a deliberately wider concept than the expression 'has with him' (*R* v *North* [2001] Crim LR 746).

There is no need for the defendant to be subsequently *convicted* of the sch. 1 offence, nor even to prove the elements of it; all that is needed is to show that the defendant, at the time of his/her arrest for a sch. 1 offence, had a firearm/imitation firearm in his/her possession (*R* v *Nelson* [2000] 3 WLR 300).

It is for the defendant to prove that the firearm was in his/her possession for a lawful purpose, presumably on the balance of probabilities.

This offence includes imitation firearms in the general sense (**see para. 3.9.2.7**).

The House of Lords has overturned the decision which allowed a defendant's use of his stiffened fingers beneath his coat to qualify as an imitation firearm for the purposes of the above offence (*R* v *Bentham* [2005] UKHL 18—**see para. 3.9.2.7**). In *Bentham* their Lordships pointed out that the above circumstances may have amounted to 'falsely pretending to have a firearm' but Parliament had not created any such offence.

Schedule 1 offences

The *main* offences listed in sch. 1 are:

- Damage—s. 1 of the Criminal Damage Act 1971.
- Assaults and woundings—ss. 20 and 47 of the Offences Against the Person Act 1861, assault police (s. 89 of the Police Act 1996) and civilian custody officers (s. 90(1) of the Criminal Justice Act 1991 and s. 13(1) of the Criminal Justice and Public Order Act 1994).
- Rape and other sexual/abduction offences—the following offences under the Sexual Offences Act 2003: s. 1 (rape), s. 2 (assault by penetration), s. 4 (causing a person to engage in sexual activity without consent), where the activity caused involved penetration within subs. (4)(a) to (d) of that section, s. 5 and s. 6 (rape and assault of a child under 13), s. 8 (causing or inciting a child under 13 to engage in sexual activity), where an activity involving penetration within subs. (3)(a) to (d) of that section was caused, s. 30 and s. 31 (sexual activity with/causing or inciting a person with a mental disorder impeding choice), where the touching involved or activity caused penetration within subs. (3)(a) to (d) of that section. Also offences under part I of the Child Abduction Act 1984.
- Theft, robbery, burglary, blackmail and taking a conveyance—Theft Act 1968. (**D.A.R.T.**)

Although covering several types of assault, sch. 1 does not extend to wounding/causing grievous bodily harm with intent. Schedule 1 also covers the aiding, abetting or attempting to commit such offences.

3.9.6.5 Trespassing with Firearms

OFFENCE: **Trespassing with firearm in building—*Firearms Act 1968, s. 20(1)***

• Triable either way (unless imitation firearm or air weapon) • Seven years' imprisonment and/or a fine on indictment • Six months' imprisonment and/or a fine summarily

The Firearms Act 1968, s. 20 states:

> (1) A person commits an offence if, while he has a firearm or imitation firearm with him, he enters or is in any building or part of a building as a trespasser and without reasonable excuse (the proof whereof lies on him).

KEYNOTE

This offence includes a specific reference to imitation firearms (**see para. 3.9.2.7**).

If the relevant firearm is an imitation or an air weapon, the offence is triable summarily.

This offence can be committed either by entering a building/part of a building or simply by *being* in such a place, in each case as a trespasser while having the firearm. As there is no need for the defendant to have 'entered' the building as a trespasser in every case, the offence might be committed after the occupier has withdrawn any permission for the defendant to be there. (Contrast the offence of trespassing with a weapon of offence.)

For the interpretation of 'has with him', **see para. 3.9.6.6**.

It will be for the defendant to prove that he/she had reasonable excuse and the standard of that proof will be judged against the balance of probabilities.

The power of entry and search under s. 47 of the 1968 Act applies to this offence (**see para. 3.9.8**).

OFFENCE: **Trespassing with firearm on land—*Firearms Act 1968, s. 20(2)***

- Triable summarily • Three months' imprisonment and/or a fine

The Firearms Act 1968, s. 20 states:

> (2) A person commits an offence if, while he has a firearm or imitation firearm with him, he enters or is on any land as a trespasser and without reasonable excuse (the proof whereof lies on him).

KEYNOTE

The elements of this offence are generally the same as those for the s. 20(1) offence above.

As with the s. 20(1) offence, there is no requirement that the defendant had the firearm/imitation firearm with him/her when entering onto the land (compare with the offence of aggravated burglary under the Theft Act 1968).

'Land' for these purposes will include land covered by water (s. 20(3)).

3.9.6.6 Having Firearm with Intent to Commit Indictable Offence or Resist Arrest

OFFENCE: **Having firearm with intent to commit an indictable offence or resist arrest—*Firearms Act 1968, s. 18(1)***

- Triable on indictment • Life imprisonment and/or a fine

The Firearms Act 1968, s. 18 states:

> (1) It is an offence for a person to have with him a firearm or imitation firearm with intent to commit an indictable offence, or to resist arrest or prevent the arrest of another, in either case while he has the firearm or imitation firearm with him.

KEYNOTE

This offence, which overlaps with that under s. 17(1) (**see para. 3.9.6.3**), requires the defendant to have the firearm 'with him'. This is a more restrictive expression than 'possession' (as to which, **see para. 3.9.3.1**), and requires that the firearm is 'readily accessible' to the defendant (e.g. in a car nearby) (*R* v *Pawlicki* [1992] 1 WLR 827).

Where a defendant left a firearm in his house which was a few miles from the scene of the relevant criminal offence, the Court of Appeal held that this was not enough to meet the requirement of 'having with him'—*R* v *Bradish* (2004) LTL 2 April.

Despite this narrower meaning, the defendant does not have to be shown to have been 'carrying' the firearm (*R* v *Kelt* [1977] 1 WLR 1365), a decision which now conflicts with the situation relating to identical statutory expressions under the Theft Act 1968 and also under the legislation relating to weapons.

Intention

This is a crime of 'specific intent' and, in proving that intent, s. 18 states:

> (2) In proceedings for an offence under this section proof that the accused had a firearm or imitation firearm with him and intended to commit an offence, or to resist or prevent arrest, is evidence that he intended to have it with him while doing so.

It is not necessary to show that the defendant intended to *use* the firearm to commit the indictable offence or to prevent/resist the arrest (*R* v *Duhaney* [1998] 2 Cr App R 25). (Contrast the offence under s. 17(1); **see para. 3.9.6.3.**)

The mental element is, however, an essential part of this offence. Therefore, if the defendant only formed the intent as a result of duress, this ingredient will not have been established—*R* v *Fisher* [2004] EWCA Crim 1190.

An indictable offence includes an offence triable either way (Interpretation Act 1978).

Section 18 does not appear to require that any arrest be 'lawful' and it may be that Parliament intended for this offence to be broader in that respect than the offence under s. 17.

This offence includes imitation firearms in the general sense (**see para. 3.9.2.7**).

The power of entry and search under s. 47 of the 1968 Act applies to this offence (**see para. 3.9.8**).

3.9.6.7 Having Firearm or Imitation Firearm in Public Place

OFFENCE: **Having firearm/imitation firearm in public place—*Firearms Act 1968, s. 19***

- Triable either way • Seven years' imprisonment and/or a fine on indictment
- Twelve months' imprisonment and/or a fine summarily

The Firearms Act 1968, s. 19 states:

> A person commits an offence if, without lawful authority or reasonable excuse (the proof whereof lies on him), he has with him in a public place—
> (a) a loaded shot gun,
> (b) an air weapon (whether loaded or not),
> (c) any other firearm (whether loaded or not) together with ammunition suitable for use in that firearm, or
> (d) an imitation firearm.

KEYNOTE

If the weapon is a shotgun it must be loaded. 'Loaded' here means if there is ammunition in the chamber or barrel (or in any magazine or other device) whereby the ammunition can be fed into the chamber or barrel by the manual or automatic operation of some part of the weapon (see s. 57(6)(b)). If the weapon is an imitation firearm (**see para. 3.9.2.7**) or an air weapon the offence is committed by the defendant having it with him/her. In the case of other firearms the offence is committed by the defendant having the firearm with him/her together with ammunition suitable for use in it.

For the meaning of 'has with him', **see para. 3.9.6.6.**

This offence is an 'absolute' offence like s. 1 (**see para. 3.9.3**). Therefore, if you can show that the defendant (X) knew he had something with him and that the 'something' was a loaded shotgun, an air weapon, an imitation firearm, or another firearm with ammunition, the offence is complete (*R* v *Vann* [1996] Crim LR 52). It is for the defendant to show lawful authority or reasonable excuse; possession of a valid certificate does not of itself provide lawful authority for having the firearm/ammunition in a public place (*Ross* v *Collins* [1982] Crim LR 368).

3.9.6.8 Using Someone to Mind a Weapon

OFFENCE: **Using someone to mind a weapon—*Violent Crime Reduction Act 2006, s. 28(1)***

- Triable on indictment • Ten years' imprisonment and/or a fine (firearms, etc.)
- Four years' imprisonment and/or a fine (offensive weapons, etc.)

The Violent Crime Reduction Act 2006, s. 28 states:

(1) A person is guilty of an offence if—
 (a) he uses another to look after, hide or transport a dangerous weapon for him; and
 (b) he does so under arrangements or in circumstances that facilitate, or are intended to facilitate, the weapon's being available to him for an unlawful purpose.

(2) For the purposes of this section the cases in which a dangerous weapon is to be regarded as available to a person for an unlawful purpose include any case where—
 (a) the weapon is available for him to take possession of it at a time and place; and
 (b) his possession of the weapon at that time and place would constitute, or be likely to involve or to lead to, the commission by him of an offence.

KEYNOTE

The offence was introduced by the 2006 Act to close a perceived loophole in the law where people have escaped prosecution by entrusting their weapon to another person, in particular to a child. Using children in this way may risk injury to them and in the longer term draw them into gun and knife crime as a result of their early association with weapons. Using a minor to mind a firearm is an aggravating factor attracting harsher sentences (s. 29(3)(a)).

A 'dangerous weapon' means a firearm other than an air weapon or a component part of, or accessory to, an air weapon; or a weapon to which s. 141 or 141A of the Criminal Justice Act 1988 applies (specified offensive weapons, knives and bladed weapons (s. 28(3)).

3.9.6.9 Firing an Air Weapon Beyond Premises

OFFENCE: **Firing an air weapon beyond premises—*Firearms Act 1968, s. 21A***

- Triable summarily • Fine

The Firearms Act 1968, s. 21A states:

(1) A person commits an offence if—
 (a) he has with him an air weapon on any premises; and
 (b) he uses it for firing a missile beyond those premises.

(2) In proceedings against a person for an offence under this section it shall be a defence for him to show that the only premises into or across which the missile was fired were premises the occupier of which had consented to the firing of the missile (whether specifically or by way of a general consent).

KEYNOTE

This offence was inserted by the Violent Crime Reduction Act 2006 to close a loophole in the law by making it an offence for a person of *any* age to fire an air weapon beyond the boundary of premises. Prior to the introduction of this section the offence only related to persons under the age of 17. Note that a defence is provided to cover the situation where the person shooting has the consent of the occupier of the land over or into which he/she shoots.

3.9.7 Possession or Acquisition of Firearms by Certain People

Sections 21 to 24 of the Firearms Act 1968 place further restrictions on the people who can possess, acquire, receive or otherwise have involvement with firearms. Section 21 deals with people who have been convicted of certain offences while ss. 22 to 24 set out minimum ages in respect of certain firearms and transactions.

Section 21 generally provides that any person who has been sentenced to:

- custody for life, or
- to preventive detention, imprisonment, corrective training, youth custody or detention in a young offender institution for three years or more

must not, *at any time*, have a firearm or ammunition in his/her possession.

Section 21 goes on to provide that any person who has been sentenced to imprisonment, youth custody, detention in a young offender institution or a secure training order for three months or more, *but less than three years*, must not have a firearm or ammunition in his/her possession at any time before the end of a five-year period beginning on the date of his/her release.

Date of release means, for a sentence partly served and partly suspended, the date on which the offender completes the part to be served and, in the case of a person subject to a secure training order, the date on which he/she is released from detention (under the various relevant statutes) or the date halfway through the total specified by the court making the order, whichever is the latest (s. 21(2A)).

A person holding a licence under the Children and Young Persons Act 1933 or a person subject to a recognisance to keep the peace or be of good behaviour with a condition relating to the possession of firearms, must not, *at any time during the licence or the recognisance*, have a firearm or ammunition in his/her possession (s. 21(3)).

Where sentences or court orders are mentioned, their Scottish equivalents will also apply and a person prohibited in Northern Ireland from possessing a firearm/ammunition will also be prohibited in Great Britain (s. 21(3A)).

Section 21 does not apply to imitation firearms as there is no express reference to them in the section and because the reference in the Firearms Act 1982 does not apply (**see para. 3.9.2.7**).

3.9.7.1 Supplying Firearm to Person Prohibited by Section 21

OFFENCE: **Selling or transferring firearm to person prohibited by s. 21—*Firearms Act 1968, s. 21(5)***

- Triable either way • Five years' imprisonment and/or a fine on indictment
- Six months' imprisonment and/or a fine summarily

The Firearms Act 1968, s. 21 states:

> (5) It is an offence for a person to sell or transfer a firearm or ammunition to, or to repair, test or prove a firearm or ammunition for, a person whom he knows or has reasonable ground for believing to be prohibited by this section from having a firearm or ammunition in his possession.

KEYNOTE

Given that all people are presumed to know the law once it is published, it would seem that the knowledge or belief by the defendant would apply to the *convictions of* the other person, not the fact that possession by that person was an offence.

What you must show is knowledge by the defendant or at least *reasonable ground for believing*; this latter requirement is stronger than mere cause to *suspect*.

3.9.7.2 Other Restrictions on Possession or Acquisition

In addition to the general provisions relating to possession, acquisition etc., ss. 22 to 24 create a number of summary offences restricting the involvement of people of various ages in their dealings with certain types of firearm and ammunition. The Violent Crime Reduction Act 2006 amended ss. 22 to 24 of the Firearms Act 1968, so that the age limit for the purchase and possession of air weapons is now higher than for other firearms. The 2006 Act also inserted a new s. 24A in relation to the sale and purchase of imitation firearms.

In summary the age restrictions are as follows:

- a person under 18:
  - (i) must not purchase or hire an air weapon or ammunition for an air weapon (s. 22(1)(a));
  - (ii) must not have with them an air weapon or ammunition for an air weapon (s. 22(4)). An exception to this is where the person is under the supervision of another who is at least 21 years old. However, if the person under 18 fires the weapon beyond the relevant premises they will commit an offence under s. 21A (**see para. 3.9.6.9**) and the person supervising them will be guilty of an offence under s. 23(1)). Generally it is not an offence under this section for a person aged 14 or over to have with them an air weapon or ammunition on private premises with the consent of the owner (s. 23(3));
  - (iii) it is an offence to sell or let on hire an air weapon or ammunition for an air weapon to a person under the age of 18 (s. 24(1)(a)), or to make a gift/part with possession of an air weapon or ammunition for an air weapon to such a person (unless under the permitted circumstances above) (s. 24(4));
  - (iv) it is an offence to sell an imitation firearm to a person under the age of 18 (s. 24A(2)), or for a person under 18 to purchase one (s. 24A(1)). It is a defence to show that the vendor believed that the purchaser was 18 or over and had reasonable grounds for that belief (s. 24A(3));
- a person under 17:
  - (i) must not purchase or hire any firearm or ammunition (s. 22(1)(b)); or
  - (ii) it is an offence to sell or let on hire to a person under 17 any firearm or ammunition (s. 24(1)(b));
- a person under 15:
  - (i) must not have with them an assembled shotgun unless supervised by a person aged at least 21 or while the shotgun is securely covered so it cannot be fired (s. 22(3)); and
  - (ii) it is an offence to make a gift of a shotgun/ammunition to such a person (s. 24(3));
- a person under 14:
  - (i) must not have in their possession a section 1 firearm or ammunition (s. 22(2)); and
  - (ii) it is an offence to make a gift/part with possession of such a firearm/ammunition to such a person (s. 24(2)) (subject to some exceptions relating to sports and shooting clubs—see s. 11 of the Firearms Act 1968 and s. 15 of the Firearms (Amendment) Act 1988).

There is a further provision creating an offence for a person under 18 who is the holder of a certificate using a firearm for a purpose not authorised by the European Weapons Directive (s. 22(1A)).

This is merely a summary of what are relatively convoluted provisions regarding ages and permitted circumstances. For the full extent of these restrictions and their exemptions, reference should be made to the 1968 and 1988 Acts. Note that s. 24(5) of the Firearms Act 1968 provides that it is a defence to prove that the person charged with an offence believed that other person to be of or over the age mentioned and had reasonable grounds for the belief.

It is a summary offence (punishable by one month's imprisonment and/or a fine) to be in possession of *any* loaded firearm when drunk (s. 12 of the Licensing Act 1872). There is no requirement that the person be in a public place.

3.9.8 Police Powers

Section 47 of the Firearms Act 1968 states:

(1) A constable may require any person whom he has reasonable cause to suspect—
(a) of having a firearm, with or without ammunition, with him in a public place; or
(b) to be committing or about to commit, elsewhere than in a public place, an offence relevant for the purposes of this section,
to hand over the firearm or any ammunition for examination by the constable.

KEYNOTE

This power has two distinct elements. The first applies where the officer has reasonable cause to suspect that a person has a firearm with him/her in a public place. The second relates to a situation where the officer has reasonable cause to suspect that the person is committing or is about to commit an offence relevant to this section anywhere else.

An 'offence relevant to this section' appears to be an offence unders ss. 18(1), 18(2) and 20 (see s. 47(6)).

It is a summary offence to fail to hand over a firearm when required under this section (s. 47(2)).

In order to exercise this power, a police officer may search the person and may detain him/her for that purpose (s. 47(3)). The officer may also enter *any place* (s. 47(5)).

If the officer has reasonable cause to suspect that:

- there is a firearm in a vehicle in a public place, or
- that a vehicle is being/about to be used in connection with the commission of an 'offence relevant to this section' (see above)

he/she may search the vehicle and, for that purpose, may require the person driving or in control of the vehicle to stop it (s. 47(4)).

The provisions of the PACE Codes of Practice, Code A, will apply to the exercise of these powers of stop and search (see appendix 1).

3.9.8.1 Power to Demand Documentation

Section 48 of the Firearms Act 1968 states:

(1) A constable may demand, from any person whom he believes to be in possession of a firearm or ammunition to which section 1 of this Act applies, or of a shot gun, the production of his firearm certificate or, as the case may be, his shot gun certificate.

KEYNOTE

The demand for the relevant documentation may be made where the police officer 'believes' that a person is in possession of a section 1 firearm or ammunition or a shotgun. There is no requirement that the officer's belief be reasonable.

Where the person fails to:

- produce the relevant certificate or
- show that he/she is not entitled to be issued with such a certificate or
- show that he/she is in possession of the firearm exclusively in connection with recognised purposes (collecting/historical/cultural) under the law of another EU Member State

the officer may demand the production of the relevant valid documentation issued in another member State under any corresponding provisions (s. 48(1A)).

Failing to produce any of the required documents *and* to let the officer read it, or failing to show an entitlement to possess the firearm or ammunition triggers (!) the power of seizure under s. 48(2). It also gives the officer the power to demand the person's name and address. This requirement is similar to the provision under s. 170 of the Road Traffic Act 1988 (duty to give details after an accident) where it has been held that the name and address of the person's solicitor would suffice (*DPP* v *McCarthy* [1999] RTR 323). That decision was based on the purpose behind the Road Traffic Act requirement, namely to allow the respective parties to the accident to get in touch with each other in the future. It is suggested that the purpose of the Firearms Act power is a very different one of regulating the possession of weapons and that the furnishing of details of some convenient administrative location for correspondence would not be enough to satisfy the requirements of this section.

If the person refuses to give his/her name or address or gives a false name and address, he/she commits a summary offence (s. 48(3)).

A person from another Member State who is in possession of a firearm and who fails to comply with a demand under s. 48(1A) also commits a separate summary offence (s. 48(4)).

3.9.9 Shortening and Conversion of Firearms

OFFENCE: **Shortening barrel of shotgun to less than 24 inches—*Firearms Act 1968, s. 4(1)***

- Triable either way • Five years' imprisonment and/or a fine on indictment
- Six months' imprisonment and/or a fine summarily

The Firearms Act 1968, s. 4 states:

> (1) Subject to this section, it is an offence to shorten the barrel of a shot gun to a length less than 24 inches.

OFFENCE: **Shortening barrel of other smooth-bore section 1 firearm to less than 24 inches—*Firearms (Amendment) Act 1988 s. 6(1)***

- Triable either way • Five years' imprisonment and/or a fine on indictment
- Six months' imprisonment and/or a fine summarily

The Firearms (Amendment) Act 1988, s. 6 states:

> (1) Subject to subsection (2) below, it is an offence to shorten to a length less than 24 inches the barrel of any smooth-bore gun to which section 1 of the principal Act applies other than one which has a barrel with a bore exceeding 2 inches in diameter;...

OFFENCE: **Converting imitation firearm—*Firearms Act 1968, s. 4(3)***

- Triable either way • Five years' imprisonment and/or a fine on indictment
- Six months' imprisonment and/or a fine summarily

The Firearms Act 1968, s. 4 states:

(3) It is an offence for a person other than a registered firearms dealer to convert into a firearm anything which, though having the appearance of being a firearm, is so constructed as to be incapable of discharging any missile through its barrel.

KEYNOTE

The relevant definitions are considered at **para. 3.9.2**.

The first two offences are concerned with the shortening of barrels while the third involves conversion of anything which has the appearance of a firearm so that it can be fired. Registered firearms dealers (**see para. 3.9.3.4**) are excluded from the wording of the conversion offence. They are also exempted by ss. 4(2) and 6(2) from the relevant offences involving shortening barrels provided the shortening is done *for the sole purpose* of replacing a defective part of the barrel *so as to produce a new barrel having an overall length of at least 24 inches.*

The length of the barrel of a weapon will be measured from its muzzle to the point at which the charge is exploded (s. 57(6)(a) of the 1968 Act).

Once the shortening or conversion has taken place, the nature of the firearm will have changed (e.g. from a shotgun into a section 1 firearm or from an imitation into a real firearm), in which case the person will also commit the relevant possession offences unless he/she has the appropriate authorisation.

PART FOUR

Sexual Offences

4.1 Sexual Offences

4.1.1 Introduction

Sexual offences represent a particularly important area of criminal law for two main reasons: the sensitivity required in their investigation and prosecution and their potential effect on the victim. Such offences can cause significant emotional harm to the victim, harm which may take far longer to 'heal' than many physical injuries. For that reason, together with the growth in the range of legal provisions that have been created to tackle the behaviour of sex offenders, sexual offences have been addressed in this separate chapter.

It is important to note that there is overlap between many of the offences, for example a mentally disordered person could be raped under s. 1 (because of his/her lack of ability to give true consent) or subjected to sexual activity contrary to s. 30 (due to an inability to refuse). In all circumstances it is essential that the most appropriate option is chosen.

4.1.2 Human Rights Considerations

A factor affecting this area of criminal law is the relevance of the European Convention on Human Rights. It is clear that sexual activities are aspects of a person's 'private life' as protected by article 8 of the Convention (see *Dudgeon* v *United Kingdom* (1981) 4 EHRR 149 and *ADT* v *United Kingdom* [2000] Crim LR 1009). This concept applies to homosexual and heterosexual relationships (*X* v *United Kingdom* (1997) 24 EHRR 143).

Any attempt by the criminal law to place restrictions on the consensual sexual activities of individuals has to be considered very carefully in light of the Human Rights Act 1998.

The Sexual Offences Act 2003 and its compatibility with the European Convention on Human Rights were considered in *R* v *G & Secretary of State for the Home Department* [2006] EWCA Crim 821. The Court of Appeal held that the imposition of strict liability in relation to the offence under s. 5 of the Act (rape of a child under 13) did not infringe article 6.2 of the Convention (presumption of innocence).

4.1.3 Anonymity

Under the Sexual Offences (Amendment) Act 1992, victims of most sexual offences (including rape, incest, and indecency with children) are entitled to anonymity throughout their lifetime. This means that there are restrictions on the way in which trials and cases may be reported and the courts have powers to enforce these provisions. Further protection preventing victims from cross-examination by their alleged attackers is provided by the Youth Justice and Criminal Evidence Act 1999. The 1999 Act also imposes restrictions on the introduction of evidence in most of the sexual offences covered in this chapter.

4.2 The Sexual Offences Act 2003

The Sexual Offences Act creates a whole series of sexual offences and sets out the elements that will be needed in proving the relevant offences and also introduces some further practical measures such as the presumptions about consent that will be made by a court under certain circumstances. In many of the mainstream offences it creates, the Act uses the approach of describing actions of a hypothetical offender 'A' towards the victim 'B'. This approach has generally worked well in discrimination legislation.

The Act has some recurring themes and terms; in order to understand—and prove—many of the offences set out in the Act, it is necessary to understand some of the themes and terms first.

4.2.1 The Definition of 'Sexual'

This is an important concept in the statutory framework. Some activities carried out in order to gain sexual gratification are difficult to classify—and certainly to prove—as 'sexual' in the ordinary meaning of the word. Fetishes in particular—for things such as feet and shoes—have caused difficulties in this regard.

What a Reasonable Person would Consider

Section 78 provides that penetration, touching or any other activity will be sexual if a reasonable person would consider that:

(a) whatever its circumstances or any person's purpose in relation to it, it is sexual by its very nature or,
(b) because of its nature it *may* be sexual and because of its circumstances or the purpose of any person in relation to it, it is sexual.

Therefore, activity under (a) covers things that a reasonable person would always consider to be sexual (for example, masturbation), while activity under (b) covers things that may or may not be considered sexual by a reasonable person depending on the circumstances or the intentions of the person carrying it out (or both). For instance, a doctor inserting a finger into a vagina might be sexual under certain circumstances, but if done for a purely medical purpose in a hospital, it would not be.

If the activity would not appear to a reasonable person to be sexual, then it will not meet either criterion and, irrespective of any sexual gratification the person might derive from it, the activity will not be 'sexual'. Therefore weird or exotic fetishes that no ordinary person would regard as being sexual or potentially sexual will not be covered. This pretty well follows the common law developments in this area (see for example *R* v *Court* [1989] AC 28 and *R* v *Tabassum* [2000] Crim LR 686).

4.2.2 The Definition of 'Touching'

This activity is relevant to a number of specific offences. Section 79(8) states that touching includes touching:

- with any part of the body
- with anything else
- through anything

and in particular, touching amounting to penetration.

'Touching' for the purposes of an offence under s. 3 (**see para. 4.4.2**) includes the touching of a victim's clothing. This is clear from the Court of Appeal's decision in *R* v *H* (2005) *The Times*, 8 February. There it was held that it was not Parliament's intention to preclude the touching of a victim's clothing from amounting to a sexual 'assault'. Where touching was not automatically by its nature 'sexual' the test under s. 78(b) applies (**see para. 4.2.1**). In a case where that section applies it will be appropriate for a trial judge to ask the jury to determine whether touching was 'sexual' by answering two questions. First, would the jury, as 12 reasonable people, consider that the touching could be sexual and, if so, whether in all the circumstances of the case, they would consider that the purpose of the touching *had in fact been* sexual.

4.3 Rape

OFFENCE: **Rape—*Sexual Offences Act 2003, s.1***

- Triable on indictment • Life imprisonment

The Sexual Offences Act 2003, s. 1 states:

(1) A person (A) commits an offence if—
 (a) he intentionally penetrates the vagina, anus or mouth of another person (B) with his penis,
 (b) B does not consent to the penetration, and
 (c) A does not reasonably believe that B consents

KEYNOTE

Rape is an offence that can *only* be committed via the use of the penis. It can be committed if the defendant penetrates the vagina, anus or mouth of the victim with the penis.

Consent is a key aspect of rape. In proving rape you must show that the victim did not in fact consent at the time and that the defendant did not reasonably believe that she/he consented. The wording is supported by the further provision that whether or not the defendant's belief is reasonable will be determined having regard to all the circumstances (s. 1(2)). Both this, and the aspects of the criminal conduct required to prove rape are considered in greater detail below.

Sections 75 and 76 apply to this offence (**see paras 4.3.3 and 4.3.4**).

If the victim is a child under 13, you simply have to prove intentional penetration and the child's age. No issue of 'consent' arises and a specific offence under s. 5 is committed.

Section 103(2)(b) of the Criminal Justice Act 2003 provides that a defendant's propensity to commit offences of the kind with which he/she is charged may (without prejudice to any other way of doing so) be established by evidence that he/she has been convicted of an offence of 'the same category'. An offence under s. 1, if committed in relation to a person under the age of 16, or under s. 5 (including aiding, abetting, counselling, procuring, inciting or attempting the commission of such an offence) falls within the relevant sexual offences category (see the Criminal Justice Act 2003 (Categories of Offences) Order 2004 (SI 2004/3346)). Many of the other offences that follow in this chapter, along with their predecessors under earlier legislation, are also covered and will fall within the relevant sexual offences category.

4.3.1 Criminal Conduct

To prove rape you must show that the defendant penetrated the vagina, mouth or anus of the victim. It should be noted that penetration is a continuing act from entry to withdrawal (s. 79(2)). The 'continuing' nature of this act is of practical importance when considering the issue of consent and the statutory presumptions (see below). While it is not necessary to prove ejaculation, clearly the presence of semen or sperm is important in proving the elements of a sexual offence, as is other scientific evidence recovered from the victim, the offender and the scene etc. References to a part of the body (for example, penis, vagina) will include references to a body part which has been surgically constructed, particularly if it is through gender reassignment (s. 79(3)).

4.3.2 Consent

The issue of consent is a question of fact and is critical to proving the offence of rape. It is also potentially the most difficult aspect of the offence to prove and that is why the legislation has included some specific sections raising presumptions and conclusions in certain circumstances. Whereas an act of intercourse or physical intimacy may be proved or corroborated by forensic evidence, the true wishes of the victim at the time of the offence are much more difficult to prove beyond a reasonable doubt. Any consent given must be 'true' consent, not simply a *submission* induced by fear or fraud. Some people however are not capable of giving the required consent—these are generally addressed in the following chapter.

The starting point in examining consent is s. 74 which states that a person consents if he or she agrees by choice and has the freedom and capacity to make that choice. Therefore, if the person does not have any real choice in the matter, or their choice is not a genuine exercise of their free will, then they have not 'consented'.

In *R* v *B* (2006) unreported, the Court of Appeal stated that whether an individual had a sexual disease or condition, such as being HIV positive, was not an issue as far as consent was concerned. The case related to a man who was alleged to have raped a woman after they had met outside a nightclub in the early hours of the morning. When arrested, the man informed the custody officer that he was HIV positive, a fact he had not disclosed to the victim prior to sexual intercourse. At the original trial, the judge directed that this non-disclosure was relevant to the issue of consent. On appeal the court stated that this was not the case and that the consent issue for a jury to consider was whether or not the victim consented to sexual intercourse, not whether she consented to sexual intercourse with a person suffering from a sexually transmitted disease.

The next key considerations in relation to consent are the important provisions set out at ss. 75 and 76. These are presumptions about consent and can be divided into *evidential* presumptions and *conclusive* presumptions. They are of considerable practical significance in evidence gathering and interviewing suspects.

4.3.3 Section 75—Evidential Presumptions and Consent

The Sexual Offences Act 2003, s. 75 states:

(1) If in proceedings for an offence to which this section applies it is proved—
  (a) that the defendant did the relevant act,
  (b) that any of the circumstances specified in subsection (2) existed, and
  (c) that the defendant knew that those circumstances existed,
  the complainant is to be taken not to have consented to the relevant act unless sufficient evidence is adduced to raise an issue as to whether he consented, and the defendant is to be taken not to have reasonably believed that the complainant consented unless sufficient evidence is adduced to raise an issue as to whether he reasonably believed it.

KEYNOTE

This means that, if the prosecution can show that the defendant carried out the relevant act in relation to certain specified sexual offences (for example, penetration in rape) and that any of the circumstances below existed and the defendant knew they existed, it will be presumed that the victim did not consent. Then the defendant will have to satisfy the court, by reference to evidence, that this presumption should not be made.

The circumstances are that:

(a) *any person* was, at the time of the relevant act (or immediately before it began), using violence against *the complainant* or causing *the complainant* to fear that immediate violence would be used against him/her;

(b) *any person* was, at the time of the relevant act or immediately before it began, causing *the complainant* to fear that violence was being used, or that immediate violence would be used, against *another person*;

(c) *the complainant* was, and the defendant was not, unlawfully detained at the time of the relevant act;
(d) *the complainant* was asleep or otherwise unconscious at the time of the relevant act;
(e) because of *the complainant's* physical disability, *the complainant* would not have been able at the time of the relevant act to communicate to the defendant whether the complainant consented;
(f) *any person* had administered to or caused to be taken by the complainant, without the complainant's consent, a substance which, having regard to when it was administered or taken, was capable of causing or enabling the complainant to be stupefied or overpowered at the time of the relevant act.

It can be seen that these conditions cover a range of circumstances, including the use or threat of violence by any person (not just the defendant) against the victim of the sexual offence and circumstances where the victim was asleep or had been drugged.

The 'relevant act' for each offence covered by s. 75 will generally be obvious but is set out specifically at s. 77. The use of the term 'sufficient evidence' is a new feature in criminal legislation and comes about as a result of the Human Rights Act 1998 and article 6(2) of the European Convention on Human Rights. Provisions where the burden to adduce 'sufficient evidence' is on the defendant, as in s. 75(1), may not breach article 6 provided the public interest is sufficient to warrant it (for example, *R* v *Lambert* [2001] 3 WLR 206; *Attorney-General's Reference (No. 4 of 2002)* [2003] HRLR 15). In the case of rape there are strong public interest and policy considerations to support this presumption.

4.3.4 Conclusive Presumptions about Consent

Section 76 of the Sexual Offences Act 2003 states that, if it is proved in some sexual offences (listed in s. 77) that the defendant did the relevant act and that he/she:

(a) intentionally deceived the complainant as to the nature or purpose of the relevant act or
(b) intentionally induced the complainant to consent to the relevant act by impersonating a person known personally to the complainant,

there will be a *conclusive* presumption both that the victim did not consent and also that the defendant did not believe she or he consented.

These provisions deal with the problems where the defendant either misrepresents the nature or purpose of what he or she is doing (for example, pretending that inserting a finger into the victim's vagina is for medical reasons) or impersonates the victim's partner. Section 76 requires that a misunderstanding was created by the defendant and that it was done deliberately. Once it is proved, beyond a reasonable doubt, that these circumstances existed then it is conclusive and the defendant cannot argue against them. An example of a deception as to the purpose of the act comes from the case of *R* v *Devonald* [2008] EWCA Crim 527. In this case, the defendant (a male) posed as a young woman and induced the complainant to masturbate in front of a web cam. The complainant only did so because he thought that he was masturbating for the sexual gratification of a young woman. The court held that the complainant had been deceived as to the purpose of the masturbation.

It is important to emphasise the fact that s. 76 deals with situations where the defendant either:

- deceives the victim regarding the nature and purpose of the act, or
- deceives the victim regarding the identity of the person who is carrying out the act.

If the deception does not relate to either of these aims then s. 76 has no application. For example, in *R* v *Harvinder Jheeta* [2007] EWCA Crim 1699, the defendant deceived the complainant into having sex more frequently than she would have done otherwise. In these circumstances the conclusive presumptions under the Sexual Offences Act 2003 had no relevance as the complainant had not been deceived as to the nature or purpose of the sexual intercourse.

As with s. 75, the 'relevant act' for each offence covered by s. 76 will generally be obvious but is set out specifically at s. 77.

Even if freely given, consent may still be withdrawn at any time. Once the 'passive' party to sexual penetration withdraws consent, any continued activity (for example, penetration in rape—*R* v *Cooper* [1994] Crim LR 531) can amount to a sexual offence provided all the other ingredients are present.

4.4 Sexual Assault

There are several specific, accurate and easy to prove offences: these are discussed below.

4.4.1 Assault by Penetration

OFFENCE: **Assault by Penetration—*Sexual Offences Act 2003, s. 2***

- Triable on indictment • Life imprisonment

The Sexual Offences Act 2003, s. 2 states:

(1) A person (A) commits an offence if—
  (a) he intentionally penetrates the vagina or anus of another person (B) with a part of his body or anything else,
  (b) the penetration is sexual,
  (c) B does not consent to the penetration, and
  (d) A does not reasonably believe that B consents.

KEYNOTE

As with all the offences in the Sexual Offences Act 2003 except rape, this offence can be committed by a male or a female against a male or female.

While the offence of rape considered in **para. 4.3** above involves penetration by the penis, this offence involves penetration by any part of the body or anything else whatsoever. It is therefore a very broad offence covering insertion into the vagina or anus (though not the mouth) of *anything*, provided that the penetration is 'sexual' (**see para. 4.2.1**). Penetration must be intentional, made without the consent of the victim and you must show that the defendant did not reasonably believe that the victim did consent. Whether a belief is reasonable is to be determined having regard to all the circumstances, including any steps the defendant has taken to ascertain whether the victim consents (s. 2(2)).

The introduction of the series of sexual offences under the 2003 Act has raised some questions as to the extent to which they mirror or replace similar offences under the former regime. The Court of Appeal has held that, so far as the above offence is concerned, its introduction attracting a potential sentence of life imprisonment means that it must be dealt with at a higher level than the previous generic offence of indecent assault. The ingredient of penetration has always been regarded by the law as being particularly serious and the starting point in s. 2 offences for sentencing ought to be in the region of four years (*Attorney-General's Reference (No. 104 of 2004)* [2004] EWCA Crim 2672).

Sections 75 and 76 apply to this offence (**see paras 4.3.3 and 4.3.4**).

If the victim is a child under 13, you simply have to prove intentional, sexual penetration and the child's age. No issue of 'consent' arises and a specific offence under s. 6 is committed.

An offence under s. 2, if committed in relation to a person under the age of 16 or under s. 6 (including aiding, abetting, counselling, procuring, inciting or attempting the commission of such an offence), falls within the relevant sexual offences category for the purposes of s. 103(2)(b) of the Criminal Justice Act 2003 (a defendant's propensity to commit offences of the kind with which he/she is charged—**see para. 4.3**).

4.4.2 Sexual Assault by Touching

OFFENCE: **Sexual Touching—*Sexual Offences Act 2003, s. 3***

• Triable either way • If victim is child under 13—fourteen years' imprisonment; otherwise ten years' imprisonment on indictment • Six months' imprisonment summarily

The Sexual Offences Act 2003, s. 3 states:

(1) A person (A) commits an offence if—
  (a) he intentionally touches another person (B),
  (b) the touching is sexual,
  (c) B does not consent to the touching, and
  (d) A does not reasonably believe that B consents.

KEYNOTE

The part of the body touched does not have to be a sexual organ or orifice. Touching for the purposes of the above offence includes touching a person's clothing. Therefore, where a man approached a woman and asked '*Do you fancy a shag?*', grabbing at a pocket on her tracksuit bottoms as she tried to walk away, he was properly convicted of the s. 3 offence (*R* v *H* (2005) *The Times*, 8 February).

As with the offence under s. 2, you need to prove that the conduct was intentional (rather than accidental), that it was sexual (**see para. 4.2.1**), that the victim did not consent and that the defendant did not reasonably believe that the victim consented.

Whether a belief is reasonable is to be determined having regard to all the circumstances, including any steps the defendant has taken to ascertain whether the victim consents (s. 3(2)).

Sections 75 and 76 apply to this offence (**see paras 4.3.3 and 4.3.4**).

If the victim is a child under 13, you simply have to prove intentional, sexual touching and the child's age. No issue of 'consent' arises and a specific offence under s. 7 is committed.

An offence under s. 3, if committed in relation to a person under the age of 16 or under s. 7 (including aiding, abetting, counselling, procuring, inciting or attempting the commission of such an offence), falls within the relevant sexual offences category—**see para. 4.3**.

4.4.3 Causing Sexual Activity without Consent

OFFENCE: **Causing a Person to Engage in Sexual Activity without Consent—*Sexual Offences Act 2003, s. 4***

• If involves penetration: of the victim's anus or vagina, of victim's mouth with penis, of any other person's anus or vagina with a part of victim's body or by victim, or of any person's mouth by victim's penis—triable on indictment; life imprisonment

• Otherwise triable either way; ten years' imprisonment on indictment; six months' imprisonment summarily

The Sexual Offences Act 2003, s. 4 states:

(1) A person (A) commits an offence if—
  (a) he intentionally causes another person (B) to engage in an activity,
  (b) the activity is sexual,
  (c) B does not consent to engaging in the activity, and
  (d) A does not reasonably believe that B consents.

KEYNOTE

The offence can involve a number of permutations—for example a woman making a man penetrate her, a man forcing someone else to masturbate him or a woman making another woman masturbate a third person. Apart from the defendant and the victim, there may be others involved who also consent. Clearly they may be liable for aiding and abetting under the right circumstances. If the permutations involve penetration, the chances are it will carry life imprisonment. You need to prove that the conduct was intentional, that the 'activity' engaged in was sexual (**see para. 4.2.1**), that the *victim* (rather than any other participant) did not consent and that the defendant did not reasonably believe that the victim consented.

Whether a belief is reasonable is to be determined having regard to all the circumstances, including any steps the defendant has taken to ascertain whether the victim consents (s. 4(2)).

Sections 75 and 76 apply to this offence (**see paras 4.3.3 and 4.3.4**).

There is a specific offence of causing or *inciting* a child under 13 to engage in sexual activity (s. 8). It is important to remember that an individual can commit an offence of incitement even if the activity he/she is encouraging, etc. does not take place. In *R* v *Walker* (2006) unreported, the Court of Appeal held that s. 8 of the Act created two offences: (i) intentionally causing, and (ii) intentionally inciting a child under 13 to engage in sexual activity. The offence was centred on the concept of incitement and the acts had to be intentional or deliberate, but it was not a necessary ingredient for incitement of sexual activity that the defendant had intended the sexual activity to take place.

An offence under s. 4, if committed in relation to a person under the age of 16 or under s. 8 (including aiding, abetting, counselling, procuring, inciting or attempting the commission of such an offence), falls within the relevant sexual offences category for the purposes of s. 103(2)(b) of the Criminal Justice Act 2003 (a defendant's propensity to commit offences of the kind with which he/she is charged—**see para. 4.3**).

4.5 Child Sex Offences

In addition to the generic sexual offences above (such as rape) where the victim is a child, the Sexual Offences Act 2003 creates several specific offences relating to sexual activity involving or directed towards children. These are set out below. In considering each offence it is important to remember the relevant ages, both of offenders and victims. In addition, the Act makes special exceptions to some offences of aiding, abetting or counselling some offences involving children. In summary a person will not be guilty of aiding, abetting or counselling the specified offence against a child if he/she acts for the purpose of:

- protecting the child from sexually transmitted infection,
- protecting the physical safety of the child,
- preventing the child from becoming pregnant, or
- promoting the child's emotional well-being by the giving of advice,

and not for the purpose of obtaining sexual gratification or for the purpose of causing or encouraging the activity constituting the offence or the child's participation in it (s. 73).

The full list of offences is set out in s. 73(2); basically it covers specific offences against children under 13 and offences involving sexual activity with a child under 16.

4.5.1 Sexual Activity with a Child

OFFENCE: **Sexual Activity with a Child—*Sexual Offences Act 2003, s. 9***

• If involves penetration: of victim's anus or vagina by a part of defendant's body or anything else, of victim's mouth with defendant's penis, of defendant's anus or vagina by a part of victim's body or of defendant's mouth by victim's penis—triable on indictment; 14 years' imprisonment • Otherwise triable either way; 14 years' imprisonment on indictment; six months' imprisonment summarily

The Sexual Offences Act 2003, s. 9 states:

(1) A person aged 18 or over (A) commits an offence if—
 (a) he intentionally touches another person (B),
 (b) the touching is sexual, and
 (c) either—
  (i) B is under 16 and A does not reasonably believe that B is 16 or over, or
  (ii) B is under 13.

KEYNOTE

The person committing this offence must be at least 18. If the defendant is under 18, he or she commits a specific offence, punishable by 5 years' imprisonment (if tried on indictment) under s. 13. Similarly, if the person committing the offence is in a position of trust in relation to the victim, he/she commits a specific offence under s. 16.

You must show that the defendant intentionally touched the victim sexually (**see para. 4.2.1**) and either that the victim was under 13 (in which case the offence is complete) or that the victim was under 16 and that the defendant did not reasonably believe he/she was 16 or over. In either case consent is irrelevant.

There is a further specific offence (s. 10) of a person aged 18 or over intentionally causing or inciting another to engage in the type of sexual activity set out above. The sexual activity caused or envisaged may be with the defendant or with a third person. In the case of incitement there is no need for the sexual activity itself to take place. If the person committing the offence is in a position of trust in relation to the victim, he/she commits a specific offence under s. 17.

An offence under s. 9 or 10 (including aiding, abetting, counselling, procuring, inciting or attempting the commission of such an offence) falls within the relevant sexual offences category for the purposes of s. 103(2)(b) of the Criminal Justice Act 2003 (a defendant's propensity to commit offences of the kind with which he/she is charged—**see para. 4.3**).

4.5.2 Sexual Activity in Presence of a Child

OFFENCE: **Engaging in Sexual Activity in the Presence of a Child—*Sexual Offences Act 2003, s. 11***

• Triable either way • Ten years' imprisonment on indictment • Six months' imprisonment summarily

The Sexual Offences Act 2003, s. 11 states:

(1) A person aged 18 or over (A) commits an offence if—
 (a) he intentionally engages in an activity,
 (b) the activity is sexual,
 (c) for the purpose of obtaining sexual gratification, he engages in it—

(i) when another person (B) is present or is in a place from which A can be observed, and
(ii) knowing or believing that B is aware, or intending that B should be aware, that he is engaging in it, and

(d) either—

(i) B is under 16 and A does not reasonably believe that B is 16 or over, or
(ii) B is under 13.

KEYNOTE

The person committing this offence must be at least 18. If the defendant is under 18, he/she commits a specific offence, punishable by 5 years' imprisonment (if tried on indictment) under s. 13. Similarly, if the person committing the offence is in a position of trust in relation to the victim, he/she commits a specific offence under s. 18.

The activity in which the offender is engaged must be 'sexual' (**see para. 4.2.1**) and intentional and must be in order to obtain sexual gratification (for the defendant). The display of sexual images or sexual activity might, in certain circumstances, be appropriate, for example, for medical or educational reasons, hence the requirement that the offence depended on the corrupt purpose of 'sexual gratification'. However, the offence under s. 12 of the Act does not require that such gratification has to be taken immediately; i.e. the section does not require that the offence can only be committed if the purposed sexual gratification and the viewed sexual act, or display of images, were simultaneous, contemporaneous or synchronised. For example, the defendant may cause a child to watch a sexual act to put the child in a frame of mind for future sexual abuse, as well as where the defendant does so to obtain enjoyment from seeing the child watch the sexual act (*R* v *Abdullahi* [2006] EWCA Crim 2060). The approach to 'sexual gratification' taken in *Abdullahi* appears equally applicable to other offences where this phrase appears (the offence under s. 11 of the Act, for example).

You must show that a person under 16 is present or is in a place from which the defendant can be observed *and* that the defendant knew, believed or intended that the child was aware that he/she was engaging in that activity. Therefore, it is not necessary to show that the child was in fact aware of the activity in every case (although that would clearly help in terms of proving the defendant's state of mind). Because of the wording in s. 79(7), 'observation' includes direct observation or by looking at any image.

In relation to the child you must show also that either the child was under 13 (in which case the offence is complete) or that he/she was under 16 and that the defendant did not reasonably believe him/her to be 16 or over.

This offence is aimed at, for example, people masturbating in front of children or performing sexual acts with others where they know they can be seen (or they want to be seen) by children directly or via a camera/video phone etc.

4.5.3 Causing a Child to Watch a Sex Act

OFFENCE: **Causing a Child to Watch a Sexual Act—*Sexual Offences Act 2003, s. 12***

• Triable either way • Ten years' imprisonment on indictment • Six months' imprisonment summarily

The Sexual Offences Act 2003, s. 12 states:

(1) A person aged 18 or over (A) commits an offence if—

(a) for the purpose of obtaining sexual gratification, he intentionally causes another person (B) to watch a third person engaging in an activity, or to look at an image of any person engaging in an activity,
(b) the activity is sexual, and
(c) either—

(i) B is under 16 and A does not reasonably believe that B is 16 or over, or
(ii) B is under 13.

KEYNOTE

The person committing this offence must be at least 18. If the defendant is under 18, he/she commits a specific offence, punishable by 5 years' imprisonment (if tried on indictment) under s. 13. Similarly, if the person committing the offence is in a position of trust in relation to the victim, he/she commits a specific offence under s. 19.

While the related offence under s. 11 is concerned with the engaging in sexual activity which the person knows, believes or intends to be observed by a child, the above offence is concerned with intentionally causing a child to watch a third person engaging in such activity *or* to look at an image of a person *engaging in such activity.* 'Image' includes a moving or still image and includes an image produced by any means and, where the context permits, a three-dimensional image (s. 79(4)); it also includes images of an imaginary person (s. 79(5)).

As with the s. 11 offence, you must show that the defendant acted for the purposes of obtaining sexual gratification. For issues in relation to the term 'sexual gratification' see the explanation given in para. 4.5.2. Similarly, you must also show that either the child was under 13 (in which case the offence is complete) or that he/she was under 16 and that the defendant did not reasonably believe him/her to be 16 or over.

4.5.4 Arranging Intended Child Sex Offences

OFFENCE: **Arranging or Facilitating Commission of Child Sex Offences—*Sexual Offences Act 2003, s. 14***

• Triable either way • 14 years' imprisonment on indictment • Six months' imprisonment summarily

The Sexual Offences Act 2003, s. 14 states:

(1) A person commits an offence if—
(a) he intentionally arranges or facilitates something that he intends to do, intends another person to do, or believes that another person will do, in any part of the world, and
(b) doing it will involve the commission of an offence under any of sections 9 to 13.

KEYNOTE

This offence addresses the activities of those who arrange or facilitate child sex offences. The relevant offences are those set out in ss. 9–13 of the Act set out in the earlier paragraphs of this chapter.

The offence applies to activities by which the defendant intends to commit one of those relevant child sex offences him/herself, or by which the defendant intends or believes another person will do so, in either case in any part of the world. The offence is complete whether or not the sexual activity actually takes place. Examples of the offence would include a defendant approaching a third person to procure a child to take part in sexual activity with him or where the defendant makes travel arrangements for another in the belief that the other person will commit a relevant child sex offence.

This part of the Act specifically excludes the actions of those who are protecting the child in question. The exception will apply to a person acting for the child's protection who arranges or facilitates something that he/she believes another person will do, but that he/she does not intend to do or intend another person to do. Acting for the child's protection must fall within one of the following:

- protecting the child from sexually transmitted infection,
- protecting the physical safety of the child,

- preventing the child from becoming pregnant, or
- promoting the child's emotional well-being by the giving of advice,

and not for obtaining sexual gratification or for causing or encouraging the activity constituting the relevant child sex offence or the child's participation in it. This statutory exception (contained in s. 14(2) and (3)) covers activities such as health workers supplying condoms to people under 16 who are intent on having sex in any event and need protection from infection; it also potentially extends to covert investigative operations.

If carrying out the above offence will involve the commission of an offence under s. 9 or 10 (arranging or facilitating the commission of a child sex offence—**see para. 4.5.1**) it will fall within the relevant sexual offences category for the purposes of s. 103(2)(b) of the Criminal Justice Act 2003 (a defendant's propensity to commit offences of the kind with which he/she is charged—**see para. 4.3**). So too will aiding, abetting, counselling, procuring, inciting or attempting the commission of such an offence.

OFFENCE: **Meeting a Child Following Sexual Grooming—*Sexual Offences Act 2003, s. 15***

- Triable either way • Ten years' imprisonment on indictment • Six months' imprisonment summarily

The Sexual Offences Act 2003, s. 15 states:

(1) A person aged 18 or over (A) commits an offence if—
- (a) A has met or communicated with another person (B) on at least two occasions and subsequently—
  - (i) A intentionally meets B,
  - (ii) A travels with the intention of meeting B in any part of the world or arranges to meet B in any part of the world, or
  - (iii) B travels with the intention of meeting A in any part of the world,
- (b) A intends to do anything to or in respect of B, during or after the meeting mentioned in paragraph (a)(i) to (iii) and in any part of the world, which if done will involve the commission by A of a relevant offence,
- (c) B is under 16, and
- (d) A does not reasonably believe that B is 16 or over.

KEYNOTE

This offence is designed to deal with the increase in child grooming as a result of developments in communications technology (such as the Internet). The initial behaviour by the defendant involves either a communication with the victim (who must be under 16) on at least two previous occasions *or* a meeting with the victim on at least two previous occasions. The communications or meetings can (and often will) be innocuous, such as family occasions or during the course of youth activities, sports fixtures and so on. The communications can include text messaging or interactions on Internet 'chat rooms'. The meetings or communications can have taken place in any part of the world (s. 15(2)).

Once these earlier meetings or communications have taken place, the offence itself is triggered by either:

- an intentional meeting with the victim, or
- the defendant travelling with the intention of meeting the victim.

At the time of either of the above, the defendant must intend to do anything to or in respect of the victim, during or even after the meeting, that would amount to a relevant offence. A relevant offence here is generally any offence under part I of the Act (all the offences covered in this chapter). Note that the intended offence does not have to take place.

You must show that the victim was under 16 and that the defendant did not reasonably believe that he/she was 16 or over.

4.5.5 Sex Offences with Family Members

OFFENCE: **Sexual Activity with Child Family Member—*Sexual Offences Act* 2003, *ss.* 25 *and* 26**

• Where defendant is 18 or over at the time of the offence and if involves penetration: of victim's anus or vagina by a part of defendant's body or anything else, of victim's mouth with defendant's penis, of defendant's anus or vagina by a part of victim's body or of defendant's mouth by victim's penis—triable on indictment: 14 years' imprisonment • Otherwise triable either way; 14 years' imprisonment on indictment; six months' imprisonment and/or fine summarily • Or, where defendant is under 18 at the time of the offence; five years' imprisonment on indictment; six months' imprisonment and/or fine summarily

The Sexual Offences Act 2003, s. 25 states:

(1) A person (A) commits an offence if—
 (a) he intentionally touches another person (B),
 (b) the touching is sexual,
 (c) the relation of A to B is within section 27,
 (d) A knows or could reasonably be expected to know that his relation to B is of a description falling within that section, and
 (e) either—
  (i) B is under 18 and A does not reasonably believe that B is 18 or over, or
  (ii) B is under 13.

KEYNOTE

Where the defendant intentionally incites another person (the victim) to touch him/her or to allow him/herself to be touched by the defendant, there is a specific—and to all practical purposes identically worded—offence under s. 26.

For the relevant definitions of touching and sexual see the earlier paragraphs in this chapter.

There are two further elements that must be proved in relation to these offences. The first is the existence of the relevant family relationship between the defendant and the victim, the second is the age of the victim.

Note that, where the relevant family relationship is proved, it will be presumed that the defendant knew or could reasonably have been expected to know that he or she was related to the victim in that way. Similarly where it is proved that the victim was under 18, there will be a presumption that the defendant did not reasonably believe that the victim was 18 or over. In respect of both the relationship and the age of the defendant under these circumstances, the defendant will have an evidential burden to discharge in that regard (see s. 25(2) and (3)).

The relevant family relationships are set out in s. 27. These cover all the close family relationships that you would expect, along with adoptive relationships. In summary the relationships are where:

- the defendant or the victim is the other's parent, grandparent, brother, sister, half-brother, half-sister, aunt or uncle or
- the defendant is or has been the victim's foster parent.

Additional categories are where the defendant and victim live or have lived in the same household, or the defendant is or has been regularly involved in caring for, training, supervising or being in sole charge of the victim and:

- one of them is or has been the other's step-parent,
- they are cousins,
- one of them is or has been the other's stepbrother or stepsister, or
- they have the same parent or foster parent.

For a full definition of the various familial relationships and their application to the specific offences, reference should be made to the statutory text.

There are exceptions for situations where the defendant and the victim are lawfully married at the time or where (under certain circumstances) the sexual relationship pre-dates the family one—for example, where two divorcees each have a child of 17 who are engaged in a sexual relationship before their respective parents marry and move all four of them into the same household.

An offence under s. 25 or 26 if committed in relation to a person under the age of 16 (including aiding, abetting, counselling, procuring, inciting or attempting the commission of such an offence) will fall within the relevant sexual offences category for the purposes of s. 103(2)(b) of the Criminal Justice Act 2003 (a defendant's propensity to commit offences of the kind with which he/she is charged—**see para. 4.3**).

4.5.6 Other Offences with Family Members

The Sexual Offences Act goes on to clarify and extend a number of other sexual offences involving adult family members (see ss. 64–65). These replace the former offences of incest and generally create either way offences punishable by up to two years' imprisonment. They can be committed by both parties where one relative (who is 16 or over) intentionally penetrates the vagina or anus of another relative (aged 18 or over) with anything, or penetrates their mouth with his penis and in each case the relative knows (or could reasonably be expected to know) that he/she is related to the other in the way described. The relatives are parent, grandparent, child, grandchild, brother, sister, half-brother, half-sister, aunt, uncle, nephew or niece (this does not include adopted children).

4.5.7 Indecent Photographs

OFFENCE: **Indecent Photographs—*Protection of Children Act 1978, s. 1***

• Triable either way • Ten years' imprisonment on indictment • Six months' imprisonment and/or a fine summarily

The Protection of Children Act 1978, ss. 1, 1A and 1B state:

1 Indecent photographs of children

(1) Subject to sections 1A and 1B, it is an offence for a person—
  (a) to take, or permit to be taken or to make, any indecent photograph or pseudo-photograph of a child...; or
  (b) to distribute or show such indecent photographs or pseudo-photographs; or
  (c) to have in his possession such indecent photographs or pseudo-photographs, with a view to their being distributed or shown by himself or others; or
  (d) to publish or cause to be published any advertisement likely to be understood as conveying that the advertiser distributes or shows such indecent photographs or pseudo-photographs, or intends to do so.

(2) For purposes of this Act, a person is to be regarded as distributing an indecent photograph or pseudo-photograph if he parts with possession of it to, or exposes or offers it for acquisition by, another person.

(3) . . .

(4) Where a person is charged with an offence under subsection (1)(b) or (c), it shall be a defence for him to prove—

(a) that he had a legitimate reason for distributing or showing the photographs or pseudo-photographs or (as the case may be) having them in his possession; or

(b) that he had not himself seen the photographs or pseudo-photographs and did not know, nor had any cause to suspect, them to be indecent.

(5) References in the Children and Young Persons Act 1933 (except in sections 15 and 99) to the offences mentioned in Schedule 1 to that Act shall include an offence under subsection (1)(a) above.

1A Marriage and other relationships

(1) This section applies where, in proceedings for an offence under section 1(1)(a) of taking or making an indecent photograph of a child, or for an offence under section 1(1)(b) or (c) relating to an indecent photograph of a child, the defendant proves that the photograph was of the child aged 16 or over, and that at the time of the offence charged the child and he—

(a) were married, or civil partners of each other or

(b) lived together as partners in an enduring family relationship.

(2) Subsections (5) and (6) also apply where, in proceedings for an offence under section 1(1)(b) or (c) relating to an indecent photograph of a child, the defendant proves that the photograph was of the child aged 16 or over, and that at the time when he obtained it the child and he—

(a) were married, or civil partners of each other or

(b) lived together as partners in an enduring family relationship.

(3) This section applies whether the photograph showed the child alone or with the defendant, but not if it showed any other person.

(4) In the case of an offence under section 1(1)(a), if sufficient evidence is adduced to raise an issue as to whether the child consented to the photograph being taken or made, or as to whether the defendant reasonably believed that the child so consented, the defendant is not guilty of the offence unless it is proved that the child did not so consent and that the defendant did not reasonably believe that the child so consented.

(5) In the case of an offence under section 1(1)(b), the defendant is not guilty of the offence unless it is proved that the showing or distributing was to a person other than the child.

1B Exception for criminal proceedings, investigations etc.

(1) In proceedings for an offence under section 1(1)(a) of making an indecent photograph or pseudo-photograph of a child, the defendant is not guilty of the offence if he proves that—

(a) it was necessary for him to make the photograph or pseudo-photograph for the purposes of the prevention, detection or investigation of crime, or for the purposes of criminal proceedings, in any part of the world,

(b) at the time of the offence charged he was a member of the Security Service, and it was necessary for him to make the photograph or pseudo-photograph for the exercise of any of the functions of the Service, or

(c) at the time of the offence charged he was a member of GCHQ, and it was necessary for him to make the photograph or pseudo-photograph for the exercise of any of the functions of GCHQ.

What is a photograph?

Section 7 of the Protection of Children Act 1978 (as amended by the Criminal Justice and Immigration Act 2008) provides a definition of a photograph for the purposes of the Act and states:

(1) The following subsections apply for the interpretation of this Act.

(2) References to an indecent photograph include an indecent film, a copy of an indecent film, and an indecent photograph comprised in a film.

(3) Photographs (including those comprised in a film) shall, if they show children and are indecent, be treated for all purposes of this Act as indecent photographs of children and so as respects of pseudo-photographs.

(4) References to a photograph include—
 (a) the negative as well as the positive version; and
 (b) data stored on a computer disc or by other electronic means which is capable of conversion into a photograph.

(4A) References to a photograph also include—
 (a) a tracing or other image, whether made by electronic or other means (of whatever nature)—
  (i) which is not itself a photograph or pseudo-photograph, but
  (ii) which is derived from the whole or part of a photograph or pseudo-photograph (or a combination of either or both); and
 (b) data stored on a computer disc or by other electronic means which is capable of conversion into an image within paragraph (a);

and subsection (8) applies in relation to such an image as it applies in relation to a pseudo-photograph.

(5) 'Film' includes any form of video-recording.

(6) 'Child', subject to subsection (8), means a person under the age of 18.

(7) 'Pseudo-photograph' means an image, whether made by computer graphics or otherwise howsoever, which appears to be a photograph.

(8) If the impression conveyed by a pseudo-photograph is that the person shown is a child, the pseudo-photograph shall be treated for all purposes of this Act as showing a child and so shall a pseudo-photograph where the predominant impression conveyed is that the person shown is a child notwithstanding that some of the physical characteristics shown are those of an adult.

(9) References to an indecent pseudo-photograph include—
 (a) a copy of an indecent pseudo-photograph; and
 (b) data stored on a computer disc or by other electronic means which is capable of conversion into a pseudo-photograph.

OFFENCE: **Indecent Photographs—*Criminal Justice Act 1988, s. 160***

• Triable either way • Five years' imprisonment on indictment • Six months' imprisonment and/or a fine

The Criminal Justice Act 1988, ss. 160 and 160A state:

160 Possession of indecent photograph of child

(1) Subject to subsecton (1A) it is an offence for a person to have any indecent photograph or pseudo-photograph of a child in his possession.

(2) Where a person is charged with an offence under subsection (1) above, it shall be a defence for him to prove—
 (a) that he had a legitimate reason for having the photograph or pseudo-photograph in his possession; or
 (b) that he had not himself seen the photograph or pseudo-photograph and did not know, nor had any cause to suspect, it to be indecent; or
 (c) that the photograph or pseudo-photograph was sent to him without any prior request made by him or on his behalf and that he did not keep it for an unreasonable time.

160A Marriage and other relationships

(1) This section applies where, in proceedings for an offence under section 160 relating to an indecent photograph of a child, the defendant proves that the photograph was of the child aged 16 or over, and that at the time of the offence charged the child and he—
 (a) were married, or civil partners of each other or
 (b) lived together as partners in an enduring family relationship.

(2) This section also applies where, in proceedings for an offence under section 160 relating to an indecent photograph of a child, the defendant proves that the photograph was of the child aged 16 or over, and that at the time when he obtained it the child and he—
  (a) were married, or civil partners of each other or
  (b) lived together as partners in an enduring family relationship.
(3) This section applies whether the photograph showed the child alone or with the defendant, but not if it showed any other person.
(4) If sufficient evidence is adduced to raise an issue as to whether the child consented to the photograph being in the defendant's possession, or as to whether the defendant reasonably believed that the child so consented, the defendant is not guilty of the offence unless it is proved that the child did not so consent and that the defendant did not reasonably believe that the child so consented.

KEYNOTE

Once the defendant realises, *or should realise*, that material is indecent, any distribution, showing or retention of the material with a view to its being distributed will result in a *prima facie* offence being made out under the 1978 Act if the person depicted turns out to be a child (*R* v *Land* [1999] QB 65). This is because s. 160(4) provides no defence of mistake as to a child's age.

A person will be a 'child' for the purposes of both Acts above if it appears from the evidence as a whole that he/she was, at the material time, under the age of 18 (Protection of Children Act 1978, s. 2(3) and Criminal Justice Act 1988, s. 160(4)).

However, if the impression conveyed by a pseudo-photograph is that the person shown is a child or where the predominant impression is that the person is a child, that pseudo-photograph will be treated for these purposes as a photograph of a child, notwithstanding that some of the physical characteristics shown are those of an adult (s. 7(8) of the 1978 Act).

'Pseudo-photographs' include computer images and the above offences will cover the situation where part of the photograph is made up of an adult form. Downloading images from the Internet will amount to 'making' a photograph for the purposes of s. 1(1)(a) of the 1978 Act (*R* v *Bowden* [2000] 2 WLR 1083). 'Making' pseudo-photographs includes voluntarily browsing through indecent images of children on and from the Internet (*R* v *Smith and Jayson* [2002] EWCA Crim 683). In *Smith and Jayson* the Court of Appeal held that a person receiving an unsolicited e-mail attachment containing an indecent image of a child would not commit an offence under s. 1(1) by opening it if he/she was unaware that it contained or was likely to contain an indecent image. This was because s. 1(1)(a) does not create an absolute offence (see also *Atkins* v *DPP* [2000] 1 WLR 1427). This may create a potential 'loophole' for paedophiles using the Internet, but all the relevant circumstances of their viewing will need to be considered. In proving the 1978 Act offence you have to show that the act of 'making' the image was deliberate and intentional with the knowledge that it was, or was likely to be, an indecent photograph or pseudo-photograph of a child. Any title that accompanied the e-mail, along with the level of IT literacy of the defendant and any subsequent e-mail correspondence that he/she had with the sender after opening the attachment, will be directly relevant to the issue of the defendant's state of mind (*mens rea*) in this offence. These issues were relevant in the case of *R* v *Harrison* [2007] EWCA Crim 2976. In this case the defendant was convicted for possessing indecent photographs of a child. The defendant was a regular user of pornographic websites and was aware that illegal photographs appeared on those websites by way of automatic 'pop-up' mechanisms. These pop-ups would then be stored to the hard drive of his computer. The Crown alleged that the defendant was aware of this and was therefore in possession of them. The Crown conceded that in order to obtain a conviction on the possession count it needed to prove not only that the defendant was in possession of the images but that he made them by copying them to his hard drive via the pop-ups. The defendant argued that a person could not be said to make an illegal image if, when using a computer to access websites comprised of lawful pornographic material, without further action on his part, the programming associated with the site caused illegal material to pop up and that it was the website creators that had caused the image to appear and not the end user. Although there were difficulties in applying the law to the rapidly changing nature of the Internet, the appeal was dismissed. The notion that it was the website designer, not the user, that made the image was contrary to authority and to the ordinary meaning of the language. The court concluded that the jury must have decided against the defendant in relation to the existence and function of the computer in storing information automatically and that he would have known that the images he accessed were so stored. It was common ground that the defendant knew that pop-ups or redirections to other sites would occur when accessing legal pornographic websites and the issue for the jury had been whether he knew of the likelihood that in accessing certain sites, illegal material would be accessed in that way. There was an evidential basis for the jury to be sure, based on the defendant's previous use of particular sites, that they were likely to contain illegal images.

In *Smith and Jayson* the Court of Appeal went on to say that, once an image is downloaded, the length of time it remains on the screen is irrelevant.

In *R* v *Porter* [2006] EWCA Crim 560, the court considered the issues surrounding retrieval. The defendant had been charged with offences under s. 160 of the Act following the seizure of his computer. On the hard drive of the computer there were images of child pornography. However, these files had been deleted and the recycle bin emptied so that the deleted images could only be retrieved using specialist software which the defendant did not have. Although originally convicted, the defendant's conviction was quashed. The Court stated that if a person cannot gain access to retrieve deleted images on a computer then he was no longer in custody or control of those images. It could not be said that an image that a person cannot retrieve from a computer hard drive is in that person's possession simply because it is on the hard drive. Whether the defendant is in custody or control of the image is a question for the jury, but if at the material time the image is beyond the defendant's control then he cannot be in possession of it.

The statutory defence under s. 160(2)(b) of the 1988 Act above is broader than it seems at first. Although the wording requires that the defendant (1) has not seen the material and (2) did not know or have *any* cause to suspect it was indecent, the defendant will be acquitted of the offence under s. 160 if he/she proves that (1) he/she had not seen the material and (2) did not know (and had no cause to suspect) that it was *an indecent photograph of a child*. This was confirmed by the Court of Appeal in *R* v *Collier* [2004] EWCA Crim 1411 and arose from an argument where the material relating to children had been among other adult material that the defendant *did* know was indecent—he just did not know that it was an indecent photograph *of a child*. While this is a very technical distinction, it is very relevant when evidence gathering and interviewing suspects for the s. 160 offence.

Evidence indicating an interest in paedophile material generally can also be relevant to show that it was more likely than not that a file containing an indecent image of a child *had* been created deliberately. Such evidence has been held by the Court of Appeal to be relevant for this purpose, along with evidence showing how a computer had been used to access paedophile news groups, chatlines and websites (*R* v *Mould* [2001] 2 Crim App R(S) 8). A further decision on the making of a 'pseudo-photograph' has held that an image consisting of two parts of two different photographs taped together (the naked body of a woman taped to the head of a child) would not suffice (*Goodland* v *DPP* [2000] 1 WLR 1427). In that case the Divisional Court accepted that such an image, *if photocopied*, could fall within the meaning of a 'pseudo-photograph'. The Court of Appeal has confirmed that the offence under s. 1(1)(a) is justified by the requirement to protect children from being exploited and does not contravene article 8 or article 10 of the European Convention on Human Rights (*R* v *Smethurst* [2001] Crim LR 657). The finer IT issues that are typically involved in these cases were further considered in *R* v *Dooley* [2005] EWCA Crim 3093. In that case the defendant appealed against convictions on six counts of possession of indecent photographs of a child with a view to their being distributed (contrary to s. 1(1)(c) of the 1978 Act, above). The defendant belonged to an Internet-based file sharing network that allowed users to share files stored in a folder named 'my shared folder' on their computer. The defendant's computer was found to have six indecent images of children stored in the shared folder but many thousands of other such images were stored elsewhere on the computer. The defendant maintained that he had intended to remove the pictures from the shared folder. The appeal turned on the judge's preliminary ruling on the meaning of 'with a view to' under s. 1(1)(c). The Court of Appeal agreed with the judge's ruling that there was a distinction between 'with the intention of' and 'with a view to'—where a defendant had knowledge that images were likely to be accessed by other people, any images would be downloaded 'with a view to distribute'. If one of the reasons the defendant left the pictures in the shared folder was so others could have access to them, he would be in possession of the images 'with a view to their being distributed'. However, as the court accepted that the defendant did *not* leave the pictures in the shared folder for that reason, his conviction could not stand.

A legitimate purpose for possessing such material might be where someone has the material as an exhibits officer or as a training aid for police officers or social workers.

The consent of the DPP is needed before prosecuting an offence under the Protection of Children Act 1978.

Distributing will include lending or offering to another. Clearly cases falling within the above legislation will vary significantly and there needs to be some distinction between the seriousness of different types of material. The Court of Appeal has set out five broad levels of seriousness and these are of use, not only in helping police officers and investigators understand how the offences will be dealt with by the criminal courts, but also in explaining this to victims and witnesses. The levels are:

(1) images depicting erotic posing with no sexual activity;
(2) sexual activity between children, or solo masturbation by a child;
(3) non-penetrative sexual activity between adults and children;
(4) penetrative sexual activity between children and adults, and;
(5) sadism or bestiality.

(*R* v *Oliver* [2003] 1 Cr App R 28).

The Court of Appeal also recognised that much of this material involves abuse of the child featuring in it and held that, so far as an offender's involvement was concerned, the seriousness of an offence increased with his/her proximity to, and responsibility for, the original abuse. In considering all these factors, courts will distinguish between pseudo-photographs which had involved no abuse or exploitation of children, and photographic images that involved real children. The Court of Appeal indicated that the imprisonment would normally follow where the material had been shown or distributed to others or where the offender had been in possession of a large amount of level 2 material or a small amount of material of level 3 or above.

Note that although the offences include video recordings, possession of exposed but undeveloped film (i.e. film in the form in which it is taken out of a camera) does not appear to be covered. The offence at s. 1(1)(b) and (c) of the 1978 Act can only be proved if the defendant showed/distributed the photograph etc. or intended to show or distribute the photograph etc. *to someone else.* This is clear from the decisions in *R* v *Fellows* [1997] 1Cr App R 244 and *R* v *T* [1999] 163 JP 349. If no such intention can be proved, or if the defendant only had the photographs etc. for his/her own use, the appropriate charge would be under the 1988 Act.

Sections 1 and 2 of the Criminal Evidence (Amendment) Act 1997 apply to an offence under s. 1 of the Protection of Children Act 1978 (and to conspiracies, attempts or incitements in the circumstances set out in the 1997 Act) (see **para. 1.9.8.1**).

4.5.8 Defences to Indecent Photographs of Marriage and Other Relationships

There is a specific defence to offences under s. 1(1) (a), (b) and (c) of the Protection of Children Act 1978 (making, distributing or possessing with a view to distributing). This defence arises where the defendant can prove that the photograph was of a child aged 16 or over, the photograph only showed the defendant and the child, and that, at the time of the offence, they were married, in a civil partnership or lived together as partners in an enduring family relationship (s. 1A). This is a very narrow defence, restricted to photographs (as opposed to pseudo-photographs, which are not covered) in the restricted circumstances set out. If the defendant cannot show these elements, the defence will not apply. If the defendant *can* show these elements, then the following further conditions of the defence will apply:

- In the case of an offence under s. 1(1)(a) (taking or permitting to be taken etc.), the defendant will have an evidential burden of showing that the child consented or that the defendant reasonably believed that the child consented to the making of the photograph (s. 1A(4)).
- In the case of an offence under s. 1(1)(b) (distributing or showing), you must prove that the distributing or showing was to a person other than the child in the photograph (s. 1A(5)).
- In the case of an offence under s. 1(1)(c) (possession with a view to distribution or showing etc.), the defendant will have an evidential burden of demonstrating that the image was to be shown/distributed to no person other than the child and that the child consented to the defendant's possession of the photograph (s. 1A(6)).

Similar provisions are made in relation to the offence under s. 160 of the Criminal Justice Act 1988 (possession)—see s. 160A.

4.5.9 Exception of Indecent Photographs for Criminal Proceedings and Investigations

There is a limited defence in relation to the making of an indecent photograph or pseudo-photograph under s. 1(1)(a) of the Protection of Children Act 1978 where the defendant proves that:

- it was *necessary* for him/her to make the photograph or pseudo-photograph for the purposes of the prevention, detection or investigation of crime or for criminal proceedings in any part of the world, or
- at the time, he/she was a member of the Security Service or GCHQ (Government Communications Headquarters) and it was *necessary* for the exercise of any of the functions of the Service/GCHQ (s. 1B).

In order to assist police officers and prosecutors the Association of Chief Police Officers (ACPO) and the Crown Prosecution Service (CPS) have published a Memorandum of Understanding. This Memorandum sets out the factors that will be taken into account in deciding whether the intention of someone accused of an offence under s. 1(1)(a) attracted criminal liability when 'making' a photograph etc. As the Memorandum points out:

> This reverse burden is intended to allow those people who need to be able to identify and act to deal with such images to do so. It also presents a significant obstacle to would-be abusers and those who exploit the potential of technology to gain access to paedophilic material for unprofessional (or personal) reasons.

The purpose of the Memorandum is therefore twofold: to reassure those whose duties properly involve the prevention, detection or investigation of this type of crime and also as a warning to others who might claim this defence having taken it upon themselves to investigate such offences. In summary the following criteria will be considered:

- How soon after its discovery the image was reported and to whom.
- The circumstances in which it was discovered.
- The way in which the image was stored and dealt with, and whether it was copied.
- Whether the person's actions were reasonable, proportionate and necessary.

4.5.10 Harmful Publications

OFFENCE: **Harmful Publications—*Children and Young Persons (Harmful Publications) Act 1955, s. 2***

- Triable summarily • Four months' imprisonment and/or a fine

The Children and Young Persons (Harmful Publications) Act 1955, s. 2 states:

> (1) A person who prints, publishes, sells or lets on hire a work to which this Act applies, or has any such work in his possession for the purpose of selling it or letting it on hire, shall be guilty of an offence...

KEYNOTE

A prosecution for this offence can only be brought with the consent of the Attorney-General (or Solicitor-General). The sort of 'works' to which the Act applies are set out in s. 1 and include books, magazines or other like works of a kind likely to fall into the hands of children or young persons which consist wholly or mainly of stories told in pictures which portray:

- the commission of crimes, or
- acts of violence or cruelty, or
- incidents of a repulsive or horrible nature,

in such a way that the work as a whole would tend to corrupt a child or young person.

Power of Search

A search warrant may be issued under s. 3 of the 1955 Act.

Defence

The Children and Young Persons (Harmful Publications) Act 1955, s. 2 states:

> (1) ... in any proceedings taken under this subsection against a person in respect of selling or letting on hire a work or of having it in his possession for the purpose of selling it or letting it on hire, it shall be a defence for him to prove that he had not examined the contents of the work and had no reasonable cause to suspect that it was one to which this Act applies.

KEYNOTE

For a possible alternative charge it is worth considering s. 2(1) of the Obscene Publications Act 1959. In such a case a jury only has to be satisfied that there was a likelihood of vulnerable persons seeing the relevant obscene material and there is no need to show that a vulnerable person actually saw the material or would have seen it. This means that the charge may be particularly suitable where obscene material is made generally available on the Internet (see *R* v *Perrin* [2002] EWCA Crim 747). Where video recordings are involved, the provisions of the Video Recordings Act 1984 may also be of use. For further detail on both statutes, **see Blackstone's Criminal Practice 2008, Part B.**

4.5.11 Offences Outside the United Kingdom

Following commencement of s. 72 of the Sexual Offences Act 2003 it will be possible to prosecute a British national or a resident of the UK who travels abroad to commit sexual offences against children, regardless of whether their actions amount to a criminal offence in the country concerned. In addition, the new offence will apply to sexual offences committed against anyone under 18. The exception to this would be those age-specific offences where the victim must be under 16 or under 13 in order for the offence to be committed.

4.6 Protection of Children

Although many of the general provisions restricting the behaviour of sex offenders have been targeted at paedophiles, there are several significant areas of legislation which are aimed specifically at the protection of children, in both a sexual context and in other areas where their well-being is jeopardised.

4.6.1 Children Act 1989

When first enacted the Children Act 1989 was the most comprehensive piece of legislation affecting children ever seen in England and Wales. The Act has been supplemented by a further substantial and far-reaching statute, the Children Act 2004. Throughout the 1989 Act, which makes provision for the care and treatment of children in virtually every aspect of their development, there is a common theme of the child's rights.

Among those rights are the right to protection from harm and the Act imposes many duties on local authorities. It also provides powers for the protection of children and, in particular, for situations where emergency protection is needed.

4.6.2 Police Protection

The police have specific statutory powers to deal with the threat of significant harm posed to children and these are set out below.

Section 46 of the Children Act 1989 states:

(1) Where a constable has reasonable cause to believe that a child would otherwise be likely to suffer significant harm, he may—
   (a) remove the child to suitable accommodation and keep him there; or
   (b) take such steps as are reasonable to ensure the the child's removal from any hospital, or other place, in which he is then being accommodated is prevented.

(2) For the purposes of this Act, a child with respect to whom a constable has exercised his powers under this section is referred to as having been taken into police protection.

KEYNOTE

For most purposes of the 1989 Act, someone who is under 18 years old is a 'child' (s. 105).

The wording of s. 46(1) means that an officer may use the powers at s. 46(1)(a) and (b) if he/she has reasonable cause to believe that, if he/she does not use them, a child is likely to suffer significant harm. The issues arising from similar wording in relation to powers of arrest have been considered by the courts on a number of occasions. Generally, tests of reasonableness impose an element of objectivity and the courts will consider whether, in the circumstances, a reasonable and sober person might have formed a similar view to that of the officer.

'Harm' is a very broad term and is defined under s. 31(9). It covers all forms of ill treatment including sexual abuse and forms of ill treatment that are not physical. It also covers the impairment of health (physical or mental) and also physical, intellectual, emotional, social or behavioural development. The definition also extends to impairment suffered from seeing or hearing the ill-treatment *of any other person.*

When determining whether harm to a child's health or development is '*significant*', the child's development will be compared with that which could reasonably be expected of a similar child (s. 31(10)).

The power under s. 46 is split into two parts:

- a power to *remove* a child to suitable accommodation and keep him/her there, and
- a power to take reasonable steps to *prevent* the child's removal from a hospital or other place.

The longest a child can spend in police protection is 72 hours (s. 46(6)). It should be remembered that this is the *maximum* time that a child can be kept in police protection, not the norm.

As soon as is reasonably practicable after taking a child into police protection, the police officer must do a number of things as set out above. These things generally include:

- telling the local authority within whose area the child was found what steps have been, and are proposed to be, taken and why this aspect of communicating with the local authority is a critical part of the protective powers;
- giving details to the local authority within whose area the child is ordinarily resident of the place at which the child is being kept;
- telling the child (if he/she appears capable of understanding) of what steps have been taken and why, and what further steps may be taken;
- taking such steps as are reasonably practicable to discover the wishes and feelings of the child;
- making sure that the case is inquired into by a 'designated officer' (see below);
- taking such steps as are reasonably practicable to inform:
    - ♦ the child's parents
    - ♦ every person who is not his/her parent but who has parental responsibility for the child and
    - ♦ any other person with whom the child was living immediately before being taken into police protection,

  of the steps that the officer has taken under this section, the reasons for taking them and the further steps that may be taken with respect to the child. This element of informing the child, parent and/or relevant carers of what is happening and why is also a vital part of the protective process.

Where the child was taken into police protection by being removed to accommodation which is not provided by or on behalf of a local authority or as a refuge (under s. 51), the officer must, as soon as is reasonably practicable after taking a child into police protection, make sure that the child is moved to accommodation provided by the local authority. Every local authority must receive and provide accommodation for children in police protection where such a request is made (s. 21).

The requirement under s. 46(3)(c) to give the child information, reflects the 1989 Act's theme that children should have some influence over their own destiny.

Note that, when considering action under s. 46, it is possible that the child may already be the subject of an Emergency Protection Order (EPO) applied for by a local authority or authorised body under s. 44.

In considering the proper approach under these circumstances the Court of Appeal has held that:

- There is no express provision in the Act prohibiting the police from invoking s. 46 where an EPO is in place and it is not desirable to imply a restriction which prohibits a constable

from removing a child under s. 46 he/she has reasonable cause to believe that the child would otherwise be likely to suffer significant harm.
- The s. 46 power to remove a child can therefore be exercised even where an EPO is in force in respect of the child.
- Where a police officer knows that an EPO is in force, he/she should not exercise the power of removing a child under s. 46, unless there are compelling reasons to do so.
- The statutory scheme accords primacy to the EPO procedure under s. 44 because removal under that section is sanctioned by the court and involves a more elaborate, sophisticated and complete process of removal than under s. 46.
- Consequently, the removal of children should usually be effected pursuant to an EPO, and s. 46 should only be invoked where it is not reasonably practicable to execute an EPO.
- In deciding whether it is practicable to execute an EPO, the police should always have regard to the paramount need to protect children from significant harm.
- Failure to follow the statutory procedure may amount to the police officer's removal of the child under s. 46 being declared unlawful.

Langley v *Liverpool City Council and Chief Constable of Merseyside* [2006] 1 WLR 375.

4.6.3 Designated Officer

The reference at s. 46(3)(e) of the Act to a 'designated officer' is a reference to the appropriate officer designated for that police station for the purposes of this legislation by the relevant chief officer of police. This is a key role in ensuring the effective use of the statutory framework set up for the protection of children in these circumstances. The responsibility for ensuring that the case is inquired into by the designated officer, together with the other responsibilities under s. 46(3) and the responsibility for taking steps to inform people under s. 46(4), clearly rest with the police officer exercising the power under s. 46.

Practically, the designated officer must inquire fully and thoroughly into the case; he/she must also do what is reasonable in all the circumstances for the purpose of safeguarding or promoting the child's welfare (having regard in particular to the length of the period during which the child will be so protected) (s. 46(9)(b)).

Where a child has been taken into police protection, the designated officer must allow:

- the child's parents
- any person who is not a parent of the child but who has parental responsibility for him
- any person with whom the child was living immediately before he/she was taken into police protection
- any person in whose favour a contact order is in force with respect to the child
- any person who is allowed to have contact with the child by virtue of an order under s. 34; and
- any person acting on behalf of any of those persons,

to have such contact (if any) with the child as, in the opinion of the designated officer, is both reasonable and in the child's best interests (s. 46(10)).

The designated officer may apply for an 'emergency protection order' under s. 44 (s. 46(7)). Such an order allows the court to order the removal of the child to certain types of accommodation and to prevent the child's removal from any other place (including a hospital) where he/she was being accommodated immediately before the making of the order (s. 44(4)). An emergency protection order gives the applicant 'parental responsibility' for the child while it is in force. It also allows the court to make certain directions in relation to contact with the child and a medical or psychiatric assessment of them. Section 44A allows the court to make an order excluding certain people from a dwellinghouse where the child lives and to attach a power of arrest accordingly.

While the designated officer can apply for an emergency protection order without the local authority's knowledge or agreement (see s. 46(8)), there should be no reason why, given proper multi-agency co-operation and a well-planned child protection strategy, this situation would come about. For further guidance on multi-agency working in the area of child protection, see *Working Together to Safeguard Children* (HMSO 1999).

On completing his/her inquiry into the case, the designated officer must release the child from police protection *unless he/she considers that there is still reasonable cause for believing that the child would be likely to suffer significant harm if released* (s. 46(5)).

While a child is in police protection, neither the officer concerned nor the designated officer will have parental responsibility for him/her (s. 46(9)(a)).

When a local authority is informed that a child is in police protection, they have a duty to make 'such enquiries as they consider necessary to enable them to decide whether they should take any action to safeguard' the child (s. 47(1)(b)). A court may issue a warrant for a constable to assist a relevant person to enter premises in order to enforce an emergency protection order.

4.6.4 Contravention of Protection Order or Police Protection

OFFENCE: **Acting in Contravention of Protection Order or Power Exercised under s. 46—*Children Act 1989, s. 49***

- Triable summarily • Six months' imprisonment

The Children Act 1989, s. 49 states:

> (1) A person shall be guilty of an offence if, knowingly and without lawful authority or reasonable excuse, he—
> (a) takes a child to whom this section applies away from the responsible person;
> (b) keeps such a child away from the responsible person; or
> (c) induces, assists or incites such a child to run away or stay away from the responsible person.
>
> (2) This section applies in relation to a child who is—
> (a) in care;
> (b) the subject of an emergency protection order; or
> (c) in police protection,
> and in this section 'the responsible person' means any person who for the time being has care of him by virtue of the care order, the emergency protection order, or section 46, as the case may be.

KEYNOTE

It is arguable that, in the case of a child who is under 16, the person would also commit an offence under the Child Abduction Act 1984.

There is also a power of entry under s. 17(1)(e) of the Police and Criminal Evidence Act 1984 for 'saving life and limb'.

Where a child is taken in contravention of s. 49 above, the court may issue a 'recovery order' under s. 50. Such an order, which is also available where a child is missing or has run away, requires certain people to produce the child to an authorised person (which includes a constable (s. 50(7)(b)) or to give certain information about the child's whereabouts to a constable or officer of the court (s. 50(3)). It can also authorise a constable to enter any premises and search for the child.

Under s. 102 of the 1989 Act a court may issue a warrant to enter premises in connection with certain provisions of the Act which regulate children's homes, foster homes, child-minding premises and nursing homes for children. Section 102 allows for constables to assist any person in the exercise of their powers under those provisions. It also makes allowances for a constable to be accompanied by a medical practitioner, nurse or health visitor (s. 102(3)).

4.6.5 Disclosure of Information Regarding Child

Where a child is reported missing problems can arise once he/she is discovered to be safe and well but one of the parents wants the police to disclose the whereabouts of the child. This situation arose in *S* v *S (Chief Constable of West Yorkshire Police Intervening)* [1999] 1 All ER 281 and the Court of Appeal provided some clarification of the issues. In that case the mother left home with her three-year-old child after a marriage breakdown. The father reported the child's absence to the police who found the child and her mother in a refuge. At the request of the mother, the police advised the father that both she and the child were safe but refused to disclose their whereabouts. The father applied 'without notice' (i.e. without telling the police) to the County Court which then made an order under s. 33 of the Family Law Act 1986, requiring the police to disclose the information. The chief constable was granted leave to intervene and, following another order from the court to disclose the child's whereabouts, the chief constable appealed. Butler-Sloss LJ (one of the key figures behind the drafting of the Children Act 1989), gave the finding of the Court of Appeal. The Court held that it was only in exceptional circumstances that the police should be asked to divulge the whereabouts of a child under a s. 33 order. Their primary role in such cases should continue to be finding missing children and ensuring their safety.

However, Butler-Sloss LJ went on to say that, in such cases:

- The police are *not* in a position to give 'categoric assurances' of confidentiality to those who provide information as to the whereabouts of a child. The most they could say is that, other than by removing the child, it would be *most unlikely* that they would have to disclose the information concerning the child's whereabouts.
- An order under s. 33 provides for the information to be disclosed to the court, not to the other party or his/her solicitor.
- An order under s. 33 should not normally be made in respect of the police without their being present (*ex parte*).

Note that the provision of information by police officers in relation to civil proceedings involving children is governed by regulations; specific advice should therefore be sought before disclosing any such information.

4.7 Preparatory Offences

In addition to the many substantive offences covered by this chapter, there are specific provisions to prevent the consequences set out in those offences from happening. These 'preparatory' offences should be considered in conjunction with the general principles applying to incomplete offences.

4.7.1 Any Offence with Intent to Commit Sexual Offence

OFFENCE: **Committing Criminal Offence with Intent to Commit a Sexual Offence—*Sexual Offences Act 2003, s. 62***

• Where the offence committed is kidnapping or false imprisonment—triable on indictment only; life imprisonment • Otherwise triable either way; ten years' imprisonment on indictment; six months' imprisonment and/or a fine summarily

The Sexual Offences Act 2003, s. 62 states:

(1) A person commits an offence under this section if he commits any offence with the intention of committing a relevant sexual offence.

KEYNOTE

Relevant sexual offence means an offence under part I of the Act (virtually all regularly occurring sexual offences) including aiding, abetting, counselling or procuring such an offence (s. 62(2)). It does not extend to other sexual offences such as those under the Protection of Children Act 1978.

This offence is designed to deal with the commission of any criminal offence where the defendant's intention is to commit a relevant sexual offence. In addition to the more obvious offences of kidnapping and blackmail, this would appear to cover a vast array of possible circumstances where the defendant's ulterior motive in committing the first offence is to carry out the relevant sexual offence. As there is no express requirement for there to be any immediate link in time between the two offences, the wording appears to cover any situation from the theft of drugs or equipment to be used in the course of the sexual offence and going equipped for burglary, to the taking of a vehicle or even dangerous driving with the intention in each case of committing the further relevant sexual offence.

4.7.2 Trespass with Intent to Commit Sexual Offence

OFFENCE: **Trespass with Intent to Commit a Relevant Sexual Offence—*Sexual Offences Act 2003, s. 63***

• Triable either way • Ten years' imprisonment on indictment • Six months' imprisonment and/or a fine summarily

The Sexual Offences Act 2003, s. 63 states:

(1) A person commits an offence if—
   (a) he is a trespasser on any premises,
   (b) he intends to commit a relevant sexual offence on the premises, and
   (c) he knows that, or is reckless as to whether, he is a trespasser.

KEYNOTE

A person is a trespasser if they are on the premises without the owner or occupier's consent, whether express or implied. Generally, the defendant ought to know whether he/she is trespassing or not and recklessness will be enough in that regard.

Premises here will include a structure or part of a structure (including a tent, vehicle or vessel or other temporary or movable structure)—s. 63(2)—which is wider than the term 'building' used in the Theft Act offence of burglary.

Relevant sexual offence has the same meaning as in the s. 62 offence (see para. 4.7.1).

This offence is one of intention rather than consequence and so there is no need to prove that the substantive sexual offence took place. There is still considerable overlap between the above offence and burglary and, if the person is caught going equipped for burglary and also has the intention of committing a relevant sexual offence at the time, he/she may commit the more general offence under s. 62.

Note that the defendant must intend to commit the relevant offence on the premises.

4.7.3 Administering Substance with Intent

OFFENCE: **Administering Substance with Intent—*Sexual Offences Act 2003, s. 61***

• Triable either way • Ten years' imprisonment on indictment • Six months' imprisonment and/or a fine summarily

The Sexual Offences Act 2003, s. 61 states:

(1) A person commits an offence if he intentionally administers a substance to, or causes a substance to be taken by, another person (B)—
  (a) knowing that B does not consent, and
  (b) with the intention of stupefying or overpowering B, so as to enable any person to engage in a sexual activity that involves B.

KEYNOTE

This offence is aimed at the use of the so-called date rape drugs but is far wider than that. For instance it would cover the spiking of a victim's soft drinks with alcohol if done with the relevant intent.

'Administering or causing to be taken' covers a broader range of conduct than the parallel offences of poisoning.

The key elements are the defendant's intentionally administering the substance (*any* substance), in the knowledge that the victim does not consent and with the intention of overpowering or stupefying the victim in order that *any person* can engage in sexual activity involving the victim.

As this is an offence of intent rather than consequence there is no need for the victim to be stupefied or overpowered or for the sexual activity to take place.

So far as proof of the relevant elements is concerned **see para. 4.3.3.**

Appendix 1

PACE Code of Practice for the Exercise by Police Officers of Statutory Powers of Stop and Search; Police Officers and Police Staff of Requirements to Record Public Encounters (Code A)

This code applies to any search by a police officer and the requirement to record public encounters taking place after midnight on 31 January 2008.

General

This code of practice must be readily available at all police stations for consultation by police officers, police staff, detained persons and members of the public.

The notes for guidance included are not provisions of this code, but are guidance to police officers and others about its application and interpretation. Provisions in the annexes to the code are provisions of this code.

This code governs the exercise by police officers of statutory powers to search a person or a vehicle without first making an arrest. The main stop and search powers to which this code applies are set out in Annex A, but that list should not be regarded as definitive. [See Note 1] In addition, it covers requirements on police officers and police staff to record encounters not governed by statutory powers. This code does not apply to:

(a) the powers of stop and search under;
  (i) Aviation Security Act 1982, section 27(2);
  (ii) Police and Criminal Evidence Act 1984, section 6(1) (which relates specifically to powers of constables employed by statutory undertakers on the premises of the statutory undertakers).

(b) searches carried out for the purposes of examination under Schedule 7 to the Terrorism Act 2000 and to which the Code of Practice issued under paragraph 6 of Schedule 14 to the Terrorism Act 2000 applies.

1 Principles governing stop and search

1.1 Powers to stop and search must be used fairly, responsibly, with respect for people being searched and without unlawful discrimination. The Race Relations (Amendment) Act 2000 makes it unlawful for police officers to discriminate on the grounds of race, colour, ethnic origin, nationality or national origins when using their powers.

1.2 The intrusion on the liberty of the person stopped or searched must be brief and detention for the purposes of a search must take place at or near the location of the stop.

1.3 If these fundamental principles are not observed the use of powers to stop and search may be drawn into question. Failure to use the powers in the proper manner reduces their effectiveness. Stop and search can play an important role in the detection and prevention of crime, and using the powers fairly makes them more effective.

1.4 The primary purpose of stop and search powers is to enable officers to allay or confirm suspicions about individuals without exercising their power of arrest. Officers may be required to justify the use or authorisation of such powers, in relation both to individual searches and the overall pattern of their activity in this regard, to their supervisory officers or in court. Any misuse of the powers is likely to be harmful to policing and lead to mistrust of the police. Officers must also be able to explain their actions to the member of the public searched. The misuse of these powers can lead to disciplinary action.

1.5 An officer must not search a person, even with his or her consent, where no power to search is applicable. Even where a person is prepared to submit to a search voluntarily, the person must not be searched unless the necessary legal power exists, and the search must be in accordance with the relevant power and the provisions of this Code. The only exception, where an officer does not require a specific power, applies to searches of persons entering sports grounds or other premises carried out with their consent given as a condition of entry.

2 Explanation of powers to stop and search

2.1 This code applies to powers of stop and search as follows:

(a) powers which require reasonable grounds for suspicion, before they may be exercised; that articles unlawfully obtained or possessed are being carried, or under Section 43 of the Terrorism Act 2000 that a person is a terrorist;

(b) authorised under section 60 of the Criminal Justice and Public Order Act 1994, based upon a reasonable belief that incidents involving serious violence may take place or that people are carrying dangerous instruments or offensive weapons within any locality in the police area;

(c) authorised under section 44(1) and (2) of the Terrorism Act 2000 based upon a consideration that the exercise of one or both powers is expedient for the prevention of acts of terrorism;

(d) powers to search a person who has not been arrested in the exercise of a power to search premises (see Code B paragraph 2.4).

Searches requiring reasonable grounds for suspicion

2.2 Reasonable grounds for suspicion depend on the circumstances in each case. There must be an objective basis for that suspicion based on facts, information, and/or intelligence which are relevant to the likelihood of finding an article of a certain kind or, in the case of searches under section 43 of the Terrorism Act 2000, to the likelihood that the person is a terrorist. Reasonable suspicion can never be supported on the basis of personal factors alone without reliable supporting intelligence or information or some specific behaviour by the person concerned. For example, a person's race, age, appearance, or the fact that the person is known to have a previous conviction, cannot be used alone or in combination with each other as the reason for searching that person. Reasonable suspicion cannot be based on generalisations or stereotypical images of certain groups or categories of people as more likely to be involved in criminal activity. A person's religion cannot be considered as reasonable grounds for suspicion and should never be considered as a reason to stop or stop and search an individual.

2.3 Reasonable suspicion can sometimes exist without specific information or intelligence and on the basis of some level of generalisation stemming from the behaviour of a person. For example, if an officer encounters someone on the street at night who is obviously trying to hide something, the officer may (depending on the other surrounding circumstances) base such suspicion on the fact that this kind of behaviour is often linked to stolen or prohibited articles being carried. Similarly, for the purposes of section 43 of the Terrorism Act 2000, suspicion that a person is a terrorist may arise from the person's behaviour at or near a location which has been identified as a potential target for terrorists.

2.4 However, reasonable suspicion should normally be linked to accurate and current intelligence or information, such as information describing an article being carried, a suspected offender, or a person who has been seen carrying a type of article known to have been stolen recently from premises in the area. Searches based on accurate and current intelligence or information are more likely to be effective. Targeting searches in a particular area at specified crime problems increases their effectiveness and minimises inconvenience to law-abiding members of the public. It also helps in justifying the use of searches both to those who are searched and to the public. This does not however prevent stop and search powers being exercised in other locations where such powers may be exercised and reasonable suspicion exists.

2.5 Searches are more likely to be effective, legitimate, and secure public confidence when reasonable suspicion is based on a range of factors. The overall use of these powers is more likely to be effective when up to date and accurate intelligence or information is communicated to officers and they are well-informed about local crime patterns.

2.6 Where there is reliable information or intelligence that members of a group or gang habitually carry knives unlawfully or weapons or controlled drugs, and wear a distinctive item of clothing or other means of identification to indicate their membership of the group or gang, that distinctive item of clothing or other means of identification may provide reasonable grounds to stop and search a person. [See *Note 9*]

2.7 A police officer may have reasonable grounds to suspect that a person is in innocent possession of a stolen or prohibited article or other item for which he or she is empowered to search. In that case the officer may stop and search the person even though there would be no power of arrest.

2.8 Under section 43(1) of the Terrorism Act 2000 a constable may stop and search a person whom the officer reasonably suspects to be a terrorist to discover whether the person is in possession of anything which may constitute evidence that the person is a terrorist. These searches may only be carried out by an officer of the same sex as the person searched.

2.9 An officer who has reasonable grounds for suspicion may detain the person concerned in order to carry out a search. Before carrying out a search the officer may ask questions about the person's behaviour or presence in circumstances which gave rise to the suspicion. As a result of questioning the detained person, the reasonable grounds for suspicion necessary to detain that person may be confirmed or, because of a satisfactory explanation, be eliminated. [See *Notes 2* and *3*] Questioning may also reveal reasonable grounds to suspect the possession of a different kind of unlawful article from that originally suspected. Reasonable grounds for suspicion however cannot be provided retrospectively by such questioning during a person's detention or by refusal to answer any questions put.

2.10 If, as a result of questioning before a search, or other circumstances which come to the attention of the officer, there cease to be reasonable grounds for suspecting that an article is being carried of a kind for which there is a power to stop and search, no search may take place. [See *Note 3*] In the absence of any other lawful power to detain, the person is free to leave at will and must be so informed.

2.11 There is no power to stop or detain a person in order to find grounds for a search. Police officers have many encounters with members of the public which do not involve detaining people against their will. If reasonable grounds for suspicion emerge during such an encounter, the officer may search the person, even though no grounds existed when the encounter began. If an officer is detaining someone for the purpose of a search, he or she should inform the person as soon as detention begins.

Searches authorised under section 60 of the Criminal Justice and Public Order Act 1994

2.12 Authority for a constable in uniform to stop and search under section 60 of the Criminal Justice and Public Order Act 1994 may be given if the authorising officer reasonably believes:

(a) that incidents involving serious violence may take place in any locality in the officer's police area, and it is expedient to use these powers to prevent their occurrence, or

(b) that persons are carrying dangerous instruments or offensive weapons without good reason in any locality in the officer's police area.

2.13 An authorisation under section 60 may only be given by an officer of the rank of inspector or above, in writing, specifying the grounds on which it was given, the locality in which the powers may be exercised and the period of time for which they are in force. The period authorised shall be no longer than appears reasonably necessary to prevent, or seek to prevent incidents of serious violence, or to deal with the problem of carrying dangerous instruments or offensive weapons. It may not exceed 24 hours. [See *Notes 10–13*]

2.14 If an inspector gives an authorisation, he or she must, as soon as practicable, inform an officer of or above the rank of superintendent. This officer may direct that the authorisation shall be extended for a further 24 hours, if violence or the carrying of dangerous instruments or offensive weapons has occurred, or is suspected to have occurred, and the continued use of the powers is considered necessary to prevent or deal with further such activity. That direction must also be given in writing at the time or as soon as practicable afterwards. [See *Note 12*]

Powers to require removal of face coverings

2.15 Section 60AA of the Criminal Justice and Public Order Act 1994 also provides a power to demand the removal of disguises. The officer exercising the power must reasonably believe that someone is wearing an item wholly or mainly for the purpose of concealing identity. There is also a power to seize such items where the officer believes that a person intends to wear them for this purpose. There is no power to stop and search for disguises. An officer may seize any such item which is discovered when exercising a power of search for something else, or which is being carried, and which the officer reasonably believes is intended to be used for concealing anyone's identity. This power can only be used if an authorisation under section 60 or an authorisation under section 60AA is in force.

2.16 Authority for a constable in uniform to require the removal of disguises and to seize them under section 60AA may be given if the authorising officer reasonably believes that activities may take place in any locality in the officer's police area that are likely to involve the commission of offences and it is expedient to use these powers to prevent or control these activities.

2.17 An authorisation under section 60AA may only be given by an officer of the rank of inspector or above, in writing, specifying the grounds on which it was given, the locality in which the powers may be exercised and the period of time for which they are in force. The period authorised shall be no longer than appears reasonably necessary to prevent, or seek to prevent the commission of offences. It may not exceed 24 hours. [See *Notes 10–13*]

2.18 If an inspector gives an authorisation, he or she must, as soon as practicable, inform an officer of or above the rank of superintendent. This officer may direct that the authorisation shall be extended for a further 24 hours, if crimes have been committed, or is suspected to have been committed, and the continued use of the powers is considered necessary to prevent or deal with further such activity. This direction must also be given in writing at the time or as soon as practicable afterwards. [See *Note 12*]

Searches authorised under section 44 of the Terrorism Act 2000

2.19 An officer of the rank of assistant chief constable (or equivalent) or above, may give authority for the following powers of stop and search under section 44 of the Terrorism Act 2000 to be exercised in the whole or part of his or her police area if the officer considers it is expedient for the prevention of acts of terrorism:

(a) under section 44(1) of the Terrorism Act 2000, to give a constable in uniform power to stop and search any vehicle, its driver, any passenger in the vehicle and anything in or on the vehicle or carried by the driver or any passenger; and

(b) under section 44(2) of the Terrorism Act 2000, to give a constable in uniform power to stop and search any pedestrian and anything carried by the pedestrian.

An authorisation under section 44(1) may be combined with one under section 44(2).

2.20 If an authorisation is given orally at first, it must be confirmed in writing by the officer who gave it as soon as reasonably practicable.

2.21 When giving an authorisation, the officer must specify the geographical area in which the power may be used, and the time and date that the authorisation ends (up to a maximum of 28 days from the time the authorisation was given). [See *Notes 12* and *13*]

2.22 The officer giving an authorisation under section 44(1) or (2) must cause the Secretary of State to be informed, as soon as reasonably practicable, that such an authorisation has been given. An authorisation which is not confirmed by the Secretary of State within 48 hours of its having been given, shall have effect up until the end of that 48 hour period or the end of the period specified in the authorisation (whichever is the earlier). [See *Note 14*]

2.23 Following notification of the authorisation, the Secretary of State may:

(i) cancel the authorisation with immediate effect or with effect from such other time as he or she may direct;

(ii) confirm it but for a shorter period than that specified in the authorisation; or

(iii) confirm the authorisation as given.

2.24 When an authorisation under section 44 is given, a constable in uniform may exercise the powers:

(a) only for the purpose of searching for articles of a kind which could be used in connection with terrorism (see paragraph 2.25);

(b) whether or not there are any grounds for suspecting the presence of such articles.

2.24A When a Community Support Officer on duty and in uniform has been conferred powers under Section 44 of the Terrorism Act 2000 by a Chief Officer of their force, the exercise of this power must comply with the requirements of this Code of Practice, including the recording requirements.

2.25 The selection of persons stopped under section 44 of Terrorism Act 2000 should reflect an objective assessment of the threat posed by the various terrorist groups active in Great Britain. The powers must not be used to stop and search for reasons unconnected with terrorism. Officers must take particular care not to discriminate against members of minority ethnic groups in the exercise of these powers. There may be circumstances, however, where it is appropriate for officers to take account of a person's ethnic origin in selecting persons to be stopped in response to a specific terrorist threat (for example, some international terrorist groups are associated with particular ethnic identities). [See *Notes 12* and *13*]

2.26 The powers under sections 43 and 44 of the Terrorism Act 2000 allow a constable to search only for articles which could be used for terrorist purposes. However, this would not prevent a search being carried out under other powers if, in the course of exercising these powers, the officer formed reasonable grounds for suspicion.

Powers to search in the exercise of a power to search premises

2.27 The following powers to search premises also authorise the search of a person, not under arrest, who is found on the premises during the course of the search:

(a) section 139B of the Criminal Justice Act 1988 under which a constable may enter school premises and search the premises and any person on those premises for any bladed or pointed article or offensive weapon; and

(b) under a warrant issued under section 23(3) of the Misuse of Drugs Act 1971 to search premises for drugs or documents but only if the warrant specifically authorises the search of persons found on the premises.

2.28 Before the power under section 139B of the Criminal Justice Act 1988 may be exercised, the constable must have reasonable grounds to believe that an offence under section 139A of the Criminal Justice Act 1988 (having a bladed or pointed article or offensive weapon on school premises) has been or is being committed. A warrant to search premises and persons found therein may be issued under section 23(3) of the Misuse of Drugs Act 1971 if there are reasonable grounds to suspect that controlled drugs or certain documents are in the possession of a person on the premises.

2.29 The powers in paragraph 2.27(a) or (b) do not require prior specific grounds to suspect that the person to be searched is in possession of an item for which there is an existing power to search. However, it is still necessary to ensure that the selection and treatment of those searched under these powers is based upon objective factors connected with the search of the premises, and not upon personal prejudice.

3 Conduct of searches

3.1 All stops and searches must be carried out with courtesy, consideration and respect for the person concerned. This has a significant impact on public confidence in the police. Every reasonable effort must be made to minimise the embarrassment that a person being searched may experience. [See *Note 4*]

3.2 The co-operation of the person to be searched must be sought in every case, even if the person initially objects to the search. A forcible search may be made only if it has been established that the person is unwilling to co-operate or resists. Reasonable force may be used as a last resort if necessary to conduct a search or to detain a person or vehicle for the purposes of a search.

3.3 The length of time for which a person or vehicle may be detained must be reasonable and kept to a minimum. Where the exercise of the power requires reasonable suspicion, the thoroughness and extent of a search must depend on what is suspected of being carried, and by whom. If the suspicion relates to a particular article which is seen to be slipped into a person's pocket, then, in the absence of other grounds for suspicion or an opportunity for the article to be moved elsewhere, the search must be confined to that pocket. In the case of a small article which can readily be concealed, such as a drug, and which might be concealed anywhere on the person, a more extensive search may be necessary. In the case of searches mentioned in paragraph 2.1(b), (c), and (d), which do not require reasonable grounds for suspicion, officers may make any reasonable search to look for items for which they are empowered to search. [See *Note 5*]

3.4 The search must be carried out at or near the place where the person or vehicle was first detained. [See *Note 6*]

3.5 There is no power to require a person to remove any clothing in public other than an outer coat, jacket or gloves except under section 45(3) of the Terrorism Act 2000 (which empowers a constable conducting a search under section 44(1) or 44(2) of that Act to require a person to remove headgear and footwear in public) and under section 60AA of the Criminal Justice and Public Order Act 1994 (which empowers a constable to require a person to remove any item worn to conceal identity). [See *Notes 4* and *6*] A search in public of a person's clothing which has not been removed must be restricted to superficial examination of outer garments. This does not, however, prevent an officer from placing his or her hand inside the pockets of the outer clothing, or feeling round the inside of collars, socks and shoes if this is reasonably necessary in the circumstances to look for the object of the search or to remove and examine any item reasonably suspected to be the object of the search. For the same reasons, subject to the restrictions on the removal of headgear, a person's hair may also be searched in public (see paragraphs 3.1 and 3.3).

3.6 Where on reasonable grounds it is considered necessary to conduct a more thorough search (e.g. by requiring a person to take off a T-shirt), this must be done out of public view, for example, in a police van unless paragraph 3.7 applies, or police station if there is one nearby. [See *Note 6*] Any search involving the removal of more than an outer coat, jacket, gloves, headgear or footwear, or any other item concealing identity, may only be made by an officer of the same sex as the person searched and may not be made in the presence of anyone of the opposite sex unless the person being searched specifically requests it. [See *Notes 4, 7* and *8*]

3.7 Searches involving exposure of intimate parts of the body must not be conducted as a routine extension of a less thorough search, simply because nothing is found in the course of the initial search. Searches involving exposure of intimate parts of the body may be carried out only at a nearby police station or other nearby location which is out of public view (but not a police vehicle). These searches must be conducted in accordance with paragraph 11 of Annex A to Code C except that an intimate search mentioned in paragraph 11(f) of Annex A to Code C may not be authorised or carried out under any stop and search powers. The other provisions of Code C do not apply to the conduct and recording of searches of persons detained at police stations in the exercise of stop and search powers. [See *Note 7*]

Steps to be taken prior to a search

3.8 Before any search of a detained person or attended vehicle takes place the officer must take reasonable steps to give the person to be searched or in charge of the vehicle the following information:

(a) that they are being detained for the purposes of a search

(b) the officer's name (except in the case of enquiries linked to the investigation of terrorism, or otherwise where the officer reasonably believes that giving his or her name might put him or her in danger, in which case a warrant or other identification number shall be given) and the name of the police station to which the officer is attached;

(c) the legal search power which is being exercised; and

(d) a clear explanation of:

 (i) the purpose of the search in terms of the article or articles for which there is a power to search; and

 (ii) in the case of powers requiring reasonable suspicion (see paragraph 2.1(a)), the grounds for that suspicion; or

 (iii) in the case of powers which do not require reasonable suspicion (see paragraph 2.1(b), and (c)), the nature of the power and of any necessary authorisation and the fact that it has been given.

3.9 Officers not in uniform must show their warrant cards. Stops and searches under the powers mentioned in paragraphs 2.1(b), and (c) may be undertaken only by a constable in uniform.

3.10 Before the search takes place the officer must inform the person (or the owner or person in charge of the vehicle that is to be searched) of his or her entitlement to a copy of the record of the search, including his entitlement to a record of the search if an application is made within 12 months, if it is wholly impracticable to make a record at the time. If a record is not made at the time the person should also be told how a copy can be obtained (see section 4). The person should also be given information about police powers to stop and search and the individual's rights in these circumstances.

3.11 If the person to be searched, or in charge of a vehicle to be searched, does not appear to understand what is being said, or there is any doubt about the person's ability to understand English, the officer must take reasonable steps to bring information regarding the person's rights and any relevant provisions of this Code to his or her attention. If the person is deaf or cannot understand English and is accompanied by someone, then the officer must try to establish whether that person can interpret or otherwise help the officer to give the required information.

4 Recording requirements

4.1 An officer who has carried out a search in the exercise of any power to which this Code applies, must make a record of it at the time, unless there are exceptional circumstances which would make this wholly impracticable (e.g. in situations involving public disorder or when the officer's presence is urgently required elsewhere). If a record is not made at the time, the officer must do so as soon as practicable afterwards. There may be situations in which it is not practicable to obtain the information necessary to complete a record, but the officer should make every reasonable effort to do so. [See *Note 21.*]

4.2 A copy of a record made at the time must be given immediately to the person who has been searched. The officer must ask for the name, address and date of birth of the person searched, but there is no obligation on a person to provide these details and no power of detention if the person is unwilling to do so.

4.3 The following information must always be included in the record of a search even if the person does not wish to provide any personal details:

(i) the name of the person searched, or (if it is withheld) a description;
(ii) a note of the person's self-defined ethnic background; [*See Note 18*]
(iii) when a vehicle is searched, its registration number; [*See Note 16*]
(iv) the date, time, and place that the person or vehicle was first detained;
(v) the date, time and place the person or vehicle was searched (if different from (iv));
(vi) the purpose of the search;
(vii) the grounds for making it, or in the case of those searches mentioned in paragraph 2.1(b) and (c), the nature of the power and of any necessary authorisation and the fact that it has been given; [*See Note 17*]
(viii) its outcome (e.g. arrest or no further action);
(ix) a note of any injury or damage to property resulting from it;
(x) subject to paragraph 3.8(b), the identity of the officer making the search. [*See Note 15*]

4.4 Nothing in paragraph 4.3 (x) or 4.10A requires the names of police officers to be shown on the search record or any other record required to be made under this code in the case of enquiries linked to the investigation of terrorism or otherwise where an officer reasonably believes that recording names might endanger the officers. In such cases the record must show the officers' warrant or other identification number and duty station.

4.5 A record is required for each person and each vehicle searched. However, if a person is in a vehicle and both are searched, and the object and grounds of the search are the same, only one record need be completed. If more than one person in a vehicle is searched, separate records for each search of a person must be made. If only a vehicle is searched, the name of the driver and his or her self-defined ethnic background must be recorded, unless the vehicle is unattended.

4.6 The record of the grounds for making a search must, briefly but informatively, explain the reason for suspecting the person concerned, by reference to the person's behaviour and/or other circumstances.

4.7 Where officers detain an individual with a view to performing a search, but the search is not carried out due to the grounds for suspicion being eliminated as a result of questioning the person detained, a record must still be made in accordance with the procedure outlined in Paragraph 4.12.

4.8 After searching an unattended vehicle, or anything in or on it, an officer must leave a notice in it (or on it, if things on it have been searched without opening it) recording the fact that it has been searched.

4.9 The notice must include the name of the police station to which the officer concerned is attached and state where a copy of the record of the search may be obtained and where any application for compensation should be directed.

4.10 The vehicle must if practicable be left secure.

4.10A When an officer makes a record of the stop electronically and is unable to produce a copy of the form at the time, the officer must explain how the person can obtain a full copy of the record of the stop or search and give the person a receipt which contains:

- a unique reference number and guidance on how to obtain a full copy of the stop or search;
- the name of the officer who carried out the stop or search (unless paragraph 4.4 applies); and
- the power used to stop and search them. [See *Note 21*]

Recording of encounters not governed by Statutory Powers

4.11 Not used.

4.12 When an officer requests a person in a public place to account for themselves, i.e. their actions, behaviour, presence in an area or possession of anything, a record of the encounter must be completed at the time and a copy given to the person who has been questioned. The record must identify the name of the officer who has made the stop and conducted the encounter. This does not apply under the exceptional circumstances outlined in paragraph 4.1 of this code.

4.13 This requirement does not apply to general conversations such as when giving directions to a place, or when seeking witnesses. It also does not include occasions on which an officer is seeking general information or questioning people to establish background to incidents which have required officers to intervene to keep the peace or resolve a dispute.

4.14 A separate record need not be completed when:

— stopping a person in a vehicle when an HORT/1 form, a Vehicle Defect Rectification Scheme Notice, or a Fixed Penalty Notice is issued. It also does not apply when a specimen of breath is required under Section 6 of the Road Traffic Act 1988.

— stopping a person when a Penalty Notice is issued for an offence.

4.15 Officers must inform the person of their entitlement to a copy of a record of the encounter.

4.16 The provisions of paragraph 4.4 of this code apply equally when the encounters described in 4.12 and 4.13 are recorded.

4.17 The following information must be included in the record

(i) the date, time and place of the encounter;
(ii) if the person is in a vehicle, the registration number;
(iii) the reason why the officer questioned that person; [See *Note 17*]
(iv) a note of the person's self-defined ethnic background; [See *Note 18*]
(v) the outcome of the encounter.

4.18 There is no power to require the person questioned to provide personal details. If a person refuses to give their self-defined ethnic background, a form must still be completed, which includes a description of the person's ethnic background. [See *Note* 18]

4.19 A record of an encounter must always be made when the criteria set out in 4.12 have been met. If the criteria are not met but the person requests a record, the officer should provide a copy of the form but record on it that the encounter did not meet the criteria. The officer can refuse to issue the form if he or she reasonably believes that the purpose of the request is deliberately aimed at frustrating or delaying legitimate police activity. [See *Note 20*]

4.20 All references to officers in this section include police staff designated as Community Support Officers under section 38 of the Police Reform Act 2002.

5 Monitoring and supervising the use of stop and search powers

5.1 Supervising officers must monitor the use of stop and search powers and should consider in particular whether there is any evidence that they are being exercised on the basis of stereotyped images or inappropriate generalisations. Supervising officers should satisfy themselves that the practice of officers under their supervision in stopping, searching and recording is fully in accordance with this Code. Supervisors must also examine whether the records reveal any trends or patterns which give cause for concern, and if so take appropriate action to address this.

5.2 Senior officers with area or force-wide responsibilities must also monitor the broader use of stop and search powers and, where necessary, take action at the relevant level.

5.3 Supervision and monitoring must be supported by the compilation of comprehensive statistical records of stops and searches at force, area and local level. Any apparently disproportionate use of the powers by particular officers or groups of officers or in relation to specific sections of the community should be identified and investigated.

5.4 In order to promote public confidence in the use of the powers, forces in consultation with police authorities must make arrangements for the records to be scrutinised by representatives of the community, and to explain the use of the powers at a local level. [See *Note 19*].

Notes for Guidance

Officers exercising stop and search powers

1 This code does not affect the ability of an officer to speak to or question a person in the ordinary course of the officer's duties without detaining the person or exercising any element of compulsion. It is not the purpose of the code to prohibit such encounters between the police and the community with the co-operation of the person concerned and neither does it affect the principle that all citizens have a duty to help police officers to prevent crime and discover offenders. This is a civic rather than a legal duty; but when a police officer is trying to discover whether, or by whom, an offence has been committed he or she may question any person from whom useful information might be obtained, subject to the restrictions imposed by Code C. A person's unwillingness to reply does not alter this entitlement, but in the absence of a power to arrest, or to detain in order to search, the person is free to leave at will and cannot be compelled to remain with the officer.

2 In some circumstances preparatory questioning may be unnecessary, but in general a brief conversation or exchange will be desirable not only as a means of avoiding unsuccessful searches, but to explain the grounds for the stop/search, to gain cooperation and reduce any tension there might be surrounding the stop/search.

3 Where a person is lawfully detained for the purpose of a search, but no search in the event takes place, the detention will not thereby have been rendered unlawful.

4 Many people customarily cover their heads or faces for religious reasons—for example, Muslim women, Sikh men, Sikh or Hindu women, or Rastarfarian men or women. A police officer cannot order the removal of a head or face covering except where there is reason to believe that the item is being worn by the individual wholly or mainly for the purpose of disguising identity, not simply because it disguises identity. Where there may be religious sensitivities about ordering the removal of such an item, the officer should permit the item to be removed out of public view. Where practicable, the item should be removed in the presence of an officer of the same sex as the person and out of sight of anyone of the opposite sex .

5 A search of a person in public should be completed as soon as possible.

6 A person may be detained under a stop and search power at a place other than where the person was first detained, only if that place, be it a police station or elsewhere, is nearby. Such a place should be located within a reasonable travelling distance using whatever mode of travel (on foot or by car) is appropriate. This applies to all searches under stop and search powers, whether or not they involve the removal of clothing or exposure of intimate parts of the body (see paragraphs 3.6 and 3.7) or take place in or out of public view. It means, for example, that a search under the stop and search power in section 23 of the Misuse of Drugs Act 1971 which involves the compulsory removal of more than a person's outer coat, jacket or gloves cannot be carried out unless a place which is both nearby the place they were first detained and out of public view, is available. If a search involves exposure of intimate parts of the body and a police station is not nearby, particular care must be taken to ensure that the location is suitable in that it enables the search to be conducted in accordance with the requirements of paragraph 11 of Annex A to Code C.

7 *A search in the street itself should be regarded as being in public for the purposes of paragraphs 3.6 and 3.7 above, even though it may be empty at the time a search begins. Although there is no power to require a person to do so, there is nothing to prevent an officer from asking a person voluntarily to remove more than an outer coat, jacket or gloves (and headgear or footwear under section 45(3) of the Terrorism Act 2000) in public.*

8 *Where there may be religious sensitivities about asking someone to remove headgear using a power under section 45(3) of the Terrorism Act 2000, the police officer should offer to carry out the search out of public view (for example, in a police van or police station if there is one nearby).*

9 *Other means of identification might include jewellery, insignias, tattoos or other features which are known to identify members of the particular gang or group.*

Authorising officers

10 *The powers under section 60 are separate from and additional to the normal stop and search powers which require reasonable grounds to suspect an individual of carrying an offensive weapon (or other article). Their overall purpose is to prevent serious violence and the widespread carrying of weapons which might lead to persons being seriously injured by disarming potential offenders in circumstances where other powers would not be sufficient. They should not therefore be used to replace or circumvent the normal powers for dealing with routine crime problems. The purpose of the powers under section 60AA is to prevent those involved in intimidatory or violent protests using face coverings to disguise identity.*

11 *Authorisations under section 60 require a reasonable belief on the part of the authorising officer. This must have an objective basis, for example: intelligence or relevant information such as a history of antagonism and violence between particular groups; previous incidents of violence at, or connected with, particular events or locations; a significant increase in knife-point robberies in a limited area; reports that individuals are regularly carrying weapons in a particular locality; or in the case of section 60AA previous incidents of crimes being committed while wearing face coverings to conceal identity.*

12 *It is for the authorising officer to determine the period of time during which the powers mentioned in paragraph 2.1 (b) and (c) may be exercised. The officer should set the minimum period he or she considers necessary to deal with the risk of violence, the carrying of knives or offensive weapons, or terrorism. A direction to extend the period authorised under the powers mentioned in paragraph 2.1(b) may be given only once. Thereafter further use of the powers requires a new authorisation. There is no provision to extend an authorisation of the powers mentioned in paragraph 2.1(c); further use of the powers requires a new authorisation.*

13 *It is for the authorising officer to determine the geographical area in which the use of the powers is to be authorised. In doing so the officer may wish to take into account factors such as the nature and venue of the anticipated incident, the number of people who may be in the immediate area of any possible incident, their access to surrounding areas and the anticipated level of violence. The officer should not set a geographical area which is wider than that he or she believes necessary for the purpose of preventing anticipated violence, the carrying of knives or offensive weapons, acts of terrorism, or, in the case of section 60AA, the prevention of commission of offences. It is particularly important to ensure that constables exercising such powers are fully aware of where they may be used. If the area specified is smaller than the whole force area, the officer giving the authorisation should specify either the streets which form the boundary of the area or a divisional boundary within the force area. If the power is to be used in response to a threat or incident that straddles police force areas, an officer from each of the forces concerned will need to give an authorisation.*

14 *An officer who has authorised the use of powers under section 44 of the Terrorism Act 2000 must take immediate steps to send a copy of the authorisation to the National Joint Unit, Metropolitan Police Special Branch, who will forward it to the Secretary of State. The Secretary of State should be informed of the reasons for the authorisation. The National Joint Unit will inform the force concerned, within 48 hours of the authorisation being made, whether the Secretary of State has confirmed or cancelled or altered the authorisation.*

Recording

15 *Where a stop and search is conducted by more than one officer the identity of all the officers engaged in the search must be recorded on the record. Nothing prevents an officer who is present but not directly involved in searching from completing the record during the course of the encounter.*

16 *Where a vehicle has not been allocated a registration number (e.g. a rally car or a trials motorbike) that part of the requirement under 4.3(iii) does not apply.*

17 *It is important for monitoring purposes to specify whether the authority for exercising a stop and search power was given under section 60 of the Criminal Justice and Public Order Act 1994, or under section 44(1) or 44(2) of the Terrorism Act 2000.*

18 *Officers should record the self-defined ethnicity of every person stopped according to the categories used in the 2001 census question listed in Annex B. Respondents should be asked to select one of the five main categories representing broad ethnic groups and then a more specific cultural background from within this group. The ethnic classification should be coded for recording purposes using the coding system in Annex B. An additional "Not stated" box is available but should not be offered to respondents explicitly. Officers should be aware and explain to members of the public, especially where concerns are raised, that this information is required to obtain a true picture of stop and search activity and to help improve ethnic monitoring, tackle discriminatory practice, and promote effective use of the powers. If the person gives what appears to the officer to be an "incorrect" answer (e.g. a person who appears to be white states that they are black), the officer should record the response that has been given. Officers should also record their own perception of the ethnic background of every person stopped and this must be done by using the PNC/Phoenix classification system. If the "Not stated" category is used the reason for this must be recorded on the form.*

19 *Arrangements for public scrutiny of records should take account of the right to confidentiality of those stopped and searched. Anonymised forms and/or statistics generated from records should be the focus of the examinations by members of the public.*

20 *Where an officer engages in conversation which is not pertinent to the actions or whereabouts of the individual (e.g. does not relate to why the person is there, what they are doing or where they have been or are going) then issuing a form would not meet the criteria set out in paragraph 4.12. Situations designed to impede police activity may arise, for example, in public order situations where individuals engage in dialogue with the officer but the officer does not initiate or engage in contact about the person's individual circumstances.*

21 *In situations where it is not practicable to provide a written record of the stop or stop and search at that time, the officer should consider providing the person with details of the station to which the person may attend for a record. This may take the form of a simple business card, adding the date of the stop or stop and search.*

Definition of Offensive Weapon

22 *'Offensive weapon' is defined as any article made or adapted for use for causing injury to the person, or intended by the person having it with him for such use or by someone else. There are three categories of offensive weapons: those made for causing injury to the person; those adapted for such a purpose; and those not so made or adapted, but carried with the intention of causing injury to the person. A firearm, as defined by section 57 of the Firearms Act 1968, would fall within the definition of offensive weapon if any of the criteria above.*

ANNEX A—SUMMARY OF MAIN STOP AND SEARCH POWERS

THIS TABLE RELATES TO STOP AND SEARCH POWERS ONLY. INDIVIDUAL STATUTES BELOW MAY CONTAIN OTHER POLICE POWERS OF ENTRY, SEARCH AND SEIZURE

Power	Object of search	Extent of search	Where exercisable
Unlawful articles general			
1. Public Stores Act 1875, s6	HM Stores stolen or unlawfully obtained	Persons, vehicles and vessels	Anywhere where the constabulary powers are exercisable
2. Firearms Act 1968, s47	Firearms	Persons and vehicles	A public place, or anywhere in the case of reasonable suspicion of offences of carrying firearms with criminal intent or trespassing with firearms
3. Misuse of Drugs Act 1971, s23	Controlled drugs	Persons and vehicles	Anywhere
4. Customs and Excise Management Act 1979, s163	Goods: (a) on which duty has not been paid; (b) being unlawfully removed, imported or exported; (c) otherwise liable to forfeiture to HM Customs and Excise	Vehicles and vessels only	Anywhere
5. Aviation Security Act 1982, s27(1)	Stolen or unlawfully obtained goods	Airport employees and vehicles carrying airport employees or aircraft or any vehicle in a cargo area whether or not carrying an employee	Any designated airport
6. Police and Criminal Evidence Act 1984, s1	Stolen goods; articles for use in certain Theft Act offences; offensive weapons, including bladed or sharply-pointed articles (except folding pocket knives with a bladed cutting edge not exceeding 3 inches); prohibited possession of a category 4 (display grade) firework, any person under 18 in possession of an adult firework in a public place.	Persons and vehicles	Where there is public access

Power	Object of search	Extent of search	Where exercisable
	Criminal Damage: articles made, adapted or intended for use in destroying or damaging property	Persons and vehicles	Where there is public access
Police and Criminal Evidence Act 1984, s6(3) (by a constable of the United Kingdom Atomic Energy Authority Constabulary in respect of property owned or controlled by British Nuclear Fuels plc)	HM Stores (in the form of goods and chattels belonging to British Nuclear Fuels plc)	Persons, vehicles and vessels	Anywhere where the constabulary powers are exercisable
7. Sporting events (Control of Alcohol etc.) Act 1985, s7	Intoxicating liquor	Persons, coaches and trains	Designated sports grounds or coaches and trains travelling to or from a designated sporting event
8. Crossbows Act 1987, s4	Crossbows or parts of crossbows (except crossbows with a draw weight of less than 1.4 kilograms)	Persons and vehicles	Anywhere except dwellings
9. Criminal Justice Act 1988 s139B	Offensive weapons, bladed or sharply pointed article	Persons	School premises
Evidence of game and wildlife offences			
10. Poaching Prevention Act 1862, s2	Game or poaching equipment	Persons and vehicles	A public place
11. Deer Act 1991, s12	Evidence of offences under the Act	Persons and vehicles	Anywhere except dwellings
12. Conservation of Seals Act 1970, s4	Seals or hunting equipment	Vehicles only	Anywhere
13. Badgers Act 1992, s11	Evidence of offences under the Act	Persons and vehicles	Anywhere
14. Wildlife and Countryside Act 1981, s19	Evidence of wildlife offences	Persons and vehicles	Anywhere except dwellings
Other			
15. Terrorism Act 2000, s.43	*Evidence of liability to arrest under section 41 of the Act*	Persons	Anywhere

Power	Object of search	Extent of search	Where exercisable
16. Terrorism Act 2000, s.44(1)	articles which could be used for a purpose connected with the commission, preparation or instigation of acts of terrorism	*Vehicles, driver and passengers*	Anywhere within the area or locality authorised under subsection (1)
17. Terrorism Act 2000, s.44(2)	*articles which could be used for a purpose connected with the commission, preparation or instigation of acts of terrorism*	*Pedestrians*	Anywhere within the area of locality authorised
18. Paragraphs 7 and 8 of Schedule 7 to the Terrorism Act 2000	*Anything relevant to determining if a person being examined falls within paragraph 2(1)(a) to (c) of Schedule 5*	Persons, vehicles, vessels etc.	*Ports and airports*
19. Section 60 Criminal Justice and Public Order Act 1994 , *as amended by s.8 of the Knives Act 1997*	Offensive weapons or dangerous instruments to prevent incidents of serious violence *or to deal with the carrying of such items*	Persons and vehicles	Anywhere within a locality authorised under subsection (1)

ANNEX B—SELF-DEFINED ETHNIC CLASSIFICATION CATEGORIES

White	**W**
A. White—British	W1
B. White—Irish	W2
C. Any other White background	W9
Mixed	**M**
D. White and Black Caribbean	M1
E. White and Black African	M2
F. White and Asian	M3
G. Any other Mixed Background	M9
Asian/Asian—British	**A**
H. Asian—Indian	A1
I. Asian—Pakistani	A2
J. Asian—Bangladeshi	A3
K. Any other Asian background	A9
Black/Black—British	**B**
L. Black—Caribbean	B1
M. Black African	B2
N. Any other Black background	B9

Other	**O**
O. Chinese	O1
P. Any other	O9
Not Stated	**NS**

ANNEX C—SUMMARY OF POWERS OF COMMUNITY SUPPORT OFFICERS TO SEARCH AND SEIZE

The following is a summary of the search and seizure powers that may be exercised by a community support officer (CSO) who has been designated with the relevant powers in accordance with Part 4 of the Police Reform Act 2002.

When exercising any of these powers, a CSO must have regard to any relevant provisions of this Code, including section 3 governing the conduct of searches and the steps to be taken prior to a search.

1. Powers to stop and search not requiring consent

Designation	Power conferred	Object of Search	Extent of Search	Where Exercisable
Police Reform Act 2002, Schedule 4, paragraph 15	*(a) Terrorism Act 2000, s.44(1)(a) and (d) and 45(2);*	Items intended to be used in connection with terrorism.	(a) Vehicles or anything carried in or on the vehicle and anything carried by driver or passenger.	Anywhere within area of locality authorised and in the company and under the supervision of a constable.
	(b) Terrorism Act 2000, s.44 (2)(b) and 45(2).		(b) Anything carried by a pedestrian.	

2. Powers to search requiring the consent of the person and seizure

A CSO may detain a person using reasonable force where necessary as set out in Part 1of Schedule 4 to the Police Reform Act 2002. If the person has been lawfully detained, the CSO may search the person provided that person gives consent to such a search in relation to the following:

Designation	Power conferred	Object of Search	Extent of Search	Where Exercisable
Police Reform Act 2002, Schedule 4, paragraph 7A	(a) Criminal Justice and Police Act 2001, s12(2)	a) Alcohol or a container for alcohol	a) Persons	a) Designated public place

Designation	Power conferred	Object of Search	Extent of Search	Where Exercisable
	(b) Confiscation of Alcohol (Young Persons) Act 1997, s1	b) Alcohol	b) Persons under 18 years old	b) Public place
	(c) Children and Young Persons Act 1933, section 7(3)	(c) Tobacco or cigarette papers	(c) Persons under 16 years old found smoking	(c) Public place

3. Powers to search not requiring the consent of the person and seizure

A CSO may detain a person using reasonable force where necessary as set out in Part 1 of Schedule 4 to the Police Reform Act 2002. If the person has been lawfully detained, the CSO may search the person without the need for that person's consent in relation to the following:

Designation	Power conferred	Object of Search	Extent of Search	Where Exercisable
Police Reform Act 2002, Schedule 4, paragraph 2A	Police and Criminal Evidence Act 1984, s.32	a) Objects that might be used to cause physical injury to the person or the CSO. b) Items that might be used to assist escape.	Persons made subject to a requirement to wait.	Any place where the requirement to wait has been made.

4. Powers to seize without consent

This power applies when drugs are found in the course of any search mentioned above.

Designation	Power conferred	Object of Seizure	Where Exercisable
Police Reform Act 2002, Schedule 4, paragraph 7B	*Police Reform Act 2002, Schedule 4, paragraph 7B*	Controlled drugs in a person's possession.	Any place where the person is in possession of the drug.

Appendix 2

PACE Code of Practice for Searches of Premises by Police Officers and the Seizure of Property found by Police Officers on Persons or Premises (Code B)

This Code applies to applications for warrants made after midnight 31 January 2008 and to searches and seizures taking place after midnight on 31 January 2008.

1 Introduction

1.1 This Code of Practice deals with police powers to:
- search premises
- seize and retain property found on premises and persons

1.1A These powers may be used to find:
- property and material relating to a crime
- wanted persons
- children who abscond from local authority accommodation where they have been remanded or committed by a court

1.2 A justice of the peace may issue a search warrant granting powers of entry, search and seizure, e.g. warrants to search for stolen property, drugs, firearms and evidence of serious offences. Police also have powers without a search warrant. The main ones provided by the Police and Criminal Evidence Act 1984 (PACE) include powers to search premises:
- to make an arrest
- after an arrest

1.3 The right to privacy and respect for personal property are key principles of the Human Rights Act 1998. Powers of entry, search and seizure should be fully and clearly justified before use because they may significantly interfere with the occupier's privacy. Officers should consider if the necessary objectives can be met by less intrusive means.

1.4 In all cases, police should:
- exercise their powers courteously and with respect for persons and property
- only use reasonable force when this is considered necessary and proportionate to the circumstances

1.5 If the provisions of PACE and this Code are not observed, evidence obtained from a search may be open to question.

2 General

2.1 This Code must be readily available at all police stations for consultation by:

- police officers
- police staff
- detained persons
- members of the public

2.2 The *Notes for Guidance* included are not provisions of this Code.

2.3 This Code applies to searches of premises:

(a) by police for the purposes of an investigation into an alleged offence, with the occupier's consent, other than:

- routine scene of crime searches;
- calls to a fire or burglary made by or on behalf of an occupier or searches following the activation of fire or burglar alarms or discovery of insecure premises;
- searches when *paragraph 5.4* applies;
- bomb threat calls;

(b) under powers conferred on police officers by PACE, sections 17, 18 and 32;

(c) undertaken in pursuance of search warrants issued to and executed by constables in accordance with PACE, sections 15 and 16. See *Note 2A*;

(d) subject to *paragraph 2.6*, under any other power given to police to enter premises with or without a search warrant for any purpose connected with the investigation into an alleged or suspected offence. See *Note 2B*.

For the purposes of this Code, 'premises' as defined in PACE, section 23, includes any place, vehicle, vessel, aircraft, hovercraft, tent or movable structure and any offshore installation as defined in the Mineral Workings (Offshore Installations) Act 1971, section 1. See *Note 2D*

2.4 A person who has not been arrested but is searched during a search of premises should be searched in accordance with Code A. See *Note 2C*

2.5 This Code does not apply to the exercise of a statutory power to enter premises or to inspect goods, equipment or procedures if the exercise of that power is not dependent on the existence of grounds for suspecting that an offence may have been committed and the person exercising the power has no reasonable grounds for such suspicion.

2.6 This Code does not affect any directions of a search warrant or order, lawfully executed in England or Wales that any item or evidence seized under that warrant or order be handed over to a police force, court, tribunal, or other authority outside England or Wales. For example, warrants and orders issued in Scotland or Northern Ireland, see *Note 2B(f)* and search warrants issued under the Criminal Justice (International Co-operation) Act 1990, section 7.

2.7 When this Code requires the prior authority or agreement of an officer of at least inspector or superintendent rank, that authority may be given by a sergeant or chief inspector authorised to perform the functions of the higher rank under PACE, section 107.

2.8 Written records required under this Code not made in the search record shall, unless otherwise specified, be made:

- in the recording officer's pocket book ('pocket book' includes any official report book issued to police officers) or
- on forms provided for the purpose

2.9 Nothing in this Code requires the identity of officers, or anyone accompanying them during a search of premises, to be recorded or disclosed:

(a) in the case of enquiries linked to the investigation of terrorism; or

(b) if officers reasonably believe recording or disclosing their names might put them in danger.

In these cases officers should use warrant or other identification numbers and the name of their police station. Police staff should use any identification number provided to them by the police force. See *Note 2E*

2.10 The 'officer in charge of the search' means the officer assigned specific duties and responsibilities under this Code. Whenever there is a search of premises to which this Code applies one officer must act as the officer in charge of the search. See *Note 2F*

2.11 In this Code:

(a) 'designated person' means a person other than a police officer, designated under the Police Reform Act 2002, Part 4 who has specified powers and duties of police officers conferred or imposed on them. See *Note 2G*.

(b) any reference to a police officer includes a designated person acting in the exercise or performance of the powers and duties conferred or imposed on them by their designation.

(c) a person authorised to accompany police officers or designated persons in the execution of a warrant has the same powers as a constable in the execution of the warrant and the search and seizure of anything related to the warrant. These powers must be exercised in the company and under the supervision of a police officer. See *Note 3C*.

2.12 If a power conferred on a designated person:

(a) allows reasonable force to be used when exercised by a police officer, a designated person exercising that power has the same entitlement to use force;

(b) includes power to use force to enter any premises, that power is not exercisable by that designated person except:

(i) in the company and under the supervision of a police officer; or

(ii) for the purpose of:

- saving life or limb; or
- preventing serious damage to property.

2.13 Designated persons must have regard to any relevant provisions of the Codes of Practice.

Notes for guidance

2A PACE sections 15 and 16 apply to all search warrants issued to and executed by constables under any enactment, e.g. search warrants issued by a:

(a) justice of the peace under the:

- *Theft Act 1968, section 26—stolen property;*
- *Misuse of Drugs Act 1971, section 23—controlled drugs;*
- *PACE, section 8—evidence of an indictable offence;*
- *Terrorism Act 2000, Schedule 5, paragraph 1;*

(b) a Circuit judge under:

- *PACE, Schedule 1;*
- *Terrorism Act 2000, Schedule 5, paragraph 11.*

2B Examples of the other powers in paragraph 2.3(d) include:

(a) Road Traffic Act 1988, section 6E(1) giving police power to enter premises under section 6E(1) to:

- *require a person to provide a specimen of breath; or*
- *arrest a person following*
  - *— a positive breath test;*
  - *— failure to provide a specimen of breath;*

(b) Transport and Works Act 1992, section 30(4) giving police powers to enter premises mirroring the powers in (a) in relation to specified persons working on transport systems to which the Act applies;

(c) Criminal Justice Act 1988, section 139B giving police power to enter and search school premises for offensive weapons, bladed or pointed articles;

(d) Terrorism Act 2000, Schedule 5, paragraphs 3 and 15 empowering a superintendent in urgent cases to give written authority for police to enter and search premises for the purposes of a terrorist investigation;

(e) Explosives Act 1875, section 73(b) empowering a superintendent to give written authority for police to enter premises, examine and search them for explosives;

(f) search warrants and production orders or the equivalent issued in Scotland or Northern Ireland endorsed under the Summary Jurisdiction (Process) Act 1881 or the Petty Sessions (Ireland) Act 1851 respectively for execution in England and Wales.

2C *The Criminal Justice Act 1988, section 139B provides that a constable who has reasonable grounds to believe an offence under the Criminal Justice Act 1988, section 139A has or is being committed may enter school premises and search the premises and any persons on the premises for any bladed or pointed article or offensive weapon. Persons may be searched under a warrant issued under the Misuse of Drugs Act 1971, section 23(3) to search premises for drugs or documents only if the warrant specifically authorises the search of persons on the premises.*

2D *The Immigration Act 1971, Part III and Schedule 2 gives immigration officers powers to enter and search premises, seize and retain property, with and without a search warrant. These are similar to the powers available to police under search warrants issued by a justice of the peace and without a warrant under PACE, sections 17, 18, 19 and 32 except they only apply to specified offences under the Immigration Act 1971 and immigration control powers. For certain types of investigations and enquiries these powers avoid the need for the Immigration Service to rely on police officers becoming directly involved. When exercising these powers, immigration officers are required by the Immigration and Asylum Act 1999, section 145 to have regard to this Code's corresponding provisions. When immigration officers are dealing with persons or property at police stations, police officers should give appropriate assistance to help them discharge their specific duties and responsibilities.*

2E *The purpose of paragraph 2.9(b) is to protect those involved in serious organised crime investigations or arrests of particularly violent suspects when there is reliable information that those arrested or their associates may threaten or cause harm to the officers or anyone accompanying them during a search of premises. In cases of doubt, an officer of inspector rank or above should be consulted.*

2F *For the purposes of paragraph 2.10, the officer in charge of the search should normally be the most senior officer present. Some exceptions are:*

(a) a supervising officer who attends or assists at the scene of a premises search may appoint an officer of lower rank as officer in charge of the search if that officer is:

- *more conversant with the facts;*
- *a more appropriate officer to be in charge of the search;*

(b) when all officers in a premises search are the same rank. The supervising officer if available must make sure one of them is appointed officer in charge of the search, otherwise the officers themselves must nominate one of their number as the officer in charge;

(c) a senior officer assisting in a specialist role. This officer need not be regarded as having a general supervisory role over the conduct of the search or be appointed or expected to act as the officer in charge of the search.

Except in (c), nothing in this Note diminishes the role and responsibilities of a supervisory officer who is present at the search or knows of a search taking place.

2G *An officer of the rank of inspector or above may direct a designated investigating officer not to wear a uniform for the purposes of a specific operation.*

3 Search warrants and production orders

(a) Before making an application

3.1 When information appears to justify an application, the officer must take reasonable steps to check the information is accurate, recent and not provided maliciously or irresponsibly. An application may not be made on the basis of information from an anonymous source if corroboration has not been sought. See *Note 3A*

3.2 The officer shall ascertain as specifically as possible the nature of the articles concerned and their location.

3.3 The officer shall make reasonable enquiries to:

(i) establish if:

- anything is known about the likely occupier of the premises and the nature of the premises themselves;

- the premises have been searched previously and how recently;

(ii) obtain any other relevant information.

3.4 An application:

(a) to a justice of the peace for a search warrant or to a Circuit judge for a search warrant or production order under PACE, Schedule 1 must be supported by a signed written authority from an officer of inspector rank or above:

Note: If the case is an urgent application to a justice of the peace and an inspector or above is not readily available, the next most senior officer on duty can give the written authority.

(b) to a circuit judge under the Terrorism Act 2000, Schedule 5 for

- a production order;
- search warrant; or
- an order requiring an explanation of material seized or produced under such a warrant or production order

must be supported by a signed written authority from an officer of superintendent rank or above.

3.5 Except in a case of urgency, if there is reason to believe a search might have an adverse effect on relations between the police and the community, the officer in charge shall consult the local police/community liaison officer:

- before the search; or
- in urgent cases, as soon as practicable after the search

(b) Making an application

3.6 A search warrant application must be supported in writing, specifying:

(a) the enactment under which the application is made, see *Note 2A;*

(b) (i) whether the warrant is to authorise entry and search of:

- one set of premises; or
- if the application is under PACE section 8, or Schedule 1, paragraph 12, more than one set of specified premises or all premises occupied or controlled by a specified person, and

(ii) the premises to be searched;

(c) the object of the search, see *Note 3B;*

(d) the grounds for the application, including, when the purpose of the proposed search is to find evidence of an alleged offence, an indication of how the evidence relates to the investigation;

(da) where the application is under PACE section 8, or Schedule 1, paragraph 12 for a single warrant to enter and search:

(i) more than one set of specified premises, the officer must specify each set of premises which it is desired to enter and search

(ii) all premises occupied or controlled by a specified person, the officer must specify;

- as many sets of premises which it is desired to enter and search as it is reasonably practicable to specify
- the person who is in occupation or control of those premises and any others which it is desired to search
- why it is necessary to search more premises than those which can be specified
- why it is not reasonably practicable to specify all the premises which it is desired to enter and search

(db) whether an application under PACE section 8 is for a warrant authorising entry and search on more than one occasion, and if so, the officer must state the grounds for this and whether the desired number of entries authorised is unlimited or a specified maximum.

(e) there are no reasonable grounds to believe the material to be sought, when making application to a:

(i) justice of the peace or a Circuit judge consists of or includes items subject to legal privilege;

(ii) justice of the peace, consists of or includes excluded material or special procedure material;

Note: this does not affect the additional powers of seizure in the Criminal Justice and Police Act 2001, Part 2 covered in paragraph 7.7, see *Note 3B*;

(f) if applicable, a request for the warrant to authorise a person or persons to accompany the officer who executes the warrant, see *Note 3C*.

3.7 A search warrant application under PACE, Schedule 1, paragraph 12(a), shall if appropriate indicate why it is believed service of notice of an application for a production order may seriously prejudice the investigation. Applications for search warrants under the Terrorism Act 2000, Schedule 5, paragraph 11 must indicate why a production order would not be appropriate.

3.8 If a search warrant application is refused, a further application may not be made for those premises unless supported by additional grounds.

Notes for guidance

3A The identity of an informant need not be disclosed when making an application, but the officer should be prepared to answer any questions the magistrate or judge may have about:

- *the accuracy of previous information from that source*
- *any other related matters*

3B The information supporting a search warrant application should be as specific as possible, particularly in relation to the articles or persons being sought and where in the premises it is suspected they may be found. The meaning of 'items subject to legal privilege', 'excluded material' and 'special procedure material' are defined by PACE, sections 10, 11 and 14 respectively.

3C Under PACE, section 16(2), a search warrant may authorise persons other than police officers to accompany the constable who executes the warrant. This includes, e.g. any suitably qualified or skilled person or an expert in a particular field whose presence is needed to help accurately identify the material sought or to advise where certain evidence is most likely to be found and how it should be dealt with. It does not give them any right to force entry, but it gives them the right to be on the premises during the search and to search for or seize property without the occupier's permission.

4 Entry without warrant—particular powers

(a) Making an arrest etc

4.1 The conditions under which an officer may enter and search premises without a warrant are set out in PACE, section 17. It should be noted that this section does not create or confer any powers of arrest. See other powers in *Note 2B(a)*.

(b) Search of premises where arrest takes place or the arrested person was immediately before arrest

4.2 When a person has been arrested for an indictable offence, a police officer has power under PACE, section 32 to search the premises where the person was arrested or where the person was immediately before being arrested.

(c) Search of premises occupied or controlled by the arrested person

4.3 The specific powers to search premises occupied or controlled by a person arrested for an indictable offence are set out in PACE, section 18. They may not be exercised, except if section 18(5) applies, unless an officer of inspector rank or above has given written authority. That authority should only be given when the authorising officer is satisfied the necessary grounds exist. If possible the authorising officer should record the authority on the Notice of Powers and Rights and, subject to *paragraph 2.9*, sign the Notice. The record of the grounds for the search and the nature of the evidence sought as required by section 18(7) of the Act should be made in:

- the custody record if there is one, otherwise
- the officer's pocket book, or
- the search record

5 Search with consent

5.1 Subject to *paragraph 5.4*, if it is proposed to search premises with the consent of a person entitled to grant entry the consent must, if practicable, be given in writing on the Notice of Powers and Rights before the search. The officer must make any necessary enquiries to be satisfied the person is in a position to give such consent. See *Notes 5A* and *5B*

5.2 Before seeking consent the officer in charge of the search shall state the purpose of the proposed search and its extent. This information must be as specific as possible, particularly regarding the articles or persons being sought and the parts of the premises to be searched. The person concerned must be clearly informed they are not obliged to consent and anything seized may be produced in evidence. If at the time the person is not suspected of an offence, the officer shall say this when stating the purpose of the search.

5.3 An officer cannot enter and search or continue to search premises under *paragraph 5.1* if consent is given under duress or withdrawn before the search is completed.

5.4 It is unnecessary to seek consent under *paragraphs 5.1* and *5.2* if this would cause disproportionate inconvenience to the person concerned. See *Note 5C*

Notes for guidance

5A In a lodging house or similar accommodation, every reasonable effort should be made to obtain the consent of the tenant, lodger or occupier. A search should not be made solely on the basis of the landlord's consent unless the tenant, lodger or occupier is unavailable and the matter is urgent.

5B If the intention is to search premises under the authority of a warrant or a power of entry and search without warrant, and the occupier of the premises co-operates in accordance with paragraph 6.4, there is no need to obtain written consent.

5C Paragraph 5.4 is intended to apply when it is reasonable to assume innocent occupiers would agree to, and expect, police to take the proposed action, e.g. if:

- *a suspect has fled the scene of a crime or to evade arrest and it is necessary quickly to check surrounding gardens and readily accessible places to see if the suspect is hiding*
- *police have arrested someone in the night after a pursuit and it is necessary to make a brief check of gardens along the pursuit route to see if stolen or incriminating articles have been discarded*

6 Searching premises—general considerations

(a) Time of searches

6.1 Searches made under warrant must be made within three calendar months of the date of the warrant's issue.

6.2 Searches must be made at a reasonable hour unless this might frustrate the purpose of the search.

6.3 When the extent or complexity of a search mean it is likely to take a long time, the officer in charge of the search may consider using the seize and sift powers referred to in *section 7*.

6.3A A warrant under PACE, section 8 may authorise entry to and search of premises on more than one occasion if, on the application, the justice of the peace is satisfied that it is necessary to authorise multiple entries in order to achieve the purpose for which the warrant is issued. No premises may be entered or searched on any subsequent occasions without the prior written authority of an officer of the rank of inspector who is not involved in the investigation. All other warrants authorise entry on one occasion only.

6.3B Where a warrant under PACE section 8, or Schedule 1, paragraph 12 authorises entry to and search of all premises occupied or controlled by a specified person, no premises which are not specified in the warrant may be entered and searched without the prior written authority of an officer of the rank of inspector who is not involved in the investigation.

(b) Entry other than with consent

6.4 The officer in charge of the search shall first try to communicate with the occupier, or any other person entitled to grant access to the premises, explain the authority under which entry is sought and ask the occupier to allow entry, unless:

(i) the search premises are unoccupied;
(ii) the occupier and any other person entitled to grant access are absent;
(iii) there are reasonable grounds for believing that alerting the occupier or any other person entitled to grant access would frustrate the object of the search or endanger officers or other people.

6.5 Unless *sub-paragraph 6.4(iii)* applies, if the premises are occupied the officer, subject to *paragraph 2.9*, shall, before the search begins:

(i) identify him or herself, show their warrant card (if not in uniform) and state the purpose of and grounds for the search;
(ii) identify and introduce any person accompanying the officer on the search (such persons should carry identification for production on request) and briefly describe that person's role in the process.

6.6 Reasonable and proportionate force may be used if necessary to enter premises if the officer in charge of the search is satisfied the premises are those specified in any warrant, or in exercise of the powers described in *paragraphs 4.1* to *4.3*, and if:

(i) the occupier or any other person entitled to grant access has refused entry;
(ii) it is impossible to communicate with the occupier or any other person entitled to grant access; or
(iii) any of the provisions of *paragraph 6.4* apply.

(c) Notice of Powers and Rights

6.7 If an officer conducts a search to which this Code applies the officer shall, unless it is impracticable to do so, provide the occupier with a copy of a Notice in a standard format:

(i) specifying if the search is made under warrant, with consent, or in the exercise of the powers described in *paragraphs 4.1* to *4.3*. Note: the notice format shall provide for authority or consent to be indicated, see *paragraphs 4.3* and *5.1*;
(ii) summarising the extent of the powers of search and seizure conferred by PACE;
(iii) explaining the rights of the occupier, and the owner of the property seized;
(iv) explaining compensation may be payable in appropriate cases for damages caused entering and searching premises, and giving the address to send a compensation application, see *Note 6A*;
(v) stating this Code is available at any police station.

6.8 If the occupier is:

- present, copies of the Notice and warrant shall, if practicable, be given to them before the search begins, unless the officer in charge of the search reasonably believes this would frustrate the object of the search or endanger officers or other people

- not present, copies of the Notice and warrant shall be left in a prominent place on the premises or appropriate part of the premises and endorsed, subject to *paragraph 2.9* with the name of the officer in charge of the search, the date and time of the search

The warrant shall be endorsed to show this has been done.

(d) Conduct of searches

6.9 Premises may be searched only to the extent necessary to achieve the object of the search, having regard to the size and nature of whatever is sought.

6.9A A search may not continue under:

- a warrant's authority once all the things specified in that warrant have been found
- any other power once the object of that search has been achieved

6.9B No search may continue once the officer in charge of the search is satisfied whatever is being sought is not on the premises. See *Note 6B*. This does not prevent a further search of the same premises if additional grounds come to light supporting a further application for a search warrant or exercise or further exercise of another power. For example, when, as a result of new information, it is believed articles previously not found or additional articles are on the premises.

6.10 Searches must be conducted with due consideration for the property and privacy of the occupier and with no more disturbance than necessary. Reasonable force may be used only when necessary and proportionate because the co-operation of the occupier cannot be obtained or is insufficient for the purpose. See *Note 6C*

6.11 A friend, neighbour or other person must be allowed to witness the search if the occupier wishes unless the officer in charge of the search has reasonable grounds for believing the presence of the person asked for would seriously hinder the investigation or endanger officers or other people. A search need not be unreasonably delayed for this purpose. A record of the action taken should be made on the premises search record including the grounds for refusing the occupier's request.

6.12 A person is not required to be cautioned prior to being asked questions that are solely necessary for the purpose of furthering the proper and effective conduct of a search, see Code C, *paragraph 10.1(c)*. For example, questions to discover the occupier of specified premises, to find a key to open a locked drawer or cupboard or to otherwise seek co-operation during the search or to determine if a particular item is liable to be seized.

6.12A If questioning goes beyond what is necessary for the purpose of the exemption in Code C, the exchange is likely to constitute an interview as defined by Code C, *paragraph 11.1A* and would require the associated safeguards included in Code C, *section 10*.

(e) Leaving premises

6.13 If premises have been entered by force, before leaving the officer in charge of the search must make sure they are secure by:

- arranging for the occupier or their agent to be present
- any other appropriate means

(f) Searches under PACE Schedule 1 or the Terrorism Act 2000, Schedule 5

6.14 An officer shall be appointed as the officer in charge of the search, see *paragraph 2.10*, in respect of any search made under a warrant issued under PACE Act 1984, Schedule 1 or the Terrorism Act 2000, Schedule 5. They are responsible for making sure the search is conducted with discretion and in a manner that causes the least possible disruption to any business or other activities carried out on the premises.

6.15 Once the officer in charge of the search is satisfied material may not be taken from the premises without their knowledge, they shall ask for the documents or other records concerned. The officer in charge of the search may also ask to see the index to files held on the premises, and the officers conducting the search may inspect any files which, according to the index, appear to contain the material sought. A more extensive search of the premises may be made only if:

- the person responsible for them refuses to:
  — produce the material sought, or
  — allow access to the index
- it appears the index is:
  — inaccurate, or
  — incomplete
- for any other reason the officer in charge of the search has reasonable grounds for believing such a search is necessary in order to find the material sought

Notes for guidance

6A *Whether compensation is appropriate depends on the circumstances in each case. Compensation for damage caused when effecting entry is unlikely to be appropriate if the search was lawful, and the force used can be shown to be reasonable, proportionate and necessary to effect entry. If the wrong premises are searched by mistake everything possible should be done at the earliest opportunity to allay any sense of grievance and there should normally be a strong presumption in favour of paying compensation.*

6B *It is important that, when possible, all those involved in a search are fully briefed about any powers to be exercised and the extent and limits within which it should be conducted.*

6C *In all cases the number of officers and other persons involved in executing the warrant should be determined by what is reasonable and necessary according to the particular circumstances.*

7 Seizure and retention of property

(a) Seizure

7.1 Subject to *paragraph 7.2*, an officer who is searching any person or premises under any statutory power or with the consent of the occupier may seize anything:

(a) covered by a warrant

(b) the officer has reasonable grounds for believing is evidence of an offence or has been obtained in consequence of the commission of an offence but only if seizure is necessary to prevent the items being concealed, lost, disposed of, altered, damaged, destroyed or tampered with

(c) covered by the powers in the Criminal Justice and Police Act 2001, Part 2 allowing an officer to seize property from persons or premises and retain it for sifting or examination elsewhere

See *Note 7B*

7.2 No item may be seized which an officer has reasonable grounds for believing to be subject to legal privilege, as defined in PACE, section 10, other than under the Criminal Justice and Police Act 2001, Part 2.

7.3 Officers must be aware of the provisions in the Criminal Justice and Police Act 2001, section 59, allowing for applications to a judicial authority for the return of property seized and the subsequent duty to secure in section 60, see *paragraph 7.12(iii).*

7.4 An officer may decide it is not appropriate to seize property because of an explanation from the person holding it but may nevertheless have reasonable grounds for believing it was obtained in consequence of an offence by some person. In these circumstances, the officer should identify the property to the holder, inform the holder of their suspicions and explain the holder may be liable to civil or criminal proceedings if they dispose of, alter or destroy the property.

7.5 An officer may arrange to photograph, image or copy, any document or other article they have the power to seize in accordance with *paragraph 7.1*. This is subject to specific restrictions on the examination, imaging or copying of certain property seized under the Criminal Justice and Police Act 2001, Part 2. An officer must have regard to their statutory obligation to retain an original document or other article only when a photograph or copy is not sufficient.

7.6 If an officer considers information stored in any electronic form and accessible from the premises could be used in evidence, they may require the information to be produced in a form:

- which can be taken away and in which it is visible and legible; or
- from which it can readily be produced in a visible and legible form

(b) Criminal Justice and Police Act 2001: Specific procedures for seize and sift powers

7.7 The Criminal Justice and Police Act 2001, Part 2 gives officers limited powers to seize property from premises or persons so they can sift or examine it elsewhere. Officers must be careful they only exercise these powers when it is essential and they do not remove any more material than necessary. The removal of large volumes of material, much of which may not ultimately be retainable, may have serious implications for the owners, particularly when they are involved in business or activities such as journalism or the provision of medical services. Officers must carefully consider if removing copies or images of relevant material or data would be a satisfactory alternative to removing originals. When originals are taken, officers must be prepared to facilitate the provision of copies or images for the owners when reasonably practicable. See *Note 7C*

7.8 Property seized under the Criminal Justice and Police Act 2001, sections 50 or 51 must be kept securely and separately from any material seized under other powers. An examination under section 53 to determine which elements may be retained must be carried out at the earliest practicable time, having due regard to the desirability of allowing the person from whom the property was seized, or a person with an interest in the property, an opportunity of being present or represented at the examination.

7.8A All reasonable steps should be taken to accommodate an interested person's request to be present, provided the request is reasonable and subject to the need to prevent harm to, interference with, or unreasonable delay to the investigatory process. If an examination proceeds in the absence of an interested person who asked to attend or their representative, the officer who exercised the relevant seizure power must give that person a written notice of why the examination was carried out in those circumstances. If it is necessary for security reasons or to maintain confidentiality officers may exclude interested persons from decryption or other processes which facilitate the examination but do not form part of it. See *Note 7D*

7.9 It is the responsibility of the officer in charge of the investigation to make sure property is returned in accordance with sections 53 to 55. Material which there is no power to retain must be:

- separated from the rest of the seized property
- returned as soon as reasonably practicable after examination of all the seized property

7.9A Delay is only warranted if very clear and compelling reasons exist, e.g. the:

- unavailability of the person to whom the material is to be returned
- need to agree a convenient time to return a large volume of material

7.9B Legally privileged, excluded or special procedure material which cannot be retained must be returned:

- as soon as reasonably practicable
- without waiting for the whole examination

7.9C As set out in section 58, material must be returned to the person from whom it was seized, except when it is clear some other person has a better right to it. See *Note 7E*

7.10 When an officer involved in the investigation has reasonable grounds to believe a person with a relevant interest in property seized under section 50 or 51 intends to make an application under section 59 for the return of any legally privileged, special procedure or excluded material, the officer in charge of the investigation should be informed as soon as practicable and the material seized should be kept secure in accordance with section 61. See *Note 7C*

7.11 The officer in charge of the investigation is responsible for making sure property is properly secured. Securing involves making sure the property is not examined, copied, imaged or put to any other use except at the request, or with the consent, of the applicant or in accordance with the directions of the appropriate judicial authority. Any request, consent or directions must be recorded in writing and signed by both the initiator and the officer in charge of the investigation. See *Notes 7F* and *7G*

7.12 When an officer exercises a power of seizure conferred by sections 50 or 51 they shall provide the occupier of the premises or the person from whom the property is being seized with a written notice:

(i) specifying what has been seized under the powers conferred by that section;

(ii) specifying the grounds for those powers;

(iii) setting out the effect of sections 59 to 61 covering the grounds for a person with a relevant interest in seized property to apply to a judicial authority for its return and the duty of officers to secure property in certain circumstances when an application is made;

(iv) specifying the name and address of the person to whom:

- notice of an application to the appropriate judicial authority in respect of any of the seized property must be given;
- an application may be made to allow attendance at the initial examination of the property.

7.13 If the occupier is not present but there is someone in charge of the premises, the notice shall be given to them. If no suitable person is available, so the notice will easily be found it should either be:

- left in a prominent place on the premises
- attached to the exterior of the premises

(c) Retention

7.14 Subject to *paragraph 7.15*, anything seized in accordance with the above provisions may be retained only for as long as is necessary. It may be retained, among other purposes:

(i) for use as evidence at a trial for an offence;

(ii) to facilitate the use in any investigation or proceedings of anything to which it is inextricably linked, see *Note 7H*;

(iii) for forensic examination or other investigation in connection with an offence;

(iv) in order to establish its lawful owner when there are reasonable grounds for believing it has been stolen or obtained by the commission of an offence.

7.15 Property shall not be retained under *paragraph 7.14(i), (ii)* or *(iii)* if a copy or image would be sufficient.

(d) Rights of owners etc

7.16 If property is retained, the person who had custody or control of it immediately before seizure must, on request, be provided with a list or description of the property within a reasonable time.

7.17 That person or their representative must be allowed supervised access to the property to examine it or have it photographed or copied, or must be provided with a photograph or copy, in either case within a reasonable time of any request and at their own expense, unless the officer in charge of an investigation has reasonable grounds for believing this would:

(i) prejudice the investigation of any offence or criminal proceedings; or

(ii) lead to the commission of an offence by providing access to unlawful material such as pornography;

A record of the grounds shall be made when access is denied.

Notes for guidance

7A *Any person claiming property seized by the police may apply to a magistrates' court under the Police (Property) Act 1897 for its possession and should, if appropriate, be advised of this procedure.*

7B *The powers of seizure conferred by PACE, sections 18(2) and 19(3) extend to the seizure of the whole premises when it is physically possible to seize and retain the premises in their totality and practical considerations make seizure desirable. For example, police may remove premises such as tents, vehicles or caravans to a police station for the purpose of preserving evidence.*

7C *Officers should consider reaching agreement with owners and/or other interested parties on the procedures for examining a specific set of property, rather than awaiting the judicial authority's determination. Agreement can sometimes give a quicker and more satisfactory route for all concerned and minimise costs and legal complexities.*

7D *What constitutes a relevant interest in specific material may depend on the nature of that material and the circumstances in which it is seized. Anyone with a reasonable claim to ownership of the material and anyone entrusted with its safe keeping by the owner should be considered.*

7E *Requirements to secure and return property apply equally to all copies, images or other material created because of seizure of the original property.*

7F *The mechanics of securing property vary according to the circumstances; "bagging up", i.e. placing material in sealed bags or containers and strict subsequent control of access is the appropriate procedure in many cases.*

7G *When material is seized under the powers of seizure conferred by PACE, the duty to retain it under the Code of Practice issued under the Criminal Procedure and Investigations Act 1996 is subject to the provisions on retention of seized material in PACE, section 22.*

7H *Paragraph 7.14 (ii) applies if inextricably linked material is seized under the Criminal Justice and Police Act 2001, sections 50 or 51. Inextricably linked material is material it is not reasonably practicable to separate from other linked material without prejudicing the use of that other material in any investigation or proceedings. For example, it may not be possible to separate items of data held on computer disk without damaging their evidential integrity. Inextricably linked material must not be examined, imaged, copied or used for any purpose other than for proving the source and/or integrity of the linked material.*

8 Action after searches

8.1 If premises are searched in circumstances where this Code applies, unless the exceptions in *paragraph 2.3(a)* apply, on arrival at a police station the officer in charge of the search shall make or have made a record of the search, to include:

(i) the address of the searched premises;

(ii) the date, time and duration of the search;

(iii) the authority used for the search:

- if the search was made in exercise of a statutory power to search premises without warrant, the power which was used for the search:
- if the search was made under a warrant or with written consent;
  — a copy of the warrant and the written authority to apply for it, see paragraph 3.4; or
  — the written consent;

shall be appended to the record or the record shall show the location of the copy warrant or consent.

(iv) subject to *paragraph 2.9*, the names of:

- the officer(s) in charge of the search;
- all other officers and any authorised persons who conducted the search;

(v) the names of any people on the premises if they are known;

(vi) any grounds for refusing the occupier's request to have someone present during the search, see *paragraph 6.11;*

(vii) a list of any articles seized or the location of a list and, if not covered by a warrant, the grounds for their seizure;

(viii) whether force was used, and the reason;

(ix) details of any damage caused during the search, and the circumstances;

(x) if applicable, the reason it was not practicable;

(a) to give the occupier a copy of the Notice of Powers and Rights, see *paragraph 6.7*;

(b) before the search to give the occupier a copy of the Notice, see *paragraph 6.8*;

(xi) when the occupier was not present, the place where copies of the Notice of Powers and Rights and search warrant were left on the premises, see *paragraph 6.8*.

8.2 On each occasion when premises are searched under warrant, the warrant authorising the search on that occasion shall be endorsed to show:

(i) if any articles specified in the warrant were found and the address where found;

(ii) if any other articles were seized;

(iii) the date and time it was executed and if present, the name of the occupier or if the occupier is not present the name of the person in charge of the premises:

(iv) subject to paragraph 2.9, the names of the officers who executed it and any authorised persons who accompanied them;

(v) if a copy, together with a copy of the Notice of Powers and Rights was:

- handed to the occupier; or
- endorsed as required by paragraph 6.8; and left on the premises and where.

8.3 Any warrant shall be returned within three calendar months of its issue or sooner on completion of the search(es) authorised by that warrant, if it was issued by a:

- justice of the peace, to the designated officer for the local justice area in which the justice was acting when issuing the warrant; or
- judge, to the appropriate officer of the court concerned,

9 Search registers

9.1 A search register will be maintained at each sub-divisional or equivalent police station. All search records required under *paragraph 8.1* shall be made, copied, or referred to in the register. See *Note 9A*

Note for guidance

9A Paragraph 9.1 also applies to search records made by immigration officers. In these cases, a search register must also be maintained at an immigration office. See also Note 2D

Appendix 3

PACE Code of Practice for the Detention, Treatment and Questioning of Persons by Police Officers (Code C)

This Code applies to people in police detention after midnight on 31 January 2008, notwithstanding that their period of detention may have commenced before that time.

1 General

1.1 All persons in custody must be dealt with expeditiously, and released as soon as the need for detention no longer applies.

1.1A A custody officer must perform the functions in this Code as soon as practicable. A custody officer will not be in breach of this Code if delay is justifiable and reasonable steps are taken to prevent unnecessary delay. The custody record shall show when a delay has occurred and the reason. See *Note 1H*

1.2 This Code of Practice must be readily available at all police stations for consultation by:

- police officers
- police staff
- detained persons
- members of the public.

1.3 The provisions of this Code:

- include the *Annexes*
- do not include the *Notes for Guidance.*

1.4 If an officer has any suspicion, or is told in good faith, that a person of any age may be mentally disordered or otherwise mentally vulnerable, in the absence of clear evidence to dispel that suspicion, the person shall be treated as such for the purposes of this Code. *See Note 1G*

1.5 If anyone appears to be under 17, they shall be treated as a juvenile for the purposes of this Code in the absence of clear evidence that they are older.

1.6 If a person appears to be blind, seriously visually impaired, deaf, unable to read or speak or has difficulty orally because of a speech impediment, they shall be treated as such for the purposes of this Code in the absence of clear evidence to the contrary.

1.7 'The appropriate adult' means, in the case of a:

(a) juvenile:

(i) the parent, guardian or, if the juvenile is in local authority or voluntary organisation care, or is otherwise being looked after under the Children Act 1989, a person representing that authority or organisation;

(ii) a social worker of a local authority;

(iii) failing these, some other responsible adult aged 18 or over who is not a police officer or employed by the police.

(b) person who is mentally disordered or mentally vulnerable: See *Note 1D*

(iv) a relative, guardian or other person responsible for their care or custody;

(v) someone experienced in dealing with mentally disordered or mentally vulnerable people but who is not a police officer or employed by the police;
(vi) failing these, some other responsible adult aged 18 or over who is not a police officer or employed by the police.

1.8 If this Code requires a person be given certain information, they do not have to be given it if at the time they are incapable of understanding what is said, are violent or may become violent or in urgent need of medical attention, but they must be given it as soon as practicable.

1.9 References to a custody officer include any:
- police officer; or
- designated staff custody officer acting in the exercise or performance of the powers and duties conferred or imposed on them by their designation,

performing the functions of a custody officer. See *Note 1J.*

1.9A When this Code requires the prior authority or agreement of an officer of at least inspector or superintendent rank, that authority may be given by a sergeant or chief inspector authorised to perform the functions of the higher rank under the Police and Criminal Evidence Act 1984 (PACE), section 107.

1.10 Subject to *paragraph 1.12*, this Code applies to people in custody at police stations in England and Wales, whether or not they have been arrested, and to those removed to a police station as a place of safety under the Mental Health Act 1983, sections 135 and 136. *Section 15* applies solely to people in police detention, e.g. those brought to a police station under arrest or arrested at a police station for an offence after going there voluntarily.

1.11 People detained under the Terrorism Act 2000, Schedule 8 and section 41 and other provisions of that Act are not subject to any part of this Code. Such persons are subject to the Code of Practice for detention, treatment and questioning of persons by police officers detained under that Act.

1.12 This Code's provisions do not apply to people in custody:
(i) arrested on warrants issued in Scotland by officers under the Criminal Justice and Public Order Act 1994, section 136(2), or arrested or detained without warrant by officers from a police force in Scotland under section 137(2). In these cases, police powers and duties and the person's rights and entitlements whilst at a police station in England or Wales are the same as those in Scotland;
(ii) arrested under the Immigration and Asylum Act 1999, section 142(3) in order to have their fingerprints taken;
(iii) whose detention is authorised by an immigration officer under the Immigration Act 1971;
(iv) who are convicted or remanded prisoners held in police cells on behalf of the Prison Service under the Imprisonment (Temporary Provisions) Act 1980;
(v) not used
(vi) detained for searches under stop and search powers except as required by Code A.

The provisions on conditions of detention and treatment in *sections 8* and *9* must be considered as the minimum standards of treatment for such detainees.

1.13 In this Code:
(a) 'designated person' means a person other than a police officer, designated under the Police Reform Act 2002, Part 4 who has specified powers and duties of police officers conferred or imposed on them;
(b) reference to a police officer includes a designated person acting in the exercise or performance of the powers and duties conferred or imposed on them by their designation.

1.14 Designated persons are entitled to use reasonable force as follows:-
(a) when exercising a power conferred on them which allows a police officer exercising that power to use reasonable force, a designated person has the same entitlement to use force; and
(b) at other times when carrying out duties conferred or imposed on them that also entitle them to use reasonable force, for example:

- when at a police station carrying out the duty to keep detainees for whom they are responsible under control and to assist any other police officer or designated person to keep any detainee under control and to prevent their escape.
- when securing, or assisting any other police officer or designated person in securing, the detention of a person at a police station.
- when escorting, or assisting any other police officer or designated person in escorting, a detainee within a police station.
- for the purpose of saving life or limb; or
- preventing serious damage to property.

1.15 Nothing in this Code prevents the custody officer, or other officer given custody of the detainee, from allowing police staff who are not designated persons to carry out individual procedures or tasks at the police station if the law allows. However, the officer remains responsible for making sure the procedures and tasks are carried out correctly in accordance with the Codes of Practice. Any such person must be:

(a) a person employed by a police authority maintaining a police force and under the control and direction of the Chief Officer of that force;

(b) employed by a person with whom a police authority has a contract for the provision of services relating to persons arrested or otherwise in custody.

1.16 Designated persons and other police staff must have regard to any relevant provisions of the Codes of Practice.

1.17 References to pocket books include any official report book issued to police officers or other police staff.

Notes for guidance

1A Although certain sections of this Code apply specifically to people in custody at police stations, those there voluntarily to assist with an investigation should be treated with no less consideration, e.g. offered refreshments at appropriate times, and enjoy an absolute right to obtain legal advice or communicate with anyone outside the police station.

1B A person, including a parent or guardian, should not be an appropriate adult if they:

- *are*
  - *— suspected of involvement in the offence*
  - *— the victim*
  - *— a witness*
  - *— involved in the investigation*
- *received admissions prior to attending to act as the appropriate adult.*

Note: If a juvenile's parent is estranged from the juvenile, they should not be asked to act as the appropriate adult if the juvenile expressly and specifically objects to their presence.

1C If a juvenile admits an offence to, or in the presence of, a social worker or member of a youth offending team other than during the time that person is acting as the juvenile's appropriate adult, another appropriate adult should be appointed in the interest of fairness.

1D In the case of people who are mentally disordered or otherwise mentally vulnerable, it may be more satisfactory if the appropriate adult is someone experienced or trained in their care rather than a relative lacking such qualifications. But if the detainee prefers a relative to a better qualified stranger or objects to a particular person their wishes should, if practicable, be respected.

1E A detainee should always be given an opportunity, when an appropriate adult is called to the police station, to consult privately with a solicitor in the appropriate adult's absence if they want. An appropriate adult is not subject to legal privilege.

1F A solicitor or independent custody visitor (formerly a lay visitor) present at the police station in that capacity may not be the appropriate adult.

1G 'Mentally vulnerable' applies to any detainee who, because of their mental state or capacity, may not understand the significance of what is said, of questions or of their replies. 'Mental disorder' is defined in the Mental Health Act 1983, section 1(2) as 'mental illness, arrested or incomplete development of mind, psychopathic disorder and any other disorder or disability of mind'. When the custody officer has any doubt about the mental state or capacity of a detainee, that detainee should be treated as mentally vulnerable and an appropriate adult called.

1H Paragraph 1.1A is intended to cover delays which may occur in processing detainees e.g. if:
- *a large number of suspects are brought into the station simultaneously to be placed in custody;*
- *interview rooms are all being used;*
- *there are difficulties contacting an appropriate adult, solicitor or interpreter.*

1I The custody officer must remind the appropriate adult and detainee about the right to legal advice and record any reasons for waiving it in accordance with section 6.

1J The designation of police staff custody officers applies only in police areas where an order commencing the provisions of the Police Reform Act 2002, section 38 and Schedule 4A, for designating police staff custody officers is in effect.

1K This Code does not affect the principle that all citizens have a duty to help police officers to prevent crime and discover offenders. This is a civic rather than a legal duty; but when a police officer is trying to discover whether, or by whom, an offence has been committed he is entitled to question any person from whom he thinks useful information can be obtained, subject to the restrictions imposed by this Code. A person's declaration that he is unwilling to reply does not alter this entitlement.

09/04170/1/2 — 845

2 Custody records

2.1A When a person is brought to a police station:
- under arrest
- is arrested at the police station having attended there voluntarily or
- attends a police station to answer bail

they should be brought before the custody officer as soon as practicable after their arrival at the station or, if appropriate, following arrest after attending the police station voluntarily. This applies to designated and non-designated police stations. A person is deemed to be "at a police station" for these purposes if they are within the boundary of any building or enclosed yard which forms part of that police station.

2.1 A separate custody record must be opened as soon as practicable for each person brought to a police station under arrest or arrested at the station having gone there voluntarily or attending a police station in answer to street bail. All information recorded under this Code must be recorded as soon as practicable in the custody record unless otherwise specified. Any audio or video recording made in the custody area is not part of the custody record.

2.2 If any action requires the authority of an officer of a specified rank, subject to *paragraph 2.6A*, their name and rank must be noted in the custody record.

2.3 The custody officer is responsible for the custody record's accuracy and completeness and for making sure the record or copy of the record accompanies a detainee if they are transferred to another police station. The record shall show the:
- time and reason for transfer;
- time a person is released from detention.

2.4 A solicitor or appropriate adult must be permitted to consult a detainee's custody record as soon as practicable after their arrival at the station and at any other time whilst the person is detained. Arrangements for this access must be agreed with the custody officer and may not unreasonably interfere with the custody officer's duties.

2.4A When a detainee leaves police detention or is taken before a court they, their legal representative or appropriate adult shall be given, on request, a copy of the custody record as soon as practicable. This entitlement lasts for 12 months after release.

2.5 The detainee, appropriate adult or legal representative shall be permitted to inspect the original custody record after the detainee has left police detention provided they give reasonable notice of their request. Any such inspection shall be noted in the custody record.

2.6 Subject to *paragraph 2.6A*, all entries in custody records must be timed and signed by the maker. Records entered on computer shall be timed and contain the operator's identification.

2.6A Nothing in this Code requires the identity of officers or other police staff to be recorded or disclosed:

(a) not used;

(b) if the officer or police staff reasonably believe recording or disclosing their name might put them in danger.

In these cases, they shall use their warrant or other identification numbers and the name of their police station. See *Note 2A*

2.7 The fact and time of any detainee's refusal to sign a custody record, when asked in accordance with this Code, must be recorded.

Note for guidance

2A The purpose of paragraph 2.6A(b) is to protect those involved in serious organised crime investigations or arrests of particularly violent suspects when there is reliable information that those arrested or their associates may threaten or cause harm to those involved. In cases of doubt, an officer of inspector rank or above should be consulted.

3 Initial action

(a) Detained persons—normal procedure

3.1 When a person is brought to a police station under arrest or arrested at the station having gone there voluntarily, the custody officer must make sure the person is told clearly about the following continuing rights which may be exercised at any stage during the period in custody:

(i) the right to have someone informed of their arrest as in *section 5*;
(ii) the right to consult privately with a solicitor and that free independent legal advice is available;
(iii) the right to consult these Codes of Practice. See *Note 3D*

3.2 The detainee must also be given:

- a written notice setting out:
  — the above three rights;
  — the arrangements for obtaining legal advice;
  — the right to a copy of the custody record as in *paragraph 2.4A*;
  — the caution in the terms prescribed in *section 10.*
- an additional written notice briefly setting out their entitlements while in custody, see *Notes 3A* and *3B.*

Note: The detainee shall be asked to sign the custody record to acknowledge receipt of these notices. Any refusal must be recorded on the custody record.

3.3 A citizen of an independent Commonwealth country or a national of a foreign country, including the Republic of Ireland, must be informed as soon as practicable about their rights of communication with their High Commission, Embassy or Consulate. See *section 7*

3.4 The custody officer shall:

- record the offence(s) that the detainee has been arrested for and the reason(s) for the arrest on the custody record. See *paragraph 10.3* and *Code G paragraphs 2.2 and 4.3.*
- note on the custody record any comment the detainee makes in relation to the arresting officer's account but shall not invite comment. If the arresting officer is not physically present when the detainee is brought to a police station, the arresting officer's account must be made available to the custody officer remotely or by a third party on the arresting officer's behalf. If the custody officer authorises a person's detention the detainee must be informed of the grounds as soon as practicable and before they are questioned about any offence;
- note any comment the detainee makes in respect of the decision to detain them but shall not invite comment;
- not put specific questions to the detainee regarding their involvement in any offence, nor in respect of any comments they may make in response to the arresting officer's account

or the decision to place them in detention. Such an exchange is likely to constitute an interview as in *paragraph 11.1A* and require the associated safeguards in *section 11*.

See *paragraph 11.13* in respect of unsolicited comments.

3.5 The custody officer shall:

(a) ask the detainee, whether at this time, they:

(i) would like legal advice, see *paragraph 6.5*;

(ii) want someone informed of their detention, see *section 5*;

(b) ask the detainee to sign the custody record to confirm their decisions in respect of (a);

(c) determine whether the detainee:

(i) is, or might be, in need of medical treatment or attention, see *section 9*;

(ii) requires:

- an appropriate adult;
- help to check documentation;
- an interpreter;

(d) record the decision in respect of (c).

3.6 When determining these needs the custody officer is responsible for initiating an assessment to consider whether the detainee is likely to present specific risks to custody staff or themselves. Such assessments should always include a check on the Police National Computer, to be carried out as soon as practicable, to identify any risks highlighted in relation to the detainee. Although such assessments are primarily the custody officer's responsibility, it may be necessary for them to consult and involve others, e.g. the arresting officer or an appropriate health care professional, see *paragraph 9.13*. Reasons for delaying the initiation or completion of the assessment must be recorded.

3.7 Chief Officers should ensure that arrangements for proper and effective risk assessments required by *paragraph 3.6* are implemented in respect of all detainees at police stations in their area.

3.8 Risk assessments must follow a structured process which clearly defines the categories of risk to be considered and the results must be incorporated in the detainee's custody record. The custody officer is responsible for making sure those responsible for the detainee's custody are appropriately briefed about the risks. If no specific risks are identified by the assessment, that should be noted in the custody record. See *Note 3E* and *paragraph 9.14*

3.9 The custody officer is responsible for implementing the response to any specific risk assessment, e.g.:

- reducing opportunities for self harm;
- calling a health care professional;
- increasing levels of monitoring or observation.

3.10 Risk assessment is an ongoing process and assessments must always be subject to review if circumstances change.

3.11 If video cameras are installed in the custody area, notices shall be prominently displayed showing cameras are in use. Any request to have video cameras switched off shall be refused.

(b) Detained persons—special groups

3.12 If the detainee appears deaf or there is doubt about their hearing or speaking ability or ability to understand English, and the custody officer cannot establish effective communication, the custody officer must, as soon as practicable, call an interpreter for assistance in the action under *paragraphs 3.1–3.5*. See *section 13*

3.13 If the detainee is a juvenile, the custody officer must, if it is practicable, ascertain the identity of a person responsible for their welfare. That person:

- may be:
  - — the parent or guardian;
  - — if the juvenile is in local authority or voluntary organisation care, or is otherwise being looked after under the Children Act 1989, a person appointed by that authority or organisation to have responsibility for the juvenile's welfare;
  - — any other person who has, for the time being, assumed responsibility for the juvenile's welfare.

- must be informed as soon as practicable that the juvenile has been arrested, why they have been arrested and where they are detained. This right is in addition to the juvenile's right in *section 5* not to be held incommunicado. See *Note 3C*

3.14 If a juvenile is known to be subject to a court order under which a person or organisation is given any degree of statutory responsibility to supervise or otherwise monitor them, reasonable steps must also be taken to notify that person or organisation (the 'responsible officer'). The responsible officer will normally be a member of a Youth Offending Team, except for a curfew order which involves electronic monitoring when the contractor providing the monitoring will normally be the responsible officer.

3.15 If the detainee is a juvenile, mentally disordered or otherwise mentally vulnerable, the custody officer must, as soon as practicable:

- inform the appropriate adult, who in the case of a juvenile may or may not be a person responsible for their welfare, as in *paragraph 3.13*, of:
  - — the grounds for their detention;
  - — their whereabouts.
- ask the adult to come to the police station to see the detainee.

3.16 It is imperative that a mentally disordered or otherwise mentally vulnerable person, detained under the Mental Health Act 1983, section 136, be assessed as soon as possible. If that assessment is to take place at the police station, an approved social worker and a registered medical practitioner shall be called to the station as soon as possible in order to interview and examine the detainee. Once the detainee has been interviewed, examined and suitable arrangements made for their treatment or care, they can no longer be detained under section 136. A detainee must be immediately discharged from detention under section 136 if a registered medical practitioner, having examined them, concludes they are not mentally disordered within the meaning of the Act.

3.17 If the appropriate adult is:

- already at the police station, the provisions of *paragraphs 3.1* to *3.5* must be complied with in the appropriate adult's presence;
- not at the station when these provisions are complied with, they must be complied with again in the presence of the appropriate adult when they arrive.

3.18 The detainee shall be advised that:

- the duties of the appropriate adult include giving advice and assistance;
- they can consult privately with the appropriate adult at any time.

3.19 If the detainee, or appropriate adult on the detainee's behalf, asks for a solicitor to be called to give legal advice, the provisions of *section 6* apply.

3.20 If the detainee is blind, seriously visually impaired or unable to read, the custody officer shall make sure their solicitor, relative, appropriate adult or some other person likely to take an interest in them and not involved in the investigation is available to help check any documentation. When this Code requires written consent or signing the person assisting may be asked to sign instead, if the detainee prefers. This paragraph does not require an appropriate adult to be called solely to assist in checking and signing documentation for a person who is not a juvenile, or mentally disordered or otherwise mentally vulnerable (see *paragraph 3.15*).

(c) Persons attending a police station voluntarily

3.21 Anybody attending a police station voluntarily to assist with an investigation may leave at will unless arrested. See *Note 1K*. If it is decided they shall not be allowed to leave, they must be informed at once that they are under arrest and brought before the custody officer, who is responsible for making sure they are notified of their rights in the same way as other detainees. If they are not arrested but are cautioned as in *section 10*, the person who gives the caution must, at the same time, inform them they are not under arrest, they are not obliged to remain at the station but if they remain at the station they may obtain free and independent legal advice if they want. They shall be told the right to legal advice includes the right to speak with a solicitor on the telephone and be asked if they want to do so.

3.22 If a person attending the police station voluntarily asks about their entitlement to legal advice, they shall be given a copy of the notice explaining the arrangements for obtaining legal advice. See *paragraph 3.2*.

(d) Documentation

3.23 The grounds for a person's detention shall be recorded, in the person's presence if practicable.

3.24 Action taken under *paragraphs 3.12* to *3.20* shall be recorded.

(e) Persons answering street bail

3.25 When a person is answering street bail, the custody officer should link any documentation held in relation to arrest with the custody record. Any further action shall be recorded on the custody record in accordance with paragraphs 3.23 and 3.24 above.

Notes for guidance

3A The notice of entitlements should:

- *list the entitlements in this Code, including:*
  - *— visits and contact with outside parties, including special provisions for Commonwealth citizens and foreign nationals;*
  - *— reasonable standards of physical comfort;*
  - *— adequate food and drink;*
  - *— access to toilets and washing facilities, clothing, medical attention, and exercise when practicable.*
- *mention the:*
  - *— provisions relating to the conduct of interviews;*
  - *— circumstances in which an appropriate adult should be available to assist the detainee and their statutory rights to make representation whenever the period of their detention is reviewed.*

3B In addition to notices in English, translations should be available in Welsh, the main minority ethnic languages and the principal European languages, whenever they are likely to be helpful. Audio versions of the notice should also be made available.

3C If the juvenile is in local authority or voluntary organisation care but living with their parents or other adults responsible for their welfare, although there is no legal obligation to inform them, they should normally be contacted, as well as the authority or organisation unless suspected of involvement in the offence concerned. Even if the juvenile is not living with their parents, consideration should be given to informing them.

3D The right to consult the Codes of Practice does not entitle the person concerned to delay unreasonably any necessary investigative or administrative action whilst they do so. Examples of action which need not be delayed unreasonably include:

- *procedures requiring the provision of breath, blood or urine specimens under the Road Traffic Act 1988 or the Transport and Works Act 1992;*
- *searching detainees at the police station;*
- *taking fingerprints, footwear impressions or non-intimate samples without consent for evidential purposes.*

3E Home Office Circular 32/2000 provides more detailed guidance on risk assessments and identifies key risk areas which should always be considered.

4 Detainee's property

(a) Action

4.1 The custody officer is responsible for:

(a) ascertaining what property a detainee:

(i) has with them when they come to the police station, whether on:
- arrest or re-detention on answering to bail;
- commitment to prison custody on the order or sentence of a court;
- lodgement at the police station with a view to their production in court from prison custody;
- transfer from detention at another station or hospital;
- detention under the Mental Health Act 1983, section 135 or 136;
- remand into police custody on the authority of a court

(ii) might have acquired for an unlawful or harmful purpose while in custody;

(b) the safekeeping of any property taken from a detainee which remains at the police station.

The custody officer may search the detainee or authorise their being searched to the extent they consider necessary, provided a search of intimate parts of the body or involving the removal of more than outer clothing is only made as in *Annex A*. A search may only be carried out by an officer of the same sex as the detainee. See *Note 4A*

4.2 Detainees may retain clothing and personal effects at their own risk unless the custody officer considers they may use them to cause harm to themselves or others, interfere with evidence, damage property, effect an escape or they are needed as evidence. In this event the custody officer may withhold such articles as they consider necessary and must tell the detainee why.

4.3 Personal effects are those items a detainee may lawfully need, use or refer to while in detention but do not include cash and other items of value.

(b) Documentation

4.4 It is a matter for the custody officer to determine whether a record should be made of the property a detained person has with him or had taken from him on arrest. Any record made is not required to be kept as part of the custody record but the custody record should be noted as to where such a record exists. Whenever a record is made the detainee shall be allowed to check and sign the record of property as correct. Any refusal to sign shall be recorded.

4.5 If a detainee is not allowed to keep any article of clothing or personal effects, the reason must be recorded.

Notes for guidance

4A PACE, Section 54(1) and paragraph 4.1 require a detainee to be searched when it is clear the custody officer will have continuing duties in relation to that detainee or when that detainee's behaviour or offence makes an inventory appropriate. They do not require every detainee to be searched, e.g. if it is clear a person will only be detained for a short period and is not to be placed in a cell, the custody officer may decide not to search them. In such a case the custody record will be endorsed 'not searched', paragraph 4.4 will not apply, and the detainee will be invited to sign the entry. If the detainee refuses, the custody officer will be obliged to ascertain what property they have in accordance with paragraph 4.1.

4B Paragraph 4.4 does not require the custody officer to record on the custody record property in the detainee's possession on arrest if, by virtue of its nature, quantity or size, it is not practicable to remove it to the police station.

4C Paragraph 4.4 does not require items of clothing worn by the person be recorded unless withheld by the custody officer as in paragraph 4.2.

5 Right not to be held incommunicado

(a) Action

5.1 Any person arrested and held in custody at a police station or other premises may, on request, have one person known to them or likely to take an interest in their welfare informed at public expense of their whereabouts as soon as practicable. If the person cannot be contacted the detainee may choose up to two alternatives. If they cannot be contacted, the person in charge of detention or the investigation has discretion to allow further attempts until the information has been conveyed. See *Notes 5C* and *5D*

5.2 The exercise of the above right in respect of each person nominated may be delayed only in accordance with *Annex B*.

5.3 The above right may be exercised each time a detainee is taken to another police station.

5.4 The detainee may receive visits at the custody officer's discretion. See *Note 5B*

5.5 If a friend, relative or person with an interest in the detainee's welfare enquires about their whereabouts, this information shall be given if the suspect agrees and *Annex B* does not apply. See *Note 5D*

5.6 The detainee shall be given writing materials, on request, and allowed to telephone one person for a reasonable time, see *Notes 5A* and *5E*. Either or both these privileges may be denied or delayed if an officer of inspector rank or above considers sending a letter or making a telephone call may result in any of the consequences in:

(a) *Annex B paragraphs 1* and *2* and the person is detained in connection with an indictable offence;

(b) *Not used*

Nothing in this paragraph permits the restriction or denial of the rights in *paragraphs 5.1* and *6.1*.

5.7 Before any letter or message is sent, or telephone call made, the detainee shall be informed that what they say in any letter, call or message (other than in a communication to a solicitor) may be read or listened to and may be given in evidence. A telephone call may be terminated if it is being abused. The costs can be at public expense at the custody officer's discretion.

5.7A Any delay or denial of the rights in this section should be proportionate and should last no longer than necessary.

(b) Documentation

5.8 A record must be kept of any:

(a) request made under this section and the action taken;

(b) letters, messages or telephone calls made or received or visit received;

(c) refusal by the detainee to have information about them given to an outside enquirer. The detainee must be asked to countersign the record accordingly and any refusal recorded.

Notes for guidance

5A A person may request an interpreter to interpret a telephone call or translate a letter.

5B At the custody officer's discretion, visits should be allowed when possible, subject to having sufficient personnel to supervise a visit and any possible hindrance to the investigation.

5C If the detainee does not know anyone to contact for advice or support or cannot contact a friend or relative, the custody officer should bear in mind any local voluntary bodies or other organisations who might be able to help. Paragraph 6.1 applies if legal advice is required.

5D In some circumstances it may not be appropriate to use the telephone to disclose information under paragraphs 5.1 and 5.5.

5E The telephone call at paragraph 5.6 is in addition to any communication under paragraphs 5.1 and 6.1.

6 Right to legal advice

(a) Action

6.1 Unless *Annex B* applies, all detainees must be informed that they may at any time consult and communicate privately with a solicitor, whether in person, in writing or by telephone, and that free independent legal advice is available. See *paragraph 3.1, Note 6B, 6B1, 6B2* and *Note 6J*

6.2 Not Used

6.3 A poster advertising the right to legal advice must be prominently displayed in the charging area of every police station. See *Note 6H*

6.4 No police officer should, at any time, do or say anything with the intention of dissuading a detainee from obtaining legal advice.

6.5 The exercise of the right of access to legal advice may be delayed only as in *Annex B*. Whenever legal advice is requested, and unless *Annex B* applies, the custody officer must act without delay to secure the provision of such advice. If, on being informed or reminded of this right, the detainee declines to speak to a solicitor in person, the officer should point out that the right includes the right to speak with a solicitor on the telephone. If the detainee continues to waive this right the officer should ask them why and any reasons should be recorded on the custody record or the interview record as appropriate. Reminders of the right to legal advice must be given as in *paragraphs 3.5, 11.2, 15.4, 16.4, 2B of Annex A, 3 of Annex K* and *16.5* and Code D, *paragraphs 3.17(ii)* and *6.3*. Once it is clear a detainee does not want to speak to a solicitor in person or by telephone they should cease to be asked their reasons. See *Note 6K*

6.5A In the case of a juvenile, an appropriate adult should consider whether legal advice from a solicitor is required. If the juvenile indicates that they do not want legal advice, the appropriate adult has the right to ask for a solicitor to attend if this would be in the best interests of the person. However, the detained person cannot be forced to see the solicitor if he is adamant that he does not wish to do so.

6.6 A detainee who wants legal advice may not be interviewed or continue to be interviewed until they have received such advice unless:

(a) *Annex B* applies, when the restriction on drawing adverse inferences from silence in *Annex C* will apply because the detainee is not allowed an opportunity to consult a solicitor; or

(b) an officer of superintendent rank or above has reasonable grounds for believing that:

(i) the consequent delay might:

- lead to interference with, or harm to, evidence connected with an offence;
- lead to interference with, or physical harm to, other people;
- lead to serious loss of, or damage to, property;
- lead to alerting other people suspected of having committed an offence but not yet arrested for it;
- hinder the recovery of property obtained in consequence of the commission of an offence.

(ii) when a solicitor, including a duty solicitor, has been contacted and has agreed to attend, awaiting their arrival would cause unreasonable delay to the process of investigation.

Note: In these cases the restriction on drawing adverse inferences from silence in *Annex C* will apply because the detainee is not allowed an opportunity to consult a solicitor;

(c) the solicitor the detainee has nominated or selected from a list:

(i) cannot be contacted;

(ii) has previously indicated they do not wish to be contacted; or

(iii) having been contacted, has declined to attend; and

the detainee has been advised of the Duty Solicitor Scheme but has declined to ask for the duty solicitor.

In these circumstances the interview may be started or continued without further delay provided an officer of inspector rank or above has agreed to the interview proceeding.

Note: The restriction on drawing adverse inferences from silence in *Annex C* will not apply because the detainee is allowed an opportunity to consult the duty solicitor;

(d) the detainee changes their mind, about wanting legal advice.

In these circumstances the interview may be started or continued without delay provided that:

(i) the detainee agrees to do so, in writing or on the interview record made in accordance with Code E or F; and

(ii) an officer of inspector rank or above has inquired about the detainee's reasons for their change of mind and gives authority for the interview to proceed.

Confirmation of the detainee's agreement, their change of mind, the reasons for it if given and, subject to *paragraph 2.6A*, the name of the authorising officer shall be recorded in the written interview record or the interview record made in accordance with Code E or F. See *Note 6I*.

Note: In these circumstances the restriction on drawing adverse inferences from silence in *Annex C* will not apply because the detainee is allowed an opportunity to consult a solicitor if they wish.

6.7 If *paragraph 6.6(b)(i)* applies, once sufficient information has been obtained to avert the risk, questioning must cease until the detainee has received legal advice unless *paragraph 6.6(a), (b)(ii), (c)* or *(d)* applies.

6.8 A detainee who has been permitted to consult a solicitor shall be entitled on request to have the solicitor present when they are interviewed unless one of the exceptions in *paragraph 6.6* applies.

6.9 The solicitor may only be required to leave the interview if their conduct is such that the interviewer is unable properly to put questions to the suspect. See *Notes 6D and 6E*

6.10 If the interviewer considers a solicitor is acting in such a way, they will stop the interview and consult an officer not below superintendent rank, if one is readily available, and otherwise an officer not below inspector rank not connected with the investigation. After speaking to the solicitor, the officer consulted will decide if the interview should continue in the presence of that solicitor. If they decide it should not, the suspect will be given the opportunity to consult another solicitor before the interview continues and that solicitor given an opportunity to be present at the interview. See *Note 6E*

6.11 The removal of a solicitor from an interview is a serious step and, if it occurs, the officer of superintendent rank or above who took the decision will consider if the incident should be reported to the Law Society. If the decision to remove the solicitor has been taken by an officer below superintendent rank, the facts must be reported to an officer of superintendent rank or above who will similarly consider whether a report to the Law Society would be appropriate. When the solicitor concerned is a duty solicitor, the report should be both to the Law Society and to the Legal Services Commission.

6.12 'Solicitor' in this Code means:

- a solicitor who holds a current practising certificate
- an accredited or probationary representative included on the register of representatives maintained by the Legal Services Commission.

6.12A An accredited or probationary representative sent to provide advice by, and on behalf of, a solicitor shall be admitted to the police station for this purpose unless an officer of inspector rank or above considers such a visit will hinder the investigation and directs otherwise. Hindering the investigation does not include giving proper legal advice to a detainee as in *Note 6D*. Once admitted to the police station, *paragraphs 6.6* to *6.10* apply.

6.13 In exercising their discretion under *paragraph 6.12A*, the officer should take into account in particular:

- whether:
  - — the identity and status of an accredited or probationary representative have been satisfactorily established;
  - — they are of suitable character to provide legal advice, e.g. a person with a criminal record is unlikely to be suitable unless the conviction was for a minor offence and not recent.
- any other matters in any written letter of authorisation provided by the solicitor on whose behalf the person is attending the police station. See *Note 6F*

6.14 If the inspector refuses access to an accredited or probationary representative or a decision is taken that such a person should not be permitted to remain at an interview, the inspector must notify the solicitor on whose behalf the representative was acting and give them an opportunity to make alternative arrangements. The detainee must be informed and the custody record noted.

6.15 If a solicitor arrives at the station to see a particular person, that person must, unless *Annex B* applies, be so informed whether or not they are being interviewed and asked if they would like to see the solicitor. This applies even if the detainee has declined legal advice or, having requested it, subsequently agreed to be interviewed without receiving advice.The solicitor's attendance and the detainee's decision must be noted in the custody record.

(b) Documentation

6.16 Any request for legal advice and the action taken shall be recorded.

6.17 A record shall be made in the interview record if a detainee asks for legal advice and an interview is begun either in the absence of a solicitor or their representative, or they have been required to leave an interview.

Notes for guidance

6A In considering if paragraph 6.6(b) applies, the officer should, if practicable, ask the solicitor for an estimate of how long it will take to come to the station and relate this to the time detention is permitted, the time of day (i.e. whether the rest period under paragraph 12.2 is imminent) and the requirements of other investigations. If the solicitor is on their way or is to set off immediately, it will not normally be appropriate to begin an interview before they arrive. If it appears necessary to begin an interview before the solicitor's arrival, they should be given an indication of how long the police would be able to wait before 6.6(b) applies so there is an opportunity to make arrangements for someone else to provide legal advice.

6B A detainee who asks for legal advice should be given an opportunity to consult a specific solicitor or another solicitor from that solicitor's firm or the duty solicitor. If advice is not available by these means, or they do not want to consult the duty solicitor, the detainee should be given an opportunity to choose a solicitor from a list of those willing to provide legal advice. If this solicitor is unavailable, they may choose up to two alternatives. If these attempts are unsuccessful, the custody officer has discretion to allow further attempts until a solicitor has been contacted and agrees to provide legal advice. Apart from carrying out these duties, an officer must not advise the suspect about any particular firm of solicitors. See Notes for Guidance 6B1 and 6B2 below.

6B1 ***With effect from 1 February 2008****, Note for Guidance 6B above will cease to apply in the following forces areas:*

Greater Manchester Police

West Midlands Police

West Yorkshire Police

and the following provisions will apply to those force areas: a detainee who asks for legal advice to be paid for by himself should be given an opportunity to consult a specific solicitor or another solicitor from that solicitor's firm. If this solicitor is unavailable by these means, they may choose up to two alternatives. If these attempts are unsuccessful, the custody officer has discretion to allow further attempts until a solicitor has been contacted and agrees to provide legal advice. Otherwise, publicly funded legal advice shall in the first instance be accessed by telephoning a call centre authorised by the Legal Services Commission (LSC) to deal with calls from the police station. The Defence Solicitor Call Centre will determine whether legal advice should be limited to telephone advice or whether a solicitor should attend. Legal advice will be by telephone if a detainee is:

- *detained for a non-imprisonable offence,*
- *arrested on a bench warrant for failing to appear and being held for production before the court (except where the solicitor has clear documentary evidence available that would result in the client being released from custody),*
- *arrested on suspicion of driving with excess alcohol (failure to provide a specimen, driving whilst unfit/drunk in charge of a motor vehicle), or*
- *detained in relation to breach of police or court bail conditions.*

An attendance by a solicitor for an offence suitable for telephone advice will depend on whether limited exceptions apply, such as:

- *whether the police are going to carry out an interview or an identification parade,*
- *whether the detainee is eligible for assistance from an appropriate adult,*
- *whether the detainee is unable to communicate over the telephone,*
- *whether the detainee alleges serious maltreatment by the police.*

Apart from carrying out these duties, an officer must not advise the suspect about any particular firm of solicitors. See Note for Guidance 6B2 below.

6B2 ***With effect from 21 April 2008****, the contents of Notes for Guidance 6B and 6B1 above will be superseded by this paragraph in all police forces areas in England and Wales by the following. A detainee who asks for legal advice to be paid for by himself should be given an opportunity to consult a specific solicitor or another solicitor from that solicitor's firm. If this solicitor is unavailable by these means, they may choose up to two alternatives. If these attempts are unsuccessful, the custody officer has discretion to allow further attempts until a solicitor has been contacted and agrees to provide legal advice. Otherwise, publicly funded legal advice shall in the first instance be accessed by telephoning a call centre authorised by the Legal Services Commission (LSC) to deal with calls from the police station. The Defence Solicitor Call Centre will determine whether legal advice should be limited to telephone advice or whether a solicitor should attend. Legal advice will be by telephone if a detainee is:*

- *detained for a non-imprisonable offence,*
- *arrested on a bench warrant for failing to appear and being held for production before the court (except where the solicitor has clear documentary evidence available that would result in the client being released from custody),*
- *arrested on suspicion of driving with excess alcohol (failure to provide a specimen, driving whilst unfit/drunk in charge of a motor vehicle), or*
- *detained in relation to breach of police or court bail conditions.*

An attendance by a solicitor for an offence suitable for telephone advice will depend on whether limited exceptions apply, such as:

- *whether the police are going to carry out an interview or an identification parade,*
- *whether the detainee is eligible for assistance from an appropriate adult,*
- *whether the detainee is unable to communicate over the telephone,*
- *whether the detainee alleges serious maltreatment by the police.*

Apart from carrying out these duties, an officer must not advise the suspect about any particular firm of solicitors.

6C Not Used

6D A detainee has a right to free legal advice and to be represented by a solicitor. Legal advice by telephone advice may be provided in respect of those offences listed in Note for Guidance 6B1 and 6B2 above. The Defence Solicitor Call Centre will determine whether attendance is required by a solicitor. The solicitor's only role in the police station is to protect and advance the legal rights of their client. On occasions this may require the solicitor to give advice which has the effect of the client avoiding giving evidence which strengthens a prosecution case. The solicitor may intervene in order to seek clarification, challenge an improper question to their client or the manner in which it is put, advise their client not to reply to particular questions, or if they wish to give their client further legal advice. Paragraph 6.9 only applies if the solicitor's approach or conduct prevents or unreasonably obstructs proper questions being put to the suspect or the suspect's response being recorded. Examples of unacceptable conduct include answering questions on a suspect's behalf or providing written replies for the suspect to quote.

6E An officer who takes the decision to exclude a solicitor must be in a position to satisfy the court the decision was properly made. In order to do this they may need to witness what is happening.

6F If an officer of at least inspector rank considers a particular solicitor or firm of solicitors is persistently sending probationary representatives who are unsuited to provide legal advice, they should inform an officer of at least superintendent rank, who may wish to take the matter up with the Law Society.

6G Subject to the constraints of Annex B, a solicitor may advise more than one client in an investigation if they wish. Any question of a conflict of interest is for the solicitor under their professional code of conduct. If, however, waiting for a solicitor to give advice to one client may lead to unreasonable delay to the interview with another, the provisions of paragraph 6.6(b) may apply.

6H *In addition to a poster in English, a poster or posters containing translations into Welsh, the main minority ethnic languages and the principal European languages should be displayed wherever they are likely to be helpful and it is practicable to do so.*

6I *Paragraph 6.6(d) requires the authorisation of an officer of inspector rank or above to the continuation of an interview when a detainee who wanted legal advice changes their mind. It is permissible for such authorisation to be given over the telephone, if the authorising officer is able to satisfy themselves about the reason for the detainee's change of mind and is satisfied it is proper to continue the interview in those circumstances.*

6J *Whenever a detainee exercises their right to legal advice by consulting or communicating with a solicitor, they must be allowed to do so in private. This right to consult or communicate in private is fundamental. If the requirement for privacy is compromised because what is said or written by the detainee or solicitor for the purpose of giving and receiving legal advice is overheard, listened to, or read by others without the informed consent of the detainee, the right will effectively have been denied. When a detainee chooses to speak to a solicitor on the telephone, they should be allowed to do so in private unless this is impractical because of the design and layout of the custody area or the location of telephones. However, the normal expectation should be that facilities will be available, unless they are being used, at all police stations to enable detainees to speak in private to a solicitor either face to face or over the telephone.*

6K *A detainee is not obliged to give reasons for declining legal advice and should not be pressed to do so.*

7 Citizens of independent Commonwealth countries or foreign nationals

(a) Action

7.1 Any citizen of an independent Commonwealth country or a national of a foreign country, including the Republic of Ireland, may communicate at any time with the appropriate High Commission, Embassy or Consulate. The detainee must be informed as soon as practicable of:

- this right;
- their right, upon request, to have their High Commission, Embassy or Consulate told of their whereabouts and the grounds for their detention. Such a request should be acted upon as soon as practicable.

7.2 If a detainee is a citizen of a country with which a bilateral consular convention or agreement is in force requiring notification of arrest, the appropriate High Commission, Embassy or Consulate shall be informed as soon as practicable, subject to *paragraph 7.4*. The countries to which this applies as at 1 April 2003 are listed in *Annex F*.

7.3 Consular officers may visit one of their nationals in police detention to talk to them and, if required, to arrange for legal advice. Such visits shall take place out of the hearing of a police officer.

7.4 Notwithstanding the provisions of consular conventions, if the detainee is a political refugee whether for reasons of race, nationality, political opinion or religion, or is seeking political asylum, consular officers shall not be informed of the arrest of one of their nationals or given access or information about them except at the detainee's express request.

(b) Documentation

7.5 A record shall be made when a detainee is informed of their rights under this section and of any communications with a High Commission, Embassy or Consulate.

Note for guidance

7A The exercise of the rights in this section may not be interfered with even though Annex B applies.

8 Conditions of detention

(a) Action

8.1 So far as it is practicable, not more than one detainee should be detained in each cell.

8.2 Cells in use must be adequately heated, cleaned and ventilated. They must be adequately lit, subject to such dimming as is compatible with safety and security to allow people detained overnight to sleep. No additional restraints shall be used within a locked cell unless absolutely necessary and then only restraint equipment, approved for use in that force by the Chief Officer, which is reasonable and necessary in the circumstances having regard to the detainee's demeanour and with a view to ensuring their safety and the safety of others. If a detainee is deaf, mentally disordered or otherwise mentally vulnerable, particular care must be taken when deciding whether to use any form of approved restraints.

8.3 Blankets, mattresses, pillows and other bedding supplied shall be of a reasonable standard and in a clean and sanitary condition. See *Note 8A*

8.4 Access to toilet and washing facilities must be provided.

8.5 If it is necessary to remove a detainee's clothes for the purposes of investigation, for hygiene, health reasons or cleaning, replacement clothing of a reasonable standard of comfort and cleanliness shall be provided. A detainee may not be interviewed unless adequate clothing has been offered.

8.6 At least two light meals and one main meal should be offered in any 24 hour period. See *Note 8B*. Drinks should be provided at meal times and upon reasonable request between meals. Whenever necessary, advice shall be sought from the appropriate health care professional, see *Note 9A*, on medical and dietary matters. As far as practicable, meals provided shall offer a varied diet and meet any specific dietary needs or religious beliefs the detainee may have. The detainee may, at the custody officer's discretion, have meals supplied by their family or friends at their expense. See *Note 8A*

8.7 Brief outdoor exercise shall be offered daily if practicable.

8.8 A juvenile shall not be placed in a police cell unless no other secure accommodation is available and the custody officer considers it is not practicable to supervise them if they are not placed in a cell or that a cell provides more comfortable accommodation than other secure accommodation in the station. A juvenile may not be placed in a cell with a detained adult.

(b) Documentation

8.9 A record must be kept of replacement clothing and meals offered.

8.10 If a juvenile is placed in a cell, the reason must be recorded.

8.11 The use of any restraints on a detainee whilst in a cell, the reasons for it and, if appropriate, the arrangements for enhanced supervision of the detainee whilst so restrained, shall be recorded. See *paragraph 3.9*

Notes for guidance

8A The provisions in paragraph 8.3 and 8.6 respectively are of particular importance in the case of a person likely to be detained for an extended period. In deciding whether to allow meals to be supplied by family or friends, the custody officer is entitled to take account of the risk of items being concealed in any food or package and the officer's duties and responsibilities under food handling legislation.

8B Meals should, so far as practicable, be offered at recognised meal times, or at other times that take account of when the detainee last had a meal.

9 Care and treatment of detained persons

(a) General

9.1 Nothing in this section prevents the police from calling the police surgeon or, if appropriate, some other health care professional, to examine a detainee for the purposes of obtaining evidence relating to any offence in which the detainee is suspected of being involved. See *Note 9A*

9.2 If a complaint is made by, or on behalf of, a detainee about their treatment since their arrest, or it comes to notice that a detainee may have been treated improperly, a report must be made as soon as practicable to an officer of inspector rank or above not connected with the investigation. If the matter concerns a possible assault or the possibility of the unnecessary or unreasonable use of force, an appropriate health care professional must also be called as soon as practicable.

9.3 Detainees should be visited at least every hour. If no reasonably foreseeable risk was identified in a risk assessment, see *paragraphs 3.6–3.10*, there is no need to wake a sleeping detainee. Those suspected of being intoxicated through drink or drugs or having swallowed drugs, see *Note 9CA*, or whose level of consciousness causes concern must, subject to any clinical directions given by the appropriate health care professional, see *paragraph 9.13*:

- be visited and roused at least every half hour
- have their condition assessed as in *Annex H*
- and clinical treatment arranged if appropriate

See *Notes 9B, 9C* and *9H*

9.4 When arrangements are made to secure clinical attention for a detainee, the custody officer must make sure all relevant information which might assist in the treatment of the detainee's condition is made available to the responsible health care professional. This applies whether or not the health care professional asks for such information. Any officer or police staff with relevant information must inform the custody officer as soon as practicable.

(b) Clinical treatment and attention

9.5 The custody officer must make sure a detainee receives appropriate clinical attention as soon as reasonably practicable if the person:

(a) appears to be suffering from physical illness; or

(b) is injured; or

(c) appears to be suffering from a mental disorder;

(d) appears to need clinical attention.

9.5A This applies even if the detainee makes no request for clinical attention and whether or not they have already received clinical attention elsewhere. If the need for attention appears urgent, e.g. when indicated as in *Annex H*, the nearest available health care professional or an ambulance must be called immediately.

9.5B The custody officer must also consider the need for clinical attention as set out in Note for Guidance 9C in relation to those suffering the effects of alcohol or drugs.

9.6 *Paragraph 9.5* is not meant to prevent or delay the transfer to a hospital if necessary of a person detained under the Mental Health Act 1983, section 136. See *Note 9D*. When an assessment under that Act takes place at a police station, see *paragraph 3.16*, the custody officer must consider whether an appropriate health care professional should be called to conduct an initial clinical check on the detainee. This applies particularly when there is likely to be any significant delay in the arrival of a suitably qualified medical practitioner.

9.7 If it appears to the custody officer, or they are told, that a person brought to a station under arrest may be suffering from an infectious disease or condition, the custody officer must take reasonable steps to safeguard the health of the detainee and others at the station. In deciding what action to take, advice must be sought from an appropriate health care professional. See *Note 9E*. The custody officer has discretion to isolate the person and their property until clinical directions have been obtained.

9.8 If a detainee requests a clinical examination, an appropriate health care professional must be called as soon as practicable to assess the detainee's clinical needs. If a safe and appropriate care plan cannot be provided, the police surgeon's advice must be sought. The detainee may also be examined by a medical practitioner of their choice at their expense.

9.9 If a detainee is required to take or apply any medication in compliance with clinical directions prescribed before their detention, the custody officer must consult the appropriate health care professional before the use of the medication. Subject to the restrictions in *paragraph 9.10*, the custody officer is responsible for the safekeeping of any medication and for making sure the detainee is given the opportunity to take or apply prescribed or approved medication. Any such consultation and its outcome shall be noted in the custody record.

9.10 No police officer may administer or supervise the self-administration of medically prescribed controlled drugs of the types and forms listed in the Misuse of Drugs Regulations 2001, Schedule 2 or 3. A detainee may only self-administer such drugs under the personal supervision of the registered medical practitioner authorising their use. Drugs listed in Schedule 4 or 5 may be distributed by the custody officer for self-administration if they have consulted the registered medical practitioner authorising their use, this may be done by telephone, and both parties are satisfied self-administration will not expose the detainee, police officers or anyone else to the risk of harm or injury.

9.11 When appropriate health care professionals administer drugs or other medications, or supervise their self-administration, it must be within current medicines legislation and the scope of practice as determined by their relevant professional body.

9.12 If a detainee has in their possession, or claims to need, medication relating to a heart condition, diabetes, epilepsy or a condition of comparable potential seriousness then, even though *paragraph 9.5* may not apply, the advice of the appropriate health care professional must be obtained.

9.13 Whenever the appropriate health care professional is called in accordance with this section to examine or treat a detainee, the custody officer shall ask for their opinion about:

- any risks or problems which police need to take into account when making decisions about the detainee's continued detention;
- when to carry out an interview if applicable; and
- the need for safeguards.

9.14 When clinical directions are given by the appropriate health care professional, whether orally or in writing, and the custody officer has any doubts or is in any way uncertain about any aspect of the directions, the custody officer shall ask for clarification. It is particularly important that directions concerning the frequency of visits are clear, precise and capable of being implemented. See *Note 9F*.

(c) Documentation

9.15 A record must be made in the custody record of:

(a) the arrangements made for an examination by an appropriate health care professional under *paragraph 9.2* and of any complaint reported under that paragraph together with any relevant remarks by the custody officer;

(b) any arrangements made in accordance with *paragraph 9.5*;

(c) any request for a clinical examination under *paragraph 9.8* and any arrangements made in response;

(d) the injury, ailment, condition or other reason which made it necessary to make the arrangements in (a) to (c), see *Note 9G*;

(e) any clinical directions and advice, including any further clarifications, given to police by a health care professional concerning the care and treatment of the detainee in connection with any of the arrangements made in (a) to (c), see *Note 9F*;

(f) if applicable, the responses received when attempting to rouse a person using the procedure in *Annex H, see Note 9H*.

9.16 If a health care professional does not record their clinical findings in the custody record, the record must show where they are recorded. See *Note 9G*. However, information which is necessary to custody staff to ensure the effective ongoing care and well being of the detainee must be recorded openly in the custody record, see *paragraph 3.8* and *Annex G, paragraph 7*.

9.17 Subject to the requirements of *Section 4*, the custody record shall include:

- a record of all medication a detainee has in their possession on arrival at the police station;
- a note of any such medication they claim to need but do not have with them.

Notes for guidance

9A *A 'health care professional' means a clinically qualified person working within the scope of practice as determined by their relevant professional body. Whether a health care professional is 'appropriate' depends on the circumstances of the duties they carry out at the time.*

9B *Whenever possible juveniles and mentally vulnerable detainees should be visited more frequently.*

9C *A detainee who appears drunk or behaves abnormally may be suffering from illness, the effects of drugs or may have sustained injury, particularly a head injury which is not apparent. A detainee needing or dependent on certain drugs, including alcohol, may experience harmful effects within a short time of being deprived of their supply. In these circumstances, when there is any doubt, police should always act urgently to call an appropriate health care professional or an ambulance. Paragraph 9.5 does not apply to minor ailments or injuries which do not need attention. However, all such ailments or injuries must be recorded in the custody record and any doubt must be resolved in favour of calling the appropriate health care professional.*

9CA *Paragraph 9.3 would apply to a person in police custody by order of a magistrates' court under the Criminal Justice Act 1988, section 152 (as amended by the Drugs Act 2005, section 8) to facilitate the recovery of evidence after being charged with drug possession or drug trafficking and suspected of having swallowed drugs. In the case of the healthcare needs of a person who has swallowed drugs, the custody officer subject to any clinical directions, should consider the necessity for rousing every half hour. This does not negate the need for regular visiting of the suspect in the cell.*

9D *Whenever practicable, arrangements should be made for persons detained for assessment under the Mental Health Act 1983, section 136 to be taken to a hospital. There is no power under that Act to transfer a person detained under section 136 from one place of safety to another place of safety for assessment.*

9E *It is important to respect a person's right to privacy and information about their health must be kept confidential and only disclosed with their consent or in accordance with clinical advice when it is necessary to protect the detainee's health or that of others who come into contact with them.*

9F *The custody officer should always seek to clarify directions that the detainee requires constant observation or supervision and should ask the appropriate health care professional to explain precisely what action needs to be taken to implement such directions.*

9G *Paragraphs 9.15 and 9.16 do not require any information about the cause of any injury, ailment or condition to be recorded on the custody record if it appears capable of providing evidence of an offence.*

9H *The purpose of recording a person's responses when attempting to rouse them using the procedure in Annex H is to enable any change in the individual's consciousness level to be noted and clinical treatment arranged if appropriate.*

10 Cautions

(a) When a caution must be given

10.1 A person whom there are grounds to suspect of an offence, see *Note 10A*, must be cautioned before any questions about an offence, or further questions if the answers provide the grounds for suspicion, are put to them if either the suspect's answers or silence, (i.e. failure or refusal to answer or answer satisfactorily) may be given in evidence to a court in a prosecution. A person need not be cautioned if questions are for other necessary purposes, e.g.:

(a) solely to establish their identity or ownership of any vehicle;

(b) to obtain information in accordance with any relevant statutory requirement, see *paragraph 10.9*;

(c) in furtherance of the proper and effective conduct of a search, e.g. to determine the need to search in the exercise of powers of stop and search or to seek co-operation while carrying out a search;

(d) to seek verification of a written record as in *paragraph 11.13*;

(e) Not used

10.2 Whenever a person not under arrest is initially cautioned, or reminded they are under caution, that person must at the same time be told they are not under arrest and are free to leave if they want to. See *Note 10C*

10.3 A person who is arrested, or further arrested, must be informed at the time, or as soon as practicable thereafter, that they are under arrest and the grounds for their arrest, see *paragraph 3.4, Note 10B* and *Code G, paragraphs 2.2* and *4.3*.

10.4 As per *Code G, section 3*, a person who is arrested, or further arrested, must also be cautioned unless:

(a) it is impracticable to do so by reason of their condition or behaviour at the time;

(b) they have already been cautioned immediately prior to arrest as in *paragraph 10.1*.

(b) Terms of the cautions

10.5 The caution which must be given on:

(a) arrest;

(b) all other occasions before a person is charged or informed they may be prosecuted, see *section 16*,

should, unless the restriction on drawing adverse inferences from silence applies, see *Annex C*, be in the following terms:

> 'You do not have to say anything. But it may harm your defence if you do not mention when questioned something which you later rely on in Court. Anything you do say may be given in evidence.'

Where the use of the Welsh Language is appropriate, a constable may provide the caution directly in Welsh in the following terms:

> *'Does dim rhaid i chi ddweud dim byd. Ond gall niweidio eich amddiffyniad os na fyddwch chi'n sôn, wrth gael eich holi, am rywbeth y byddwch chi'n dibynnu arno nes ymlaen yn y Llys. Gall unrhyw beth yr ydych yn ei ddweud gael ei roi fel tystiolaeth.'*

See *Note 10G*

10.6 *Annex C, paragraph 2* sets out the alternative terms of the caution to be used when the restriction on drawing adverse inferences from silence applies.

10.7 Minor deviations from the words of any caution given in accordance with this Code do not constitute a breach of this Code, provided the sense of the relevant caution is preserved. See *Note 10D*

10.8 After any break in questioning under caution, the person being questioned must be made aware they remain under caution. If there is any doubt the relevant caution should be given again in full when the interview resumes. See *Note 10E*

10.9 When, despite being cautioned, a person fails to co-operate or to answer particular questions which may affect their immediate treatment, the person should be informed of any relevant consequences and that those consequences are not affected by the caution. Examples are when a person's refusal to provide:

- their name and address when charged may make them liable to detention;
- particulars and information in accordance with a statutory requirement, e.g. under the Road Traffic Act 1988, may amount to an offence or may make the person liable to a further arrest.

(c) Special warnings under the Criminal Justice and Public Order Act 1994, sections 36 and 37

10.10 When a suspect interviewed at a police station or authorised place of detention after arrest fails or refuses to answer certain questions, or to answer satisfactorily, after due warning, see *Note 10F*, a court or jury may draw such inferences as appear proper under the Criminal Justice and Public Order Act 1994, sections 36 and 37. Such inferences may only be drawn when:

(a) the restriction on drawing adverse inferences from silence, see *Annex C*, does not apply; and

(b) the suspect is arrested by a constable and fails or refuses to account for any objects, marks or substances, or marks on such objects found:

- on their person;
- in or on their clothing or footwear;
- otherwise in their possession; or
- in the place they were arrested;

(c) the arrested suspect was found by a constable at a place at or about the time the offence for which that officer has arrested them is alleged to have been committed, and the suspect fails or refuses to account for their presence there.

When the restriction on drawing adverse inferences from silence applies, the suspect may still be asked to account for any of the matters in *(b)* or *(c)* but the special warning described in *paragraph 10.11* will not apply and must not be given.

10.11 For an inference to be drawn when a suspect fails or refuses to answer a question about one of these matters or to answer it satisfactorily, the suspect must first be told in ordinary language:

(a) what offence is being investigated;

(b) what fact they are being asked to account for;

(c) this fact may be due to them taking part in the commission of the offence;

(d) a court may draw a proper inference if they fail or refuse to account for this fact;

(e) a record is being made of the interview and it may be given in evidence if they are brought to trial.

(d) Juveniles and persons who are mentally disordered or otherwise mentally vulnerable

10.12 If a juvenile or a person who is mentally disordered or otherwise mentally vulnerable is cautioned in the absence of the appropriate adult, the caution must be repeated in the adult's presence.

(e) Documentation

10.13 A record shall be made when a caution is given under this section, either in the interviewer's pocket book or in the interview record.

Notes for guidance

10A There must be some reasonable, objective grounds for the suspicion, based on known facts or information which are relevant to the likelihood the offence has been committed and the person to be questioned committed it.

10B An arrested person must be given sufficient information to enable them to understand that they have been deprived of their liberty and the reason they have been arrested, e.g. when a person is arrested on suspicion of committing an offence they must be informed of the suspected offence's nature, when and where it was committed. The suspect must also be informed of the reason or reasons why the arrest is considered necessary. Vague or technical language should be avoided.

10C The restriction on drawing inferences from silence, see Annex C, paragraph 1, does not apply to a person who has not been detained and who therefore cannot be prevented from seeking legal advice if they want, see paragraph 3.21.

10D If it appears a person does not understand the caution, the person giving it should explain it in their own words.

10E It may be necessary to show to the court that nothing occurred during an interview break or between interviews which influenced the suspect's recorded evidence. After a break in an interview or at the beginning of a subsequent interview, the interviewing officer should summarise the reason for the break and confirm this with the suspect.

10F The Criminal Justice and Public Order Act 1994, sections 36 and 37 apply only to suspects who have been arrested by a constable or Customs and Excise officer and are given the relevant warning by the police or customs officer who made the arrest or who is investigating the offence. They do not apply to any interviews with suspects who have not been arrested.

10G Nothing in this Code requires a caution to be given or repeated when informing a person not under arrest they may be prosecuted for an offence. However, a court will not be able to draw any inferences under the Criminal Justice and Public Order Act 1994, section 34, if the person was not cautioned.

11 Interviews—general

(a) Action

11.1A An interview is the questioning of a person regarding their involvement or suspected involvement in a criminal offence or offences which, under *paragraph 10.1*, must be carried out under caution. Whenever a person is interviewed they must be informed of the nature of the offence, or further offence. Procedures under the Road Traffic Act 1988, section 7 or the Transport and Works Act 1992, section 31 do not constitute interviewing for the purpose of this Code.

11.1 Following a decision to arrest a suspect, they must not be interviewed about the relevant offence except at a police station or other authorised place of detention, unless the consequent delay would be likely to:

(a) lead to:
- interference with, or harm to, evidence connected with an offence;
- interference with, or physical harm to, other people; or
- serious loss of, or damage to, property;

(b) lead to alerting other people suspected of committing an offence but not yet arrested for it; or

(c) hinder the recovery of property obtained in consequence of the commission of an offence.

Interviewing in any of these circumstances shall cease once the relevant risk has been averted or the necessary questions have been put in order to attempt to avert that risk.

11.2 Immediately prior to the commencement or re-commencement of any interview at a police station or other authorised place of detention, the interviewer should remind the suspect of their entitlement to free legal advice and that the interview can be delayed for legal advice to be obtained, unless one of the exceptions in *paragraph 6.6* applies. It is the interviewer's responsibility to make sure all reminders are recorded in the interview record.

11.3 Not Used

11.4 At the beginning of an interview the interviewer, after cautioning the suspect, see *section 10*, shall put to them any significant statement or silence which occurred in the presence and hearing of a police officer or other police staff before the start of the interview and which have not been put to the suspect in the course of a previous interview. See *Note 11A*. The interviewer shall ask the suspect whether they confirm or deny that earlier statement or silence and if they want to add anything.

11.4A A significant statement is one which appears capable of being used in evidence against the suspect, in particular a direct admission of guilt. A significant silence is a failure or refusal to answer a question or answer satisfactorily when under caution, which might, allowing for the restriction on drawing adverse inferences from silence, see *Annex C*, give rise to an inference under the Criminal Justice and Public Order Act 1994, Part III.

11.5 No interviewer may try to obtain answers or elicit a statement by the use of oppression. Except as in *paragraph 10.9*, no interviewer shall indicate, except to answer a direct question, what action will be taken by the police if the person being questioned answers questions, makes a statement or refuses to do either. If the person asks directly what action will be taken if they answer questions, make a statement or refuse to do either, the interviewer may inform them what action the police propose to take provided that action is itself proper and warranted.

11.6 The interview or further interview of a person about an offence with which that person has not been charged or for which they have not been informed they may be prosecuted, must cease when:

(a) the officer in charge of the investigation is satisfied all the questions they consider relevant to obtaining accurate and reliable information about the offence have been put to the suspect, this includes allowing the suspect an opportunity to give an innocent explanation and asking questions to test if the explanation is accurate and reliable, e.g. to clear up ambiguities or clarify what the suspect said;

(b) the officer in charge of the investigation has taken account of any other available evidence; and

(c) the officer in charge of the investigation, or in the case of a detained suspect, the custody officer, see *paragraph 16.1*, reasonably believes there is sufficient evidence to provide a realistic prospect of conviction for that offence. See *Note 11B*

This paragraph does not prevent officers in revenue cases or acting under the confiscation provisions of the Criminal Justice Act 1988 or the Drug Trafficking Act 1994 from inviting suspects to complete a formal question and answer record after the interview is concluded.

(b) Interview records

11.7 (a) An accurate record must be made of each interview, whether or not the interview takes place at a police station

(b) The record must state the place of interview, the time it begins and ends, any interview breaks and, subject to *paragraph 2.6A*, the names of all those present; and must be made on the forms provided for this purpose or in the interviewer's pocket book or in accordance with the Codes of Practice E or F;

(c) Any written record must be made and completed during the interview, unless this would not be practicable or would interfere with the conduct of the interview, and must constitute either a verbatim record of what has been said or, failing this, an account of the interview which adequately and accurately summarises it.

11.8 If a written record is not made during the interview it must be made as soon as practicable after its completion.

11.9 Written interview records must be timed and signed by the maker.

11.10 If a written record is not completed during the interview the reason must be recorded in the interview record.

11.11 Unless it is impracticable, the person interviewed shall be given the opportunity to read the interview record and to sign it as correct or to indicate how they consider it inaccurate. If the person interviewed cannot read or refuses to read the record or sign it, the senior interviewer present shall read it to them and ask whether they would like to sign it as correct or make their mark or to indicate how they consider it inaccurate. The interviewer shall certify on the interview record itself what has occurred. See *Note 11E*

11.12 If the appropriate adult or the person's solicitor is present during the interview, they should also be given an opportunity to read and sign the interview record or any written statement taken down during the interview.

11.13 A written record shall be made of any comments made by a suspect, including unsolicited comments, which are outside the context of an interview but which might be relevant to the offence. Any such record must be timed and signed by the maker. When practicable the suspect shall be given the opportunity to read that record and to sign it as correct or to indicate how they consider it inaccurate. See *Note 11E*

11.14 Any refusal by a person to sign an interview record when asked in accordance with this Code must itself be recorded.

(c) Juveniles and mentally disordered or otherwise mentally vulnerable people

11.15 A juvenile or person who is mentally disordered or otherwise mentally vulnerable must not be interviewed regarding their involvement or suspected involvement in a criminal offence or offences, or asked to provide or sign a written statement under caution or record of interview, in the absence of the appropriate adult unless *paragraphs 11.1, 11.18* to *11.20* apply. See *Note 11C*

11.16 Juveniles may only be interviewed at their place of education in exceptional circumstances and only when the principal or their nominee agrees. Every effort should be made to notify the parent(s) or other person responsible for the juvenile's welfare and the appropriate adult, if this is a different person, that the police want to interview the juvenile and reasonable time should be allowed to enable the appropriate adult to be present at the interview. If awaiting the appropriate adult would cause unreasonable delay, and unless the juvenile is suspected of an offence against the educational establishment, the principal or their nominee can act as the appropriate adult for the purposes of the interview.

11.17 If an appropriate adult is present at an interview, they shall be informed:

- they are not expected to act simply as an observer; and
- the purpose of their presence is to:
  - — advise the person being interviewed;
  - — observe whether the interview is being conducted properly and fairly;
  - — facilitate communication with the person being interviewed.

(d) Vulnerable suspects—urgent interviews at police stations

11.18 The following persons may not be interviewed unless an officer of superintendent rank or above considers delay will lead to the consequences in *paragraph 11.1(a)* to *(c)*, and is satisfied the interview would not significantly harm the person's physical or mental state (see Annex G):

(a) a juvenile or person who is mentally disordered or otherwise mentally vulnerable if at the time of the interview the appropriate adult is not present;

(b) anyone other than in *(a)* who at the time of the interview appears unable to:
- appreciate the significance of questions and their answers; or
- understand what is happening because of the effects of drink, drugs or any illness, ailment or condition;

(c) a person who has difficulty understanding English or has a hearing disability, if at the time of the interview an interpreter is not present.

11.19 These interviews may not continue once sufficient information has been obtained to avert the consequences in *paragraph 11.1(a)* to *(c)*.

11.20 A record shall be made of the grounds for any decision to interview a person under *paragraph 11.18*.

Notes for guidance

11A Paragraph 11.4 does not prevent the interviewer from putting significant statements and silences to a suspect again at a later stage or a further interview.

11B The Criminal Procedure and Investigations Act 1996 Code of Practice, paragraph 3.4 states 'In conducting an investigation, the investigator should pursue all reasonable lines of enquiry, whether these point towards or away from the suspect. What is reasonable will depend on the particular circumstances.' Interviewers should keep this in mind when deciding what questions to ask in an interview.

11C *Although juveniles or people who are mentally disordered or otherwise mentally vulnerable are often capable of providing reliable evidence, they may, without knowing or wishing to do so, be particularly prone in certain circumstances to provide information that may be unreliable, misleading or self-incriminating. Special care should always be taken when questioning such a person, and the appropriate adult should be involved if there is any doubt about a person's age, mental state or capacity. Because of the risk of unreliable evidence it is also important to obtain corroboration of any facts admitted whenever possible.*

11D *Juveniles should not be arrested at their place of education unless this is unavoidable. When a juvenile is arrested at their place of education, the principal or their nominee must be informed.*

11E *Significant statements described in paragraph 11.4 will always be relevant to the offence and must be recorded. When a suspect agrees to read records of interviews and other comments and sign them as correct, they should be asked to endorse the record with, e.g. 'I agree that this is a correct record of what was said' and add their signature. If the suspect does not agree with the record, the interviewer should record the details of any disagreement and ask the suspect to read these details and sign them to the effect that they accurately reflect their disagreement. Any refusal to sign should be recorded.*

12 Interviews in police stations

(a) Action

12.1 If a police officer wants to interview or conduct enquiries which require the presence of a detainee, the custody officer is responsible for deciding whether to deliver the detainee into the officer's custody.

12.2 Except as below, in any period of 24 hours a detainee must be allowed a continuous period of at least 8 hours for rest, free from questioning, travel or any interruption in connection with the investigation concerned. This period should normally be at night or other appropriate time which takes account of when the detainee last slept or rested. If a detainee is arrested at a police station after going there voluntarily, the period of 24 hours runs from the time of their arrest and not the time of arrival at the police station. The period may not be interrupted or delayed, except:

(a) when there are reasonable grounds for believing not delaying or interrupting the period would:
  - (i) involve a risk of harm to people or serious loss of, or damage to, property;
  - (ii) delay unnecessarily the person's release from custody;
  - (iii) otherwise prejudice the outcome of the investigation;

(b) at the request of the detainee, their appropriate adult or legal representative;

(c) when a delay or interruption is necessary in order to:
  - (i) comply with the legal obligations and duties arising under *section 15*;
  - (ii) to take action required under *section 9* or in accordance with medical advice.

If the period is interrupted in accordance with *(a)*, a fresh period must be allowed. Interruptions under *(b)* and *(c)*, do not require a fresh period to be allowed.

12.3 Before a detainee is interviewed the custody officer, in consultation with the officer in charge of the investigation and appropriate health care professionals as necessary, shall assess whether the detainee is fit enough to be interviewed. This means determining and considering the risks to the detainee's physical and mental state if the interview took place and determining what safeguards are needed to allow the interview to take place. See *Annex G*. The custody officer shall not allow a detainee to be interviewed if the custody officer considers it would cause significant harm to the detainee's physical or mental state. Vulnerable suspects listed at *paragraph 11.18* shall be treated as always being at some risk during an interview and these persons may not be interviewed except in accordance with *paragraphs 11.18* to *11.20*.

12.4 As far as practicable interviews shall take place in interview rooms which are adequately heated, lit and ventilated.

12.5 A suspect whose detention without charge has been authorised under PACE, because the detention is necessary for an interview to obtain evidence of the offence for which they have been arrested, may choose not to answer questions but police do not require the suspect's consent or agreement to interview them for this purpose. If a suspect takes steps to prevent themselves being questioned or further questioned, e.g. by refusing to leave their cell to go to a suitable interview room or by trying to leave the interview room, they shall be advised their consent or agreement to interview is not required. The suspect shall be cautioned as in *section 10*, and informed if they fail or refuse to co-operate, the interview may take place in the cell and that their failure or refusal to co-operate may be given in evidence. The suspect shall then be invited to co-operate and go into the interview room.

12.6 People being questioned or making statements shall not be required to stand.

12.7 Before the interview commences each interviewer shall, subject to *paragraph 2.6A*, identify themselves and any other persons present to the interviewee.

12.8 Breaks from interviewing should be made at recognised meal times or at other times that take account of when an interviewee last had a meal. Short refreshment breaks shall be provided at approximately two hour intervals, subject to the interviewer's discretion to delay a break if there are reasonable grounds for believing it would:

(i) involve a:
- risk of harm to people;
- serious loss of, or damage to, property;

(ii) unnecessarily delay the detainee's release;

(iii) otherwise prejudice the outcome of the investigation.

See *Note 12B*

12.9 If during the interview a complaint is made by or on behalf of the interviewee concerning the provisions of this Code, the interviewer should:

(i) record it in the interview record;

(ii) inform the custody officer, who is then responsible for dealing with it as in *section 9*.

(b) Documentation

12.10 A record must be made of the:
- time a detainee is not in the custody of the custody officer, and why
- reason for any refusal to deliver the detainee out of that custody

12.11 A record shall be made of:

(a) the reasons it was not practicable to use an interview room; and

(b) any action taken as in *paragraph 12.5*.

The record shall be made on the custody record or in the interview record for action taken whilst an interview record is being kept, with a brief reference to this effect in the custody record.

12.12 Any decision to delay a break in an interview must be recorded, with reasons, in the interview record.

12.13 All written statements made at police stations under caution shall be written on forms provided for the purpose.

12.14 All written statements made under caution shall be taken in accordance with *Annex D*. Before a person makes a written statement under caution at a police station they shall be reminded about the right to legal advice. See *Note 12A*

Notes for guidance

12A *It is not normally necessary to ask for a written statement if the interview was recorded in writing and the record signed in accordance with paragraph 11.11 or audibly or visually recorded in accordance with Code E or F. Statements under caution should normally be taken in these circumstances only at the person's express wish. A person may however be asked if they want to make such a statement.*

12B *Meal breaks should normally last at least 45 minutes and shorter breaks after two hours should last at least 15 minutes. If the interviewer delays a break in accordance with paragraph 12.8 and prolongs the interview, a longer break should be provided. If there is a short interview, and another short interview is contemplated, the length of the break may be reduced if there are reasonable grounds to believe this is necessary to avoid any of the consequences in paragraph 12.8(i) to (iii).*

13 Interpreters

(a) General

13.1 Chief officers are responsible for making sure appropriate arrangements are in place for provision of suitably qualified interpreters for people who:

- are deaf;
- do not understand English.

Whenever possible, interpreters should be drawn from the National Register of Public Service Interpreters (NRPSI) or the Council for the Advancement of Communication with Deaf People (CACDP) Directory of British Sign Language/English Interpreters.

(b) Foreign languages

13.2 Unless *paragraphs 11.1, 11.18* to *11.20* apply, a person must not be interviewed in the absence of a person capable of interpreting if:

(a) they have difficulty understanding English;

(b) the interviewer cannot speak the person's own language;

(c) the person wants an interpreter present.

13.3 The interviewer shall make sure the interpreter makes a note of the interview at the time in the person's language for use in the event of the interpreter being called to give evidence, and certifies its accuracy. The interviewer should allow sufficient time for the interpreter to note each question and answer after each is put, given and interpreted. The person should be allowed to read the record or have it read to them and sign it as correct or indicate the respects in which they consider it inaccurate. If the interview is audibly recorded or visually recorded, the arrangements in Code E or F apply.

13.4 In the case of a person making a statement to a police officer or other police staff other than in English:

(a) the interpreter shall record the statement in the language it is made;

(b) the person shall be invited to sign it;

(c) an official English translation shall be made in due course.

(c) Deaf people and people with speech difficulties

13.5 If a person appears to be deaf or there is doubt about their hearing or speaking ability, they must not be interviewed in the absence of an interpreter unless they agree in writing to being interviewed without one or *paragraphs 11.1, 11.18* to *11.20* apply.

13.6 An interpreter should also be called if a juvenile is interviewed and the parent or guardian present as the appropriate adult appears to be deaf or there is doubt about their hearing or speaking ability, unless they agree in writing to the interview proceeding without one or *paragraphs 11.1, 11.18* to *11.20* apply.

13.7 The interviewer shall make sure the interpreter is allowed to read the interview record and certify its accuracy in the event of the interpreter being called to give evidence. If the interview is audibly recorded or visually recorded, the arrangements in Code E or F apply.

(d) Additional rules for detained persons

13.8 All reasonable attempts should be made to make the detainee understand that interpreters will be provided at public expense.

13.9 If *paragraph 6.1* applies and the detainee cannot communicate with the solicitor because of language, hearing or speech difficulties, an interpreter must be called. The interpreter may not be a police officer or any other police staff when interpretation is needed for the purposes of obtaining legal advice. In all other cases a police officer or other police staff may only interpret if the detainee and the appropriate adult, if applicable, give their agreement in writing or if the interview is audibly recorded or visually recorded as in Code E or F.

13.10 When the custody officer cannot establish effective communication with a person charged with an offence who appears deaf or there is doubt about their ability to hear, speak or to understand English, arrangements must be made as soon as practicable for an interpreter to explain the offence and any other information given by the custody officer.

(e) Documentation

13.11 Action taken to call an interpreter under this section and any agreement to be interviewed in the absence of an interpreter must be recorded.

14 Questioning—special restrictions

14.1 If a person is arrested by one police force on behalf of another and the lawful period of detention in respect of that offence has not yet commenced in accordance with PACE, section 41 no questions may be put to them about the offence while they are in transit between the forces except to clarify any voluntary statement they make.

14.2 If a person is in police detention at a hospital they may not be questioned without the agreement of a responsible doctor. See *Note 14A*

Note for guidance

14A If questioning takes place at a hospital under paragraph 14.2, or on the way to or from a hospital, the period of questioning concerned counts towards the total period of detention permitted.

15 Reviews and extensions of detention

(a) Persons detained under PACE

15.1 The review officer is responsible under PACE, section 40 for periodically determining if a person's detention, before or after charge, continues to be necessary. This requirement continues throughout the detention period and except as in *paragraph 15.10*, the review officer must be present at the police station holding the detainee. See *Notes 15A* and *15B*

15.2 Under PACE, section 42, an officer of superintendent rank or above who is responsible for the station holding the detainee may give authority any time after the second review to extend the maximum period the person may be detained without charge by up to 12 hours. Further detention without charge may be authorised only by a magistrates' court in accordance with PACE, sections 43 and 44. See *Notes 15C, 15D* and *15E*

15.2A Section 42(1) of PACE as amended extends the maximum period of detention for indictable offences from 24 hours to 36 hours. Detaining a juvenile or mentally vulnerable person for longer than 24 hours will be dependent on the circumstances of the case and with regard to the person's:

(a) special vulnerability;
(b) the legal obligation to provide an opportunity for representations to be made prior to a decision about extending detention;
(c) the need to consult and consider the views of any appropriate adult; and
(d) any alternatives to police custody.

15.3 Before deciding whether to authorise continued detention the officer responsible under *paragraphs 15.1* or *15.2* shall give an opportunity to make representations about the detention to:

(a) the detainee, unless in the case of a review as in *paragraph 15.1*, the detainee is asleep;

(b) the detainee's solicitor if available at the time; and
(c) the appropriate adult if available at the time.

15.3A Other people having an interest in the detainee's welfare may also make representations at the authorising officer's discretion.

15.3B Subject to *paragraph 15.10*, the representations may be made orally in person or by telephone or in writing. The authorising officer may, however, refuse to hear oral representations from the detainee if the officer considers them unfit to make representations because of their condition or behaviour. See *Note 15C*

15.3C The decision on whether the review takes place in person or by telephone or by video conferencing (see Note 15G) is a matter for the review officer. In determining the form the review may take, the review officer must always take full account of the needs of the person in custody. The benefits of carrying out a review in person should always be considered, based on the individual circumstances of each case with specific additional consideration if the person is:

(a) a juvenile (and the age of the juvenile); or
(b) mentally vulnerable; or
(c) has been subject to medical attention for other than routine minor ailments; or
(d) there are presentational or community issues around the person's detention.

15.4 Before conducting a review or determining whether to extend the maximum period of detention without charge, the officer responsible must make sure the detainee is reminded of their entitlement to free legal advice, see *paragraph 6.5*, unless in the case of a review the person is asleep.

15.5 If, after considering any representations, the officer decides to keep the detainee in detention or extend the maximum period they may be detained without charge, any comment made by the detainee shall be recorded. If applicable, the officer responsible under *paragraph 15.1* or *15.2* shall be informed of the comment as soon as practicable. See also *paragraphs 11.4* and *11.13*

15.6 No officer shall put specific questions to the detainee:

- regarding their involvement in any offence; or
- in respect of any comments they may make:
  - — when given the opportunity to make representations; or
  - — in response to a decision to keep them in detention or extend the maximum period of detention.

Such an exchange could constitute an interview as in *paragraph 11.1A* and would be subject to the associated safeguards in *section 11* and, in respect of a person who has been charged, *paragraph 16.5*. See also *paragraph 11.13*

15.7 A detainee who is asleep at a review, see *paragraph 15.1*, and whose continued detention is authorised must be informed about the decision and reason as soon as practicable after waking.

15.8 Not used

(b) Telephone review of detention

15.9 PACE, section 40A provides that the officer responsible under section 40 for reviewing the detention of a person who has not been charged, need not attend the police station holding the detainee and may carry out the review by telephone.

15.9A PACE, section 45A(2) provides that the officer responsible under section 40 for reviewing the detention of a person who has not been charged, need not attend the police station holding the detainee and may carry out the review by video conferencing facilities (See *Note 15G*).

15.9B A telephone review is not permitted where facilities for review by video conferencing exist and it is practicable to use them.

15.9C The review officer can decide at any stage that a telephone review or review by video conferencing should be terminated and that the review will be conducted in person. The reasons for doing so should be noted in the custody record.
See *Note 15F*

15.10 When a telephone review is carried out, an officer at the station holding the detainee shall be required by the review officer to fulfil that officer's obligations under PACE section 40 or this Code by:

(a) making any record connected with the review in the detainee's custody record;
(b) if applicable, making a record in (a) in the presence of the detainee; and
(c) giving the detainee information about the review.

15.11 When a telephone review is carried out, the requirement in *paragraph 15.3* will be satisfied:

(a) if facilities exist for the immediate transmission of written representations to the review officer, e.g. fax or email message, by giving the detainee an opportunity to make representations:
  (i) orally by telephone; or
  (ii) in writing using those facilities; and
(b) in all other cases, by giving the detainee an opportunity to make their representations orally by telephone.

(c) Documentation

15.12 It is the officer's responsibility to make sure all reminders given under *paragraph 15.4* are noted in the custody record.

15.13 The grounds for, and extent of, any delay in conducting a review shall be recorded.

15.14 When a telephone review is carried out, a record shall be made of:

(a) the reason the review officer did not attend the station holding the detainee;
(b) the place the review officer was;
(c) the method representations, oral or written, were made to the review officer, see *paragraph 15.11*.

15.15 Any written representations shall be retained.

15.16 A record shall be made as soon as practicable about the outcome of each review or determination whether to extend the maximum detention period without charge or an application for a warrant of further detention or its extension. If *paragraph 15.7* applies, a record shall also be made of when the person was informed and by whom. If an authorisation is given under PACE, section 42, the record shall state the number of hours and minutes by which the detention period is extended or further extended. If a warrant for further detention, or extension, is granted under section 43 or 44, the record shall state the detention period authorised by the warrant and the date and time it was granted.

Notes for guidance

15A Review officer for the purposes of:

- PACE, sections 40 and 40A means, in the case of a person arrested but not charged, an officer of at least inspector rank not directly involved in the investigation and, if a person has been arrested and charged, the custody officer;

15B The detention of persons in police custody not subject to the statutory review requirement in paragraph 15.1 should still be reviewed periodically as a matter of good practice. Such reviews can be carried out by an officer of the rank of sergeant or above. The purpose of such reviews is to check the particular power under which a detainee is held continues to apply, any associated conditions are complied with and to make sure appropriate action is taken to deal with any changes. This includes the detainee's prompt release when the power no longer applies, or their transfer if the power requires the detainee be taken elsewhere as soon as the necessary arrangements are made. Examples include persons:

(a) arrested on warrant because they failed to answer bail to appear at court;
(b) arrested under the Bail Act 1976, section 7(3) for breaching a condition of bail granted after charge;
(c) in police custody for specific purposes and periods under the Crime (Sentences) Act 1997, Schedule 1;

(d) *convicted, or remand prisoners, held in police stations on behalf of the Prison Service under the Imprisonment (Temporary Provisions) Act 1980, section 6;*

(e) *being detained to prevent them causing a breach of the peace;*

(f) *detained at police stations on behalf of the Immigration Service.*

(g) *detained by order of a magistrates' court under the Criminal Justice Act 1988, section 152 (as amended by the Drugs Act 2005, section 8) to facilitate the recovery of evidence after being charged with drug possession or drug trafficking and suspected of having swallowed drugs.*

The detention of persons remanded into police detention by order of a court under the Magistrates' Courts Act 1980, section 128 is subject to a statutory requirement to review that detention. This is to make sure the detainee is taken back to court no later than the end of the period authorised by the court or when the need for their detention by police ceases, whichever is the sooner.

15C *In the case of a review of detention, but not an extension, the detainee need not be woken for the review. However, if the detainee is likely to be asleep, e.g. during a period of rest allowed as in paragraph 12.2, at the latest time a review or authorisation to extend detention may take place, the officer should, if the legal obligations and time constraints permit, bring forward the procedure to allow the detainee to make representations. A detainee not asleep during the review must be present when the grounds for their continued detention are recorded and must at the same time be informed of those grounds unless the review officer considers the person is incapable of understanding what is said, violent or likely to become violent or in urgent need of medical attention.*

15D *An application to a Magistrates' Court under PACE, sections 43 or 44 for a warrant of further detention or its extension should be made between 10am and 9pm, and if possible during normal court hours. It will not usually be practicable to arrange for a court to sit specially outside the hours of 10am to 9pm. If it appears a special sitting may be needed outside normal court hours but between 10am and 9pm, the clerk to the justices should be given notice and informed of this possibility, while the court is sitting if possible.*

15E *In paragraph 15.2, the officer responsible for the station holding the detainee includes a superintendent or above who, in accordance with their force operational policy or police regulations, is given that responsibility on a temporary basis whilst the appointed long-term holder is off duty or otherwise unavailable.*

15F *The provisions of PACE, section 40A allowing telephone reviews do not apply to reviews of detention after charge by the custody officer. When video conferencing is not required, they allow the use of a telephone to carry out a review of detention before charge. The procedure under PACE, section 42 must be done in person.*

15G *The use of video conferencing facilities for decisions about detention under section 45A of PACE is subject to the introduction of regulations by the Secretary of State.*

16 Charging detained persons

(a) Action

16.1 When the officer in charge of the investigation reasonably believes there is sufficient evidence to provide a realistic prospect of conviction for the offence (see *paragraph 11.6*), they shall without delay, and subject to the following qualification, inform the custody officer who will be responsible for considering whether the detainee should be charged. See *Notes 11B and 16A*. When a person is detained in respect of more than one offence it is permissible to delay informing the custody officer until the above conditions are satisfied in respect of all the offences, but see *paragraph 11.6*. If the detainee is a juvenile, mentally disordered or otherwise mentally vulnerable, any resulting action shall be taken in the presence of the appropriate adult if they are present at the time. See *Notes 16B and 16C*

16.1A Where guidance issued by the Director of Public Prosecutions under section 37A is in force the custody officer must comply with that Guidance in deciding how to act in dealing with the detainee. See *Notes 16AA* and *16AB*.

16.1B Where in compliance with the DPP's Guidance the custody officer decides that the case should be immediately referred to the CPS to make the charging decision, consultation should take place with a Crown Prosecutor as soon as is reasonably practicable. Where the Crown Prosecutor is unable to make the charging decision on the information available at that time, the detainee may be released without charge and on bail (with conditions if necessary) under section 37(7)(a). In such circumstances, the detainee should be informed that they are being released to enable the Director of Public Prosecutions to make a decision under section 37B.

16.2 When a detainee is charged with or informed they may be prosecuted for an offence, see *Note 16B*, they shall, unless the restriction on drawing adverse inferences from silence applies, see *Annex C*, be cautioned as follows:

'You do not have to say anything. But it may harm your defence if you do not mention now something which you later rely on in court. Anything you do say may be given in evidence.'

Where the use of the Welsh Language is appropriate, a constable may provide the caution directly in Welsh in the following terms:

'Does dim rhaid i chi ddweud dim byd. Ond gall niweidio eich amddiffyniad os fyddwch chi'n sôn, yn awr, am rywbeth y byddwch chi'n dibynnu arno nes ymlaen llys. Gall unrhyw beth yr ydych yn ei ddweud gael ei roi fel tystiolaeth.'

Annex C, paragraph 2 sets out the alternative terms of the caution to be used when the restriction on drawing adverse inferences from silence applies.

16.3 When a detainee is charged they shall be given a written notice showing particulars of the offence and, subject to *paragraph 2.6A*, the officer's name and the case reference number. As far as possible the particulars of the charge shall be stated in simple terms, but they shall also show the precise offence in law with which the detainee is charged. The notice shall begin:

'You are charged with the offence(s) shown below.' Followed by the caution.

If the detainee is a juvenile, mentally disordered or otherwise mentally vulnerable, the notice should be given to the appropriate adult.

16.4 If, after a detainee has been charged with or informed they may be prosecuted for an offence, an officer wants to tell them about any written statement or interview with another person relating to such an offence, the detainee shall either be handed a true copy of the written statement or the content of the interview record brought to their attention. Nothing shall be done to invite any reply or comment except to:

(a) caution the detainee, *'You do not have to say anything, but anything you do say may be given in evidence.'*;

Where the use of the Welsh Language is appropriate, caution the detainee in the following terms:

'Does dim rhaid i chi ddweud dim byd, ond gall unrhyw beth yr ydych yn ei ddweud gael ei roi fel tystiolaeth.'

and

(b) remind the detainee about their right to legal advice.

16.4A If the detainee:

- cannot read, the document may be read to them
- is a juvenile, mentally disordered or otherwise mentally vulnerable, the appropriate adult shall also be given a copy, or the interview record shall be brought to their attention

16.5 A detainee may not be interviewed about an offence after they have been charged with, or informed they may be prosecuted for it, unless the interview is necessary:

- to prevent or minimise harm or loss to some other person, or the public
- to clear up an ambiguity in a previous answer or statement
- in the interests of justice for the detainee to have put to them, and have an opportunity to comment on, information concerning the offence which has come to light since they were charged or informed they might be prosecuted

Before any such interview, the interviewer shall:

(a) caution the detainee, *'You do not have to say anything, but anything you do say may be given in evidence.'*;

Where the use of the Welsh Language is appropriate, the interviewer shall caution the detainee, *'Does dim rhaid i chi ddweud dim byd, ond gall unrhyw beth yr ydych yn ei ddweud gael ei roi fel tystiolaeth.'*

(b) remind the detainee about their right to legal advice.

See *Note 16B*

16.6 The provisions of *paragraphs 16.2* to *16.5* must be complied with in the appropriate adult's presence if they are already at the police station. If they are not at the police station then these provisions must be complied with again in their presence when they arrive unless the detainee has been released.

See *Note 16C*

16.7 When a juvenile is charged with an offence and the custody officer authorises their continued detention after charge, the custody officer must try to make arrangements for the juvenile to be taken into the care of a local authority to be detained pending appearance in court unless the custody officer certifies it is impracticable to do so or, in the case of a juvenile of at least 12 years old, no secure accommodation is available and there is a risk to the public of serious harm from that juvenile, in accordance with PACE, section 38(6). See *Note 16D*

(b) Documentation

16.8 A record shall be made of anything a detainee says when charged.

16.9 Any questions put in an interview after charge and answers given relating to the offence shall be recorded in full during the interview on forms for that purpose and the record signed by the detainee or, if they refuse, by the interviewer and any third parties present. If the questions are audibly recorded or visually recorded the arrangements in Code E or F apply.

16.10 If it is not practicable to make arrangements for a juvenile's transfer into local authority care as in *paragraph 16.7*, the custody officer must record the reasons and complete a certificate to be produced before the court with the juvenile. See *Note 16D*

Notes for guidance

16A The custody officer must take into account alternatives to prosecution under the Crime and Disorder Act 1998, reprimands and warning applicable to persons under 18, and in national guidance on the cautioning of offenders, for persons aged 18 and over.

16AA When a person is arrested under the provisions of the Criminal Justice Act 2003 which allow a person to be re-tried after being acquitted of a serious offence which is a qualifying offence specified in Schedule 5 to that Act and not precluded from further prosecution by virtue of section 75(3) of that Act the detention provisions of PACE are modified and make an officer of the rank of superintendent or above who has not been directly involved in the investigation responsible for determining whether the evidence is sufficient to charge.

16AB Where Guidance issued by the Director of Public Prosecutions under section 37B is in force, a custody officer who determines in accordance with that Guidance that there is sufficient evidence to charge the detainee, may detain that person for no longer than is reasonably necessary to decide how that person is to be dealt with under PACE, section 37(7)(a) to (d), including, where appropriate, consultation with the Duty Prosecutor. The period is subject to the maximum period of detention before charge determined by PACE, sections 41 to 44. Where in accordance with the Guidance the case is referred to the CPS for decision, the custody officer should ensure that an officer involved in the investigation sends to the CPS such information as is specified in the Guidance.

16B The giving of a warning or the service of the Notice of Intended Prosecution required by the Road Traffic Offenders Act 1988, section 1 does not amount to informing a detainee they may be prosecuted for an offence and so does not preclude further questioning in relation to that offence.

16C There is no power under PACE to detain a person and delay action under paragraphs 16.2 to 16.5 solely to await the arrival of the appropriate adult. After charge, bail cannot be refused, or release on bail delayed, simply because an appropriate adult is not available, unless the absence of that adult provides the custody officer with the necessary grounds to authorise detention after charge under PACE, section 38.

16D Except as in paragraph 16.7, neither a juvenile's behaviour nor the nature of the offence provides grounds for the custody officer to decide it is impracticable to arrange the juvenile's transfer to local authority care. Similarly, the lack of secure local authority accommodation does not make it impracticable to transfer the juvenile. The availability of secure accommodation is only a factor in relation to a juvenile aged 12 or over when the local authority accommodation would not be adequate to protect the public from serious harm from them. The obligation to transfer a juvenile to local authority accommodation applies as much to a juvenile charged during the daytime as to a juvenile to be held overnight, subject to a requirement to bring the juvenile before a court under PACE, section 46.

17 Testing persons for the presence of specified Class A drugs

(a) Action

17.1 This section of Code C applies only in selected police stations in police areas where the provisions for drug testing under section 63B of PACE (as amended by section 5 of the Criminal Justice Act 2003 and section 7 of the Drugs Act 2005) are in force and in respect of which the Secretary of State has given a notification to the relevant chief officer of police that arrangements for the taking of samples have been made. Such a notification will cover either a police area as a whole or particular stations within a police area. The notification indicates whether the testing applies to those arrested or charged or under the age of 18 as the case may be and testing can only take place in respect of the persons so indicated in the notification. Testing cannot be carried out unless the relevant notification has been given and has not been withdrawn. See *Note 17F*

17.2 A sample of urine or a non-intimate sample may be taken from a person in police detention for the purpose of ascertaining whether he has any specified Class A drug in his body only where they have been brought before the custody officer and:

(a) either the arrest condition, see *paragraph 17.3*, or the charge condition, see *paragraph 17.4* is met;

(b) the age condition see *paragraph 17.5*, is met;

(c) the notification condition is met in relation to the arrest condition, the charge condition, or the age condition, as the case may be. (Testing on charge and/or arrest must be specifically provided for in the notification for the power to apply. In addition, the fact that testing of under 18s is authorised must be expressly provided for in the notification before the power to test such persons applies.). See *paragraph 17.1*; and

(d) a police officer has requested the person concerned to give the sample (the request condition).

17.3 The arrest condition is met where the detainee:

(a) has been arrested for a trigger offence, see *Note 17E*, but not charged with that offence; or

(b) has been arrested for any other offence but not charged with that offence and a police officer of inspector rank or above, who has reasonable grounds for suspecting that their misuse of any specified Class A drug caused or contributed to the offence, has authorised the sample to be taken.

17.4 The charge condition is met where the detainee:

(a) has been charged with a trigger offence, or

(b) has been charged with any other offence and a police officer of inspector rank or above, who has reasonable grounds for suspecting that the detainee's misuse of any specified Class A drug caused or contributed to the offence, has authorised the sample to be taken.

17.5 The age condition is met where:

(a) in the case of a detainee who has been arrested but not charged as in *paragraph 17.3*, they are aged 18 or over;

(b) in the case of a detainee who has been charged as in *paragraph 17.4*, they are aged 14 or over.

17.6 Before requesting a sample from the person concerned, an officer must:

(a) inform them that the purpose of taking the sample is for drug testing under PACE. This is to ascertain whether they have a specified Class A drug present in their body;

(b) warn them that if, when so requested, they fail without good cause to provide a sample they may be liable to prosecution;

(c) where the taking of the sample has been authorised by an inspector or above in accordance with *paragraph 17.3(b)* or *17.4(b)* above, inform them that the authorisation has been given and the grounds for giving it;

(d) remind them of the following rights, which may be exercised at any stage during the period in custody:

(i) the right to have someone informed of their arrest [see section 5];

(ii) the right to consult privately with a solicitor and that free independent legal advice is available [see section 6]; and

(iii) the right to consult these Codes of Practice [see section 3].

17.7 In the case of a person who has not attained the age of 17—

(a) the making of the request for a sample under *paragraph 17.2(d)* above;

(b) the giving of the warning and the information under *paragraph 17.6* above; and

(c) the taking of the sample,

may not take place except in the presence of an appropriate adult. (see Note 17G)

17.8 Authorisation by an officer of the rank of inspector or above within *paragraph 17.3(b)* or *17.4(b)* may be given orally or in writing but, if it is given orally, it must be confirmed in writing as soon as practicable.

17.9 If a sample is taken from a detainee who has been arrested for an offence but not charged with that offence as in *paragraph 17.3*, no further sample may be taken during the same continuous period of detention. If during that same period the charge condition is also met in respect of that detainee, the sample which has been taken shall be treated as being taken by virtue of the charge condition, see *paragraph 17.4*, being met.

17.10 A detainee from whom a sample may be taken may be detained for up to six hours from the time of charge if the custody officer reasonably believes the detention is necessary to enable a sample to be taken. Where the arrest condition is met, a detainee whom the custody officer has decided to release on bail without charge may continue to be detained, but not beyond 24 hours from the relevant time (as defined in section 41(2) of PACE), to enable a sample to be taken.

17.11 A detainee in respect of whom the arrest condition is met, but not the charge condition, see *paragraphs 17.3* and *17.4*, and whose release would be required before a sample can be taken had they not continued to be detained as a result of being arrested for a further offence which does not satisfy the arrest condition, may have a sample taken at any time within 24 hours after the arrest for the offence that satisfies the arrest condition.

(b) Documentation

17.12 The following must be recorded in the custody record:

(a) if a sample is taken following authorisation by an officer of the rank of inspector or above, the authorisation and the grounds for suspicion;

(b) the giving of a warning of the consequences of failure to provide a sample;

(c) the time at which the sample was given; and

(d) the time of charge or, where the arrest condition is being relied upon, the time of arrest and, where applicable, the fact that a sample taken after arrest but before charge is to be treated as being taken by virtue of the charge condition, where that is met in the same period of continuous detention. See *paragraph 17.9*

(c) General

17.13 A sample may only be taken by a prescribed person. See *Note 17C*.

17.14 Force may not be used to take any sample for the purpose of drug testing.

17.15 The terms "Class A drug" and "misuse" have the same meanings as in the Misuse of Drugs Act 1971. "Specified" (in relation to a Class A drug) and "trigger offence" have the same meanings as in Part III of the Criminal Justice and Court Services Act 2000.

17.16 Any sample taken:

(a) may not be used for any purpose other than to ascertain whether the person concerned has a specified Class A drug present in his body; and

(b) can be disposed of as clinical waste unless it is to be sent for further analysis in cases where the test result is disputed at the point when the result is known, or where medication has been taken, or for quality assurance purposes.

(d) Assessment of misuse of drugs

17.17 Under the provisions of Part 3 of the Drugs Act 2005, where a detainee has tested positive for a specified Class A drug under section 63B of PACE a police officer may, at any time before the person's release from the police station, impose a requirement on the detainee to attend an initial assessment of their drug misuse by a suitably qualified person and to remain for its duration. Where such a requirement is imposed, the officer must, at the same time, impose a second requirement on the detainee to attend and remain for a follow-up assessment. The officer must inform the detainee that the second requirement will cease to have effect if, at the initial assessment they are informed that a follow-up assessment is not necessary. These requirements may only be imposed on a person if:

(a) they have reached the age of 18

(b) notification has been given by the Secretary of State to the relevant chief officer of police that arrangements for conducting initial assessments and follow-up assessments have been made for those from whom samples for testing have been taken at the police station where the detainee is in custody.

17.18 When imposing a requirement to attend an initial assessment and a follow-up assessment the police officer must:

(a) inform the person of the time and place at which the initial assessment is to take place;

(b) explain that this information will be confirmed in writing; and

(c) warn the person that they may be liable to prosecution if they fail without good cause to attend the initial assessment and if they fail to attend the follow-up assessment and remain for its duration (if so required).

17.19 Where a police officer has imposed a requirement to attend an initial assessment in accordance with *paragraph 17.17*, he must, before the person is released from detention, give the person notice in writing which:

(a) confirms their requirements to attend and remain for the duration of assessments; and

(b) confirms the information and repeats the warning referred to in *paragraph 17.18*.

17.20 The following must be recorded in the custody record:

(a) that the requirement to attend an initial assessment and a follow-up assessment has been imposed; and

(b) the information, explanation, warning and notice given in accordance with *paragraphs 17.17* and *17.19*.

17.21 Where a notice is given in accordance with *paragraph 17.19*, a police officer can give the person a further notice in writing which informs the person of any change to the time or place at which the initial assessment is to take place and which repeats the warning referred to in *paragraph 17.18(c)*.

17.22 Part 3 of the Drugs Act 2005 also requires police officers to have regard to any guidance issued by the Secretary of State in respect of the assessment provisions.

Notes for guidance

17A When warning a person who is asked to provide a urine or non-intimate sample in accordance with paragraph 17.6(b), the following form of words may be used:

> *'You do not have to provide a sample, but I must warn you that if you fail or refuse without good cause to do so, you will commit an offence for which you may be imprisoned, or fined, or both'.*

Where the Welsh language is appropriate, the following form of words may be used:

> *'Does dim rhaid i chi roi sampl, ond mae'n rhaid i mi eich rhybuddio y byddwch chi'n cyflawni trosedd os byddwch chi'n methu neu yn gwrthod gwneud hynny heb reswm da, ac y gellir, oherwydd hynny, eich carcharu, eich dirwyo, neu'r ddau.'*

17B A sample has to be sufficient and suitable. A sufficient sample is sufficient in quantity and quality to enable drug-testing analysis to take place. A suitable sample is one which by its nature, is suitable for a particular form of drug analysis.

17C A prescribed person in paragraph 17.13 is one who is prescribed in regulations made by the Secretary of State under section 63B(6) of the Police and Criminal Evidence Act 1984. [The regulations are currently contained in regulation SI 2001 No. 2645, the Police and Criminal Evidence Act 1984 (Drug Testing Persons in Police Detention) (Prescribed Persons) Regulations 2001.]

17D Samples, and the information derived from them, may not be subsequently used in the investigation of any offence or in evidence against the persons from whom they were taken.

17E Trigger offences are:

1. Offences under the following provisions of the Theft Act 1968:

section 1	*(theft)*
section 8	*(robbery)*
section 9	*(burglary)*
section 10	*(aggravated burglary)*
section 12	*(taking a motor vehicle or other conveyance without authority)*
section 12A	*(aggravated vehicle-taking)*
section 22	*(handling stolen goods)*
section 25	*(going equipped for stealing etc.)*

2. Offences under the following provisions of the Misuse of Drugs Act 1971, if committed in respect of a specified Class A drug:—

section 4	*(restriction on production and supply of controlled drugs)*
section 5(2)	*(possession of a controlled drug)*
section 5(3)	*(possession of a controlled drug with intent to supply)*

3. Offences under the following provisions of the Fraud Act 2006:

section 1	*(fraud)*
section 6	*(possession etc. of articles for use in frauds)*
section 7	*(making or supplying articles for use in frauds)*

3A. An offence under section 1(1) of the Criminal Attempts Act 1981 if committed in respect of an offence under:

(a) any of the following provisions of the Theft Act 1968:

section 1	*(theft)*
section 8	*(robbery)*
section 9	*(burglary)*
section 22	*(handling stolen goods)*

(b) section 1 of the Fraud Act 2006 (fraud)

4. Offences under the following provisions of the Vagrancy Act 1824:

section 3	*(begging)*
section 4	*(persistent begging)*

17F The power to take samples is subject to notification by the Secretary of State that appropriate arrangements for the taking of samples have been made for the police area as a whole or for the particular police station concerned for whichever of the following is specified in the notification:

(a) persons in respect of whom the arrest condition is met;

(b) persons in respect of whom the charge condition is met;

(c) persons who have not attained the age of 18.

Note: Notification is treated as having been given for the purposes of the charge condition in relation to a police area, if testing (on charge) under section 63B(2) of PACE was in force immediately before section 7 of the Drugs Act 2005 was brought into force; and for the purposes of the age condition, in relation to a police area or police station, if immediately before that day, notification that arrangements had been made for the taking of samples from persons under the age of 18 (those aged 14–17) had been given and had not been withdrawn.

17G Appropriate adult in paragraph 17.7 means the person's—

(a) parent or guardian or, if they are in the care of a local authority or voluntary organisation, a person representing that authority or organisation; or

(b) a social worker of, a local authority; or

(c) if no person falling within (a) or (b) above is available, any responsible person aged 18 or over who is not a police officer or a person employed by the police.

ANNEX A—INTIMATE AND STRIP SEARCHES

A Intimate search

1. An intimate search consists of the physical examination of a person's body orifices other than the mouth. The intrusive nature of such searches means the actual and potential risks associated with intimate searches must never be underestimated.

(a) Action

2. Body orifices other than the mouth may be searched only:
   (a) if authorised by an officer of inspector rank or above who has reasonable grounds for believing that the person may have concealed on themselves:
      (i) anything which they could and might use to cause physical injury to themselves or others at the station; or
      (ii) a Class A drug which they intended to supply to another or to export;

   and the officer has reasonable grounds for believing that an intimate search is the only means of removing those items; and

   (b) if the search is under *paragraph 2(a)(ii)* (a drug offence search), the detainee's appropriate consent has been given in writing.

2A. Before the search begins, a police officer, designated detention officer or staff custody officer, must tell the detainee:
   (a) that the authority to carry out the search has been given;
   (b) the grounds for giving the authorisation and for believing that the article cannot be removed without an intimate search.

2B Before a detainee is asked to give appropriate consent to a search under *paragraph 2(a)(ii)* (a drug offence search) they must be warned that if they refuse without good cause their refusal may harm their case if it comes to trial, see *Note A6*. This warning may be given by a police officer or member of police staff. A detainee who is not legally represented must be reminded of their entitlement to have free legal advice, see Code C, *paragraph 6.5*, and the reminder noted in the custody record.

3. An intimate search may only be carried out by a registered medical practitioner or registered nurse, unless an officer of at least inspector rank considers this is not practicable and the search is to take place under *paragraph 2(a)(i)*, in which case a police officer may carry out the search. See *Notes A1* to *A5*

3A. Any proposal for a search under *paragraph 2(a)(i)* to be carried out by someone other than a registered medical practitioner or registered nurse must only be considered as a last resort and when the authorising officer is satisfied the risks associated with allowing the item to remain with the detainee outweigh the risks associated with removing it. See *Notes A1* to *A5*

4. An intimate search under:
   - *paragraph 2(a)(i)* may take place only at a hospital, surgery, other medical premises or police station
   - *paragraph 2(a)(ii)* may take place only at a hospital, surgery or other medical premises and must be carried out by a registered medical practitioner or a registered nurse

5. An intimate search at a police station of a juvenile or mentally disordered or otherwise mentally vulnerable person may take place only in the presence of an appropriate adult of the same sex, unless the detainee specifically requests a particular adult of the opposite sex who is readily available. In the case of a juvenile the search may take place in the absence of the appropriate adult only if the juvenile signifies in the presence of the appropriate adult they do not want the adult present during the search and the adult agrees. A record shall be made of the juvenile's decision and signed by the appropriate adult.
6. When an intimate search under *paragraph 2(a)(i)* is carried out by a police officer, the officer must be of the same sex as the detainee. A minimum of two people, other than the detainee, must be present during the search. Subject to *paragraph 5*, no person of the opposite sex who is not a medical practitioner or nurse shall be present, nor shall anyone whose presence is unnecessary. The search shall be conducted with proper regard to the sensitivity and vulnerability of the detainee.

(b) Documentation

7. In the case of an intimate search, the following shall be recorded as soon as practicable, in the detainee's custody record:
   (a) for searches under *paragraphs 2(a)(i)* and *(ii)*;
   - the authorisation to carry out the search;
   - the grounds for giving the authorisation;
   - the grounds for believing the article could not be removed without an intimate search
   - which parts of the detainee's body were searched
   - who carried out the search
   - who was present
   - the result.

   (b) for searches under paragraph 2(a)(ii):
   - the giving of the warning required by *paragraph 2B*;
   - the fact that the appropriate consent was given or (as the case may be) refused, and if refused, the reason given for the refusal (if any).
8. If an intimate search is carried out by a police officer, the reason why it was impracticable for a registered medical practitioner or registered nurse to conduct it must be recorded.

B Strip search

9. A strip search is a search involving the removal of more than outer clothing. In this Code, outer clothing includes shoes and socks.

(a) Action

10. A strip search may take place only if it is considered necessary to remove an article which a detainee would not be allowed to keep, and the officer reasonably considers the detainee might have concealed such an article. Strip searches shall not be routinely carried out if there is no reason to consider that articles are concealed.

The conduct of strip searches

11. When strip searches are conducted:
    (a) a police officer carrying out a strip search must be the same sex as the detainee;
    (b) the search shall take place in an area where the detainee cannot be seen by anyone who does not need to be present, nor by a member of the opposite sex except an appropriate adult who has been specifically requested by the detainee;

(c) except in cases of urgency, where there is risk of serious harm to the detainee or to others, whenever a strip search involves exposure of intimate body parts, there must be at least two people present other than the detainee, and if the search is of a juvenile or mentally disordered or otherwise mentally vulnerable person, one of the people must be the appropriate adult. Except in urgent cases as above, a search of a juvenile may take place in the absence of the appropriate adult only if the juvenile signifies in the presence of the appropriate adult that they do not want the adult to be present during the search and the adult agrees. A record shall be made of the juvenile's decision and signed by the appropriate adult. The presence of more than two people, other than an appropriate adult, shall be permitted only in the most exceptional circumstances;

(d) the search shall be conducted with proper regard to the sensitivity and vulnerability of the detainee in these circumstances and every reasonable effort shall be made to secure the detainee's co-operation and minimise embarrassment. Detainees who are searched shall not normally be required to remove all their clothes at the same time, e.g. a person should be allowed to remove clothing above the waist and redress before removing further clothing;

(e) if necessary to assist the search, the detainee may be required to hold their arms in the air or to stand with their legs apart and bend forward so a visual examination may be made of the genital and anal areas provided no physical contact is made with any body orifice;

(f) if articles are found, the detainee shall be asked to hand them over. If articles are found within any body orifice other than the mouth, and the detainee refuses to hand them over, their removal would constitute an intimate search, which must be carried out as in *Part A*;

(g) a strip search shall be conducted as quickly as possible, and the detainee allowed to dress as soon as the procedure is complete.

(b) Documentation

12. A record shall be made on the custody record of a strip search including the reason it was considered necessary, those present and any result.

Notes for guidance

A1 Before authorising any intimate search, the authorising officer must make every reasonable effort to persuade the detainee to hand the article over without a search. If the detainee agrees, a registered medical practitioner or registered nurse should whenever possible be asked to assess the risks involved and, if necessary, attend to assist the detainee.

A2 If the detainee does not agree to hand the article over without a search, the authorising officer must carefully review all the relevant factors before authorising an intimate search. In particular, the officer must consider whether the grounds for believing an article may be concealed are reasonable.

A3 If authority is given for a search under paragraph 2(a)(i), a registered medical practitioner or registered nurse shall be consulted whenever possible. The presumption should be that the search will be conducted by the registered medical practitioner or registered nurse and the authorising officer must make every reasonable effort to persuade the detainee to allow the medical practitioner or nurse to conduct the search.

A4 A constable should only be authorised to carry out a search as a last resort and when all other approaches have failed. In these circumstances, the authorising officer must be satisfied the detainee might use the article for one or more of the purposes in paragraph 2(a)(i) and the physical injury likely to be caused is sufficiently severe to justify authorising a constable to carry out the search.

A5 If an officer has any doubts whether to authorise an intimate search by a constable, the officer should seek advice from an officer of superintendent rank or above.

A6 In warning a detainee who is asked to consent to an intimate drug offence search, as in paragraph 2B, the following form of words may be used:

> *'You do not have to allow yourself to be searched, but I must warn you that if you refuse without good cause, your refusal may harm your case if it comes to trial.'*

Where the use of the Welsh Language is appropriate, the following form of words may be used:

'Nid oes rhaid i chi roi caniatâd i gael eich archwilio, ond mae'n rhaid i mi eich rhybuddio os gwrthodwch heb reswm da, y gallai eich penderfyniad i wrthod wneud niwed i'ch achos pe bai'n dod gerbron llys.'

ANNEX B—DELAY IN NOTIFYING ARREST OR ALLOWING ACCESS TO LEGAL ADVICE

A Persons detained under PACE

1. The exercise of the rights in *Section 5* or *Section 6*, or both, may be delayed if the person is in police detention, as in PACE, section 118(2), in connection with an indictable offence, has not yet been charged with an offence and an officer of superintendent rank or above, or inspector rank or above only for the rights in Section 5, has reasonable grounds for believing their exercise will:
   (i) lead to:
      - interference with, or harm to, evidence connected with an indictable offence; or
      - interference with, or physical harm to, other people; or
   (ii) lead to alerting other people suspected of having committed an indictable offence but not yet arrested for it; or
   (iii) hinder the recovery of property obtained in consequence of the commission of such an offence.
2. These rights may also be delayed if the officer has reasonable grounds to believe that:
   (i) the person detained for an indictable offence has benefited from their criminal conduct (decided in accordance with Part 2 of the Proceeds of Crime Act 2002); and
   (ii) the recovery of the value of the property constituting that benefit will be hindered by the exercise of either right.
3. Authority to delay a detainee's right to consult privately with a solicitor may be given only if the authorising officer has reasonable grounds to believe the solicitor the detainee wants to consult will, inadvertently or otherwise, pass on a message from the detainee or act in some other way which will have any of the consequences specified under *paragraphs 1 or 2*. In these circumstances the detainee must be allowed to choose another solicitor. See *Note B3*
4. If the detainee wishes to see a solicitor, access to that solicitor may not be delayed on the grounds they might advise the detainee not to answer questions or the solicitor was initially asked to attend the police station by someone else. In the latter case the detainee must be told the solicitor has come to the police station at another person's request, and must be asked to sign the custody record to signify whether they want to see the solicitor.
5. The fact the grounds for delaying notification of arrest may be satisfied does not automatically mean the grounds for delaying access to legal advice will also be satisfied.
6. These rights may be delayed only for as long as grounds exist and in no case beyond 36 hours after the relevant time as in PACE, section 41. If the grounds cease to apply within this time, the detainee must, as soon as practicable, be asked if they want to exercise either right, the custody record must be noted accordingly, and action taken in accordance with the relevant section of the Code.
7. A detained person must be permitted to consult a solicitor for a reasonable time before any court hearing.

B Not used

C Documentation

13. The grounds for action under this Annex shall be recorded and the detainee informed of them as soon as practicable.
14. Any reply given by a detainee under *paragraphs 6* or *11* must be recorded and the detainee asked to endorse the record in relation to whether they want to receive legal advice at this point.

D Cautions and special warnings

15. When a suspect detained at a police station is interviewed during any period for which access to legal advice has been delayed under this Annex, the court or jury may not draw adverse inferences from their silence.

Notes for guidance

B1 Even if Annex B applies in the case of a juvenile, or a person who is mentally disordered or otherwise mentally vulnerable, action to inform the appropriate adult and the person responsible for a juvenile's welfare if that is a different person, must nevertheless be taken as in paragraph 3.13 and 3.15.

B2 In the case of Commonwealth citizens and foreign nationals, see Note 7A.

B3 A decision to delay access to a specific solicitor is likely to be a rare occurrence and only when it can be shown the suspect is capable of misleading that particular solicitor and there is more than a substantial risk that the suspect will succeed in causing information to be conveyed which will lead to one or more of the specified consequences.

ANNEX C—RESTRICTION ON DRAWING ADVERSE INFERENCES FROM SILENCE AND TERMS OF THE CAUTION WHEN THE RESTRICTION APPLIES

(a) The restriction on drawing adverse inferences from silence

1. The Criminal Justice and Public Order Act 1994, sections 34, 36 and 37 as amended by the Youth Justice and Criminal Evidence Act 1999, section 58 describe the conditions under which adverse inferences may be drawn from a person's failure or refusal to say anything about their involvement in the offence when interviewed, after being charged or informed they may be prosecuted. These provisions are subject to an overriding restriction on the ability of a court or jury to draw adverse inferences from a person's silence. This restriction applies:
   (a) to any detainee at a police station, see *Note 10C* who, before being interviewed, see *section 11* or being charged or informed they may be prosecuted, see *section 16*, has:
      (i) asked for legal advice, see *section 6, paragraph 6.1*;
      (ii) not been allowed an opportunity to consult a solicitor, including the duty solicitor, as in this Code; and
      (iii) not changed their mind about wanting legal advice, see *section 6, paragraph 6.6(d)*
   Note the condition in (ii) will
   — apply when a detainee who has asked for legal advice is interviewed before speaking to a solicitor as in *section 6, paragraph 6.6(a)* or *(b)*.
   — not apply if the detained person declines to ask for the duty solicitor, see *section 6, paragraphs 6.6(c)* and *(d)*.

(b) to any person charged with, or informed they may be prosecuted for, an offence who:
  (i) has had brought to their notice a written statement made by another person or the content of an interview with another person which relates to that offence, see *section 16, paragraph 16.4*;
  (ii) is interviewed about that offence, see *section 16, paragraph 16.5*; or
  (iii) makes a written statement about that offence, see *Annex D paragraphs 4* and *9*.

(b) Terms of the caution when the restriction applies

2. When a requirement to caution arises at a time when the restriction on drawing adverse inferences from silence applies, the caution shall be:

   'You do not have to say anything, but anything you do say may be given in evidence.'

   Where the use of the Welsh Language is appropriate, the caution may be used directly in Welsh in the following terms:

   'Does dim rhaid i chi ddweud dim byd, ond gall unrhyw beth yr ydych chi'n ei ddweud gael ei roi fel tystiolaeth.'

3. Whenever the restriction either begins to apply or ceases to apply after a caution has already been given, the person shall be re-cautioned in the appropriate terms. The changed position on drawing inferences and that the previous caution no longer applies shall also be explained to the detainee in ordinary language. See *Note C2*

Notes for guidance

C1 *The restriction on drawing inferences from silence does not apply to a person who has not been detained and who therefore cannot be prevented from seeking legal advice if they want to, see paragraphs 10.2 and 3.15.*

C2 *The following is suggested as a framework to help explain changes in the position on drawing adverse inferences if the restriction on drawing adverse inferences from silence:*

(a) begins to apply:

'The caution you were previously given no longer applies. This is because after that caution:

(i) you asked to speak to a solicitor but have not yet been allowed an opportunity to speak to a solicitor. See paragraph 1(a); or

(ii) you have been charged with/informed you may be prosecuted.' See paragraph 1(b).

'This means that from now on, adverse inferences cannot be drawn at court and your defence will not be harmed just because you choose to say nothing. Please listen carefully to the caution I am about to give you because it will apply from now on. You will see that it does not say anything about your defence being harmed.'

(b) ceases to apply before or at the time the person is charged or informed they may be prosecuted, see paragraph 1(a);

'The caution you were previously given no longer applies. This is because after that caution you have been allowed an opportunity to speak to a solicitor. Please listen carefully to the caution I am about to give you because it will apply from now on. It explains how your defence at court may be affected if you choose to say nothing.'

ANNEX D—WRITTEN STATEMENTS UNDER CAUTION

(a) Written by a person under caution

1. A person shall always be invited to write down what they want to say.
2. A person who has not been charged with, or informed they may be prosecuted for, any offence to which the statement they want to write relates, shall:

(a) unless the statement is made at a time when the restriction on drawing adverse inferences from silence applies, see Annex C, be asked to write out and sign the following before writing what they want to say:

'I make this statement of my own free will. I understand that I do not have to say anything but that it may harm my defence if I do not mention when questioned something which I later rely on in court. This statement may be given in evidence.';

(b) if the statement is made at a time when the restriction on drawing adverse inferences from silence applies, be asked to write out and sign the following before writing what they want to say;

'I make this statement of my own free will. I understand that I do not have to say anything. This statement may be given in evidence.'

3. When a person, on the occasion of being charged with or informed they may be prosecuted for any offence, asks to make a statement which relates to any such offence and wants to write it they shall:

(a) unless the restriction on drawing adverse inferences from silence, see *Annex C*, applied when they were so charged or informed they may be prosecuted, be asked to write out and sign the following before writing what they want to say:

'I make this statement of my own free will. I understand that I do not have to say anything but that it may harm my defence if I do not mention when questioned something which I later rely on in court. This statement may be given in evidence.';

(b) if the restriction on drawing adverse inferences from silence applied when they were so charged or informed they may be prosecuted, be asked to write out and sign the following before writing what they want to say:

'I make this statement of my own free will. I understand that I do not have to say anything. This statement may be given in evidence.'

4. When a person, who has already been charged with or informed they may be prosecuted for any offence, asks to make a statement which relates to any such offence and wants to write it they shall be asked to write out and sign the following before writing what they want to say:

'I make this statement of my own free will. I understand that I do not have to say anything. This statement may be given in evidence.';

5. Any person writing their own statement shall be allowed to do so without any prompting except a police officer or other police staff may indicate to them which matters are material or question any ambiguity in the statement.

(b) Written by a police officer or other police staff

6. If a person says they would like someone to write the statement for them, a police officer, or other police staff shall write the statement.
7. If the person has not been charged with, or informed they may be prosecuted for, any offence to which the statement they want to make relates they shall, before starting, be asked to sign, or make their mark, to the following:

(a) unless the statement is made at a time when the restriction on drawing adverse inferences from silence applies, see Annex C:

'I, ..., wish to make a statement. I want someone to write down what I say. I understand that I do not have to say anything but that it may harm my defence if I do not mention when questioned something which I later rely on in court. This statement may be given in evidence.';

(b) if the statement is made at a time when the restriction on drawing adverse inferences from silence applies:

'I, ..., wish to make a statement. I want someone to write down what I say. I understand that I do not have to say anything. This statement may be given in evidence.'

8. If, on the occasion of being charged with or informed they may be prosecuted for any offence, the person asks to make a statement which relates to any such offence they shall before

starting be asked to sign, or make their mark to, the following:

(a) unless the restriction on drawing adverse inferences from silence applied, see Annex C, when they were so charged or informed they may be prosecuted:

'I, ..., wish to make a statement. I want someone to write down what I say. I understand that I do not have to say anything but that it may harm my defence if I do not mention when questioned something which I later rely on in court. This statement may be given in evidence.';

(b) if the restriction on drawing adverse inferences from silence applied when they were so charged or informed they may be prosecuted:

'I, ..., wish to make a statement. I want someone to write down what I say. I understand that I do not have to say anything. This statement may be given in evidence.'

9. If, having already been charged with or informed they may be prosecuted for any offence, a person asks to make a statement which relates to any such offence they shall before starting, be asked to sign, or make their mark to:

'I, ..., wish to make a statement. I want someone to write down what I say. I understand that I do not have to say anything. This statement may be given in evidence.'

10. The person writing the statement must take down the exact words spoken by the person making it and must not edit or paraphrase it. Any questions that are necessary, e.g. to make it more intelligible, and the answers given must be recorded at the same time on the statement form.

11. When the writing of a statement is finished the person making it shall be asked to read it and to make any corrections, alterations or additions they want. When they have finished reading they shall be asked to write and sign or make their mark on the following certificate at the end of the statement:

'I have read the above statement, and I have been able to correct, alter or add anything I wish. This statement is true. I have made it of my own free will.'

12. If the person making the statement cannot read, or refuses to read it, or to write the above mentioned certificate at the end of it or to sign it, the person taking the statement shall read it to them and ask them if they would like to correct, alter or add anything and to put their signature or make their mark at the end. The person taking the statement shall certify on the statement itself what has occurred.

ANNEX E—SUMMARY OF PROVISIONS RELATING TO MENTALLY DISORDERED AND OTHERWISE MENTALLY VULNERABLE PEOPLE

1. If an officer has any suspicion, or is told in good faith, that a person of any age may be mentally disordered or otherwise mentally vulnerable, or mentally incapable of understanding the significance of questions or their replies that person shall be treated as mentally disordered or otherwise mentally vulnerable for the purposes of this Code. See *paragraph 1.4*

2. In the case of a person who is mentally disordered or otherwise mentally vulnerable, 'the appropriate adult' means:

(a) a relative, guardian or other person responsible for their care or custody;

(b) someone experienced in dealing with mentally disordered or mentally vulnerable people but who is not a police officer or employed by the police;

(c) failing these, some other responsible adult aged 18 or over who is not a police officer or employed by the police.

See *paragraph 1.7(b) and Note 1D*

3. If the custody officer authorises the detention of a person who is mentally vulnerable or appears to be suffering from a mental disorder, the custody officer must as soon as practicable inform the appropriate adult of the grounds for detention and the person's whereabouts, and ask the adult to come to the police station to see them. If the appropriate adult:

- is already at the station when information is given as in *paragraphs 3.1* to *3.5* the information must be given in their presence

- is not at the station when the provisions of *paragraph 3.1* to *3.5* are complied with these provisions must be complied with again in their presence once they arrive.

See *paragraphs 3.15* to *3.17*

4. If the appropriate adult, having been informed of the right to legal advice, considers legal advice should be taken, the provisions of *section 6* apply as if the mentally disordered or otherwise mentally vulnerable person had requested access to legal advice. See *paragraph 3.19* and *Note E1*
5. The custody officer must make sure a person receives appropriate clinical attention as soon as reasonably practicable if the person appears to be suffering from a mental disorder or in urgent cases immediately call the nearest health care professional or an ambulance. It is not intended these provisions delay the transfer of a detainee to a place of safety under the Mental Health Act 1983, section 136 if that is applicable. If an assessment under that Act is to take place at a police station, the custody officer must consider whether an appropriate health care professional should be called to conduct an initial clinical check on the detainee. See *paragraph 9.5* and *9.6*
6. It is imperative a mentally disordered or otherwise mentally vulnerable person detained under the Mental Health Act 1983, section 136 be assessed as soon as possible. If that assessment is to take place at the police station, an approved social worker and registered medical practitioner shall be called to the station as soon as possible in order to interview and examine the detainee. Once the detainee has been interviewed, examined and suitable arrangements been made for their treatment or care, they can no longer be detained under section 136. A detainee should be immediately discharged from detention if a registered medical practitioner having examined them, concludes they are not mentally disordered within the meaning of the Act. See *paragraph 3.16*
7. If a mentally disordered or otherwise mentally vulnerable person is cautioned in the absence of the appropriate adult, the caution must be repeated in the appropriate adult's presence. See *paragraph 10.12*
8. A mentally disordered or otherwise mentally vulnerable person must not be interviewed or asked to provide or sign a written statement in the absence of the appropriate adult unless the provisions of *paragraphs 11.1* or *11.18* to *11.20* apply. Questioning in these circumstances may not continue in the absence of the appropriate adult once sufficient information to avert the risk has been obtained. A record shall be made of the grounds for any decision to begin an interview in these circumstances. See *paragraphs 11.1, 11.15* and *11.18* to *11.20*
9. If the appropriate adult is present at an interview, they shall be informed they are not expected to act simply as an observer and the purposes of their presence are to:
   - advise the interviewee
   - observe whether or not the interview is being conducted properly and fairly
   - facilitate communication with the interviewee

   See *paragraph 11.17*
10. If the detention of a mentally disordered or otherwise mentally vulnerable person is reviewed by a review officer or a superintendent, the appropriate adult must, if available at the time, be given an opportunity to make representations to the officer about the need for continuing detention. See *paragraph 15.3*
11. If the custody officer charges a mentally disordered or otherwise mentally vulnerable person with an offence or takes such other action as is appropriate when there is sufficient evidence for a prosecution this must be done in the presence of the appropriate adult. The written notice embodying any charge must be given to the appropriate adult. See *paragraphs 16.1* to *16.4A*
12. An intimate or strip search of a mentally disordered or otherwise mentally vulnerable person may take place only in the presence of the appropriate adult of the same sex, unless the detainee specifically requests the presence of a particular adult of the opposite sex. A strip search may take place in the absence of an appropriate adult only in cases of urgency when there is a risk of serious harm to the detainee or others. See *Annex A, paragraphs 5* and *11(c)*

13. Particular care must be taken when deciding whether to use any form of approved restraints on a mentally disordered or otherwise mentally vulnerable person in a locked cell. See *paragraph 8.2*

Notes for guidance

E1 The purpose of the provision at paragraph 3.19 is to protect the rights of a mentally disordered or otherwise mentally vulnerable detained person who does not understand the significance of what is said to them. If the detained person wants to exercise the right to legal advice, the appropriate action should be taken and not delayed until the appropriate adult arrives. A mentally disordered or otherwise mentally vulnerable detained person should always be given an opportunity, when an appropriate adult is called to the police station, to consult privately with a solicitor in the absence of the appropriate adult if they want.

E2 Although people who are mentally disordered or otherwise mentally vulnerable are often capable of providing reliable evidence, they may, without knowing or wanting to do so, be particularly prone in certain circumstances to provide information that may be unreliable, misleading or self-incriminating. Special care should always be taken when questioning such a person, and the appropriate adult should be involved if there is any doubt about a person's mental state or capacity. Because of the risk of unreliable evidence, it is important to obtain corroboration of any facts admitted whenever possible.

E3 Because of the risks referred to in Note E2, which the presence of the appropriate adult is intended to minimise, officers of superintendent rank or above should exercise their discretion to authorise the commencement of an interview in the appropriate adult's absence only in exceptional cases, if it is necessary to avert an immediate risk of serious harm. See paragraphs 11.1, 11.18 to 11.20

ANNEX F—COUNTRIES WITH WHICH BILATERAL CONSULAR CONVENTIONS OR AGREEMENTS REQUIRING NOTIFICATION OF THE ARREST AND DETENTION OF THEIR NATIONALS ARE IN FORCE AS AT 1 APRIL 2003

Armenia
Austria
Azerbaijan
Belarus
Belgium
Bosnia-Herzegovina
Bulgaria
China*
Croatia
Cuba
Czech Republic
Denmark
Egypt
France
Georgia
German Federal Republic
Greece
Hungary
Italy
Japan
Kazakhstan
Macedonia
Mexico
Moldova
Mongolia
Norway
Poland
Romania
Russia
Slovak Republic
Slovenia
Spain
Sweden
Tajikistan
Turkmenistan
Ukraine
USA
Uzbekistan
Yugoslavia

* Police are required to inform Chinese officials of arrest/detention in the Manchester consular district only. This comprises Derbyshire, Durham, Greater Manchester, Lancashire, Merseyside, North South and West Yorkshire, and Tyne and Wear.

ANNEX G—FITNESS TO BE INTERVIEWED

1. This Annex contains general guidance to help police officers and health care professionals assess whether a detainee might be at risk in an interview.
2. A detainee may be at risk in an interview if it is considered that:
   (a) conducting the interview could significantly harm the detainee's physical or mental state;
   (b) anything the detainee says in the interview about their involvement or suspected involvement in the offence about which they are being interviewed **might** be considered unreliable in subsequent court proceedings because of their physical or mental state.
3. In assessing whether the detainee should be interviewed, the following must be considered:
   (a) how the detainee's physical or mental state might affect their ability to understand the nature and purpose of the interview, to comprehend what is being asked and to appreciate the significance of any answers given and make rational decisions about whether they want to say anything;
   (b) the extent to which the detainee's replies may be affected by their physical or mental condition rather than representing a rational and accurate explanation of their involvement in the offence;
   (c) how the nature of the interview, which could include particularly probing questions, might affect the detainee.
4. It is essential health care professionals who are consulted consider the functional ability of the detainee rather than simply relying on a medical diagnosis, e.g. it is possible for a person with severe mental illness to be fit for interview.
5. Health care professionals should advise on the need for an appropriate adult to be present, whether reassessment of the person's fitness for interview may be necessary if the interview lasts beyond a specified time, and whether a further specialist opinion may be required.
6. When health care professionals identify risks they should be asked to quantify the risks. They should inform the custody officer:
   - whether the person's condition:
     — is likely to improve
     — will require or be amenable to treatment; and
   - indicate how long it may take for such improvement to take effect
7. The role of the health care professional is to consider the risks and advise the custody officer of the outcome of that consideration. The health care professional's determination and any advice or recommendations should be made in writing and form part of the custody record.
8. Once the health care professional has provided that information, it is a matter for the custody officer to decide whether or not to allow the interview to go ahead and if the interview is to proceed, to determine what safeguards are needed. Nothing prevents safeguards being provided in addition to those required under the Code. An example might be to have an appropriate health care professional present during the interview, in addition to an appropriate adult, in order constantly to monitor the person's condition and how it is being affected by the interview.

ANNEX H—DETAINED PERSON: OBSERVATION LIST

1. If any detainee fails to meet any of the following criteria, an appropriate health care professional or an ambulance must be called.
2. When assessing the level of rousability, consider:
   Rousability—can they be woken?
   - go into the cell
   - call their name
   - shake gently

   Response to questions—can they give appropriate answers to questions such as:
   - What's your name?
   - Where do you live?

- Where do you think you are?

Response to commands—can they respond appropriately to commands such as:

- Open your eyes!
- Lift one arm, now the other arm!

3. Remember to take into account the possibility or presence of other illnesses, injury, or mental condition, a person who is drowsy and smells of alcohol may also have the following:
   - Diabetes
   - Epilepsy
   - Head injury
   - Drug intoxication or overdose
   - Stroke

ANNEX I—NOT USED

ANNEX J—NOT USED

ANNEX K—X-RAYS AND ULTRASOUND SCANS

(a) Action

1. PACE, section 55A allows a person who has been arrested and is in police detention to have an X-ray taken of them or an ultrasound scan to be carried out on them (or both) if:
   (a) authorised by an officer of inspector rank or above who has reasonable grounds for believing that the detainee:
      (i) may have swallowed a Class A drug; and
      (ii) was in possession of that Class A drug with the intention of supplying it to another or to export; and
   (b) the detainee's appropriate consent has been given in writing.
2. Before an x-ray is taken or an ultrasound scan carried out, a police officer, designated detention officer or staff custody officer must tell the detainee:
   (a) that the authority has been given; and
   (b) the grounds for giving the authorisation.
3. Before a detainee is asked to give appropriate consent to an x-ray or an ultrasound scan, they must be warned that if they refuse without good cause their refusal may harm their case if it comes to trial, see *Notes K1* and *K2*. This warning may be given by a police officer or member of police staff. A detainee who is not legally represented must be reminded of their entitlement to have free legal advice, see *Code C, paragraph 6.5*, and the reminder noted in the custody record.
4. An x-ray may be taken, or an ultrasound scan may be carried out, only by a registered medical practitioner or registered nurse, and only at a hospital, surgery or other medical premises.

(b) Documentation

5. The following shall be recorded as soon as practicable in the detainee's custody record:
   (a) the authorisation to take the x-ray or carry out the ultrasound scan (or both);
   (b) the grounds for giving the authorisation;
   (c) the giving of the warning required by *paragraph 3*; and
   (d) the fact that the appropriate consent was given or (as the case may be) refused, and if refused, the reason given for the refusal (if any); and
   (e) if an x-ray is taken or an ultrasound scan carried out:
      - where it was taken or carried out
      - who took it or carried it out
      - who was present
      - the result

6. Paragraphs 1.4–1.7 of this Code apply and an appropriate adult should be present when consent is sought to any procedure under this Annex.

Notes for guidance

K1 If authority is given for an x-ray to be taken or an ultrasound scan to be carried out (or both), consideration should be given to asking a registered medical practitioner or registered nurse to explain to the detainee what is involved and to allay any concerns the detainee might have about the effect which taking an x-ray or carrying out an ultrasound scan might have on them. If appropriate consent is not given, evidence of the explanation may, if the case comes to trial, be relevant to determining whether the detainee had a good cause for refusing.

K2 In warning a detainee who is asked to consent to an X-ray being taken or an ultrasound scan being carried out (or both), as in paragraph 3, the following form of words may be used:

> *'You do not have to allow an x-ray of you to be taken or an ultrasound scan to be carried out on you, but I must warn you that if you refuse without good cause, your refusal may harm your case if it comes to trial.'*

Where the use of the Welsh Language is appropriate, the following form of words may be provided in Welsh:

> *'Does dim rhaid i chi ganiatáu cymryd sgan uwchsain neu belydr-x (neu'r ddau) arnoch, ond mae'n rhaid i mi eich rhybuddio os byddwch chi'n gwrthod gwneud hynny heb reswm da, fe allai hynny niweidio eich achos pe bai'n dod gerbron llys.'*

Appendix 4

PACE Code of Practice for the Identification of Persons by Police Officers (Code D)

This code has effect in relation to any identification procedure carried out after midnight on 31 January 2008.

1 Introduction

1.1 This Code of Practice concerns the principal methods used by police to identify people in connection with the investigation of offences and the keeping of accurate and reliable criminal records.

1.2 Identification by witnesses arises, e.g. if the offender is seen committing the crime and a witness is given an opportunity to identify the suspect in a video identification, identification parade or similar procedure. The procedures are designed to:

- test the witness' ability to identify the person they saw on a previous occasion
- provide safeguards against mistaken identification.

While this Code concentrates on visual identification procedures, it does not preclude the police making use of aural identification procedures such as a "voice identification parade", where they judge that appropriate.

1.3 Identification by fingerprints applies when a person's fingerprints are taken to:

- compare with fingerprints found at the scene of a crime
- check and prove convictions
- help to ascertain a person's identity.

1.3A Identification using footwear impressions applies when a person's footwear impressions are taken to compare with impressions found at the scene of a crime.

1.4 Identification by body samples and impressions includes taking samples such as blood or hair to generate a DNA profile for comparison with material obtained from the scene of a crime, or a victim.

1.5 Taking photographs of arrested people applies to recording and checking identity and locating and tracing persons who:

- are wanted for offences
- fail to answer their bail.

1.6 Another method of identification involves searching and examining detained suspects to find, e.g. marks such as tattoos or scars which may help establish their identity or whether they have been involved in committing an offence.

1.7 The provisions of the Police and Criminal Evidence Act 1984 (PACE) and this Code are designed to make sure fingerprints, samples, impressions and photographs are taken, used and retained, and identification procedures carried out, only when justified and necessary for preventing, detecting or investigating crime. If these provisions are not observed, the application of the relevant procedures in particular cases may be open to question.

2 General

2.1 This Code must be readily available at all police stations for consultation by:
- police officers and police staff
- detained persons
- members of the public

2.2 The provisions of this Code:
- include the *Annexes*
- do not include the *Notes for guidance.*

2.3 Code C, paragraph 1.4, regarding a person who may be mentally disordered or otherwise mentally vulnerable and the *Notes for guidance* applicable to those provisions apply to this Code.

2.4 Code C, paragraph 1.5, regarding a person who appears to be under the age of 17 applies to this Code.

2.5 Code C, paragraph 1.6, regarding a person who appears blind, seriously visually impaired, deaf, unable to read or speak or has difficulty orally because of a speech impediment applies to this Code.

2.6 In this Code:
- 'appropriate adult' means the same as in Code C, paragraph 1.7,
- 'solicitor' means the same as in Code C, paragraph 6.12 and the *Notes for guidance* applicable to those provisions apply to this Code.

2.7 References to custody officers include those performing the functions of custody officer, see *paragraph 1.9* of Code C.

2.8 When a record of any action requiring the authority of an officer of a specified rank is made under this Code, subject to *paragraph 2.18,* the officer's name and rank must be recorded.

2.9 When this Code requires the prior authority or agreement of an officer of at least inspector or superintendent rank, that authority may be given by a sergeant or chief inspector who has been authorised to perform the functions of the higher rank under PACE, section 107.

2.10 Subject to *paragraph 2.18*, all records must be timed and signed by the maker.

2.11 Records must be made in the custody record, unless otherwise specified. References to 'pocket book' include any official report book issued to police officers or police staff.

2.12 If any procedure in this Code requires a person's consent, the consent of a:
- mentally disordered or otherwise mentally vulnerable person is only valid if given in the presence of the appropriate adult
- juvenile, is only valid if their parent's or guardian's consent is also obtained unless the juvenile is under 14, when their parent's or guardian's consent is sufficient in its own right. If the only obstacle to an identification procedure in *section 3* is that a juvenile's parent or guardian refuses consent or reasonable efforts to obtain it have failed, the identification officer may apply the provisions of *paragraph 3.21*. See *Note 2A*.

2.13 If a person is blind, seriously visually impaired or unable to read, the custody officer or identification officer shall make sure their solicitor, relative, appropriate adult or some other person likely to take an interest in them and not involved in the investigation is available to help check any documentation. When this Code requires written consent or signing, the person assisting may be asked to sign instead, if the detainee prefers. This paragraph does not require an appropriate adult to be called solely to assist in checking and signing documentation for a person who is not a juvenile, or mentally disordered or otherwise mentally vulnerable (see Note 2B and Code C *paragraph 3.15*).

2.14 If any procedure in this Code requires information to be given to or sought from a suspect, it must be given or sought in the appropriate adult's presence if the suspect is mentally disordered, otherwise mentally vulnerable or a juvenile. If the appropriate adult is not present when the information is first given or sought, the procedure must be repeated in the presence of the appropriate adult when they arrive. If the suspect appears deaf or there is doubt about their hearing or speaking ability or ability to understand English, and effective communication cannot be established, the information must be given or sought through an interpreter.

2.15 Any procedure in this Code involving the participation of a suspect who is mentally disordered, otherwise mentally vulnerable or a juvenile must take place in the presence of the appropriate adult. See *Code C paragraph 1.4*.

2.15A Any procedure in this Code involving the participation of a witness who is or appears to be mentally disordered, otherwise mentally vulnerable or a juvenile should take place in the presence of a pre-trial support person. However, the support-person must not be allowed to prompt any identification of a suspect by a witness. See *Note 2AB*.

2.16 References to:

- 'taking a photograph', include the use of any process to produce a single, still or moving, visual image
- 'photographing a person', should be construed accordingly
- 'photographs', 'films', 'negatives' and 'copies' include relevant visual images recorded, stored, or reproduced through any medium
- 'destruction' includes the deletion of computer data relating to such images or making access to that data impossible.

2.17 Except as described, nothing in this Code affects the powers and procedures:

(i) for requiring and taking samples of breath, blood and urine in relation to driving offences, etc, when under the influence of drink, drugs or excess alcohol under the:
- Road Traffic Act 1988, sections 4 to 11
- Road Traffic Offenders Act 1988, sections 15 and 16
- Transport and Works Act 1992, sections 26 to 38;

(ii) under the Immigration Act 1971, Schedule 2, paragraph 18, for taking photographs and fingerprints from persons detained under that Act, Schedule 2, paragraph 16 (Administrative Controls as to Control on Entry etc.); for taking fingerprints in accordance with the Immigration and Asylum Act 1999; sections 141 and 142(3), or other methods for collecting information about a person's external physical characteristics provided for by regulations made under that Act, section 144;

(iii) under the Terrorism Act 2000, Schedule 8, for taking photographs, fingerprints, skin impressions, body samples or impressions from people:
- arrested under that Act, section 41,
- detained for the purposes of examination under that Act, Schedule 7, and to whom the Code of Practice issued under that Act, Schedule 14, paragraph 6, applies ('the terrorism provisions')

See *Note 2C*;

(iv) for taking photographs, fingerprints, skin impressions, body samples or impressions from people who have been:
- arrested on warrants issued in Scotland, by officers exercising powers under the Criminal Justice and Public Order Act 1994, section 136(2)
- arrested or detained without warrant by officers from a police force in Scotland exercising their powers of arrest or detention under the Criminal Justice and Public Order Act 1994, section 137(2), (Cross Border powers of arrest etc.).

Note: In these cases, police powers and duties and the person's rights and entitlements whilst at a police station in England and Wales are the same as if the person had been arrested in Scotland by a Scottish police officer.

2.18 Nothing in this Code requires the identity of officers or police staff to be recorded or disclosed:

(a) in the case of enquiries linked to the investigation of terrorism;

(b) if the officers or police staff reasonably believe recording or disclosing their names might put them in danger.

In these cases, they shall use warrant or other identification numbers and the name of their police station. See *Note 2D*

2.19 In this Code:

(a) 'designated person' means a person other than a police officer, designated under the Police Reform Act 2002, Part 4, who has specified powers and duties of police officers conferred or imposed on them;

(b) any reference to a police officer includes a designated person acting in the exercise or performance of the powers and duties conferred or imposed on them by their designation.

2.20 If a power conferred on a designated person:

(a) allows reasonable force to be used when exercised by a police officer, a designated person exercising that power has the same entitlement to use force;

(b) includes power to use force to enter any premises, that power is not exercisable by that designated person except:

(i) in the company, and under the supervision, of a police officer; or

(ii) for the purpose of:

- saving life or limb; or
- preventing serious damage to property.

2.21 Nothing in this Code prevents the custody officer, or other officer given custody of the detainee, from allowing police staff who are not designated persons to carry out individual procedures or tasks at the police station if the law allows. However, the officer remains responsible for making sure the procedures and tasks are carried out correctly in accordance with the Codes of Practice. Any such person must be:

(a) a person employed by a police authority maintaining a police force and under the control and direction of the Chief Officer of that force;

(b) employed by a person with whom a police authority has a contract for the provision of services relating to persons arrested or otherwise in custody.

2.22 Designated persons and other police staff must have regard to any relevant provisions of the Codes of Practice.

Notes for guidance

2A For the purposes of paragraph 2.12, the consent required from a parent or guardian may, for a juvenile in the care of a local authority or voluntary organisation, be given by that authority or organisation. In the case of a juvenile, nothing in paragraph 2.12 requires the parent, guardian or representative of a local authority or voluntary organisation to be present to give their consent, unless they are acting as the appropriate adult under paragraphs 2.14 or 2.15. However, it is important that a parent or guardian not present is fully informed before being asked to consent. They must be given the same information about the procedure and the juvenile's suspected involvement in the offence as the juvenile and appropriate adult. The parent or guardian must also be allowed to speak to the juvenile and the appropriate adult if they wish. Provided the consent is fully informed and is not withdrawn, it may be obtained at any time before the procedure takes place.

2AB The Youth Justice and Criminal Evidence Act 1999 guidance "Achieving Best Evidence in Criminal Proceedings" indicates that a pre-trial support person should accompany a vulnerable witness during any identification procedure. It states that this support person should not be (or not be likely to be) a witness in the investigation.

2B People who are seriously visually impaired or unable to read may be unwilling to sign police documents. The alternative, i.e. their representative signing on their behalf, seeks to protect the interests of both police and suspects.

2C Photographs, fingerprints, samples and impressions may be taken from a person detained under the terrorism provisions to help determine whether they are, or have been, involved in terrorism, as well as when there are reasonable grounds for suspecting their involvement in a particular offence.

2D The purpose of paragraph 2.18(b) is to protect those involved in serious organised crime investigations or arrests of particularly violent suspects when there is reliable information that those arrested or their associates may threaten or cause harm to the officers. In cases of doubt, an officer of inspector rank or above should be consulted.

3 Identification by witnesses

3.1 A record shall be made of the suspect's description as first given by a potential witness. This record must:

(a) be made and kept in a form which enables details of that description to be accurately produced from it, in a visible and legible form, which can be given to the suspect or the suspect's solicitor in accordance with this Code; and

(b) unless otherwise specified, be made before the witness takes part in any identification procedures under *paragraphs 3.5* to *3.10, 3.21* or *3.23*.

A copy of the record shall where practicable, be given to the suspect or their solicitor before any procedures under *paragraphs 3.5* to *3.10, 3.21* or *3.23* are carried out. See *Note 3E*

(a) Cases when the suspect's identity is not known

3.2 In cases when the suspect's identity is not known, a witness may be taken to a particular neighbourhood or place to see whether they can identify the person they saw. Although the number, age, sex, race, general description and style of clothing of other people present at the location and the way in which any identification is made cannot be controlled, the principles applicable to the formal procedures under *paragraphs 3.5* to *3.10* shall be followed as far as practicable. For example:

(a) where it is practicable to do so, a record should be made of the witness' description of the suspect, as in paragraph 3.1(a), before asking the witness to make an identification;

(b) care must be taken not to direct the witness' attention to any individual unless, taking into account all the circumstances, this cannot be avoided. However, this does not prevent a witness being asked to look carefully at the people around at the time or to look towards a group or in a particular direction, if this appears necessary to make sure that the witness does not overlook a possible suspect simply because the witness is looking in the opposite direction and also to enable the witness to make comparisons between any suspect and others who are in the area; See *Note 3F*

(c) where there is more than one witness, every effort should be made to keep them separate and witnesses should be taken to see whether they can identify a person independently;

(d) once there is sufficient information to justify the arrest of a particular individual for suspected involvement in the offence, e.g. after a witness makes a positive identification, the provisions set out from paragraph 3.4 onwards shall apply for any other witnesses in relation to that individual. Subject to *paragraphs 3.12* and *3.13*, it is not necessary for the witness who makes such a positive identification to take part in a further procedure;

(e) the officer or police staff accompanying the witness must record, in their pocket book, the action taken as soon as, and in as much detail, as possible. The record should include: the date, time and place of the relevant occasion the witness claims to have previously seen the suspect; where any identification was made; how it was made and the conditions at the time (e.g. the distance the witness was from the suspect, the weather and light); if the witness's attention was drawn to the suspect; the reason for this; and anything said by the witness or the suspect about the identification or the conduct of the procedure.

3.3 A witness must not be shown photographs, computerised or artist's composite likenesses or similar likenesses or pictures (including 'E-fit' images) if the identity of the suspect is known to the police and the suspect is available to take part in a video identification, an identification parade or a group identification. If the suspect's identity is not known, the showing of such images to a witness to obtain identification evidence must be done in accordance with *Annex E*.

(b) Cases when the suspect is known and available

3.4 If the suspect's identity is known to the police and they are available, the identification procedures set out in paragraphs 3.5 to 3.10 may be used. References in this section to a suspect being 'known' mean there is sufficient information known to the police to justify the arrest of a particular person for suspected involvement in the offence. A suspect being 'available' means they are immediately available or will be within a reasonably short time and willing to take an effective part in at least one of the following which it is practicable to arrange:

- video identification;
- identification parade; or
- group identification.

Video identification

3.5 A 'video identification' is when the witness is shown moving images of a known suspect, together with similar images of others who resemble the suspect. Moving images must be used unless:

- the suspect is known but not available (see *paragraph 3.21* of this Code); or
- in accordance with *paragraph 2A of Annex A* of this Code, the identification officer does not consider that replication of a physical feature can be achieved or that it is not possible to conceal the location of the feature on the image of the suspect.

The identification officer may then decide to make use of video identification but using still images.

3.6 Video identifications must be carried out in accordance with *Annex A*.

Identification parade

3.7 An 'identification parade' is when the witness sees the suspect in a line of others who resemble the suspect.

3.8 Identification parades must be carried out in accordance with *Annex B*.

Group identification

3.9 A 'group identification' is when the witness sees the suspect in an informal group of people.

3.10 Group identifications must be carried out in accordance with *Annex C*.

Arranging identification procedures

3.11 Except for the provisions in *paragraph 3.19*, the arrangements for, and conduct of, the identification procedures in paragraphs 3.5 to 3.10 and circumstances in which an identification procedure must be held shall be the responsibility of an officer not below inspector rank who is not involved with the investigation, 'the identification officer'. Unless otherwise specified, the identification officer may allow another officer or police staff, see *paragraph 2.21*, to make arrangements for, and conduct, any of these identification procedures. In delegating these procedures, the identification officer must be able to supervise effectively and either intervene or be contacted for advice. No officer or any other person involved with the investigation of the case against the suspect, beyond the extent required by these procedures, may take any part in these procedures or act as the identification officer. This does not prevent the identification officer from consulting the officer in charge of the investigation to determine which procedure to use. When an identification procedure is required, in the interest of fairness to suspects and witnesses, it must be held as soon as practicable.

Circumstances in which an identification procedure must be held

3.12 Whenever:

(i) a witness has identified a suspect or purported to have identified them prior to any identification procedure set out in paragraphs 3.5 to 3.10 having been held; or

(ii) there is a witness available, who expresses an ability to identify the suspect, or where there is a reasonable chance of the witness being able to do so, and they have not been given an opportunity to identify the suspect in any of the procedures set out in paragraphs 3.5 to 3.10, and the suspect disputes being the person the witness claims to have seen, an identification procedure shall be held unless it is not practicable or it would serve no useful purpose in proving or disproving whether the suspect was involved in committing the offence. For example, when it is not disputed that the suspect is already well known to the witness who claims to have seen them commit the crime.

3.13 Such a procedure may also be held if the officer in charge of the investigation considers it would be useful.

Selecting an identification procedure

3.14 If, because of paragraph 3.12, an identification procedure is to be held, the suspect shall initially be offered a video identification unless:

(a) a video identification is not practicable; or

(b) an identification parade is both practicable and more suitable than a video identification; or

(c) paragraph 3.16 applies.

The identification officer and the officer in charge of the investigation shall consult each other to determine which option is to be offered. An identification parade may not be practicable because of factors relating to the witnesses, such as their number, state of health, availability and travelling requirements. A video identification would normally be more suitable if it could be arranged and completed sooner than an identification parade.

3.15 A suspect who refuses the identification procedure first offered shall be asked to state their reason for refusing and may get advice from their solicitor and/or if present, their appropriate adult. The suspect, solicitor and/or appropriate adult shall be allowed to make representations about why another procedure should be used. A record should be made of the reasons for refusal and any representations made. After considering any reasons given, and representations made, the identification officer shall, if appropriate, arrange for the suspect to be offered an alternative which the officer considers suitable and practicable. If the officer decides it is not suitable and practicable to offer an alternative identification procedure, the reasons for that decision shall be recorded.

3.16 A group identification may initially be offered if the officer in charge of the investigation considers it is more suitable than a video identification or an identification parade and the identification officer considers it practicable to arrange.

Notice to suspect

3.17 Unless *paragraph 3.20* applies, before a video identification, an identification parade or group identification is arranged, the following shall be explained to the suspect:

(i) the purposes of the video identification, identification parade or group identification;

(ii) their entitlement to free legal advice; see Code C, paragraph 6.5;

(iii) the procedures for holding it, including their right to have a solicitor or friend present;

(iv) that they do not have to consent to or co-operate in a video identification, identification parade or group identification;

(v) that if they do not consent to, and co-operate in, a video identification, identification parade or group identification, their refusal may be given in evidence in any subsequent trial and police may proceed covertly without their consent or make other arrangements to test whether a witness can identify them, see *paragraph 3.21;*

(vi) whether, for the purposes of the video identification procedure, images of them have previously been obtained, see *paragraph 3.20*, and if so, that they may co-operate in providing further, suitable images to be used instead;

(vii) if appropriate, the special arrangements for juveniles;

(viii) if appropriate, the special arrangements for mentally disordered or otherwise mentally vulnerable people;

(ix) that if they significantly alter their appearance between being offered an identification procedure and any attempt to hold an identification procedure, this may be given in evidence if the case comes to trial, and the identification officer may then consider other forms of identification, see *paragraph 3.21* and *Note 3C*;

(x) that a moving image or photograph may be taken of them when they attend for any identification procedure;

(xi) whether, before their identity became known, the witness was shown photographs, a computerised or artist's composite likeness or similar likeness or image by the police, see *Note 3B;*

(xii) that if they change their appearance before an identification parade, it may not be practicable to arrange one on the day or subsequently and, because of the appearance change, the identification officer may consider alternative methods of identification, see *Note 3C;*

(xiii) that they or their solicitor will be provided with details of the description of the suspect as first given by any witnesses who are to attend the video identification, identification parade, group identification or confrontation, see *paragraph 3.1.*

3.18 This information must also be recorded in a written notice handed to the suspect. The suspect must be given a reasonable opportunity to read the notice, after which, they should be asked to sign a second copy to indicate if they are willing to co-operate with the making of a video or take part in the identification parade or group identification. The signed copy shall be retained by the identification officer.

3.19 The duties of the identification officer under *paragraphs 3.17* and *3.18* may be performed by the custody officer or other officer not involved in the investigation if:

(a) it is proposed to release the suspect in order that an identification procedure can be arranged and carried out and an inspector is not available to act as the identification officer, see *paragraph 3.11*, before the suspect leaves the station; or

(b) it is proposed to keep the suspect in police detention whilst the procedure is arranged and carried out and waiting for an inspector to act as the identification officer, see *paragraph 3.11*, would cause unreasonable delay to the investigation.

The officer concerned shall inform the identification officer of the action taken and give them the signed copy of the notice. See *Note 3C*

3.20 If the identification officer and officer in charge of the investigation suspect, on reasonable grounds that if the suspect was given the information and notice as in *paragraphs 3.17* and *3.18*, they would then take steps to avoid being seen by a witness in any identification procedure, the identification officer may arrange for images of the suspect suitable for use in a video identification procedure to be obtained before giving the information and notice. If suspect's images are obtained in these circumstances, the suspect may, for the purposes of a video identification procedure, co-operate in providing new images which if suitable, would be used instead, see *paragraph 3.17(vi).*

(c) Cases when the suspect is known but not available

3.21 When a known suspect is not available or has ceased to be available, see *paragraph 3.4*, the identification officer may make arrangements for a video identification (see Annex A). If necessary, the identification officer may follow the video identification procedures but using **still** images. Any suitable moving or still images may be used and these may be obtained covertly if necessary. Alternatively, the identification officer may make arrangements for a group identification. See *Note 3D*. These provisions may also be applied to juveniles where the consent of their parent or guardian is either refused or reasonable efforts to obtain that consent have failed (see *paragraph 2.12*).

3.22 Any covert activity should be strictly limited to that necessary to test the ability of the witness to identify the suspect.

3.23 The identification officer may arrange for the suspect to be confronted by the witness if none of the options referred to in paragraphs 3.5 to 3.10 or 3.21 are practicable. A "confrontation" is when the suspect is directly confronted by the witness. A confrontation does not require the suspect's consent. Confrontations must be carried out in accordance with Annex D.

3.24 Requirements for information to be given to, or sought from, a suspect or for the suspect to be given an opportunity to view images before they are shown to a witness, do not apply if the suspect's lack of co-operation prevents the necessary action.

(d) Documentation

3.25 A record shall be made of the video identification, identification parade, group identification or confrontation on forms provided for the purpose.

3.26 If the identification officer considers it is not practicable to hold a video identification or identification parade requested by the suspect, the reasons shall be recorded and explained to the suspect.

3.27 A record shall be made of a person's failure or refusal to co-operate in a video identification, identification parade or group identification and, if applicable, of the grounds for obtaining images in accordance with *paragraph 3.20.*

(e) Showing films and photographs of incidents and information released to the media

3.28 Nothing in this Code inhibits showing films or photographs to the public through the national or local media, or to police officers for the purposes of recognition and tracing suspects. However, when such material is shown to potential witnesses, including police officers, see *Note 3A*, to obtain identification evidence, it shall be shown on an individual basis to avoid any possibility of collusion, and, as far as possible, the showing shall follow the principles for video identification if the suspect is known, see *Annex A*, or identification by photographs if the suspect is not known, see *Annex E.*

3.29 When a broadcast or publication is made, see *paragraph 3.28*, a copy of the relevant material released to the media for the purposes of recognising or tracing the suspect, shall be kept. The suspect or their solicitor shall be allowed to view such material before any procedures under *paragraphs 3.5* to *3.10, 3.21 or 3.23* are carried out, provided it is practicable and would not unreasonably delay the investigation. Each witness involved in the procedure shall be asked, after they have taken part, whether they have seen any broadcast or published films or photographs relating to the offence or any description of the suspect and their replies shall be recorded. This paragraph does not affect any separate requirement under the Criminal Procedure and Investigations Act 1996 to retain material in connection with criminal investigations.

(f) Destruction and retention of photographs taken or used in identification procedures

3.30 PACE, section 64A, see *paragraph 5.12*, provides powers to take photographs of suspects and allows these photographs to be used or disclosed only for purposes related to the prevention or detection of crime, the investigation of offences or the conduct of prosecutions by, or on behalf of, police or other law enforcement and prosecuting authorities inside and outside the United Kingdom or the enforcement of a sentence. After being so used or disclosed, they may be retained but can only be used or disclosed for the same purposes.

3.31 Subject to *paragraph 3.33*, the photographs (and all negatives and copies), of suspects not taken in accordance with the provisions in *paragraph 5.12* which are taken for the purposes of, or in connection with, the identification procedures in *paragraphs 3.5* to *3.10, 3.21* or *3.23* must be destroyed unless the suspect:

(a) is charged with, or informed they may be prosecuted for, a recordable offence;
(b) is prosecuted for a recordable offence;
(c) is cautioned for a recordable offence or given a warning or reprimand in accordance with the Crime and Disorder Act 1998 for a recordable offence; or
(d) gives informed consent, in writing, for the photograph or images to be retained for purposes described in *paragraph 3.30.*

3.32 When *paragraph 3.31* requires the destruction of any photograph, the person must be given an opportunity to witness the destruction or to have a certificate confirming the destruction if they request one within five days of being informed that the destruction is required.

3.33 Nothing in *paragraph 3.31* affects any separate requirement under the Criminal Procedure and Investigations Act 1996 to retain material in connection with criminal investigations.

Notes for guidance

3A *Except for the provisions of Annex E, paragraph 1, a police officer who is a witness for the purposes of this part of the Code is subject to the same principles and procedures as a civilian witness.*

3B *When a witness attending an identification procedure has previously been shown photographs, or been shown or provided with computerised or artist's composite likenesses, or similar likenesses or pictures, it is the officer in charge of the investigation's responsibility to make the identification officer aware of this.*

3C *The purpose of paragraph 3.19 is to avoid or reduce delay in arranging identification procedures by enabling the required information and warnings, see sub-paragraphs 3.17(ix) and 3.17(xii), to be given at the earliest opportunity.*

3D *Paragraph 3.21 would apply when a known suspect deliberately makes themself 'unavailable' in order to delay or frustrate arrangements for obtaining identification evidence. It also applies when a suspect refuses or fails to take part in a video identification, an identification parade or a group identification, or refuses or fails to take part in the only practicable options from that list. It enables any suitable images of the suspect, moving or still, which are available or can be obtained, to be used in an identification procedure. Examples include images from custody and other CCTV systems and from visually recorded interview records, see Code F Note for Guidance 2D.*

3E *When it is proposed to show photographs to a witness in accordance with Annex E, it is the responsibility of the officer in charge of the investigation to confirm to the officer responsible for supervising and directing the showing, that the first description of the suspect given by that witness has been recorded. If this description has not been recorded, the procedure under Annex E must be postponed. See Annex E paragraph 2.*

3F *The admissibility and value of identification evidence obtained when carrying out the procedure under paragraph 3.2 may be compromised if:*

(a) before a person is identified, the witness' attention is specifically drawn to that person; or

(b) the suspect's identity becomes known before the procedure.

4 Identification by fingerprints and footwear impressions

(A) Taking fingerprints in connection with a criminal investigation

(a) General

4.1 References to 'fingerprints' means any record, produced by any method, of the skin pattern and other physical characteristics or features of a person's:

(i) fingers; or

(ii) palms.

(b) Action

4.2 A person's fingerprints may be taken in connection with the investigation of an offence only with their consent or if *paragraph 4.3* applies. If the person is at a police station consent must be in writing.

4.3 PACE, section 61, provides powers to take fingerprints without consent from any person over the age of ten years:

(a) under section 61(3), from a person detained at a police station in consequence of being arrested for a recordable offence, see Note 4A, if they have not had their fingerprints taken in the course of the investigation of the offence unless those previously taken fingerprints are not a complete set or some or all of those fingerprints are not of sufficient quality to allow satisfactory analysis, comparison or matching.

(b) under section 61(4), from a person detained at a police station who has been charged with a recordable offence, see Note 4A, or informed they will be reported for such an offence if they have not had their fingerprints taken in the course of the investigation of the offence unless those previously taken fingerprints are not a complete set or some or all of those fingerprints are not of sufficient quality to allow satisfactory analysis, comparison or matching.

(c) under section 61(4A), from a person who has been bailed to appear at a court or police station if the person:

(i) has answered to bail for a person whose fingerprints were taken previously and there are reasonable grounds for believing they are not the same person; or

(ii) who has answered to bail claims to be a different person from a person whose fingerprints were previously taken;

and in either case, the court or an officer of inspector rank or above, authorises the fingerprints to be taken at the court or police station;

(d) under section 61(6), from a person who has been:

(i) convicted of a recordable offence;

(ii) given a caution in respect of a recordable offence which, at the time of the caution, the person admitted; or

(iii) warned or reprimanded under the Crime and Disorder Act 1998, section 65, for a recordable offence.

4.4 PACE, section 27, provides power to:

(a) require the person as in *paragraph 4.3(d)* to attend a police station to have their fingerprints taken if the:

(i) person has not been in police detention for the offence and has not had their fingerprints taken in the course of the investigation of that offence; or

(ii) fingerprints that were taken from the person in the course of the investigation of that offence, do not constitute a complete set or some, or all, of the fingerprints are not of sufficient quality to allow satisfactory analysis, comparison or matching; and

(b) arrest, without warrant, a person who fails to comply with the requirement.

Note: The requirement must be made within one month of the date the person is convicted, cautioned, warned or reprimanded and the person must be given a period of at least 7 days within which to attend. This 7 day period need not fall during the month allowed for making the requirement.

4.5 A person's fingerprints may be taken, as above, electronically.

4.6 Reasonable force may be used, if necessary, to take a person's fingerprints without their consent under the powers as in *paragraphs 4.3* and *4.4.*

4.7 Before any fingerprints are taken with, or without, consent as above, the person must be informed:

(a) of the reason their fingerprints are to be taken;

(b) of the grounds on which the relevant authority has been given if the power mentioned in *paragraph 4.3 (c) applies;*

(c) that their fingerprints may be retained and may be subject of a speculative search against other fingerprints, see *Note 4B,* unless destruction of the fingerprints is required in accordance with *Annex F, Part (a)*; and

(d) that if their fingerprints are required to be destroyed, they may witness their destruction as provided for in *Annex F, Part (a).*

(c) Documentation

4.8 A record must be made as soon as possible, of the reason for taking a person's fingerprints without consent. If force is used, a record shall be made of the circumstances and those present.

4.9 A record shall be made when a person has been informed under the terms of *paragraph 4.7(c)*, of the possibility that their fingerprints may be subject of a speculative search.

(B) Taking fingerprints in connection with immigration enquiries

Action

4.10 A person's fingerprints may be taken for the purposes of Immigration Service enquiries in accordance with powers and procedures other than under PACE and for which the Immigration Service (not the police) are responsible, only with the person's consent in writing or if *paragraph 4.11* applies.

4.11 Powers to take fingerprints for these purposes without consent are given to police and immigration officers under the:

(a) Immigration Act 1971, Schedule 2, paragraph 18(2), when it is reasonably necessary for the purposes of identifying a person detained under the Immigration Act 1971, Schedule 2, paragraph 16 (Detention of person liable to examination or removal);

(b) Immigration and Asylum Act 1999, section 141(7)(a), from a person who fails to produce, on arrival, a valid passport with a photograph or some other document satisfactorily establishing their identity and nationality if an immigration officer does not consider the person has a reasonable excuse for the failure;

(c) Immigration and Asylum Act 1999, section 141(7)(b), from a person who has been refused entry to the UK but has been temporarily admitted if an immigration officer reasonably suspects the person might break a condition imposed on them relating to residence or reporting to a police or immigration officer, and their decision is confirmed by a chief immigration officer;

(d) Immigration and Asylum Act 1999, section 141(7)(c), when directions are given to remove a person:
- as an illegal entrant,
- liable to removal under the Immigration and Asylum Act 1999, section 10,
- who is the subject of a deportation order from the UK;

(e) Immigration and Asylum Act 1999, section 141(7)(d), from a person arrested under UK immigration laws under the Immigration Act 1971, Schedule 2, paragraph 17;

(f) Immigration and Asylum Act 1999, section 141(7)(e), from a person who has made a claim:
- for asylum
- under article 3 of the European Convention on Human Rights; or

(g) Immigration and Asylum Act 1999, section 141(7)(f), from a person who is a dependant of someone who falls into (b) to (f) above.

4.12 The Immigration and Asylum Act 1999, section 142(3), gives a police and immigration officer power to arrest, without warrant, a person who fails to comply with a requirement imposed by the Secretary of State to attend a specified place for fingerprinting.

4.13 Before any fingerprints are taken, with or without consent, the person must be informed:

(a) of the reason their fingerprints are to be taken;

(b) the fingerprints, and all copies of them, will be destroyed in accordance with *Annex F, Part B*.

4.14 Reasonable force may be used, if necessary, to take a person's fingerprints without their consent under powers as in *paragraph 4.11*.

4.15 *Paragraphs 4.1* and *4.8* apply.

(C) Taking footwear impressions in connection with a criminal investigation

(a) Action

4.16 Impressions of a person's footwear may be taken in connection with the investigation of an offence only with their consent or if *paragraph 4.17* applies. If the person is at a police station consent must be in writing.

4.17 PACE, section 61A, provides power for a police officer to take footwear impressions without consent from any person over the age of ten years who is detained at a police station:

(a) in consequence of being arrested for a recordable offence, see *Note 4A*; or if the detainee has been charged with a recordable offence, or informed they will be reported for such an offence; and

(b) the detainee has not had an impression of their footwear taken in the course of the investigation of the offence unless the previously taken impression is not complete or is not of sufficient quality to allow satisfactory analysis, comparison or matching (whether in the case in question or generally).

4.18 Reasonable force may be used, if necessary, to take a footwear impression from a detainee without consent under the power in *paragraph 4.17*.

4.19 Before any footwear impression is taken with, or without, consent as above, the person must be informed:

(a) of the reason the impression is to be taken;

(b) that the impression may be retained and may be subject of a speculative search against other impressions, see *Note 4B*, unless destruction of the impression is required in accordance with *Annex F, Part (a)*; and

(c) that if their footwear impressions are required to be destroyed, they may witness their destruction as provided for in *Annex F, Part (a)*.

(b) Documentation

4.20 A record must be made as soon as possible, of the reason for taking a person's footwear impressions without consent. If force is used, a record shall be made of the circumstances and those present.

4.21 A record shall be made when a person has been informed under the terms of *paragraph 4.19(b)*, of the possibility that their footwear impressions may be subject of a speculative search.

Notes for guidance

4A *References to 'recordable offences' in this Code relate to those offences for which convictions, cautions, reprimands and warnings may be recorded in national police records. See PACE, section 27(4). The recordable offences current at the time when this Code was prepared, are any offences which carry a sentence of imprisonment on conviction (irrespective of the period, or the age of the offender or actual sentence passed) as well as the non-imprisonable offences under the Vagrancy Act 1824 sections 3 and 4 (begging and persistent begging), the Street Offences Act 1959, section 1 (loitering or soliciting for purposes of prostitution), the Road Traffic Act 1988, section 25 (tampering with motor vehicles), the Criminal Justice and Public Order Act 1994, section 167 (touting for hire car services) and others listed in the National Police Records (Recordable Offences) Regulations 2000 as amended.*

4B *Fingerprints, footwear impressions or a DNA sample (and the information derived from it) taken from a person arrested on suspicion of being involved in a recordable offence, or charged with such an offence, or informed they will be reported for such an offence, may be subject of a speculative search. This means the fingerprints, footwear impressions or DNA sample may be checked against other fingerprints, footwear impressions and DNA records held by, or on behalf of, the police and other law enforcement authorities in, or outside, the UK, or held in connection with, or as a result of, an investigation of an offence inside or outside the UK. Fingerprints, footwear impressions and samples taken from a person suspected of committing a recordable offence but not arrested, charged or informed they will be reported for it, may be subject to a speculative search only if the person consents in writing. The following is an example of a basic form of words:*

> *"I consent to my fingerprints, footwear impressions and DNA sample and information derived from it being retained and used only for purposes related to the prevention and detection of a crime, the investigation of an offence or the conduct of a prosecution either nationally or internationally.*

I understand that my fingerprints, footwear impressions or DNA sample may be checked against other fingerprint, footwear impressions and DNA records held by or on behalf of relevant law enforcement authorities, either nationally or internationally.

I understand that once I have given my consent for my fingerprints, footwear impressions or DNA sample to be retained and used I cannot withdraw this consent."

See Annex F regarding the retention and use of fingerprints and footwear impressions taken with consent for elimination purposes.

5 Examinations to establish identity and the taking of photographs

(A) Detainees at police stations

(a) Searching or examination of detainees at police stations

5.1 PACE, section 54A (1), allows a detainee at a police station to be searched or examined or both, to establish:

(a) whether they have any marks, features or injuries that would tend to identify them as a person involved in the commission of an offence and to photograph any identifying marks, see *paragraph 5.5*; or

(b) their identity, see *Note 5A*.

A person detained at a police station to be searched under a stop and search power, see Code A, is not a detainee for the purposes of these powers.

5.2 A search and/or examination to find marks under section 54A (1) (a) may be carried out without the detainee's consent, see *paragraph 2.12*, only if authorised by an officer of at least inspector rank when consent has been withheld or it is not practicable to obtain consent, see *Note 5D*.

5.3 A search or examination to establish a suspect's identity under section 54A (1) (b) may be carried out without the detainee's consent, see *paragraph 2.12*, only if authorised by an officer of at least inspector rank when the detainee has refused to identify themselves or the authorising officer has reasonable grounds for suspecting the person is not who they claim to be.

5.4 Any marks that assist in establishing the detainee's identity, or their identification as a person involved in the commission of an offence, are identifying marks. Such marks may be photographed with the detainee's consent, see *paragraph 2.12*; or without their consent if it is withheld or it is not practicable to obtain it, see *Note 5D*.

5.5 A detainee may only be searched, examined and photographed under section 54A, by a police officer of the same sex.

5.6 Any photographs of identifying marks, taken under section 54A, may be used or disclosed only for purposes related to the prevention or detection of crime, the investigation of offences or the conduct of prosecutions by, or on behalf of, police or other law enforcement and prosecuting authorities inside, and outside, the UK. After being so used or disclosed, the photograph may be retained but must not be used or disclosed except for these purposes, see *Note 5B*.

5.7 The powers, as in *paragraph 5.1*, do not affect any separate requirement under the Criminal Procedure and Investigations Act 1996 to retain material in connection with criminal investigations.

5.8 Authority for the search and/or examination for the purposes of *paragraphs 5.2* and *5.3* may be given orally or in writing. If given orally, the authorising officer must confirm it in writing as soon as practicable. A separate authority is required for each purpose which applies.

5.9 If it is established a person is unwilling to co-operate sufficiently to enable a search and/or examination to take place or a suitable photograph to be taken, an officer may use reasonable force to:

(a) search and/or examine a detainee without their consent; and
(b) photograph any identifying marks without their consent.

5.10 The thoroughness and extent of any search or examination carried out in accordance with the powers in section 54A must be no more than the officer considers necessary to achieve the required purpose. Any search or examination which involves the removal of more than the person's outer clothing shall be conducted in accordance with Code C, Annex A, paragraph 11.

5.11 An intimate search may not be carried out under the powers in section 54A.

(b) Photographing detainees at police stations and other persons elsewhere than at a police station

5.12 Under PACE, section 64A, an officer may photograph:

(a) any person whilst they are detained at a police station; and
(b) any person who is elsewhere than at a police station and who has been:-
  (i) arrested by a constable for an offence;
  (ii) taken into custody by a constable after being arrested for an offence by a person other than a constable;
  (iii) made subject to a requirement to wait with a community support officer under *paragraph 2(3) or (3B)* of Schedule 4 to the Police Reform Act 2002;
  (iv) given a penalty notice by a constable in uniform under Chapter 1 of Part 1 of the Criminal Justice and Police Act 2001, a penalty notice by a constable under section 444A of the Education Act 1996, or a fixed penalty notice by a constable in uniform under section 54 of the Road Traffic Offenders Act 1988;
  (v) given a notice in relation to a relevant fixed penalty offence (within the meaning of paragraph 1 of Schedule 4 to the Police Reform Act 2002) by a community support officer by virtue of a designation applying that paragraph to him;
  (vi) given a notice in relation to a relevant fixed penalty offence (within the meaning of paragraph 1 of Schedule 5 to the Police Reform Act 2002) by an accredited person by virtue of accreditation specifying that that paragraph applies to him; or
  (vii) given a direction to leave and not return to a specified location for up to 48 hours by a police constable (under section 27 of the Violent Crime Reduction Act 2006).

5.12A Photographs taken under PACE, section 64A:

(a) may be taken with the person's consent, or without their consent if consent is withheld or it is not practicable to obtain their consent, see *Note 5E*; and
(b) may be used or disclosed only for purposes related to the prevention or detection of crime, the investigation of offences or the conduct of prosecutions by, or on behalf of, police or other law enforcement and prosecuting authorities inside and outside the United Kingdom or the enforcement of any sentence or order made by a court when dealing with an offence. After being so used or disclosed, they may be retained but can only be used or disclosed for the same purposes. see *Note 5B*.

5.13 The officer proposing to take a detainee's photograph may, for this purpose, require the person to remove any item or substance worn on, or over, all, or any part of, their head or face. If they do not comply with such a requirement, the officer may remove the item or substance.

5.14 If it is established the detainee is unwilling to co-operate sufficiently to enable a suitable photograph to be taken and it is not reasonably practicable to take the photograph covertly, an officer may use reasonable force, see *Note 5F*.

(a) to take their photograph without their consent; and
(b) for the purpose of taking the photograph, remove any item or substance worn on, or over, all, or any part of, the person's head or face which they have failed to remove when asked.

5.15 For the purposes of this Code, a photograph may be obtained without the person's consent by making a copy of an image of them taken at any time on a camera system installed anywhere in the police station.

(c) Information to be given

5.16 When a person is searched, examined or photographed under the provisions as in *paragraph 5.1* and *5.12*, or their photograph obtained as in *paragraph 5.15*, they must be informed of the:

(a) purpose of the search, examination or photograph;

(b) grounds on which the relevant authority, if applicable, has been given; and

(c) purposes for which the photograph may be used, disclosed or retained.

This information must be given before the search or examination commences or the photograph is taken, except if the photograph is:

(i) to be taken covertly;

(ii) obtained as in *paragraph 5.15*, in which case the person must be informed as soon as practicable after the photograph is taken or obtained.

(d) Documentation

5.17 A record must be made when a detainee is searched, examined, or a photograph of the person, or any identifying marks found on them, are taken. The record must include the:

(a) identity, subject to paragraph 2.18, of the officer carrying out the search, examination or taking the photograph;

(b) purpose of the search, examination or photograph and the outcome;

(c) detainee's consent to the search, examination or photograph, or the reason the person was searched, examined or photographed without consent;

(d) giving of any authority as in *paragraphs 5.2* and *5.3*, the grounds for giving it and the authorising officer.

5.18 If force is used when searching, examining or taking a photograph in accordance with this section, a record shall be made of the circumstances and those present.

(B) Persons at police stations not detained

5.19 When there are reasonable grounds for suspecting the involvement of a person in a criminal offence, but that person is at a police station **voluntarily** and not detained, the provisions of *paragraphs 5.1* to *5.18* should apply, subject to the modifications in the following paragraphs.

5.20 References to the 'person being detained' and to the powers mentioned in *paragraph 5.1* which apply only to detainees at police stations shall be omitted.

5.21 Force may not be used to:

(a) search and/or examine the person to:

(i) discover whether they have any marks that would tend to identify them as a person involved in the commission of an offence; or

(ii) establish their identity, see *Note 5A*;

(b) take photographs of any identifying marks, see *paragraph 5.4*; or

(c) take a photograph of the person.

5.22 Subject to *paragraph 5.24*, the photographs of persons or of their identifying marks which are not taken in accordance with the provisions mentioned in *paragraphs 5.1* or *5.12*, must be destroyed (together with any negatives and copies) unless the person:

(a) is charged with, or informed they may be prosecuted for, a recordable offence;

(b) is prosecuted for a recordable offence;

(c) is cautioned for a recordable offence or given a warning or reprimand in accordance with the Crime and Disorder Act 1998 for a recordable offence; or

(d) gives informed consent, in writing, for the photograph or image to be retained as in *paragraph 5.6*.

5.23 When *paragraph 5.22* requires the destruction of any photograph, the person must be given an opportunity to witness the destruction or to have a certificate confirming the destruction provided they so request the certificate within five days of being informed the destruction is required.

5.24 Nothing in *paragraph 5.22* affects any separate requirement under the Criminal Procedure and Investigations Act 1996 to retain material in connection with criminal investigations.

Notes for guidance

5A The conditions under which fingerprints may be taken to assist in establishing a person's identity, are described in Section 4.

5B Examples of purposes related to the prevention or detection of crime, the investigation of offences or the conduct of prosecutions include:

(a) checking the photograph against other photographs held in records or in connection with, or as a result of, an investigation of an offence to establish whether the person is liable to arrest for other offences;

(b) when the person is arrested at the same time as other people, or at a time when it is likely that other people will be arrested, using the photograph to help establish who was arrested, at what time and where;

(c) when the real identity of the person is not known and cannot be readily ascertained or there are reasonable grounds for doubting a name and other personal details given by the person, are their real name and personal details. In these circumstances, using or disclosing the photograph to help to establish or verify their real identity or determine whether they are liable to arrest for some other offence, e.g. by checking it against other photographs held in records or in connection with, or as a result of, an investigation of an offence;

(d) when it appears any identification procedure in section 3 may need to be arranged for which the person's photograph would assist;

(e) when the person's release without charge may be required, and if the release is:

(i) on bail to appear at a police station, using the photograph to help verify the person's identity when they answer their bail and if the person does not answer their bail, to assist in arresting them; or

(ii) without bail, using the photograph to help verify their identity or assist in locating them for the purposes of serving them with a summons to appear at court in criminal proceedings;

(f) when the person has answered to bail at a police station and there are reasonable grounds for doubting they are the person who was previously granted bail, using the photograph to help establish or verify their identity;

(g) when the person arrested on a warrant claims to be a different person from the person named on the warrant and a photograph would help to confirm or disprove their claim;

(h) when the person has been charged with, reported for, or convicted of, a recordable offence and their photograph is not already on record as a result of (a) to (f) or their photograph is on record but their appearance has changed since it was taken and the person has not yet been released or brought before a court.

5C There is no power to arrest a person convicted of a recordable offence solely to take their photograph. The power to take photographs in this section applies only where the person is in custody as a result of the exercise of another power, e.g. arrest for fingerprinting under PACE, section 27.

5D Examples of when it would not be practicable to obtain a detainee's consent, see paragraph 2.12, to a search, examination or the taking of a photograph of an identifying mark include:

(a) when the person is drunk or otherwise unfit to give consent;

(b) when there are reasonable grounds to suspect that if the person became aware a search or examination was to take place or an identifying mark was to be photographed, they would take steps to prevent this happening, e.g. by violently resisting, covering or concealing the mark etc and it would not otherwise be possible to carry out the search or examination or to photograph any identifying mark;

(c) in the case of a juvenile, if the parent or guardian cannot be contacted in sufficient time to allow the search or examination to be carried out or the photograph to be taken.

5E *Examples of when it would not be practicable to obtain the person's consent, see paragraph 2.12, to a photograph being taken include:*

(a) when the person is drunk or otherwise unfit to give consent;

(b) when there are reasonable grounds to suspect that if the person became aware a photograph, suitable to be used or disclosed for the use and disclosure described in paragraph 5.6, was to be taken, they would take steps to prevent it being taken, e.g. by violently resisting, covering or distorting their face etc, and it would not otherwise be possible to take a suitable photograph;

(c) when, in order to obtain a suitable photograph, it is necessary to take it covertly; and

(d) in the case of a juvenile, if the parent or guardian cannot be contacted in sufficient time to allow the photograph to be taken.

5F *The use of reasonable force to take the photograph of a suspect elsewhere than at a police station must be carefully considered. In order to obtain a suspect's consent and co-operation to remove an item of religious headwear to take their photograph, a constable should consider whether in the circumstances of the situation the removal of the headwear and the taking of the photograph should be by an officer of the same sex as the person. It would be appropriate for these actions to be conducted out of public view.*

6 Identification by body samples and impressions

(A) General

6.1 References to:

(a) an 'intimate sample' mean a dental impression or sample of blood, semen or any other tissue fluid, urine, or pubic hair, or a swab taken from any part of a person's genitals or from a person's body orifice other than the mouth;

(b) a 'non-intimate sample' means:

(i) a sample of hair, other than pubic hair, which includes hair plucked with the root, see *Note 6A*;

(ii) a sample taken from a nail or from under a nail;

(iii) a swab taken from any part of a person's body other than a part from which a swab taken would be an intimate sample;

(iv) saliva;

(v) a skin impression which means any record, other than a fingerprint, which is a record, in any form and produced by any method, of the skin pattern and other physical characteristics or features of the whole, or any part of, a person's foot or of any other part of their body.

(B) Action

(a) Intimate samples

6.2 PACE, section 62, provides that intimate samples may be taken under:

(a) section 62(1), from a person in police detention only:

(i) if a police officer of inspector rank or above has reasonable grounds to believe such an impression or sample will tend to confirm or disprove the suspect's involvement in a recordable offence, see *Note 4A*, and gives authorisation for a sample to be taken; and

(ii) with the suspect's written consent;

(b) section 62(1A), from a person not in police detention but from whom two or more non-intimate samples have been taken in the course of an investigation of an offence and the samples, though suitable, have proved insufficient if:

(i) a police officer of inspector rank or above authorises it to be taken; and

(ii) the person concerned gives their written consent. See *Notes 6B* and *6C*

6.3 Before a suspect is asked to provide an intimate sample, they must be warned that if they refuse without good cause, their refusal may harm their case if it comes to trial, see *Note 6D*. If the suspect is in police detention and not legally represented, they must also be reminded of their entitlement to have free legal advice, see Code C, *paragraph 6.5*, and the reminder noted in the custody record. If *paragraph 6.2(b)* applies and the person is attending a station voluntarily, their entitlement to free legal advice as in Code C, *paragraph 3.21* shall be explained to them.

6.4 Dental impressions may only be taken by a registered dentist. Other intimate samples, except for samples of urine, may only be taken by a registered medical practitioner or registered nurse or registered paramedic.

(b) Non-intimate samples

6.5 A non-intimate sample may be taken from a detainee only with their written consent or if *paragraph 6.6* applies.

6.6 (a) under section 63, a non-intimate sample may not be taken from a person without consent and the consent must be in writing

(aa) A non-intimate sample may be taken from a person without the appropriate consent in the following circumstances:

(i) under section 63(2A) where the person is in police detention as a consequence of his arrest for a recordable offence and he has not had a non-intimate sample of the same type and from the same part of the body taken in the course of the investigation of the offence by the police or he has had such a sample taken but it proved insufficient.

(ii) Under section 63(3) (a) where he is being held in custody by the police on the authority of a court and an officer of at least the rank of inspector authorises it to be taken.

(b) under section 63(3A), from a person charged with a recordable offence or informed they will be reported for such an offence: and

(i) that person has not had a non-intimate sample taken from them in the course of the investigation; or

(ii) if they have had a sample taken, it proved unsuitable or insufficient for the same form of analysis, see *Note 6B*; or

(c) under section 63(3B), from a person convicted of a recordable offence after the date on which that provision came into effect. PACE, section 63A, describes the circumstances in which a police officer may require a person convicted of a recordable offence to attend a police station for a non-intimate sample to be taken.

6.7 Reasonable force may be used, if necessary, to take a non-intimate sample from a person without their consent under the powers mentioned in *paragraph 6.6*.

6.8 Before any intimate sample is taken with consent or non-intimate sample is taken with, or without, consent, the person must be informed:

(a) of the reason for taking the sample;

(b) of the grounds on which the relevant authority has been given;

(c) that the sample or information derived from the sample may be retained and subject of a speculative search, see *Note 6E*, unless their destruction is required as in *Annex F*, Part A.

6.9 When clothing needs to be removed in circumstances likely to cause embarrassment to the person, no person of the opposite sex who is not a registered medical practitioner or registered health care professional shall be present, (unless in the case of a juvenile, mentally disordered or mentally vulnerable person, that person specifically requests the presence of an appropriate adult of the opposite sex who is readily available) nor shall anyone whose presence is unnecessary. However, in the case of a juvenile, this is subject to the overriding proviso that such a removal of clothing may take place in the absence of the appropriate adult only if the juvenile signifies, in their presence, that they prefer the adult's absence and they agree.

(c) Documentation

6.10 A record of the reasons for taking a sample or impression and, if applicable, of its destruction must be made as soon as practicable. If force is used, a record shall be made of the circumstances and those present. If written consent is given to the taking of a sample or impression, the fact must be recorded in writing.

6.11 A record must be made of a warning given as required by *paragraph 6.3*.

6.12 A record shall be made of the fact that a person has been informed as in *paragraph 6.8(c)* that samples may be subject of a speculative search.

Notes for guidance

6A When hair samples are taken for the purpose of DNA analysis (rather than for other purposes such as making a visual match), the suspect should be permitted a reasonable choice as to what part of the body the hairs are taken from. When hairs are plucked, they should be plucked individually, unless the suspect prefers otherwise and no more should be plucked than the person taking them reasonably considers necessary for a sufficient sample.

6B (a) An insufficient sample is one which is not sufficient either in quantity or quality to provide information for a particular form of analysis, such as DNA analysis. A sample may also be insufficient if enough information cannot be obtained from it by analysis because of loss, destruction, damage or contamination of the sample or as a result of an earlier, unsuccessful attempt at analysis.

(b) An unsuitable sample is one which, by its nature, is not suitable for a particular form of analysis.

6C Nothing in paragraph 6.2 prevents intimate samples being taken for elimination purposes with the consent of the person concerned but the provisions of paragraph 2.12 relating to the role of the appropriate adult, should be applied. Paragraph 6.2(b) does not, however, apply where the non-intimate samples were previously taken under the Terrorism Act 2000, Schedule 8, paragraph 10.

6D In warning a person who is asked to provide an intimate sample as in paragraph 6.3, the following form of words may be used:

> *"You do not have to provide this sample/allow this swab or impression to be taken, but I must warn you that if you refuse without good cause, your refusal may harm your case if it comes to trial."*

6E Fingerprints or a DNA sample and the information derived from it taken from a person arrested on suspicion of being involved in a recordable offence, or charged with such an offence, or informed they will be reported for such an offence, may be subject of a speculative search. This means they may be checked against other fingerprints and DNA records held by, or on behalf of, the police and other law enforcement authorities in or outside the UK or held in connection with, or as a result of, an investigation of an offence inside or outside the UK. Fingerprints and samples taken from any other person, e.g. a person suspected of committing a recordable offence but who has not been arrested, charged or informed they will be reported for it, may be subject to a speculative search only if the person consents in writing to their fingerprints being subject of such a search. The following is an example of a basic form of words:

> *"I consent to my fingerprints/DNA sample and information derived from it being retained and used only for purposes related to the prevention and detection of a crime, the investigation of an offence or the conduct of a prosecution either nationally or internationally.*
>
> *I understand that this sample may be checked against other fingerprint/DNA records held by or on behalf of relevant law enforcement authorities, either nationally or internationally.*
>
> *I understand that once I have given my consent for the sample to be retained and used I cannot withdraw this consent."*

See Annex F regarding the retention and use of fingerprints and samples taken with consent for elimination purposes.

6F Samples of urine and non-intimate samples taken in accordance with sections 63B and 63C of PACE may not be used for identification purposes in accordance with this Code. See Code C note for guidance 17D.

ANNEX A—VIDEO IDENTIFICATION

(a) General

1. The arrangements for obtaining and ensuring the availability of a suitable set of images to be used in a video identification must be the responsibility of an identification officer, who has no direct involvement with the case.
2. The set of images must include the suspect and at least eight other people who, so far as possible, resemble the suspect in age, general appearance and position in life. Only one suspect shall appear in any set unless there are two suspects of roughly similar appearance, in which case they may be shown together with at least twelve other people.

2A If the suspect has an unusual physical feature, e.g. a facial scar, tattoo or distinctive hairstyle or hair colour which does not appear on the images of the other people that are available to be used, steps may be taken to:

(a) conceal the location of the feature on the images of the suspect and the other people; or
(b) replicate that feature on the images of the other people.

For these purposes, the feature may be concealed or replicated electronically or by any other method which it is practicable to use to ensure that the images of the suspect and other people resemble each other. The identification officer has discretion to choose whether to conceal or replicate the feature and the method to be used. If an unusual physical feature has been described by the witness, the identification officer should, if practicable, have that feature replicated. If it has not been described, concealment may be more appropriate.

2B If the identification officer decides that a feature should be concealed or replicated, the reason for the decision and whether the feature was concealed or replicated in the images shown to any witness shall be recorded.

2C If the witness requests to view an image where an unusual physical feature has been concealed or replicated without the feature being concealed or replicated, the witness may be allowed to do so.

3. The images used to conduct a video identification shall, as far as possible, show the suspect and other people in the same positions or carrying out the same sequence of movements. They shall also show the suspect and other people under identical conditions unless the identification officer reasonably believes:

   (a) because of the suspect's failure or refusal to co-operate or other reasons, it is not practicable for the conditions to be identical; and
   (b) any difference in the conditions would not direct a witness' attention to any individual image.

4. The reasons identical conditions are not practicable shall be recorded on forms provided for the purpose.
5. Provision must be made for each person shown to be identified by number.
6. If police officers are shown, any numerals or other identifying badges must be concealed. If a prison inmate is shown, either as a suspect or not, then either all, or none of, the people shown should be in prison clothing.
7. The suspect or their solicitor, friend, or appropriate adult must be given a reasonable opportunity to see the complete set of images before it is shown to any witness. If the suspect has a reasonable objection to the set of images or any of the participants, the suspect shall be asked to state the reasons for the objection. Steps shall, if practicable, be taken to remove the grounds for objection. If this is not practicable, the suspect and/or their representative shall be told why their objections cannot be met and the objection, the reason given for it and why it cannot be met shall be recorded on forms provided for the purpose.
8. Before the images are shown in accordance with *paragraph 7,* the suspect or their solicitor shall be provided with details of the first description of the suspect by any witnesses who are to attend the video identification. When a broadcast or publication is made, as in *paragraph 3.28,* the suspect or their solicitor must also be allowed to view any material released to the media by the police for the purpose of recognising or tracing the suspect, provided it is practicable and would not unreasonably delay the investigation.

9. The suspect's solicitor, if practicable, shall be given reasonable notification of the time and place the video identification is to be conducted so a representative may attend on behalf of the suspect. If a solicitor has not been instructed, this information shall be given to the suspect. The suspect may not be present when the images are shown to the witness(es). In the absence of the suspect's representative, the viewing itself shall be recorded on video. No unauthorised people may be present.

(b) Conducting the video identification

10. The identification officer is responsible for making the appropriate arrangements to make sure, before they see the set of images, witnesses are not able to communicate with each other about the case, see any of the images which are to be shown, see, or be reminded of, any photograph or description of the suspect or be given any other indication as to the suspect's identity, or overhear a witness who has already seen the material. There must be no discussion with the witness about the composition of the set of images and they must not be told whether a previous witness has made any identification.
11. Only one witness may see the set of images at a time. Immediately before the images are shown, the witness shall be told that the person they saw on a specified earlier occasion may, or may not, appear in the images they are shown and that if they cannot make a positive identification, they should say so. The witness shall be advised that at any point, they may ask to see a particular part of the set of images or to have a particular image frozen for them to study. Furthermore, it should be pointed out to the witness that there is no limit on how many times they can view the whole set of images or any part of them. However, they should be asked not to make any decision as to whether the person they saw is on the set of images until they have seen the whole set at least twice.
12. Once the witness has seen the whole set of images at least twice and has indicated that they do not want to view the images, or any part of them, again, the witness shall be asked to say whether the individual they saw in person on a specified earlier occasion has been shown and, if so, to identify them by number of the image. The witness will then be shown that image to confirm the identification, see *paragraph 17*.
13. Care must be taken not to direct the witness' attention to any one individual image or give any indication of the suspect's identity. Where a witness has previously made an identification by photographs, or a computerised or artist's composite or similar likeness, the witness must not be reminded of such a photograph or composite likeness once a suspect is available for identification by other means in accordance with this Code. Nor must the witness be reminded of any description of the suspect.
14. After the procedure, each witness shall be asked whether they have seen any broadcast or published films or photographs, or any descriptions of suspects relating to the offence and their reply shall be recorded.

(c) Image security and destruction

15. Arrangements shall be made for all relevant material containing sets of images used for specific identification procedures to be kept securely and their movements accounted for. In particular, no-one involved in the investigation shall be permitted to view the material prior to it being shown to any witness.
16. As appropriate, *paragraph 3.30* or *3.31* applies to the destruction or retention of relevant sets of images.

(d) Documentation

17. A record must be made of all those participating in, or seeing, the set of images whose names are known to the police.
18. A record of the conduct of the video identification must be made on forms provided for the purpose. This shall include anything said by the witness about any identifications or the conduct of the procedure and any reasons it was not practicable to comply with any of the provisions of this Code governing the conduct of video identifications.

ANNEX B—IDENTIFICATION PARADES

(a) General

1. A suspect must be given a reasonable opportunity to have a solicitor or friend present, and the suspect shall be asked to indicate on a second copy of the notice whether or not they wish to do so.
2. An identification parade may take place either in a normal room or one equipped with a screen permitting witnesses to see members of the identification parade without being seen. The procedures for the composition and conduct of the identification parade are the same in both cases, subject to *paragraph 8* (except that an identification parade involving a screen may take place only when the suspect's solicitor, friend or appropriate adult is present or the identification parade is recorded on video).
3. Before the identification parade takes place, the suspect or their solicitor shall be provided with details of the first description of the suspect by any witnesses who are attending the identification parade. When a broadcast or publication is made as in *paragraph 3.28*, the suspect or their solicitor should also be allowed to view any material released to the media by the police for the purpose of recognising or tracing the suspect, provided it is practicable to do so and would not unreasonably delay the investigation.

(b) Identification parades involving prison inmates

4. If a prison inmate is required for identification, and there are no security problems about the person leaving the establishment, they may be asked to participate in an identification parade or video identification.
5. An identification parade may be held in a Prison Department establishment but shall be conducted, as far as practicable under normal identification parade rules. Members of the public shall make up the identification parade unless there are serious security, or control, objections to their admission to the establishment. In such cases, or if a group or video identification is arranged within the establishment, other inmates may participate. If an inmate is the suspect, they are not required to wear prison clothing for the identification parade unless the other people taking part are other inmates in similar clothing, or are members of the public who are prepared to wear prison clothing for the occasion.

(c) Conduct of the identification parade

6. Immediately before the identification parade, the suspect must be reminded of the procedures governing its conduct and cautioned in the terms of Code C, paragraphs 10.5 or 10.6, as appropriate.
7. All unauthorised people must be excluded from the place where the identification parade is held.
8. Once the identification parade has been formed, everything afterwards, in respect of it, shall take place in the presence and hearing of the suspect and any interpreter, solicitor, friend or appropriate adult who is present (unless the identification parade involves a screen, in which case everything said to, or by, any witness at the place where the identification parade is held, must be said in the hearing and presence of the suspect's solicitor, friend or appropriate adult or be recorded on video).
9. The identification parade shall consist of at least eight people (in addition to the suspect) who, so far as possible, resemble the suspect in age, height, general appearance and position in life. Only one suspect shall be included in an identification parade unless there are two suspects of roughly similar appearance, in which case they may be paraded together with at least twelve other people. In no circumstances shall more than two suspects be included in one identification parade and where there are separate identification parades, they shall be made up of different people.
10. If the suspect has an unusual physical feature, e.g. a facial scar, tattoo or distinctive hairstyle or hair colour which cannot be replicated on other members of the identification parade, steps may be taken to conceal the location of that feature on the suspect and the other members

of the identification parade if the suspect and their solicitor, or appropriate adult, agree. For example, by use of a plaster or a hat, so that all members of the identification parade resemble each other in general appearance.

11. When all members of a similar group are possible suspects, separate identification parades shall be held for each unless there are two suspects of similar appearance when they may appear on the same identification parade with at least twelve other members of the group who are not suspects. When police officers in uniform form an identification parade any numerals or other identifying badges shall be concealed.
12. When the suspect is brought to the place where the identification parade is to be held, they shall be asked if they have any objection to the arrangements for the identification parade or to any of the other participants in it and to state the reasons for the objection. The suspect may obtain advice from their solicitor or friend, if present, before the identification parade proceeds. If the suspect has a reasonable objection to the arrangements or any of the participants, steps shall, if practicable, be taken to remove the grounds for objection. When it is not practicable to do so, the suspect shall be told why their objections cannot be met and the objection, the reason given for it and why it cannot be met, shall be recorded on forms provided for the purpose.
13. The suspect may select their own position in the line, but may not otherwise interfere with the order of the people forming the line. When there is more than one witness, the suspect must be told, after each witness has left the room, that they can, if they wish, change position in the line. Each position in the line must be clearly numbered, whether by means of a number laid on the floor in front of each identification parade member or by other means.
14. Appropriate arrangements must be made to make sure, before witnesses attend the identification parade, they are not able to:
    (i) communicate with each other about the case or overhear a witness who has already seen the identification parade;
    (ii) see any member of the identification parade;
    (iii) see, or be reminded of, any photograph or description of the suspect or be given any other indication as to the suspect's identity; or
    (iv) see the suspect before or after the identification parade.
15. The person conducting a witness to an identification parade must not discuss with them the composition of the identification parade and, in particular, must not disclose whether a previous witness has made any identification.
16. Witnesses shall be brought in one at a time. Immediately before the witness inspects the identification parade, they shall be told the person they saw on a specified earlier occasion may, or may not, be present and if they cannot make a positive identification, they should say so. The witness must also be told they should not make any decision about whether the person they saw is on the identification parade until they have looked at each member at least twice.
17. When the officer or police staff (see paragraph 3.11) conducting the identification procedure is satisfied the witness has properly looked at each member of the identification parade, they shall ask the witness whether the person they saw on a specified earlier occasion is on the identification parade and, if so, to indicate the number of the person concerned, see *paragraph 28.*
18. If the witness wishes to hear any identification parade member speak, adopt any specified posture or move, they shall first be asked whether they can identify any person(s) on the identification parade on the basis of appearance only. When the request is to hear members of the identification parade speak, the witness shall be reminded that the participants in the identification parade have been chosen on the basis of physical appearance only. Members of the identification parade may then be asked to comply with the witness' request to hear them speak, see them move or adopt any specified posture.
19. If the witness requests that the person they have indicated remove anything used for the purposes of *paragraph 10* to conceal the location of an unusual physical feature, that person may be asked to remove it.

20. If the witness makes an identification after the identification parade has ended, the suspect and, if present, their solicitor, interpreter or friend shall be informed. When this occurs, consideration should be given to allowing the witness a second opportunity to identify the suspect.
21. After the procedure, each witness shall be asked whether they have seen any broadcast or published films or photographs or any descriptions of suspects relating to the offence and their reply shall be recorded.
22. When the last witness has left, the suspect shall be asked whether they wish to make any comments on the conduct of the identification parade.

(d) Documentation

23. A video recording must normally be taken of the identification parade. If that is impracticable, a colour photograph must be taken. A copy of the video recording or photograph shall be supplied, on request, to the suspect or their solicitor within a reasonable time.
24. As appropriate, *paragraph 3.30* or *3.31*, should apply to any photograph or video taken as in *paragraph 23*.
25. If any person is asked to leave an identification parade because they are interfering with its conduct, the circumstances shall be recorded.
26. A record must be made of all those present at an identification parade whose names are known to the police.
27. If prison inmates make up an identification parade, the circumstances must be recorded.
28. A record of the conduct of any identification parade must be made on forms provided for the purpose. This shall include anything said by the witness or the suspect about any identifications or the conduct of the procedure, and any reasons it was not practicable to comply with any of this Code's provisions.

ANNEX C—GROUP IDENTIFICATION

(a) General

1. The purpose of this Annex is to make sure, as far as possible, group identifications follow the principles and procedures for identification parades so the conditions are fair to the suspect in the way they test the witness' ability to make an identification.
2. Group identifications may take place either with the suspect's consent and cooperation or covertly without their consent.
3. The location of the group identification is a matter for the identification officer, although the officer may take into account any representations made by the suspect, appropriate adult, their solicitor or friend.
4. The place where the group identification is held should be one where other people are either passing by or waiting around informally, in groups such that the suspect is able to join them and be capable of being seen by the witness at the same time as others in the group. For example people leaving an escalator, pedestrians walking through a shopping centre, passengers on railway and bus stations, waiting in queues or groups or where people are standing or sitting in groups in other public places.
5. If the group identification is to be held covertly, the choice of locations will be limited by the places where the suspect can be found and the number of other people present at that time. In these cases, suitable locations might be along regular routes travelled by the suspect, including buses or trains or public places frequented by the suspect.
6. Although the number, age, sex, race and general description and style of clothing of other people present at the location cannot be controlled by the identification officer, in selecting the location the officer must consider the general appearance and numbers of people likely to be present. In particular, the officer must reasonably expect that over the period the witness observes the group, they will be able to see, from time to time, a number of others whose appearance is broadly similar to that of the suspect.

7. A group identification need not be held if the identification officer believes, because of the unusual appearance of the suspect, none of the locations it would be practicable to use satisfy the requirements of *paragraph 6* necessary to make the identification fair.
8. Immediately after a group identification procedure has taken place (with or without the suspect's consent), a colour photograph or video should be taken of the general scene, if practicable, to give a general impression of the scene and the number of people present. Alternatively, if it is practicable, the group identification may be video recorded.
9. If it is not practicable to take the photograph or video in accordance with *paragraph 8,* a photograph or film of the scene should be taken later at a time determined by the identification officer if the officer considers it practicable to do so.
10. An identification carried out in accordance with this Code remains a group identification even though, at the time of being seen by the witness, the suspect was on their own rather than in a group.
11. Before the group identification takes place, the suspect or their solicitor shall be provided with details of the first description of the suspect by any witnesses who are to attend the identification. When a broadcast or publication is made, as in *paragraph 3.28*, the suspect or their solicitor should also be allowed to view any material released by the police to the media for the purposes of recognising or tracing the suspect, provided that it is practicable and would not unreasonably delay the investigation.
12. After the procedure, each witness shall be asked whether they have seen any broadcast or published films or photographs or any descriptions of suspects relating to the offence and their reply recorded.

(b) Identification with the consent of the suspect

13. A suspect must be given a reasonable opportunity to have a solicitor or friend present. They shall be asked to indicate on a second copy of the notice whether or not they wish to do so.
14. The witness, the person carrying out the procedure and the suspect's solicitor, appropriate adult, friend or any interpreter for the witness, may be concealed from the sight of the individuals in the group they are observing, if the person carrying out the procedure considers this assists the conduct of the identification.
15. The person conducting a witness to a group identification must not discuss with them the forthcoming group identification and, in particular, must not disclose whether a previous witness has made any identification.
16. Anything said to, or by, the witness during the procedure about the identification should be said in the presence and hearing of those present at the procedure.
17. Appropriate arrangements must be made to make sure, before witnesses attend the group identification, they are not able to:
    (i) communicate with each other about the case or overhear a witness who has already been given an opportunity to see the suspect in the group;
    (ii) see the suspect; or
    (iii) see, or be reminded of, any photographs or description of the suspect or be given any other indication of the suspect's identity.
18. Witnesses shall be brought one at a time to the place where they are to observe the group. Immediately before the witness is asked to look at the group, the person conducting the procedure shall tell them that the person they saw may, or may not, be in the group and that if they cannot make a positive identification, they should say so.The witness shall be asked to observe the group in which the suspect is to appear. The way in which the witness should do this will depend on whether the group is moving or stationary.

Moving group

19. When the group in which the suspect is to appear is moving, e.g. leaving an escalator, the provisions of *paragraphs 20* to *24* should be followed.
20. If two or more suspects consent to a group identification, each should be the subject of separate identification procedures. These may be conducted consecutively on the same occasion.

21. The person conducting the procedure shall tell the witness to observe the group and ask them to point out any person they think they saw on the specified earlier occasion.
22. Once the witness has been informed as in *paragraph 21* the suspect should be allowed to take whatever position in the group they wish.
23. When the witness points out a person as in *paragraph 21* they shall, if practicable, be asked to take a closer look at the person to confirm the identification. If this is not practicable, or they cannot confirm the identification, they shall be asked how sure they are that the person they have indicated is the relevant person.
24. The witness should continue to observe the group for the period which the person conducting the procedure reasonably believes is necessary in the circumstances for them to be able to make comparisons between the suspect and other individuals of broadly similar appearance to the suspect as in *paragraph 6*.

Stationary groups

25. When the group in which the suspect is to appear is stationary, e.g. people waiting in a queue, the provisions of *paragraphs 26* to *29* should be followed.
26. If two or more suspects consent to a group identification, each should be subject to separate identification procedures unless they are of broadly similar appearance when they may appear in the same group. When separate group identifications are held, the groups must be made up of different people.
27. The suspect may take whatever position in the group they wish. If there is more than one witness, the suspect must be told, out of the sight and hearing of any witness, that they can, if they wish, change their position in the group.
28. The witness shall be asked to pass along, or amongst, the group and to look at each person in the group at least twice, taking as much care and time as possible according to the circumstances, before making an identification. Once the witness has done this, they shall be asked whether the person they saw on the specified earlier occasion is in the group and to indicate any such person by whatever means the person conducting the procedure considers appropriate in the circumstances. If this is not practicable, the witness shall be asked to point out any person they think they saw on the earlier occasion.
29. When the witness makes an indication as in *paragraph 28,* arrangements shall be made, if practicable, for the witness to take a closer look at the person to confirm the identification. If this is not practicable, or the witness is unable to confirm the identification, they shall be asked how sure they are that the person they have indicated is the relevant person.

All cases

30. If the suspect unreasonably delays joining the group, or having joined the group, deliberately conceals themselves from the sight of the witness, this may be treated as a refusal to co-operate in a group identification.
31. If the witness identifies a person other than the suspect, that person should be informed what has happened and asked if they are prepared to give their name and address. There is no obligation upon any member of the public to give these details. There shall be no duty to record any details of any other member of the public present in the group or at the place where the procedure is conducted.
32. When the group identification has been completed, the suspect shall be asked whether they wish to make any comments on the conduct of the procedure.
33. If the suspect has not been previously informed, they shall be told of any identifications made by the witnesses.

(c) Identification without the suspect's consent

34. Group identifications held covertly without the suspect's consent should, as far as practicable, follow the rules for conduct of group identification by consent.
35. A suspect has no right to have a solicitor, appropriate adult or friend present as the identification will take place without the knowledge of the suspect.

36. Any number of suspects may be identified at the same time.

(d) Identifications in police stations

37. Group identifications should only take place in police stations for reasons of safety, security or because it is not practicable to hold them elsewhere.
38. The group identification may take place either in a room equipped with a screen permitting witnesses to see members of the group without being seen, or anywhere else in the police station that the identification officer considers appropriate.
39. Any of the additional safeguards applicable to identification parades should be followed if the identification officer considers it is practicable to do so in the circumstances.

(e) Identifications involving prison inmates

40. A group identification involving a prison inmate may only be arranged in the prison or at a police station.
41. When a group identification takes place involving a prison inmate, whether in a prison or in a police station, the arrangements should follow those in *paragraphs 37* to *39*. If a group identification takes place within a prison, other inmates may participate. If an inmate is the suspect, they do not have to wear prison clothing for the group identification unless the other participants are wearing the same clothing.

(f) Documentation

42. When a photograph or video is taken as in *paragraph 8* or *9*, a copy of the photograph or video shall be supplied on request to the suspect or their solicitor within a reasonable time.
43. *Paragraph 3.30* or *3.31*, as appropriate, shall apply when the photograph or film taken in accordance with *paragraph 8* or *9* includes the suspect.
44. A record of the conduct of any group identification must be made on forms provided for the purpose. This shall include anything said by the witness or suspect about any identifications or the conduct of the procedure and any reasons why it was not practicable to comply with any of the provisions of this Code governing the conduct of group identifications.

ANNEX D—CONFRONTATION BY A WITNESS

1. Before the confrontation takes place, the witness must be told that the person they saw may, or may not, be the person they are to confront and that if they are not that person, then the witness should say so.
2. Before the confrontation takes place the suspect or their solicitor shall be provided with details of the first description of the suspect given by any witness who is to attend. When a broadcast or publication is made, as in *paragraph 3.28*, the suspect or their solicitor should also be allowed to view any material released to the media for the purposes of recognising or tracing the suspect, provided it is practicable to do so and would not unreasonably delay the investigation.
3. Force may not be used to make the suspect's face visible to the witness.
4. Confrontation must take place in the presence of the suspect's solicitor, interpreter or friend unless this would cause unreasonable delay.
5. The suspect shall be confronted independently by each witness, who shall be asked "Is this the person?". If the witness identifies the person but is unable to confirm the identification, they shall be asked how sure they are that the person is the one they saw on the earlier occasion.
6. The confrontation should normally take place in the police station, either in a normal room or one equipped with a screen permitting a witness to see the suspect without being seen. In both cases, the procedures are the same except that a room equipped with a screen may be used only when the suspect's solicitor, friend or appropriate adult is present or the confrontation is recorded on video.

7. After the procedure, each witness shall be asked whether they have seen any broadcast or published films or photographs or any descriptions of suspects relating to the offence and their reply shall be recorded.

ANNEX E—SHOWING PHOTOGRAPHS

(a) Action

1. An officer of sergeant rank or above shall be responsible for supervising and directing the showing of photographs. The actual showing may be done by another officer or police staff, see *paragraph 3.11*.
2. The supervising officer must confirm the first description of the suspect given by the witness has been recorded before they are shown the photographs. If the supervising officer is unable to confirm the description has been recorded they shall postpone showing the photographs.
3. Only one witness shall be shown photographs at any one time. Each witness shall be given as much privacy as practicable and shall not be allowed to communicate with any other witness in the case.
4. The witness shall be shown not less than twelve photographs at a time, which shall, as far as possible, all be of a similar type.
5. When the witness is shown the photographs, they shall be told the photograph of the person they saw may, or may not, be amongst them and if they cannot make a positive identification, they should say so. The witness shall also be told they should not make a decision until they have viewed at least twelve photographs. The witness shall not be prompted or guided in any way but shall be left to make any selection without help.
6. If a witness makes a positive identification from photographs, unless the person identified is otherwise eliminated from enquiries or is not available, other witnesses shall not be shown photographs. But both they, and the witness who has made the identification, shall be asked to attend a video identification, an identification parade or group identification unless there is no dispute about the suspect's identification.
7. If the witness makes a selection but is unable to confirm the identification, the person showing the photographs shall ask them how sure they are that the photograph they have indicated is the person they saw on the specified earlier occasion.
8. When the use of a computerised or artist's composite or similar likeness has led to there being a known suspect who can be asked to participate in a video identification, appear on an identification parade or participate in a group identification, that likeness shall not be shown to other potential witnesses.
9. When a witness attending a video identification, an identification parade or group identification has previously been shown photographs or computerised or artist's composite or similar likeness (and it is the responsibility of the officer in charge of the investigation to make the identification officer aware that this is the case), the suspect and their solicitor must be informed of this fact before the identification procedure takes place.
10. None of the photographs shown shall be destroyed, whether or not an identification is made, since they may be required for production in court. The photographs shall be numbered and a separate photograph taken of the frame or part of the album from which the witness made an identification as an aid to reconstituting it.

(b) Documentation

11. Whether or not an identification is made, a record shall be kept of the showing of photographs on forms provided for the purpose. This shall include anything said by the witness about any identification or the conduct of the procedure, any reasons it was not practicable to comply with any of the provisions of this Code governing the showing of photographs and the name and rank of the supervising officer.
12. The supervising officer shall inspect and sign the record as soon as practicable.

ANNEX F—FINGERPRINTS, FOOTWEAR IMPRESSIONS AND SAMPLES—DESTRUCTION AND SPECULATIVE SEARCHES

(a) Fingerprints, footwear impressions and samples taken in connection with a criminal investigation

1. When fingerprints, footwear impressions or DNA samples are taken from a person in connection with an investigation and the person is not suspected of having committed the offence, see *Note F1*, they must be destroyed as soon as they have fulfilled the purpose for which they were taken unless:

   (a) they were taken for the purposes of an investigation of an offence for which a person has been convicted; and

   (b) fingerprints, footwear impressions or samples were also taken from the convicted person for the purposes of that investigation.

   However, subject to *paragraph 2*, the fingerprints, footwear impressions and samples, and the information derived from samples, may not be used in the investigation of any offence or in evidence against the person who is, or would be, entitled to the destruction of the fingerprints, footwear impressions and samples, see *Note F2*.

2. The requirement to destroy fingerprints, footwear impressions and DNA samples, and information derived from samples, and restrictions on their retention and use in paragraph 1 do not apply if the person gives their written consent for their fingerprints, footwear impressions or sample to be retained and used after they have fulfilled the purpose for which they were taken, see *Note F1*.

3. When a person's fingerprints, footwear impressions or sample are to be destroyed:

   (a) any copies of the fingerprints and footwear impressions must also be destroyed;

   (b) the person may witness the destruction of their fingerprints, footwear impressions or copies if they ask to do so within five days of being informed destruction is required;

   (c) access to relevant computer fingerprint data shall be made impossible as soon as it is practicable to do so and the person shall be given a certificate to this effect within three months of asking; and

   (d) neither the fingerprints, footwear impressions, the sample, or any information derived from the sample, may be used in the investigation of any offence or in evidence against the person who is, or would be, entitled to its destruction.

4. Fingerprints, footwear impressions or samples, and the information derived from samples, taken in connection with the investigation of an offence which are not required to be destroyed, may be retained after they have fulfilled the purposes for which they were taken but may be used only for purposes related to the prevention or detection of crime, the investigation of an offence or the conduct of a prosecution in, as well as outside, the UK and may also be subject to a speculative search. This includes checking them against other fingerprints, footwear impressions and DNA records held by, or on behalf of, the police and other law enforcement authorities in, as well as outside, the UK.

(b) Fingerprints taken in connection with Immigration Service enquiries

5. Fingerprints taken for Immigration Service enquiries in accordance with powers and procedures other than under PACE and for which the Immigration Service, not the police, are responsible, must be destroyed as follows:

   (a) fingerprints and all copies must be destroyed as soon as practicable if the person from whom they were taken proves they are a British or Commonwealth citizen who has the right of abode in the UK under the Immigration Act 1971, section 2(1)(b);

   (b) fingerprints taken under the power as in *paragraph 4.11(g)* from a dependant of a person in *4.11 (b)* to *(f)* must be destroyed when that person's fingerprints are to be destroyed;

   (c) fingerprints taken from a person under any power as in *paragraph 4.11* or with the person's consent which have not already been destroyed as above, must be destroyed within ten years of being taken or within such period specified by the Secretary of State under the Immigration and Asylum Act 1999, section 143(5).

Notes for guidance

F1 Fingerprints, footwear impressions and samples given voluntarily for the purposes of elimination play an important part in many police investigations. It is, therefore, important to make sure innocent volunteers are not deterred from participating and their consent to their fingerprints, footwear impressions and DNA being used for the purposes of a specific investigation is fully informed and voluntary. If the police or volunteer seek to have the fingerprints, footwear impressions or samples retained for use after the specific investigation ends, it is important the volunteer's consent to this is also fully informed and voluntary.

Examples of consent for:

- *DNA/fingerprints/footwear impressions - to be used only for the purposes of a specific investigation;*
- *DNA/fingerprints/footwear impressions - to be used in the specific investigation* ***and*** *retained by the police for future use.*

To minimise the risk of confusion, each consent should be physically separate and the volunteer should be asked to sign ***each consent****.*

(a) DNA:

(i) DNA sample taken for the purposes of elimination or as part of an intelligence-led screening and to be used only for the purposes of that investigation and destroyed afterwards:

"I consent to my DNA/mouth swab being taken for forensic analysis. I understand that the sample will be destroyed at the end of the case and that my profile will only be compared to the crime stain profile from this enquiry. I have been advised that the person taking the sample may be required to give evidence and/or provide a written statement to the police in relation to the taking of it."

(ii) DNA sample to be retained on the National DNA database and used in the future:

"I consent to my DNA sample and information derived from it being retained and used only for purposes related to the prevention and detection of a crime, the investigation of an offence or the conduct of a prosecution either nationally or internationally."

"I understand that this sample may be checked against other DNA records held by, or on behalf of, relevant law enforcement authorities, either nationally or internationally."

"I understand that once I have given my consent for the sample to be retained and used I cannot withdraw this consent."

(b) Fingerprints:

(i) Fingerprints taken for the purposes of elimination or as part of an intelligence-led screening and to be used only for the purposes of that investigation and destroyed afterwards:

"I consent to my fingerprints being taken for elimination purposes. I understand that the fingerprints will be destroyed at the end of the case and that my fingerprints will only be compared to the fingerprints from this enquiry. I have been advised that the person taking the fingerprints may be required to give evidence and/or provide a written statement to the police in relation to the taking of it."

(ii) Fingerprints to be retained for future use:

"I consent to my fingerprints being retained and used only for purposes related to the prevention and detection of a crime, the investigation of an offence or the conduct of a prosecution either nationally or internationally."

"I understand that my fingerprints may be checked against other records held by, or on behalf of, relevant law enforcement authorities, either nationally or internationally."

"I understand that once I have given my consent for my fingerprints to be retained and used I cannot withdraw this consent."

(c) Footwear impressions:

(i) Footwear impressions taken for the purposes of elimination or as part of an intelligence-led screening and to be used only for the purposes of that investigation and destroyed afterwards:

"I consent to my footwear impressions being taken for elimination purposes. I understand that the footwear impressions will be destroyed at the end of the case and that my footwear impressions will only be compared to the footwear impressions from this enquiry. I have been advised that the person taking the footwear impressions may be required to give evidence and/or provide a written statement to the police in relation to the taking of it."

(ii) Footwear impressions to be retained for future use:

"I consent to my footwear impressions being retained and used only for purposes related to the prevention and detection of a crime, the investigation of an offence or the conduct of a prosecution, either nationally or internationally."

"I understand that my footwear impressions may be checked against other records held by, or on behalf of, relevant law enforcement authorities, either nationally or internationally."

"I understand that once I have given my consent for my footwear impressions to be retained and used I cannot withdraw this consent."

F2 The provisions for the retention of fingerprints, footwear impressions and samples in paragraph 1 allow for all fingerprints, footwear impressions and samples in a case to be available for any subsequent miscarriage of justice investigation.

Appendix 5

PACE Code of Practice on Audio Recording Interviews with Suspects (Code E)

This code applies to interviews carried out after midnight on 31 January 2008, notwithstanding that the interview may have commenced before that time.

1 General

1.1 This Code of Practice must be readily available for consultation by:
- police officers
- police staff
- detained persons
- members of the public.

1.2 The *Notes for Guidance* included are not provisions of this Code.

1.3 Nothing in this Code shall detract from the requirements of Code C, the Code of Practice for the detention, treatment and questioning of persons by police officers.

1.4 This Code does not apply to those people listed in Code C, *paragraph 1.12.*

1.5 The term:
- 'appropriate adult' has the same meaning as in Code C, *paragraph 1.7*
- 'solicitor' has the same meaning as in Code C, *paragraph 6.12.*

1.6 In this Code:

(aa) 'recording media' means any removable, physical audio recording medium (such as magnetic type, optical disc or solid state memory) which can be played and copied.

(a) 'designated person' means a person other than a police officer, designated under the Police Reform Act 2002, Part 4 who has specified powers and duties of police officers conferred or imposed on them;

(b) any reference to a police officer includes a designated person acting in the exercise or performance of the powers and duties conferred or imposed on them by their designation.

(c) 'digital network solution' means the use of platform architecture that secures a network by providing each user with a digital identity and is managed by a central digital certificate authority (see section 7 of this Code).

1.7 If a power conferred on a designated person:

(a) allows reasonable force to be used when exercised by a police officer, a designated person exercising that power has the same entitlement to use force;

(b) includes power to use force to enter any premises, that power is not exercisable by that designated person except:

(i) in the company, and under the supervision, of a police officer; or

(ii) for the purpose of:
- saving life or limb; or
- preventing serious damage to property.

1.8 Nothing in this Code prevents the custody officer, or other officer given custody of the detainee, from allowing police staff who are not designated persons to carry out individual procedures or tasks at the police station if the law allows. However, the officer remains responsible for making sure the procedures and tasks are carried out correctly in accordance with these Codes. Any such police staff must be:

(a) a person employed by a police authority maintaining a police force and under the control and direction of the Chief Officer of that force; or

(b) employed by a person with whom a police authority has a contract for the provision of services relating to persons arrested or otherwise in custody.

1.9 Designated persons and other police staff must have regard to any relevant provisions of the Codes of Practice.

1.10 References to pocket book include any official report book issued to police officers or police staff.

1.11 References to a custody officer include those performing the functions of a custody officer as in *paragraph 1.9* of Code C.

2 Recording and sealing master recordings

2.1 Recording of interviews shall be carried out openly to instil confidence in its reliability as an impartial and accurate record of the interview.

2.2 One recording, the master recording, will be sealed in the suspect's presence. A second recording will be used as a working copy. The master recording is either of the two recordings used in a twin deck/drive machine or the only recording in a single deck/drive machine. The working copy is either the second/third recording used in a twin/triple deck/drive machine or a copy of the master recording made by a single deck/drive machine. See *Notes 2A* and *2B*

2.3 Nothing in this Code requires the identity of officers or police staff conducting interviews to be recorded or disclosed:

(a) in the case of enquiries linked to the investigation of terrorism; or

(b) if the interviewer reasonably believes recording or disclosing their name might put them in danger.

In these cases interviewers should use warrant or other identification numbers and the name of their police station. See Note 2C

Notes for guidance

2A The purpose of sealing the master recording in the suspect's presence is to show the recording's integrity is preserved. If a single deck/drive machine is used the working copy of the master recording must be made in the suspect's presence and without the master recording leaving their sight. The working copy shall be used for making further copies if needed.

2B Not used.

2C The purpose of paragraph 2.3(b) is to protect those involved in serious organised crime investigations or arrests of particularly violent suspects when there is reliable information that those arrested or their associates may threaten or cause harm to those involved. In cases of doubt, an officer of inspector rank or above should be consulted.

3 Interviews to be audio recorded

3.1 Subject to *paragraphs 3.3* and *3.4*, audio recording shall be used at police stations for any interview:

(a) with a person cautioned under Code C, *section 10* in respect of any indictable offence, including an offence triable either way; see *Note 3A*

(b) which takes place as a result of an interviewer exceptionally putting further questions to a suspect about an offence described in *paragraph 3.1(a)* after they have been charged with, or told they may be prosecuted for, that offence, see Code C, *paragraph 16.5*

(c) when an interviewer wants to tell a person, after they have been charged with, or informed they may be prosecuted for, an offence described in *paragraph 3.1(a)*, about any written statement or interview with another person, see Code C, *paragraph 16.4*.

3.2 The Terrorism Act 2000 makes separate provision for a Code of Practice for the audio recording of interviews of those arrested under Section 41 or detained under Schedule 7 of the Act. The provisions of this Code do not apply to such interviews.

3.3 The custody officer may authorise the interviewer not to audio record the interview when it is:

(a) not reasonably practicable because of equipment failure or the unavailability of a suitable interview room or recording equipment and the authorising officer considers, on reasonable grounds, that the interview should not be delayed; or

(b) clear from the outset there will not be a prosecution.

Note: In these cases the interview should be recorded in writing in accordance with Code C, *section 11*. In all cases the custody officer shall record the specific reasons for not audio recording. See *Note 3B*

3.4 If a person refuses to go into or remain in a suitable interview room, see Code C *paragraph 12.5*, and the custody officer considers, on reasonable grounds, that the interview should not be delayed the interview may, at the custody officer's discretion, be conducted in a cell using portable recording equipment or, if none is available, recorded in writing as in Code C, *section 11*. The reasons for this shall be recorded.

3.5 The whole of each interview shall be audio recorded, including the taking and reading back of any statement.

Notes for guidance

3A Nothing in this Code is intended to preclude audio recording at police discretion of interviews at police stations with people cautioned in respect of offences not covered by paragraph 3.1, or responses made by persons after they have been charged with, or told they may be prosecuted for, an offence, provided this Code is complied with.

3B A decision not to audio record an interview for any reason may be the subject of comment in court. The authorising officer should be prepared to justify that decision.

4 The interview

(a) General

4.1 The provisions of Code C: 4

- *sections 10 and 11*, and the applicable *Notes for Guidance* apply to the conduct of interviews to which this Code applies
- *paragraphs 11.7 to 11.14* apply only when a written record is needed.

4.2 Code C, *paragraphs 10.10, 10.11* and Annex C describe the restriction on drawing adverse inferences from a suspect's failure or refusal to say anything about their involvement in the offence when interviewed or after being charged or informed they may be prosecuted, and how it affects the terms of the caution and determines if and by whom a special warning under sections 36 and 37 can be given.

(b) Commencement of interviews

4.3 When the suspect is brought into the interview room the interviewer shall, without delay but in the suspect's sight, load the recorder with new recording media and set it to record. The recording media must be unwrapped or opened in the suspect's presence.

4.4 The interviewer should tell the suspect about the recording process. The interviewer shall:

(a) say the interview is being audibly recorded

(b) subject to *paragraph 2.3*, give their name and rank and that of any other interviewer present

(c) ask the suspect and any other party present, e.g. a solicitor, to identify themselves
(d) state the date, time of commencement and place of the interview
(e) state the suspect will be given a notice about what will happen to the copies of the recording.

See *Note 4A*

4.5 The interviewer shall:

- caution the suspect, see Code C, *section 10*
- remind the suspect of their entitlement to free legal advice, see Code C, *paragraph 11.2*.

4.6 The interviewer shall put to the suspect any significant statement or silence; see Code C, *paragraph 11.4*.

(c) Interviews with deaf persons

4.7 If the suspect is deaf or is suspected of having impaired hearing, the interviewer shall make a written note of the interview in accordance with Code C, at the same time as audio recording it in accordance with this Code. See *Notes 4B* and *4C*

(d) Objections and complaints by the suspect

4.8 If the suspect objects to the interview being audibly recorded at the outset, during the interview or during a break, the interviewer shall explain that the interview is being audibly recorded and that this Code requires the suspect's objections to be recorded on the audio recording. When any objections have been audibly recorded or the suspect has refused to have their objections recorded, the interviewer shall say they are turning off the recorder, give their reasons and turn it off. The interviewer shall then make a written record of the interview as in Code C, *section 11*. If, however, the interviewer reasonably considers they may proceed to question the suspect with the audio recording still on, the interviewer may do so. This procedure also applies in cases where the suspect has previously objected to the interview being visually recorded, see *Code F 4.8*, and the investigating officer has decided to audibly record the interview. See *Note 4D*

4.9 If in the course of an interview a complaint is made by or on behalf of the person being questioned concerning the provisions of this Code or Code C, the interviewer shall act as in Code C, *paragraph 12.9*. See *Notes 4E* and *4F*

4.10 If the suspect indicates they want to tell the interviewer about matters not directly connected with the offence and they are unwilling for these matters to be audio recorded, the suspect should be given the opportunity to tell the interviewer at the end of the formal interview.

(e) Changing recording media

4.11 When the recorder shows the recording media only has a short time left, the interviewer shall tell the suspect the recording media are coming to an end and round off that part of the interview. If the interviewer leaves the room for a second set of recording media, the suspect shall not be left unattended. The interviewer will remove the recording media from the recorder and insert the new recording media which shall be unwrapped or opened in the suspect's presence. The recorder should be set to record on the new media. To avoid confusion between the recording media, the interviewer shall mark the media with an identification number immediately after they are removed from the recorder.

(f) Taking a break during interview

4.12 When a break is taken, the fact that a break is to be taken, the reason for it and the time shall be recorded on the audio recording.

4.12A When the break is taken and the interview room vacated by the suspect, the recording media shall be removed from the recorder and the procedures for the conclusion of an interview followed, see *paragraph 4.18*.

4.13 When a break is a short one and both the suspect and an interviewer remain in the interview room, the recording may be stopped. There is no need to remove the recording media and when the interview recommences the recording should continue on the same recording media. The time the interview recommences shall be recorded on the audio recording.

4.14 After any break in the interview the interviewer must, before resuming the interview, remind the person being questioned that they remain under caution or, if there is any doubt, give the caution in full again. See *Note 4G*

(g) Failure of recording equipment

4.15 If there is an equipment failure which can be rectified quickly, e.g. by inserting new recording media, the interviewer shall follow the appropriate procedures as in *paragraph 4.11*. When the recording is resumed the interviewer shall explain what happened and record the time the interview recommences. If, however, it will not be possible to continue recording on that recorder and no replacement recorder is readily available, the interview may continue without being audibly recorded. If this happens, the interviewer shall seek the custody officer's authority as in *paragraph 3.3*. See *Note 4H*

(h) Removing recording media from the recorder

4.16 When recording media is removed from the recorder during the interview, they shall be retained and the procedures in *paragraph 4.18* followed.

(i) Conclusion of interview

4.17 At the conclusion of the interview, the suspect shall be offered the opportunity to clarify anything he or she has said and asked if there is anything they want to add.

4.18 At the conclusion of the interview, including the taking and reading back of any written statement, the time shall be recorded and the recording shall be stopped. The interviewer shall seal the master recording with a master recording label and treat it as an exhibit in accordance with force standing orders. The interviewer shall sign the label and ask the suspect and any third party present during the interview to sign it. If the suspect or third party refuse to sign the label an officer of at least inspector rank, or if not available the custody officer, shall be called into the interview room and asked, subject to *paragraph 2.3*, to sign it.

4.19 The suspect shall be handed a notice which explains:

- how the audio recording will be used
- the arrangements for access to it
- that if the person is charged or informed they will be prosecuted, a copy of the audio recording will be supplied as soon as practicable or as otherwise agreed between the suspect and the police.

Notes for guidance

4A For the purpose of voice identification the interviewer should ask the suspect and any other people present to identify themselves.

4B This provision is to give a person who is deaf or has impaired hearing equivalent rights of access to the full interview record as far as this is possible using audio recording.

4C The provisions of Code C, section 13 on interpreters for deaf persons or for interviews with suspects who have difficulty understanding English continue to apply. However, in an audibly recorded interview the requirement on the interviewer to make sure the interpreter makes a separate note of the interview applies only to paragraph 4.7 (interviews with deaf persons).

4D The interviewer should remember that a decision to continue recording against the wishes of the suspect may be the subject of comment in court.

4E If the custody officer is called to deal with the complaint, the recorder should, if possible, be left on until the custody officer has entered the room and spoken to the person being interviewed. Continuation or termination of the interview should be at the interviewer's discretion pending action by an inspector under Code C, paragraph 9.2.

4F If the complaint is about a matter not connected with this Code or Code C, the decision to continue is at the interviewer's discretion. When the interviewer decides to continue the interview, they shall tell the suspect the complaint will be brought to the custody officer's attention at the conclusion of the interview. When the interview is concluded the interviewer must, as soon as practicable, inform the custody officer about the existence and nature of the complaint made.

4G *The interviewer should remember that it may be necessary to show to the court that nothing occurred during a break or between interviews which influenced the suspect's recorded evidence. After a break or at the beginning of a subsequent interview, the interviewer should consider summarising on the record the reason for the break and confirming this with the suspect.*

4H *Where the interview is being recorded and the media or the recording equipment fails the officer conducting the interview should stop the interview immediately. Where part of the interview is unaffected by the error and is still accessible on the media, that media shall be copied and sealed in the suspect's presence and the interview recommenced using new equipment/media as required. Where the content of the interview has been lost in its entirety the media should be sealed in the suspect's presence and the interview begun again. If the recording equipment cannot be fixed or no replacement is immediately available the interview should be recorded in accordance with Code C, section 11.*

5 After the interview

5.1 The interviewer shall make a note in their pocket book that the interview has taken place, was audibly recorded, its time, duration and date and the master recording's identification number.

5.2 If no proceedings follow in respect of the person whose interview was recorded, the recording media must be kept securely as in *paragraph 6.1* and *Note 6A*.

Note for guidance

5A *Any written record of an audibly recorded interview should be made in accordance with national guidelines approved by the Secretary of State.*

6 Media security

6.1 The officer in charge of each police station at which interviews with suspects are recorded shall make arrangements for master recordings to be kept securely and their movements accounted for on the same basis as material which may be used for evidential purposes, in accordance with force standing orders. See *Note 6A*

6.2 A police officer has no authority to break the seal on a master recording required for criminal trial or appeal proceedings. If it is necessary to gain access to the master recording, the police officer shall arrange for its seal to be broken in the presence of a representative of the Crown Prosecution Service. The defendant or their legal adviser should be informed and given a reasonable opportunity to be present. If the defendant or their legal representative is present they shall be invited to reseal and sign the master recording. If either refuses or neither is present this should be done by the representative of the Crown Prosecution Service. See *Notes 6B* and *6C*

6.3 If no criminal proceedings result or the criminal trial and, if applicable, appeal proceedings to which the interview relates have been concluded, the chief officer of police is responsible for establishing arrangements for breaking the seal on the master recording, if necessary.

6.4 When the master recording seal is broken, a record must be made of the procedure followed, including the date, time, place and persons present.

Notes for guidance

6A *This section is concerned with the security of the master recording sealed at the conclusion of the interview. Care must be taken of working copies of recordings because their loss or destruction may lead to the need to access master recordings.*

6B If the recording has been delivered to the crown court for their keeping after committal for trial the crown prosecutor will apply to the chief clerk of the crown court centre for the release of the recording for unsealing by the crown prosecutor.

6C Reference to the Crown Prosecution Service or to the crown prosecutor in this part of the Code should be taken to include any other body or person with a statutory responsibility for prosecution for whom the police conduct any audibly recorded interviews.

7 Recording of Interviews by Secure Digital Network

7.1 This section of the Code applies only in the following area:

- Lancashire Constabulary, Eastern Division as defined at 1 September 2007

7.2 This section of the Code does not extend to the audio recording of interviews with suspects by secure digital network (SDN) to any other Division of the Lancashire Constabulary nor to any other police force area in England and Wales. Any interviews with suspects subject to recording by secure digital network in an area other than that listed in *paragraph 7.1* above must be simultaneously recorded, and any recordings used, in accordance with *sections 1 to 6* above.

7.3 The following requirements are solely applicable to the use of a secure digital network for the recording of interviews.

Application of section 1 to 6 of Code E

7.4 Sections 1 to 6 of Code E above apply except for the following paragraphs:

- Paragraph 2.2
- Paragraph 4.3
- Paragraph 4.4 (e)
- Paragraphs 4.11 – 4.19
- Paragraphs 6.1 – 6.4

Commencement of Interview

7.5 When the suspect is brought into the interview room, the interviewer shall without delay and in the sight of the suspect, switch on the recording equipment and enter his or her digital identifier.

7.6 The interviewer must then provide the appropriate case reference for the interview and inform the suspect that the interview is being recorded via a secure digital network and that recording commenced when the interviewer inserted the digital identifier.

7.7 In addition to the requirements of paragraph 4.4 (a–d) above, the interviewer must inform the person that the recording of the interview can only be accessed on the order of a court; that copies of the recording will be made available in the event that he or she is charged or informed that they will prosecuted; and that a written notice will be provided to them at the end of the interview setting out their access rights and what will happen to the recording.

Taking a break during interview

7.8 When a break is taken and the interview room vacated by the suspect, the recording shall be stopped and the procedures for the conclusion of an interview followed.

7.9 When a break is a short one and either the suspect or the interviewer or both remain in the interview room, the recording must be stopped. There is no need to create a new secure digital network file. When the interview recommences the recording should continue on the same secure network file. The time the interview recommences shall be recorded on the audio recording.

7.10 After any break in the interview the interviewer must, before resuming the interview, remind the person being questioned that they remain under caution or, if there is any doubt, give the caution in full again. See *Note for Guidance 4G*.

Failure of recording equipment

7.11 If there is an equipment failure which can be rectified quickly, e.g. by commencing a new secure digital network recording, the interviewer shall follow the appropriate procedures as in *paragraph 7.8*. When the recording is resumed the interviewer shall explain what happened and record the time the interview recommences. If, however, it is not possible to continue recording on the secure digital network the interview should be recorded on removable media as in *paragraph 4.3* unless the necessary equipment is not available. If this happens the interview may continue without being audibly recorded and the interviewer shall seek the custody officer's authority as in *paragraph 3.3*. See *Note for Guidance 4H*.

Conclusion of interview

7.12 At the conclusion of the interview, the suspect shall be offered the opportunity to clarify anything he or she has said and asked if there is anything they want to add.

7.13 At the conclusion of the interview, including the taking and reading back of any written statement:

(a) the time shall be orally recorded

(b) the suspect shall be handed a notice which explains:
- how the audio recording will be used
- the arrangements for access to it
- that if the person is charged or informed they will be prosecuted, a copy of the audio recording will be supplied as soon as practicable or as otherwise agreed between the suspect and the police.

See *Note for Guidance 7A*.

(c) the suspect must be asked to confirm that he or she has received a copy of the notice at *paragraph 7.13(b)* above. If the suspect fails to accept or to acknowledge receipt of the notice, the interviewer will state for the recording that a copy of the notice has been provided to the suspect and that he or she has refused to take a copy of the notice or has refused to acknowledge receipt.

(d) the time shall be recorded and the interviewer shall notify the suspect that the recording is being saved to the secure network. The interviewer must save the recording in the presence of the suspect. The suspect should then be informed that the interview is terminated.

Note for Guidance

7A *The notice at paragraph 7.13 above should provide a brief explanation on the secure digital network and how access is strictly limited to the recording. The notice should also explain the access rights of the suspect, his or her legal representative, the police and the prosecutor to copies of the recording of the interview. Space should be provided on the form to insert the date and the file reference number for the interview.*

Appendix 6

PACE Code of Practice on Visual Recording with Sound of Interviews with Suspects (Code F)

The contents of this code should be considered if an interviewing officer decides to make a visual recording with sound of an interview with a suspect after midnight on 31 December 2005.

There is no statutory requirement to visually record interviews.

1 General

1.1 This code of practice must be readily available for consultation by police officers and other police staff, detained persons and members of the public.

1.2 The notes for guidance included are not provisions of this code. They form guidance to police officers and others about its application and interpretation.

1.3 Nothing in this code shall be taken as detracting in any way from the requirements of the Code of Practice for the Detention, Treatment and Questioning of Persons by Police Officers (Code C). [See *Note 1A*].

1.4 The interviews to which this Code applies are set out in paragraphs 3.1–3.3.

1.5 In this code, the term "appropriate adult", "solicitor" and "interview" have the same meaning as those set out in Code C. The corresponding provisions and Notes for Guidance in Code C applicable to those terms shall also apply where appropriate.

1.6 Any reference in this code to visual recording shall be taken to mean visual recording with sound.

1.7 References to "pocket book" in this Code include any official report book issued to police officers.

Note for Guidance

1A As in paragraph 1.9 of Code C, references to custody officers include those carrying out the functions of a custody officer.

2 Recording and sealing of master tapes

2.1 The visual recording of interviews shall be carried out openly to instil confidence in its reliability as an impartial and accurate record of the interview. [See *Note 2A*].

2.2 The camera(s) shall be placed in the interview room so as to ensure coverage of as much of the room as is practicably possible whilst the interviews are taking place.

2.3 The certified recording medium will be of a high quality, new and previously unused. When the certified recording medium is placed in the recorder and switched on to record, the correct date and time, in hours, minutes and seconds, will be superimposed automatically, second by second, during the whole recording. [See *Note 2B*].

2.4 One copy of the certified recording medium, referred to in this code as the master copy, will be sealed before it leaves the presence of the suspect. A second copy will be used as a working copy. [See *Note 2C and 2D*].

2.5 Nothing in this code requires the identity of an officer to be recorded or disclosed if:

(a) the interview or record relates to a person detained under the Terrorism Act 2000; or

(b) otherwise where the officer reasonably believes that recording or disclosing their name might put them in danger.

In these cases, the officer will have their back to the camera and shall use their warrant or other identification number and the name of the police station to which they are attached. Such instances and the reasons for them shall be recorded in the custody record. [See *Note 2E*]

Notes for Guidance

2A *Interviewing officers will wish to arrange that, as far as possible, visual recording arrangements are unobtrusive. It must be clear to the suspect, however, that there is no opportunity to interfere with the recording equipment or the recording media.*

2B *In this context, the certified recording media will be of either a VHS or digital CD format and should be capable of having an image of the date and time superimposed upon them as they record the interview.*

2C *The purpose of sealing the master copy before it leaves the presence of the suspect is to establish their confidence that the integrity of the copy is preserved.*

2D *The recording of the interview may be used for identification procedures in accordance with paragraph 3.21 or Annex E of Code D.*

2E *The purpose of the paragraph 2.5 is to protect police officers and others involved in the investigation of serious organised crime or the arrest of particularly violent suspects when there is reliable information that those arrested or their associates may threaten or cause harm to the officers, their families or their personal property.*

3 Interviews to be visually recorded

3.1 Subject to paragraph 3.2 below, if an interviewing officer decides to make a visual recording these are the areas where it might be appropriate:

(a) with a suspect in respect of an indictable offence (including an offence triable either way) [see *Notes 3A and 3B*];

(b) which takes place as a result of an interviewer exceptionally putting further questions to a suspect about an offence described in sub-paragraph (a) above after they have been charged with, or informed they may be prosecuted for, that offence [see *Note 3C*];

(c) in which an interviewer wishes to bring to the notice of a person, after that person has been charged with, or informed they may be prosecuted for an offence described in sub-paragraph (a) above, any written statement made by another person, or the content of an interview with another person [see *Note 3D*]

(d) with, or in the presence of, a deaf or deaf/blind or speech impaired person who uses sign language to communicate;

(e) with, or in the presence of anyone who requires an "appropriate adult"; or

(f) in any case where the suspect or their representative requests that the interview be recorded visually.

3.2 The Terrorism Act 2000 makes separate provision for a code of practice for the video recording of interviews in a police station of those detained under Schedule 7 or section 41 of the Act. The provisions of this code do not therefore apply to such interviews [see *Note 3E*].

3.3 The custody officer may authorise the interviewing officer not to record the interview visually:

(a) where it is not reasonably practicable to do so because of failure of the equipment, or the non-availability of a suitable interview room, or recorder, and the authorising officer considers on reasonable grounds that the interview should not be delayed until the failure has been rectified or a suitable room or recorder becomes available. In such cases the custody officer may authorise the interviewing officer to audio record the interview in accordance with the guidance set out in Code E;

(b) where it is clear from the outset that no prosecution will ensue; or

(c) where it is not practicable to do so because at the time the person resists being taken to a suitable interview room or other location which would enable the interview to be recorded, or otherwise fails or refuses to go into such a room or location, and the authorising officer considers on reasonable grounds that the interview should not be delayed until these conditions cease to apply.

3.4 When a person who is voluntarily attending the police station is required to be cautioned in accordance with Code C prior to being interviewed, the subsequent interview shall be recorded, unless the custody officer gives authority in accordance with the provisions of paragraph 3.3 above for the interview not to be so recorded.

3.5 The whole of each interview shall be recorded visually, including the taking and reading back of any statement.

3.6 A visible illuminated sign or indicator will light and remain on at all times when the recording equipment is activated or capable of recording or transmitting any signal or information.

Notes for Guidance

3A Nothing in the code is intended to preclude visual recording at police discretion of interviews at police stations with people cautioned in respect of offences not covered by paragraph 3.1, or responses made by interviewees after they have been charged with, or informed they may be prosecuted for, an offence, provided that this code is complied with.

3B Attention is drawn to the provisions set out in Code C about the matters to be considered when deciding whether a detained person is fit to be interviewed.

3C Code C sets out the circumstances in which a suspect may be questioned about an offence after being charged with it.

3D Code C sets out the procedures to be followed when a person's attention is drawn after charge, to a statement made by another person. One method of bringing the content of an interview with another person to the notice of a suspect may be to play him a recording of that interview.

3E When it only becomes clear during the course of an interview which is being visually recorded that the interviewee may have committed an offence to which paragraph 3.2 applies, the interviewing officer should turn off the recording equipment and the interview should continue in accordance with the provisions of the Terrorism Act 2000.

3F A decision not to record an interview visually for any reason may be the subject of comment in court. The authorising officer should therefore be prepared to justify their decision in each case.

4 The Interview

(a) General

4.1 The provisions of Code C in relation to cautions and interviews and the Notes for Guidance applicable to those provisions shall apply to the conduct of interviews to which this Code applies.

4.2 Particular attention is drawn to those parts of Code C that describe the restrictions on drawing adverse inferences from a suspect's failure or refusal to say anything about their involvement in the offence when interviewed, or after being charged or informed they may be prosecuted and how those restrictions affect the terms of the caution and determine whether a special warning under Sections 36 and 37 of the Criminal Justice and Public Order Act 1994 can be given.

(b) Commencement of interviews

4.3 When the suspect is brought into the interview room the interviewer shall without delay, but in sight of the suspect, load the recording equipment and set it to record. The recording media must be unwrapped or otherwise opened in the presence of the suspect. [See *Note 4A*]

4.4 The interviewer shall then tell the suspect formally about the visual recording. The interviewer shall:

(a) explain the interview is being visually recorded;

(b) subject to paragraph 2.5, give his or her name and rank, and that of any other interviewer present;

(c) ask the suspect and any other party present (e.g. his solicitor) to identify themselves.

(d) state the date, time of commencement and place of the interview; and

(e) state that the suspect will be given a notice about what will happen to the recording.

4.5 The interviewer shall then caution the suspect, which should follow that set out in Code C, and remind the suspect of their entitlement to free and independent legal advice and that they can speak to a solicitor on the telephone.

4.6 The interviewer shall then put to the suspect any significant statement or silence (i.e. failure or refusal to answer a question or to answer it satisfactorily) which occurred before the start of the interview, and shall ask the suspect whether they wish to confirm or deny that earlier statement or silence or whether they wish to add anything. The definition of a "significant" statement or silence is the same as that set out in Code C.

(c) Interviews with the deaf

4.7 If the suspect is deaf or there is doubt about their hearing ability, the provisions of Code C on interpreters for the deaf or for interviews with suspects who have difficulty in understanding English continue to apply.

(d) Objections and complaints by the suspect

4.8 If the suspect raises objections to the interview being visually recorded either at the outset or during the interview or during a break in the interview, the interviewer shall explain the fact that the interview is being visually recorded and that the provisions of this code require that the suspect's objections shall be recorded on the visual recording. When any objections have been visually recorded or the suspect has refused to have their objections recorded, the interviewer shall say that they are turning off the recording equipment, give their reasons and turn it off. If a separate audio recording is being maintained, the officer shall ask the person to record the reasons for refusing to agree to visual recording of the interview. Paragraph 4.8 of Code E will apply if the person objects to audio recording of the interview. The officer shall then make a written record of the interview. If the interviewer reasonably considers they may proceed to question the suspect with the visual recording still on, the interviewer may do so. See *Note 4G*.

4.9 If in the course of an interview a complaint is made by the person being questioned, or on their behalf, concerning the provisions of this code or of Code C, then the interviewer shall act in accordance with Code C, record it in the interview record and inform the custody officer. [See *4B and 4C*].

4.10 If the suspect indicates that they wish to tell the interviewer about matters not directly connected with the offence of which they are suspected and that they are unwilling for these matters to be recorded, the suspect shall be given the opportunity to tell the interviewer about these matters after the conclusion of the formal interview.

(e) Changing the recording media

4.11 In instances where the recording medium is not of sufficient length to record all of the interview with the suspect, further certified recording medium will be used. When the recording equipment indicates that the recording medium has only a short time left to run, the interviewer shall advise the suspect and round off that part of the interview. If the interviewer wishes to continue the interview but does not already have further certified recording media with him, they shall obtain a set. The suspect should not be left unattended in the interview room. The interviewer will remove the recording media from the recording equipment and insert the new ones which have been unwrapped or otherwise opened in the suspect's presence. The recording equipment shall then be set to record. Care must be taken, particularly when a number of sets of recording media have been used, to ensure that there is no confusion between them. This could be achieved by marking the sets of recording media with consecutive identification numbers.

(f) Taking a break during the interview

4.12 When a break is to be taken during the course of an interview and the interview room is to be vacated by the suspect, the fact that a break is to be taken, the reason for it and the time shall be recorded. The recording equipment must be turned off and the recording media removed. The procedures for the conclusion of an interview set out in paragraph 4.19, below, should be followed.

4.13 When a break is to be a short one, and both the suspect and a police officer are to remain in the interview room, the fact that a break is to be taken, the reasons for it and the time shall be recorded on the recording media. The recording equipment may be turned off, but there is no need to remove the recording media. When the interview is recommenced the recording shall continue on the same recording media and the time at which the interview recommences shall be recorded.

4.14 When there is a break in questioning under caution, the interviewing officer must ensure that the person being questioned is aware that they remain under caution. If there is any doubt, the caution must be given again in full when the interview resumes. [See *Notes 4D and 4E*].

(g) Failure of recording equipment

4.15 If there is a failure of equipment which can be rectified quickly, the appropriate procedures set out in paragraph 4.12 shall be followed. When the recording is resumed the interviewer shall explain what has happened and record the time the interview recommences. If, however, it is not possible to continue recording on that particular recorder and no alternative equipment is readily available, the interview may continue without being recorded visually. In such circumstances, the procedures set out in paragraph 3.3 of this code for seeking the authority of the custody officer will be followed. [See *Note 4F*].

(h) Removing used recording media from recording equipment

4.16 Where used recording media are removed from the recording equipment during the course of an interview, they shall be retained and the procedures set out in paragraph 4.18 below followed.

(i) Conclusion of interview

4.17 Before the conclusion of the interview, the suspect shall be offered the opportunity to clarify anything he or she has said and asked if there is anything that they wish to add.

4.18 At the conclusion of the interview, including the taking and reading back of any written statement, the time shall be recorded and the recording equipment switched off. The master tape or CD shall be removed from the recording equipment, sealed with a master copy label and treated as an exhibit in accordance with the force standing orders. The interviewer shall sign the label and also ask the suspect and any appropriate adults or other third party present during the interview to sign it. If the suspect or third party refuses to sign the label, an officer of at least the rank of inspector, or if one is not available, the custody officer, shall be called into the interview room and asked to sign it.

4.19 The suspect shall be handed a notice which explains the use which will be made of the recording and the arrangements for access to it. The notice will also advise the suspect that a copy of the tape shall be supplied as soon as practicable if the person is charged or informed that he will be prosecuted.

Notes for Guidance

4A The interviewer should attempt to estimate the likely length of the interview and ensure that an appropriate quantity of certified recording media and labels with which to seal the master copies are available in the interview room.

4B Where the custody officer is called immediately to deal with the complaint, wherever possible the recording equipment should be left to run until the custody officer has entered the interview room and spoken to the person being interviewed. Continuation or termination of the interview should be at the discretion of the interviewing officer pending action by an inspector as set out in Code C.

4C Where the complaint is about a matter not connected with this code of practice or Code C, the decision to continue with the interview is at the discretion of the interviewing officer. Where the interviewing officer decides to continue with the interview, the person being interviewed shall be told that the complaint will be brought to the attention of the custody officer at the conclusion of the interview. When the interview is concluded, the interviewing officer must, as soon as practicable, inform the custody officer of the existence and nature of the complaint made.

4D In considering whether to caution again after a break, the officer should bear in mind that he may have to satisfy a court that the person understood that he was still under caution when the interview resumed.

4E The officer should bear in mind that it may be necessary to satisfy the court that nothing occurred during a break in an interview or between interviews which influenced the suspect's recorded evidence. On the re-commencement of an interview, the officer should consider summarising on the tape or CD the reason for the break and confirming this with the suspect.

4F If any part of the recording media breaks or is otherwise damaged during the interview, it should be sealed as a master copy in the presence of the suspect and the interview resumed where it left off. The undamaged part should be copied and the original sealed as a master tape in the suspect's presence, if necessary after the interview. If equipment for copying is not readily available, both parts should be sealed in the suspect's presence and the interview begun again.

4G The interviewer should be aware that a decision to continue recording against the wishes of the suspect may be the subject of comment in court.

5 After the Interview

5.1 The interviewer shall make a note in his or her pocket book of the fact that the interview has taken place and has been recorded, its time, duration and date and the identification number of the master copy of the recording media.

5.2 Where no proceedings follow in respect of the person whose interview was recorded, the recording media must nevertheless be kept securely in accordance with paragraph 6.1 and Note 6A.

Note for Guidance

5A Any written record of a recorded interview shall be made in accordance with national guidelines approved by the Secretary of State, and with regard to the advice contained in the Manual of Guidance for the preparation, processing and submission of files.

6 Master copy security

(a) General

6.1 The officer in charge of the police station at which interviews with suspects are recorded shall make arrangements for the master copies to be kept securely and their movements accounted for on the same basis as other material which may be used for evidential purposes, in accordance with force standing orders [See *Note 6A*].

(b) Breaking master copy seal for criminal proceedings

6.2 A police officer has no authority to break the seal on a master copy which is required for criminal trial or appeal proceedings. If it is necessary to gain access to the master copy, the police officer shall arrange for its seal to be broken in the presence of a representative of the Crown Prosecution Service. The defendant or their legal adviser shall be informed and given a reasonable opportunity to be present. If the defendant or their legal representative is present they shall be invited to reseal and sign the master copy. If either refuses or neither is present, this shall be done by the representative of the Crown Prosecution Service. [See *Notes 6B and 6C*].

(c) Breaking master copy seal: other cases

6.3 The chief officer of police is responsible for establishing arrangements for breaking the seal of the master copy where no criminal proceedings result, or the criminal proceedings, to which the interview relates, have been concluded and it becomes necessary to break the seal. These arrangements should be those which the chief officer considers are reasonably necessary to demonstrate to the person interviewed and any other party who may wish to use or refer to the interview record that the master copy has not been tampered with and that the interview record remains accurate. [See *Note 6D*]

6.4 Subject to paragraph 6.6, a representative of each party must be given a reasonable opportunity to be present when the seal is broken, the master copy copied and re-sealed.

6.5 If one or more of the parties is not present when the master copy seal is broken because they cannot be contacted or refuse to attend or paragraph 6.6 applies, arrangements should be made for an independent person such as a custody visitor, to be present. Alternatively, or as an additional safeguard, arrangement should be made for a film or photographs to be taken of the procedure.

6.6 Paragraph 6.5 does not require a person to be given an opportunity to be present when:

(a) it is necessary to break the master copy seal for the proper and effective further investigation of the original offence or the investigation of some other offence; and

(b) the officer in charge of the investigation has reasonable grounds to suspect that allowing an opportunity might prejudice any such an investigation or criminal proceedings which may be brought as a result or endanger any person. [See *Note 6E*]

(d) Documentation

6.7 When the master copy seal is broken, copied and re-sealed, a record must be made of the procedure followed, including the date time and place and persons present.

Notes for Guidance

6A This section is concerned with the security of the master copy which will have been sealed at the conclusion of the interview. Care should, however, be taken of working copies since their loss or destruction may lead unnecessarily to the need to have access to master copies.

6B If the master copy has been delivered to the Crown Court for their keeping after committal for trial the Crown Prosecutor will apply to the Chief Clerk of the Crown Court Centre for its release for unsealing by the Crown Prosecutor.

6C *Reference to the Crown Prosecution Service or to the Crown Prosecutor in this part of the code shall be taken to include any other body or person with a statutory responsibility for prosecution for whom the police conduct any recorded interviews.*

6D *The most common reasons for needing access to master copies that are not required for criminal proceedings arise from civil actions and complaints against police and civil actions between individuals arising out of allegations of crime investigated by police.*

6E *Paragraph 6.6 could apply, for example, when one or more of the outcomes or likely outcomes of the investigation might be: (i) the prosecution of one or more of the original suspects, (ii) the prosecution of someone previously not suspected, including someone who was originally a witness; and (iii) any original suspect being treated as a prosecution witness and when premature disclosure of any police action, particularly through contact with any parties involved, could lead to a real risk of compromising the investigation and endangering witnesses.*

Appendix 7

PACE Code of Practice for the Statutory Power of Arrest by Police Officers (Code G)

This Code applies to any arrest made by a police officer after midnight on 31 December 2005

1 Introduction

1.1 This Code of Practice deals with statutory power of police to arrest persons suspected of involvement in a criminal offence.

1.2 The right to liberty is a key principle of the Human Rights Act 1998. The exercise of the power of arrest represents an obvious and significant interference with that right.

1.3 The use of the power must be fully justified and officers exercising the power should consider if the necessary objectives can be met by other, less intrusive means. Arrest must never be used simply because it can be used. Absence of justification for exercising the powers of arrest may lead to challenges should the case proceed to court. When the power of arrest is exercised it is essential that it is exercised in a non- discriminatory and proportionate manner.

1.4 Section 24 of the Police and Criminal Evidence Act 1984 (as substituted by section 110 of the Serious Organised Crime and Police Act 2005) provides the statutory power of arrest. If the provisions of the Act and this Code are not observed, both the arrest and the conduct of any subsequent investigation may be open to question.

1.5 This code of practice must be readily available at all police stations for consultation by police officers and police staff, detained persons and members of the public.

1.6 The notes for guidance are not provisions of this code.

2 Elements of Arrest under section 24 PACE

2.1 A lawful arrest requires two elements:

A person's involvement or suspected involvement or attempted involvement in the commission of a criminal offence;

AND

Reasonable grounds for believing that the person's arrest is necessary.

2.2 Arresting officers are required to inform the person arrested that they have been arrested, even if this fact is obvious, and of the relevant circumstances of the arrest in relation to both elements and to inform the custody officer of these on arrival at the police station. See Code C paragraph 3.4.

Involvement in the commission of an offence'

2.3 A constable may arrest without warrant in relation to any offence, except for the single exception listed in Note for Guidance 1. A constable may arrest anyone:

- who is about to commit an offence or is in the act of committing an offence
- whom the officer has reasonable grounds for suspecting is about to commit an offence or to be committing an offence

- whom the officer has reasonable grounds to suspect of being guilty of an offence which he or she has reasonable grounds for suspecting has been committed
- anyone who is guilty of an offence which has been committed or anyone whom the officer has reasonable grounds for suspecting to be guilty of that offence.

Necessity criteria

2.4 The power of arrest is only exercisable if the constable has reasonable grounds for believing that it is necessary to arrest the person. The criteria for what may constitute necessity are set out in paragraph 2.9. It remains an operational decision at the discretion of the arresting officer as to:

- what action he or she may take at the point of contact with the individual;
- the necessity criterion or criteria (if any) which applies to the individual; and
- whether to arrest, report for summons, grant street bail, issue a fixed penalty notice or take any other action that is open to the officer.

2.5 In applying the criteria, the arresting officer has to be satisfied that at least one of the reasons supporting the need for arrest is satisfied.

2.6 Extending the power of arrest to all offences provides a constable with the ability to use that power to deal with any situation. However applying the necessity criteria requires the constable to examine and justify the reason or reasons why a person needs to be taken to a police station for the custody officer to decide whether the person should be placed in police detention.

2.7 The criteria below are set out in section 24 of PACE as substituted by section 110 of the Serious Organised Crime and Police Act 2005. The criteria are exhaustive. However, the circumstances that may satisfy those criteria remain a matter for the operational discretion of individual officers. Some examples are given below of what those circumstances may be.

2.8 In considering the individual circumstances, the constable must take into account the situation of the victim, the nature of the offence, the circumstances of the suspect and the needs of the investigative process.

2.9 The criteria are that the arrest is necessary:

(a) to enable the name of the person in question to be ascertained (in the case where the constable does not know, and cannot readily ascertain, the person's name, or has reasonable grounds for doubting whether a name given by the person as his name is his real name)

(b) correspondingly as regards the person's address
an address is a satisfactory address for service of summons if the person will be at it for a sufficiently long period for it to be possible to serve him or her with a summons; or, that some other person at that address specified by the person will accept service of the summons on their behalf.

(c) to prevent the person in question—

(i) causing physical injury to himself or any other person;
(ii) suffering physical injury;
(iii) causing loss or damage to property;
(iv) committing an offence against public decency (only applies where members of the public going about their normal business cannot reasonably be expected to avoid the person in question); or
(v) causing an unlawful obstruction of the highway;

(d) to protect a child or other vulnerable person from the person in question

(e) to allow the prompt and effective investigation of the offence or of the conduct of the person in question.
This may include cases such as:

(i) Where there are reasonable grounds to believe that the person:

- has made false statements;
- has made statements which cannot be readily verified;
- has presented false evidence;
- may steal or destroy evidence;
- may make contact with co-suspects or conspirators;

- may intimidate or threaten or make contact with witnesses;
- where it is necessary to obtain evidence by questioning; or

(ii) when considering arrest in connection with an indictable offence, there is a need to:
- enter and search any premises occupied or controlled by a person
- search the person
- prevent contact with others
- take fingerprints, footwear impressions, samples or photographs of the suspect

(iii) ensuring compliance with statutory drug testing requirements.

(f) to prevent any prosecution for the offence from being hindered by the disappearance of the person in question.

This may arise if there are reasonable grounds for believing that
- if the person is not arrested he or she will fail to attend court
- street bail after arrest would be insufficient to deter the suspect from trying to evade prosecution

3 Information to be given on Arrest

(a) Cautions—when a caution must be given (taken from Code C section 10)

3.1 A person whom there are grounds to suspect of an offence (see Note 2) must be cautioned before any questions about an offence, or further questions if the answers provide the grounds for suspicion, are put to them if either the suspect's answers or silence, (i.e. failure or refusal to answer or answer satisfactorily) may be given in evidence to a court in a prosecution. A person need not be cautioned if questions are for other necessary purposes e.g.:

(a) solely to establish their identity or ownership of any vehicle;

(b) to obtain information in accordance with any relevant statutory requirement;

(c) in furtherance of the proper and effective conduct of a search, e.g. to determine the need to search in the exercise of powers of stop and search or to seek cooperation while carrying out a search;

(d) to seek verification of a written record as in *Code C paragraph 11.13*;

(e) when examining a person in accordance with the Terrorism Act 2000, Schedule 7 and the Code of Practice for Examining Officers issued under that Act, Schedule 14, paragraph 6.

3.2 Whenever a person not under arrest is initially cautioned, or reminded they are under caution, that person must at the same time be told they are not under arrest and are free to leave if they want to.

3.3 A person who is arrested, or further arrested, must be informed at the time, or as soon as practicable thereafter, that they are under arrest and the grounds for their arrest, see *Note 3*.

3.4 A person who is arrested, or further arrested, must also be cautioned unless:

(a) it is impracticable to do so by reason of their condition or behaviour at the time;

(b) they have already been cautioned immediately prior to arrest as in *paragraph 3.1*.

(c) Terms of the caution (Taken from Code C section 10)

3.5 The caution, which must be given on arrest, should be in the following terms:

"You do not have to say anything. But it may harm your defence if you do not mention when questioned something which you later rely on in Court. Anything you do say may be given in evidence."

See *Note 5*

3.6 Minor deviations from the words of any caution given in accordance with this Code do not constitute a breach of this Code, provided the sense of the relevant caution is preserved. See *Note 6*

3.7 When, despite being cautioned, a person fails to co-operate or to answer particular questions which may affect their immediate treatment, the person should be informed of any relevant consequences and that those consequences are not affected by the caution. Examples are when a person's refusal to provide:

- their name and address when charged may make them liable to detention;
- particulars and information in accordance with a statutory requirement, e.g. under the Road Traffic Act 1988, may amount to an offence or may make the person liable to a further arrest.

4 Records of Arrest

(a) General

4.1 The arresting officer is required to record in his pocket book or by other methods used for recording information:
- the nature and circumstances of the offence leading to the arrest
- the reason or reasons why arrest was necessary
- the giving of the caution
- anything said by the person at the time of arrest

4.2 Such a record should be made at the time of the arrest unless impracticable to do. If not made at that time, the record should then be completed as soon as possible thereafter.

4.3 On arrival at the police station, the custody officer shall open the custody record (see paragraph 1.1A and section 2 of Code C). The information given by the arresting officer on the circumstances and reason or reasons for arrest shall be recorded as part of the custody record. Alternatively, a copy of the record made by the officer in accordance with paragraph 4.1 above shall be attached as part of the custody record. See *paragraph 2.2* and *Code C paragraphs 3.4 and 10.3.*

4.4 The custody record will serve as a record of the arrest. Copies of the custody record will be provided in accordance with paragraphs 2.4 and 2.4A of Code C and access for inspection of the original record in accordance with paragraph 2.5 of Code C.

(b) Interviews and arrests

4.5 Records of interview, significant statements or silences will be treated in the same way as set out in sections 10 and 11 of Code C and in Code E (tape recording of interviews).

Notes for guidance

1 *The powers of arrest for offences under sections 4(1) and 5(1) of the Criminal Law Act 1967 require that the offences to which they relate must carry a sentence fixed by law or one in which a first time offender aged 18 or over could be sentenced to 5 years or more imprisonment.*

2 *There must be some reasonable, objective grounds for the suspicion, based on known facts or information which are relevant to the likelihood the offence has been committed and the person to be questioned committed it.*

3 *An arrested person must be given sufficient information to enable them to understand they have been deprived of their liberty and the reason they have been arrested, e.g. when a person is arrested on suspicion of committing an offence they must be informed of the suspected offence's nature, when and where it was committed. The suspect must also be informed of the reason or reasons why arrest is considered necessary. Vague or technical language should be avoided.*

4 *Nothing in this Code requires a caution to be given or repeated when informing a person not under arrest they may be prosecuted for an offence. However, a court will not be able to draw any inferences under the Criminal Justice and Public Order Act 1994, section 34, if the person was not cautioned.*

5 *If it appears a person does not understand the caution, the people giving it should explain it in their own words.*

6 *The powers available to an officer as the result of an arrest—for example, entry and search of premises, holding a person incommunicado, setting up road blocks—are only available in respect of indictable offences and are subject to the specific requirements on authorisation as set out in the 1984 Act and relevant PACE Code of Practice.*

Appendix 8

Summary of PACE Code of Practice for the Detention, Treatment and Questioning of Persons under s. 41 of, and sch. 8 to, the Terrorism Act 2000 (Code H)

As stated at the start of chapter 11, Code H has been introduced and applies to people in police detention following their arrest under the Terrorism Act 2000, s. 41; it has effect from midnight on 24 July 2006 notwithstanding that the person has been arrested before that time. This has led to a number of revisions to Code C which include the following paragraphs:

- 1.11 making reference to Code H
- 1.12(v)—not used
- 2.6A(a)—not used
- 5.6(b)—amended to remove references to terrorism detainees
- 8A—amended to remove references to terrorism detainees
- 10.1(e)—not used
- 15.8—not used
- 15A—amended to remove references to terrorism detainees
- Annex B para B—not used

Code H is not reproduced within the manual but should be available in custody suites and at police stations. Generally Code H mirrors much of Code C; however in relation to reviews and extensions of detention there are significant changes from the equivalent provisions in PACE Code C owing to the changes made to maximum detention times by the Terrorism Act 2006. These can be found in Code H in section 14.

Section 1—General

This section covers the scope and applicability of the Code (which are, by definition, different from the equivalent provisions of Code C); it also covers the availability of the Code, definitions, applicability to the deaf, blind and speech impaired and the use of reasonable force, and in these respects follows Code C.

Section 2—Custody Records

This section follows Code C. It covers general requirements for making custody records, including the exemption for counter terrorism officers from disclosing their identities on custody records and provisions as to access to custody records by detainees' solicitors and disclosure of those records to them.

Section 3—Initial Action in respect of arrested individuals

Code H broadly follows Code C in respect of detainees' rights and arrangements for exercising them but differs in a number of respects:

(a) the record will indicate that the arrest was under s. 41 as opposed to indicating the offence in respect of which the arrest was made—Note 3G indicates that, where an arrest is made on grounds of sensitive information which cannot be disclosed, the recorded grounds 'may be given in terms of the interpretation of "terrorist"' set out in s. 40(1)(a) or 40(1)(b);

(b) there is a specific provision to the effect that risk assessments do not form part of the custody record and should not be shown to the detainee or their legal representative;

(c) there are provisions relating to the initial steps that may be taken in connection with the identification of suspects.

Section 4—Detainees' Property

This section of Code H includes a simplification of the circumstances in which a custody officer should search a detainee to ascertain what they have in their possession but there is no material change in comparison with Code C.

Section 5—Right not to be Held Incommunicado

The detainee's right to have someone informed of his whereabouts closely follows the equivalent section of Code C but there is much more detailed guidance on visiting rights. A requirement is imposed for custody officers to liaise with the investigation team to ascertain the risks presented by visits. Where visits from relatives etc. present a risk, consideration of more frequent visits from independent visitor schemes is suggested. Visits from official visitors ('official visitors' may include accredited faith representatives and MPs) may be allowed subject to consultation with the officer in charge of the investigation. Note 5B indicates that custody officers should bear in mind the effects of prolonged detention under the Act and consider the health and welfare benefits that visits bring to the health and welfare of detainees who are held for extended periods. However, Note 5G reminds officers that the nature of terrorist investigations means that they need to have 'particular regard to the possibility of suspects attempting to pass information which may be detrimental to public safety, or to an investigation'.

Section 6—Right to Legal Advice

The principal difference from Code C is that there is provision for an authorisation to be given whereby a detainee may only consult a solicitor within sight and hearing of a qualified officer (a uniformed officer of at least the rank of inspector who has no connection with the investigation).

Section 7—Citizens of Independent Commonwealth Countries or Foreign Nationals

Section 7 shows no material change from the equivalent Code C provisions.

Section 8—Conditions of Detention

The main differences from Code C are that there is specific reference to allowing detainees to practise religious observance and to the provision of reading material, including religious texts. Police should consult with representatives of religious communities on provision of facilities for religious observance and handling of religious texts and other articles. The benefits of exercise for detainees, particularly in the cases of prolonged detention, are emphasised. If facilities exist, indoor exercise is to be offered if requested or if outdoor exercise is not practicable. Although the same restrictions on putting a juvenile in a cell apply as under Code C, there is no requirement to include occasions when a juvenile is so confined on the custody record.

Section 9—Care and Treatment of Detained Persons

Section 9 of Code H begins by requiring that, notwithstanding other requirements for medical attention, 'detainees who are held for more than 96 hours must be visited by a healthcare professional at least once every 24 hours'. In all other material respects, the provisions are the same as under Code C.

Section 10—Cautions

Insofar as relevant, the provisions on cautions closely follow those of Code C.

Section 11—Interviews (General)

There are no material differences from Code C under this section. The Code H equivalent is however much shorter, reflecting the fact that not all instances covered by the Code C equivalent are relevant to detention of terrorist suspects

Section 12—Interviews in Police Stations

The only material difference here is set out at para. 12.9:

12.9 During extended periods where no interviews take place, because of the need to gather further evidence or analyse existing evidence, detainees and their legal representative shall be informed that the investigation into the relevant offence remains ongoing. If practicable, the detainee and legal representative should also be made aware in general terms of any reasons for long gaps between interviews. Consideration should be given to allowing visits, more frequent exercise, or for reading or writing materials to be offered. *See paragraph 5.4, section 8* and *Note 12C.*

Note 12C indicates that consideration should be given to the matters referred to in para. 12.9 after a period of over 24 hours without questioning.

Section 13—Interpreters

The requirements for accredited interpreters to be provided for deaf or non-English speakers, for both general custody procedures and interviews are the same as under Code C.

Section 14—Reviews and Extensions of Detention

This section contains significant changes from the equivalent provisions in PACE Code C (PACE Code C, section 15), owing to the changes made to maximum detention times by the Terrorism Act 2006. It is set out in full below.

14 Reviews and Extensions of Detention

(a) Reviews and Extensions of Detention

14.1 The powers and duties of the review officer are in the Terrorism Act 2000, Schedule 8, Part II. See *Notes 14A* and *14B*. A review officer should carry out his duties at the police station where the detainee is held, and be allowed such access to the detainee as is necessary for him to exercise those duties.

14.2 For the purposes of reviewing a person's detention, no officer shall put specific questions to the detainee:
- regarding their involvement in any offence; or
- in respect of any comments they may make:
  - when given the opportunity to make representations; or
  - in response to a decision to keep them in detention or extend the maximum period of detention.

Such an exchange could constitute an interview as in *paragraph 11.1* and would be subject to the associated safeguards in *section 11* and, in respect of a person who has been charged. See *PACE Code C Section 16.8.*

14.3 If detention is necessary for longer than 48 hours, a police officer of at least superintendent rank, or a Crown Prosecutor may apply for warrants of further detention under the Terrorism Act 2000, Schedule 8, Part III.

14.4 When an application for a warrant of further or extended detention is sought under Paragraph 29 or 36 of Schedule 8, the detained person and their representative must be informed of their rights in respect of the application. These include:

(a) the right to a written or oral notice of the warrant. See *Note 14G.*
(b) the right to make oral or written representations to the judicial authority about the application.
(c) the right to be present and legally represented at the hearing of the application, unless specifically excluded by the judicial authority.
(d) their right to free legal advice (see section 6 of this Code).

(b) Transfer of Detained Persons to Prison

14.5 Where a warrant is issued which authorises detention beyond a period of 14 days from the time of arrest (or if a person was being detained under TACT Schedule 7, from the time at which the examination under Schedule 7 began), the detainee must be transferred from detention in a police station to detention in a designated prison as soon as is practicable, unless:

(a) the detainee specifically requests to remain in detention at a police station and that request can be accommodated, or
(b) there are reasonable grounds to believe that transferring a person to a prison would:
  (i) significantly hinder a terrorism investigation;
  (ii) delay charging of the detainee or his release from custody, or
  (iii) otherwise prevent the investigation from being conducted diligently and expeditiously.

If any of the grounds in (b)(i) to (iii) above are relied upon, these must be presented to the judicial authority as part of the application for the warrant that would extend detention beyond a period of 14 days from the time of arrest (or if a person was being detained under

TACT Schedule 7, from the time at which the examination under Schedule 7 began). *See Note 14J.*

14.6 If a person remains in detention at a police station under a warrant of further detention as described at section 14.5, they must be transferred to a prison as soon as practicable after the grounds at (b)(i) to (iii) of that section cease to apply.

14.7 Police should maintain an agreement with the National Offender Management Service (NOMS) that stipulates named prisons to which individuals may be transferred under this section. This should be made with regard to ensuring detainees are moved to the most suitable prison for the purposes of the investigation and their welfare, and should include provision for the transfer of male, female and juvenile detainees. Police should ensure that the Governor of a prison to which they intend to transfer a detainee is given reasonable notice of this. Where practicable, this should be no later than the point at which a warrant is applied for that would take the period of detention beyond 14 days.

14.8 Following a detained person's transfer to a designated prison, their detention will be governed by the terms of Schedule 8 and Prison Rules, and this Code of Practice will not apply during any period that the person remains in prison detention. The Code will once more apply if a detained person is transferred back from prison detention to police detention. In order to enable the Governor to arrange for the production of the detainee back into police custody, police should give notice to the governor of the relevant prison as soon as possible of any decision to transfer a detainee from prison back to a police station. Any transfer between a prison and a police station should be conducted by police, and this Code will be applicable during the period of transit. See *Note 14K*. A detainee should only remain in police custody having been transferred back from a prison, for as long as is necessary for the purpose of the investigation.

14.9 The investigating team and custody officer should provide as much information as necessary to enable the relevant prison authorities to provide appropriate facilities to detain an individual. This should include, but not be limited to:
   (i) medical assessments
   (ii) security and risk assessments
   (iii) details of the detained person's legal representatives
   (iv) details of any individuals from whom the detained person has requested visits, or who have requested to visit the detained person.

14.10 Where a detainee is to be transferred to prison, the custody officer should inform the detainee's legal adviser beforehand that the transfer is to take place (including the name of the prison). The custody officer should also make all reasonable attempts to inform:
- family or friends who have been informed previously of the detainee's detention; and
- the person who was initially informed of the detainee's detention as at *paragraph 5.1.*

(c) Documentation

14.11 It is the responsibility of the officer who gives any reminders as at *paragraph 14.4*, to ensure that these are noted in the custody record, as well any comments made by the detained person upon being told of those rights.

14.12 The grounds for, and extent of, any delay in conducting a review shall be recorded.

14.13 Any written representations shall be retained.

14.14 A record shall be made as soon as practicable about the outcome of each review or determination whether to extend the maximum detention period without charge or an application for a warrant of further detention or its extension.

14.15 Any decision not to transfer a detained person to a designated prison under paragraph *14.5,* must be recorded, along with the reasons for this decision. If a request under paragraph *14.5(a)* is not accommodated, the reasons for this should also be recorded.

Notes for guidance

14A TACT Schedule 8 Part II sets out the procedures for review of detention up to 48 hours from the time of arrest under TACT section 41 (or if a person was being detained under TACT Schedule 7, from the time at which the examination under Schedule 7 began). These include provisions for the requirement to review detention, postponing a review, grounds for continued detention, designating a review officer, representations, rights of the detained person and keeping a record. The review officer's role ends after a warrant has been issued for extension of detention under Part III of Schedule 8.

14B *Section 24(1) of the Terrorism Act 2006, amended the grounds contained within the 2000 Act on which a review officer may authorise continued detention. Continued detention may be authorised if it is necessary—*

- *(a) to obtain relevant evidence whether by questioning him or otherwise*
- *(b) to preserve relevant evidence*
- *(c) while awaiting the result of an examination or analysis of relevant evidence*
- *(d) for the examination or analysis of anything with a view to obtaining relevant evidence*
- *(e) pending a decision to apply to the Secretary of State for a deportation notice to be served on the detainee, the making of any such application, or the consideration of any such application by the Secretary of State*
- *(f) pending a decision to charge the detainee with an offence.*

14C *Applications for warrants to extend detention beyond 48 hours, may be made for periods of 7 days at a time (initially under TACT Schedule 8 paragraph 29, and extensions thereafter under TACT Schedule 8, paragraph 36), up to a maximum period of 28 days from the time of arrest (or if a person was being detained under TACT Schedule 7, from the time at which the examination under Schedule 7 began). Applications may be made for shorter periods than 7 days, which must be specified. The judicial authority may also substitute a shorter period if he feels a period of 7 days is inappropriate.*

14D *Unless Note 14F applies, applications for warrants that would take the total period of detention up to 14 days or less should be made to a judicial authority, meaning a District Judge (Magistrates' Court) designated by the Lord Chancellor to hear such applications.*

14E *Any application for a warrant which would take the period of detention beyond 14 days from the time of arrest (or if a person was being detained under TACT Schedule 7, from the time at which the examination under Schedule 7 began), must be made to a High Court Judge.*

14F *If an application has been made to a High Court Judge for a warrant which would take detention beyond 14 days, and the High Court Judge instead issues a warrant for a period of time which would not take detention beyond 14 days, further applications for extension of detention must also be made to a High Court Judge, regardless of the period of time to which they refer.*

14G *TACT Schedule 8 paragraph 31 requires a notice to be given to the detained person if a warrant is sought for further detention. This must be provided before the judicial hearing of the application for that warrant and must include:*

- *(a) notification that the application for a warrant has been made*
- *(b) the time at which the application was made*
- *(c) the time at which the application is to be heard*
- *(d) the grounds on which further detention is sought.*

A notice must also be provided each time an application is made to extend an existing warrant.

14H *An officer applying for an order under TACT Schedule 8 paragraph 34 to withhold specified information on which he intends to rely when applying for a warrant of further detention, may make the application for the order orally or in writing. The most appropriate method of application will depend on the circumstances of the case and the need to ensure fairness to the detainee.*

14I *Where facilities exist, hearings relating to extension of detention under Part III of Schedule 8 may take place using video conferencing facilities provided that the requirements set out in Schedule 8 are still met. However, if the judicial authority requires the detained person to be physically present at any hearing, this should be complied with as soon as practicable. Paragraphs 33(4) to 33(9) of TACT Schedule 8 govern the relevant conduct of hearings.*

14J *Transfer to prison is intended to ensure that individuals who are detained for extended periods of time are held in a place designed for longer periods of detention than police stations. Prison will provide detainees with a greater range of facilities more appropriate to longer detention periods.*

14K *The Code will only apply as is appropriate to the conditions of detention during the period of transit. There is obviously no requirement to provide such things as bed linen or reading materials for the journey between prison and police station.*

General

There are no equivalents to PACE Code C, sections 16 and 17, which cannot apply in the context of a terrorist investigation. The annexes to Code H are in terms which closely follow Code C—changes are only to remove or amend references that are not applicable to terrorism detention.

Appendix 9

Disclosure Extracts

Criminal Procedure and Investigations Act 1996: Code of Practice Under Part II

Preamble

This code of practice is issued under Part II of the Criminal Procedure and Investigations Act 1996 ('the Act'). It sets out the manner in which police officers are to record, retain and reveal to the prosecutor material obtained in a criminal investigation and which may be relevant to the investigation, and related matters.

Introduction

1.1 This code of practice applies in respect of criminal investigations conducted by police officers which begin on or after the day on which this code comes into effect. Persons other than police officers who are charged with the duty of conducting an investigation as defined in the Act are to have regard to the relevant provisions of the code, and should take these into account in applying their own operating procedures.

1.2 This code does not apply to persons who are not charged with the duty of conducting an investigation as defined in the Act.

1.3 Nothing in this code applies to material intercepted in obedience to a warrant issued under section 5 of the Regulation of Investigatory Powers Act 2000, or to any copy of that material as defined in section 15 of the 2000 Act.

1.4 This code extends only to England and Wales.

Definitions

2.1 In this code:

- *a criminal investigation* is an investigation conducted by police officers with a view to it being ascertained whether a person should be charged with an offence, or whether a person charged with an offence is guilty of it. This will include:
  - investigations into crimes that have been committed;
  - investigations whose purpose is to ascertain whether a crime has been committed, with a view to the possible institution of criminal proceedings; and
  - investigations which begin in the belief that a crime may be committed, for example when the police keep premises or individuals under observation for a period of time, with a view to the possible institution of criminal proceedings;

- charging a person with an offence includes prosecution by way of summons;
- *an investigator* is any police officer involved in the conduct of a criminal investigation. All investigators have a responsibility for carrying out the duties imposed on them under this code, including in particular recording information, and retaining records of information and other material;
- the *officer in charge of an investigation* is the police officer responsible for directing a criminal investigation. He is also responsible for ensuring that proper procedures are in place for recording information, and retaining records of information and other material, in the investigation;
- the *disclosure officer* is the person responsible for examining material retained by the police during the investigation; revealing material to the prosecutor during the investigation and any criminal proceedings resulting from it, and certifying that he has done this; and disclosing material to the accused at the request of the prosecutor;
- the *prosecutor* is the authority responsible for the conduct, on behalf of the Crown, of criminal proceedings resulting from a specific criminal investigation;
- *material* is material of any kind, including information and objects, which is obtained in the course of a criminal investigation and which may be relevant to the investigation. This includes not only material coming into the possession of the investigator (such as documents seized in the course of searching premises) but also material generated by him (such as interview records);
- material may be *relevant to an investigation* if it appears to an investigator, or to the officer in charge of an investigation, or to the disclosure officer, that it has some bearing on any offence under investigation or any person being investigated, or on the surrounding circumstances of the case, unless it is incapable of having any impact on the case;
- *sensitive material* is material, the disclosure of which, the disclosure officer believes, would give rise to a real risk of serious prejudice to an important public interest;
- references to *prosecution disclosure* are to the duty of the prosecutor under sections 3 and 7A of the Act to disclose material which is in his possession or which he has inspected in pursuance of this code, and which might reasonably be considered capable of undermining the case against the accused, or of assisting the case for the accused;
- references to the disclosure of material to a person accused of an offence include references to the disclosure of material to his legal representative;
- references to police officers and to the chief officer of police include those employed in a police force as defined in section 3(3) of the Prosecution of Offences Act 1985.

General responsibilities

3.1 The functions of the investigator, the officer in charge of an investigation and the disclosure officer are separate. Whether they are undertaken by one, two or more persons will depend on the complexity of the case and the administrative arrangements within each police force. Where they are undertaken by more than one person, close consultation between them is essential to the effective performance of the duties imposed by this code.

3.2 In any criminal investigation, one or more deputy disclosure officers may be appointed to assist the disclosure officer, and a deputy disclosure officer may perform any function of a disclosure officer as defined in paragraph 2.1.

3.3 The chief officer of police for each police force is responsible for putting in place arrangements to ensure that in every investigation the identity of the officer in charge of an investigation and the disclosure officer is recorded. The chief officer of police for each police force shall ensure that disclosure officers and deputy disclosure officers have sufficient skills and authority, commensurate with the complexity of the investigation, to discharge their functions effectively. An individual must not be appointed as disclosure officer, or continue in that role, if that is likely to result in a conflict of interest, for instance, if the disclosure officer is the victim of the alleged crime which is the subject of the investigation. The advice of a more senior officer must always be sought if there is doubt as to whether a conflict of interest precludes an individual acting as disclosure officer. If thereafter the doubt remains, the advice of a prosecutor should be sought.

3.4 The officer in charge of an investigation may delegate tasks to another investigator, to civilians employed by the police force, or to other persons participating in the investigation under arrangements for joint investigations, but he remains responsible for ensuring that these have been carried out and for accounting for any general policies followed in the investigation. In particular, it is an essential part of his duties to ensure that all material which may be relevant to an investigation is retained, and either made available to the disclosure officer or (in exceptional circumstances) revealed directly to the prosecutor.

3.5 In conducting an investigation, the investigator should pursue all reasonable lines of inquiry, whether these point towards or away from the suspect. What is reasonable in each case will depend on the particular circumstances. For example, where material is held on computer, it is a matter for the investigator to decide which material on the computer it is reasonable to inquire into, and in what manner.

3.6 If the officer in charge of an investigation believes that other persons may be in possession of material that may be relevant to the investigation, and if this has not been obtained under paragraph 3.5 above, he should ask the disclosure officer to inform them of the existence of the investigation and to invite them to retain the material in case they receive a request for its disclosure. The disclosure officer should inform the prosecutor that they may have such material. However, the officer in charge of an investigation is not required to make speculative enquiries of other persons; there must be some reason to believe that they may have relevant material. That reason may come from information provided to the police by the accused or from other inquiries made or from some other source.

3.7 If, during a criminal investigation, the officer in charge of an investigation or disclosure officer for any reason no longer has responsibility for the functions falling to him, either his supervisor or the police officer in charge of criminal investigations for the police force concerned must assign someone else to assume that responsibility. That person's identity must be recorded, as with those initially responsible for these functions in each investigation.

Recording of information

4.1 If material which may be relevant to the investigation consists of information which is not recorded in any form, the officer in charge of an investigation must ensure that it is recorded in a durable or retrievable form (whether in writing, on video or audio tape, or on computer disk).

4.2 Where it is not practicable to retain the initial record of information because it forms part of a larger record which is to be destroyed, its contents should be transferred as a true record to a durable and more easily-stored form before that happens.

4.3 Negative information is often relevant to an investigation. If it may be relevant it must be recorded. An example might be a number of people present in a particular place at a particular time who state that they saw nothing unusual.

4.4 Where information which may be relevant is obtained, it must be recorded at the time it is obtained or as soon as practicable after that time. This includes, for example, information obtained in house-to-house enquiries, although the requirement to record information promptly does not require an investigator to take a statement from a potential witness where it would not otherwise be taken.

Retention of material

(a) Duty to retain material

5.1 The investigator must retain material obtained in a criminal investigation which may be relevant to the investigation. Material may be photographed, video-recorded, captured digitally or otherwise retained in the form of a copy rather than the original at any time, if the original is perishable; the original was supplied to the investigator rather than generated by him and is to be returned to its owner; or the retention of a copy rather than the original is reasonable in all the circumstances.

5.2 Where material has been seized in the exercise of the powers of seizure conferred by the Police and Criminal Evidence Act 1984, the duty to retain it under this code is subject to the provisions on the retention of seized material in section 22 of that Act.

5.3 If the officer in charge of an investigation becomes aware as a result of developments in the case that material previously examined but not retained (because it was not thought to be relevant) may now be relevant to the investigation, he should, wherever practicable, take steps to obtain it or ensure that it is retained for further inspection or for production in court if required.

5.4 The duty to retain material includes in particular the duty to retain material falling into the following categories, where it may be relevant to the investigation:

— crime reports (including crime report forms, relevant parts of incident report books or police officers' notebooks);
— custody records;
— records which are derived from tapes of telephone messages (for example, 999 calls) containing descriptions of an alleged offence or offender;
— final versions of witness statements (and draft versions where their content differs from the final version), including any exhibits mentioned (unless these have been returned to their owner on the understanding that they will be produced in court if required);
— interview records (written records, or audio or video tapes, of interviews with actual or potential witnesses or suspects);
— communications between the police and experts such as forensic scientists, reports of work carried out by experts, and schedules of scientific material prepared by the expert for the investigator, for the purposes of criminal proceedings;
— records of the first description of a suspect by each potential witness who purports to identify or describe the suspect, whether or not the description differs from that of subsequent descriptions by that or other witnesses;
— any material casting doubt on the reliability of a witness.

5.5 The duty to retain material, where it may be relevant to the investigation, also includes in particular the duty to retain material which may satisfy the test for prosecution disclosure in the Act, such as:

— information provided by an accused person which indicates an explanation for the offence with which he has been charged;
— any material casting doubt on the reliability of a confession;
— any material casting doubt on the reliability of a prosecution witness.

5.6 The duty to retain material falling into these categories does not extend to items which are purely ancillary to such material and possess no independent significance (for example, duplicate copies of records or reports).

(b) Length of time for which material is to be retained

5.7 All material which may be relevant to the investigation must be retained until a decision is taken whether to institute proceedings against a person for an offence.

5.8 If a criminal investigation results in proceedings being instituted, all material which may be relevant must be retained at least until the accused is acquitted or convicted or the prosecutor decides not to proceed with the case.

5.9 Where the accused is convicted, all material which may be relevant must be retained at least until:

— the convicted person is released from custody, or discharged from hospital, in cases where the court imposes a custodial sentence or a hospital order;
— six months from the date of conviction, in all other cases.

If the court imposes a custodial sentence or hospital order and the convicted person is released from custody or discharged from hospital earlier than six months from the date of conviction, all material which may be relevant must be retained at least until six months from the date of conviction.

5.10 If an appeal against conviction is in progress when the release or discharge occurs, or at the end of the period of six months specified in paragraph 5.9, all material which may be relevant must be retained until the appeal is determined. Similarly, if the Criminal Cases Review Commission is considering an application at that point in time, all material which may be relevant must be retained at least until the Commission decides not to refer the case to the Court of Appeal, or until the Court determines the appeal resulting from the reference by the Commission.

5.11 Material need not be retained by the police as required in paragraph 5.8 if it was seized and is to be returned to its owner.

Preparation of material for prosecutor

(a) Introduction

6.1 The officer in charge of the investigation, the disclosure officer or an investigator may seek advice from the prosecutor about whether any particular item of material may be relevant to the investigation.

6.2 Material which may be relevant to an investigation, which has been retained in accordance with this code, and which the disclosure officer believes will not form part of the prosecution case, must be listed on a schedule.

6.3 Material which the disclosure officer does not believe is sensitive must be listed on a schedule of non-sensitive material. The schedule must include a statement that the disclosure officer does not believe the material is sensitive.

6.4 Any material which is believed to be sensitive must be either listed on a schedule of sensitive material or, in exceptional circumstances, revealed to the prosecutor separately. If there is no sensitive material, the disclosure officer must record this fact on a schedule of sensitive material.

6.5 Paragraphs 6.6 to 6.11 below apply to both sensitive and non-sensitive material. Paragraphs 6.12 to 6.14 apply to sensitive material only.

(b) Circumstances in which a schedule is to be prepared

6.6 The disclosure officer must ensure that a schedule is prepared in the following circumstances:

- the accused is charged with an offence which is triable only on indictment;
- the accused is charged with an offence which is triable either way, and it is considered either that the case is likely to be tried on indictment or that the accused is likely to plead not guilty at a summary trial;
- the accused is charged with a summary offence, and it is considered that he is likely to plead not guilty.

6.7 In respect of either way and summary offences, a schedule may not be needed if a person has admitted the offence, or if a police officer witnessed the offence and that person has not denied it.

6.8 If it is believed that the accused is likely to plead guilty at a summary trial, it is not necessary to prepare a schedule in advance. If, contrary to this belief, the accused pleads not guilty at a summary trial, or the offence is to be tried on indictment, the disclosure officer must ensure that a schedule is prepared as soon as is reasonably practicable after that happens.

(c) Way in which material is to be listed on schedule

6.9 The disclosure officer should ensure that each item of material is listed separately on the schedule, and is numbered consecutively. The description of each item should make clear the nature of the item and should contain sufficient detail to enable the prosecutor to decide whether he needs to inspect the material before deciding whether or not it should be disclosed.

6.10 In some enquiries it may not be practicable to list each item of material separately. For example, there may be many items of a similar or repetitive nature. These may be listed in a block and described by quantity and generic title.

6.11 Even if some material is listed in a block, the disclosure officer must ensure that any items among that material which might satisfy the test for prosecution disclosure are listed and described individually.

(d) Treatment of sensitive material

6.12 Subject to paragraph 6.13 below, the disclosure officer must list on a sensitive schedule any material, the disclosure of which he believes would give rise to a real risk of serious prejudice to an important public interest, and the reason for that belief. The schedule must include a statement that the disclosure officer believes the material is sensitive. Depending on the circumstances, examples of such material may include the following among others:

— material relating to national security;
— material received from the intelligence and security agencies;
— material relating to intelligence from foreign sources which reveals sensitive intelligence gathering methods;
— material given in confidence;
— material relating to the identity or activities of informants, or undercover police officers, or witnesses, or other persons supplying information to the police who may be in danger if their identities are revealed;
— material revealing the location of any premises or other place used for police surveillance, or the identity of any person allowing a police officer to use them for surveillance;
— material revealing, either directly or indirectly, techniques and methods relied upon by a police officer in the course of a criminal investigation, for example covert surveillance techniques, or other methods of detecting crime;
— material whose disclosure might facilitate the commission of other offences or hinder the prevention and detection of crime;
— material upon the strength of which search warrants were obtained;
— material containing details of persons taking part in identification parades;
— material supplied to an investigator during a criminal investigation which has been generated by an official of a body concerned with the regulation or supervision of bodies corporate or of persons engaged in financial activities, or which has been generated by a person retained by such a body;
— material supplied to an investigator during a criminal investigation which relates to a child or young person and which has been generated by a local authority social services department, an Area Child Protection Committee or other party contacted by an investigator during the investigation.
— material relating to the private life of a witness.

6.13 In exceptional circumstances, where an investigator considers that material is so sensitive that its revelation to the prosecutor by means of an entry on the sensitive schedule is inappropriate, the existence of the material must be revealed to the prosecutor separately. This will apply only where compromising the material would be likely to lead directly to the loss of life, or directly threaten national security.

6.14 In such circumstances, the responsibility for informing the prosecutor lies with the investigator who knows the detail of the sensitive material. The investigator should act as soon as is reasonably practicable after the file containing the prosecution case is sent to the prosecutor. The investigator must also ensure that the prosecutor is able to inspect the material so that he can assess whether it is disclosable and, if so, whether it needs to be brought before a court for a ruling on disclosure.

Revelation of material to prosecutor

7.1 The disclosure officer must give the schedules to the prosecutor. Wherever practicable this should be at the same time as he gives him the file containing the material for the prosecution case (or as soon as is reasonably practicable after the decision on mode of trial or the plea, in cases to which paragraph 6.8 applies).

7.2 The disclosure officer should draw the attention of the prosecutor to any material an investigator has retained (including material to which paragraph 6.13 applies) which may satisfy the test for prosecution disclosure in the Act, and should explain why he has come to that view.

7.3 At the same time as complying with the duties in paragraphs 7.1 and 7.2, the disclosure officer must give the prosecutor a copy of any material which falls into the following categories (unless such material has already been given to the prosecutor as part of the file containing the material for the prosecution case):

— information provided by an accused person which indicates an explanation for the offence with which he has been charged;
— any material casting doubt on the reliability of a confession;
— any material casting doubt on the reliability of a prosecution witness;
— any other material which the investigator believes may satisfy the test for prosecution disclosure in the Act.

7.4 If the prosecutor asks to inspect material which has not already been copied to him, the disclosure officer must allow him to inspect it. If the prosecutor asks for a copy of material which has not already been copied to him, the disclosure officer must give him a copy. However, this does not apply where the disclosure officer believes, having consulted the officer in charge of the investigation, that the material is too sensitive to be copied and can only be inspected.

7.5 If material consists of information which is recorded other than in writing, whether it should be given to the prosecutor in its original form as a whole, or by way of relevant extracts recorded in the same form, or in the form of a transcript, is a matter for agreement between the disclosure officer and the prosecutor.

Subsequent action by disclosure officer

8.1 At the time a schedule of non-sensitive material is prepared, the disclosure officer may not know exactly what material will form the case against the accused, and the prosecutor may not have given advice about the likely relevance of particular items of material. Once these matters have been determined, the disclosure officer must give the prosecutor, where necessary, an amended schedule listing any additional material:

— which may be relevant to the investigation,
— which does not form part of the case against the accused,
— which is not already listed on the schedule, and
— which he believes is not sensitive,

unless he is informed in writing by the prosecutor that the prosecutor intends to disclose the material to the defence.

8.2 Section 7A of the Act imposes a continuing duty on the prosecutor, for the duration of criminal proceedings against the accused, to disclose material which satisfies the test for disclosure (subject to public interest considerations). To enable him to do this, any new material coming to light should be treated in the same way as the earlier material.

8.3 In particular, after a defence statement has been given, the disclosure officer must look again at the material which has been retained and must draw the attention of the prosecutor to any material which might reasonably be considered capable of undermining the case for the prosecution against the accused or of assisting the case for the accused; and he must reveal it to him in accordance with paragraphs 7.4 and 7.5 above.

Certification by disclosure officer

9.1 The disclosure officer must certify to the prosecutor that to the best of his knowledge and belief, all relevant material which has been retained and made available to him has been revealed to the prosecutor in accordance with this code. He must sign and date the certificate. It will be necessary to certify not only at the time when the schedule and accompanying material is submitted to the prosecutor, and when relevant material which has been retained is reconsidered after the accused has given a defence statement, but also whenever a schedule is otherwise given or material is otherwise revealed to the prosecutor.

Disclosure of material to accused

10.1 If material has not already been copied to the prosecutor, and he requests its disclosure to the accused on the ground that:

— it satisfies the test for prosecution disclosure, **or**

— the court has ordered its disclosure after considering an application from the accused,

the disclosure officer must disclose it to the accused.

10.2 If material has been copied to the prosecutor, and it is to be disclosed, whether it is disclosed by the prosecutor or the disclosure officer is a matter of agreement between the two of them.

10.3 The disclosure officer must disclose material to the accused either by giving him a copy or by allowing him to inspect it. If the accused person asks for a copy of any material which he has been allowed to inspect, the disclosure officer must give it to him, unless in the opinion of the disclosure officer that is either not practicable (for example because the material consists of an object which cannot be copied, or because the volume of material is so great), or not desirable (for example because the material is a statement by a child witness in relation to a sexual offence).

10.4 If material which the accused has been allowed to inspect consists of information which is recorded other than in writing, whether it should be given to the accused in its original form or in the form of a transcript is matter for the discretion of the disclosure officer. If the material is transcribed, the disclosure officer must ensure that the transcript is certified to the accused as a true record of the material which has been transcribed.

10.5 If a court concludes that an item of sensitive material satisfies the prosecution disclosure test and that the interests of the defence outweigh the public interest in withholding disclosure, it will be necessary to disclose the material if the case is to proceed. This does not mean that sensitive documents must always be disclosed in their original form: for example, the court may agree that sensitive details still requiring protection should be blocked out, or that documents may be summarised, or that the prosecutor may make an admission about the substance of the material under section 10 of the Criminal Justice Act 1967.

Attorney-General's Guidelines on Disclosure: Disclosure of Unused Material in Criminal Proceedings

Introduction

1. Every accused person has a right to a fair trial, a right long embodied in our law and guaranteed under article 6 of the European Convention on Human Rights (ECHR). A fair trial is the proper object and expectation of all participants in the trial process. Fair disclosure to an accused is an inseparable part of a fair trial.

2. What must be clear is that a fair trial consists of an examination not just of all the evidence the parties wish to rely on but also all other relevant subject matter. A fair trial should not require consideration of irrelevant material and should not involve spurious applications or arguments which serve to divert the trial process from examining the real issues before the court.
3. The scheme set out in the Criminal Procedure and Investigations Act 1996 (as amended by the Criminal Justice Act 2003) (the Act) is designed to ensure that there is fair disclosure of material which may be relevant to an investigation and which does not form part of the prosecution case. Disclosure under the Act should assist the accused in the timely preparation and presentation of their case and assist the court to focus on all the relevant issues in the trial. Disclosure which does not meet these objectives risks preventing a fair trial taking place.
4. This means that the disclosure regime set out in the Act must be scrupulously followed. These Guidelines build upon the existing law to help to ensure that the legislation is operated more effectively, consistently and fairly.
5. Disclosure must not be an open ended trawl of unused material. A critical element to fair and proper disclosure is that the defence play their role to ensure that the prosecution are directed to material which might reasonably be considered capable of undermining the prosecution case or assisting the case for the accused. This process is key to ensuring prosecutors make informed determinations about disclosure of unused material.
6. Fairness does recognise that there are other interests that need to be protected, including those of victims and witnesses who might otherwise be exposed to harm. The scheme of the Act protects those interests. It should also ensure that material is not disclosed which overburdens the participants in the trial process, diverts attention from the relevant issues, leads to unjustifiable delay, and is wasteful of resources.
7. Whilst it is acknowledged that these Guidelines have been drafted with a focus on Crown Court proceedings the spirit of the Guidelines must be followed where they apply to proceedings in the magistrates' court.

General principles

8. Disclosure refers to providing the defence with copies of, or access to, any material which might reasonably be considered capable of undermining the case for the prosecution against the accused, or of assisting the case for the accused, and which has not previously been disclosed.
9. Prosecutors will only be expected to anticipate what material might weaken their case or strengthen the defence in the light of information available at the time of the disclosure decision, and this may include information revealed during questioning.
10. Generally, material which can reasonably be considered capable of undermining the prosecution case against the accused or assisting the defence case will include anything that tends to show a fact inconsistent with the elements of the case that must be proved by the prosecution. Material can fulfil the disclosure test:
    (a) by the use to be made of it in cross-examination; or
    (b) by its capacity to support submissions that could lead to:
        (i) the exclusion of evidence; or
        (ii) a stay of proceedings; or
        (iii) a court or tribunal finding that any public authority had acted incompatibly with the accused's rights under the ECHR, or
    (c) by its capacity to suggest an explanation or partial explanation of the accused's actions.
11. In deciding whether material may fall to be disclosed under paragraph 10, especially (b)(ii), prosecutors must consider whether disclosure is required in order for a proper application to be made. The purpose of this paragraph is not to allow enquiries to support speculative arguments or for the manufacture of defences.
12. Examples of material that might reasonably be considered capable of undermining the prosecution case or of assisting the case for the accused are:
    i. Any material casting doubt upon the accuracy of any prosecution evidence.

ii. Any material which may point to another person, whether charged or not (including a co-accused) having involvement in the commission of the offence.
iii. Any material which may cast doubt upon the reliability of a confession.
iv. Any material that might go to the credibility of a prosecution witness.
v. Any material that might support a defence that is either raised by the defence or apparent from the prosecution papers.
vi. Any material which may have a bearing on the admissibility of any prosecution evidence.

13. It should also be borne in mind that while items of material viewed in isolation may not be reasonably considered to be capable of undermining the prosecution case or assisting the accused, several items together can have that effect.
14. Material relating to the accused's mental or physical health, intellectual capacity, or to any ill treatment which the accused may have suffered when in the investigator's custody is likely to fall within the test for disclosure set out in paragraph 8 above.

Defence statements

15. A defence statement must comply with the requirements of section 6A of the Act. A comprehensive defence statement assists the participants in the trial to ensure that it is fair. The trial process is not well served if the defence make general and unspecified allegations and then seek far-reaching disclosure in the hope that material may turn up to make them good. The more detail a defence statement contains the more likely it is that the prosecutor will make an informed decision about whether any remaining undisclosed material might reasonably be considered capable of undermining the prosecution case or of assisting the case for the accused, or whether to advise the investigator to undertake further enquiries. It also helps in the management of the trial by narrowing down and focussing on the issues in dispute. It may result in the prosecution discontinuing the case. Defence practitioners should be aware of these considerations when advising their clients.
16. Whenever a defence solicitor provides a defence statement on behalf of the accused it will be deemed to be given with the authority of the solicitor's client.

Continuing duty of prosecutor to disclose

17. Section 7A of the Act imposes a continuing duty upon the prosecutor to keep under review at all times the question of whether there is any unused material which might reasonably be considered capable of undermining the prosecution case against the accused or assisting the case for the accused and which has not previously been disclosed. This duty arises after the prosecutor has complied with the duty of initial disclosure or purported to comply with it and before the accused is acquitted or convicted or the prosecutor decides not to proceed with the case. If such material is identified, then the prosecutor must disclose it to the accused as soon as is reasonably practicable.
18. As part of their continuing duty of disclosure, prosecutors should be open, alert and promptly responsive to requests for disclosure of material supported by a comprehensive defence statement. Conversely, if no defence statement has been served or if the prosecutor considers that the defence statement is lacking specificity or otherwise does not meet the requirements of section 6A of the Act, a letter should be sent to the defence indicating this. If the position is not resolved satisfactorily, the prosecutor should consider raising the issue at a hearing for directions to enable the court to give a warning or appropriate directions.
19. When defence practitioners are dissatisfied with disclosure decisions by the prosecution and consider that they are entitled to further disclosure, applications to the court should be made pursuant to section 8 of the Act and in accordance with the procedures set out in the Criminal Procedure Rules. Applications for further disclosure should not be made as ad hoc applications but dealt with under the proper procedures.

Applications for non-disclosure in the public interest

20. Before making an application to the court to withhold material which would otherwise fall to be disclosed, on the basis that to disclose would give rise to a real risk of serious prejudice to an important public interest, prosecutors should aim to disclose as much of the material as they properly can (for example, by giving the defence redacted or edited copies or summaries). Neutral material or material damaging to the defendant need not be disclosed and must *not* be brought to the attention of the court. It is only in truly borderline cases that the prosecution should seek a judicial ruling on the disclosability of material in its possession.
21. Prior to or at the hearing, the court must be provided with full and accurate information. Prior to the hearing the prosecutor and the prosecution advocate must examine all material, which is the subject matter of the application and make any necessary enquiries of the investigator. The prosecutor (or representative) and/or investigator should attend such applications.
22. The principles set out at paragraph 36 of *R v H & C* should be rigorously applied firstly by the prosecutor and then by the court considering the material. It is essential that these principles are scrupulously attended to to ensure that the procedure for examination of material in the absence of the accused is compliant with article 6 of ECHR.

Responsibilities

Investigators and disclosure officers

23. Investigators and disclosure officers must be fair and objective and must work together with prosecutors to ensure that disclosure obligations are met. A failure to take action leading to inadequate disclosure may result in a wrongful conviction. It may alternatively lead to a successful abuse of process argument, an acquittal against the weight of the evidence or the appellate courts may find that a conviction is unsafe and quash it.
24. Officers appointed as disclosure officers must have the requisite experience, skills, competence and resources to undertake their vital role. In discharging their obligations under the Act, code, common law and any operational instructions, investigators should always err on the side of recording and retaining material where they have any doubt as to whether it may be relevant.
25. An individual must not be appointed as disclosure officer, or continue in that role, if that is likely to result in a conflict of interest, for instance, if the disclosure officer is the victim of the alleged crime which is the subject of investigation. The advice of a more senior investigator must always be sought if there is doubt as to whether a conflict of interest precludes an individual acting as the disclosure officer. If thereafter a doubt remains, the advice of a prosecutor should be sought.
26. There may be a number of disclosure officers, especially in large and complex cases. However, there must be a lead disclosure officer who is the focus for enquiries and whose responsibility it is to ensure that the investigator's disclosure obligations are complied with. Disclosure officers, or their deputies, must inspect, view or listen to all relevant material that has been retained by the investigator, and the disclosure officer must provide a personal declaration to the effect that this task has been undertaken.
27. Generally this will mean that such material must be examined in detail by the disclosure officer or the deputy, but exceptionally the extent and manner of inspecting, viewing or listening will depend on the nature of material and its form. For example, it might be reasonable to examine digital material by using software search tools, or to establish the contents of large volumes of material by dip sampling. If such material is not examined in detail, it must nonetheless be described on the disclosure schedules accurately and as clearly as possible. The extent and manner of its examination must also be described together with justification for such action.

28. Investigators must retain material that may be relevant to the investigation. However, it may become apparent to the investigator that some material obtained in the course of an investigation because it was considered potentially relevant, is in fact incapable of impact. It need not then be retained or dealt with in accordance with these Guidelines, although the investigator should err on the side of caution in coming to this conclusion and seek the advice of the prosecutor as appropriate.
29. In meeting the obligations in paragraphs 6.9 and 8.1 of the Code, it is crucial that descriptions by disclosure officers in non-sensitive schedules are detailed, clear and accurate. The descriptions may require a summary of the contents of the retained material to assist the prosecutor to make an informed decision on disclosure. Sensitive schedules must contain sufficient information to enable the prosecutor to make an informed decision as to whether or not the material itself should be viewed, to the extent possible without compromising the confidentiality of the information.
30. Disclosure officers must specifically draw material to the attention of the prosecutor for consideration where they have any doubt as to whether it might reasonably be considered capable of undermining the prosecution case or of assisting the case for the accused.
31. Disclosure officers must seek the advice and assistance of prosecutors when in doubt as to their responsibility as early as possible. They must deal expeditiously with requests by the prosecutor for further information on material, which may lead to disclosure.

Prosecutors

32. Prosecutors must do all that they can to facilitate proper disclosure, as part of their general and personal professional responsibility to act fairly and impartially, in the interests of justice and in accordance with the law. Prosecutors must also be alert to the need to provide advice to, and where necessary probe actions taken by, disclosure officers to ensure that disclosure obligations are met.
33. Prosecutors must review schedules prepared by disclosure officers thoroughly and must be alert to the possibility that relevant material may exist which has not been revealed to them or material included which should not have been. If no schedules have been provided, or there are apparent omissions from the schedules, or documents or other items are inadequately described or are unclear, the prosecutor must at once take action to obtain properly completed schedules. Likewise schedules should be returned for amendment if irrelevant items are included. If prosecutors remain dissatisfied with the quality or content of the schedules they must raise the matter with a senior investigator, and if necessary, persist, with a view to resolving the matter satisfactorily.
34. Where prosecutors have reason to believe that the disclosure officer has not discharged the obligation in paragraph 26 to inspect, view or listen to relevant material, they must at once raise the matter with the disclosure officer and, if it is believed that the officer has not inspected, viewed or listened to the material, request that it be done.
35. When prosecutors or disclosure officers believe that material might reasonably be considered capable of undermining the prosecution case or assisting the case for the accused, prosecutors must always inspect, view or listen to the material and satisfy themselves that the prosecution can properly be continued having regard to the disclosability of the material reviewed. Their judgement as to what other material to inspect, view or listen to will depend on the circumstances of each case.
36. Prosecutors should copy the defence statement to the disclosure officer and investigator as soon as reasonably practicable and prosecutors should advise the investigator if, in their view, reasonable and relevant lines of further enquiry should be pursued.
37. Prosecutors cannot comment upon, or invite inferences to be drawn from, failures in defence disclosure otherwise than in accordance with section 11 of the Act. Prosecutors may cross-examine the accused on differences between the defence case put at trial and that set out in his or her defence statement. In doing so, it may be appropriate to apply to the judge

under section 6E of the Act for copies of the statement to be given to a jury, edited if necessary to remove inadmissible material. Prosecutors should examine the defence statement to see whether it points to other lines of enquiry. If the defence statement does point to other reasonable lines of inquiry further investigation is required and evidence obtained as a result of these enquiries may be used as part of the prosecution case or to rebut the defence.

38. Once initial disclosure is completed and a defence statement has been served, requests for disclosure should ordinarily only be answered if the request is in accordance with and relevant to the defence statement. If it is not, then a further or amended defence statement should be sought and obtained before considering the request for further disclosure.
39. Prosecutors must ensure that they record in writing all actions and decisions they make in discharging their disclosure responsibilities, and this information is to be made available to the prosecution advocate if requested or if relevant to an issue.
40. If the material does not fulfil the disclosure test there is no requirement to disclose it. For this purpose, the parties' respective cases should not be restrictively analysed but must be carefully analysed to ascertain the specific facts the prosecution seek to establish and the specific grounds on which the charges are resisted. Neutral material or material damaging to the defendant need not be disclosed and must not be brought to the attention of the court. Only in truly borderline cases should the prosecution seek a judicial ruling on the disclosability of material in its hands.
41. If prosecutors are satisfied that a fair trial cannot take place where material which satisfies the disclosure test cannot be disclosed, and that this cannot or will not be remedied including by, for example, making formal admissions, amending the charges or presenting the case in a different way so as to ensure fairness or in other ways, they must not continue with the case.

Prosecution advocates

42. Prosecution advocates should ensure that all material that ought to be disclosed under the Act is disclosed to the defence. However, prosecution advocates cannot be expected to disclose material if they are not aware of its existence. As far as is possible, prosecution advocates must place themselves in a fully informed position to enable them to make decisions on disclosure.
43. Upon receipt of instructions, prosecution advocates should consider as a priority all the information provided regarding disclosure of material. Prosecution advocates should consider, in every case, whether they can be satisfied that they are in possession of all relevant documentation and that they have been instructed fully regarding disclosure matters. Decisions already made regarding disclosure should be reviewed. If as a result, the advocate considers that further information or action is required, written advice should be promptly provided setting out the aspects that need clarification or action. Prosecution advocates must advise on disclosure in accordance with the Act. If necessary and where appropriate a conference should be held to determine what is required.
44. The prosecution advocate must keep decisions regarding disclosure under review until the conclusion of the trial. The prosecution advocate must in every case specifically consider whether he or she can satisfactorily discharge the duty of continuing review on the basis of the material supplied already, or whether it is necessary to inspect further material or to reconsider material already inspected. Prosecution advocates must not abrogate their responsibility under the Act by disclosing material which could not be considered capable of undermining the prosecution case or of assisting the case for the accused.
45. Prior to the commencement of a trial, the prosecuting advocate should always make decisions on disclosure in consultation with those instructing him or her and the disclosure officer. After a trial has started, it is recognised that in practice consultation on disclosure issues may not be practicable; it continues to be desirable, however, whenever this can be achieved without affecting unduly the conduct of the trial.
46. There is no basis in law or practice for disclosure on a 'counsel to counsel' basis.

Involvement of other agencies

Material held by Government departments or other Crown bodies

47. Where it appears to an investigator, disclosure officer or prosecutor that a Government department or other Crown body has material that may be relevant to an issue in the case, reasonable steps should be taken to identify and consider such material. Although what is reasonable will vary from case to case, the prosecution should inform the department or other body of the nature of its case and of relevant issues in the case in respect of which the department or body might possess material, and ask whether it has any such material.
48. It should be remembered that investigators, disclosure officers and prosecutors cannot be regarded to be in constructive possession of material held by Government departments or Crown bodies simply by virtue of their status as Government departments or Crown bodies.
49. Departments in England and Wales should have identified personnel as established Enquiry Points to deal with issues concerning the disclosure of information in criminal proceedings.
50. Where, after reasonable steps have been taken to secure access to such material, access is denied the investigator, disclosure officer or prosecutor should consider what if any further steps might be taken to obtain the material or inform the defence.

Material held by other agencies

51. There may be cases where the investigator, disclosure officer or prosecutor believes that a third party (for example, a local authority, a social services department, a hospital, a doctor, a school, a provider of forensic services) has material or information which might be relevant to the prosecution case. In such cases, if the material or information might reasonably be considered capable of undermining the prosecution case or of assisting the case for the accused prosecutors should take what steps they regard as appropriate in the particular case to obtain it.
52. If the investigator, disclosure officer or prosecutor seeks access to the material or information but the third party declines or refuses to allow access to it, the matter should not be left. If despite any reasons offered by the third party it is still believed that it is reasonable to seek production of the material or information, and the requirements of section 2 of the Criminal Procedure (Attendance of Witnesses) Act 1965 or as appropriate section 97 of the Magistrates Courts Act 1980[1] are satisfied, then the prosecutor or investigator should apply for a witness summons causing a representative of the third party to produce the material to the Court.
53. Relevant information which comes to the knowledge of investigators or prosecutors as a result of liaison with third parties should be recorded by the investigator or prosecutor in a durable or retrievable form (for example, potentially relevant information revealed in discussions at a child protection conference attended by police officers).
54. Where information comes into the possession of the prosecution in the circumstances set out in paragraphs 51–53 above, consultation with the other agency should take place before disclosure is made: there may be public interest reasons which justify withholding disclosure and which would require the issue of disclosure of the information to be placed before the court.

Other disclosure

Disclosure prior to initial disclosure

55. Investigators must always be alive to the potential need to reveal and prosecutors to the potential need to disclose material, in the interests of justice and fairness in the particular circumstances of any case, after the commencement of proceedings but before their duty arises

[1] The equivalent legislation in Northern Ireland is section 51A of the Judicature (Northern Ireland) Act 1978 and article 118 of the Magistrates' Courts (Northern Ireland) Order 1981.

under the Act. For instance, disclosure ought to be made of significant information that might affect a bail decision or that might enable the defence to contest the committal proceedings.

56. Where the need for such disclosure is not apparent to the prosecutor, any disclosure will depend on what the accused chooses to reveal about the defence. Clearly, such disclosure will not exceed that which is obtainable after the statutory duties of disclosure arise.

Summary trial

57. The prosecutor should, in addition to complying with the obligations under the Act, provide to the defence all evidence upon which the Crown proposes to rely in a summary trial. Such provision should allow the accused and their legal advisers sufficient time properly to consider the evidence before it is called.

Material relevant to sentence

58. In all cases the prosecutor must consider disclosing in the interests of justice any material, which is relevant to sentence (e.g. information which might mitigate the seriousness of the offence or assist the accused to lay blame in part upon a co-accused or another person).

Post-conviction

59. The interests of justice will also mean that where material comes to light after the conclusion of the proceedings, which might cast doubt upon the safety of the conviction, there is a duty to consider disclosure. Any such material should be brought immediately to the attention of line management.

60. Disclosure of any material that is made outside the ambit of the Act will attract confidentiality by virtue of *Taylor v SFO* [1998].

Applicability of these guidelines

61. Although the relevant obligations in relation to unused material and disclosure imposed on the prosecutor and the accused are determined by the date on which the investigation began, these Guidelines should be adopted with immediate effect in relation to all cases submitted to the prosecuting authorities in receipt of these Guidelines save where they specifically refer to the statutory or Code provisions of the Criminal Justice Act 2003 that do not yet apply to the particular case.

Index

A

B

C

D

E

F

G

H

N

O

P

Q

R

S

T